**The Dow Jones-Irwin Guide to
Personal Financial Planning**

The Dow Jones-Irwin Guide to Personal Financial Planning

FREDERICK AMLING, Ph.D.

WILLIAM G. DROMS, D.B.A., C.F.A.

DOW JONES-IRWIN
Homewood, Illinois 60430

ISBN 0-87094-265-4
Library of Congress Catalog Card No. 81–67117
Printed in the United States of America

4 5 6 7 8 9 0 K 9 8 7 6 5 4 3

To our wives and children,
Gwen, Scott, Terry, and Jeff Amling
JoAnn, Courtney, and Justin Droms

Foreword

It is very important for the economic health of the nation and world economies to have individuals and households who manage their financial resources competently. The stronger the personal financial position of the family and individual, the stronger the nation.

Consumers who continually over extend themselves financially weaken the basic foundation of the financial structure of the economy. This makes it difficult to generate savings that provide capital investment which will increase productivity. Both savings and investment are needed to fight inflation and bring stability to our economic and financial system.

The basic financial principles discussed in this book should provide individuals with a framework for making rational and sensible financial decisions. The sequence of the chapters provides a preview of what individuals can expect in the future. From establishing financial goals to the transference of wealth, the reader is provided with a life-cycle approach to financial security.

Ideally, as a result of reading this book individuals will be better able to achieve financial security at all stages of their lives. To the authors I would like to extend a word of encouragement, keep up the good work.

William McChesney Martin, Jr.
Counselor to the Bank and
Board of Directors of The Riggs
National Bank of Washington, D.C.
Formerly Chairman of the Federal
Reserve Board and President of the
New York Stock Exchange

Preface

The material in this book will help you develop a realistic approach to managing your personal finances. It is the result of extensive experience dealing with institutional and personal finance. Its purpose is to provide a direction for your personal financial planning which will ultimately lead you to financial independence.

Effective financial planning requires that you attempt to anticipate future events. If you anticipate and plan for your future financial commitments, you will act more responsibly in the use of your present income. You should use this book as a guide for financial planning and controlling your current financial actions to reach your future goals. As you will learn in the pages which follow, even a person or family of moderate means can achieve financial security through careful resource allocation.

This book is not a "get rich quick" guide or a "doom and gloom" prescription for making money during some forecasted economic debacle. There is no guarantee that you will become a millionaire if you follow the principles advanced here. But you can achieve balance in your financial life that will lead you to a more secure financial future.

This book is organized to cover the most important areas of personal financial management. Part I deals with the important topic of setting personal financial objectives.

Part II deals with financial planning and control. Part III deals with financing consumer expenditures. Part IV covers the topic of risk control through insurance. Part V deals with investing for the future. Part VI is the final section of the book and deals with retirement and estate planning.

Some chapters introduce financial terms which may be unfamiliar to you. These chapters include a glossary of terms as an appendix to the chapter. The glossaries provide a means of ready reference to aid your understanding of new terms in such areas as insurance and investments.

Acknowledgements

As is usual in an undertaking of this size, a number of thank yous are owed. At George Washington University, we would like to thank Joe Borreli for research assistance and Pamela Britnell and Bilge N. Criss for typing assistance. At Georgetown, Mary Cuddeback, Marsha Hill, Mary

Stuart Kilner, Peggy ("Coy") Long, and Jetta Prescott deserve our thanks for suffering through a number of drafts. Thanks are also due Professors Tom Cooke, Mike Skigen, and John Sauter for their review of various chapters. A special note of appreciation goes to Steve Apkon for his meticulous research assistance in many areas.

Our respective deans also deserve our thanks. To Dean Norma Maine Loeser of The George Washington University School of Government and Business Administration and Dean Ronald L. Smith of Georgetown University's School of Business Administration, a sincere thank you for supporting our efforts on this book. A number of finance professors also took the time to review early drafts of the manuscript. Our thanks for this difficult chore go to Professors James Agresta, Prince Georges Community College; Jefferson Hooper, Mesa Community College; Theodore Mah, Diablo Valley College; Ester McCabe, The University of Connecticut; Roger Potter, Illinois State University; and William Weller, Modesto Junior College.

Finally, a special note of appreciation goes to Francis J. Lyons, executive vice president—Trust and George R. Adams, vice president and trust officer at the Riggs National Bank of Washington, D.C. We are particularly indebted to George Adams for his detailed help on the estate planning chapter.

Of course no expression of appreciation is complete without recognizing the very special contribution made by our wives who have put up with book after book with hardly a complaint. We extend, therefore, our deepest appreciation for the time stolen from them and the children, to Gwen Stewart Amling and JoAnn Gilberti Droms.

Frederick Amling
William G. Droms

Contents

PART **1**

Setting
objectives

1

Personal financial planning

- Planning for financial independence
- Setting financial goals
- The financial planning cycle
- A personal balance sheet
- Lesson learned from the balance sheet
- Summary

It is a sad fact of life that many people make personal financial decisions by chance. Investment decisions are based on tips or casual observations of friends or relatives; insurance is purchased from a friend in the business; and savings plans are based on how much money is left over at the end of the month. It should be obvious that there is a better way to plan for the future.

It is the central thesis of this book that all of us can achieve greater wealth and financial security for the future by clearly defining our financial goals and developing definite plans to achieve them. Establishing your own personal financial goals requires careful planning and close monitoring of your progress toward those goals. As you will learn, the benefits from this process make the effort well worthwhile.

In this book you will learn about the interrelated topics of career planning, budgeting, taxes, savings, housing, credit, insurance, investments, retirement, and estate planning. In all these areas our overriding objective is to show you how to maximize your personal wealth and achieve financial independence. Our conception of financial independence does not necessarily imply great wealth. Rather it requires that you make maximum use of your income, whatever its level. With careful planning even people who earn moderate incomes can achieve financial independence. Higher-income people will, of course, achieve higher levels of absolute wealth, and may achieve financial independence earlier in life. However, eventual financial independence can be achieved by most people who are willing to work for it.

Planning for financial independence

As an illustration of this principle, consider the case of Paul and Carol, a retired couple. When they retired in 1975, Paul was 65 years old and Carol was 62. Neither Paul nor Carol had earned a particularly high income during their working years. They were certainly not wealthy people, but by the time they retired, they had achieved financial independence. They had both participated in automatic savings plans through payroll deductions where they worked, and had accumulated substantial amounts of savings through these programs. Some of these savings had been kept in liquid form, and some had been invested in stocks and bonds. In addition to their savings, they also participated in employer-sponsored pension plans and in the Social Security system. Thus when they retired, they each received two monthly retirement checks—one from Social Security and one from a private pension.

They had also managed to pay off the mortgage on their home during their working years. Their retirement income is more than adequate to pay the cost of real estate taxes, utilities, and maintenance on their home. They are still not wealthy, but they are living well within their means, and they have a substantial savings nest egg.

Paul and Carol did not achieve financial independence through sheer good fortune. Neither did they achieve independence by scrimping and saving and sacrificing all present consumption to insure a future pension. They worked hard and planned carefully for the future, but they also lived in the present and enjoyed their lives. The real key to their financial independence was that they established financial goals for themselves and worked toward those goals. They saved a modest percentage of their incomes over a long period of time, and they did so automatically. They invested in a home and in pension plans to provide for their future needs. At the same time they provided themselves with an adequate income to support a moderate lifestyle during their working years.

Paul and Carol were lucky in some respects. They were lucky mainly to be healthy enough to work steadily until retirement age. They were also lucky to have stable employment. As you will learn, it is critically important for you to plan to protect yourself against the possibility of physical disability or unstable employment. With proper planning, even these problems can be overcome.

Setting financial goals

You can begin the financial planning process at any age, but the sooner the better. If you learn to establish financial goals early in life, you can improve the quality of your life by making maximum use of your income. You probably already have many financial goals you would like to achieve. You may want to buy a home of your own, a new car, or an expensive stereo system. You have probably also realized that you cannot afford to reach all these objectives at once. You will have to plan how to spend your income so that you can reach these goals.

Even when you are working full-time and earning a full-time income, you will find that you will not have enough money to reach all your financial goals. If you are like most people, you will find your wants and needs growing as your income grows. You will have to single out those goals that are most important to you, and you will have to make sacrifices to reach them.

You should give a great deal of thought to selecting the goals toward which you are willing to work. You will need to select out those goals that are most important to you, and then concentrate on reaching them. If you set reasonable goals and exercise some self-discipline, you will achieve them. Therefore, you want to be certain that the goals you set are what you really want. It would be a shame to work to reach a goal only to find out that it wasn't really important to you.

Chapter 3, which deals with budgeting and control, introduces a system of management by objectives for personal financial planning. You can use this system to establish your goals and work toward them efficiently. You can use the system throughout your life to plan your financial objectives and control your progress toward those objectives. In addition to this kind of planning and control, you must also give some thought to your overall financial planning cycle.

The financial planning cycle

Financial planning requires the anticipation of future events. As you plan for the future, you should take a long-run perspective. You will find that as you grow older, and grow intellectually and emotionally, your needs and desires will change. Your major financial priorities will change along with changes in your life cycle. Figure 1–1 illustrates the changing nature of your planning cycle.

Figure 1–1
Financial planning cycle

Formative years	High-school and college years	Working years	Retirement years
	Career planning Budgeting Savings	Budgeting Housing Savings Investments Credit Taxes Retirement planning Estate planning Insurance	Budgeting Investment management Estate planning

In your formative years you will probably not pay much attention to financial planning. When you reach your high-school and college years, your primary focus of attention will probably be on career planning, budgeting, and savings. Most college students live on fairly tight budgets, so budgeting may emerge as a major concern. You will find that it will probably be a major concern for much of the rest of your life.

Your working years may overlap your education years. More and more Americans are continuing their education on a part-time basis after completing college. During your working years you will have many financial concerns. Budgeting will continue to be important. You will have to plan for housing, savings, investment, insurance, taxes, credit control, retirement, and estate planning. You will also have to plan for the education of your children if you have a family. In your later working years you will begin to give major attention to investment management and retirement planning. As you get closer to retirement, you will find that you will have to live with planning decisions made earlier in your working years. This is why it is important to begin retirement planning with your first job. The decisions you make as a young person will play a major role in your retirement outlook when you are older.

Finally, in your retirement years, you will be concerned with budgeting to live within your retirement income. If you follow the advice in this book, you will also be concerned with managing your accumulated investments. At this stage in your life, estate planning will also be a major priority. You will want to plan and control the transfer of your accumulated assets to your children or other heirs.

Of all the many factors affecting personal financial planning, your financial planning cycle and life-style are probably the most important. Your goals will undoubtedly change as you progress through your financial planning cycle. Because of this natural growth cycle, your financial goals must be established within a flexible framework that will allow for change as your needs and objectives change.

Your goals also will be influenced by your family situation. A young couple without children will have radically different financial goals than a middle-aged couple with three children in college. Similarly, a high-income family will have different goals than a low- or moderate-income family, and single people will have different goals than married couples.

Your nonfinancial goals also must be taken into account as you set your financial goals. Individuals differ in a myriad of ways, and financial planning is no exception. Thus no one set of financial goals can be made to fit everyone. To some people consumption of income is much more important than saving of income. Many people prefer to spend the majority or even all of their income on such things as expensive clothing, elegant restaurants, or fancy automobiles. Other people, with different types of needs and objectives, may elect to save and invest a large portion of their income and spend very little on consumption.

Before you can establish meaningful financial goals, you must first determine your current financial position. Drawing up a personal balance sheet is one convenient way to show where you stand financially.

A personal balance sheet

As an example of a balance sheet, the financial position of John Diamond and Carla Gilberti will be examined. John and Carla are seniors at a leading state university who plan to marry immediately after graduation. They are at the point in their lives where they need to determine their current position and begin planning for the future.

John and Carla have different financial value systems and hence have rather different-looking balance sheets. Both John and Carla have been employed part-time during their first three years of college and expect to continue working through their senior year. Both are responsible for providing their own spending money from these part-time jobs. All other expenses are paid through scholarships, student loans, summer earnings, and money from their parents. John is working as a waiter in a popular restaurant near the university campus. Carla is employed on-campus as a student grader and research assistant for one of her professors.

John likes to dress well and spends a great deal of money on clothing. Carla has much less expensive taste in clothing but is a collector of antique silver jewelry. John and Carla's current financial position may be conveniently summarized through the use of a balance sheet. Tables 1–1 and 1–2 portray John and Carla's respective balance sheets. The balance sheets present a "snapshot" of their financial position. Assets, things they own, are listed on the left-hand side. Liabilities, or money owed, are listed on the right-hand side. Net worth is also listed on the right-hand side. By definition, net worth is equal to the difference between the value of what you own and the amount of money, if any, that you owe. Thus the balance sheets as presented in Tables 1–1 and 1–2 must balance because by definition:

$$\text{Assets} = \text{Liabilities} + \text{Net worth}$$

Table 1–1
John's balance sheet

JOHN
Balance Sheet

Assets		Liabilities and Net Worth	
Cash in bank	$ 150	Charge account—College Shop	$ 200
Books	200	Net worth	1,000
Clothing	850	Total liabilities and	
Total assets	$1,200	net worth	$1,200

Table 1–2
Carla's balance sheet

CARLA
Balance Sheet

Assets		Liabilities and Net Worth	
Cash in bank	$ 100	Charge account—Silver Shop	$ 50
Books	200		
Clothing	600	Net worth	1,550
Silver collection	700	Total liabilities and	
Total assets	$1,600	net worth	$1,600

From John's balance sheet it can be seen that John has a total of $1,200 in assets. He has $150 cash in the bank (in his checking account), $200 worth of books, and $850 worth of clothing. The clothing is listed at its current value. Since clothing depreciates rather rapidly after purchase, the clothing's current value of $850 is quite a bit less than the total amount paid for the clothes. On the liabilities side John owes $200 to the College Shop on his revolving charge account. The difference between John's $1,200 in assets and $200 in liabilities leaves John with a net worth of $1,000.

On Carla's balance sheet it can be seen that Carla has a total of

$1,600 in assets, consisting of $100 in cash, $200 in books, $600 worth of clothing and $700 worth of silver. Since silver appreciates over time, the silver's current value of $700 is somewhat more than the total amount Carla paid for it. On the liabilities side Carla has a $50 charge account at the Silver Shop. The difference between her assets and liabilities leaves a net worth of $1,550.

Lesson learned from the balance sheet

An important lesson may be learned from John and Carla's balance sheets in Tables 1–1 and 1–2. Carla's spending decisions, although unplanned, are directed toward building value with a focus on increasing net worth. Her purchases of silver have resulted in the accumulation of assets that are increasing in value over time, thereby increasing her net worth. John has spent most of his income on so-called "wasting assets," or assets that decrease in value over time. The result is that John, who earns roughly the same income as Carla, has not built up his net worth to the extent Carla has, even though he has purchased a large dollar amount of assets. These assets, however, have declined in value. Although John may get as much personal satisfaction from his clothing collection, it is obvious that Carla is far ahead from a financial point of view.

It is important to note from the personal balance sheet that assets are always listed at their current market value. Accountants will note that this practice is different from that employed in business. For this reason John's clothing assets are listed at quite a bit less than what John actually paid for the clothing. Carla's assets, on the other hand, have appreciated in value and are listed at more than their original cost. After liabilities are subtracted, the resulting calculation of net worth will reflect the current value of John and Carla's assets.

John and Carla intend to marry at the end of this year. A single balance sheet combining their two separate balance sheets shows their combined financial position as they start out their marriage. This combined balance sheet is shown in Table 1–3.

John and Carla's combined balance sheet shows a division of assets between financial assets and nonfinancial assets. Financial assets generally are liquid assets, such as cash in checking and savings accounts, or investments in stocks and bonds. In John and Carla's case, their only financial asset is the $250 in their checking account.

Nonfinancial assets generally encompass relatively unliquid assets that are purchased for personal use or for long-term investment. In John and Carla's case, their clothing, books, and silver collection fall in this category. Other major assets in this category would include automobiles and real estate. John and Carla do not currently own an automobile or home, but these important asset acquisitions must be planned in their

Table 1–3
John and Carla's balance sheet

JOHN AND CARLA'
Balance Sheet

Assets		Liabilities and Net Worth	
Financial Assets:		Charge Account—College Shop ..	$ 200
Cash in bank	$ 250	Charge Account—Silver Shop	50
Nonfinancial Assets:			
Books	400		
Clothing	1,450		
Silver Collection	700	Net worth	2,550
		Total Liabilities and	
Total assets	$2,800	net worth	$2,800

future budgeting decisions. In Chapter 3 a budget will be developed for John and Carla that will help them plan for these purchases.

John and Carla can also use their balance sheet to help them with their long-term planning. One of the principles you will learn in this book is to force yourself into a position where your expenditures will cause you to increase your net worth in an automatic way. For example, if you buy a house, the value of the house will generally increase as years go by. Your mortgage payments and other expenses will lead to an increase in your net worth as the value of your house increases. This is only one way of forcing yourself to increase your net worth over time. You will see this increase in your net worth on your balance sheet.

In John and Carla's case, suppose we could look into the future and see their balance sheet 10 years from now. It might look like the balance sheet in Table 1–4. In the table their financial assets have increased to $7,000. Their $3,000 retirement fund is a company-sponsored program in which they both participate. This program is a means of forced saving because their payments are automatically deducted from their paychecks each month.

Their nonfinancial assets show a tremendous increase over the next 10 years. They bought a house that has a current market value of $97,500. They also own two cars that are worth $5,350. In addition, they have accumulated home furnishings over the years, increased their silver collection, and increased their investment in books and clothing. Altogether, they now have a total of $116,150 in nonfinancial assets. Their total assets, financial and nonfinancial, amount to $123,150.

On the liabilities side they have $2,500 in short-term debts. They also have a long-term mortgage on their house in the amount of $80,000, and a long-term personal loan of $1,500. Their total liabilities amount to $84,000.

Subtracting their total liabilities from their total assets yields John and Carla's net worth of $39,150. This is a dramatic increase over their current net worth position. Much of this increase is due to the automatic increases

Table 1–4
John and Carla's balance sheet 10 years
from now

JOHN AND CARLA
Balance Sheet

Assets		*Liabilities and Net Worth*	
Financial assets:		Short-term liabilities:	
Cash in Bank	$ 1,250	Charge accounts	$ 850
Retirement Fund	3,000	Automobile loan	1,650
Mutual Funds	2,750	Total short-term	2,500
Total financial assets	7,000	Long-term liabilities:	
Nonfinancial assets:		House mortgage	$ 80,000
House	$ 97,500	Personal loan	1,500
Automobiles	5,350	Total long-term	81,500
Silver collection	3,000	Total liabilities	84,000
Home furnishings	7,000	Net worth	39,150
Clothing	2,400		
Books	900		
Total Nonfinancial			
assets	116,150	Total liabilities	
Total assets	$123,150	and net worth	$123,150

of the kind discussed: their retirement fund, house, and silver collection have all slowly increased in value over the years. They have obviously planned carefully over the past 10 years and are now reaping the benefits of this planning. In the chapters that follow, you will learn how to benefit from this kind of planning.

Summary

It is the central thesis of this book that everyone can achieve greater wealth and financial security for the future by clearly defining financial goals and developing definite plans to achieve them. Eventual financial independence can be achieved by nearly everyone who is willing to work for it.

Regardless of your future success and income level, you probably will not have enough money to do everything you might like to do. Your wants and needs will probably grow with your income. You will have to carefully define the goals you wish to work toward and make sacrifices to reach them.

Effective financial planning requires the anticipation of future events. As you plan for the future, you must consider the long term as well as your current position in your financial planning cycle. Your goals will be influenced by your life cycle, family situation, and preferred life-style.

You will need to assess your current financial position when defining your future goals. The best way to do this is to construct a personal balance sheet. As you plan for the future, you can then focus on maximizing your net worth when making financial decisions.

2

Career planning and financial success

- Plan where you are going
- Investing in education and training
- The employment outlook
- Career selection criteria
- Career choices for John and Carla
- Some pointers toward a career
- Summary

Careful career planning is an important step along the road to financial independence and the buildup of your net worth. To reach your goals, you need to learn about the earnings potential of various job opportunities. You will also need to learn about the education, training, and personality requirements of each occupation. Finally, you need to know something about the mental capacities required and the cost of pursuing a given career field. Brain surgeons, for example, can earn $200,000 or more per year, but the education and training for such a career is difficult and expensive. This occupation also requires extraordinary mental capacity and physical dexterity. Therefore, most of us will probably eliminate this occupation from our career choices early in life. However, this does not mean that you cannot have a satisfying and profitable career in some other field.

There are virtually thousands of jobs for men and women that will provide excellent incomes, satisfying work, and a financially secure future. You might begin your career search by seeking a position that offers high immediate rewards. However, you must also consider the long term and think of where you may be 5, 10, 20, or even 30 years from now. You should seek out an occupation that you can enjoy for the long run, since you will probably be working for most of your adult life.

This chapter will present some career alternatives for you to consider, and will provide information on career requirements and potential income. In planning your career, you should consider other factors in addition to how you will make your living. Your future financial plans will be intimately related to your career plans. You must begin to think of future savings and investment, future income and expenditures, and planning your lifetime financial goals. Without this type of planning, you risk ending up with nothing to show for a lifetime of work. Career planning is the essential first step in beginning your lifetime financial planning.

Plan where you are going

Your choice of occupation is a key component of your financial planning system. Many conscious and unconscious decisions must be made as you progress up the career ladder. Often career choices are made as the result of careful thought and planning, but it is also true that many people blunder into a career field as a result of simply doing whatever turns up. Since such a large portion of your life will be spent working, it is important that your selection of a career be preceeded by careful thought and planning.

Survey your career choices

A logical first step in the career selection process would be to survey the possible choices available. One of the best sources of information is the *Occupational Outlook Handbook* published by the U.S. Department of Labor's Bureau of Labor Statistics. This publication is available in most public libraries. It provides extensive information about careers and projections of where tomorrow's jobs will be. The *Handbook* summarizes 300 Occupational Briefs, which are grouped into 13 clusters of related jobs. It also provides 35 Industry Briefs grouped into 9 major industrial groupings.

Tables 2–1 and 2–2 provide an overview of the range of material in the *Handbook*. Table 2–1 lists the 13 occupational groupings, along with

**Table 2–1
Occupational groupings**

1. Industrial production and related:
   - Foundry
   - Machining
   - Printing
   - Other industrial production
2. Office:
   - Clerical
   - Computer related
   - Banking
   - Insurance
   - Administrative
3. Service:
   - Cleaning
   - Food service
   - Personal service
   - Private household service
   - Protective and related service (police)
4. Education and related:
   - Teaching
   - Library
5. Sales:
   - Automobile parts
   - Automobile sales and service
   - Gasoline service
   - Insurance agents and brokers
   - Manufacturing sales
   - Models
   - Real estate agents and brokers
   - Route drivers
   - Securities sales
   - Travel agents
   - Wholesale trade sales
6. Construction:
   - Bricklayers, stone masons, marble setters
   - Carpenters
   - Cement masons and terrazzo works
   - Construction Laborers
   - Drywall installers and finishers
   - Electrician
   - Floor-covering installers
   - Glaziers
   - Insulation workers
   - Iron workers
   - Lathers
   - Machinery operators
   - Painters
   - Plasterers
   - Plumbers and pipefitters
   - Roofers
   - Sheetmetal workers
   - Tilesetters
7. Transportation
   - Airline flight attendants
   - Airline reservation, ticket, and passenger agents
   - Air traffic controller
   - Airline mechanics
   - Airplane pilots
   - Drivers (bus, truck, taxicab)
   - Merchant marine officers and sailors
   - Railroad workers
8. Scientific and technical
   - Biochemists
   - Chemists
   - Conservation workers
   - Engineers
   - Environmental scientists
   - Life Scientists
   - Mathematicians
   - Physical scientists
   - Statisticians
   - Technicians
9. Mechanics and repairers
   - Air conditioning, heating, and refrigeration mechanics
   - Automobile mechanics
   - Computer service technicians
   - Diesel mechanics
   - Industrial machinery repairers
   - Instrument repairers
   - Jewelers
   - Locksmiths
   - Maintenance electricians

Table 2–1 *(continued)*

Shoe repairers
Television and radio service
  technicians
Watch repairers
10. Health
Dentists
Dental hygienists
Dental laboratory technicians
Nurses
Nurses aides, orderlies, and
  attendants
Optometrists
Pharmacists
Physical therapists
Physicians
11. Social scientists
Anthropologists
Economists
Geographers
Historians
Political scientists
Psychologists
Sociologists

12. Social service
Counselors
Clergymen
Home economists
Social service aides
Social workers
13. Art, design, and communication
Actors and actresses
Architects
Commercial artists
Dancers
Floral designers
Industrial designers
Interior designers
Interpreters
Musicians
Newspaper reporters
Photographers
Radio and television announcers
Singers
Technical writers

SOURCE   Bureau of Labor Statistics, *Occupational Outlook Handbook* (Washington, D.C.: U.S. Government Printing Office, 1978–79).

some of the subcategories within each group. Table 2–2 lists the nine major industrial groupings used in the *Handbook*. A good deal of detailed information about individual occupations is provided within this broad range of material. Each occupational brief contains six major sections of information: nature of the work; place of employment; training, other qualifications, and advancement; employment outlook; earnings and working conditions; and sources of further information. Overall, each occupational brief provides important information for planning to meet the

Table 2-2
Major industrial groupings

1. Agriculture
2. Mining and petroleum
3. Construction
4. Manufacturing
5. Transportation, communication, and public utilities
6. Wholesale and retail trade
7. Finance, insurance, and real estate
8. Service industries
9. Government

SOURCE   Bureau of Labor Statistics, *Occupational Outlook Handbook* (Washington, D.C.: U.S. Government Printing Office, 1978–79).

education and training for a particular career, for assessing the employment outlook in areas of interest, and for understanding the typical duties and working conditions of each career field.

To provide a concrete example of the value of the information in the *Handbook*, Figure 2–1 presents the occupational brief for advertising workers as it appears in the *Handbook*. A careful reading of the Figure provides an excellent demonstration of the value of the information.

Figure 2–1
Occupational brief for advertising workers

Nature of the work

Almost every business, from a small grocery store to a large bank, does some form of advertising to persuade people to buy its products or use its services. Advertising requires the talents of people in many different kinds of jobs. Creative workers such as writers, artists, and designers develop and produce advertisements, while people with business and sales ability handle the arrangements for broadcasting the advertisements on radio and television, publishing them in newspapers or magazines, mailing them directly, or posting them on billboards. The following occupations are those most commonly associated with advertising.

Advertising managers direct the advertising program of the businesses for which they work. They determine the size of the advertising budget, the type of ad and the media to use, and what advertising agency, if any, to employ. Managers who decide to employ an agency work closely with the advertising specialists from the agency. These managers may supervise the preparation of pamphlets, brochures, or other materials developed to promote the firm's products or services. Advertising managers working for newspapers, radio stations, and other communications media have somewhat different duties. They are responsible for selling advertising time or space, and do work that is similar to the work of sales managers in other businesses.

Account executives are employed by advertising agencies to develop advertising programs for client firms and individuals. They first study the client's sales, public image, and advertising problems, and then create a program that suits the client's needs. In most agencies, artists and copywriters are responsible for developing the actual artwork and advertising copy, but in some small agencies, the account executives have this responsibility.

Research directors and their assistants study the market. They review possible uses for the product or service being sold, compare its advantages or disadvantages with those of competitors, and suggest ways of reaching potential buyers. To develop market information, these workers may survey buying habits and motives of customers, or try out sample ads to find the theme or medium that best sells the product. (See the statement on marketing research workers for more information on this occupation.)

Figure 2–1 *(continued)*

Advertising copywriters develop the headlines and text to be used in the ads. By studying information about the product and its potential customers, they are able to write copy aimed at the particular group of customers the advertiser seeks to attract. They may specialize in writing copy for a certain group of people, such as business managers, teenagers, or sports lovers, or for a class of products, such as cars or computer equipment. Copywriters usually work closely with account executives. In some agencies, they may be supervised by copy chiefs.

Artists and *layout workers* create the visual impact of an ad by selecting photographs, drawing illustrations or figures, and selecting the size or type of print to be used in a magazine or newspaper ad. When television commercials are planned, they usually sketch sample scenes for the client to consider. (See the statements on commercial artists and photographers for more information on this type of work.)

Media directors (or *space buyers* and *time buyers*) negotiate contracts for advertising space or air time. They determine the day and time when a television commercial will reach the largest group of prospective buyers at the lowest cost. To select the best medium for the advertiser, media directors must know the costs of using various media and the characteristics of the audience reached by specific publications or television stations.

Production managers and their assistants arrange to have the ad printed for publication, filmed for television, or recorded for radio. They must know which firms or freelance workers will be able to produce the best ad for the least cost.

Places of employment

In 1976, about 180,000 people worked in jobs requiring considerable knowledge of advertising. Those employed in advertising agencies were heavily concentrated in New York City, Los Angeles, and Chicago.

Many others worked in the advertising departments of manufacturing firms, retail stores, banks, power companies, professional and trade associations, and many other organizations. Some people had advertising jobs with television or radio stations, newspapers, and magazines. Still other people in the advertising field worked for printers, art studios, letter shops, package design firms, and similar businesses.

Training, other qualifications, and advancement

Most employers prefer college graduates. Some employers seek persons with degrees in advertising with heavy emphasis on marketing, business, and journalism; others prefer graduates with a liberal arts background (social science, literature, art, and other disciplines); some employers place little emphasis on the type of degree.

Figure 2-1 *(continued)*

No particular educational background is equated with success in advertising. In fact, relevant work experience may be more important than educational background. Experience selling ads for school publications or radio stations, or on a summer job with a marketing research service, can be a distinct advantage to the jobseeker.

Some organizations recruit outstanding college graduates for training programs that cover all aspects of advertising work. In other firms, employees immediately enter a specialty and do not gain such all-round experience. Some beginners start as research or production assistants or as space or time buyers. A few begin as junior copywriters.

Many advertising jobs require imagination, creativity and a flair for language. These traits are especially important to artists, layout workers, and account executives. All creative effort must be directed toward the sales function. People interested in becoming advertising managers, account executives, media buyers, and production managers must be able to get along well with people and be able to sell their ideas. Research directors and their assistants must have an understanding of human behavior. All advertising workers must be able to accept criticism of their work and be able to function as part of a team.

Opportunities for advancement in this field generally are excellent for creative, talented, and hard-working people. For example, copywriters and account executives may advance to more responsible work in their specialties, or to managerial jobs, if they demonstrate ability in dealing with clients. Some especially capable workers may become partners in an existing agency, or they may establish their own agency.

Employment outlook

Employment of advertising workers is expected to increase faster than the average for all occupations through the mid-1980's. Most openings, however, will result from the need to replace workers who die, retire, or leave the occupation for other reasons.

The growing number of consumer and industrial goods and increasing competition in many product and service markets will cause advertising expenditures to rise. Such expenditures also may be spurred by the growing tendency toward self service in retail marketing. An additional factor is the growing need of small businesses for professional advertising services. Employment in advertising occupations is strongly affected by general business conditions because firms expand or contract their advertising budgets according to their financial success. Although opportunities should be favorable for highly qualified applicants, particularly in retail advertising, others seeking entry jobs will face keen competition because the glamorous nature of the field attracts many people.

Local television, radio, and newspapers are expected to increase their share

Figure 2-1 *(continued)*

of total advertising expenditures while direct mail, magazines, and national newspapers continue to lose ground. The few very large agencies that account for nearly all national advertising are expected to maintain fast growth because of their expanding international business.

Earnings and working conditions

Based on limited information, annual salaries for beginning advertising workers with bachelor's degrees ranged from $8,000 to $10,000 in 1976. Higher starting salaries generally were paid by the largest firms or advertising agencies to outstanding applicants, particularly those with advertising experience.

Salaries of experienced advertising workers varied by size and type of firm as well as by type of job. According to a survey of advertising agencies taken in 1975, average annual salaries of workers in selected occupations were as follows: Chief executive officer, $45,300; account supervisor, $28,400; account executive, $18,500; executive art director, $24,400; art director, $17,100; senior layout artist, $12,900; junior layout artist, $9,300; copy chief, $22,300; senior copywriter, $16,600; junior copywriter, $10,500; media director, $16,800; space or time buyer, $9,400; research director, $24,000; research analyst, $13,500; production manager, $14,400. Several other surveys yielded these results: In 1976, the top advertising officers in large retail firms averaged over $32,000 a year; in 1975, the median salary of advertising directors in large banks ranged from $16,000 to $17,000 a year; in 1975, the average salary of advertising managers in a wide variety of companies ranged from $18,000 to $34,000 a year, depending upon the annual sales volume of the firm. Salaries of advertising managers generally are higher in consumer than industrial product firms, and many receive incentive compensation.

People in advertising work under great pressure, and do not have the job security enjoyed by workers in many other occupations. These workers are expected to produce quality ads in as short a time as possible. Sometimes they must work long or irregular hours to meet deadlines or make last-minute changes. Account executives, copywriters, and layout workers may become frustrated by a client's inability to define the type of ad he or she wants for a product.

Advertising can be a satisfying career for persons who enjoy variety, excitement, creative challenges, and competition. Unlike workers in many other occupations, advertising workers experience the satisfaction of having their work in print, on television, or on radio, even though they remain unknown to the public at large.

Sources of additional information

Information on advertising agencies and the careers they offer is available from:

Figure 2-1 *(concluded)*

American Association of Advertising Agencies, 200 Park Ave. New York, N.Y. 10017.

For additional information on careers and a list of colleges that provide training in advertising, contact:

American Advertising Federation, 1225 Connecticut Ave. NW, Washington, D.C. 20036.

SOURCE   Bureau of Labor Statistics, *Occupational Outlook Handbook* (Washington, D.C.: U.S. Government Printing Office, 1978–79).

Plan for education

The wide variety of career choices available and the broad range of educational requirements clearly illustrate the need for careful advance planning. In particular, the broad range of skills required to qualify for various entry-level positions highlights the need to plan your education well in advance. One major consideration in undertaking this kind of advance planning is an analysis of your investment in education and training. In short, you must answer the question "Does education really pay?"

Investing in education and training

In recent years the employment demand for college graduates has changed significantly. The major effect of this change is that a college degree is no longer an automatic passport to an attractive and high-salaried career. College students and graduates have had to be a bit more selective in choosing major fields of study as a means of preparation for employment. However, the old maxim "to get a good job, get a good education" still holds. The available data indicate that education is still a good investment. Students who select their education programs with care will reap handsome dividends.

Education as an investment

Education alone will not provide adequate preparation to enter many fields. However, it is still true that there is a strong and positive relationship between income and educational attainment. Figure 2–2 and Table 2–3 provide some insights into the nature of this relationship. Figure 2–2 shows average family income according to the number of years of school completed by the head of the household. These data provide a dramatic illustration of how income increases with education. Households headed by a high-school graduate earn a family income 54 percent higher than that earned by elementary-school graduates. Moving on to the college level, families headed by college graduates have an average income

Figure 2–2
Total money income of families in 1977

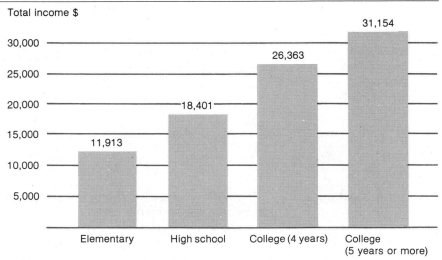

SOURCE   Bureau of the Census, *Current Population Reports,* U.S. Department of Commerce, March 1979.

Table 2–3
Income and occupation of year-round, full-time workers in the experienced civilian labor force
(1977 income data)

	Median income	
Occupational group	Male workers	Female workers
Professional and technical workers	$17,520	$12,009
Managers and administrators, except farm	18,704	10,203
Sales workers	15,798	7,098
Clerical workers	13,915	8,598
Craft workers	14,666	8,981
Operatives, including transport workers	12,599	7,362
Private household workers	n.a.	2,975
Laborers, except farm	10,826	7,433
Service workers, except private household	10,354	6,431
Farmers and farm managers	2,829	n.a.
Farm laborers and supervisors	7,002	n.a.

n.a. = not available.
SOURCE   Bureau of the Census, *Current Population Reports,* U.S. Department of Commerce, March 1979.

level 43 percent higher than families headed by high-school graduates. For households whose heads have completed five or more years of college, average income levels are 18 percent higher than families headed by a college graduate.

The data indicate that the largest percentage increase in family income comes from obtaining a high-school education. There is also a substantial percentage increase in income for college graduates over high-school graduates. This increase is the largest dollar amount ($7,962). The differential between incomes of high-school graduates and college graduates has been narrowing in recent years, but it is still a substantial amount. The percentage increase in income if you have more than a four-year college education is smallest of any of the other differentials, but the dollar amount of increase is quite large. The average income of households headed by someone with five or more years of college is $4,791 higher than households headed by a college graduate.

Table 2–3 shows income data for male and female workers in various occupational groups. Two important conclusions may be drawn from the data. First, those occupations requiring more education pay higher average salaries than occupations requiring little or no education. Among male workers, for example, the highest income goes to managers and administrators. For females, professional and technical workers earn the highest income.

Women still underpaid

The second conclusion is that the median income for female workers is substantially below that for male workers in the same industry groups. This state of affairs holds true for all occupational groups. Two logical explanations come to mind that would account for this observed differential. The first is the obvious and unpleasant conclusion that women have been and are discriminated against in determining salary levels in relation to salaries of their male counterparts. Much progress has been made in overcoming such discrimination in recent years, but we still have a long way to go. The second reason for the differential is that, on the average, many women have not been in the work force as long as their male counterparts. Equal participation in the work force is still a relatively recent phenomenon. Since workers with more seniority in a career generally earn higher salaries, the seniority differential may well account for a large part of the salary differential.

Education isn't everything

Thus far, the data presented strongly support a positive answer to the question of whether or not education really pays. However, it is important to keep in mind that a high-school diploma and even a college degree by itself are often not sufficient to prepare you for entry into a given career field. Neither is it true that the mere possession of a degree will guarantee you any kind of a job at all. You still need experience and training. Once again, careful advance planning is critical. Of utmost importance is for you to assess the career prospects in fields of interest. Then you should match the educational and training efforts required to the career field you intend to enter. To begin this planning process, you must carefully study current market conditions. The Bureau of Labor Statistics' *Occupational Outlook Handbook* is an excellent source of such information.

You should also consider that although college graduates do earn substantially more on the average than high-school graduates, there are a number of highly paid occupations that do not require a college degree. For example, skilled construction workers, electricians, and plumbers normally are not college graduates. However, they often earn more than many people in occupations that require a degree. High-school graduates who complete additional education or training programs, such as apprenticeship programs required by many craft unions, often earn very satisfactory incomes.

A final caveat is in order with regard to investment in higher education. As more and more Americans elect to attend college, an increasing number of college graduates find themselves underemployed and working in areas that traditionally have not required a college degree. In a number of areas, entry-level requirements have risen to meet the supply of college graduates. A college degree is now required to apply for a job that a few years ago required only a high-school diploma. This trend argues strongly in favor of investment in higher education in order to develop yourself into a more competitive "product" in the work force.

Data gathered by the Bureau of Labor Statistics indicate that the number of college graduates in the 1980s is expected to exceed the number of jobs available that normally require a college degree. This trend is also expected to exist for advanced degree holders. Colleges and universities, the primary employers of advanced degree holders, are faced with declining enrollments and budget cutbacks. They are expected to employ fewer advanced degree holders in the future. The Bureau of Labor Statistics warns that except for persons whose degrees are in areas demanded by business and industry, advanced degree holders may have to take jobs that formerly went to graduates with only a bachelor's degree.

Nonmonetary rewards of education

In addition to considering the financial pros and cons of investment in higher education, you should also consider the nonfinancial rewards of a college degree. A college education often provides a great deal of personal satisfaction in terms of meeting your need for achievement and broadening your intellectual horizons. There are also a variety of social advantages to a college education. In fact, a college degree may often serve as a social prerequisite to a number of job opportunities. For example, a particular job may not actually require a bachelor's degree for technical competence. However, if everyone employed in the organization has a degree, a new entrant to the organization will almost certainly be required to have a degree. Finally, a degree often provides you with an added degree of flexibility in the work force. It is fairly easy to move from a management position in a bank to the finance department of a large corporation, for example. But it is relatively difficult to change from a job as an electrician to a job as a plumber. Many jobs requiring a degree are much more flexible in this respect than jobs requiring a high-school education and some additional technical training.

Financing your education

Some people say they cannot afford a college education. If you have the ability and determination, this should not stop you. Private funds, government grants, merit scholarships, help from universities, and loans are available. Without listing all sources of aid for college tuition, room, and board, just remember that help is available. The cost of four years education at a private college or university ranges from $20,000 to $30,000. At a state university the cost might range from $12,000 to $16,000 for four years. If you seek the sources of money for a college education, you really will find them.

In addition, you can work during the summer and part-time during the school year. Your work will pay off financially and improve your life.

The employment outlook

Given that you accept the general proposition that education is a worth-while investment, the selection of an appropriate major field of study requires careful advance planning. This planning requires you to consider the employment outlook for the 1980s.

Figures 2–3 through 2–7 and Table 2–4 provide a variety of interesting statistical data relative to the employment outlook for the upcoming decade. The civilian labor force is expected to grow to nearly 105 million persons by 1985. A good deal of this rather dramatic increase in the size of the labor force is due to an increase in the number of women entering the labor market. Figure 2–4 shows that the percentage of men in the labor force has declined rather steadily since 1950, while the percentage of women in the labor force has increased by a substantial margin. This decreasing trend for men and increasing trend for women is expected to continue through 1985.

Table 2–4 shows the industry concentration of working people in the United States. The data are classified according to the customary division of the economy into nine industry categories organized under two broad industry groups: service-producing industries (five industry categories) and goods-producing industries (four industry categories). Service indus-

Figure 2–3
Civilian labor force growth projections

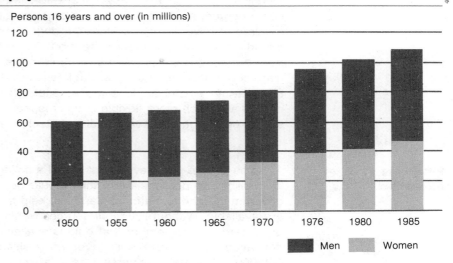

Persons 16 years and over (in millions)

SOURCE   Bureau of Labor Statistics, *Occupational Outlook Handbook* (Washington, D.C.: U.S. Government Printing Office, 1978–79).

Figure 2–4
Women in the labor force

Percent of persons 16 and over in the civilian labor force

SOURCE   Bureau of Labor Statistics, *Occupational Outlook Handbook* (Washington, D.C.: U.S. Government Printing Office, 1978–79).

Figure 2–5
Percent change in employment growth by industry, 1976–1985

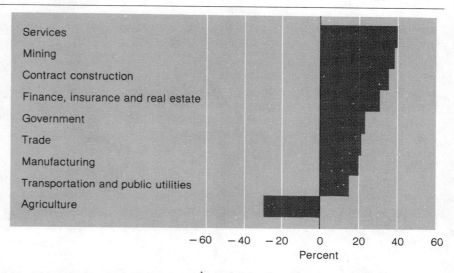

SOURCE Bureau of Labor Statistics, *Occupational Outlook Handbook* (Washington, D.C.: U.S. Government Printing Office, 1978–79).

Figure 2–6
Employment in major occupational groups

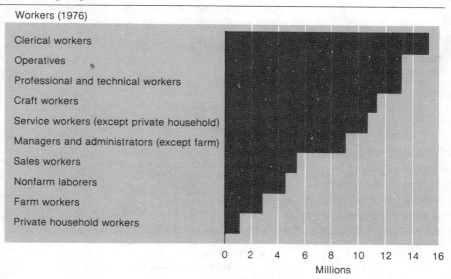

SOURCE Bureau of Labor Statistics, *Occupational Outlook Handbook* (Washington, D.C.: U.S. Government Printing Office, 1978–79).

Figure 2–7
Percent change in employment,
1976–1985

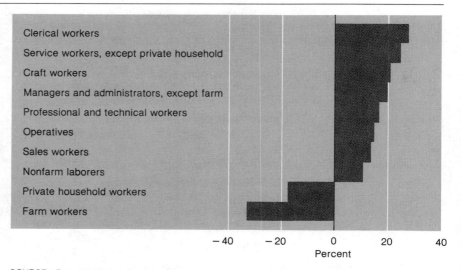

SOURCE   Bureau of Labor Statistics, *Occupational Outlook Handbook* (Washington, D.C.: U.S. Government Printing Office, 1978–79).

tries employ approximately two thirds of all U.S. workers. Goods-producing industries, which include manufacturing, contract construction, agriculture, and mining and petroleum, employ the other one third. The four largest employers are manufacturing (23 percent), wholesale and retail trade (22 percent), government (18 percent), and services (18 per-

Table 2–4
Where people work

Industries	Percent of workforce
Service:	
Wholesale and retail trade	22%
Government	18
Services	18
Finance, insurance, and real estate	5
Transportation and public utilities	5
Total service industries	68%
Goods-producing:	
Manufacturing	23%
Contract construction	4
Agriculture	4
Mining and petroleum	1
Total goods-producing industries	32%

SOURCE   Bureau of Labor Statistics, *Occupational Outlook Handbook* (Washington, D.C.: U.S. Government Printing Office, 1978–79).

cent). The smallest employer is mining and petroleum, which employs only 1 percent of the work force.

Projections for employment growth in these industries through 1985 are illustrated in Figure 2–5. The largest area of expected growth is in the service group. The projected growth rate of this group is nearly double that for service-producing industries as a whole. Major growth sectors in this group include health care services, maintenance and repair, advertising, and commercial cleaning. Rapid growth is also anticipated in business services, including accounting, data processing, and maintenance.

In the other service-producing industries, wholesale and retail trade are expected to continue the substantial growth of past years. Employment growth in government is expected to continue its slowdown and be less than the growth of service-producing industries overall. Growth of state and local government is expected to be particularly slow. This reflects the recent phenomenon of taxpayer unwillingness to finance ever increasing government services. The "Proposition 13 mentality," referring to the tax-limitation bill voted into effect in California, has severely limited the taxing power of state and local governments. This attitude appears to be spreading throughout the United States and may be expected to continue into the foreseeable future.

The remaining group within the service-producing industries is the area of transportation and public utilities. This group is expected to exhibit the slowest growth of all the service-producing industries.

The goods-producing industries are expected to exhibit rapid growth on a percentage basis, but the actual number of new job openings will be small. Since mining and petroleum employ only 1 percent of the total work force, even a very high percentage increase in employment will result in a rather limited number of new job opportunities. The Bureau of Labor Statistics forecasts a 39 percent increase in jobs over the 1976 to 1985 period. This results in an overall numerical increase of only 300,000 jobs spread over nine years.

Contract construction is expected to exhibit strong growth, with employment expected to increase at almost as high a rate as mining and petroleum. Since contract construction employs approximately four times as many people as mining and petroleum, job growth will be significant.

Employment growth in manufacturing should be strong but mainly concentrated in the manufacture of durable goods. Growth will be rather slow in the nondurable goods area. Growth in the final goods-producing category, agriculture, will actually be negative. Agriculture employment, which has been declining for many years, is expected to continue its decline.

Career selection criteria

Working within the context of a general employment outlook, there are a number of additional key decision variables that must be considered in planning your career. The single most important factor is to match your abilities and interests to a career pattern that allows you to use these abilities and interests. As the old saying goes, be yourself. You should pick a career pattern that allows for personal fulfillment. Regardless of the employment outlook, no long-term personal or financial gain can be expected from trying to fit a round peg into a square hole. If, for example, you have a strong dislike for working with numbers, the fact that accountants are in strong demand will not make accounting a satisfying career for you. The increasing number of mid-life career changes provides strong support for the position that entering a career that is inherently satisfying should be a prime criterion for a career selection. If it is not possible to match your personality to a career that also provides high income, then serious consideration must be given to sacrificing some income in order to engage in a preferred line of work. Your personal financial planning system will then have to be adjusted to conform with this choice.

It is worth emphasizing that the choice described above is a very real choice. It is a choice that confronts nearly everyone at one time or another. The central point of this chapter is that career choice implies a choice of income level. Once your career objectives and income level are established, sound personal financial planning requires that you develop a system that allows you to live within your anticipated income level. There is no suggestion here that career choices should be dictated solely by financial considerations. However, the broader your knowledge of career opportunities, the greater the likelihood of finding the ideal match of a high-income career that also provides personally satisfying work.

An additional important career consideration is the issue of comparing the cost of obtaining the necessary education to enter a given career field with the expected income in that field. The cost of education is an important career consideration. For example, future employment opportunities in teaching are expected to grow very slowly, both at the high-school and college levels. Some fields, such as college-level teaching in the humanities, have particularly gloomy employment prospects. As a result of this, it is very difficult to justify the expense of obtaining a Ph.D. degree in the humanities as preparation for entering the teaching profession. On the other hand, the very high cost of obtaining an M.D. degree is quite easily justified by the explosive demand expected in the health care field and the traditionally high-income levels of doctors. Although these strictly financial considerations should not be the sole deciding factors in assessing educational options, they clearly cannot be ignored. They should be major considerations in any rational assessment of your educational options.

A final important variable to consider is the risk-reward pattern of a given career path. For example, you might want to consider starting your own business. Although entrepreneurs face great risks in beginning a new business, the potential rewards of owning your own business are exceptional. It is very difficult to make a direct comparison of the very risky rewards of entrepreneurship to the relatively secure rewards of a job with a large corporation. However, you should at least make some subjective comparison. The library of the nearest branch office of the U.S. Small Business Administration would provide a good starting point to learn more about the possibilities of beginning a new business.

One interesting way to conceptualize the many career choices available is through an "opportunity map" of career choices. Such a map is shown in Figure 2–8. The map begins with high-school graduation and illustrates the wide variety of career choices available. Each circle represents a choice point where a decision must be made about which road to travel. Needless to say, the size of the paper limits the number of roads that are shown. The total number of choices is much larger than those illustrated. You should also bear in mind that many adults are now choosing to combine advanced education with work by attending school on a part-time basis. Thus the work road may often include some additional education along with your job.

**Figure 2–8
Career opportunity map**

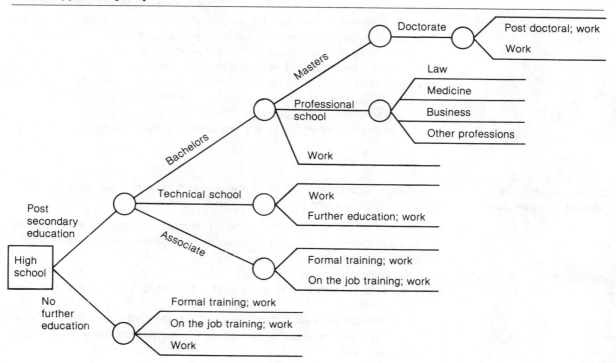

Despite the limitations of Figure 2–8, it is a useful conceptual device. The map graphically illustrates the need to broaden your horizons in evaluating career choices. It is extremely important to search as widely as possible in looking for a career field. The road maps of Figure 2–8 provide a good starting point for this process.

In the final section of this chapter, we will travel down the career roads selected by John and Carla, the couple introduced in Chapter 1. They recently married, and are looking forward to their new careers after graduation from college.

Career choices for John and Carla

After surveying available career options, John and Carla have decided to combine a low-risk job for John with a high-risk job for Carla. With his new bachelor's degree in business administration, John has decided to begin his career in commercial banking, specifically in corporate lending. John feels that this type of a job will provide him with broad industry exposure and allow him to gain valuable business experience. John also intends to work on his M.B.A. in night school in order to increase his business skills.

Carla has elected to take the entrepreneur's risk. She is going to open an antique business. Although both Carla and John realize that opening a new business is a very risky venture, they believe that the potential long-term rewards of a successful business outweigh the risk of failure. In addition, since they are both young and do not have children to support, they are in the best possible position to assume such a risk. John's stable employment will provide the necessary income to allow them to accept the risk of receiving no income from the new business.

John and Carla's career choices will obviously have major implications for their future financial planning. These implications will be dealt with in detail in the next chapter, which is concerned with personal budgeting.

Some pointers toward a career

It seems appropriate to offer a few pointers towards your goal of selecting a profitable career:

1. Obtain the right amount of education and training so that you are flexible. Don't let a lack of money stand in your way. An investment in education pays.
2. Choose an occupation you will enjoy.
3. Select an occupation in an industry and area of the economy that are growing.
4. Think about the salary level you will be at in 10, 20, and 30 years. It is important to know what you can expect—you do want to avoid dead-end jobs.

5. Make certain you will continue to learn and train.
6. Consider the possibility of going into business for yourself.
7. Continue to be flexible in your career plans. If you get off the track, change direction and start moving ahead.

Summary

In planning your career, you should strive to select a field that will provide you with satisfying work and an adequate level of income. Your career choice will have a major impact on your progress toward building up your net worth and achieving financial independence. The important first step in this process is to carefully survey your career choices. A great deal of information is available in the publications of the Department of Labor. These publications are readily available in most libraries.

As a general rule, education is still a good investment. Data gathered by the Census Bureau indicate that incomes generally increase as education increases. The average income of a college graduate is over 40 percent higher than that of a high-school graduate. In addition to the financial payoff of a college degree, there are also a number of nonmonetary rewards that must be considered. Chief of these rewards is the added degree of job flexibility that higher education often brings.

When planning your career, it is important for you to carefully survey the employment outlook for the industries in which you are interested. Service industries are expected to grow rapidly in the coming decade, with wholesale and retail trade in the lead.

PART **2**

Financial planning and control

3

Budgeting as a financial planning technique

- What is a budget?
- Budgeting as a financial planning technique
- Establishing financial objectives
- Setting financial goals and objectives
- John and Carla's personal financial objectives
- General guidelines for budgeting
- Principles of personal budgeting
- John and Carla's budget
- Impact of financial planning on net worth
- Controlling expenditures
- Impact of inflation on financial planning
- Summary

Achieving financial independence through the acquisition of financial and real assets does not come about by accident. It requires thought and planning and control. It requires that individuals and families establish acceptable and realistic goals and objectives on the basis of their available income in the present and their expected future income. How you spend your income is just as important as how much income you receive.

The budgeting process is an excellent way to develop your financial plan. It requires a knowledge of what a budget is and the kind of budget systems suitable for a particular individual or family. The budgeting process begins with an agreement on your financial objectives. Then budgeting guidelines are established. Once the budget objectives and system have been set up, a way to control expenditures must be devised. The control process will allow you to consciously improve your net worth. It will also protect you against the effects of inflation so prevalent in our society.

If you want to improve your net worth, you will spend your income on assets that will increase in value. Expenditures for housing and some household furnishings tend to increase your net worth and act as a hedge against inflation. Expenditures for food, gasoline, heating, water, electricity, and similar consumption expenditures tend to reduce your net worth.

These subjects will be discussed in this chapter. In addition, the chapter will show how a budget for financial planning and control can help you achieve your objectives.

What is a budget?

In essence, a budget is simply a personal plan, set down in terms of dollars and cents, as to how you will spend your current and future income. An effective budget will allow you to answer the question "How shall I spend my income?" You will avoid focusing on the more common question many people face: "How can I pay for what I already owe?" Budgeting is a simple approach to the common and recurring problem of the allocation of scarce resources; that is, money is scarce for almost all of us. With the exception of a few fortunate people who are born to great wealth or who achieve it suddenly, hardly anyone has enough money.

Even people with great wealth can be spendthrifts and overspend their resources. Many people believe that if they could just earn 10 percent more, they would finally balance their budget. However, experience has shown that desires generally expand with income. That additional 10 percent doesn't quite balance the budget either. Families unable to balance a $20,000 per year budget do not seem to be any more successful at balancing a $25,000 per year budget.

The purpose of a budget is to maximize benefits received from your expenditures and maximize your net worth. This requires a conscious effort to balance current expenditures with your long-term financial goals.

Budgeting as a financial planning technique

A budget and control system is a key requirement for long-range financial planning. Every family or individual expecting to achieve eventual financial security must develop such a system. The system may be an informal one kept in your head, or it may be a very elaborate system complete with formal written financial objectives, income forecasts, expense projections, and estimates of future net worth. Lessons learned from the business affairs of well-run corporations indicate that a formal written system will probably be the most successful one for you. As is true for most important business undertakings, a formal written budget will lead to the development of a formal financial plan for the future.

It is also important not to overplan. You should not devise a plan that is so elaborate and time-consuming that you lose interest in following the plan. A simple but effective system requiring a small amount of attention each week or month is the most effective. The most important point is that there be a plan in existence. The single most important way to build financial security and to maximize net worth is to develop a plan that enables you to reach your financial goals over time in a more or less automatic way. By *automatic*, what is meant is that by following your plan, short-term, intermediate-term, and long-term goals and objectives will be achieved as a by-product of following the guidelines set down in the financial plan. This assumes, of course, that the real world as it unfolds for you is consistent with the assumptions you made in your financial plan.

Controlling credit

One of the most important aspects of budgeting and control is the control of credit. Chapter 7 provides consumer credit guidelines. Personal credit should be carefully controlled. The budget will help you do this. As a general rule, the use of credit should be minimized, and all charge purchases should be carefully planned in advance as part of the budget. Only planned expenditures should be charged. Payment of these charges should be planned in advance as part of the budget.

Before moving on to general budget principles, one final word of advice: learn and use the four little words "I can't afford it." You should never be embarrassed to admit that you cannot afford to buy everything that strikes your fancy. The effective use of "I can't afford it" may save hundreds or even thousands of dollars per year. A good personal budget and financial plan will aid you in taking the emotion out of spending decisions and substituting reason and logic in its place.

Establishing financial objectives

The most important step in beginning the budgeting process is to establish a set of personal financial objectives. You should keep in mind the idea that the goal of budgeting is to enable you to meet your financial objectives, not just to engage in a bookkeeping exercise. You must establish both long-run and short-run financial objectives, and then develop budget guidelines to meet those objectives.

In contrast to many individuals' financial planning, most successful businesses have well-defined goals and objectives. One very successful management planning system that has stood the test of time is a system known as Management by Objectives (MBO). This system was originally suggested by Peter Drucker,[1] a famous management consultant and professor of management. As a consultant to many large multinational corporations, including General Motors, Drucker has had a major influence on corporate planning systems as well as on personal planning for many people who have studied his work.

Much of the usefulness of the MBO approach to planning stems from its inherent clarity of concept and relative ease of implementation. An MBO system may be quite complex and require a great deal of administrative skill to implement, or it may be designed and implemented in a very streamlined fashion. For personal budgeting, a streamlined version of the MBO technique can be used.

The critical elements for a personal finance MBO system may be identified as follows:

1. Define personal financial goals and objectives in terms of results to be accomplished within a given period of time.
2. Rank objectives in order or priority.
3. Develop realistic action plans and strategies to determine how and when each objective will be achieved.
4. Implement action plans.
5. Monitor progress toward goals, with specific intermediate objectives specified.
6. Evaluate results, taking corrective action where necessary.
7. Revise and replace objectives as goals are achieved or changed.

The heart of the MBO system lies in developing clearly specified objectives that are understandable and achievable. A well-defined financial objective must clearly specify the action to be taken, the results to be achieved, and the time period in which these results are to be attained. Objectives should be developed only for important areas of concern. Attempting to accomplish too many objectives at once will result in dilution of effort and frustration. As a general rule, no more than five objectives should be pursued at one time. Furthermore, objectives should be challenging, but attainable. Goals should neither be too high nor too low. Useful objectives should challenge and stretch individuals, but must be attainable with appropriate effort.

---

[1] Professor Drucker, an extremely prolific writer, published a comprehensive text entitled *Management: Tasks, Principles and Functions* (San Francisco: Harper & Row, 1974).

As an overall guide, well-written objectives should begin with an action verb that specifies a clear result. A good objective would be "to purchase a home of our own three years from now by saving $2,000 per year toward the required downpayment."

Setting financial goals and objectives

If you are to profit from the MBO approach, then it would seem useful to carefully define one overriding goal to guide all subsequent financial planning. In other words, one major principle can serve as the foundation upon which subsequent objectives may be built. Building a firm financial planning foundation is just as important to personal financial success as building a firm concrete foundation is to the longevity of a modern skyscraper. Without a firm foundation both structures will collapse sooner or later. Careful thought must be given to the formulation of the financial foundation.

As noted in Chapter 1, many consumers concentrate on the acquisition of assets rather than the maximization of value. In many cases the assets acquired are assets that gradually decline in value, such as automobiles or clothing, rather than assets that increase in value, such as real estate, stocks, or bonds. Of course, many expenditures on so-called wasting assets (assets that decline in value) are necessary because such expenses are unavoidable. But expenditures on these unavoidable items can be carefully planned and controlled.

Instead of maximizing assets, you should strive instead toward maximizing net worth. You will then be striving for the same goal as a well-run business: maximization of value. In attempting to maximize net worth, you will be forced to consider both sides of your personal balance sheet. You will focus not only on ownership of assets but also on liabilities and the choices made in financing these assets.

Effective planning and control are the two key elements in any successful financial planning system. While a well-written set of financial objectives will provide an excellent planning system, these objectives will never be reached without an effective means of control. You must constantly compare your progress with the goals toward which you are striving. You can then take action to either get back on track or revise your objectives whenever necessary.

In personal financial management, controlling expenditures to achieve your objectives is always difficult and sometimes impossible. As an abstract planning exercise, personal financial management always assumes clear goals and rational decisions. But when the new car models or new spring fashions arrive, goals sometimes become cloudy. Purely financial decisions often become complicated by emotion. And human frailty being what it is, giving in to temptation is often one of life's great joys! However, for personal financial success, you should plan well and assume that clear-headed, calculated decisions will always be made. Then an occasional "falling off the wagon" should not totally disrupt the system, and it should be fairly easy to get back on track.

As an example of these principles, John and Carla's budgeting and control system will be carefully constructed to aid them in achieving both their financial and personal objectives. You can modify John and Carla's modest life-style and conservative financial planning system to meet your individual needs and objectives. The planning structure used for John and Carla will thus fit a wide variety of individual needs and tastes.

John and Carla's personal financial objectives

Using their combined balance sheet from Table 3–1 as a basis for planning, John and Carla decided on three major financial objectives to guide their personal budgeting and control system for the years immediately following graduation. Since John and Carla married right after graduation, they decided that their first objective would have to be to purchase a car. Both John and Carla intended to seek employment upon graduation. But they decided that they could not afford to own a car for each of them to drive back and forth to work. They therefore decided to buy one car for one of them to use to commute to work; the other spouse would take public transportation. Since they had very little cash in the bank, they intended to finance the car with a bank loan that they would pay off over the next two years. Thus their first objective is to purchase a used car for less than $2,500, using a bank loan to be paid off over a two-year period.

Table 3–1
John and Carla's budget objectives

Objective in order of priority	Annual cost	Monthly cost	Time horizon
1. Purchase a used car for less than $2,500 using a bank loan that will be paid off over a two-year period	$1,200	$100	2 years
2. Save $125 per month for the next five years toward the downpayment on a home in the $50,000 to $60,000 price range	$1,500	$125	5 years
3. Save 5 percent of combined income every year for the foreseeable future to provide for a long-term savings and investment program	5 percent of income	5 percent of income	indefinite
4. Save $1,200 over the next three years to pay for a luxury ski vacation in Aspen	$ 400	35	3 years
5. Save $300 per year over the next five years as the downpayment on a new sports car	$ 300	$ 25	5 years

John and Carla's second major financial objective is to begin saving toward the downpayment on a home of their own. They expect to be able to save $1,500 per year for the next five years. Their savings objective is expressed as follows: to save $125 per month for the next five years toward the downpayment on a home or condominium in the $50,000 to $60,000 price range.

A final financial objective relates to John and Carla's plans for a general savings and investment program. As part of their overall financial planning system, John and Carla expect to provide some savings for unexpected contingencies and for eventual investment. This objective is as follows: to save 5 percent of our combined income every year for the forseeable future in order to provide for a rainy day and a long-term investment program.

Given these three objectives as the cornerstones of their financial planning system, John and Carla are now well armed to confront their future financial decisions. These objectives will serve as the foundation upon which they will build their future financial plans and budgets.

John and Carla have one fairly short-run objective, that of purchasing a used car and paying off a bank loan on the car in the next two years. They also have one very long-run objective, to save 5 percent of their combined income every year in order to provide an emergency fund and fund a long-term investment program. Finally, they have one objective that may be classified as of intermediate term. This objective is their goal of saving $125 per month toward the downpayment on a new home five years from now.

In thinking through your objectives and providing budget guidelines, it is easiest to first develop long-run objectives. You can then establish short-run objectives consistent with the long-run objectives. Two additional objectives will be established for John and Carla, and added to the three objectives already specified.

In reviewing their first three objectives, John and Carla could see that these objectives related primarily to the necessities of life. In order to provide some flexibility in their budget and allow them to "stop and smell the roses," they decided to develop two additional objectives related to luxury items. They decided that each of them would specify one of the additional objectives, subject to the consideration that they must both agree that the objective was reasonable.

Carla chose an objective with a three-year time horizon. She had always wanted to "ski the West" and therefore specified a one-week ski vacation in Aspen, Colorado, as her luxury objective. In order to achieve this objective, John and Carla agreed that they would have to save a total of $1,200 over the next three years. They would therefore have to save $400 per year toward this objective.

John specified an objective with a five-year time horizon. Since he was a car buff, John decided to specify as an objective that he and

Carla would save $300 per year over the next five years as a downpayment on their first sports car. John and Carla agreed that it was simply not possible for them to save enough cash to pay in full for a new car five years from now. So they decided to accumulate a substantial downpayment and to finance the balance.

John and Carla's next step is to rank their complete set of budget objectives in order of priority and translate the objectives into annual and monthly financial goals. The result of this process is shown in Table 3–1.

The cost of achieving these five major objectives must be integrated into John and Carla's overall annual and monthly budgets. As an aid in developing an annual or operating budget, some general guidelines must be specified to provide John and Carla with budgeting benchmarks.

General guidelines for budgeting

In developing general guidelines for budgeting, some guidance is available from various government studies that show the expenditure patterns for typical families. The largest percentage of the consumer dollar is allocated to services, including such items as housing, household operations, and transportation. The next largest fraction of the consumer dollar is allocated to nondurable goods such as food and beverages, gasoline and oil, and clothing and shoes. The smallest percentage is allocated to such durable goods items as furniture, household equipment, and automobiles.

A look at other budgets

Table 3–2 illustrates typical annual budgets for four-person families at three different levels of income. Table 3–3 translates this information into percentage figures. Table 3–4 shows how the cost of living varies according to the geographic area in which you live.

Tables 3–2 through 3–4 provide a number of interesting insights into how American families spend their money. Lower- and intermediate-budget families spend the largest proportion of their income on the monthly grocery bill. Lower-budget families spend 31.0 percent and intermediate-level families spend 24.8 percent of their budget on the food category. Housing absorbed 19.3 percent of the lower-income and 22.5 percent of the intermediate-income groups' expenditures. As you move up the economic scale, the grocery bill begins to absorb a smaller percentage of the consumption budget, although a larger dollar amount is spent. The food category accounts for 21.2 percent of the total family budget of higher-budget families.

The largest single expense category for higher budget families is housing. Food is ranked second and personal income taxes third. For these families the percentage of the budget allocated to personal income taxes

Table 3-2
Annual budgets for a family of four at three
income levels urban United States
(fall 1978)

	Lower budget ($11,546)	Intermediate budget ($18,622)	Higher budget ($27,420)
Total budget			
Family Consumption:			
Food	$3,574	$ 4,609	$ 5,806
Transportation	856	1,572	2,043
Housing	2,233	4,182	6,345
Clothing	847	1,209	1,768
Personal care	301	403	570
Medical care	1,065	1,070	1,116
Other family consumption	515	956	1,578
Total family consumption*	$9,391	$14,000	$19,225
Social security and disability payments	719	1,073	1,091
Personal income taxes	935	2,738	5,739
Other costs	$ 502	$ 810	$ 1,365

* Totals may not add due to rounding.
SOURCE Derived from Bureau of Labor Statistics, U.S. Department of Labor, *BLS News,* (USDL: 79-305), April 29, 1979.

Table 3-3
Consumption expenditures as a percent-
age of income urban United States
(fall 1978)

	Lower Budget ($11,546)	Intermediate budget ($18,622)	Higher budget ($27,420)
Family consumption:			
Food	31.0%	24.8%	21.2%
Transportation	7.4	8.4	7.5
Housing	19.3	22.5	23.1
Clothing	7.3	6.5	6.4
Personal care	2.6	2.2	2.1
Medical care	9.2	5.7	4.1
Other family consumption	4.5	5.1	5.8
Total family consumption	81.3%	75.2%	70.2%
Social security and disability payments	6.3	5.8	4.0
Personal income taxes	8.1	14.7	20.9
Other costs	4.4	4.3	5.0
Total consumption expenditures	100.0%	100.0%	100.0%

Totals may not add due to rounding.
SOURCE Derived from Bureau of Labor Statistics, U.S. Department of Labor, *BLS News,* (USDL: 79-305), April 29, 1979.

Table 3–4
Cost of living comparisons in urban areas

	Average living expenses (autumn 1978)		
Metropolitan area	Lower budget	Intermediate budget	Higher budget
Anchorage	$19,030	$26,329	$38,406
Honolulu	14,870	23,099	35,602
San Francisco	12,710	19,427	28,719
Boston	12,501	22,117	33,596
Washington, D.C.	12,398	20,105	29,584
New York	12,063	21,587	34,252
Philadelphia	11,903	19,416	28,291
Chicago	11,829	18,794	27,169
Metropolitan average	11,685	18,982	28,186
Detroit	11,596	19,145	28,172
Denver	11,475	18,565	27,089
Minneapolis-St. Paul	11,421	19,389	28,629
St. Louis	11,150	17,897	25,847
Nonmetropolitan average	10,925	17,016	24,000
Houston	10,906	17,114	24,787
Dallas	10,699	16,714	24,492
Atlanta	10,495	16,897	24,666

SOURCE: Bureau of Labor Statistics, U.S. Department of Labor, *BLS News,* (USDL: 79–305), April 29, 1979.

rises substantially. It is well above that for intermediate and lower budgets. For higher budgets 20.9 percent is allocated to personal income taxes, whereas the percentages for intermediate and lower budgets are 14.7 and 8.1 percent, respectively. This increasing percentage of consumption expenditures allocated to personal income taxes is due to the progressive nature of the personal income tax structure in the United States. Under this progressive structure the percentage tax levied on your income increases as your income increases.

Where you live has an effect on budget

The comparative figures provided in Table 3–4 show the wide variation in the cost of living according to the geographic area in which you live. The average consumption expenditures for an intermediate budget in a U.S. metropolitan area are $18,982. In a nonmetropolitan area, U.S. average consumption expenditures drop to $17,016, a decrease of 10.4 percent. The lowest budget cost for the 15 cities listed is $16,714 in Dallas, Texas, and the highest cost is $26,329 in Anchorage, Alaska. The cost of an intermediate-level budget in Anchorage is higher than the cost of a higher budget in St. Louis, Houston, Dallas, or Atlanta. The data in Table 3–4 clearly support the position that your standard of living is dependent on location as well as income. In general, urban living costs are lower than average in southern and midwestern cities and higher than average in northeastern cities. The four most expensive cities in the United States are Anchorage, Honolulu, San Francisco, and Boston.

Principles of personal budgeting

Several general budgeting principles should be followed in developing your personal financial plan. The most important consideration in drawing up a family budget is to recognize that budgeting is a joint effort. It must be approached with equal concern by and for all members of the family. Family agreement on important goals and objectives must be obtained if the family is to take the job seriously and respect preplanned budget and financial decisions. Developing the necessary discipline to follow your preplanned decisions is the single most important requirement for successful planning. An unplanned expenditure is the most common cause of a derailed financial plan.

A budget is flexible

A second important principle is that a personal budget should provide only rough, flexible guidelines. You should avoid the temptation to over-control your spending. The most often cited reason for abandoning the budget effort is that the family soon loses interest in attempting to follow it.

To begin the process, you need to know where you are spending your current income. The easiest way to do this is to keep a record of your expenditures for a month or two. Then consolidate the records into a summary of your consumption pattern similar to the family consumption patterns illustrated in Tables 3–2 and 3–3. In addition, checkbook records should be examined for the past few months and past expenditures recorded. You may be able to estimate general expenditure patterns from memory, which will save a lot of work.

Budgeting must recognize priorities

A third general budgeting principle to be followed is that the financial plan must recognize priorities responsive to your family's objectives, lifestyle, and personal tastes. It is a totally useless strategy to attempt to force yourself to follow some preconceived notion of correct budgeting standards. General guidelines and the experiences of other families are helpful in setting up an initial budget. But you must tailor the budget to your own personal tastes and habits. Be certain to include all items of importance in the budget, and make sure that some allocation, however large or small, is made to each of these items. Every budget should have a miscellaneous account to allow some room for unplanned and unaccountable expenditures. Every member of the family should be allocated some amount of money in this category. This money may be spent without regard to the overall budget. This account may be considered "safety-valve" money. It will provide a release from the danger of an overly controlled budget.

Records and control are essential

The fourth and final guideline for successful budgeting is to keep a record of actual expenditures after the budget is established. These actual expenditures should then be compared to planned expenditures and revisions made, when necessary. The revisions may be made either to the budget guidelines or to your spending habits. Select the type of revision that is most appropriate. This process is known as "controlling to plan." It is a crucial step in the execution of any fiancial plan.

John and Carla's budget

In setting up their budget, John and Carla began with a forecast of their monthly cash income after all taxes and other deductions are taken into account. On John's job his take-home pay is $980 per month. In addition to his annual salary, John anticipates receiving a year-end Christmas bonus of $500. His total take-home pay for the year will therefore amount to $11,760.

Profits from Carla's new business are expected to be fairly modest in the first year. A majority of the money earned by the business will have to be reinvested to help finance future growth. Carla plans to draw only $4,450 from her business for personal use during the upcoming year. No personal money at all will be drawn from the business during the first three months of operation. After April Carla expects to be able to increase the amount drawn by a small amount each month as the business prospers. This type of a cash flow pattern is not at all unusual for a new business. Early profits must often be reinvested to cover the initial expenses associated with a new venture.

The results of John and Carla's projections show that they will have a total income (after tax and other deductions) of $16,710 next year. The timing of income is shown in Table 3–5. Their income will grow from a monthly level of $980 in January to $1,780 in December (not counting John's bonus, which is a one-time income item). The growth

Table 3–5
Forecasted income worksheet
(after taxes)

	Jan.	Feb.	Mar.	Apr.	May	Jun.	Jul.	Aug.	Sep.	Oct.	Nov.	Dec.	Total
John's salary	980	980	980	980	980	980	980	980	980	980	980	980	11,760
John's bonus	—	—	—	—	—	—	—	—	—	—	—	500	500
Carla's profits . . .	—	—	—	250	250	300	400	500	600	650	700	800	4,450
Total income	980	980	980	1230	1230	1280	1380	1480	1580	1630	1680	2280	16,710

in monthly income is, of course, the result of Carla's growing business venture. Some allowance for the risk involved in a new venture should be made in designing the overall budget for next year.

John and Carla's expected expenses are summarized in Table 3–6. The expense forecast shown has three major sections. The first section indicates the monthly and annual cost of meeting the five major financial objectives specified earlier. These costs amount to a total of $4,275 for the year. The second section of the budget lists all expected day-to-day expenses, such as rent, groceries, utilities, and so forth. These items total $11,720 for the year. The third and final section of the budget provides an allocation for three extra items: a few local ski trips during the winter months, a summer vacation at the beach, and some new furniture for the apartment. These three items total $1,435 for the year.

The projections in John and Carla's expense forecast indicate three major problem areas. The most obvious problem is that their anticipated expenses for the year exceed their expected income. They expect to earn $16,710 in income and incur $17,430 in expenses—obviously something's gotta give! Since their projections indicate that they will be $720 short next year, they must take some action to either increase their income or decrease their expenses.

The second problem facing John and Carla is that, in addition to the problem of an overall shortage, they have a cash flow problem. Several months show abnormally high levels of expenses that cannot be paid out of only one month's income. For example, in January John's bill for tuition and books for his part-time M.B.A. program will fall due, and Carla's business will provide no income at all. As a result of these two factors, total expenses in January will exceed income by $740. This is obviously a serious problem. In fact, this problem of expenses exceeding income is expected to occur in all months except May, August, October, November, and December.

The final budgeting problem is the uncertainty surrounding the income expected from Carla's business and John's bonus. Neither of these expected cash receipts is as certain as John's salary, although the bonus is more secure than the income expected from the business. This uncertainty is just as important as the other two problems. Some means of dealing with this problem will have to be devised when the final budget is structured.

In working out solutions to the three budgeting problems, John and Carla put first priority on eliminating the expected shortfall of $720 for the year. They did not see any way to increase their overall level of income since they felt that work, part-time school, and running a new business would absorb all of their time. Because of these time constraints, a part-time job for one of them was eliminated as a possibility, and no other source of increased income seemed possible. So they decided

Table 3–6
Forecasted expense worksheet ($ signs omitted)

	Jan.	Feb.	Mar.	Apr.	May	Jun.	Jul.	Aug.	Sep.	Oct.	Nov.	Dec.	Total	Monthly average
Cost to meet five objectives:														
1. Car loan	100	100	100	100	100	100	100	100	100	100	100	100	1,200	100
2. House downpayment	125	125	125	125	125	125	125	125	125	125	125	125	1,500	125
3. Aspen trip	35	35	35	35	35	35	35	35	35	35	35	35	420	35
4. Long-term savings	45	45	45	60	60	65	70	75	80	85	90	135	855	71
5. Sports car	25	25	25	25	25	25	25	25	25	25	25	25	300	25
Subtotal	330	330	330	345	345	350	355	360	365	370	375	420	4,275	356
Monthly expenses:														
1. Rent	250	250	250	250	250	250	250	250	250	250	250	250	3,000	250
2. Groceries	200	200	200	200	200	200	200	200	200	200	200	200	2,400	200
3. Utilities	60	60	55	55	50	45	60	60	50	50	55	60	660	55
4. Food away from home	35	35	35	35	35	35	35	35	35	35	35	35	420	35
5. Recreation	60	60	60	60	60	60	60	60	60	60	60	60	720	60
6. Clothing	100	100	100	100	100	100	100	100	100	100	100	100	1,200	100
7. Medical care	35	35	35	35	35	35	35	35	35	35	35	35	420	35
8. Tuition and books	450	—	—	—	—	200	—	—	450	—	—	—	1,100	92
9. Life insurance	30	30	30	30	30	30	30	30	30	30	30	30	360	30
10. Charitable contributions	20	20	20	20	20	20	20	20	20	20	20	20	240	20
11. Transportation	60	60	60	60	60	60	60	60	60	60	60	60	720	60
12. Miscellaneous	40	40	40	40	40	40	40	40	40	40	40	40	480	40
Subtotal	1340	890	885	885	880	1075	890	890	1330	880	885	890	11,720	977
Extras:														
1. Local ski trips	50	50	25	—	—	—	—	—	—	—	50	85	260	22
2. Beach vacation	—	—	—	—	—	—	500	—	—	—	—	—	500	42
3. Furniture	—	—	—	75	—	—	—	100	—	200	—	300	675	56
Subtotal	50	50	25	75	—	—	500	100	—	200	50	385	1,435	120
Total monthly expenses	1720	1270	1240	1305	1225	1425	1745	1350	1695	1450	1310	1695	17,430	1453

that they would have to solve this problem by decreasing their level of expenses.

In looking around for ways to reduce the total amount of annual expenses, John and Carla felt that it was not possible to reduce or eliminate any items listed in the category monthly expenses in the second section of the expense worksheet. They therefore focused their attention on the five long-term objectives they hoped to achieve over the next few years. They also took a good look at the extras category in the budget. Their first decision was not to cancel their vacation and skiing plans. The final item in the extras category, the planned purchase of furniture, was also retained. John and Carla intended to use the next few years to build up their stock of furniture for the eventual move to a home of their own. Having retained the extras, they moved their attention to the five objectives in the top section of the expense worksheet.

In this category John and Carla considered the car loan, the savings program for a house downpayment, and the long-term savings and investment program to be their most important objectives. As a result, they decided that these items could not be reduced. The remaining long-term objectives—the trip to Aspen and the savings program for a sports car— were thus selected through a process of elimination as the best ways to reduce expenses. Although unwilling to abandon these objectives altogether, the couple agreed that it would be possible to postpone them for one year. They decided that these items could be worked back into the budget after Carla's business had the opportunity to become established and to contribute more income. Removing the costs of the Aspen trip and sports car from the budget resulted in an annual savings of $720, an amount exactly equal to the expected shortfall. The annual budget is now balanced.

Now that John and Carla have solved the problem of getting their annual budget to balance, they must come to grips with their cash flow and uncertainty problems. Even though the budget does balance on an annual basis, there are still some months ahead when expected expenses will exceed expected income. In other months expected income will exceed expected expenses. Thus on the average everything will even out by the end of the year. Since the budget will now show a cash deficit in some months and a cash surplus in others, some means will have to be devised to smooth out this cash flow problem.

Fortunately, John and Carla have a small nest egg that they built up immediately after their graduation and wedding. Their combined balance sheet reported in Table 1–3 of Chapter 1 showed a savings account of $250. Since then, they have added a fairly substantial amount of cash received as graduation and wedding gifts. They used part of this cash to buy some furniture for their first apartment, and put the remainder in their savings account. The net result is that they now have a balance of $1,350 in their savings account. As will be seen shortly, this account can be used as a buffer to help solve the cash flow problem.

John and Carla decided on two courses of action which, taken together, would effectively solve the problem. First, it was obvious that they would have to either borrow money from a bank or use their savings to cover cash deficits in the months for which deficits were expected. However, it was equally obvious that the cumulative deficit could become quite large as the budget was now planned. They therefore decided as a first step to move postponable cash expenses into later months when surpluses were expected. The most easily postponable items were, of course, their two long-run savings goals. In effect, these objectives represent obligations to themselves that are postponable at their option. Their first decision, then, was that surplus months would be used to fund their savings objectives, and deficits would only be incurred for expenses that could not possibly be postponed.

To cover these deficits, John and Carla both agreed that they would strongly prefer to avoid the use of debt. They therefore decided that they would borrow from their current savings account in deficit months and pay back this loan to themselves in surplus months. They also decided to open a second savings account into which deposits for their house downpayment and long-term savings would be made. They consider this their long-term account and treat their present account as a rainy day account.

The result of this line of reasoning can be seen in John and Carla's summary budget worksheet in Table 3–7. In making up this worksheet, the monthly expenses from the center section of their original expense forecast were grouped together and treated as fixed, nonpostponable expenses. The car loan was listed next, since this item was also not a postponable item. To these two items was added the cost of monthly extras to arrive at a total figure for each month's fixed expenses. This total was then compared to expected income for the month to determine whether a surplus or deficit would be incurred. In deficit months they planned to borrow from savings and then repay this loan in surplus months. As can be seen from the exhibit, deficits were expected in January, February, and March, followed by three surplus months in April, May, and June. The last deficit month would occur in July, and by August, all borrowings from their savings would be repaid and they could begin depositing money in their long-term savings account.

John and Carla will have to borrow $510 in January, mainly due to the cost of John's tuition and books for his part-time M.B.A. program. They will have to borrow another $60 in February, and an additional $30 in March. By the end of March, their total borrowings will be $600. During April, May, and June, they will be able to repay a total of $525 from the surpluses in those months, but they will have to borrow an

Table 3–7
John and Carla's summary budget worksheet

	Jan.	Feb.	Mar.	Apr.	May	Jun.	Jul.	Aug.	Sep.	Oct.	Nov.	Dec.	Annual total
Monthly expenses	1340	890	885	885	880	1075	890	890	1330	880	885	890	11,720
Car loan	100	100	100	100	100	100	100	100	100	100	100	100	1,200
Extras	50	50	25	75	—	—	500	100	—	200	50	385	1,435
Total fixed expenses	1490	1040	1010	1060	980	1175	1490	1090	1430	1180	1035	1375	14,355
Total income	980	980	980	1230	1230	1280	1380	1480	1580	1630	1680	2280	16,710
Surplus	—	—	—	170	250	105	—	390	150	450	645	905	3,065
Deficit	510	60	30	—	—	—	110	—	—	—	—	—	710
Borrow from savings	510	60	30	—	—	—	110	—	—	—	—	—	710
Repay to savings	—	—	—	170	250	105	—	185	—	—	—	—	710
House downpayment	—	—	—	—	—	—	—	205	150	450	645	50	1,500
Long-term savings	—	—	—	—	—	—	—	—	—	—	—	855	855

Annual totals

Total fixed expenses	$14,355
House downpayment	1,500
Long-term savings	855
Annual total	$16,710

John's salary	$11,760
John's bonus	500
Carla's business	4,450
Annual total:	$16,710

additional $110 in July. Thus, by the end of July they will still owe them-selves $185. In August they will have a surplus of $390, part of which will be used to pay off the $180 owed to savings. The remaining $205 of the August surplus will be deposited into their long-term savings ac-count. After August the surpluses for the rest of the year will be deposited into the long-term account.

By the end of the year, all accounts balance out! The total of $710 borrowed from savings will be repaid, and the savings account will not be depleted. The savings goals for the house downpayment and the long-term savings account will be achieved. And most important, expendi-tures for the year will equal income. We should note that achieving these objectives will call for a good deal of control. John and Carla have allo-cated themselves a reasonable amount of money for normal living ex-penses as well as some extras. Even though they have arranged to fund their long-term savings goals from surplus months, they must not forget that these savings goals are just as important as meeting their monthly expense requirements. In fact, from the point of view of their long-term financial security, these goals are even more important. Carla and John must recall that their possession of a modest savings account has saved them from the inconvenience and expense of having to borrow money somewhere else. Their savings account has turned what could have been a serious problem into a minor inconvenience.

The problem of uncertainty

The only remaining problem facing John and Carla is that of uncertainty. As mentioned earlier, a new business is a somewhat risky venture. They cannot be certain of Carla's income. Yet they do not feel that Carla should abandon her plans to be an independent business person just because it is risky. In reality, there is almost nothing they can do about the risk involved. But they must accept the fact that their plans may have to be changed in the future if adequate income is not generated from the business. They have decided to give the business one full year to get established. Carla will then seek employment elsewhere if their plans do not work out. Beyond this acceptance of the necessary risks and their contingency planning, there is very little else to be done.

The last step in John and Carla's budget process is to set up a monthly budget control worksheet. This worksheet will be used to keep track of their actual monthly expenditures and the relationship of actual expendi-tures to planned expenditures. This simple document is illustrated in Table 3–8. As can be seen from the exhibit, the only requirement for using this document is for John and Carla to fill in their actual expenditures as the month progresses. Note that they don't have to record every penny. The budget control worksheet is designed as an overall control method. It may be filled in either at the end of the month or during the

Table 3-8
Monthly budget control worksheet

Month of: _____

Expenditure category	Planned expenditure	Actual expenditure	Reason for difference
Fixed monthly expenses:			
Rent.........................	_____	_____	_____
Groceries	_____	_____	_____
Utilities	_____	_____	_____
Food away from home	_____	_____	_____
Recreation	_____	_____	_____
Clothing	_____	_____	_____
Medical care	_____	_____	_____
Tuition and books	_____	_____	_____
Life insurance	_____	_____	_____
Charitable contributions	_____	_____	_____
Transportation	_____	_____	_____
Miscellaneous .....:.........	_____	_____	_____
Car loan	_____	_____	_____
Extras:			
Local ski trips	_____	_____	_____
Beach vacation	_____	_____	_____
Furniture	_____	_____	_____
Long-term objectives:			
House downpayment...........	_____	_____	_____
Long-term savings	_____	_____	_____
Total expenditures	_____	_____	_____
Total income.................	_____	_____	_____
Savings borrowing.............	_____	_____	_____
Savings repayment	_____	_____	_____
Total	_____	_____	_____

month as expenditures occur. Use of this worksheet will enable John and Carla to keep track of major categories of expenditures.

Two important comments should be made about the budget control worksheet:

1. Columns are provided to record actual expenditures as well as planned expenditures and a reason for any difference between the two figures. This comparison is essential if the budget is to be used in an intelligent manner to revise spending plans as necessary and to control expenditures in accordance with the previously established plan. In the final analysis, the budget's most important use is as a planning and control device. Use of comparisons and explanations for differences as a basis for revising plans or changing spending patterns provides the key control step.

2. How much time is required to use the budget control worksheet? Of all the documents presented here, only the budget control worksheet needs to be updated on a monthly basis. The other planning documents may be updated either quarterly or annually. Once the quarterly or annual planning effort is made, use of the system requires about one hour's work per month to keep the budget control worksheet up to date. This

hour is certainly time well spent, and it may pay large dividends in return for the effort expended. As noted at the beginning of this chapter, effective financial planning is the single most important way to build financial security and maximize net worth. The system outlined in this chapter for John and Carla provides a simple but effective system for personal financial planning.

Impact of financial planning on net worth

The final important consideration in reviewing John and Carla's financial planning system is to evaluate the impact that their budget plans will have on their net worth. Table 3–9 shows John and Carla's current

Table 3–9
John and Carla's balance sheets

JOHN AND CARLA
Current Balance Sheet

Assets		Liabilities and Net Worth	
Financial assets:		Liabilities:	
Cash in checking	$ 200	Charge accounts	$ 150
Cash in savings	1,350	Car loan	2,400
Total financial assets	1,550	Total liabilities	2,550
Nonfinancial assets:			
Automobile	2,400	Net worth	3,100
Clothing	500		
Silver collection	800		
Furniture	400		
Total nonfinancial assets	4,100		
Total assets	$5,650	Total liabilities and net worth	$5,650

JOHN AND CARLA
Forecasted Balance Sheet
(one year from now)

Assets		Liabilities and Net Worth	
Financial assets:		Liabilities:	
Cash in checking	$ 200	Charge accounts	$ 150
		Car loan	1,400
Cash in short-term savings	1,400	Total liabilities	1,550
Cash in long-term savings	2,355		
Total financial assets	3,955		
Nonfinancial assets:			
Automobile	1,800	Net worth	6,705
Clothing	800		
Silver collection	900		
Furniture	800		
Total nonfinancial assets	4,300		
Total assets	$8,255	Total liabilities and net worth	$8,255

balance sheet and their forecasted balance sheet one year from now. By comparing the two sheets, we can see the impact of their budget on their net worth.

John and Carla's current net worth is $3,100. Their net worth is expected to increase substantially during the upcoming year, to $6,955. There are a number of reasons for this dramatic increase. Their savings account balances are expected to increase a lot. This is due to the deposits they expect to make late in the year to meet their house downpayment and long-term savings objectives. They also will see a slight increase in their short-term savings account as a result of the interest earned on this account. The net result is that the total amount of cash in savings will be $3,955 at the end of next year.

Nonfinancial assets will increase by only $200 during the year. This is the result of several factors. The value of their car decreased, as is normally true for most cars. The decline in the value of the car was offset by an increase in the value of their silver collection and by the additional purchase of clothing and furniture. The value of John and Carla's clothing and furniture is not expected to increase by as much as they expect to spend on these two items during the year. These items represent wasting assets that depreciate in value over time. Their automobile is also a wasting asset that depreciates over time. Clothing and furniture depreciate much more rapidly over time than cars because the second-hand markets for these items are not nearly as strong and active as the used-car market.

The decrease in liabilities that can be seen on the right-hand side of the balance sheet also contributes to the expected increase in John and Carla's net worth. Their charge account balance is expected to remain the same. As they pay off older charges, they create some new liabilities by charging a few new items. The lack of a decrease in their overall charge account indebtedness is no cause for alarm, however, since the total amount they owe is quite small in relation to their income.

The large decrease in liabilities is due solely to the drop in the amount they owe on their car loan. They will have paid this loan down to $1,400 by the end of the year. Of the $1,200 they paid on the loan during the year, $1,000 will reduce the principal and $200 will be for interest. This causes net worth to increase by $1,000 because the change in the principal value will show up in the difference between total assets and total liabilities.

This effort on the part of John and Carla to increase their net worth requires control. Let's see what they had to do to control expenditures.

Controlling expenditures

Once the budget system is established, efforts must begin to control expenditures according to the plan laid out in the budget. It is obviously important to pay some attention to the categories of consumer expenditures listed in Table 3–3 that absorb the largest percentage of the consumer dollar. Some brief comments will therefore by made about the categories of food, housing, transportation, and personal income taxes.

Keep food costs low

Since food costs absorb the largest percentage of the consumer dollar for most families, this item provides a logical starting point. A few general budgeting guidelines may be useful here. As a general rule, you should attempt to minimize expenses in this category, subject to the consideration that you need a nutritious and appetizing diet. To do this, the most important rule to follow is to avoid buying impulse items at the grocery store. This means that you should not buy unnecessary items on impulse as a result of an attractive display or a sudden craving.

Stick to your budget

The easiest way to avoid impulse buying is to draw up a complete shopping list before going to the store. Then buy only the items on that list. Consumer behavior studies show that significant savings in food expenditures can be achieved just by this simple device. Studies also show that it is generally more costly to shop in a grocery store when you are hungry than when you are not hungry! Therefore, it is a good idea to follow the rule of never going grocery shopping when hungry. These two simple ideas will pay large dividends in the form of a reduced food budget.

A final hint for reducing food expenditures is to seek out and use discount coupons for grocery shopping. The grocery industry is the most active business in the country in coupon marketing and price reduction specials. By following newspaper advertisements for weekly specials and using available coupons, you may be able to reduce your monthly grocery budget by as much as 10 percent. The suggestions offered here for reducing grocery expenditures may seem rather simple. Yet they can achieve substantial savings in the largest item in most consumer budgets.

Housing as an inflation hedge

The two next largest items of consumer expenditures, housing and personal taxes, are dealt with at length in two future chapters. Housing expenditures and home financing are discussed in Chapter 6. Personal taxes are given extensive treatment in Chapter 5. A third important area of consumer expenditure, insurance, will be described in Chapters 8, 9, and 10. The last remaining major area of consumer expenditure, transportation, will be discussed in this chapter.

Cars will not increase net worth

It is a fact of life that most consumers own cars. The great American romance with the automobile is far from dead! Car transportation is a major expense for most families, and car purchase decisions are often influenced as much by emotion as by reason. Tables 3–10 through 3–12 provide some interesting insights into the cost of the American car.

Table 3–10 shows the national average costs to own and operate a 1979 Chevrolet, eight-cylinder, Malibu Classic Sedan. Variable costs of operation include gas and oil, maintenance, and tires. These costs average out to 5.86 cents for each mile driven. Fixed costs, which assume that the car is financed by a standard auto loan, include finance charges, insurance, license fee, registration fee, taxes, and depreciation. These total $1,811 per year, or almost $5 per day. Annual costs, assuming the car is driven 15,000 miles per year, total $2,690. For most families, this is a great deal of money, and it would certainly be appropriate to ask how to reduce this expense area.

Table 3–10
Car ownership expenses: the national average*

Variable costs:	Average per mile
Gasoline (unleaded) and oil	4.11 cents
Maintenance	1.10 cents
Tires	.65 cents
	5.86 cents

Fixed costs:	Annually
Comprehensive insurance ($100 ded.)	$ 74.00
$250 ded. collision insurance	168.00
Property damage and liability (100/300/25M)	241.00
License, registration, taxes	90.00
Depreciation	942.00
Finance charge	296.00
	$1,811.00
	(or $4.96 per day)

Add-ons:
Air conditioning: .2 cent per mile and 20 cents per day.
Depreciation for excess mileage: $41 per thousand miles over 15,000 annually. (The $942 is an average based on trade-in at the end of four years or 60,000 miles, whichever comes first. This is the period during which the car is expected to deliver the greatest economy.)

Average annual driving costs:
Based on the figures above, the motorist driving 15,000 miles a year would pay:

15,000 miles at 5.86 cents	$ 879.00
365 days at $4.96	1,811.00
	$2,690.00
	(or 17.9 cents per mile)

* The figures above represent national average costs computed by Runzheimer and Company for a 1979 Chevrolet, eight-cylinder (305 cu. in.) Malibu Classic four-door sedan with standard accessories, automatic transmission, power steering, power disc brakes, and radio, driven up to 15,000 miles per year. All insurance is based on a pleasure-use category where the vehicle is driven less than 10 miles to or from work and there is no youthful operator.

SOURCE *Your Driving Costs, 1979 Edition,* American Automobile Association, 1979.

Table 3-11
Cost variation by type of car

Type of car	Rural area		Metropolitan area	
	Cost per mile	Total per year*	Cost per mile	Total per year*
Subcompact .... (four-cylinder)	12.8¢	$1,923	16.4¢	$2,462
Compact .... (six-cylinder)	14.6¢	$2,190	18.7¢	$2,808
Intermediate .... (eight-cylinder)	16.6¢	$2,486	21.1¢	$3,170
Standard .... (eight-cylinder)	17.7¢	$2,659	22.6¢	$3,391

* Assumes car driven 15,000 miles per year.
SOURCE *Your Driving Costs, 1979 Edition,* American Automobile Association, 1979.

One obvious way to reduce the level of expense is through the careful selection of the type of car you drive. Table 3–11 provides some useful information in this area. As can be seen from the exhibit, the cost of a smaller car is much lower than that of a larger car.

In a metropolitan area the difference between annual operating costs of a four-cylinder, subcompact car and an eight-cylinder, standard size car is over $900 per year. Smaller cars save money not only by using less gas. They also are less expensive to purchase, require less costly tires, and generally cost less to insure. These cars are not called economy

Table 3-12
Worksheet to compute annual driving costs

	Annual total
Annual fixed costs	
Depreciation	_____
Insurance	_____
Taxes	_____
License and registration	_____
Finance charges	_____
Total annual fixed costs	_____
Annual variable costs:	
Gas and oil	_____
Maintenance	_____
Tires	_____
Total annual variable costs	_____
Other costs:	
Repairs	_____
Miscellaneous	_____
Total other costs	_____
Grand total annual costs	

Grand total annual costs ÷ Miles driven = Cost per mile

_____ ÷ _____ = _____

SOURCE *Your Driving Costs, 1979 Edition,* American Automobile Association, 1979.

cars without reason. Given the nation's continuing oil shortage, it is also no exaggeration to say that what's good for economical consumers is also good for the country.

In any event, whether you drive a large or small car, it is important to know what it costs to own and operate that car. Table 3–12 provides a worksheet that can be used to calculate these costs. Knowing the actual costs is the first important step in cost control.

Another obvious and highly effective option—public transportation—will substantially reduce your transportation costs. Most metropolitan areas have public transportation systems that can reduce expenses and also contribute to the solution of the nation's energy crisis. In rural areas and outer suburbs it may not be possible to use public transportation. But where it is available, it makes good fiscal sense to do so.

Other control devices

Two simple methods are widely used as an effective aid to expenditure control. One is the so-called envelope system whereby your paycheck is divided among a number of envelopes. The evelopes are labeled to correspond to each major expenditure category in the budget. The amount of money allocated to each category is then deposited in the appropriate envelope. When the envelope is empty, no further expenditures can be made in that category. The envelopes also provide a very convenient method of keeping track of how much money is spent in each category. In an emergency, of course, money may be lent from one envelope to another and paid back the next month. Budget allocations to envelopes that consistently operate at a surplus or deficit may be adjusted as appropriate.

Another system involves the use of multiple checkbooks. Instead of envelopes, a number of checkbooks may be set up, all of which draw on the same account. This account is effectively partitioned into a number of subaccounts. Each subaccount corresponds to a major budget expenditure category. When one account is empty, no further expenditures may be made from that account. Since all checkbooks are based on the same bank account, the actual account will not have a zero balance unless all subaccounts have zero balances. Similarly, one subaccount may be overdrawn as long as there is enough money in one or more other subaccounts to cover the overdrawn subaccount. Once again, this system provides a convenient record of expenditures.

Impact of inflation on financial planning

In recent years one of the most important factors in financial planning has been the impact of inflation. This has been especially true in such important areas as housing, savings and investment programs, tax planning, and planning for eventual retirement and estate transfer. The double-digit inflation of recent years has so eroded purchasing power that any realistic plan must take notice of this erosion.

The impact of inflation on planning to meet housing needs, on savings and investments programs, on insurance programs, and on retirement planning will be treated in detail as these topics are examined in later chapters of this book. For the present we need to emphasize two major points.

Inflation increases taxes

The first major point is the substantial impact that continued inflation has on your tax position. As noted earlier, when your income expands, the percentage you pay in federal and state income taxes also expands. As inflation causes salaries to continually rise at rather rapid rates, individuals find themselves pushed into higher and higher tax brackets. The net effect is that individuals—even middle-class individuals—increasingly need to consider various investment strategies to reduce their tax liability.

Defending yourself against inflation

The second major point is that all financial planning efforts must explicitly recognize the impact of inflation on your long-term plans. For example, in John and Carla's budget, their savings and investment objective was expressed in terms of a percentage of their income rather than in terms of a fixed dollar amount. Therefore, as the years go by and their income grows along with inflation, the amount of money allocated to meet their long-term savings and investment goals will grow too. Additionally, in planning their investment strategy, they should devise a responsible investment program that will try to provide a rate of return commensurate with the rate of inflation. In this way they can preserve the purchasing power of their invested dollars.

Table 3–13 provides some interesting insights into the impact of inflation over long periods of time. The table shows John and Carla's current budget and what their budget might look like 20 years from now, assuming an average inflation rate of 7 percent. If their income keeps pace with inflation, their annual income will increase from its current level of $16,710 to $65,663. This is the income they would have to earn just to maintain their current purchasing power. If they are to have a higher level of real income, their income would have to be above $64,663. Their annual expenses would also inflate dramatically; for example, rent would increase from its current level of $3,000 per year to more than $11,000 per year. Their grocery bill would increase from its current annual level of $2,400 to slightly above $9,000. Tuition and books for John as a part-time student would run in excess of $4,000, and their annual transportation costs would increase to nearly $3,000. They would also be saving somewhere in the neighborhood of $9,000 per year and making annual car payments of nearly $5,000. Expectations of 7 percent inflation over the long run do not appear too unreasonable. The figures in Table 3–13 provide a rather startling illustration of the impact of inflation on our long-term financial plans.

Table 3–13
John and Carla's budget with 7 percent inflation

	Current ($16,710)	20 years later ($64,663)
Annual income		
Annual Expenses:		
Rent.........................	$ 3,000	$11,609
Groceries	2,400	9,287
Utilities	660	2,554
Food away from home	420	1,625
Recreation	720	2,786
Clothing	1,200	4,644
Medical care	420	1,625
Tuition and books	1,100	4,257
Life insurance	360	1,393
Charitable contributions...........	240	929
Transportation	720	2,786
Miscellaneous	480	1,857
Subtotal....................	11,720	45,353
Car loan	1,200	4,644
House and long-term savings......	2,355	9,113
Extras	1,435	5,553
Grand total	$16,710	$64,663

The moral of this inflation story is that you must plan carefully for the future and work diligently toward achieving your objectives. Subsequent chapters of this book will attempt to provide information and guidance to help you steer a clear path around the many bumps and potholes along your road to financial security.

Summary

A budget and control system is a key requirement for long-range financial planning to provide you with financial security and independence. The budget helps you allocate your income to reach your financial goals and objectives. In the process you first establish your short-term and long-term objectives. Then you estimate your income and decide on how best to spend your income to reach these goals. While you can compare your goals with other family budgets, you can also retain flexibility on the basis of your life-style and habits. Make certain you follow the budgeting principles: budgeting is a joint effort; it should be inclusive and flexible; and it must meet your life-style. You need to keep records and controls. Your budget might be formal or informal, but it should never be too detailed.

Sound budgeting and planning should lead to an increase in your net worth. But you must control your expenditures to meet your budget goals. This requires restraint. In the budget process you must give recognition to inflation. Some of your expenditures will not only allow you to save and preserve your net worth, they will also protect you from the ravages of inflation.

Savings institutions and savings instruments

- National savings rate
- Establishing a savings plan
- Savings institutions
- Commercial banks
- Savings and loan associations
- Mutual savings banks
- Credit unions
- NOW accounts
- Interest rates on savings deposits
- Other savings media
- Savings and the magic of compound interest
- Other banking services
- Checking accounts
- Summary

You cannot achieve your personal and financial objectives without saving. You cannot buy a car or a house without first saving enough money to meet the downpayment requirement. You also cannot begin an investment plan until you have saved an adequate amount of money. Thus you need to spend less than you earn to provide for the long-run goal of financial independence. You must also save to meet some of your short-run goals. You will need savings to take a vacation, buy new clothes, or buy a new set of golf clubs. And you must save to provide protection from possible loss of income due to unemployment or illness. Savings will also give you an opportunity to take advantage of a bargain price on something you have always wanted.

You should save even if you expect your income to increase in the future. As your income increases, so does your need for ready cash. Your liquidity needs also increase. Savings can provide an important buffer for those occasions when your monthly cash outflow may exceed your inflow.

Saving requires discipline and a philosophy about the future. You might think of saving as a battle between current and future needs. You must learn to give up some of your current income in order to accumulate savings that will provide for future needs. You should not spend all of your income on current consumption. Some income should be saved to provide for future planned committments and unforeseen contingencies. In this chapter, you will learn why you should save, how to save, and where to save.

National savings rate

A monthly savings allocation should be an important part of everyone's budget. Unfortunately, the rate at which Americans currently save is at an all-time low. As Figure 4–1 shows, the personal savings rate is normally between 5 and 10 percent. But the rate in 1980 was well below 5 percent. The reason for this low rate seems to be related to consumers' attitudes toward inflation. Consumers reacted to the double digit inflation of 1973–74 by reducing their spending and increasing savings. Consumer attitude surveys indicated that they did this because they expected the rate of inflation to slow down in the near future. Inflation did in fact slow down in the 1976–79 period. However, double-digit inflation reared its ugly head again in 1979–80. This time around, consumer attitude surveys showed that consumers expected high inflation to persist. Consumers then began to speed up purchases in the hopes of beating future price increases. People reasoned that they should buy a new car this year rather than wait and pay a higher price next year. To pay for these kinds of purchases, consumers reduced savings and went more heavily into debt. This was not good for the economy and was not good for consumers.

Figure 4–1
Seasonally adjusted personal savings rate*

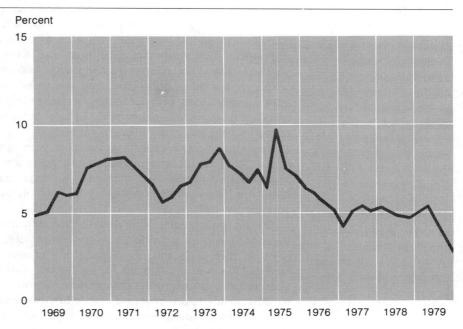

Percent

* Personal savings as a percent of disposable income.
SOURCE   Department of Commerce, 1980.

Establishing a savings plan

There are many good reasons to save. Most people save at one of four major financial institutions: a commercial bank, mutual savings bank, savings and loan association, or credit union. All these institutions offer a variety of savings plans. All of them are eligible to join federal programs that will insure your savings up to $100,000. Some caution must be exercised, however, since not all institutions choose to join a federal insurance program. You must make certain that your savings will be insured before opening an account. Even before you open an account, however, you must first establish your savings plan.

Savings versus investment

In establishing a savings plan, it is important to recognize the distinction between savings and investment. The distinction is a simple but important one. Your savings account provides a fund that is available to meet short-term needs or to provide money quickly in the event of a financial emergency. Because of the short time horizon, your primary savings objective should be safety and liquidity. You want to be sure that your money is available when you need it. You also want to minimize or eliminate the possiblity of losing any of your principal. The amount of interest you earn on your savings, although important, should be considered as secondary to the need for safety and liquidity. The need for safety and liquidity is the reason that most people choose to save with a federally insured account at one of the four financial institutions mentioned above.

In comparison to your savings objectives, your investment objectives will have a longer time horizon. Money you invest should be money for which you do not expect to have any immediate need. In short, investment capital should be money you feel you can put away for the long term. Thus, when investing, liquidity has a much lower priority. Safety is still important, but when investing, the long time horizon allows you to take more risk in return for a higher yield. The main objective you should pursue in your investment strategy is to earn the highest possible return consistent with the risk you are willing to take. The topic of investing will be explored in detail later in the book.

The need for saving
People save for many reasons. One of the primary purposes of saving is to provide an emergency fund in the event of unexpected illness, a sudden unanticipated expense, or a period of unemployment. An emergency fund can be a real lifesaver when unexpected expenses pop up. Similarly, an emergency fund can take some of the panic out of a sudden period of unemployment. If you are suddenly fired or laid off, the knowledge that you can still meet your financial obligations will enable you to search more calmly for another job. As a senior executive in an industry well-known for sudden firings commented, "In this business your bankbook is your best friend!"

Most people save for a specific purpose. You may wish to set up a savings program to accumulate the downpayment on a house, for example. You may also wish to save to buy a car or a boat or to take a special vacation. Whatever the reason, a short-term savings goal is appropriate and consistent with a long-term investment plan. You must save in order to invest.

You may also want to save to meet various liquidity needs. As you learned in the chapter on budgeting, a savings account can be the key to making a budget plan work. You may know that a month is coming up in which your cash outflow will exceed your cash income. You can then use your savings as a temporary source of funds to balance your monthly budget. This is one example of a liquidity need. You may want to build up some liquid funds in savings in order to invest this money later. There may also be other liquidity needs in which you are particularly interested.

Establishing savings objectives

The first step in your savings plan should be to establish savings objectives. Your first objective will probably be to provide an emergency fund. According to a conventional rule of thumb, you should have a savings account equal to about six month's aftertax income to meet this need. This conservative standard is probably more than most people need. Even if you lose your job, unemployment compensation will replace part of your lost income. If you do lose your job, you will probably not be unemployed for anywhere near six months.

The need for an emergency fund to pay medical bills or replace lost income due to accident or illness probably does not require six month's income, either. In fact, if you follow the insurance planning guidelines given in Part 4 of this book, three month's income should be more than adequate.

The important point is that you should set a definite upper and lower limit on your emergency fund. As a general guideline, you should have no less than three month's aftertax income in your emergency fund. This should provide an adequate cushion for any sudden emergency. To this sum you should add one month's aftertax income to meet any liquidity needs. You can regard this additional month's income as a part of an emergency fund available for short-term loans to yourself.

At the other end of the spectrum, six months' aftertax income should be the maximum amount saved for an emergency fund. Any funds accumulated above this level should be invested to earn a higher rate of return. Since it is highly unlikely that these funds will be needed in an emergency, some risk may be accepted with them. If you do establish a six-months' emergency fund, you may want to consider investing part of it in more permanent investments.

Any additional savings objectives to meet a specific purpose will be solely a matter of individual preference. You may wish to save for any of the purposes mentioned earlier or for some other purpose. Whatever these objectives are, you should consider them in addition to, not in place of, your emergency fund objective. Your emergency fund is a key part of your overall financial plan and is an absolute must for any prudent financial planner.

Meeting savings objectives

Once you establish your savings objectives, you must then begin the difficult process of meeting them. Obviously, you cannot save four to six months' income overnight. If you are starting on your first job, or if you currently have little or no savings, it will take a good bit of time to accumulate such a sum. As an initial objective, you should try to save 5 percent of your aftertax income toward this goal. At that rate it would take about five years to accumulate a substantial emergency fund. By that time your savings habits should be firmly entrenched. Additional savings accumulated each month could then be invested for the long run.

Pay yourself first

Most successful savers adopt a pay-yourself-first policy. This means that you should pay your savings account before you pay any other bills or obligations. Every payday deposit 5 percent of your paycheck in a savings account when you take your check to the bank. Other expenses then become secondary to meeting your savings objective. People who are not successful at saving generally follow the opposite of this policy— they pay themselves last. In other words they pay all their expenses first. Then if any money is left over, they put it in savings. Most unsuccessful savers find very little money left over at the end of the month for saving. As one popular saying describes this policy, "I throw all my cash up to the ceiling. What sticks goes into my savings account."

Savings discipline

Saving 5 percent of your income each month requires a great deal of self-discipline. One of the most effective ways of enforcing this discipline on yourself is to engage in some sort of an automatic savings plan. Check with the payroll department where you work to explore this possibility. Many payroll departments offer a plan whereby a designated sum of money can be deducted automatically from your paycheck and deposited in a savings account. Since this money will never show up in your paycheck, you will probably never miss it. Systematic saving through some type of automatic plan is probably the most effective means of enforcing saving discipline.

Many banks also offer an automatic savings plan. You can designate a fixed sum of money to be automatically transferred each month from your checking account to your savings account. In this way the bank helps you enforce your pay-yourself-first plan. Money for savings is deducted before you have a chance to spend it for anything else. Use of this plan will cause your savings account to grow systematically to meet your objectives.

You may also want to try some of the successful tricks or games used by successful savers. For example, you can make a habit of saving all your coins. At the end of each day, empty all your change into a jar. When the jar is full, wrap the coins up and deposit them in your savings account. If you do, you will probably accumulate $100 or more in extra savings by the end of each year.

There are many variations on the coin game. Nearly everyone saves pennies. You can save them separately in a large jar or bottle and wrap them up once or twice a year. You may also want to save specific types of coins separately, such as Susan B. Anthony dollars. Or you can obtain coin-saver cards at many banks or savings and loan associations. When the cards are full, deposit them in your savings account.

Other savings games may also be useful. If you earn any extra money from moonlighting or a part-time job, you may want to designate that money for saving. You may also try "kick-the-habit" saving. For example, you may have recently quit smoking. Take the money you would normally spend on tobacco and pay it to your savings account. Or cut out the doughnut with your morning coffee break and pay the money into a dough-nut jar. When the jar fills up, deposit the money in savings.

Whatever techniques you use to save, the most important point is for you to work toward your goals in a systematic manner. Even small amounts saved over a long period of time will grow into substantial balances. Continued progress toward your financial goals requires a long-term commitment to your savings program.

Savings institutions

You can choose from a variety of savings institutions in establishing a savings account. Commercial banks, savings and loan associations, mutual savings banks, and credit unions offer a number of services in addition to savings accounts. In this chapter we will examine how these institutions can play a role in your savings program.

Commercial banks

Commercial banks are by far the most popular savings institutions used by American consumers. These banks offer the following savings plans as well as a vast array of other services.

Passbook accounts

You may already be familiar with the regular savings account offered by commercial banks. This is often called a passbook account. You can open it with almost any amount of money. Some banks may require a minimum opening deposit, but the amount is usually very small—normally $10 or less. This type of savings account normally requires no prior notice or waiting period for withdrawal. Technically, banks have a legal right to demand 30 days notice of withdrawal, but they seldom exercise this right. It is thus a highly liquid form of savings.

A passbook account, like all other commercial bank accounts, is also a very safe form of savings. Nearly all commercial banks are insured by the Federal Deposit Insurance Corporation (FDIC). The FDIC insures any type of deposit in a commercial bank up to a maximum of $100,000. This $100,000 limit applies to the total of all accounts in the same name at any one bank. For example, you might have two separate savings accounts and one checking account with a bank. The total amount of money deposited in all three accounts would be insured by the federal government up to $100,000. This insurance provides a federal guarantee that you will not lose your money (or your interest) if the bank should go bankrupt. This is obviously a very important guarantee. You should not even consider depositing money in a bank not insured by the FDIC.

Certificates of deposit

Commercial banks also offer a number of time deposit accounts. These accounts require you to leave your money on deposit for some minimum amount of time. The accounts are commonly called certificates of deposit or CDs. A CD offers a higher interest rate than a passbook account. However, if you withdraw your money before the time limit is up, there are substantial interest penalties. Certificates are available with maturity dates ranging from 90 days to eight years. Longer maturities normally offer higher rates of return, but they are also less liquid.

Savings clubs

In addition to regular accounts and certificates of deposit, many commercial banks also offer club plans. Christmas clubs and vacation clubs are examples of such plans. When you enroll in this type of plan, the bank gives you a payment book. The book contains coupons that indicate the required payment dates for your club. Payments are typically made every two weeks. For example, a $10 Christmas club account requires you to deposit $10 every two weeks. When you make each $10 deposit, you turn in a coupon for the appropriate due date. At the end of a year, you will have made 25 payments. The bank will then send you a check for $250 plus interest. Christmas clubs normally require you to make the first payment in October and the last payment the following September. The amount saved is thus available in time for Christmas shopping.

The primary advantage of a club account is its forced savings aspect. The payment book serves as a constant reminder to make your payments on time. It also helps you reach your savings goal. The primary disadvantage is that the interest rate paid on a club plan is fairly low. Most people using club plans find that the convenience of forced saving outweighs the sacrifice of lower interest payment. Since the dollars involved are relatively small, the dollar sacrifice is quite modest. However, if you are a well-disciplined saver, you may not want to use a club savings plan.

Savings and loan associations

Savings and loan associations (S & Ls) may be either a mutual or a corporate association. The mutual association, which is the most common form of association, is owned by the depositors. The depositors are legally the association's shareholders. Interest paid on deposits is considered to be a dividend paid to the shareholders. From a tax point of view, however, the dividends are treated as interest. Corporate associations are organized like any other corporation; most of them pay interest instead of dividends, just like a commercial bank does.

Unlike bank interest, dividends paid by an S & L are not guaranteed. These dividends are paid out of operating profits, and the board of directors has a legal right to reduce the dividend, if necessary. In reality, however, S & L dividends are almost never reduced. As a practical matter, they are virtually guaranteed. If a corporate association pays interest, the interest is guaranteed.

Savings and loan associations are the second most popular type of savings institution. Current federal law allows savings and loans to pay slightly higher interest rates than that paid by commercial banks. However, savers still prefer commercial banks to S & Ls as judged by the total dollars deposited in savings accounts in these two types of institutions. The reason for this seems to lie in the greater familiarity of consumers with commercial banks.

Savings and loan associations exist primarily to provide financing for the housing industry. Recent legal changes, however, allow S & Ls to make some consumer loans in addition to housing loans. Current federal law allows S & Ls to pay interest rates approximately one quarter of 1 percent higher than commercial banks. This law was passed in order to help S & Ls accumulate capital to invest in the housing industry. At present, however, the interest rate differential is being phased out. Details of this phaseout will be provided in the section of this chapter dealing with interest rates.

Savings and loans offer essentially the same selection of savings plans as do commercial banks. Passbook accounts as well as time deposits are available. Many S & Ls also now offer a "bill-payer" service, which arranges for certain specified bills to be paid directly from your savings account. This is a convenient method of paying recurring monthly expenses.

Most savings and loans are federally insured by the Federal Savings and Loan Insurance Corporation (FSLIC). In some states S & L deposits are insured by a state association up to a maximum of $100,000. If you open an account at a savings and loan, be certain to open it at a federally or state insured association.

Mutual savings banks

Mutual savings banks enjoy limited popularity in the United States. They exist in a total of only 17 states, with most of them concentrated in New York and New England. In fact, of the 465 mutual savings banks in the United States, approximately 75 percent are located in New York or Massachusetts. Outside New England, there are a few mutual savings banks in Pennsylvania, New Jersey, Washington, Indiana, and Minnesota.

Like S & Ls, mutual savings banks fall in the broad category of thrift institutions. Their purpose and operation is similar to that of a mutual savings and loan association. They offer similar savings plans and are subject to the same interest rate ceilings as are S & Ls. Savings deposits in mutual savings banks are insured by the FDIC.

Credit unions

Credit unions are mutual associations of people sharing some common interest or characteristic. This interest is most often a common place of employment. For example, one of the world's largest credit unions is the Navy Federal Credit Union, headquartered in Washington, D.C. Membership in this credit union is open only to civilian and military employees of the U.S. Navy. Many private firms and organizations have a credit union.

The main purpose of a credit union is to provide an association for members to invest their savings and to make low-cost consumer loans. You can open an account at a credit union by buying shares, usually in $5 units. You can normally redeem your shares immediately by selling them back to the credit union. Dividends are paid on your shares out of earnings of the credit union. The board of directors, which is elected by the members, is responsible for overseeing the operation of the credit union.

Deposits in federal credit unions are insured up to $100,000 by the National Credit Union Association (NCUA). Dividends and the safety of your principal are dependent upon the successful operation of the credit union. Because of the risk involved (the bankruptcy rate for credit unions is much higher than for banks, S & Ls, and mutual savings banks), you should not save at any credit union not insured by the NCUA.

Current federal law allows credit unions to pay a maximum of 7 percent interest on regular accounts. In addition to regular and certificate accounts, credit unions offer share draft accounts. These accounts function just like NOW accounts, which are available at commercial banks, savings and loans, and mutual savings banks.

NOW accounts

Negotiable order of withdrawal (NOW) accounts are relatively new offerings of financial institutions. A NOW account is a checking account that pays interest. Actually a NOW certificate is not the legal equivalent of a check, but it looks just like a check. Legally a NOW is a negotiable order to withdraw money from your savings account. Even though it is not the exact legal equivalent of a check, a NOW is acceptable nearly everywhere as the same as a check.

NOW accounts were originally available only in Massachusetts and

New Hampshire. In the mid-70s they spread to the rest of New England and New York. However, with the passage of the Depository Institutions Deregulation and Monetary Control Act of 1980, NOW accounts are now authorized in all 50 states. Beginning in 1981, the act granted authority for all federally insured commercial banks, S & Ls, mutual savings banks, and credit unions to offer NOW accounts. The act also continued authority to offer automatic transfer accounts. These accounts offer automatic transfer of money from your savings account to your checking account. In effect, you can keep your checking account at a zero balance. Whenever a check is presented for payment, money is automatically transferred from your savings account to cover the check. This combined checking-savings plan offers the equivalent of an interest-bearing checking account.

The chief disadvantage of an automatic transfer account is that the interest rate paid on a combined saving-checking plan is typically very low if your average balance is less than $1,000 to $1,500. Each individual plan differs, so it is not possible to generalize about rates. If your bank offers such a plan, read it carefully. You may actually be better off keeping your savings and checking accounts separate. Your savings will then earn a higher rate of interest than the combined savings-checking plan, but your checking will earn no interest. On the average, however, you may end up better off. The answer to which is better for you depends on your particular situation and the terms offered by your bank.

Interest rates on savings deposits

For many years the maximum interest rate payable on savings deposits has been regulated by federal law. The law controlling interest rates is known as Regulation Q. At present, however, Regulation Q is being slowly phased out over the 1980–86 period. This phasing out is the result of the Depository Institution Deregulation and Monetary Control Act of 1980. Under the act, the 1980 ceilings were increased by 0.25 percent in 1981. From 1982 to 1986 the ceilings will be increased by approximately 0.50 percent per year until 1986. Ceilings will be removed completely after 1986.

The ceiling guidelines are fairly clear for regular accounts, but the guidelines are a bit complex for time deposits. The rate payable on some time deposits is linked to the rate payable on U.S. Treasury obligations of similar duration. Since Treasury obligations are generally referred to as money market instruments, these certificates are called Money Market Certificates (MMC). Interest rates on MMCs will vary widely depending upon current money market rates. For specific rates payable currently, you should contact your bank or thrift institution for up-to-the-minute information. Table 4–1 summarizes the 1981 ceilings on regular accounts and approximate rates payable on time deposits.

Table 4-1
Maximum interest rates on savings
accounts at federally insured institutions
(1981)

	Commercial banks	Savings and loan associations	Mutual savings banks	Credit unions
Regular accounts	5.50%	5.75%	5.75%	7.00%
NOW accounts*	5.25%	5.25%	5.25%	7.00%
Time deposits (approximate):				
30-89 days	6.00%	6.00%	6.00%	6.00%
6-month MMC†	7-9%	7-9%	7-9%	7-9%
30-month MMC†	9-12%	9-12%	9-12%	9-12%
1-2½ years	6.25%	6.75%	6.75%	9.50%
2½-4 years	6.75%	7.00%	7.00%	9.50%
4-6 years	7.50%	7.75%	7.75%	9.50%
6-8 years	7.75%	8.00%	8.00%	9.50%
8 years or more	8.00%	8.25%	8.25%	9.50%

* Share draft accounts at credit union.
† Rates payable on MMCs vary with money market conditions.
SOURCE   Federal Reserve Board National, Credit Union Administration.

Other savings media

In addition to the financial institutions discussed above, three additional savings media should be noted here: U.S. savings bonds, life insurance, and money market funds.

U.S. savings bonds

The United States government offers two types of savings bonds that may be purchased by individuals: Series EE and Series HH bonds. These replaced the old Series E and Series H bonds that were sold prior to January 1980.

Series EE bonds are sold at one half of face value and yield 6.5 percent interest if held to maturity (11 years and 9 months). These bonds are sold in minimum units of $50. Thus you can buy a $50 bond today for $25 and redeem it for $50 in 11 years and 9 months. Series EE must be held for a minimum period of six months before they can be cashed.

Series HH bonds are current income bonds. They may be purchased in minimum denominations of $500 and pay interest semiannually at the rate of 6.5 percent per year. Series HH bonds have a 10-year maturity and may be subject to an interest penalty if cashed prior to maturity. Bonds bought with cash are subject to the early redemption penalty. Bonds bought by trading in Series E or Series EE bonds are not subject to an early redemption penalty.

Savings bonds can be purchased and redeemed at any federally insured commercial bank, savings and loan, or mutual savings bank. Many employers also offer systematic Series EE bond purchases through a payroll savings plan. This type of plan can be very helpful as part of a forced saving plan for people who find saving difficult. In fact, the forced saving aspect of the savings bond deduction is the bond's major attraction to many people.

There are a number of other advantages to savings bonds. They are a totally safe means of saving because the principal and interest payments are fully guaranteed by the federal government. If a bond is lost or stolen, it can be replaced easily through your local bank. There are also some tax advantages to savings bonds. For one, interest on the bonds is exempt from state and local taxes. You also can defer the tax on a Series E or EE bond until you cash it. Finally, if you buy Series HH bonds with your Series E or EE bonds, you can defer the tax another 10 years until the HH bonds mature.

There are also some disadvantages to savings bonds. The six-month waiting period before cashing a Series EE is one disadvantage because it reduces your liquidity. The potential interest penalty on Series HH bonds is an obvious disadvantage. However, the biggest disadvantage is the relatively low interest rate paid. You can normally find a similar time deposit at a financial institution that will yield a higher rate.

Life insurance

Certain types of life insurance policies have built-in savings features. These policies, generally called whole life, build cash values over the years. The advantages and disadvantages of whole life policies are explained in detail in Chapter 10, which is devoted entirely to life insurance.

Money market mutual funds

Money market mutual funds have grown enormously in recent years. They invest your money in short-term debt certificates of various types. Many people find these funds an excellent place to keep all or part of their savings. Money market funds are explained in detail in Chapter 12, which deals with investment in debt securities. Money market funds can be used for savings and for temporary investments.

Savings and the magic of compound interest

When you open a savings account, it is important for you to understand how interest payments will be computed on your account. There are four generally used methods to compute interest payments on a savings account. These methods differ according to how the savings institution computes the account balance on which interest is computed.

Minimum balance method

One method is the minimum balance or low balance method. In this case the account pays interest on only the lowest balance on deposit during a specified interest period. The interest period most often used is one calendar quarter (three months). If you withdraw a portion of your money at or near the end of the quarter, you will receive no interest on it. This method pays the lowest amount of interest of any of the four methods.

Table 4–2 presents an interest computation example. The example assumes that the account is opened on the first day of the quarter with $5,000. An additional $1,000 is added on day 30, and $4,000 is withdrawn on day 80. On day 90, the last day of the quarter, the account has a balance of $2,000. Under the minimum balance method, interest would be paid only on the $2,000 lowest balance. At 6 percent per year (1.5 percent per quarter), interest would amount to $30.00.

Table 4–2
Interest rate calculations

Day of quarter	Transaction	Balance
1	+ $5,000	$5,000
30	+ $1,000	$6,000
80	− $4,000	$2,000
90	closing balance	$2,000

Method	Interest paid at end of quarter (6 percent)
Minimum balance	$30.00
Fifo	$25.00
Lifo	$30.00
Day of deposit to day of withdrawal	$78.33

Fifo method

A second method of interest calculation is called Fifo (first-in, first-out). Under this method the bank assumes that any withdrawals come from the earliest deposits. In our example the $4,000 withdrawal on day 80 would be assumed to come from the $5,000 deposited on day 1. Interest would also be paid on the remaining $1,000 for 90 days. Sixty days' interest would also be paid on the $1,000 deposited on day 30. The total interest paid would thus be $25.00.

Lifo method

A third common method of interest computation is called last-in, first-out or Lifo. Using Lifo, the bank assumes that any withdrawals are made from the latest deposit. In the example the $4,000 would be deducted first from the $1,000 deposit on day 30. The remaining $3,000 would be deducted from the $5,000 deposited on day 1. The end result would be that interest would be paid on $2,000 for 90 days. A total of $30.00 interest would be paid for the quarter.

Day of deposit to day of withdrawal

The final computational method is day of deposit to day of withdrawal interest. Using this method interest is computed daily on the basis of the balance for that day. In our example the calculation is as follows:

1. (30 days) ($5,000) (6%/360 days) = $24.99
2. (50 days) ($6,000) (6%/360 days) = $49.98
3. (10 days) ($2,000) (6%/360 days) = $ 3.33

    Total interest $78.30

As this example dramatically illustrates, day of deposit to day of withdrawal interest pays substantially more interest than any of the other three methods. This will always be true. Day of deposit to day of withdrawal interest is fairly common. When shopping for a savings account, you should select a financial institution using this method of interest calculation.

Effect of compounding periods

The number of times per year that your savings interest is compounded is also important. The stated rate of interest paid on your account is called the nominal rate. However, the effective rate of interest is the rate actually paid. The effective rate takes into account the payment of interest on interest. A simple example will illustrate the difference.

Table 4–3 shows the difference that compounding makes at a nominal rate of 6 percent. When compounded annually, the effective rate is equal to the nominal rate. When compounded semiannually, the effective rate increases to 6.09 percent. The reason for this is simple. With semiannual compounding, you are paid 3 percent (one half year's interest) for the first six months of the year on your original $1,000. You now have a total of $1,030 in your account. For the second six months you are paid 3 percent on this $1,030 balance. As Ben Franklin is reported to have said, "The magic of compound interest is that you are paid interest on your principal and then paid interest on the interest."

The more often your interest is compounded, the higher is your effective rate of interest. With quarterly compounding, the effective rate increases to 6.14 percent. When interest is compounded daily, the effective rate increases to 6.27 percent.

Table 4–3
Nominal and effective rates of interest
(Nominal rate = 6 percent)

Compounding periods	Beginning balance	Ending balance	Effective rate
Annual	$1,000	$1,060.00	6.00%
Semiannual	$1,000	$1,060.90	6.09%
Quarterly	$1,000	$1,061.36	6.14%
Daily	$1,000	$1,062.70	6.27%

A few simple calculations can also dramatically illustrate the effect of systematic savings earning compound interest over long periods of time. For example, Table 4–4 illustrates the effect of various systematic savings plans. You can see that a systematic plan is the key to accumulating a substantial savings account.

Table 4–4
Systematic savings plan

Save <u>Weekly</u> Now for Your Retirement

Retiring at age 65? Here's what you can accumulate, if you save weekly. These figures are projected at 5¼% a year, compounded daily.

Begin Saving at Age	AMOUNT SAVED WEEKLY					
	$1	$2	$3	$5	$10	$20
20	9523.53	19052.41	28575.93	47630.13	95260.25	190434.87
30	5229.34	10461.62	15690.96	26153.56	52307.12	104567.22
40	2689.03	5379.57	8068.60	13448.68	26897.35	53770.52
50	1186.26	2373.18	3559.44	5932.85	11865.70	23720.73
60	297.26	594.70	891.96	1486.71	2973.43	5944.18

How a Fixed Investment GROWS with Compounded Earnings

This chart shows how given amounts grow when left in your savings account for various periods of time. Figures are projected at 5¼% a year, compounded daily.

HOW SAVINGS GROW	$50	$100	$500	$1,000	$5,000	$10,000
6 mos	51.34	102.69	513.47	1026.95	5134.75	10269.50
1 year	52.70	105.39	526.95	1053.90	5269.50	10539.00
2 years	55.54	111.07	555.35	1110.71	5553.53	11107.05
3 years	58.53	117.06	585.29	1170.57	5852.86	11705.72
4 years	61.68	123.37	616.83	1233.67	6168.33	12336.66
5 years	65.01	130.02	650.08	1300.16	6500.80	13001.61
10 years	84.52	169.04	845.21	1690.42	8452.09	16904.18
20 years	142.88	285.75	1428.76	2857.51	14287.56	28575.12

Save <u>Weekly</u> for Future Buying or for an Emergency Fund

This schedule, showing how weekly savings accumulate, is projected at 5¼% a year, compounded daily.

HOW SAVINGS GROW	$1 Weekly	$2 Weekly	$3 Weekly	$5 Weekly	$10 Weekly	$20 Weekly
6 mos.	26.69	53.39	80.08	133.48	266.97	533.70
1 yr.	53.38	106.79	160.17	266.97	533.94	1067.40
2 yrs.	109.64	219.34	328.97	548.33	1096.66	2192.33
3 yrs.	168.93	337.95	506.87	844.85	1689.71	3377.90
4 yrs.	231.41	462.95	694.37	1157.36	2314.72	4627.37
5 yrs.	297.26	594.70	891.96	1486.71	2973.43	5944.18
10 yrs.	683.76	1367.90	2051.66	2419.68	6839.36	13672.58
15 yrs.	1186.26	2373.18	3559.44	5932.85	11865.70	23720.73
20 yrs.	1839.59	3680.22	5519.81	9200.37	18400.74	36784.94

Save <u>Monthly</u> Now for College for Your Youngsters

Use this chart to plan your college fund. These figures are projected at 5¼% a year, compounded daily.

Starting at Child's Present Age	Here's how various amounts build up by the time your child is 18					
	$5 monthly	$10 monthly	$20 monthly	$25 monthly	$50 monthly	$100 monthly
0	1801.75	3603.50	7207.09	9009.04	18018.07	36036.15
1	1651.01	3302.02	6604.31	8255.32	16510.63	33021.26
2	1507.98	3015.96	6032.16	7540.14	15080.28	30160.57
3	1372.26	2744.53	5489.28	6861.54	13723.09	27446.18
4	1243.49	2486.98	4974.16	6217.65	12435.31	24870.61
5	1121.30	2242.60	4485.39	5606.69	11213.39	22426.77
6	1005.36	2010.73	4021.62	5026.98	10053.96	20107.91
7	895.35	1790.71	3581.56	4476.91	8953.83	17907.65
8	790.97	1581.94	3164.01	3954.98	7909.96	15819.92
9	691.93	1383.85	2767.81	3459.74	6919.48	13838.96
10	597.95	1195.89	2391.88	2989.83	5979.66	11959.31
11	508.77	1017.55	2035.18	2543.95	5087.90	10175.80
12	424.16	848.32	1696.71	2120.87	4241.75	8483.49
13	343.88	687.75	1375.56	1719.44	3438.87	6877.74
14	267.70	535.39	1070.83	1338.53	2677.06	5354.12
15	195.41	390.83	781.69	977.10	1954.21	3908.41
16	126.83	253.66	507.33	634.16	1268.32	2536.65
17	61.75	123.50	247.01	308.76	617.52	1235.04

SOURCE First American Savings and Loan Association.

Other banking services

Until the mid-1970s commercial banks had a large competitive edge over other financial institutions in terms of the extent of services offered. In the 80s, however, all this has changed. In many states thrift institutions offer almost the same array of services as do commercial banks. Recent surveys have shown, however, that commercial banks still are seen as superior to thrift institutions in three main areas. First, banks offer greater locational convenience. There are more than twice as many banking locations in the United States as thrift institution locations.

Better service is the second advantage of commercial banks. An American Bankers Association survey showed that many people feel that banks offer more services and have the experience to back them up. This experience factor is a key to banks' third advantage over thrift institutions—giving people financial advice. Bankers have a great deal of credibility, and people often turn to them for advice. People trust their banker, and experience has shown that this trust is usually well deserved.

The American Bankers Association has been the driving force behind advertising the Full Service Bank. (*Full Service Bank* is a registered trademark of the ABA.) Banks considered Full Service Banks offer over 100 financial services. These services include checking accounts, savings plans, loan services, trust services, business loans and services, municipal financial services, and international banking services. Table 4–5 summarizes the range of services offered by a Full Service Bank.

Checking accounts

One major banking service you may already be familiar with is a checking account. Checks are widely used and provide a great deal of convenience and safety for monetary transactions. A series of five helpful illustrations explaining how a checking account works are provided for you. These illustrations are reproduced courtesy of the Riggs National Bank of Washington, D.C.

Checking account costs

The cost of a checking account varies widely, depending on the rate structure offered by your bank and the number of checks you write each month. Many banks offer free checking accounts as a means of attracting business. Obviously, if you can find a conveniently located bank that offers free checking, a free account would normally be preferred to an account that has a service charge.

Selection criteria

Most banks offer one of the six types of checking plans summarized in Figure 4–6. In selecting a bank, your main criteria should be convenience, cost and service. You should shop for a reasonable cost account and compare cost alternatives for the number of checks you expect to write each month. You should also consider the convenience of the bank

Table 4–5
Services available at full service banks

1. Checking accounts (individual or joint):
   Instant cash checking account service
   Scenic checks, other styles
2. Savings plans (individual, joint, or trustee):
   Regular savings
   Passbook accounts
   Time certificates of deposit
   Christmas club savings accounts
   Automatic savings
   For the children: Trustee savings accounts
   For business: Time deposits—open account and certificates
3. Loan Services
   Personal loans
   Auto loans
   Home improvement loans
   Household goods financing (appliances, furniture, etc.)
   Travel loans
   Aircraft loans
   Mobile home loans
   Boat loans
   Vacation home loans
   Insurance premium financing
   Loans for legal services
   Dental care loans
   Health care loans
   Education loans
   Real estate loans (homes, apartments, stores, other improved property)
   Escrow service
   Credit life and disability insurance
4. Trust services*
   Executor of wills
   Trustee of living or testamentary trust
   Guardian of minor children's property
   Investment management
   Custodianship of securities
   Pension and profit-sharing plans
5. Other personal services
   Charge cards

   Safe deposit boxes
   Money orders
   Cashier checks
   Bank drafts
   Foreign drafts
   Automatic transfer of funds
   Travelers cheques
   Travelers letters of credit
   Foreign exchange
   Bank-by-mail
   Account transfer
   Buy and sell tax-exempt securities
6. Farm loans†
   Crop production loans
   Farm equipment loans
   Livestock loans
   Farm equipment leasing
7. Loans for business purposes
   Commercial loans
   Term loans to small business
   Industrial equipment loans
   Truck loans
   Aircraft loans
   Real estate loans
   Accounts receivable financing
   Factoring
   Commercial property improvement loans
   Commodity loans
8. Services for Business
   Time deposits—open account and certificates
   Federal tax deposit service
   Insurance premium financing
   Payroll service
   Payables and management information service
   Regional collection plan (lock box service)
   Foreign collections & discounts
   Domestic credit information
   Foreign credit information

Table 4–5 *(continued)*

Bank wire service

Checking account reconciliation service

Freight payment service

Direct billing service

Customer billing service

Automatic payroll deposit service

Employee benefit trusts: pension, profit sharing, thrift & welfare plans

Corporate trust services: transfer agent, register, subscription agent

Investment services

Escrow services

Safe deposit boxes

Foreign exchange

Commercial letters of credit

Travelers cheques

Foreign drafts

Professional billing service

Plant location service

Industrial investment services

9. Municipal financial services

Public funds deposit—demand and time

Checking accounts—reconciliation service

Loans to political subdivisions

Equipment financing—political subdivisions

Equipment leasing—political subdivisions

Purchase & sale of municipal securities

Payroll service

Trust services: pension, thrift and welfare plans

Automatic payroll deposit

Municipal financing consulting

Municipal credit analysis

10. International banking services

Import-export financing

Foreign exchange

Commercial letters of credit

Foreign drafts

Collections & discounts

Foreign credit information

Foreign trade information

Letters of introduction

Travelers cheques

(A total of 107 services)

* If the bank does not have these trust services on-premise but does provide them through correspondent services, the bank can be considered Full Service.

† Provided on-premise or through correspondent relationships.

In some states some of these services won't be found because of state laws and regulations.

SOURCE *Florida Banker,* November–December 1979. Publication of the Florida Bankers Association.

location. Finally, you should give some weight to the range of other services offered. All other things equal, a Full Service Bank is probably a better choice than a bank offering fewer services.

Summary

You must save to meet your financial goals. Most people save at one of four major financial institutions: a commercial bank, savings and loan association, mutual savings bank, or credit union. In establishing your savings plan, you need to understand clearly the difference between savings and investment. Because of the short-term time horizon of your savings account, your primary savings objective should be safety and

Figure 4–2
How to write a check

How to WRITE a check

On the face of your check are:
- Your name and address
- Riggs' name and the address of your branch
- The Federal Reserve check routing symbol for banks located in Washington, D.C.   0540
- Riggs Bank number   0003
- Your account number   12 34567890
- Check number for your records   No. 681
- Riggs Bank transit symbol identifying the bank and Federal Reserve District   15-3/540

When writing a check, you fill in with *ink:*
- Date. Do not date ahead. It is legal to date a check on Sundays and holidays.

- The name of the person or firm to whom the check is payable — payee. Avoid making a check payable to cash, because if lost or stolen it may be cashed by anyone. It is better to make the check payable to yourself.
- The amount in numerals, close to the dollar sign to prevent the insertion of numbers to increase the amount.
- The amount in words beginning at the far left edge of the check adding the cents as 00/100. Fill in the remaining space to DOLLARS with a line.
- Signature. Sign your check exactly as you did your signature card.

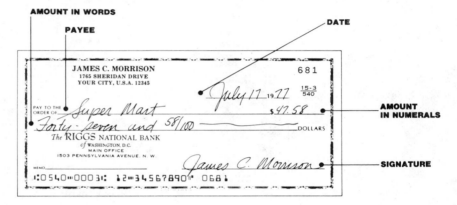

SOURCE   Riggs National Bank.

liquidity. For long-term investments your primary objective should be earning the highest possible return consistent with the risk you are willing to take.

One major objective of savings should be to establish an emergency fund equal to three to six month's aftertax income. You may also want to save for additional specific purposes or to provide for liquidity needs. To meet your savings objectives, you should adopt a pay-yourself-first policy. A goal of saving 5 percent of your aftertax income is reasonable.

Commercial banks are by far the most popular savings institutions used by American consumers. Savings and loan associations are the next most popular. Mutual savings banks and credit unions claim a much smaller share of the savings dollar. These institutions offer a variety of savings plans, including passbook accounts, certificates of deposit, club accounts, and NOW accounts. Many people also use U.S. savings bonds,

Figure 4-3
How to make a deposit

How to make a DEPOSIT

Deposit slips are provided free with your checks. Complete a deposit slip in the following manner:

- Date of deposit.
- Cash — total all currency and/or bond coupons enter by CASH.
- Checks — list each check separately. Enter the ABA number (fraction in upper right corner of each check or draft) in the column on the left.
- Total — add cash and checks.

Record the deposit in your checkbook register and keep your receipt from the teller for your records.

If your deposit is a check drawn on another bank, it may take several days for the check to clear and for funds to be available. Therefore, do not write checks on this deposit for a few days.

Be sure not to write a check for more funds than in your account. This would cause an overdraft or returned check for which you may be charged a penalty.

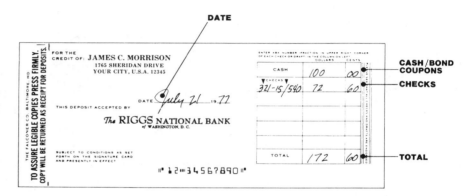

SOURCE   Riggs National Bank.

whole life insurance, and money market mutual funds as savings media.

The manner in which interest is computed on your account and the number of compounding periods play a major role in determining the actual dollars of interest paid. An account that compounds interest daily and pays from day of deposit to day of withdrawal will pay the most annual interest for a given stated interest rate.

Full Service Banks offer a broad array of services in addition to savings. Checking accounts are one of the most important of these services. In selecting a bank for your checking acccunt, you should consider cost, convenience, and service.

The following pointers are offered to guide your savings plans.

Figure 4–4
How to record your checks and deposits

How to RECORD your checks and deposits

It is a good habit to record check and deposit information in your check register *before* writing each check or deposit.

Also keep a current balance by adding deposits and subtracting checks written. Record the following in your check register when you write a check:

1. Check number
2. Date of check
3. Payee
4. Amount of check
5. Date of deposit
6. Amount of deposit
7. Balance

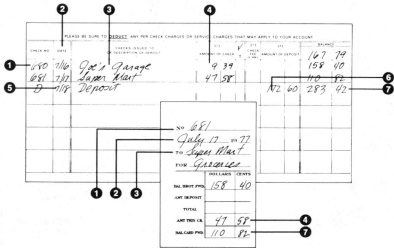

SOURCE   Riggs National Bank.

1. You must save to reach financial independence.
2. Establish your saving objectives to first meet your liquidity and emergency needs.
3. Save 5 percent of each paycheck to develop a habit of thrift.
4. Pay yourself first.
5. Play the savings game—savings requires discipline.
6. Select the savings institution that offers the highest yield for the shortest period of time.
7. You may want to save with U.S. savings bonds through a payroll deduction plan.
8. Life insurance and money market funds also offer a way to save.

Figure 4–5
How to endorse checks

How to
ENDORSE
checks

Checks made payable to you must be endorsed with your signature on the back before you can cash or use them. Sign your name on the back exactly as it is on the face of the check.

There are three types of endorsements:

- **Blank.** This type is used to cash a check payable to you. Be sure to use extreme caution; because, once a check is endorsed in this manner, it can be cashed by anyone if lost or stolen.
- **Special.** This endorsement is used for checks payable to you which you would like to turn over to someone else. Write on the back, "Pay to the order of (Payee's name)," and then sign.
- **Restrictive.** Write, "For Deposit Only to Account Number . . .," and sign. This endorsement authorizes the bank to deposit the check, not to cash it. This protects you, because no one can cash this check once it is endorsed. Always endorse your checks for deposit in this manner.

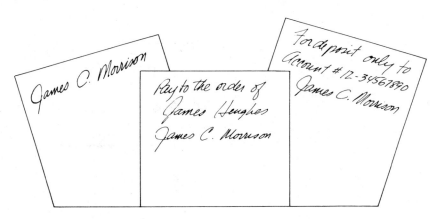

SOURCE   Riggs National Bank.

9. There is a magic in compounding of interest on savings accounts.
10. Select a savings account that pays the highest interest from day of deposit to day of withdrawal.
11. A checking account at a full service bank may be to your advantage.
12. Select a checking account that gives you moderate cost, convenience, and service.

Figure 4-6
How to balance your bank statement

How to BALANCE your bank statement

Each month you will receive in the mail a Riggs Bank statement listing checks, deposits, bank charges, if any, and a new balance, plus your canceled checks (i.e., checks paid against your account). To balance your account make sure that the figures in your check register agree with the figures on your statement.

The steps you should follow are:

1. Place your checks in order by check number or issue date.
2. Compare your canceled checks with the information in your check register, correcting any errors in recording. Place a check mark by each figure in your check register.

3. Subtract any bank charges which appear on your statement from your checkbook register.
4. Add all "outstanding" checks (those which you have written but which were not presented for payment in time to appear in your statement).
5. Total all deposits in your check register which are not shown on your statement and add that to your statement balance and then subtract total of outstanding checks. The balance in your check register should now agree with the balance on your statement. If the balances do not agree, recheck your statement and check register following the same steps. Also note

if the amount of the check corresponds with the amount encoded in the lower right hand corner of the canceled check. Once your statement is balanced mark your check register to indicate where this statement ends and a new statement begins. Keep your canceled checks and statements in a safe place, because they will be handy for tax purposes.

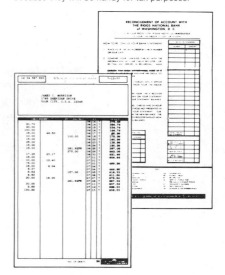

SOURCE   Riggs National Bank.

Table 4-6
Typical checking account costs

Type of account	Minimum balance required	Monthly maintenance charge	Transaction charge
Free checking	None	None	None
Analysis plan	None	$1	$.10 to $.15 per transaction (check or deposit)
Activity or special plan	None	None	$.10 to $.15 per transaction
Minimum balance plan	$100 to $1,000 in checking or saving	N.C.*	N.C.*
Package plan	None	$2 to $3	None
NOW	None	Interest paid on balance	0 to $.15

* N.C. = no charge if minimum balance maintained.

5

The tax environment

- The federal tax structure
- Federal income tax details
- Additional tax considerations
- A sample tax return
- Tax audits
- Tax shelters
- Summary

Government at all levels, federal, state, and local, is financed through a variety of tax levies. One of the most important and most painful obligations of each citizen is the obligation to pay a fair share of the taxes necessary to run the community, state, and country. Almost everyone recognizes the importance of providing the revenue necessary to finance essential government services. Virtually no one, however, is overly eager to "kick in" his or her share of the bill. Although we are all obligated to pay a fair share of the expense, no one is required to pay more than the law demands. Therefore, it is critical that you understand the basic nature of the tax environment. The objective of this chapter is to provide you with the background material necessary to develop that understanding.

Effective personal financial planning requires you to be familiar with the tax environment and its effect on your income assets and net worth. Keeping your tax bill to the legal minimum will maximize your aftertax income. Holding down your taxes will help you build your net worth and make progress toward financial independence.

The burden imposed by taxes is partially controllable and partially uncontrollable. Your federal and state tax liability, for example, is partially controllable through proper tax management and various tax-reduction strategies. On the other hand, the Social Security tax, officially know as the Federal Insurance Contributions Act or FICA tax, is a completely uncontrollable expense. If you are subject to FICA tax, the tax is levied as a flat percentage of your salary. Other taxes, such as sales taxes and personal property taxes, are only partially controllable as a function of your choice of where you live and how you spend your income.

An example will illustrate the overwhelming importance of the "tax bite" to your financial position. Let us examine the case of a young married couple, who both graduated from college one year ago. Both are currently employed, and each earns a salary of $13,500. Thus their combined income is $27,000 per year. They elect the "married filing jointly" option on their federal tax return. They claim two exemptions, and do not itemize their deductions. (Further details of tax terms and computations will be provided later.) In their situation their federal tax liability would be $4,641.

As large as $4,641 seems, it is only the beginning. If both parties are subject to FICA tax, as are most employees, they each pay an additional 6.13 percent of their salary for Social Security withholding (1980 rates). This amounts to $827.55 each, or a total of approximately $1,655. One more large bite remains. If they live in one of the majority of the states that have a state income tax, they may pay as high as an additional 15 percent of income in state income taxes. If the couple live in Virginia, for example, their state income tax liability will come to approximately $830. Their total tax bill for federal and state income taxes and FICA contributions is thus a whooping $7,126. This amounts to approximately 26 percent of their total income.

In addition to the $7,126, the couple is subject to a variety of other taxes. Personal property taxes are levied in approximately 20 states. Sales taxes are levied in varying amounts in most states. City income taxes are levied by some municipalities. Federal taxes are levied on such "luxury" items as gasoline, automobiles, and telephone service. Finally, taxes on real estate and a variety of other taxes might also be paid. The federal income tax will be dealt with in some detail. It is the most widely levied, most complex, and largest of the taxes we all must pay. A discussion of the costs and benefits of the FICA system will be undertaken in Part 6, which discusses retirement and estate planning. The remaining taxes mentioned vary widely in applicability according to locality. The federal tax environment is clearly an issue of most concern to you.

The federal tax structure

The Internal Revenue code comprises the basis of federal tax law. It consists of over 2,000 pages detailing federal tax rules governing individuals and corporations. Original authority for the United States government to tax individual income without apportionment among the states according to population was granted by the 16th amendment to the Constitution, adopted on February 25, 1913. This amendment provided:

> The congress shall have the power to lay and collect taxes on income from whatever source derived, without apportionment among the several states, and without regard to any census or enumeration.

The first law implementing this tax on individuals was passed by Congress in October 1913. The law has been codified, revised, and amended ever since.

The first systematic detailing of the tax laws was in the Internal Revenue Code of 1939. This code was revised and amended over the years until replaced by a new comprehensive code, the Internal Revenue Code of 1954. The most important revisions of the 1954 Code occurred with Tax Reform Acts of 1959 and 1976, and the Tax Reduction and Simplification Act of 1977.

Tax law is quite complex and subject to continual change. Three major sources of information interpret and implement the legal provision of the code. They are the various regulations issued by the Treasury Department, administrative rulings issued by the Internal Revenue Service, and a very large number of federal tax rulings issued by courts. Of the three sources, court rulings are the most numerous. Tax rulings are handed down by the Supreme Court, the United States Court of Appeals, the United States of Claims, the United State District Courts, and the United States Tax Courts. These court rulings resolve tax disputes between the taxpayer and the Internal Revenue Service.

Progressive nature of federal tax

The federal tax rate is progressive. As your income increases, the percentage of your income payable in taxes also increases. Thus a person earning $20,000 per year not only pays more tax dollars per year than a person earning $10,000 but also pays a higher percentage of income. For example, a single person earning $10,000 per year who claims one exemption and does not itemize deductions would be liable for a tax of $1,172 or 11.7 percent of income. The same person earning $20,000 per year would be liable for a tax of $3,829, or 19.1 percent of income. This progressive system is based on the theory that as your income increases, so does your ability to shoulder a greater relative proportion of the tax burden.

A tax that impacts lower-income people more than higher-income people is said to be regressive as compared to the progressive structure of the federal income tax system. One common objection used against the use of state lotterys to increase state tax revenues is that low-income people are more likely to buy lottery tickets on a regular basis. This type of indirect tax is therefore said to be regressive in nature. On the average, a low-income person is likely to spend a higher budget percentage on lottery tickets than a high-income person.

Overview of the tax system

In looking at the big picture of the federal income tax structure, you can see that the essential nature of the tax system is actually quite simple. However, as you delve deeper and deeper into the rules surrounding tax computations, problems can become increasingly complex. To illustrate basic requirements of the system, the determination of your federal tax liability may be simplified to six steps. These six steps will be outlined first and filled in with details later.

In step one of the process you must determine your filing status and number of personal exemptions. Each taxpayer must file under one of five filing statuses: (1) single; (2) married filing a joint return; (3) married filing separate returns, (4) unmarried head of household; or (5) qualifying widow or widower with a dependent child. Once your correct filing status is determined, you are allowed one exemption of $1,000 in income from taxation (1980 rates) for yourself. You are also allowed one exemption for your spouse (if married and filing jointly), one for each dependent child living with you, and one for any other qualifying dependent. In addition, one extra exemption is allowed if you are age 65 or over, and one additional exemption is allowed if you are blind.

In step two you must determine your total income. Total income includes income from all sources, the most common of which are wages, tips, interest, and dividends.

If you work for a salary, your employer is required to provide you with a W–2 Form at the end of the year. The W–2 contains a statement of your total wages for the year and the amount of federal, state, and

FICA taxes withheld from your wages. The taxes withheld are the result of the "pay-as-you-go basis" of the income tax system. The law requires that income taxes be paid as wages are received. Taxes are withheld by employers when paychecks are issued weekly, bimonthly, or monthly. The amounts withheld are forwarded by the employer to the government weekly or monthly, depending on the amount withheld. The amount of tax withheld depends upon the number of exemptions to which you are entitled. You may claim entitlements by filing a W–4 Form with your employer.

Total income will reflect the profit or loss from a venture owned by a self-employed person if the business organization is organized as a sole proprietorship or partnership. A proprietorship or partnership is a simple form of business organization in which the sole owner (sole proprietorship) or group of partners (partnership) own and operate an unincorporated business enterprise. For a proprietorship, all the profits from the business are considered taxable income to the sole owner. For partnerships, each partner's share in the profits of the business is considered as taxable income to each partner. In the case of a self-employed person who owns a business organized as a corporation, the owner is considered an employee of the corporation for tax purposes and pays a tax on his or her corporate salary.

Regardless of whether you are self-employed or work for a salary, the income from your job will probably be your largest single source of income. To this income you would add other sources of income such as tips, dividends, and interest. The total income from all sources is your total income for tax purposes.

Step three in determining your tax liability is to calculate your adjusted gross income. Adjusted gross income is determined by deducting certain adjustments to income from total income. Such adjustments include deductions for moving expenses, alimony, travel, gift and entertainment expenses incurred by employees, and certain exclusions for disability income. A variety of special rules apply to these deductions. For most individuals a sufficient amount of detail to determine eligibility is included in the Internal Revenue Services' publication *Your Federal Income Tax.* This publication is issued annually without charge. A copy may be obtained by writing directly to the IRS.

The fourth step in the process requires the determination of your taxable income. Taxable income is determined by deducting excess itemized deductions from adjusted gross income. Excess itemized deductions are allowable deductions in excess of the zero bracket amount built into the tax tables. If the system *seems* to be getting a bit complicated at this point it is because it *is* getting a bit complicated. A brief historical review may serve to clarify this step.

The historical origin of the zero bracket amount and excess itemized deductions is related to the Tax Reduction and Simplification Act of 1977.

Prior to the filing of 1977 tax returns, you were allowed a choice between deducting a standard amount from adjusted gross income or itemizing deductions. Itemized deductions include items such as medical and dental expenses, state and local taxes, interest expense, charitable contributions, and casualty and theft losses. You simply deducted the larger of the standard deduction or the sum of all itemized deductions from your adjusted gross income to determine your taxable income.

Following the 1977 Act, the standard deduction was built into the tax tables. Only that portion of total itemized deductions exceeding the amount already allowed for by the tables can now be deducted from your adjusted gross income. The amount allowed varies according to your filing status. The current amounts (1980 rates) are $2,300 if single or an unmarried head of household, $3,400 if married filing jointly or a qualifying widow or widower with dependent children, and $1,700 if married and filing a separate return. Itemized deductions in excess of these limits may be deducted from adjusted gross income to arrive at taxable income. If your itemized deductions are less than these limits, your taxable income is equal to your adjusted gross income. The limits of $2,300, $3,400 or $1,700 are referred to as the *zero bracket amount*. This is the income level on which zero tax is levied for the appropriate filing status.

Once taxable income is determined, step five requires the computation of your tax. For most people the amount of tax due may be determined by looking up the tax in one of four tables provided in the tax return. Whether or not you may use the tables depends upon your filing status, income, and number of personal exemptions claimed. Four basic tables identified as Tables A, B, C, and D are provided by the IRS. The tables reflect the four different tax rates imposed according to your filing status and zero bracket amount. Table A applies to single taxpayers with three or fewer personal exemptions and taxable income less than or equal to $20,000. Table B applies to married taxpayers filing a joint return and qualifying widows or widowers who claim nine or fewer personal exemptions and have taxable income of $40,000 or less. Table C applies to married taxpayers filing separate returns who claim three or fewer personal exemptions and have personal income of $20,000 or less. Table D applies to unmarried heads of household who claim eight or fewer personal exemptions and have $20,000 or less of taxable income.

For taxpayers who exceed the guidelines above for the use of the tables, the IRS provides Tax Rate Schedules X, Y, and Z. Tax rate schedules are used in conjunction with Schedule TC (Tax Computation) to calculate your tax. Thus, for example, if you are single with taxable income of more than $20,000, you could not use Table A. You would have to use Schedule TC in conjunction with the Tax Rate Schedule X. Schedule X applies to single taxpayers. Schedule Y applies to married taxpayers and qualifying widows and widowers. Schedule Z applies to unmarried heads of household. Table 5–1 summarizes the selection criteria to choose the appropriate table or schedule.

For the majority of taxpayers, one of the seven tables or schedules described above will suffice. One or more schedules or forms may be needed for some taxpayers, mainly those eligible for income averaging or subject to the maximum tax on earned income. Further details on these two major exceptions to the general rule will be provided later on in this chapter.

Table 5–1
Selection of tax table or tax-rate schedule

Use tax table or tax rate schedule	If your filing status is:
A	Single; income ⩽ $20,000; exemptions ⩽ 3
B	Married or qualifying widow or widower; income ⩽ $40,000; exemptions ⩽ 9
C	Married filing separate return; income ⩽ $20,000; exemptions ⩽ 3
D	Unmarried head of household; income ⩽ $20,000; exemptions ⩽ 8
X	Single, income > $20,000 or exemptions > 3
Y	Married (joint or separate) or qualifying widow or widower; income > $40,000 or exemptions > 9
Z	Unmarried head of household; income > $20,000 or exemptions > 8

The final step in the process is to deduct any available tax credits from your tax liability determined in step five. Tax credits are certain items the law allows to be deducted directly from your final bill. Examples of available tax credits include such items as child-care expenses under some circumstances, contributions to candidates for public office, residential energy credits, and investment tax credits.

At the conclusion of step six, your final bill is determined. In most cases you need only compare this final bill to the amount of tax withheld from your regular paycheck. You will then know whether a refund is due or whether an additional tax payment is required. The result may bring you great joy or great sorrow at tax time.

Table 5–2 briefly outlines the six steps in determining your tax. In

Table 5–2
Simplified federal income tax steps

1. Determine filing status and personal exemptions.
2. Determine total income from all sources.
3. Adjusted gross income = total income minus adjustments to income.
4. Taxable income = adjusted gross income minus excess itemized deductions.
5. Compute tax using appropriate table or schedule.
6. Deduct tax credits.

the following pages additional details will be provided to fill in the outline in Table 5–2.

Federal income tax details

More detail must be provided to fill in the overview of the tax system. You should not rely completely on this necessarily brief presentation to file an actual tax return. It is simply not possible to provide a comprehensive treatment of tax return requirements in one chapter. To file your actual tax return, you must read carefully the directions and guidelines published by the Internal Revenue Service. You may even need to consult a professional tax adviser. The present objective is simply to provide a basic guide to the income tax system. There is sufficient information so that you may develop a clear understanding of how the system works.

Filing requirements

The first requirement in understanding the system is to determine whether or not you are required to file a return. The requirement to file depends upon your income level, marital status, whether or not tax was withheld from your paycheck, and a variety of other factors. Fortunately, the Internal Revenue Service provides a very useful table to help you determine your filing requirements. The filing requirements are reproduced in Table 5–3.

As you can see from the table, determining your filing requirement is actually quite simple. For example, suppose you are an employed college student earning $2,000 per year and are claimed on your parents' return as an exemption. You would not have to file a return at the end of the year. The law requires a return only if you had $1,000 or more of unearned income, such as interest or dividends. If income tax was withheld from your paycheck, however, you should file a return to obtain a refund.

Once your filing requirement is determined, you are ready to follow the simplified steps listed in Table 5–2.

Step one: filing status and personal exemptions

Step one is certainly the easiest of the six steps. Your filing status determines which tax table (A, B, C, or D) or tax rate schedule (X, Y, or Z) you will use. Married taxpayers may elect to file either a joint return or separate returns. Filing a joint return simply means that a husband and wife file only one return to cover the income earned by both spouses. Filing separate returns means that the husband and wife each file their own return to cover their individual incomes.

The choice of whether to file separate or joint returns is an important one. The total tax paid under each method may not be the same. In some cases it may be advantageous for the husband and wife to file jointly. In other cases it may be advantageous for husband and wife to file separately. If only one spouse has income, less tax will be paid filing

Table 5-3
Who must file

Your income and your filing status generally determine whether or not you must file a tax return.

You must file a return for 1980, even if you owe no tax:	And your income was at least:
If you were single (this also means legally separated, divorced, or married with a dependent child and living apart from your spouse for all of 1980) and:	
Under 65	$3,300
65 or over	4,300
If you were married filing a joint return and were living with your spouse at the end of 1980 (or on the date your spouse died), and:	
Both were under 65	5,400
One was 65 or over	6,400
Both were 65 or over	7,400
If you were married filing a separate return or married but were not living with your spouse at the end of 1980 ..	1,000
If you could be claimed as a dependent on your parents' return, and had taxable dividends, interest, or other unearned income of $1,000 or more...........................	1,000
If you were a qualifying widow(er) with a dependent child and:	
Under 65	4,440
65 or over	5,400
If you could exclude income from sources within U.S. possessions	1,000
If you were self-employed and your net earnings from this work were at least $400	
If you received any advance earned income credit (EIC) payments from your employer(s) during 1980	

Even if your income was less than the amounts shown, you must file a return if you owe any taxes, such as:

- FICA (Social Security) on tips you did not report to your employer.
- Minimum Tax.
- Tax on an IRA (Individual Retirement Arrangement).
- Tax from recomputing a prior year investment credit.

These rules apply to all U.S. citizens and resident aliens, including those under 21 years of age. They also apply to those nonresident aliens and resident aliens who are married to citizens or residents of the United States at the end of 1980 and who file a joint return as discussed on page 6, under *Special Rule for Aliens*.

Note: *Different rules apply if you were a nonresident alien at any time during 1980 (unless you file a joint return as mentioned above). You may have to file* Form 1040NR. *U.S. Nonresident Alien Income Tax Return. Also get* Publication 519, *U.S. Tax Guide for Aliens.*

Who should file

Even if you do not have to file, you should file to get a refund if income tax was withheld from your pay. Also file if you can take the earned income credit. If you file for either of these reasons only, you may be able to use Form 1040A.

SOURCE: Internal Revenue Service

jointly than separately. If both spouses have income, separate returns may be an advantage. The tax should be computed both ways to be certain that the lowest possible tax will be paid.

Unmarried taxpayers may file in one of three categories: single, unmarried head of household, or as a qualifying widow or widower with a dependent child. If you are single, you may qualify as an unmarried head of household if you meet either one of two criteria. One is that you pay more than half of the cost of maintaining a home that is the principal residence for the entire year of a dependent parent. The other is that you pay more than half of the cost of maintaining a home that is the principal residence for the entire year for yourself and an unmarried child, grandchild, foster child, stepchild, or other dependent relative.

Some widows and widowers are entitled to pay the tax rate for married taxpayers filing jointly. If the widow's or widower's spouse died within the two tax years preceding the year for which the return is being filed, four tests must be met to qualify for this benefit. In general, the widow or widower qualifies if he or she was entitled to file a joint return during the year of the spouse's death, did not remarry before the close of the tax year, had a child or stepchild who qualified as a dependent, and provided more than half the cost of maintaining the home that is the principal residence of a dependent child or stepchild for the entire year (except for temporary absences). All single taxpayers who do not qualify as unmarried heads of household or qualifying widows or widowers file as single persons.

In summary, five possible filing statuses are available:

1. Single.
2. Married filing joint return.
3. Married filing separate return.
4. Unmarried head of household.
5. Qualifying widow or widower with dependent child.

Once your filing status is determined, the number of personal exemptions to which you are entitled must be determined. As noted previously, you are allowed one exemption from taxation of $1,000 in income (1980 rates) for yourself. You are allowed one exemption for each dependent child living with you and one for any other qualifying dependent. In addition, one additional exemption is allowed if you are age 65 or older, and one additional exemption is allowed if you are blind.

The rules governing whether or not a given individual may be claimed as your dependent can be summarized by five dependency tests. All five tests must be met in order for a person to qualify as your dependent:

1. Support test.
2. Gross-income test.
3. Member of household or relationship test.

4. Citizenship test.
5. Joint-return test.

The support test simply requires you to furnish more than half of your dependent's total support during the calendar year. The gross-income test says that, in general, you may not claim a person as a dependent if that person had gross income of $1,000 or more during the year. This test is of particular interest to teenagers and students. Two important exceptions to the gross-income test have been written into the law. The first is that if a taxpayer's child is less than 19 years of age at the end of the year, the gross-income test does not apply. The second important exemption is for students. If a taxpayer's child is a full-time student during some part of each of five calendar months of the calendar year, then the gross-income test does not apply, regardless of the age of the student.

The third dependency test, the member-of-household or relationship test, states that a person who is a member of your household and lives with you for the entire year (except for temporary absences) does not have to be related to you in order to be claimed as a dependent. Conversely, a dependent who is related to you need not live with you in order for the exemption to be claimed.

The fourth test requires that a dependent must be a U.S. citizen, resident, or national, or a resident of Canada or Mexico for some part of the calendar year in which your year begins. The last test, the joint-return test, states that you may not claim an exemption for a dependent if the dependent files a joint return. Thus, for example, a married daughter who files a joint return with her husband may not be claimed as an exemption on her parents' return even if the parents provide more than one half of her support.

Once your filing status and total personal exemptions are determined, you must determine your total income.

Step two: determining total income

The detailed regulations surrounding the determination of income are rather lengthy. Only a brief overview is provided here. You should consult the previously cited *IRS Publication 17* or one of the many commercial tax preparation guides for complete details.

In general, all compensation for personal services must be included in gross income. Sources of unearned income must also be considered. Total sources include but are not limited to wages, salaries, certain fringe benefits and allowances, tips, interest, dividends, rents, royalties, retirement plans, pensions, annuities, prizes and awards, partnership or proprietorship income, and estate and trust income. A myriad of rules and regulations surround the determination of whether or not income from sources other than compensation for personal services is taxable or nontaxable. If any doubt exists, you must consult a competent tax reference service.

Step three: adjusted gross income

Adjusted gross income is total income less various allowable expenses that may be deducted from total income prior to the determination of taxable income. Treating an expense as an adjustment instead of a deduction provides a tax advantage if you do not have sufficient deductions to itemize. The advantage arises because you may deduct allowable adjustments even if you do not itemize your deductions. Without the option to treat an expense as an adjustment, you would loose the expense as a deduction from income if your total deductions did not exceed the zero bracket amount.

Once again, it must be noted that a large number of rules apply to the determination of how the various adjustments are determined. However, we may generalize by categorizing the allowable adjustments to income into five major categories:

1. Moving expenses.
2. Employee's travel, gift, and entertainment.
3. Alimony payments.
4. Disability income exclusion.
5. Depreciation, amortization, and depletion.

The moving-expense adjustment allows you to deduct the cost of moving to a new residence when the move is caused by a change in your principal place of work. Certain other criteria also must be met. You must have made the move as a result of being an employee or self-employed individual. You also must have moved to a new principal place of work which is at least 25 miles farther from your old residence than the old residence was from your former place of work. If you had no former place of work, your new place of work must be at least 35 miles from your old residence. If the distance is less than 35 miles, the moving expenses are not deductible. Furthermore, you must be employed full-time for at least 39 weeks during the 12-month period immediately following the move. The move must be closely related to the start of work (within one year, in most cases). The expenses incurred must be reasonable. The cost of moving should be by the shortest, most direct route available by conventional means of transportation.

Deductions for an employee's travel, gift, and entertainment expenses are subject to a vast array of limitations, and generalization is difficult. In general, however, if you are required by the nature of your employment to incur expenses for travel, business gifts, and entertainment, you may deduct these expenses from total income. Of course, expenses for which you are reimbursed are not deductible. You should keep careful records of your travel and entertainment expenses. If you incur expenses greater than the amount for which you are reimbursed, you may deduct the excess expenses.

The rules surrounding alimony payments are fairly straightforward. Payments made to a former spouse for alimony, separate maintenance, or similar periodic payments are deductible. Spouses receiving such payments must claim the payments as income. Payments made to a former spouse for child support are not deductible.

Adjustments to income for disability income are also relatively straightforward. To qualify, you must be under age 65, have retired on disability, be permanently and totally disabled, and not have reached mandatory retirement age. Up to $5,200 a year of disability payments may be excluded from income subject to one limitation. The amount excluded must be reduced dollar-for-dollar for each dollar of adjusted gross income above $15,000. Disability income payments received from the Veterans Administration are not subject to this limitation. Disability payments to certain government employees that are the result of combat-related injuries are also exempt from this limitation. Similarly, sickness and injury payments from workers' compensation and black-lung benefits are fully exempt from tax.

The final category of adjustments to income is adjustments for depreciation, amortization, and depletion. These adjustments apply to property used in a trade or business, or property held for the production of income. A reasonable proportion of the cost of such property may be deducted each year as an allowance for the exhaustion, wear and tear, and obsolescence of such property. The determination of each year's allowable depreciation is subject to a variety of complex rules. Interpretation of the rules requires reference to a detailed tax guide. Only business property or property held for the production of income may be depreciated. Property used exclusively for personal or pleasure purposes may not be deducted. Examples of such personal property include your personal residence, home furnishings, and personal automobiles. Land may never be depreciated under any circumstances.

Amortization is similar to depreciation. In an accounting sense, amortization applies to the depreciation of business expenditures such as capital improvements to leased property that are made by the lessee. Depletion applies to the amortization of an economic interest in mineral deposits, oil and gas wells, geo-thermal deposits, or standing timber. The cost of such an economic interest may be amortized over the economic life of the property. An economic interest is defined as an investment by which you have acquired an interest in minerals in place or standing timber, and have received income from extracting the minerals or cutting the timber.

Any adjustments resulting from the five categories outlined above may be deducted from your total income to determine adjusted gross income. Your next step requires you to determine your tax table income.

Step four: determining taxable income

Your tax table income is determined by subtracting excess itemized deductions from adjusted gross income. If the total of your itemized deductions are less than your zero bracket amount, then tax table income is simply equal to adjusted gross income. You may proceed directly to the appropriate tax table. If total deductions exceed the zero bracket amount, then excess itemized deductions must be subtracted first before consulting the table. Table 5–4 summarizes the zero bracket amounts according to filing status. Table 5–5 lists the general types of expenses allowable as deductions.

Table 5–4
Zero bracket amount and itemized deductions

Zero bracket (1980 rates)	Amount
Single	$2,300
Married, filing joint return	$3,400
Married, filing separate return	$1,700
Unmarried head of household	$2,300
Qualifying widow or widower with dependent child	$3,400

It should be emphasized that the list given in Table 5–5 is by no means all-inclusive. The list only provides a brief outline of the general categories of deductions. You may need additional reference material for the preparation of a list of itemized deductions when filing an actual tax return. Once all of your deductions are itemized, you may then compute the actual tax due.

Step five: computing the tax due

The tax due on your tax table income may be determined quite easily in most cases. You can either look up the tax due in the appropriate tax table or compute the tax due from the appropriate tax schedule.

Consider the case of a single taxpayer claiming one exemption who has tax table income of $10,000 and does not itemize deductions. Since the single person's income is less than $20,000, Table A, a portion of which is illustrated in Figure 5–1, may be used. From the figure it can be seen that the tax due on $10,000 is $1,172. This amount is listed in column three of the table and is the amount due on income of more than $9,950 but not over $10,000.

If the single taxpayer earned $30,000 in taxable income, Schedule X would have to be used since $30,000 exceeds the limits of Table A. Because personal exemptions are not built into Schedule X, the one $1,000 exemption would have to be subtracted from the $30,000 income before computing the tax due. On an actual tax return, a Schedule TC would be used to do this. For this illustration we may simply reduce taxable income to $29,000 and compute the tax on that amount. From Schedule X, illustrated in Figure 5–2, it can be seen that the tax due on $29,000 is $7,434 plus 44 percent of the amount earned above

Table 5–5
General categories of itemized deductions

1. **Medical and dental expenses**

   Fees for doctors, dentists, optometrists, etc.
   Hospital and nurses services, therapy, and similar services.
   Meals and lodging furnished to a patient by hospital or therapeutic center.
   Special medical equipment and medical items.
   Transportation essential to medical care.

   Note: With the exception of medical insurance premiums, medical expenses may be deducted only to the extent that they exceed 3 percent of adjusted gross income. One half of medical insurance premiums, up to a maximum of $150, may be deducted regardless of income. The balance is then added to other medical expenses. Expenses for medicine and drugs may be deducted only to the extent that they exceed one percent of adjusted gross income.

2. **Taxes**

   State, local, or foreign income taxes.
   Real property tax (state, local, or foreign).
   Personal property tax (state or local).
   General sales tax (state or local).

3. **Interest expenses**

   Mortgage interest.
   Points charged to a home buyer on a personal residence.
   Mortgage prepayment penalty.
   Finance charges on charge accounts.
   Bank credit card interest.
   Interest paid on loan.
   Installment plan interest.
   Redeemable ground rents.

4. **Contributions to qualified organizations**

   U.S. state, possession, or the District of Columbia location required.
   Community chest, corporation, trust, fund or foundation organized and operated exclusively for charitable, religious, educational, scientific, or literary purposes.

5. **Casualty and theft losses**

   Complete or partial destruction or loss of property resulting from an identifiable event that is damaging to property *and* is sudden, unexpected, or unusual in nature.
   Business casualty losses are deductible in full.

Table 5–5 *(continued)*

Personal casualty losses are deductible to the extent they exceed $100. Examples of casualty losses include loss due to hurricane, tornado, flood, storm, shipwreck, fire, accident, mine cave-in, sonic boom, or vandalism.

6. Employee's educational expense

Expenses for education that meets the express requirements of employer or requirements of law or regulation to maintain present position.

Educational expenses that maintain or improve skills required in performing the duties of present employment.

Education must have a bona fide business purpose.

7. Miscellaneous itemized deductions

College professor's research, lecturing, and writing expenses.

Research chemist's laboratory breakage fee.

Certain employment agency fees.

Dues to professional societies.

Malpractice insurance premiums.

Physical examinations required by employer.

Portion of home used regularly and exclusively in work.

Small tools and supplies.

Subscription to professional journals.

Uniforms not adaptable to general use.

Union dues and expenses.

Political or newsletter fund contribution.

Tax counsel and assistance.

$28,800. The total tax is thus $7,434 plus 44 percent of $200, which amounts to $7,522.

Two important concepts are illustrated by this example. First, the difference between the average and marginal tax rate is illustrated. For the $30,000 single person, the $7,522 tax represents 25 percent of taxable income. This 25 percent rate is referred to as the taxpayer's average tax rate. However, note that each dollar earned above $28,800 is taxed at the 44 percent rate. This rate is referred to as the marginal tax rate. The marginal rate represents the rate assessed on each additional dollar of income for single persons in the $28,800 to $34,100 income bracket. This marginal rate is the rate commonly referred to as "my tax bracket." Note that the tax at the upper limit of the 44 percent bracket is the same as the tax at the lower limit of the 49 percent bracket. The tax due on $34,100 is $9,766 whether you compute it as $7,434 plus 44

Figure 5-1
Tax table A

1980 Tax Table A

Single (Filing Status Box 1)

(For single persons with income of $20,000 or less on Form 1040A, line 11, who claim 3 or fewer exemptions)

To find your tax: Read down the income column until you find your income as shown on Form 1040A, line 11. Read across to the column headed by the total number of exemptions claimed on

Form 1040A, line 6. The amount shown where the two lines meet is your tax. Enter on Form 1040A, line 14a.

The $2,300 zero bracket amount and your deduction for exemptions have been taken into account in figuring the tax shown in this table. Do not take a separate deduction for them.

Caution: *If you can be claimed as a dependent on your parent's return AND you have unearned income (interest, dividends, etc.) of $1,000 or more AND your earned income is less than $2,300, you must use Form 1040.*

If Form 1040A, line 11, is—		And the total number of exemptions claimed on line 6—			If Form 1040A, line 11, is—		And the total number of exemptions claimed on line 6—			If Form 1040A, line 11, is—		And the total number of exemptions claimed on line 6—		
Over	But not over	1	2	3	Over	But not over	1	2	3	Over	But not over	1	2	3
		Your tax is—					Your tax is—					Your tax is—		
If $3,300 or less your tax is 0					5,900	5,950	409	238	88	8,500	8,550	887	697	517
3,300	3,350	4	0	0	5,950	6,000	418	246	95	8,550	8,600	896	706	526
3,350	3,400	11	0	0	6,000	6,050	427	254	102	8,600	8,650	906	716	535
3,400	3,450	18	0	0	6,050	6,100	436	262	109	8,650	8,700	915	725	544
3,450	3,500	25	0	0										
					6,100	6,150	445	270	116	8,700	8,750	925	735	553
3,500	3,550	32	0	0	6,150	6,200	454	278	123	8,750	8,800	934	744	562
3,550	3,600	39	0	0	6,200	6,250	463	286	130	8,800	8,850	944	754	571
3,600	3,650	46	0	0	6,250	6,300	472	294	137	8,850	8,900	953	763	580
3,650	3,700	53	0	0										
					6,300	6,350	481	302	144	8,900	8,950	963	773	589
3,700	3,750	60	0	0	6,350	6,400	490	310	151	8,950	9,000	972	782	598
3,750	3,800	67	0	0	6,400	6,450	499	319	158	9,000	9,050	982	792	607
3,800	3,850	74	0	0	6,450	6,500	508	328	166	9,050	9,100	991	801	616
3,850	3,900	81	0	0										
					6,500	6,550	517	337	174	9,100	9,150	1,001	811	625
3,900	3,950	88	0	0	6,550	6,600	526	346	182	9,150	9,200	1,010	820	634
3,950	4,000	95	0	0	6,600	6,650	535	355	190	9,200	9,250	1,020	830	643
4,000	4,050	102	0	0	6,650	6,700	544	364	198	9,250	9,300	1,029	839	652
4,050	4,100	109	0	0										
					6,700	6,750	553	373	206	9,300	9,350	1,039	849	661
4,100	4,150	116	0	0	6,750	6,800	562	382	214	9,350	9,400	1,048	858	670
4,150	4,200	123	0	0	6,800	6,850	571	391	222	9,400	9,450	1,058	868	679
4,200	4,250	130	0	0	6,850	6,900	580	400	230	9,450	9,500	1,067	877	688
4,250	4,300	137	0	0										
					6,900	6,950	589	409	238	9,500	9,550	1,077	887	697
4,300	4,350	144	4	0	6,950	7,000	598	418	246	9,550	9,600	1,088	896	706
4,350	4,400	151	11	0	7,000	7,050	607	427	254	9,600	9,650	1,098	906	716
4,400	4,450	158	18	0	7,050	7,100	616	436	262	9,650	9,700	1,109	915	725
4,450	4,500	166	25	0										
					7,100	7,150	625	445	270	9,700	9,750	1,119	925	735
4,500	4,550	174	32	0	7,150	7,200	634	454	278	9,750	9,800	1,130	934	744
4,550	4,600	182	39	0	7,200	7,250	643	463	286	9,800	9,850	1,140	944	754
4,600	4,650	190	46	0	7,250	7,300	652	472	294	9,850	9,900	1,151	953	763
4,650	4,700	198	53	0										
					7,300	7,350	661	481	302	9,900	9,950	1,161	963	773
4,700	4,750	206	60	0	7,350	7,400	670	490	310	9,950	10,000	1,172	972	782
4,750	4,800	214	67	0	7,400	7,450	679	499	319	10,000	10,050	1,182	982	792
4,800	4,850	222	74	0	7,450	7,500	688	508	328	10,050	10,100	1,193	991	801
4,850	4,900	230	81	0										
					7,500	7,550	697	517	337	10,100	10,150	1,203	1,001	811
4,900	4,950	238	88	0	7,550	7,600	706	526	346	10,150	10,200	1,214	1,010	820
4,950	5,000	246	95	0	7,600	7,650	716	535	355	10,200	10,250	1,224	1,020	830
5,000	5,050	254	102	0	7,650	7,700	725	544	364	10,250	10,300	1,235	1,029	839
5,050	5,100	262	109	0										
					7,700	7,750	735	553	373	10,300	10,350	1,245	1,039	849
5,100	5,150	270	116	0	7,750	7,800	744	562	382	10,350	10,400	1,256	1,048	858
5,150	5,200	278	123	0	7,800	7,850	754	571	391	10,400	10,450	1,266	1,058	868
5,200	5,250	286	130	0	7,850	7,900	763	580	400	10,450	10,500	1,277	1,067	877
5,250	5,300	294	137	0										
					7,900	7,950	773	589	409	10,500	10,550	1,287	1,077	887
5,300	5,350	302	144	4	7,950	8,000	782	598	418	10,550	10,600	1,298	1,088	896
5,350	5,400	310	151	11	8,000	8,050	792	607	427	10,600	10,650	1,308	1,098	906
5,400	5,450	319	158	18	8,050	8,100	801	616	436	10,650	10,700	1,319	1,109	915
5,450	5,500	328	166	25										
					8,100	8,150	811	625	445	10,700	10,750	1,329	1,119	925
5,500	5,550	337	174	32	8,150	8,200	820	634	454	10,750	10,800	1,340	1,130	934
5,550	5,600	346	182	39	8,200	8,250	830	643	463	10,800	10,850	1,350	1,140	944
5,600	5,650	355	190	46	8,250	8,300	839	652	472	10,850	10,900	1,361	1,151	953
5,650	5,700	364	198	53										
					8,300	8,350	849	661	481	10,900	10,950	1,371	1,161	963
5,700	5,750	373	206	60	8,350	8,400	858	670	490	10,950	11,000	1,382	1,172	972
5,750	5,800	382	214	67	8,400	8,450	868	679	499	11,000	11,050	1,392	1,182	982
5,800	5,850	391	222	74	8,450	8,500	877	688	508	11,050	11,100	1,403	1,193	991
5,850	5,900	400	230	81										

Continued next column • Continued next column • Continued on next page

percent of $5,300 or simply pick it off the schedule as the tax due on $34,100 from the $34,100 to $41,500 income bracket.

The second important concept illustrated by this example is the progressive nature of the income tax system. The $30,000 single person earned exactly three times as much as the $10,000 single person. However, the tax on $30,000 ($7,522) is 6.4 times as much as the tax due

Figure 5-2
Tax rate schedules X, Y, and Z

1980 Tax Rate Schedules

If you cannot use one of the Tax Tables, figure your tax on the amount on Schedule TC, Part I, line 3, by using the appropriate Tax Rate Schedule on this page. Enter the tax on Schedule TC, Part I, line 4.

Note: *Your zero bracket amount has been built into these Tax Rate Schedules.*

SCHEDULE X—Single Taxpayers			SCHEDULE Y—Married Taxpayers and Qualifying Widows and Widowers						SCHEDULE Z—Heads of Household (including certain married persons who live apart (and abandoned spouses)—see page 6 of the Instructions)		
			Married Filing Joint Returns and Qualifying Widows and Widowers			**Married Filing Separate Returns**					
Use this schedule if you checked **Filing Status Box 1** on Form 1040—			Use this schedule if you checked **Filing Status Box 2 or 5** on Form 1040—			Use this schedule if you checked **Filing Status Box 3** on Form 1040—			Use this schedule if you checked **Filing Status Box 4** on Form 1040—		
If the amount on Schedule TC, Part I, line 3, is:	Enter on Schedule TC, Part I, line 4:		If the amount on Schedule TC, Part I, line 3, is:	Enter on Schedule TC, Part I, line 4:		If the amount on Schedule TC, Part I, line 3, is:	Enter on Schedule TC, Part I, line 4:		If the amount on Schedule TC, Part I, line 3, is:	Enter on Schedule TC, Part I, line 4:	
Not over $2,300........	—0—		Not over $3,400........	—0—		Not over $1,700........	—0—		Not over $2,300........	—0—	
Over—	But not over—	of the amount over—	Over—	But not over—	of the amount over—	Over—	But not over—	of the amount over—	Over—	But not over—	of the amount over—
$2,300	$3,400	14%	$2,300	$3,400	$5,500	14%	$3,400	$1,700	$2,750	14%	$1,700	$2,300	$4,400	14%	$2,300
$3,400	$4,400	$154+16%	$3,400	$5,500	$7,600	$294+16%	$5,500	$2,750	$3,800	$147.00+16%	$2,750	$4,400	$6,500	$294+16%	$4,400
$4,400	$6,500	$314+18%	$4,400	$7,600	$11,900	$630+18%	$7,600	$3,800	$5,950	$315.00+18%	$3,800	$6,500	$8,700	$630+18%	$6,500
$6,500	$8,500	$692+19%	$6,500	$11,900	$16,000	$1,404+21%	$11,900	$5,950	$8,000	$702.00+21%	$5,950	$8,700	$11,800	$1,026+22%	$8,700
$8,500	$10,800	$1,072+21%	$8,500	$16,000	$20,200	$2,265+24%	$16,000	$8,000	$10,100	$1,132.50+24%	$8,000	$11,800	$15,000	$1,708+24%	$11,800
$10,800	$12,900	$1,555+24%	$10,800	$20,200	$24,600	$3,273+28%	$20,200	$10,100	$12,300	$1,636.50+28%	$10,100	$15,000	$18,200	$2,476+26%	$15,000
$12,900	$15,000	$2,059+26%	$12,900	$24,600	$29,900	$4,505+32%	$24,600	$12,300	$14,950	$2,252.50+32%	$12,300	$18,200	$23,500	$3,306+31%	$18,200
$15,000	$18,200	$2,605+30%	$15,000	$29,900	$35,200	$6,201+37%	$29,900	$14,950	$17,600	$3,100.50+37%	$14,950	$23,500	$28,800	$4,951+36%	$23,500
$18,200	$23,500	$3,565+34%	$18,200	$35,200	$45,800	$8,162+43%	$35,200	$17,600	$22,900	$4,081.00+43%	$17,600	$28,800	$34,100	$6,859+42%	$28,800
$23,500	$28,800	$5,367+39%	$23,500	$45,800	$60,000	$12,720+49%	$45,800	$22,900	$30,000	$6,360.00+49%	$22,900	$34,100	$44,700	$9,085+46%	$34,100
$28,800	$34,100	$7,434+44%	$28,800	$60,000	$85,600	$19,678+54%	$60,000	$30,000	$42,800	$9,839.00+54%	$30,000	$44,700	$60,600	$13,961+54%	$44,700
$34,100	$41,500	$9,766+49%	$34,100	$85,600	$109,400	$33,502+59%	$85,600	$42,800	$54,700	$16,751.00+59%	$42,800	$60,600	$81,800	$22,547+59%	$60,600
$41,500	$55,300	$13,392+55%	$41,500	$109,400	$162,400	$47,544+64%	$109,400	$54,700	$81,200	$23,772.00+64%	$54,700	$81,800	$108,300	$35,055+63%	$81,800
$55,300	$81,800	$20,982+63%	$55,300	$162,400	$215,400	$81,464+68%	$162,400	$81,200	$107,700	$40,732.00+68%	$81,200	$108,300	$161,300	$51,750+68%	$108,300
$81,800	$108,300	$37,677+68%	$81,800	$215,400	....	$117,504+70%	$215,400	$107,700	....	$58,752.00+70%	$107,700	$161,300	....	$87,790+70%	$161,300
$108,300	....	$55,697+70%	$108,300												

on $10,000 ($1,172). This is the meaning of a progressive tax structure. As your income increases, a higher percentage of that income must be paid in income taxes.

After calculating your tax, only one final step remains. You must subtract any tax credits for which you are eligible from the amount of tax you owe.

Step six: deduct tax credits

A variety of tax credits are available that allow you to deduct eligible credit items directly from the amount of tax due. The various rules governing eligibility for and computation of these tax credits are somewhat complex. The credits may be grouped into the following categories:

1. Child care and disabled dependent care: for eligible individuals up to 20 percent of such expenses may be credited.

2. Credit for the elderly: 15 percent of a portion of income received by persons over 65 years old (or under age 65 who are receiving a taxable pension or annuity from a public retirement system) may be credited.

3. Residential energy credit: a variety of tax incentives to encourage energy conservation may be credited.

4. Jobs credit: employers who hire members of special targeted groups may qualify for this credit.

5. Credit for political contributions: You may take one half of such contributions as a credit. The credit limit is $50 for single persons, $100 for married filing jointly.

6. Foreign tax credit: income taxes paid to a foreign country or U.S. possession may be treated as a credit or an itemized deduction.

7. Investment credit: up to 10 percent of the cost of certain new or used personal property acquired for use in a trade or business may be creditable. The property must have an expected useful life of at least three years.

8. Work incentive (WIN) program credit: 20 percent of a portion of wages paid certain eligible nonbusiness employees who are recipients of financial assistance under Part A of Title IV of the Social Security Act may be treated as a credit.

9. Earned income credit: if earned income is less than $10,000, a credit may be allowable.

10. Credit for excess social security tax or railroad retirement tax withheld: excess withholding resulting from working for two or more employers is refundable as a credit.

11. Credit from a regulated investment company: capital gains taxes paid by a regulated investment company on dividends credited to an individual taxpayer are refundable as a credit.

12. Alcohol fuels credit: special credits may be available for persons using alcohol fuel in a trade or business.

Determining the total amount of tax credits completes the process. However, before presenting a sample tax-return form, four additional tax considerations require at least a brief discussion: the treatment of capital gains and losses, sale of a personal residence, limitations on earned income taxation, and the possibility of tax averaging.

Additional tax considerations

Capital gains and losses

Capital gains and losses result from the sale or other disposal of capital assets such as real property or investment securities. These gains and losses are treated differently than income derived from ordinary income sources such as salaries and wages. Once again, the laws surrounding this area are quite complex. The essential point here is that long-term capital gains (gains on assets held more than one year) are accorded favorable tax treatment. Subject to a variety of special considerations and limitations, your ordinary tax rate is paid on only 40 percent of a long-term capital gain. Gains from short-term capital gains (gains on assets held less than one year) are essentially treated the same as ordinary income.

Capital losses are deducted from capital gains in determining the amount of tax owed. However, there is one exception to this rule. Capital losses from sales or exchanges of property held for personal use, such as a personal residence, are not deductible. If total capital losses exceed capital gains, a capital-loss deduction may be claimed, subject to some limitations on the maximum amount that may be deducted.

Deductions of capital losses are subject to two important limitations. First, if you have net long-term losses, you may only deduct one half of these losses from ordinary income. In comparison, short-term capital losses may be deducted in full from net income. Second, you may not deduct more than $3,000 in net capital losses from ordinary income in any given year. Losses in excess of $3,000 may be carried forward to future years.

Sale of a personal residence

The sale of a personal residence is subject to special rules within the general guidelines for treatment of capital gains and losses. If you sell your home at a profit, the capital-gains tax may be deferred if a new home is purchased within 18 months before or after the sale of the old home. In order to qualify for the deferral, the new home must cost at least as much as the sale price of the old home. If the new home costs less than the old one, the gain can be partially deferred. The 18-month time limit is extended to two years if a new home is being constructed. For military personnel the time limit is suspended while serving on extended active duty. Extended active duty is more than 90 days. The maximum time limit for military personnel is four years, including the period during which the limit is suspended.

It is important to recognize that the capital gains tax is only deferred, not forgiven. Eventually, when you sell your last home, the tax on accumulated capital gains will have to be paid. However, persons aged 55 or over are entitled to a "once-in-a-lifetime" exclusion from capital gains tax of up to $100,000 in profit from the sale of personal residence. This provision of the law allows older persons the opportunity to sell their home and preserve their capital for retirement.

Maximum tax on earned income

The maximum tax on personal-service income is of interest to high-income taxpayers. Personal-service income is earned income received for personal services. It is also any income received as a pension or annuity resulting from an employment position or from prior tax-deductible contributions to a retirement plan. Examples of personal-services income include wages, salaries, professional fees, commissions, and tips. The law states that personal-service income may not be taxed at a rate higher than 50 percent. You can see that this is a provision of great interest to persons whose marginal tax rate exceeds 50 percent.

Income averaging

The final special provision of interest is the possibility of income averaging. This provision of the law is important to individuals who have had a substantial increase in income in one year. United States citizens who have furnished more than 50 percent of their own support during the four years preceding the year of the substantial increase may income average. Income averaging allows part of the increase to be "averaged back" and taxed in the lower brackets of the previous years. To be eligible to average, your averageable income must exceed $3,000. Your averageable income is the amount by which your taxable income in the current year exceeds 30 percent of your total taxable income for the preceeding four years. Income averaging effectively allows you to average back this income to the earlier years when you were in a lower tax bracket.

A sample tax return

You are now ready to put your tax knowledge to work. A sample tax return will be presented for Nick and Gincy, a married couple with three children who reside in a small town. Nick is employed as vice president of a local building-supply wholesale firm. Gincy is a full-time homemaker and also works part-time as a tax consultant in an accounting firm. Their combined annual salaries total $34,500. Additionally, they receive income of $380 per year from interest on savings accounts and $400 in stock dividends.

Nick and Gincy's tax return is illustrated in Figures 5–3 and 5–4. Their total income, including salary, interest, dividends, and a $180 state tax refund, amounts to $35,260. Since they have no adjustments to income, $35,260 is also their adjusted gross income. The tax computation section of their return (page 2 of Form 1040) shows excess itemized deductions of $6,020. To see the source of these deductions, Figure 5–4, a summary of their itemized deductions, must be examined.

They have a number of deductions, as might be expected of a family of their size and relatively high income level. Allowable medical and dental expenses come to $150. Deductible taxes amount to $3,308. Their largest deduction ($4,490) comes from interest expense. Most of the interest is attributable to their home-mortgage loan. Contributions total $950 and represent contributions to their local church. Finally, they have one miscel-

Figure 5–3
Sample form 1040

Form **1040** Department of the Treasury—Internal Revenue Service
U.S. Individual Income Tax Return **1980**

For Privacy Act Notice, see Instructions | For the year January 1–December 31, 1980, or other tax year beginning _____ 1980, ending _____ 19 _____

Use IRS label. Otherwise, please print or type.
Your first name and initial (if joint return, also give spouse's name and initial) — *Nicholas and Virginia* — Last name *Carasi*
Your social security number **999 89 7969**
Present home address (Number and street, including apartment number, or rural route) — *942 Cove Drive*
Spouse's social security no. **999 98 9796**
City, town or post office, State and ZIP code — *Waterview, Virginia 22914*
Your occupation ▶ *Executive*
Spouse's occupation ▶ *Tax Consultant*

Presidential Election Campaign Fund ▶
Do you want $1 to go to this fund? . . . . ✓ Yes ☐ No
If joint return, does your spouse want $1 to go to this fund? . . . ✓ Yes ☐ No
Note: Checking "Yes" will not increase your tax or reduce your refund.

Requested by Census Bureau for Revenue Sharing ▶
A Where do you live (actual location of residence)? (See page 2 of Instructions.) State: *Va* City, village, borough, etc.: *Waterview*
B Do you live within the legal limits of a city, village, etc.? ☐ Yes ☑ No
C In what county do you live? *Prince*
D In what township do you live? *Williams*

Filing Status
Check only one box.
1 ☐ Single
2 ✓ Married filing joint return (even if only one had income)
3 ☐ Married filing separate return. Enter spouse's social security no. above and full name here ▶ _____
4 ☐ Head of household. (See page 6 of Instructions.) If qualifying person is your unmarried child, enter child's name ▶ _____
5 ☐ Qualifying widow(er) with dependent child (Year spouse died ▶ 19 ___). (See page 6 of Instructions.)
For IRS use only

Exemptions
Always check the box labeled Yourself. Check other boxes if they apply.
6a ✓ Yourself ☐ 65 or over ☐ Blind
b ✓ Spouse ☐ 65 or over ☐ Blind
Enter number of boxes checked on 6a and b ▶ **2**
c First names of your dependent children who lived with you ▶ *Lee, Joy, Nicholas*
Enter number of children listed on 6c ▶ **3**

d Other dependents:
(1) Name | (2) Relationship | (3) Number of months lived in your home | (4) Did dependent have income of $1,000 or more? | (5) Did you provide more than one-half of dependent's support?
Enter number of other dependents ▶
Add numbers entered in boxes above ▶ **5**

7 Total number of exemptions claimed . . . .

Income
Please attach Copy B of your Forms W–2 here.
If you do not have a W–2, see page 5 of Instructions.

8 Wages, salaries, tips, etc. | 8 | **34,500** ✓
9 Interest income (attach Schedule B if over $400) | 9 | **380**
10a Dividends (attach Schedule B if over $400) **400** ✓ , 10b Exclusion **20** ✓
c Subtract line 10b from line 10a | 10c | **200** ✓
11 Refunds of State and local income taxes (do not enter an amount unless you deducted those taxes in an earlier year—see page 9 of Instructions) . . . . | 11 | **180** ✓
12 Alimony received . . . . | 12 | **—0—**
13 Business income or (loss) (attach Schedule C) | 13 | **—0—**
14 Capital gain or (loss) (attach Schedule D) . . . . | 14 | **—0—**
15 40% of capital gain distributions not reported on line 14 (See page 9 of Instructions) . | 15 | **—0—**
16 Supplemental gains or (losses) (attach Form 4797) | 16 | **—0—**
17 Fully taxable pensions and annuities not reported on line 18 . . . . | 17 | **—0—**
18 Pensions, annuities, rents, royalties, partnerships, etc. (attach Schedule E) . . . | 18 | **—0—**
19 Farm income or (loss) (attach Schedule F) . . . . | 19 | **—0—**
20a Unemployment compensation (insurance). Total received _____
b Taxable amount, if any, from worksheet on page 10 of Instructions . . . . | 20b | **—0—**
21 Other income (state nature and source—see page 10 of Instructions) ▶ _____ | 21 | **—0—**

22 Total income. Add amounts in column for lines 8 through 21 . . . . ▶ | 22 | **35,260** ✓

Adjustments to Income
(See Instructions on page 10)
23 Moving expense (attach Form 3903 or 3903F) . . . . | 23 |
24 Employee business expenses (attach Form 2106) . . | 24 |
25 Payments to an IRA (enter code from page 10 ....) . | 25 |
26 Payments to a Keogh (H.R. 10) retirement plan . . . | 26 |
27 Interest penalty on early withdrawal of savings . . . | 27 |
28 Alimony paid . . . . | 28 |
29 Disability income exclusion (attach Form 2440) . . . | 29 |
30 Total adjustments. Add lines 23 through 29 . . . . ▶ | 30 | **—0—**

Adjusted Gross Income
31 Adjusted gross income. Subtract line 30 from line 22. If this line is less than $10,000, see "Earned Income Credit" (line 57) on pages 13 and 14 of Instructions. If you want IRS to figure your tax, see page 3 of Instructions . . . . ▶ | 31 | **35,260** ✓

☆ U.S. GOVERNMENT PRINTING OFFICE: 1980—O-313-250 13-2687299
Form **1040** (1980)

Figure 5–3 *(continued)*

Form 1040 (1980)   Page 2

Tax Computation (See Instructions on page 11)	32 Amount from line 31 (adjusted gross income)	32	35,260
	33 If you do not itemize deductions, enter zero . . . . }	33	6,020
	If you itemize, complete Schedule A (Form 1040) and enter the amount from Schedule A, line 41		
	Caution: If you have unearned income and can be claimed as a dependent on your parent's return, check here ▶ ☐ and see page 11 of the Instructions. Also see page 11 of the Instructions if: • You are married filing a separate return and your spouse itemizes deductions, OR • You file Form 4563, OR • You are a dual-status alien.		
	34 Subtract line 33 from line 32. Use the amount on line 34 to find your tax from the Tax Tables, or to figure your tax on Schedule TC, Part I . . . . Use Schedule TC, Part I, and the Tax Rate Schedules ONLY if: • Line 34 is more than $20,000 ($40,000 if you checked Filing Status Box 2 or 5), OR • You have more exemptions than are shown in the Tax Table for your filing status, OR • You use Schedule G or Form 4726 to figure your tax. Otherwise, you MUST use the Tax Tables to find your tax.	34	29,240
	35 Tax. Enter tax here and check if from ☑ Tax Tables or ☐ Schedule TC	35	4,400
	36 Additional taxes. (See page 12 of Instructions.) Enter here and check if from ☐ Form 4970, } ☐ Form 4972, ☐ Form 5544, ☐ Form 5405, or ☐ Section 72(m)(5) penalty tax . . .	36	–0–
	37 **Total.** Add lines 35 and 36 . . . . ▶	37	4,400

Credits (See Instructions on page 12)	38 Credit for contributions to candidates for public office . . .	38	50	
	39 Credit for the elderly (attach Schedules R&RP)	39	–0–	
	40 Credit for child and dependent care expenses (attach Form 2441) .	40	–0–	
	41 Investment credit (attach Form 3468)	41	–0–	
	42 Foreign tax credit (attach Form 1116)	42	–0–	
	43 Work incentive (WIN) credit (attach Form 4874)	43	–0–	
	44 Jobs credit (attach Form 5884)	44	–0–	
	45 Residential energy credits (attach Form 5695)	45	–0–	
	46 Total credits. Add lines 38 through 45	46		50
	47 **Balance.** Subtract line 46 from line 37 and enter difference (but not less than zero). ▶	47		4,350

Other Taxes (Including Advance EIC Payments)	48 Self-employment tax (attach Schedule SE)	48		–0–
	49a Minimum tax. Attach Form 4625 and check here ▶ ☐	49a		–0–
	49b Alternative minimum tax. Attach Form 6251 and check here ▶ ☐	49b		–0–
	50 Tax from recomputing prior-year investment credit (attach Form 4255)	50		–0–
	51a Social security (FICA) tax on tip income not reported to employer (attach Form 4137) . .	51a		–0–
	51b Uncollected employee FICA and RRTA tax on tips (from Form W–2)	51b		–0–
	52 Tax on an IRA (attach Form 5329)	52		–0–
	53 Advance earned income credit (EIC) payments received (from Form W–2)	53		–0–
	54 **Balance.** Add lines 47 through 53 . . . . ▶	54		4,350

Payments Attach Forms W–2, W–2G, and W–2P to front.	55 Total Federal income tax withheld . . .	55	5,240	
	56 1980 estimated tax payments and amount applied from 1979 return . .	56	–0–	
	57 Earned income credit. If line 32 is under $10,000, see pages 13 and 14 of Instructions	57	–0–	
	58 Amount paid with Form 4868	58	–0–	
	59 Excess FICA and RRTA tax withheld (two or more employers)	59	–0–	
	60 Credit for Federal tax on special fuels and oils (attach Form 4136 or 4136–T)	60	–0–	
	61 Regulated Investment Company credit (attach Form 2439)	61	–0–	
	62 **Total.** Add lines 55 through 61	62		5,240

Refund or Balance Due	63 If line 62 is larger than line 54, enter amount **OVERPAID** . . . . ▶	63	890
	64 Amount of line 63 to be **REFUNDED TO YOU** . . . . ▶	64	890
	65 Amount of line 63 to be applied to your 1981 estimated tax . . . ▶	65 –0–	
	66 If line 54 is larger than line 62, enter **BALANCE DUE.** Attach check or money order for full amount payable to "Internal Revenue Service." Write your social security number on check or money order . . ▶ (Check ▶ ☐ if Form 2210 (2210F) is attached. See page 15 of Instructions.) ▶ $	66	–0–

Please Sign Here	Under penalties of perjury, I declare that I have examined this return, including accompanying schedules and statements, and to the best of my knowledge and belief, it is true, correct, and complete. Declaration of preparer (other than taxpayer) is based on all information of which preparer has any knowledge. ▶ *Nicholas Carosi* 3/19/81 ▶ *Virginia Carosi* 3/19/81 Your signature Date Spouse's signature (if filing jointly, BOTH must sign even if only one had income)
Paid Preparer's Use Only	Preparer's signature and date ▶ Check if self-employed ▶ ☐ Preparer's social security no. Firm's name (or yours, if self-employed) and address ▶ E.I. No. ▶ ZIP code ▶

laneous deduction of $22, the cost of two tax publications purchased during the year. Total deductions come to $9,420 from which is subtracted the zero bracket amount of $3,400. The difference, $6,020, is deducted from total income to obtain their tax table income.

Using the appropriate tax table yields a tax bill of $4,400. They have

Figure 5-4
Sample schedule A

Schedules A&B—Itemized Deductions AND
(Form 1040) Interest and Dividend Income

Department of the Treasury
Internal Revenue Service

▶ Attach to Form 1040. ▶ See Instructions for Schedules A and B (Form 1040).

1980
08

Name(s) as shown on Form 1040
Nicholas and Virginia Carosi

Your social security number
999 89 7969

Schedule A—Itemized Deductions *(Schedule B is on back)*

Medical and Dental Expenses (not paid or reimbursed by insurance or otherwise) (See page 16 of Instructions.)

1 One-half (but not more than $150) of insurance premiums you paid for medical care. (Be sure to include in line 10 below.) . ▶	150
2 Medicine and drugs .	50
3 Enter 1% of Form 1040, line 31 . . .	353
4 Subtract line 3 from line 2. If line 3 is more than line 2, enter zero . . .	-0-
5 Balance of insurance premiums for medical care not entered on line 1 . .	290
6 Other medical and dental expenses:	
a Doctors, dentists, nurses, etc. . . .	120
b Hospitals	52
c Other (itemize—include hearing aids, dentures, eyeglasses, transportation, etc.) ▶ *Eyeglasses*	124
Transportation	56
7 Total (add lines 4 through 6c)	242
8 Enter 3% of Form 1040, line 31 . . .	1058
9 Subtract line 8 from line 7. If line 8 is more than line 7, enter zero	-0-
10 Total medical and dental expenses (add lines 1 and 9). Enter here and on line 33 ▶	150

Taxes *(See page 17 of Instructions.)*
Note: Gasoline taxes are no longer deductible.

11 State and local income	1694
12 Real estate	980
13 General sales (see sales tax tables) . .	354
14 Personal property	280
15 Other (itemize) ▶	
16 Total taxes (add lines 11 through 15). Enter here and on line 34 . . . ▶	3308

Interest Expense *(See page 17 of Instructions.)*

17 Home mortgage	4650
18 Credit and charge cards	120
19 Other (itemize) ▶ *Bank Loan*	250
20 Total interest expense (add lines 17 through 19). Enter here and on line 35 ▶	4990

Contributions *(See page 17 of Instructions.)*

21 a Cash contributions for which you have receipts or cancelled checks	950
b Other cash contributions (show to whom you gave and how much you gave) ▶	
22 Other than cash (see page 17 of Instructions for required statement) . . .	
23 Carryover from prior years	
24 Total contributions (add lines 21a through 23). Enter here and on line 36 . ▶	950

Casualty or Theft Loss(es) *(See page 18 of Instructions.)*

25 Loss before insurance reimbursement .	
26 Insurance reimbursement	
27 Subtract line 26 from line 25. If line 26 is more than line 25, enter zero . . .	
28 Enter $100 or amount from line 27, whichever is smaller	
29 Total casualty or theft loss(es) (subtract line 28 from line 27). Enter here and on line 37 . ▶	-0-

Miscellaneous Deductions *(See page 18 of Instructions.)*

30 Union dues	
31 Other (itemize) ▶ *Tax Publications*	22
32 Total miscellaneous deductions (add lines 30 and 31). Enter here and on line 38 ▶	22

Summary of Itemized Deductions
(See page 19 of Instructions.) **A**

33 Total medical and dental—from line 10 .	150
34 Total taxes—from line 16	3308
35 Total interest—from line 20	4990
36 Total contributions—from line 24 . . .	950
37 Total casualty or theft loss(es)—from line 29 .	-0-
38 Total miscellaneous—from line 32 . .	22
39 Add lines 33 through 38	9420
40 If you checked Form 1040, Filing Status box: 2 or 5, enter $3,400 . . . . 1 or 4, enter $2,300 . . . . 3, enter $1,700	3400
41 Subtract line 40 from line 39. Enter here and on Form 1040, line 33. (If line 40 is more than line 39, see the Instructions for line 41 on page 19.) . . . . ▶	6020

one tax credit of $50 for a contribution to a candidate for public office, reducing the final tax due to $4,350. Since a total of $5,240 has been withheld from their paychecks, they are due a refund of $890.

Tax audits

If you itemize your deductions, you are likely to be audited sometime in your tax life. Your return may be selected for audit through two common procedures. First, the IRS has a regular program of selecting returns at random. You might be one of the people randomly selected. If you are selected by the random process, it is likely that each line of your return will be checked by auditors.

Returns may also be selected for audit if itemized deductions are out of line with average deductions taken by people in the same income category. A person earning $15,000 per year, for example, might claim $4,000 in interest expense. Interest deductions of $4,000 are much higher than normal for this income category. The return might be selected for audit because of this discrepancy. Table 5–6 provides some average deductions based on 1978 tax returns. If your deductions are substantially greater than these levels, you might be audited. Normally only the deductions questioned are checked in this type of audit.

Table 5–6
Average itemized deductions

	Adjusted gross income ($000)						
	8–12	12–20	20–25	25–30	30–50	50–100	Over 100
Medical expense	$ 980	$ 680	$ 500	$ 520	$ 550	$ 750	$ 1,070
Taxes..............	1,170	1,500	1,950	2,300	3,124	5,500	14,000
Contributions........	530	520	560	680	900	1,970	9,700
Interest	1,560	1,880	2,090	2,270	2,640	4,230	9,360

SOURCE   Linda Small, "How to Survive a Tax Audit," *McCalls Magazine*, January 1980.

There are several types of audits you can expect. You might receive a letter from the IRS asking for more information. Or you might receive notification of an error in your return. This is the simplest type of audit. All you have to do is send the IRS what they want. You might have to pay a few more dollars in tax or you might even get a refund.

A more complicated audit will ask you to explain how you arrived at your figures for deduction and expenses. Usually the IRS will review your records in this type of audit. If this happens, there is no need to panic. It just takes time to explain how you arrived at your numbers. The better your records, the easier it will be to explain your position. If you disagree with the IRS, there are procedures for review and adjudication. In some cases you might even have to go to court. You have nothing to fear from this process if you have filed an honest return. If fraud is involved, you can be prosecuted on criminal charges.

A few simple rules will help take the worry and panic out of tax time. Like any good business person, you should plan ahead for tax time. You should be familiar with the tax system and have a good idea of what your tax liability will be. You can then insure that your tax withholding or quarterly payments are adequate to cover the amount you owe. In this way a large unexpected bill on April 15 can be avoided. You should also keep good records and maintain these records for at least three years. Be sure to report all income subject to tax and to take all deductions to which you are entitled. When in doubt, research your problem carefully or seek professional assistance.

Tax shelters

The topic of tax shelters is important to income tax planning. You have seen the importance of the income tax to personal financial management. A discussion of strategies to reduce your personal tax liability seems most appropriate.

Stated in most general terms, a tax shelter is any device or investment that provides a legal means for you to reduce, defer, or escape taxation. Most tax shelters are the result of legal provisions written by the Congress to encourage investment in certain areas. These areas are regarded as important to the national interest. For example, a number of tax incentives are provided to people who invest in a variety of real estate ventures, oil- and gas-drilling ventures, equipment leasing, and cattle-feeding plans. In its most narrowly interpreted sense, a tax shelter is often defined as any investment that allows you to convert earned income into a long-term capital gain. The classic tax shelter is one that allows invested funds to be deducted from ordinary income at the time the investment is made. Later profits on the investment are taken in the form of long-term capital gains.

It should be emphasized that nearly all such tax shelters are quite risky. The tax incentives have been written into the law in order to attract investments that otherwise might not be made. One tax-shelter specialist defines a tax shelter as any investment so risky that a prudent person would not invest without the added tax incentive. Great care must be exercised in selecting a tax shelter for possible investment. Not only are these investments risky, but they can also be questionable from a legal viewpoint. Many swindles have been perpetrated on unsuspecting investors who thought they were investing in a legitimate tax shelter.

In a broader sense a number of investments that provide tax-sheltered income are considered to be tax shelters. If you invest in municipal bonds, the original investment does not provide a tax deduction. But the income earned on a municipal bond is free of federal income tax. In some cases the interest earned may also be exempt from state taxes. More will be said about municipal bond investments in the investments section of the text (Part 5).

Owning a personal residence is considered by many middle-income families to be the most important tax shelter available. The interest portion of your monthly mortgage payment and your annual property taxes are tax-deductible. In our current inflationary times these major deductions, coupled with an expected increase in the value of a home, make home ownership extremely attractive. A great deal of detailed information is provided about the pros and cons of home ownership in Chapter 6, "Housing Expenditures and Home Financing." Home ownership is a major income tax shelter for taxpayers of moderate means.

Summary

The subject of income taxes is very complicated. The functioning of our federal tax system depends largely on the voluntary cooperation and reporting of income by taxpayers. The IRS maintains a very active audit service to aid you in carrying out your voluntary duties. Approximately 2 percent of all returns filed are audited, and the chances of being audited increase as your income increases. As might be expected from the complexity of the tax laws, a rather high percentage of errors are discovered during the auditing process. Most taxpayers who are audited end up owing more money, but a small percentage of people do obtain a refund. A number of stiff penalties are provided in the event an audit turns up a fraudulent return. If you are honest and keep good records, you need not fear any audit.

Most taxpayers who derive their major source of income from a salary can file their own tax return without professional assistance. When in doubt, professional advice should be sought. A professional counselor, accountant, or attorney may be consulted for a fee. The local IRS office will provide assistance free of charge. In any event you should not hesitate to take all legitimate deductions to which you feel entitled. Criminal penalties are provided only in the case of fraud. As millions of Americans can attest, it is no crime to disagree with the Internal Revenue Service.

PART **3**

Financing consumer expenditures

6

Home ownership—the buying and care of your own home

- Should you buy a home?
- Some good reasons for home ownership
- A life cycle of renting and home ownership
- A need to rent
- Buying a house: What can you afford?
- Locating the downpayment money
- Finding a house you can afford
- The process of buying a house
- What is a mortgage?
- A deed represents ownership and title
- How you must pay operating costs and repairs
- Be a "Harry Homeowner"
- Should you sell a house yourself?
- Don't lose your home!
- Summary

The selection of a house or an apartment is one of the most exciting activities in which you will become involved. Adequate housing is a part of our lives, and reflects how we live and how we think about life. The purchase of a house also is one of your most important financial transactions. Certainly for most of us, it is our largest financial transaction. It will probably add the most money to your financial net worth and provide you with the greatest enjoyment. To make certain that you get your money's worth, you must understand the process involved in buying a house. This includes the mechanics of buying, where to obtain the downpayment, and how to finance the house. Finally, you must understand what it will cost you to live in the house and maintain it.

Should you buy a home?

At one time when a young couple contemplated the purchase of a house, a question would be raised: "Is it cheaper to own your own house or to rent?" When that question is raised today, there is little reason to pause. The answer is simple and direct. It is almost always better to own your own home than to rent. Support for that answer requires a discussion of the financial and economic advantages of home ownership, the tax advantages it brings, and the protection it gives you against inflation. Lastly, you need to consider the emotional stability and security of home ownership. Let's examine each of these reasons.

Some good reasons for home ownership

A house is an inflation hedge

One reason home ownership is so attractive is inflation. Housing prices in most metropolitan areas of the United States have risen dramatically since the end of World War II. During the 70s they went up with a vengeance. In Washington, D.C., for example, although this is not a typical American city, a house that sold for $19,000 in the late 1960s sold for $90,000 in 1980. A house that sold for $70,000 in 1970 sold for $224,000 in 1980. (Prices did ease in the 1980 recession. But past economic downturns only postponed the rise in housing prices.) This dramatic rise in real estate values has been duplicated in other cities. Figure 6–1 provides an example of the dramatic rise in average price of a house over a period of time. This information clearly shows not only that housing prices have risen dramatically but that home ownership has been a good hedge against inflation.

Some people who look at today's housing prices may raise the following questions: "But will prices of housing increase forever?" "Can we afford

**Figure 6–1
Average price of new and existing homes,
1970–1978**

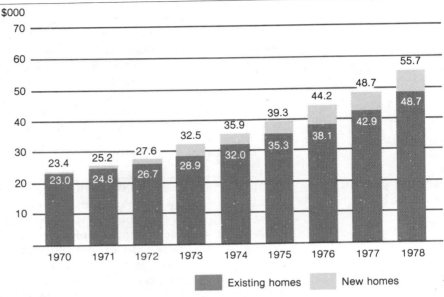

SOURCE   National Association of Home Builders

to take the risk of home ownership after such a dramatic rise in the prices of houses in the United States?'' Certainly if you raise these questions, you are worried about the future. In fact, you have a reason to worry. But we have had periods of recession in housing before, and we will have them again. Yet somehow we have survived as individuals and as a nation. Even though there is a reason to be concerned, chances are that prices of housing, both old and new, will continue to rise. This is simply because the inflationary pressures in the world created by our need for shelter will continue to force housing prices up in the future, much as they have done in the past. Michael Sumichrast, chief economist of the National Association of Home Builders, thinks that housing prices will continue to rise in the 1980s. Figure 6–2 reflects his estimate of the expected trend in housing prices. The average price of an existing home in 1979 was $55,800 and is expected to reach $136,000 in 1989. The average price of a new house for the same period will increase from $63,300 to $156,537. This means that housing prices for new homes will rise at an average simple rate of return of 14.7 percent, compared to 14.4 percent for existing homes. If you accept Sumichrast's estimate, you would be foolish not to consider the purchase of a house as both an inflationary hedge and a way of increasing capital and net worth. Of course, this assumes that you can afford the mortgage payments.

Figure 6–2
Estimate of future home prices, 1979–1989

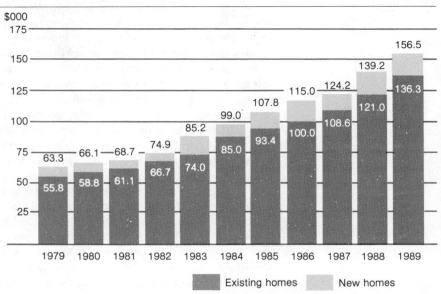

SOURCE   National Association of Home Builders, *Econometric Forecasting Service.*

Tax advantage of home ownership

Another financial reason for buying a house is the tax break you get from Uncle Sam. It's nice to have a wealthy uncle who will help you buy your own house! The federal government allows you to deduct the interest you pay on your mortgage from your income tax. This results in a lower aftertax cost. Interest on the mortgage is also deducted as a legitimate expense from state income taxes. You can also deduct the real estate taxes you pay from your federal, state, and municipal income taxes. Many people who never itemized their income tax deductions will begin to do so after they buy a house. This is because of the substantial tax write-offs they receive for interest payments and taxes. Such write-offs reduce the amount of tax paid and make home ownership very worthwhile.

It is estimated that a couple earning $22,500 a year pays slightly over 12 percent of their income to the federal government. In addition, they must pay Social Security taxes, property taxes, sales taxes, and other kinds of taxes. When you add all these items together, they pay approximately one third of their annual income in taxes. And the amount of taxes people pay has risen over the years because of inflation. It has also risen because the federal government has not revised its tax-rate schedule downward to reflect inflation. Therefore, the fact that interest and taxes on real estate are deductible from income taxes makes home ownership all the more attractive.

Those hit hardest by taxes are people who do not own a house, who are unmarried, and who are middle-income taxpayers. A single person pays one third more in taxes for the same income as does a married couple. Single people usually do not buy a house—they rent. This prevents them from obtaining deductions that could reduce their income tax substantially. Therefore, if you are a single, middle-income person, consider the tax benefits of home ownership.

You would have enough income tax deductions because of your property deduction to allow you to itemize all deductions and thus reduce your tax bill. And this is where the tax savings occur. If you pay $4,000 interest the first year, this can be written off as a tax-deductible expense. If you are in the 30 percent tax bracket, your taxes are reduced by $1,200. This is because your income subject to the tax is $4,000 lower than it would have been if you had not purchased a house. This, in effect, reduces the cost of home ownership by $1,200 because of the tax deductibility of interest. If you pay $1,000 in property taxes, that amount will actually cost 30 percent less because of the tax deductibility of property taxes. Therefore, the $1,000 property taxes will cost only $700 after income taxes are considered. In addition, as the price of the property increases, you benefit from an increase in the value of the house.

Stability of costs

Another financial advantage of home ownership is not as direct as the tax advantage. Usually when you borrow $50,000 to buy a house, the principal and interest payments are constant over the life of the mortgage. Such payments, as a rule, cannot be increased by the lending organization. Therefore, one advantage in buying your own house is that you can keep your payment for housing constant. By contrast, if you rented a house, the rent would tend to increase over time. (Property taxes are likely to increase, but they usually represent only a small part of your housing cost.) Therefore, you tend to reduce housing costs by buying rather than renting because your costs stay relatively constant. In recent years lending institutions have introduced variable rate mortgages that change with the level of interest rates. Under such a mortgage costs do not remain constant and will increase if mortgage rates increase.

Forced savings

Another side effect of the financial aspects of real estate ownership should be understood. You will probably pay a greater percentage of your income for housing if you buy your own house than if you rent. If you own your own house, you are likely to put more money into furnishings, decorations, bookshelves, landscaping, and other improvements. There is also a tendency to "stretch" your budget for a house of your dreams.

But in the long run, even though you spend more for a house, you will end up with more. You will have a greater net worth and more real assets. Of course, this is one of your goals in financial planning—to maximize your net worth. Buying a house is a way to do so.

Ownership adds to your security and peace of mind

The financial attractiveness of home ownership and the fact that it provides basic shelter are only a part of the many advantages of home ownership. Another major advantage relates to the basic security you derive in living in your own home. Although you spend more money, you have the advantage of enjoying your own home. You also have a feeling of pride of ownership that you do not obtain from renting. Home ownership provides a sense of belonging, a feeling of permanence, and a sense of security that are achieved in no other way. Therefore, a strong case may be made for the idea of home ownership versus renting. However as we look at the life cycle of our need for shelter, we will find that there is a definite place for renting.

A life cycle of renting and home ownership

Most people begin life in a family unit. They live with loved ones until they go off to college or leave home. So the first type of shelter you know as a rule is the home environment of your family. This may be followed by a rented room, probably in a strange city. If you serve in the military, you might even have to put up with a small cot in a room shared with a hundred other people. College isn't usually that bad. At worst you might have to share a room with four or five other people.

From the rented room people often move to a furnished apartment. This is because many cannot afford to furnish a first apartment. And then as housing needs grow, you may go through the following events: a move to an unfurnished efficiency apartment with no bedrooms; an unfurnished apartment with one bedroom; and then an unfurnished apartment with two bedrooms. And as your proprietary instinct and demand for space increase, you may move to an unfurnished house or to a series of unfurnished houses.

If you are wise, you will buy a small house or condominium at first. Then you may buy a larger house, and afterward you may try to buy or build the house of your dreams. Once that dream has been accomplished, if your fortunes increase and prosper, you may begin to rent a vacation apartment or house. If you continue to prosper, you may even buy a vacation house. (This topic is discussed in detail in a later chapter on real estate investment.) Next, as children grow older and leave the nest you may find that your dream house has become too large. You may decide to sell it and buy either a house with less space or a maintenance-provided condominium.

A need to rent

At some point in this housing cycle there is a great need for people to rent. Many people cannot buy and must rent because of economic necessity. There is nothing wrong with renting if you can't afford to buy. Therefore, renting plays a very important place in planning your housing needs. It allows you to go from the family home to your own house in a transitional way. You thus become gradually used to the idea of the additional expense and cost of home ownership. So a major reason for you to rent is that you cannot afford to buy.

A second reason to rent is when you are only temporarily located in a city and do not wish to make a financial commitment. You know it is expensive to buy and sell in a short period of time, except in very dynamic housing market where prices move up substantially in a very short period. So you decide to rent because it is to your advantage to do so.

A third reason to rent is that you may not be able to locate a house where you wish to live. Many people coming to Washington, D.C., for example, would like to live in the Georgetown area, even though houses there are expensive. While houses may not be available for purchase, some may still be available as rentals. It makes sense to rent under these circumstances. Finally, you may decide to rent for a half dozen different reasons. You may not wish to commit money to a house in spite of the advantages of home ownership. You may like the convenience of renting. Or you may just not want the responsibility of owning your own place. All of these reasons are good and legitimate grounds for renting. On the other hand, over the long term owning your own house is very profitable and satisfying.

Buying a house: What can you afford?

Before you start looking for a house or apartment to buy, you should ask yourself how much you can afford to pay. You will save yourself a lot of time and effort if you have a clear idea about this point. You also need to know *all* the financial commitments related to the ownership of a house. Essentially there are three aspects to keep in mind. First, how much money do you have available as a downpayment? Second, how much do you earn and have available for the principal, interest, and taxes? Third, if you do borrow mortgage money, what is the interest rate you must pay? How many years do you have to repay the mortgage? All these factors will influence how much you can afford to spend on a house. Generally speaking, the greater the amount of money available as a downpayment, the bigger and the better will be the house you can afford. Second, the higher your income and the more money you have available for the mortgage, the more impressive will be the house you can buy. Third, the lower the interest rate on the mortgage, the more money you can afford to borrow, and the bigger the house you can afford to buy.

The mortgage you can afford at each income level

Some detailed financial data will help you understand a bit more about the financial requirements of paying the principal and interest on a house. Table 6–1 indicates the size of mortgage and the price of house you can afford on the basis of income level. In this table the annual income figures increase in $6,000 increments, from $6,000 all the way up to $84,000. In the second column monthly incomes are listed. In the third column monthly incomes available for payment of principal and interest are listed. Here the conventional guideline used is that principal and interest payments should not exceed 25 percent of your gross income. In some locations this might be high because in addition to the principal and interest payments, you must pay real estate taxes on your property. You must also pay for the cost of electricity, heating, maintenance, water and sewage, and telephone service for your residence.

Even though the figures in the third column show only an approximate amount of money available for principal and interest, they can serve as a guide to the kind of mortgage you can support with the money available to you. Therefore, if you feel you can afford $500 a month for principal and interest, Table 6–1 tells you how much of a mortgage you can support, depending on the current mortgage interest rate.

The mortgage payments in Table 6–1 are based on a 30–year mortgage at 10, 12, 14, and 16 percent. It is assumed that a 20 percent downpayment will be made. The amount below each of these columns represents the amount of mortgage that can be supported by the income available for principal and interest. Thus, for example, if you have $500 a month available for principal and interest and can obtain a 30–year, 10 percent mortgage, $500 a month will support a mortgage of $56,947. Notice the dramatic effect that an increase in the interest rate has on the amount of mortgage money you can borrow, assuming that you have $500 a month available. At 12 percent, the $500 available for principal and interest supports a mortgage of $48,592; at 14 percent, $42,942; and at 16 percent, $37,340. Therefore, the higher the interest rate, the less house you can buy on the basis of a given level of income.

Since the 30–year mortgage represents 80 percent of the value of the house (a 20 percent downpayment is assumed), the next questions are: What price house can you afford? How much can you pay for a house? If you have $500 a month available for principal and interest and convert the mortgage value into house value, you will be able to afford a house valued at $71,184 if interest rates are at 10 percent. You could afford a $60,740 house at 12 percent, a $52,740 house at 14 percent, and only a $46,676 house at 16 percent. The higher the mortgage interest rate you pay, the less you can afford.

Let's now assume that you want to buy a bigger house. You must either increase the amount of money for principal and interest, or you must come up with a larger downpayment. To determine the downpayment required, the last column in Table 6–1 shows the various downpay-

Table 6-1
Home ownership: What can you afford?

Annual income	Monthly income	Income available for P & I*	Mortgage you can afford				Price of home you can afford (80% mortgage)				Down payment required (20% downpayment)			
			10%	12%	14%	16%	10%	12%	14%	16%	10%	12%	14%	16%
6,000	500	125	14,237	12,148	10,548	9,335	17,796	15,185	13,185	11,669	3,559	3,037	2,637	2,334
12,000	1,000	250	28,474	24,296	21,097	18,670	35,592	30,370	26,370	23,338	7,118	6,074	5,274	4,668
18,000	1,500	375	42,711	36,444	31,644	28,005	53,388	45,555	39,555	35,007	10,677	9,111	7,911	7,002
24,000	2,000	500	56,948	48,592	42,192	37,340	71,184	60,740	52,740	46,676	14,236	12,148	10,548	9,336
30,000	2,500	625	71,825	60,740	52,740	46,675	88,980	75,925	65,925	58,345	17,795	15,185	13,185	11,670
36,000	3,000	750	85,422	72,888	63,288	56,010	106,776	91,110	75,110	70,014	21,354	18,222	15,822	14,004
42,000	3,500	875	99,659	85,036	73,826	65,346	124,572	106,295	92,296	81,683	24,913	21,259	18,459	16,338
48,000	4,000	1,000	113,896	97,184	81,384	74,681	142,368	121,480	105,480	93,352	28,472	24,296	21,096	18,672
54,000	4,500	1,125	128,133	109,332	94,932	81,016	160,164	136,665	118,666	105,021	32,031	27,333	23,733	21,006
60,000	5,000	1,250	142,370	121,480	105,480	93,351	177,960	151,850	131,850	116,690	35,590	30,370	26,370	23,340
66,000	5,500	1,375	156,607	133,628	116,028	102,686	195,756	167,035	145,035	128,359	39,149	33,407	29,007	25,674
72,000	6,000	1,500	170,844	145,776	136,576	112,021	213,552	182,220	158,220	140,028	42,708	36,444	31,644	28,007
78,000	6,500	1,625	185,081	157,924	137,124	121,356	231,351	197,405	171,405	151,697	46,270	39,481	34,281	30,341
84,000	7,000	1,750	199,318	170,072	147,672	130,691	249,147	212,590	184,590	163,366	49,829	42,518	36,918	32,675

* P & I = principal and interest.

ments required on the basis of the price of the house and a 20 percent downpayment. For the $71,184 house at 10 percent, you need $14,236 down. For the $60,740 house at 12 percent, you need a downpayment of $12,148. For the $52,740 house at 14 percent, you need a downpayment of $10,548, and for the $46,676 house at 16 percent, you can afford—on a monthly income of $500—$9,336 downpayment. Therefore, the higher the mortgage interest rate, the smaller the house you can afford. At the same time, fortunately, you will need less in the way of a downpayment, assuming again a 20 percent downpayment rate.

Now assume that you have $500 a month available for housing and that interest rates are 14 percent. You want to know how much of a house you can afford with a $20,000 downpayment. First, look at the column of monthly income in Table 6–1. If you have $500 a month available for principal and interest and if the mortgage interest rate is 14 percent, you can support a mortgage of $42,192. So if you wish to put down $20,000, you can buy a house worth $62,192 and handle the mortgage payments very readily. If you do not have $20,000, then you will have to buy a smaller house. If you have $15,000 available, you can buy a house worth $57,192.

The data in Table 6–1 clearly demonstrate the impact of high interest rates on your ability to finance and buy a house. There have been periods of very dramatic increases in interest. For example, between the end of 1979 and the end of the first quarter of 1980 mortgage interest increased from 12 percent to approximately 16 percent. This was a 33 percent increase in the cost of mortgage money. As shown in Table 6–1, an increase of this size has a dramatic impact on the amount you can pay at any income level. If you earn $30,000 a year, for example, you will be severely hurt by rising interest rates. At an income level of $30,000 a year, you can afford a mortgage of $60,740 at 12 percent interest. The amount of mortgage you can afford at 16 percent interest will be $46,675. Therefore, as a result of a 33 percent increase in mortgage rates, the amount of a mortgage you can support declines from $60,740 to $46,675. This is approximately a 30 percent decrease in the amount of mortgage you can afford. With a 20 percent downpayment, if you earn $30,000, you can afford a house worth only $58,345 at 16 percent interest instead of a house worth $75,925 at 12 percent. Not only can you see in this way how much more expensive a mortgage is at a higher interest rate but you can also realize the pressure on prices when mortgage rates increase. Since everyone can afford less, prices tend to decline.

The summary of our discussion so far indicates that you can afford a more impressive house if you have a larger downpayment, a lower interest rate, and a greater income. If you expect your income to increase, you should try to buy a more expensive house that you will eventually be able to grow into. If you can do this, you can save a later move.

This means that you won't have to buy a small house first, and then move up to a larger one. However, it seems reasonable to assume that regardless of your income level, you may be able to afford to buy some kind of a house. You will almost always be better off buying something you can afford and selling later, that is "moving up," than simply trying to save your money for the house of your dreams. By getting involved in the home ownership process, you will learn to adopt your life-style and your budget to home ownership. You can build up your home equity through the increase in the value of the house. In that way you will ultimately reach a position where you can afford a more expensive house. This will add to your net worth. If you wait until you can afford a downpayment on a very expensive house, you may never catch up to the price increases on that house.

For example, it may take you two years to save $5,000 for the downpayment on a $50,000 house. At the end of that time, that $50,000 house may well be selling for $60,000. You will then have to get a $55,000 mortgage on the home that sold for only $50,000 when you first started saving money for the downpayment! One way to avoid this inflation trap is to find a way to accumulate a downpayment as quickly as possible.

Locating the downpayment money

Where to get the money for a downpayment is an age-old problem. It is dramatically harsh when housing prices are rising rapidly. Yet if you lived in the United States in the 40s, 50s, 60s, and 70s, you faced the problem of finding enough money for the downpayment on a house. Everyone is affected by this very real and frustrating problem. There is just no easy solution. Housing prices have continued to increase rapidly in the last decade. If you own a house, apartment, or condominium, you are pleasantly surprised by the increase in your equity and net worth as a result of the increase in housing prices. You consider yourself fortunate. But what if you are trying to save money to buy a house? Every time you look for one, you find prices just a little bit higher. You have too little in the way of a downpayment, and your income is too low to allow you to afford the house you want. Actually it would be better if you could borrow the downpayment money in some way just to get started on the home ownership process. Otherwise you may be forever unable to buy.

If you are a young person who needs housing, you will find buying a house difficult. When you enter the job market, you may be lucky to find a good job that will provide an income of $15,000 a year. But you will not have enough money for the downpayment to buy a house. An income of $15,000 a year represents a monthly income of $1,250, which provides approximately $312.50 for principal and interest. That means that at a 14 percent interest rate you can afford a mortgage of $26,370.

With that income you can afford a $32,960 house. But if you do not have $6,590 as downpayment, you will be unable to buy the house. And of course this raises the problem of where to obtain the downpayment money. It can come from savings, gifts, loans, and what sometimes is referred to as "sweat equity." Let's examine each of these sources of the downpayment money.

Savings The most common way to obtain the downpayment money is through regular savings. This is difficult for a young couple to do because they have not been working long enough to save. It is difficult to save $6,000 to $7,000 at any income level but worse if you earn a low salary. In fact, if you can save 10 percent of your gross salary, it will take approximately four years to save $6,000 for a downpayment if you earn $15,000 a year. If your household has two incomes (and earns more), this will accelerate the savings process. Yet having two incomes and earning more income than $15,000 puts you in a higher tax bracket. This means that it still will be difficult to save.

So the conclusion is that you should plan ahead to buy. You must recognize the fact that the faster you can buy a house and start paying for it, the better off you are going to be. Even when you are young, you must understand that savings can be used to buy a whole list of assets you will need in the future. Shelter is such an important asset that, if possible, you should start saving early. You will accomplish two things by this: you will develop an attitude of thrift, and you will provide for the shelter you will need as you get older.

Gifts Gifts represent another source of money for a downpayment. Many young couples buy their first house by using gift money from their parents to make the downpayment. You may be making $15,000 a year but may not have the $6,000 downpayment necessary to buy a house. Parents who have money might give $3,000 per parent to their child or children. Under the Internal Revenue Code, they are allowed to give up to $3,000 a year away without paying a gift tax. (Of course, this gift would then reduce the parents' estate for tax purposes.)

Loans A third source of funds for a downpayment is loans. Personal loans at reasonable interest rates from parents can be paid back later when you are able to save some money. When you make an application for a mortgage loan with a lender, you need to identify the source of your downpayment. This requires approval from the lending institution. The personal loan, at least, would provide you with a way of buying a house. Second, bank loans on a short-term basis, if not too large, are another way to obtain downpayment money. This assumes that money is available, and that banks are willing to lend it for this purpose. Some banks may be willing to lend money for up to two years for the purpose of making a downpayment on a house. Such a loan also must receive approval from the mortgage-lending institution.

Second trusts The seller of the house, whether a private person or a builder, is another source of funds. Sellers often provide a second trust to be paid off over a shorter period of time than the mortgage. Assume that a young couple has only $3,000 for a downpayment. This means that they have a 10 percent instead of a 20 percent downpayment on a $30,000 house. The owner might give them a second trust payable over the next several years. With a second trust, or second mortgage as these loans are also known, the owner of the house forgoes part of the cash downpayment. Instead of taking all the downpayment in cash, the owner gives the buyer a loan for part of it. The house acts as collateral, or security, for the loan. The buyer then pays the loan off in three to seven or more years. The following chapter, which deals with consumer credit, provides additional information about second trusts.

Using a second trust gives people an opportunity to buy a house, begin to pay for it, and use money from salary to pay off the second trust to the builder or owner of the house. Of course, buyers have to find a builder or an owner willing to provide a loan in place of downpayment money.

"Sweat equity" Sweat equity is a way for you to earn your downpayment money. One form of sweat equity is if the builder of your house allows you to do some work to complete the house. This adds to the value of the house and increases your equity or ownership in it. For example, an allowance of $5,000 for painting and landscaping labor may be included in the price of the house. You might do the painting and landscaping yourself and earn $5,000. This becomes part of your equity in the house as well as part of your downpayment. You would need less money in cash since part of your downpayment would be in the form of your labor. Sweat equity would reduce the amount of cash you need for the downpayment from $6,000 to $1,000.

You can also earn sweat equity on an existing house if the house needs a substantial amount of work. You can do this if the mortgage lender is willing to make a loan on the finished and improved value of the house rather than on the value of the house before it is completely renovated. You can earn sweat equity by finding a house in need of substantial repair, moving in, and making improvements that increase its value. The financial institution making the loan recognizes this increase in value. The increase becomes part of the equity or downpayment money you need in order to obtain the loan.

There are, therefore, many ways in which you can come up with downpayment money to buy a house. This has always been the major hurdle for young people buying their first house. Once you have bought your first house, it is an easy matter from then on to obtain equity which will allow you to buy your next house. That means that you can trade in your old house and buy a new one. But coming up with a downpayment is the all-important first step. Because there are many ways to do it, consider *all* the opportunities to find the downpayment if you really want to buy a house or condominium.

Source of real estate mortgages

When you think about buying a house, you should become familiar with the individuals and businesses that make mortgage loans. A list of sources of mortgage loans would include savings and loan associations, commercial banks, mutual savings banks, credit unions, life insurance companies, real estate investment trusts, mortgage banks, pension funds, private individuals, and home sellers. In other words, the people with whom you do business as a savings depositor in a bank, as an owner of a savings account, or as an owner of an ordinary life insurance policy may provide loans to buy a house.

Savings and loan associations

Savings and loan associations are one of the most important sources of mortgage funds in the United States. They perhaps account for as much as one third of the total mortgage debt outstanding. They also account for the largest part of conventional first mortgages on one- to four-family houses. They tend to concentrate their loans in communities where they are located. They also tend to have the most liberal lending policies of all lenders, although their lending policy will be a function of the overall condition of the mortgage market.

Commercial banks

Ordinarily commercial banks are not a major source of mortgage loans. The reason is that commercial banks exist to make relatively short-term loans and are limited in the amount of mortgage money they can extend. However, commercial banks have become an important source of mortgage money. They perhaps finance almost 20 percent of one- to four-family housing units. Commercial banks are a source of construction money for those who are going to build a house themselves or for those who are in the building industry. They provide short-term loans to put up the building. Then some other source supplies the long-term mortgage money.

Mutual savings banks

Mutual savings banks are best known in New England and the Middle Atlantic region. They are called mutual savings banks because they are owned by the depositors. Insured by the Federal Deposit Insurance Corporation, they emphasize savings and make mortgage loans. In addition, they are not limited to one particular region and can make loans out of state. Their mortgage interest rates tend to be lower than those of savings and loan associations. Mutual savings banks are dependent upon individual savings as sources of mortgage money.

Life insurance companies

At one time life insurance companies were a very important source of mortgage funds for the housing industry, particularly for single-family units. Today approximately 30 percent of their investments are in mortgages. But over the years they have tended to concentrate on commercial mortgage and multifamily dwellings rather than the one- to four-family dwellings stressed by the savings and loans and mutual savings banks. Certainly if you are looking for funds, you might consider life insurance companies if they have available funds. However, the amount a life insurance company will lend as a percent of the value of the house tends to be lower than for savings and loans, whose primary business is to make mortgage loans.

Real estate investment trusts

Real estate investment trusts are a source of funds for real estate ventures. The money lent by a real estate investment trust is obtained from stockholders of the trust, from short-term loans from commercial banks, and from long-term loans to finance the purchase of mortgages. The trusts invest approximately 80 percent of the total money available for mortgage loans. The remaining 20 percent represents equity ownership and properties. Essentially the trusts invest four fifths of their money in first mortgages on real estate. If you examine the breakdown of their investments, you will find half used for first mortgage construction, approximately 10 percent for first mortgages on land, 15 percent for first mortgages on development, 10 percent for junior mortgages, and 10 percent short-term mortgages. The remaining amount represents long-term mortgages on properties. In obtaining a mortgage on a house, you may do business with a firm owned by a real-estate investment trust and/or one that makes a mortgage loan for a single-family residence.

Mortgage banks

Mortgage bankers obtain funds from owners of the bank and money that they borrow. They in turn lend the money to people who wish to build homes, businesses, shopping centers, and other real-estate ventures. Mortgage bankers really serve as intermediaries between persons needing a mortgage and sources of funds. They might work as loan correspondents to life insurance companies, mutual savings banks, or pension funds. Mortgage bankers really originate a loan, and then service the loan for lenders or owners. You might look on them as possible sources of mortgage money in a particular market.

Pension funds

Pension funds accumulate a substantial amount of money for the purpose of providing retirement income for workers, managers, and executives. Pension funds generally invest in securities, both common stocks and bonds. To a certain extent they also invest in mortgages. However, the amount of money for this last purpose is relatively small in relation to the total amount of money available.

Private individuals

From time to time private individuals well known in a local community make mortgage loans to other individuals. You may wish to find out who these people are and obtain financing from them. Sometimes mortgages can be provided by friends or relatives who have a substantial amount of money available in savings accounts and are willing to make personal loans on real estate to others. Certainly, if you are interested in obtaining mortgage financing and discover that mortgage money is unavailable, you would be wise to look for individuals willing to make you a mortgage loan.

Often house owners or sellers who do not need the money represented by their ownership in a house may be willing to make a mortgage loan to purchasers. In a sense, the purchasers give back to the owners what is referred to as a purchase money mortgage. It is a private financing arrangement whereby buyers pay to sellers principal and interest payments just as they would to any lending institutions. Of course, the sellers or owners hold a first mortgage on the property. If the buyers default, the house will revert back to the sellers. This is not a source of funds that you can depend on regularly. But from time to time owners will indeed give back mortgages on their properties because they want to sell at a time when mortgage money is unavailable.

In addition, owners who have mortgages on their property can sell the property to a buyer who then assumes the existing mortgage. As long as the buyer meets all credit requirements, the seller may take a second trust on the property. This will allow the buyer to purchase the property with a smaller downpayment. Therefore, a buyer might very well be able to buy a property with only a 10 percent or even smaller downpayment. You, as the new buyer, assume the old mortgage. You also assume the responsibility for paying off a second trust on the property. All you need to do is to come up with the downpayment money. Nice work if you get it and afford it!

Creative financing

Much of our discussion about ways of finding downpayment money and a mortgage is related to *creative financing*. This is a term used by real estate professionals to describe the purchase of a piece of real estate with little or no money. An example of creative financing would be the use of all borrowed money to purchase a $50,000 home on which a $35,000 first mortgage exists. For a 10 percent downpayment the buyer would need to put down $5,000 as downpayment. The buyer would assume a mortgage of $35,000, and would have to come up with an additional $10,000. In a creative solution to this problem, the buyer borrows the $5,000 down payment against a commercial bank line of credit. This is paid off at the rate of $250 per month, with interest at the going rate charged by the bank. The $35,000 mortgage is an 11 percent, 30-year mortgage requiring principal and interest payments of $333 a month. The buyer then gives back a second trust note to the seller. This requires a $100 monthly payment for interest only for five years at 12 percent, with the final payment of $10,000 due in five years. Thus the buyer buys the house with none of his or her own money. All the buyer needs is the income to support a debt of $50,000. And this is the rub in creative financing—you might become so creative that you go broke!

Special mortgage features—VA and FHA

If you are a veteran, you can take advantage of a special program to buy a house. You apply for what is referred to as Veteran's Administration financing (VA financing). This allows you to pay an interest rate somewhat below the market rate. VA financing came about after World War II as a benefit to veterans. It was designed to help them find inexpensive money for housing at a time when such money was not available. Essentially the government said to the lending institution, "You make the loan. If anything happens and the person cannot repay, we will guarantee that loan."

Ordinarily VA mortgages are extended to 90 or 95 percent of the value of the property, particularly on lower-priced properties. Mortgages financed through VA are not available for properties costing over $150,000. Historically VA loans have been attractive, but there is a substantial amount of administrative work involved in obtaining them. Often money is not available for VA loans because the conventional mortgage rate is substantially higher than the rate established for VA loans. Lenders are not willing to finance VA loans if they cannot earn a rate of return comparable to that earned on other mortgages.

The Federal Housing Administration administers the FHA home financing program. This program provides a way for people to borrow money at attractive rates. Certain lenders are allowed to loan under conditions established by the FHA. Essentially the FHA program combines the first and second mortgage. It provides a system of mortgage insurance. In this way money is available on an FHA loan to repay the lender in case the buyer of the house defaults on the loan. The cost of the FHA loan program is borne by the borrowers. A fee is charged for the FHA benefit. Under an FHA contract you can take out a mortgage loan from any of the lending institutions previously discussed. Your mortgage will be based on a smaller downpayment for a longer term and at a lower interest rate than you can obtain under a conventional mortgage. However, more red tape is involved in getting an FHA loan. You also have to pay an insurance premium for the risk that you are imposing on the lending institution. Sometimes money is not readily available under FHA loans. This is because the FHA interest limit is below the market rate of interest charged for conventional loans.

Variable rate mortgages (VRM)

We all tend to think that mortgage payments are a fixed amount and reduce the mortgage. But in the 1920s and 30s in the United States, people did not reduce the amount of their mortgage loan; they simply paid interest on the mortgage. When the mortgage debt matured, they were required to pay it off or borrow again an amount equal to the mortgage on the property. This meant that many people never repaid their mortgage debt. When the mortgage loan matured and they didn't have the money, they lost their house. Many unscrupulous lenders, primarily individuals, would not allow borrowers to refinance. The lenders would take the house back for the amount of the mortgage. To stop this practice, the FHA established a direct loan reduction schedule under which the mortgage payment included a payment on both principal and interest. Over a 20 year period the borrower would pay interest as well as principal until the mortgage debt was repaid. The idea of fixed payments has been with us since the beginning of the FHA program in the United States.

In recent times, because of the high price of real estate and the high interest rates on mortgage loans, young families have not been able to afford the high principal and interest payments needed to reduce their mortgage loans. There has developed a system whereby buyers can pay less in the early life of the mortgage. Then they can pay more later on when they are better able to afford higher payments. This assumes, of course, that the buyers' income goes up. This change in the mortgage or housing industry has been introduced within the last 10 years.

Another change has come about because some lenders have lost substantial sums of money when rates of interest on mortgages went up. In some cases lenders can increase the interest rate after giving notification to the borrower. But generally savings associations and mortgage lenders have not raised interest rates nor have they increased payments. The only reason for your mortgage payment to increase would be because your taxes or insurance fees have gone up. For this reason your mortgage payment might indeed go up. But as interest rates continue to rise, borrowers are reluctant to borrow money at very high rates. This is because they don't want to lock themselves into a 30-year mortgage at an extremely high interest rate when interest rates may come down in a few years. Therefore the mortgage lending industry has developed a variable rate mortgage (VRM) that fluctuates on the basis of interest rates in the market. With a VRM, automatic changes occur in the interest rate and the mortgage repayment on the basis of what is happening in the marketplace. It makes sense for borrowers to pay more when the general level of interest rates go up and to pay less when they go down. Since individuals prefer to borrow money as cheaply and for as long a time as possible, the VRM is a disadvantage for lenders. Its main advantage is that it does not prevent people from borrowing when interest rates are high. This is because the borrowers know that when rates decline, their principal and interest costs for mortgage repayment will be reduced. Otherwise people attempting to buy a house at a time of high interest rates would want to use short-term financing. Then when rates come down, they would arrange a permanent mortgage at a reasonable rate that would allow them to pay the loan back over the usual 25 to 30 years. The variable mortgage rate is not yet a common practice. But if interest rates remain high, the VRM might very well become so in the next decade.

Availability of mortgage money

You need to examine all sources of funds if you are going into the marketplace to buy a house. In various areas information is provided through the professional real estate brokerage community. Real estate brokers can provide an up-to-date report of who is making mortgage loans, at what rate, the maximum amount available, and whether or not they are charging points. *Points* is a term everyone going into the mortgage market should understand. Essentially points paid by borrowers add to the loan interest cost, but they are paid at the time of settlement, that is, when the sale of the house is concluded. One point is simply 1 percent of the face value of the loan. If the lender charges you one point, that means that you have to pay a fee of 1 percent of the loan value. This fee is paid at the settlement.

An example will explain how points work. Let's assume that a lender is willing to make a mortgage loan at 11 percent with two points. If you borrow $50,000, you will have to pay $1,000 for points. That $1,000 represents an additional interest rate cost in the first year and actually increases the rate of interest you pay. The reason for the points is to increase the amount of interest received by the lender. This is done in markets where money is tight and the interest rate does not really reflect the going rate of interest. In addition, if there is a limit on the rate of interest that can be charged, the lender may charge points to avoid the usury limit imposed by the state government.

Let's assume that the lender cannot charge points and that there's a limit on the interest rate that can be charged. In this case let's assume a 15 percent interest rate ceiling, while mortgage rates in the current marketplace are up to 17 percent. In these circumstances a lender would be unwilling to lend at 15 percent. Since the lender cannot charge the

17 percent rate, no loan can be made. A way of getting around the difficulty is for the lender to charge enough points to bring the rate up to 17 percent. The rate on the contract will still be listed as 15 percent. In the past some states have insisted on maintaining a maximum limit on the amount of mortgage interest that can be charged. In addition, some states have refused to allow any charges for points. The point system, in effect, raises the interest rate to borrowers and provides a higher compensation to lenders. The more points, the higher the cost of your mortgage.

Finding a house you can afford

Now we will assume that you have saved your downpayment money. You also have some idea of where money can be borrowed. The next step is to find a house you can afford. And this is where you begin to interface with the professional brokerage community, the professional lending community, and people who own houses. As a basic guide to the selection of a house or condominium, you should strive to find one in the best possible location. This can be determined by asking the question "Where is the best area to buy in our city?" The second question, then, is "Can I afford to buy in the best area?"

You should stress quality and good location in your search for housing. You want a house that is close to transportation and shopping and one that is energy-efficient. You must consider the costs of operating the house and getting to and from your place of work.

Information about housing

The way you find out about location, desirability, and cost begins with reading notices about houses offered for sale in the weekly real estate section of your local newspaper. All professionals advertise in the weekly and daily issues of the newspaper. They list houses and tell when the houses are open. They provide pictures that give you some idea of what the houses look like. This is a basic source of information about the real estate market.

A second source of information is establishing good relationships with professional real estate agents in your area. They can explain the real estate market and give you straightforward information about the pros and cons of various areas. They can give you an idea of what you can afford in the best location. As a matter of course you need to take time to read about what is going on in the local market. You also need to begin the process of looking at houses that may meet your needs. All this takes time. But if you take the time, read newspapers, and ask questions, you will very quickly find desirable areas for living, for working, and for playing. Such areas will also add to your long-term financial security and increase your net worth.

The process of buying a house

The open house

As you look at your local newspaper, notice the houses offered for sale. Many are listed by real estate brokerage firms throughout the city. Many are open over the weekend, usually in the afternoon, on occasions referred to as "open houses." On Saturday and Sunday afternoon in many major metropolitan areas, houses may be open for you and other prospective customers to look at. Some owners list their houses for sale with brokerage firms, and agents of these firms are ready to answer questions and show prospective clients houses in various price ranges. Other owners advertise their houses for sale, but show them only by appointment. Not all cities follow the same procedures. In some areas open house programs are not very extensive. In other places there is no such thing as an open house. You have to find out what is listed for sale through advertisements in newspapers or through brokers.

The role of the real estate agent

Let's make the assumption that you know approximately what you can afford to pay for a house. You're driving around on a beautiful Sunday afternoon and looking at houses. You find a house you like. After you learn all you need to know about the house from the agent, you decide that you want to buy it. You need to be aware of the relationships among the parties in the transaction so that you can better understand the entire process of buying a property.

First, let's look at the agent who is dealing with you. He or she will try to explain in detail the qualities of the house. When its owner listed the property with a specific brokerage firm, the owner provided listing information. The listing sheet describes the street address, the amount of taxes, the number and size of rooms on the different floors as well as in the basement and attic. It identifies the type of heating and cooling system and tells whether there are storm doors and windows, decks, patios, and a pool. The list includes information on the existence (or absence) of the following features: dishwasher, dryer, disposal, freezer, internal TV system, alarm system, oven, hardwood floors, and carpeting. It provides all the information you would want to know about the house, including its asking price, operating expenses, school district, and similar details. The listing information for single-family houses is an agreement entered into between the owner and broker. Because the owner signs it, the assumption is that all information in the listing agreement is correct.

The agent you talk with is most likely a real estate associate of a brokerage firm. He or she is a professional engaged in the business of selling houses for the listor. As you talk to the agent, you must understand that he or she really represents the owner. However, the agent will try to answer all your questions thoroughly and correctly. After all, he or she does wish to sell the house for the owner.

The asking price— Making an offer

The listing agreement includes the asking price for the house. It also states whether or not a mortgage exists on the property as well as the rate of interest. The listing price is the owner's asking price. It is the agent's responsibility to sell the house for that price or as close to it as possible. This price has usually been established by a professional agent after studying comparable listings of similar houses. Ordinarily the price on a house seems to reflect the market conditions of similarly situated houses in a particular market at a particular time. Certainly all prices are subject to negotiation. This depends on competitive conditions in the market at the time, the availability of funds, and the urgency on the part of the seller to sell and of the buyer to buy the property.

The commission—Who pays it?

The agent or broker earns a fee on the sale of a house, referred to as a *commission*. Typical commissions are 5, 6, or 7 percent of the selling price, depending upon the region. This means if a broker or a real estate associate of a broker sells a $100,000 home, a commission or a fee of $5,000 to $7,000 is paid by the seller of the house. This amount is divided among the broker, realtor associate, and listing agent. In a typical real estate transaction 20 percent of the commission goes to the listor. (The listor is the person who originally listed the house for sale). The remaining 80 percent is divided between the brokerage firm and the real estate associate of the brokerage firm that sells the house. Therefore, out of a $6,000 commission, $1,200 goes to the listor and $4,800 is essentially divided between agent and broker. If divided equally, $2,400 goes to the broker and $2,400 to the selling agent.

The higher the price of the house, the higher the commission. This is essentially the economics of a real estate transaction. It is the responsibility of the listing agent to bring together buyer and seller at a price close to what the owner is asking.

The contract of sale

Once you decide to make an offer on a house, you must do so in a formal way. All offers of purchase must be in writing. You have to complete a contract of sale with the real estate associate and present this document formally to the owner for acceptance or rejection. The contract of sale must be accompanied by a deposit which is usually 10 percent of the selling price of the house. This earnest money or good-faith money is in the form of a check. When the seller accepts the contract for sale, the earnest money is deposited in an interest-bearing escrow account. There it accrues interest until the date of settlement.

Let us review the major items on a contract for sale. We assume that you have found a house you can afford. Its sales price is $60,000. You have $20,000 in savings and earn $24,000 a year. On the basis of your income, you can support a mortgage of $42,192 according to Table 6–1. Therefore, you need $17,808 in downpayment money to buy the house. You do have enough in savings to make the purchase. After examining the house, you find that it has all the attributes you are looking for. You ask the agent if the owner is firm on the $60,000 price. Generally, the listing price of the house is higher than the final price a buyer is willing to accept. If the market is not too competitive, it might be a good idea for you to make an offer somewhat below the asking price. If the owner does not accept your offer, you can raise your price in subsequent negotiations. Therefore, you offer $58,000 for the house, stating that you will put down earnest money of $5,800 and will supply the rest of the money at the settlement.

Settlement is the formal process by which ownership of real property passes from seller to buyer. It is the end of the home-buying process, the time when title to the property is transferred from the seller to the buyer.

Ordinarily you would ask for an 80 percent loan. Because the mortgage market is tight, you want to keep the mortgage in line with your ability to pay. You calculate that you can afford a $42,000 mortgage. Therefore, assuming that the $58,000 offer is accepted, you will pay an additional cash downpayment of $10,200 from your savings. This means that your total downpayment on the house will be $16,000. You will then have a first mortgage of $42,000. That keeps the financial transaction in line with the data provided by Table 6–1. All of this will be formally written down in the contract for sale.

The first item in the contract for sale reads as follows: "Received from John and Mary Doe a deposit of $5,800 in the form of a check to be applied as part of the purchase of. . . ." The address of the house follows. The contract indicates the total price of the property in dollars that the purchaser agrees to pay. It adds that an additional $10,200 in cash will be paid at settlement. The remaining $42,000 will be financed by a first trust. At that point you indicate your willingness to pay interest and principal over a 30-year period at the rate of interest of 12 percent (if that is indeed the agreed rate of interest). You also state how much money you will pay monthly to retire the debt. Ordinarily, if you know exactly the interest rate on mortgage money at the time the contract of sale is indicated, the contract will specify this rate. In a rapidly changing mortgage market you might prudently state your intention to arrange the best possible financing within a given period of time. Usually an addendum to the contract affirms that the entire contract is subject to the availability of mortgage money at a price not to exceed, say, 14 percent. In this way, if you can't obtain proper financing, the entire contract is null and void, and the associate or agent has to return the deposit check to you.

In the part of the contract concerned with financing, a traditional first trust or first mortgage is assumed. Perhaps a second trust or second mortgage is to be placed on the property. If this is so and if the arrangement is agreeable to the first mortgage lender, this fact will be stated. If a mortgage already exists on the house and if the seller is going to take back a second trust, this fact will also be indicated.

Next the contract describes the type of loan to be placed against the house. If it is by conventional financing or by an FHA or VA loan, this will be stated. If loan fees exist for the original amount of the loan, this fact will be noted as well.

The contract of sale next takes up the examination of the title and cost, and states the name of the buyer to whom the property is to be conveyed. This is followed by a settlement date, which is usually determined by the seller. But it may be decided on by negotiation between buyer and seller. Ordinarily an interval of 45 days is adequate, provided the purchaser can obtain the necessary financing and reach a settlement agreement. As a rule, the seller gives the purchaser an opportunity to determine if suitable financial arrangements can be made to raise the money to buy the house.

Your contract may contain other provisions dealing with special conditions or added provisions with regard to the house. Such details are usually contained in addendums. You are well advised to include an addendum to the effect that the contract is subject to a termite inspection, a structural inspection, and a mechanical inspection of all the moving parts of the house. If any part of the house, including the sewage or septic system and the foundations or structural parts, are defective, the contract is declared null and void. This is also the case if termites are found. This addendum gives you an opportunity to make certain that your future house is in working order. In all too many cases a person may buy a house, move in, and then two weeks later find that the furnace doesn't work. Then $5,000 is needed to put in a new furnace. This is tragic. But once you move into the house, there is nothing you can do about the situation. On the other hand, let's assume you include an inspection clause in your purchase contract. (This is particularly recommended when buying a used house.) If you then find that the furnace does not work after it has been inspected, the seller of the house has to put the furnace back in good repair.

A sample contract for purchase is provided in Figure 6–3. Although the print is small, you can see that it is a legal document. Included are standard clauses with respect to performance, title, termite inspection, and general financing provisions. It would be a good idea for you to

Figure 6–3
Sample real estate contract

STUART and MAURY, INC.

REALTORS

REALTOR®

5010 Wisconsin Ave., N.W.
Washington, D.C. 20016
(202) 244-1000

10220 River Road
Potomac, Md. 20854
(301) 983-9700

EQUAL HOUSING OPPORTUNITY

William C. Stuart, III
President

Deane Maury
Vice President & Secretary

William C. Stuart, IV
Vice President & Treasurer

RESALE CONTRACT FOR SINGLE FAMILY HOMES

1. **THIS CONTRACT OF SALE,** made this _______ day of ____________________, 198____, by and between ____, hereinafter referred to as Seller, and ____, hereinafter referred to as Purchaser.

WITNESSETH, that for and in consideration of the mutual covenants herein, Seller agrees to sell and Purchaser agrees to buy the property legally described as Lot ____________, Block ____________, Subdivision ____ or ____, located in ____________ County, Maryland, with improvements thereon, including built-in heating plant and air-conditioning system, all plumbing and lighting fixtures, kitchen equipment including range, refrigerator, built-in dishwasher and disposal, all wall-to-wall carpeting, cornices, curtain rods and drapery rods, awnings, screens, storm doors and windows, venetian blinds, shades and indoor shutters, trees, shrubs, and plants, all as now installed on the premises known as (address) ____ upon the following terms of sale:

TOTAL PRICE OF PROPERTY IS ____ Dollars ($____________).

Deposit has been received from the Purchaser with this contract in the form of ________________________________ in the amount of ________________________________ Dollars ($____________).

THE PURCHASER AGREES TO PAY ________________________________ Dollars ($____________) at settlement (by cash or certified, treasurer's or cashier's check) of which sum the deposit shall be a part. If the deposit exceeds the down payment, any excess of the deposit shall apply first to settlement costs and the balance shall be refunded to the Purchaser at settlement.

2. **FINANCING a. FIRST TRUST.** (To be Placed or Assumed) The Purchaser is to ____________ a ________________________ first deed of trust in lender's usual form secured on said premises of $ ________________________ due in ____________ years and bearing interest at the rate of ________ percent per annum, or the maximum rate prevailing at the time of settlement, payable approximately $ ________________ per month, plus one-twelfth (1/12) of annual taxes, fire insurance and mortgage insurance, if required by the lender.

b. **SECOND TRUST.** (To be Placed or Assumed) The Purchaser is to ________________________ a second deed of trust in lender's usual form secured on said premises of $ ________________________ due in ________ years and bearing interest at the rate of ________ percent per annum, payable approximately $ ________________________ per month.

c. **TRUST.** (Seller to Take Back) **The deferred purchase money amounting to $**________________________ is to be secured by a ____________ deed of trust in usual form **on said premises to be paid in monthly installments of $**________________________ or more, without penalty, at maker's option, including **interest at the rate of** ____________ **percent per annum, each installment when so paid is to be applied first to the payment** of interest on the amount of principal remaining **and the balance thereof credited to the principal, which deed of trust the Seller agrees to accept** as a part of the purchase price. In case of default in any payment, **the entire amount then remaining unpaid shall immediately become due and payable. Said trust** and note may not be assumed or title taken subject to said trust **and note without** the prior written consent of the **note holder.** The entire unpaid **balance shall be due and payable in full within** ____________.

d. **FINANCING APPLICATION.** Purchaser placing financing (**regardless of type**) agrees to make **application therefor within fourteen** (14) calendar days of the final ratification of **this contract** and agrees to promptly file any **supplemental** information or papers **later requested by the lender** and agrees that failure to comply with the terms **of this provision** shall give the Seller the right **to declare the** deposit forfeited or avail **himself of any legal or equitable** rights as provided in the paragraph labeled "**FORFEITURE** OF DEPOSIT/LEGAL REMEDIES."

3. **CONVENTIONAL LOAN.** This contract is contingent on the **ability of the** Purchaser to secure or receive **a commitment for the** herein described conventional financing, or **lender's approval** of assumption, if required, and **furnish evidence** of commitment or approval **to the listing and selling** Agents within forty-five (45) calendar days from **the date of final** ratification of this contract, **which commitment** or approval the Purchaser **agrees to pursue diligently.** (See Paragraph 2d hereof). The Purchaser **reserves the right** to increase the cash down **payment and/or** accept a modified commitment **for financing and shall** so notify the Seller and Agents in writing **within the term of this** contingency. In the event the **Purchaser does** not obtain the specified financing **or increase the cash** down payment and/or accept a modified **commitment for financing** within the specified time **period, then** this contract shall be null and void **and the Purchaser's deposit** shall be refunded in full. By accepting **a loan commitment** which bears an interest rate **or loan amount** other than the rate(s) or loan **amount designated in** Paragraph 2 above, the financing contingency **contained herein** shall be deemed satisifed and the **Purchaser** nereby waives any rights which **Purchaser may have** to declare this contract null and void for failure to **obtain acceptable** financing.

4. **FHA LOAN. a. It is expressly** agreed that, notwithstanding **any other provisions** of this contract, the Purchaser **shall not be obligated** to complete the purchase of the property **described herein** or to incur any penalty by **forfeiture of earnest** money deposit or otherwise **unless the Seller has** delivered to the Purchaser a written statement **issued by the** Federal Housing Commissioner **setting forth** the appraised value of the pro**perty (excluding closing** costs) of not less than $ ________________________ **which statement** the Seller hereby agrees to **deliver to the** Purchaser promptly after such **appraised value statement** is made available to the Seller. The Purchaser **shall, however,** have the privilege and option of pro**ceeding with** consummation of the contract **without regard to the** amount of the appraised valuation made by the **Federal Housing** Commissioner. The appraised **valuation is** arrived at to determine the **maximum mortgage** the Department of Housing and Urban Development **will insure. HUD** does not warrant the value or the **condition** of the property. The **Purchaser should satisfy himself** that the price and the condition of the property **are acceptable.**

b. Paragraph 4a **is applicable** only in the event that Purchaser **places a Federal Housing Administration (FHA) insured loan.** Purchaser shall exercise the above-mentioned privil**ege and option** to proceed at the contract price **which is over and above the FHA appraisal by giving the Seller** notice of his intention to do so by the method provid**ed in Paragr**aph 30 hereof. Said Notice **shall be given** within **FIVE days after Purchaser receives the FHA** appraisal. This contract is subject to FHA and **lender's approval.** If the aforesaid approval is no**t obtained,** it is **expressly agreed that the Purchaser shall be refunded** his deposit and the contract shall be null **and void.**

5. **LOAN FEES. If a new loan is** to be placed pursuant to this con**tract, the Purchaser agrees to pay a loan origination fee of one percent** (1%) of the principal sum of the loan on FHA **and VA LOANS** and ________% of the principal **sum of ANY** OTHER LOAN. **The Seller agrees to pay a loan placement** fee of ________% of the principal sum of **said loan. If the** existing loan is to be assumed, **the Purchaser** agrees to pay **any loan assumption fees, charges or** expenses required by the lender. The above loan **origination and** placement fees are based upon **current FHA** or VA regulations **and/or the present mortgage** money market. It is further agreed that the parties **will comply with** any reasonable change in said **fees at the time** of settlement, **provided said change is permitted** by FHA or VA regulations (if FHA or VA loan) **and/or is due to a** change in the mortgage money ma**rket. Lender's** inspection fee, if **applicable, shall be paid by the Seller.** Purchaser agrees to pay mortgage insurance **premiums as** required by the lender.

6. **EXAMINATION OF TITLE AND COSTS.** Property is to be con**veyed in the** name of ____. THE PURCHASER HAS A RIGHT TO SELECT THE TITLE INSUR**ANCE COMPANY,** SETTLEMENT OR **ESCROW COMPANY,** OR TITLE ATTORNEY, and Purchaser hereby **authorizes the** undersigned agent to order the **examination** of title and the preparation **of all necessary convey**ancing papers through ________________________, **and** agrees to pay the settlement ch**arges in con**nection therewith, tax certificate, **transfer and recorda**tion taxes (except that Seller shall pay D.C. tra**nsfer tax if the** property is located in the District **of Columbia**), conveyancing, notary fees, survey **where required, lender's** fees (exclusive of inspection fee), and **recording charges** except those incident to clearing **existing encum**brances. The Seller hereby agrees to **pay any above** mentioned costs incurred if upon examination th**e title should be** found defective and it is not r**emedied as** herein stated, and to pay a reasonable clo**sing fee for se**rvices rendered to him.

7. **SETTLEMENT.** The **Seller** and Purchaser are required and agr**ee to make full** settlement in accordance with the terms he**reof on or before the** ______ day of ____________________, **198____, or as soon thereafter as a report of the title and a survey, if required, can be secured if promptly orde**red, and/or a FHA or VA loan, if applicable, can **be processed, if applied for immediately.**

8. **ADDITIONAL PROVISIONS. SPECIAL PROVISIONS IN THE ATTACHED ADDENDUM, BEARING THE SIGNATURES** OF ALL PARTIES CONCERNED, ARE HERE**BY MADE A PART OF THIS CONTRACT. ADDENDUM ATTACHED: ( ) Yes ( ) No**

____

____

____

9. **AGENCY.** The Seller recognizes ____ as the Agent(s) negotiating this contract and agrees to pay such Agent(s) a brokerage fee for services rendered as specified in a separate Listing Agreement. If not previously paid by the Seller, the party making settlement is hereby irrevocably authorized and directed to deduct and pay the aforesaid brokerage fee from the proceeds of the sale. However, should settlement fail to occur within the time herein set forth, the Agent(s) shall still be entitled to the brokerage fee herein provided. THE ENTIRE DEPOSIT, RECEIPT OF WHICH IS ACKNOWLEDGED, SHALL BE HELD BY THE UNDERSIGNED AGENT AND DEPOSITED IN AN ESCROW ACCOUNT IN ACCORDANCE WITH THE MARYLAND REAL ESTATE LICENSE LAW UPON RATIFICATION OF THIS CONTRACT BY BOTH PURCHASER AND SELLER.

________________________ Sales Associate

________________________ Broker or Sales Manager

10. **AGREEMENT OF PRINCIPALS.** We, the undersigned, hereby ratify, accept and agree to this contract and acknowledge receipt of a copy thereof. The principals to this contract mutually agree that it shall be binding upon them, their heirs, executors, administrators, personal representatives, successors and assigns; that the provisions hereof shall survive the execution and delivery of the deed herein stated and shall not be merged therein; that this contract contains the final and entire agreement between the parties hereto, and neither they nor their Agents shall be bound by any terms, conditions, statements, warranties or representations, oral or written, not herein contained.

ADDITIONAL PARAGRAPHS NUMBERED 11 THROUGH 30 SET FORTH ON THE REVERSE SIDE HEREOF ARE INCORPORATED HEREIN AND MADE A PART HEREOF AND ALL PARTIES ACKNOWLEDGE THAT THEY HAVE READ SAID PARAGRAPHS.

________________________ Seller	________________________ Purchaser
________________________ Seller	________________________ Purchaser
________________________ Date of Acceptance	________________________ Address of Purchaser
Phone: Residence ____________ Office	Phone: Residence ____________ Office

IMPORTANT—READ REVERSE SIDE

This is the Resale Contract for Single Family Homes recommended by the Montgomery County Board of REALTORS®, Inc.
This form is the property of the Montgomery County Board of REALTORS®, Inc. and is for Members use only.

Form #1301 12/80

Figure 6–3 *(continued)*

11. **SPECIAL NOTICE.** THE AGENTS ASSUME NO RESPONSIBILITY FOR THE CONDITION OF THE PROPERTY NOR FOR THE PERFORMANCE OF
THIS CONTRACT BY ANY OR ALL PARTIES HERETO. PURCHASER HEREBY WARRANTS AND REPRESENTS UNTO THE SELLER AND THE REAL
ESTATE BROKERS HEREIN THAT NO AGENT, SERVANT OR EMPLOYEE OF SAID REAL ESTATE BROKERS HAS MADE ANY STATEMENT, REPRE-
SENTATION OR WARRANTY TO THEM REGARDING THE CONDITION OF THE PREMISES OR ANY PART THEREOF UPON WHICH PURCHASER HAS
RELIED AND WHICH IS NOT CONTAINED IN THIS CONTRACT.

12. **FORFEITURE OF DEPOSIT/LEGAL REMEDIES.** If the Purchaser shall fail to make full settlement, the deposit herein provided for may be forfeited at
the option of the Seller, in which event the Purchaser shall be relieved from further liability hereunder. If the Seller elects not to forfeit the deposit, Seller shall
notify the Purchaser and the Agent in writing within 30 days from the date provided for settlement herein of his election to avail himself of any legal or equitable
rights which he may have under this contract, other than the said forfeiture. In the event that the Seller elects not to forfeit the deposit, said deposit shall be returned by the Agent holding the same to the Purchaser, and the Agent shall not be liable to the Seller for return of said deposit. In the event of the forfeiture of the
deposit, or if the Seller shall fail to take any action or fail to pursue any legal or equitable remedies, then and in that event, the Seller shall pay the Agent as compensation for his services one-half of the amount of the deposit, said amount not to exceed the amount of the full brokerage fee. If after a breach by the Purchaser,
the Seller shall release the Purchaser from liability hereunder or authorize refund of the deposit monies, the Seller shall pay the Agent as compensation for his
services one-half of the amount of the Purchaser's deposit not to exceed the amount of the full brokerage fee. If after a breach by the Purchaser, the Seller obtains
an award of damages by a court, or enters into a compromise agreement with the Purchaser, the Seller shall pay the Agent one-half thereof, said amount not to
exceed the amount of the full brokerage fee, but said amount shall not be less than one-half of the deposit in the event of a compromise agreement. If the Agent is
required to participate in any legal proceedings, either as Plaintiff, Defendant or Third Party, Seller agrees to pay reasonable attorneys' fees for Agent's own attorney.

13. **TITLE.** The property, including the aforesaid chattels, is sold free of encumbrances except as stated herein. Any financing statements will be paid and
released by Seller at time of settlement. Title is to be good of record, merchantable and insurable, subject however, to the covenants, rights of way, easements,
conditions and restrictions of record, if any, otherwise the deposit is to be returned and sale declared off at the option of the Purchaser, unless the defects are of
such a character that they may be remedied by legal action within a reasonable time, but the Seller and Agent(s) are hereby expressly released from all liability to
the Purchaser for damages by reason of any defect in the title. In case legal steps are necessary to perfect the title such action must be taken promptly by the Seller
at his own expense, whereupon the time herein specified for full settlement by the Purchaser will thereby be extended for the period necessary for such prompt
action.

14. **PERFORMANCE.** Settlement is to be made at the office of the Attorney or the Title Company examining the title. Delivery to the Attorney or to the
Title Company of the cash payment and settlement costs as herein stated, the executed deed of conveyance and such other papers as required of either party by the
terms of this contract shall be considered good and sufficient tender of performance in accordance with the terms hereof. It is agreed that funds arising out of this
transaction at settlement may be used to pay off any existing encumbrances, including interest, as required by the appropriate lender.

15. **ADJUSTMENTS.** Rents, taxes, water, sewer charges, oil, escrow, insurance and interest on existing encumbrances, if any, are to be adjusted to date of
settlement. Taxes, general and special, are to be adjusted according to the certificate of taxes issued by the collector of taxes, if any, except that assessments for
improvements completed prior to the date of acceptance hereof, whether assessment therefor has been levied or not, shall be paid by the Seller or allowance made
therefor at time of settlement. If the property is serviced by the Washington Suburban Sanitary Commission or a local government, annual benefit charges and sewer
and water tap fees of said Commission or local government are to be adjusted to date of settlement and assumed thereafter by Purchaser. PURCHASER HEREBY
ACKNOWLEDGES THAT HE IS ASSUMING OUTSTANDING AND UNPAID SEWER AND WATER CONNECTION FEES (TAP FEES) WHICH WILL BE PAID
ANNUALLY (EXCEPT AS PROVIDED IN PARAGRAPH 27.) For initial purchases of improved residential real property in Maryland, the estimated cost of any
deferred water and sewer charges for which the Purchaser assumes liability are disclosed under paragraph 8 hereof, or in the addendum attached hereto.

16. **CONVEYANCE.** Seller agrees to execute and deliver a good and sufficient special warranty deed. Purchaser agrees to have the deed of conveyance recorded
promptly.

17. **INSURANCE.** The risk of loss or damage to said property by fire or other casualty until the deed of conveyance is recorded is assumed by the Seller.

18. **PROPERTY CONDITION.** At the time of settlement or occupancy (whichever occurs first) Seller will leave premises free and clear of trash and debris and
broom clean and have the electrical, plumbing, heating, air conditioning (excluding portable unit) and any other mechanical systems and related equipment included
in this contract in operating condition. The Seller will deliver the premises in substantially the same physical condition as of the date of final ratification. Purchaser
has the privilege of one (1) inspection of all the premises prior to settlement or occupancy (whichever occurs first). Except as expressly contained herein, no other
warranties have been made by the Seller, nor relied upon by the Purchaser.

19. **POSSESSION.** Seller agrees to give possession and occupancy at time of settlement and in the event he shall fail to do so, he shall become and be thereafter
a tenant by sufferance of the Purchaser and hereby waives all notice to quit as provided by laws effective in the state in which the property is located. All notices
of violations of orders or requirements noted or issued by any governmental authority, or actions in any court on account thereof, against or affecting the property
at the date of settlement of this contract, shall be complied with by the Seller, and the property conveyed free thereof.

20. **SUBDIVISION PLAT (MONTGOMERY COUNTY, MARYLAND ONLY).** The Purchaser hereby waives the receipt of an entire copy of the single
recorded subdivision plat. Prior to or at the time of settlement, the Purchaser shall be provided with a copy of said subdivision plat where required. If the property
sold herein is an unimproved lot or a new dwelling, the Purchaser acknowledges receipt of said subdivision plat prior to execution of the contract.

21. **GENERAL/MASTER PLAN (MONTGOMERY COUNTY, MARYLAND ONLY).** The Purchaser acknowledges that he has been apprised of his rights to
review the applicable Master Plan and the Wedges and Corridors General Plan for the Bicounty Region, including maps showing planned land uses, roads and highways, and the location and nature of proposed parks and other public facilities affecting the property herein described prior to execution of this contract. He acknowledges that he has reviewed said applicable plans prior to executing this contract or does hereby waive his right to do so. The Purchaser also acknowledges that
the real estate Agent has advised him of the relative location of any airport or heliport existing within a five (5) mile radius of the property.
The Purchaser acknowledges that he is aware that the applicable Master Plan or General Plan for Montgomery County is available at the Maryland—National Capital Park and Planning Commission and that at no time did the Agent explain to him the intent or meaning of such a Plan, nor did he rely on any representations
made by the Agent pertaining to the applicable Master Plan or General Plan.

22. **THE PLAN, GENERAL/MASTER PLANS (CITY OF ROCKVILLE, MARYLAND ONLY).** The Purchaser acknowledges that he has been afforded the
opportunity to examine the Plan for the City of Rockville, including maps showing planned land uses, roads and highways, and the location and nature of proposed
parks and other public facilities affecting the property herein described prior to the execution of this contract. Purchaser further acknowledges that the property
Owner's real estate Agent has provided said opportunity to examine the Plan by either producing and making available for examination a copy of the Plan or escort-
ing the Purchaser to a place where the Plan is available for examination by the Purchaser. The Purchaser also acknowledges that the property Owner's real estate
Agent has advised him of the relative location of any airport or heliport existing within a five (5) mile radius of the property. The Purchaser acknowledges that at
no time did the Agent explain to him the intent or meaning of such a Plan, nor did he rely on any representations made by the Agent pertaining to the applicable
Plan. (This paragraph supersedes paragraph 21 hereof only when the property being sold is in the City of Rockville.)

23. **NOTICE AND DISCLOSURE OF AVAILABILITY OF SEWAGE DISPOSAL SYSTEM AND DESIGNATED AREAS (MONTGOMERY COUNTY, MARY-
LAND ONLY).**

a. Notice is hereby given, pursuant to the Montgomery County Code, to the prospective Purchaser of the obligation of the Seller, or his duly authorized agent,
to disclose to the Purchaser any information known to the Seller as to whether the property is connected to, or has been authorized for connection to, a community
sewage system, and if not, whether an individual sewage disposal system has been constructed on the property, whether an individual sewage disposal system has
been approved by the county for such property, or whether the property has been disapproved by the county for the installation of an individual sewage disposal
system.

b. The Purchaser hereby acknowledges that, prior to entering into this contract of sale, Seller or his duly authorized agent, provided the above information, as
known to the Seller or his agent.

c. If an individual sewage disposal system has been or is to be installed upon this property, and if said property is located in a subdivision, and if Purchaser
received a copy of the subdivision record plat, as provided in Paragraph 20 above, Purchaser indicates that he has reviewed the said record plat, including any
provisions thereon with regard to areas restricted for the initial and reserve well locations and the individual sewage disposal system, and the restricted area in
which construction of the building to be served by the individual sewage disposal system is permitted.

24. **TERMITE INSPECTION.** Prior to settlement, the Seller shall order a termite inspection of the house and no later than the time of settlement, Seller shall
pay the cost of the termite inspection and provide to Purchaser a written certification issued in Purchaser's name or for Purchaser's benefit from a licensed exterm-
inator that, based upon a careful visual inspection of accessible areas of the house, there is no evidence of infestation by termites or wood-boring insects. If such
infestation exists, the Seller is to exterminate. The Seller at his own expense and prior to settlement shall repair any prior or current visible damage caused by termites or woodboring insects.

25. **GENERAL FINANCING PROVISIONS.** (a) In the event that mortgages are used rather than deeds of trust, the word "mortgage" shall be substituted
automatically. (b) If the contract provides for the assumption of existing trusts, it is understood that the balance of such trusts and the cash down payment are
approximate amounts. (c) Trustees in all deeds of trust are to be named by the parties secured thereby. (d) Seller shall allow inspections of all of the premises and
furnish any pertinent information required by the Purchaser or his financing agency in reference to obtaining a loan commitment. (e) Proceeds of loans acquired
pursuant to Paragraph 2 shall be applied to the purchase price.

26. **VA LOAN.** In the event the Purchaser is placing a Veterans Administration guaranteed loan, the Veteran Purchaser's deposit shall be placed in an escrow
account as required by Title 38, US Code, Section 1806. It is expressly agreed that, notwithstanding any other provisions of this contract, the Purchaser shall not
incur any penalty by forfeiture of earnest money or otherwise or be obligated to complete the purchase of the property described herein, if the contract purchase
price or cost exceeds the reasonable value of the property established by the Veterans Administration or the Purchaser is not approved by the Veterans Administration and the lending institution. In the event the Certificate of Reasonable Value is less than the amount of the contract price the Purchaser shall have the privilege
and option for five (5) days after receipt of the VA appraisal to proceed with the consummation of this contract without regard to the amount of reasonable value
established by the Veterans Administration by giving the Seller notice of his intention to do so by the method provided in Paragraph 30 hereof within said five
days. In the event that he shall not so elect, then the Seller shall have the privilege and option of reducing the contract price to the VA appraised value. This option
must be exercised by the Seller, within seven (7) days after delivery to the Purchaser of the VA appraisal, by giving the Purchaser notice of his intention to do so by
the method provided in Paragraph 30 hereof. If the Seller elects to reduce the contract price to the appraised valuation, the Purchaser covenants and agrees to be
bound to proceed with consummation hereof at the appraised valuation price. If the Seller does not elect to reduce the price after the Purchaser's refusal to con-
summate this contract at its full price, then this contract shall be null and void. This contract is contingent on the approval of the house and the Purchaser by the
Veterans Administration and the lending institution. If the aforesaid approval is not obtained, it is expressly agreed that the Purchaser shall be refunded his deposit,
and the contract shall be null and void.

27. **FHA/VA/CONV. REQUIREMENTS.** Seller agrees to comply with reasonable FHA, VA or CONV requirements or repairs where applicable. If FHA
financing is provided for herein, any outstanding sewer and water connection fees (tap fees) shall be paid in full by the Seller if said Agency requires pay-off of such
fees as a condition of financing.

28. **CONSUMER REPORT AUTHORIZATION.** The Purchaser hereby authorizes the Agent(s) to disclose to the Seller or any lender the credit information
provided to the Agent(s) by the Purchaser. In the event that terms of this contract require the Seller to take back financing from the Purchaser, and Seller desires to
obtain a Consumer Report (Credit Report) regarding the Purchaser, Seller must notify the listing Agent within five (5) days of the date of ratification of this contract, in writing, that the Agent is authorized and directed to order said report. In the event such a report is ordered within the stated time period, then this contract
of sale shall be contingent upon approval of a satisfactory Consumer Report (Credit Report) by Seller within five (5) days after receipt of said report by Seller. If
Seller does not approve the credit standing of the Purchaser, Seller shall notify the listing Agent in writing within five (5) days after receipt of the report of his
rejection of the Purchaser's credit. In that event this contract shall be null and void and deposit returned to the Purchaser. Failure to notify the listing Agent of the
rejection of the Purchaser's credit within the time provided shall constitute a waiver of the benefits of this provision and/or an approval of the Purchaser's credit.
Additionally, if Seller shall fail to order the said report within the five (5) days following the date of ratification of this contract, Seller waives the benefits provided
in this paragraph. The Purchaser hereby authorizes the Agent to order and obtain a Credit Report from a credit reporting agency to be used in connection with this
transaction where the Purchaser has applied for an extension of credit. Further, in the event the Agent is acting on behalf of a Creditor, Seller or other party
directly or indirectly affected by this transaction, the Purchaser hereby authorizes the Agent to forward all or any portion of the information contained in the said
report to the Creditor, Seller, or any other party directly involved. The cost of said report is to be borne by the Purchaser.

29. **IN COMPLIANCE WITH SECTION 45-308 OF THE DISTRICT OF COLUMBIA CODE (ACT OF SEPTEMBER 28, 1977, D.C. LAW 2-23) THE FOL-
LOWING INFORMATION IS PROVIDED (DISTRICT OF COLUMBIA ONLY):**

a. The characteristic of the soil on the subject property as described by the Soil Conservation Service of the United States Department of Agriculture in the
Soil Survey of the District of Columbia published in 1976 and as shown on the Soil Maps of the District of Columbia at the back of that publication is provided
in paragraph 8 hereof.

b. For further information, the Purchaser can contact a soil testing laboratory, the District of Columbia Department of Environmental Services or the Soil
Conservation Service of the Department of Agriculture.

30. **NOTICES.** Notices required to be given to Seller by this contract shall be in writing and effective as of the date on which such notice is delivered to one of
the Agents of the Seller named in Paragraph 9 hereof at the principal place of business of said Agent(s). Notice required to be given to Purchaser by this contract
shall also be in writing and effective either when delivered to Purchaser or when mailed to Purchaser's address as shown on page one hereof.

This is the Resale Contract for Single Family Homes recommended by the Montgomery County Board of REALTORS®, Inc.

FORM #1301 12/80

Courtesy of the Montgomery County Board of Realtors,® *Inc., Kensington, Maryland.*

read over the contract carefully. If you have any questions for the agent, make sure that you receive satisfactory answers before you sign.

Getting a mortgage

Let us continue the assumption that you have made an offer for $58,000, and that the seller, through the agent, has agreed to accept your terms. This procedure may take a day or two. You must then go to a financial institution and find out if you can get a loan. In applying for the mortgage, you will need a contract of sale.

At this time the real estate agent will ask you to fill out a credit information sheet. This is not a loan application. It is simply a method of giving to the real estate associate some idea of your credit worthiness. Figure 6–4 shows a typical credit information sheet for purchasers to complete. Among the details to be provided are your name and address, your age, how long you have lived at your present address, your base salary, any bonuses, and other sources of income. If your spouse works, you need to give his or her place of employment, salary, and income. Indicate the number of dependent children you have. Also list your present rent or mortgage on your property and the equity you have in that property. Describe the amount of installment payments on your automobile as well as the details of other loans outstanding that require monthly payments. You should list any child support or alimony payments as well as payments resulting from a lawsuit. References and a brief balance sheet are also required. You should fill out the credit information system completely and accurately.

The information supplied gives the agent some idea of whether you have enough money to handle the contract. If you do not, the seller of the house may reject you for credit reasons before you even go to the bank. Let's assume that you are successful in your offer to purchase the house and that you have a good credit position. Now to obtain mortgage financing, you have to ask your proposed mortgage lender what assets they expect you to have in order to provide you with a mortgage commitment. In applying for a mortgage, you have to fill out a mortgage credit sheet. The lender is especially interested in finding out the amount of your monthly income available for the payment of principal, interest, taxes, and operating expenses of the property.

Here a piece of advice seems desirable. If you are going into a housing transaction, you must make sure before you try to buy a house that your automobile payments, charge accounts, and outstanding loans are at a minimum. If you do, then you will have a maximum amount of income to satisfy your mortgage commitment. The higher your afterloan income or afterpayment income, the more the lender will be willing to lend you.

The mortgage lender will want a complete history or your financial and work experience. Officials of the lender also need certain documents before they will process the loan application. First, they need a completed

Figure 6-4

FINANCIAL INFORMATION SHEET

PURCHASER (Full Name) _____ AGE _____ SOC. SEC. # _____
RESIDENCE PHONE ( ) _____ BUSINESS PHONE ( ) _____ OTHER ( ) _____
PRESENT ADDRESS _____
YEARS AT PRESENT ADDRESS _____ ( ) OWN $ _____ PITI OR ( ) RENT $ _____ PER MONTH
PREVIOUS ADDRESS _____
MARITAL STATUS: ( ) MARRIED ( ) SEPARATED ( ) UNMARRIED (Including single, divorced or widowed)
OCCUPATION (Position & Title) _____ No. of Years _____
PLACE OF EMPLOYMENT (Name & Address) _____
PREVIOUS EMPLOYER (Name & Address) _____

CO-PURCHASER (Full Name) _____ AGE _____ SOC. SEC. # _____
RESIDENCE PHONE ( ) _____ BUSINESS PHONE ( ) _____ OTHER ( ) _____
PRESENT ADDRESS _____
YEARS AT PRESENT ADDRESS _____ ( ) OWN $ _____ PITI OR ( ) RENT $ _____ PER MONTH
PREVIOUS ADDRESS _____
MARITAL STATUS: ( ) MARRIED ( ) SEPARATED ( ) UNMARRIED (Including single, divorced or widowed)
OCCUPATION (Position & Title) _____ No. of Years _____
PLACE OF EMPLOYMENT (Name & Address) _____
PREVIOUS EMPLOYER (Name & Address) _____

GROSS ANNUAL INCOME:

	PURCHASER	CO-PURCHASER
BASE SALARY:	$	$
OVERTIME:	$	$
BONUSES:	$	$
COMMISSIONS:	$	$
DIVIDENDS:	$	$
NET RENTAL INCOME:	$	$
OTHER: _____	$	$
_____	$	$
TOTAL -	$	$

PURCHASER SELF EMPLOYED?
( ) Yes   ( ) No
CO-PURCHASER SELF EMPLOYED?
( ) Yes   ( ) No
DO YOU INTEND TO OCCUPY THIS
PROPERTY? ( ) Yes ( ) No
NUMBER OF CHILDREN _____
AGES _____
OTHER DEPENDENTS _____

ASSETS:
CHECKING: $ _____ BANK _____
                $ _____ BANK _____
SAVINGS: $ _____ BANK _____
                $ _____ BANK _____
CREDIT UNION: $ _____ BANK _____
STOCKS: $ _____ BONDS $ _____ LIFE INSURANCE $ _____
PRESENT RESIDENCE (If owned): Mkt. value $ _____ Mtge. Balance $ _____ Lender _____
OTHER ASSETS: (SPECIFY) _____

LIABILITIES: (List outstanding obligations including auto loans, mortgage payments, credit cards, personal loans and all other loans.)

TYPE	CREDITORS NAME	UNPAID BALANCE	DUE DATE	MONTHLY PAYMENT
_____	_____	$ _____	_____	$ _____
_____	_____	$ _____	_____	$ _____
_____	_____	$ _____	_____	$ _____
	TOTAL	$ _____		$ _____

ADDITIONAL MONTHLY OBLIGATIONS: ALIMONY $ _____ CHILD SUPPORT $ _____ CHILD CARE $ _____

ARE THERE ANY JUDGEMENTS OR LAWSUITS CURRENT? YES ( )   NO ( )   AMOUNT $ _____
(If YES, use reverse side for details)

IS ANY PART OF THE DOWN PAYMENT OR SETTLEMENT COSTS BEING OBTAINED FROM A SOURCE OTHER THAN FROM
ASSETS LISTED ABOVE? YES ( )   NO ( )   (If YES, use reverse side for details.)

THIS INFORMATION IS PRESENTED WITH THE UNDERSTANDING THAT IT MAY BE USED AS A BASIS FOR THE ACCEPTANCE OF
A CONTRACT BY THE SELLER, AND ALSO MAY BE USED AS INFORMATION FOR THE PLACEMENT OF A LOAN. THE UNDER-
SIGNED HEREBY AUTHORIZES THE AGENT TO DISCLOSE TO THE SELLER, COOPERATING BROKERS AND ANY LENDER ALL OR
ANY PORTION OF THE INFORMATION CONTAINED IN THIS FINANCIAL INFORMATION SHEET.

I (we) certify the above information to be true and accurate to the best of my (our) knowledge and by our signature(s) acknowledge receipt of
a copy of this Financial Information Sheet.

PURCHASER _____ CO-PURCHASER _____

DATE _____ DATE _____

contract for sale that has been signed by you and the seller of the property. Other details that should be provided are the following: a copy of the house location plat; your Social Security number; your bank account number; verification of your employment and salary; the amount of your installment debt; all sources of income for you and your spouse.

When the loan application and all attached documents are received, the lender will send an appraiser to examine the property. The appraiser's report will determine whether the mortgage lender can indeed make a loan on that property in the amount you have asked. When the loan commitment is obtained, the lending institution will send it to you so that you know that you may purchase the property. Then the real estate agent, in consultation with buyer and seller, will establish a settlement date, noting that all contingencies of the loan have been met. After the final inspection and formality of settlement, the house is yours.

The most important aspect in the whole process is for you to convince the mortgage lender that you are worthy of credit and that you can and will repay the loan. Here is a list of items the lender is interested in:

1. Gross monthly income from all sources including the income of both husband and wife. This includes:
   a. Base employment income.
   b. Overtime.
   c. Bonuses.
   d. Commissions.
   e. Dividends/interest.
   f. Net rental income.
   g. Other.
2. Your present and proposed housing expenses, including:
   a. Rent (P & I).
   b. Other financing (P & I).
   c. Hazard insurance.
   d. Real estate taxes.
   e. Mortgage insurance.
   f. Homeowner association dues.
   g. Utilities.
   h. Other.
3. Your assets, including:
   a. Cash toward purchase of house.
   b. Checking and savings.
   c. Stocks and bonds.
   d. Life insurance net cash value.
   e. Real estate owned.
   f. Retirement funds.
   g. Automobile.
   h. Furniture and personal property.
   i. Other assets.

4. Your liabilities, including:
    a. Installment debts.
    b. Charge accounts.
    c. Credit lines.
    d. Credit card purchases.
    e. Department store purchases.
    f. Other debts.
    g. Loans with stock pledged.
    h. Life insurance loans.
    i. Real estate loans.
    j. Automobile loans.
    k. Boat loans.
    l. Airplane loans.
    m. Alimony.
    n. Child support.
    o. Other.

When the lender has this information, he or she can judge whether you are worthy of credit. Ordinarily a bank or other mortgage lender does not wish your total current payments on debt to exceed 38 percent of your income. Therefore, you should give yourself a credit check before you go out to buy a house. If you have enough income to support a mortgage, fine. If not, cut back on your debt and payments, and wait until your debt is at a minimum. It is a good idea to keep a current statement of your income, expenses, assets, and liabilities. This means that you should update the statement each year. That way you know where you stand, and a lender can be quickly informed about your financial position.

Settlement costs

The settlement procedures were strengthened when Congress passed the Real Estate Settlement Procedures Act of 1974 (RESPA), which was amended in 1975. This act established a procedure for closing loans on one- to four-family residential properties. Its aim was to provide to all consumers greater and more timely information on the nature of settlement costs. Settlement fees given here are only illustrative of the costs involved in settling a house. You will find fuller coverage on this point in Chapter 15 of this book, "Investment in Real Assets." The following estimated fees are based on those current in Montgomery County, Maryland:

1. A recording fee, which amounts to $2.50 on all instruments.
2. Revenue stamps on the basis of $4.40 per $1,000 of purchase price.
3. A transfer tax, which is based on the purchase price of the property.
4. A tax certificate must be paid.

5. A survey must be paid, which comes to a minimum of $60 or $70.
6. There is a cost of platting.
7. Title examination, which might amount to $90 plus $2.50 per $1,000 up to $7,500. Then it goes down to $2.00 per $1,000 up to a $100,000. Over $100,000, it is $1.00 per $1,000. These are explained more fully in Chapter 15.
8. A settlement fee of $1.00 per $1,000.
9. The cost of preparation of the papers.
10. The title insurance, which must be paid. Usually it's required on all loans based on the amount of the loan.
11. All taxes owed on the property must be included in the settlement fees.
12. Finally, notary fees must be paid.

RESPA provides for notification about all of these settlement costs.

In addition, according to the Truth in Lending Law, when you close on your property, the lending agency has to give you a statement of how much interest you will pay on the loan over the next 30 years. For example, a $42,000 loan at 14 percent for 30 years requires 360 payments at $497.65. You will pay out a total of $179,154, of which $42,000 is principal repayment and $137,154 is interest. You are probably shocked by the amount you will pay in interest. Some unwary, unsuspecting buyers may panic when they see how high the interest payments are. But just remember a few things: (1) you are going to have a job; (2) you are going to be able to make your payments; (3) you will be able to write the interest off against your income for tax purposes; and (4) the value of your property will probably go up, and you will get the money back later when you sell. So when you see the amount at settlement time, don't panic and don't be frightened.

The three main items in a settlement are the taxes that must be paid, the cost of title examination, and miscellaneous transfer costs. If points are given, points must also be paid at closing. The main idea is that you must be prepared to pay the costs of settlement that are sometimes hidden in the negotiations to buy a house. Not only must you come up with the downpayment at closing but also with the settlement costs.

Furnishing costs

In addition, you should not forget one other cost. How much will it cost you to furnish the house? Here you have to consider what you already have in the way of rugs, carpets, and furniture. Next, what else will you need? What will the move cost? Certainly if your house is brand new, it will be wonderful. But in the first few years of living in the house, you will have to spend a lot of money to decorate. Make sure you have enough money to cover closing costs, moving expenses, and decorating.

What is a mortgage?   You might need a word of advice about the mortgage you are repaying and your rights and obligations under the mortgage agreement. The mortgage is a document in writing that represents a claim on the property. The parties entering into the mortgage must be legally competent to do so. What you are doing essentially is pledging your property as security. To keep title to it from passing to the lender, you must meet all of the commitments of the mortgage. You must pay your interest and principal on time. You must maintain the premises and value of the house. The debt is, to be repaid in specific amounts. The mortgage agreement is a legal description of the house. The person borrowing the money must really be the owner of the house. The mortgage must be properly witnessed, acknowledged, and accepted according to state law. In addition, as the borrower you must pay all taxes and assessments that become due.

A deed represents ownership and title   Your ownership of the house is represented by a deed. This is simply a written document conveying interest in the property. A warranty deed is usually the highest form of deed offered (apart from a special warranty deed). It states that the seller owns the property and gives complete warranty of its title. The seller affirms that the purchaser will have the use of the property free of claims by other persons and that there are no encumbrances against the property. In addition, it contains a covenant of further assurance to the effect that the seller will provide any additional information needed to protect the buyer's rights. In essence, the warranty deed you receive at the purchase of the house affirms legally to the world that you own the property and that the seller will protect your property interest.

Operating costs and repairs   Once you move in and start enjoying your new house, you will have to pay monthly operating expenses. You should itemize them and be prepared to pay for them. In fact, they are listed in your loan application. Because such costs may differ from your former expenses, you should estimate them in advance for your new house. These costs will be in addition to your furnishing and moving expenses. They include the following items: heat; electricity; telephone; water and sewage; trash removal; lawn care; costs of maintenance, painting, and repairing. Your budget should provide for these standard items.

As a basic principle, try to make your house efficient in all aspects of operation. While you want to keep your maintenance costs as low as possible, you still need to maintain the property. Keep two points in mind: (1) provide for all your needs in your budget, and (2) don't become "house poor." If you put all of your money into the house you will be angry when all you can do is just live in it. Try to economize on all expenses. Heating costs that go up the chimney will not add to your net worth!

There are two other expense items to consider. Ordinarily, you must set up an escrow account with your lending institution to pay real estate taxes. Real estate taxes are, of course, tax-deductible. In addition, you must carry property insurance. The mortgage lender will provide you with an escrow account for paying property insurance. If you move into a house from an apartment, you are probably not accustomed to carrying a substantial amount of insurance. But your budget must now provide for it. While you should keep such costs fairly low, you still must protect your property.

Fix it yourself

You need to become a "Harry Homeowner" with regard to maintenance. A person with a little skill and some tools can save substantial sums of money for simple repairs. This includes such tasks as replacing electrical fuses and light fixtures, repairing panes of glass, painting the house, handling general repairs, and taking care of the lawn and yard. You probably cannot repair a TV set because you may not have the required amount of expertise. But you can do the simple chores around the house and save substantial amounts of money.

Should you sell a house yourself?

Let's suppose you live in your house a while. Property values go up. You enjoy living in your home, which has become a successful financial venture. Suddenly you decide to move on to bigger and better things—the house of your dreams. People often move every seven years or so, depending on their careers and their housing needs. One question to raise is "Should I try to sell the house myself and save the real estate commission?" There are pros and cons on this matter. Many people think that they can save a substantial amount on the broker's commission, which is usually about 6 percent. On the other hand, if you are not familiar with the market, you might price your house too low and lose money when you sell. Or you may ask too high a price. Because the house does not sell, you are left sitting on it for some time. Of course, we are assuming an ordinary market, that is, one not plagued by either a super-abundance of mortgage money or such a lack of it that no houses can be bought or sold.

One major advantage in having an agent list the house is that in this way your property is carried on the local community's multiple listing service. The agent places the house in the marketplace, where it becomes known to other agents. You are more likely to sell the house faster, quicker, and at a fair price if you use an agent. If you try to sell it yourself, you can advertise it by putting up "Home for Sale" signs on the lawn, and advertising in your local newspaper. But in a difficult market it will take some time to sell it because you are not receiving wide advertising and other kinds of exposure.

An agent's commission is worthwhile if you consider how hard some agents work to sell real estate for their clients and the extra services they perform. They relieve the owner of the responsibility of finding a buyer. They insure a pleasant experience rather than an adversary relationship with the people that come to see your house. A third party helps. Using an agent takes some of the emotion out of selling your house. For example, you might show the house to many different people before someone decides to buy. As an owner-seller you must listen to their criticisms of the house, which can be emotionally trying. The professionalism of some brokerage firms seems to make the 6 percent commission a rather small price to pay to sell an asset that has increased in value. So think carefully if you decide to sell your house without an agent.

Don't lose your home!

Let's assume that you purchase a house. But suddenly you find that you can't continue your payments on the principal and interest. You become ill and cannot work. Perhaps you have had unexpected expenses. You may have had some difficulty with your children. How can you handle this situation? The federal government has a pamphlet entitled *Having Problems Paying Your Mortgage?* It is published by the Department of Housing and Urban Development (HUD). They recommend that a homeowner who cannot pay a mortgage should open up an honest dialogue with the lender. Explain how you got into trouble, indicate all of the resources that you have available to pay the loan, and work out some solution for repayment of your debt. And by all means make it clear that you have every intention of fulfilling your obligations. If you hold an FHA mortgage, HUD may be willing to assume it. HUD may pay the lender, and then you as the borrower can later repay HUD.

Another solution is possible for you if you hold a FHA or conventional mortgage. The lender may be willing to let you stop payments temporarily until you get out of your difficulties. Under these circumstances, of course, the duration of the mortgage would be extended for a longer period. But eventually you can pay it off.

Do not try to borrow more money to pay off your mortgage. That only increases your indebtedness and makes it more difficult for you in the long run. Do not hire an outsider to represent you, but deal on your own with the lending agents. If you need more detailed advice, you can get the government's pamphlet by writing to the Publications Distribution,

Room B258, Department of Housing and Urban Development, Washington, D.C. 20140. Or visit any HUD field office near you, and ask there for this information.

Summary

In this chapter we have examined the following advantages of owning a home: (1) the increasing value of a house acts as a hedge against inflation; (2) income tax is reduced as a result of the deductibility of interest and tax payments; (3) the size of mortgage payments remains fixed as a rule while other costs go up; (4) home ownership is a form of forced savings that adds to net worth more than do most other investments; and (5) home ownership provides peace of mind.

The house you can afford is a function of the amount of income you have available for home ownership and the size of all your financial obligations. Generally speaking, one fourth of your monthly income can be used to pay for principal and interest on your mortgage. A mortgage lender has a different formula for calculating the cost of the house you can buy and the size of your mortgage. The higher your downpayment on a house, the more impressive the house you can afford. And the lower the interest rate you pay, the more you can spend on housing. Therefore, with interest rates at 14 percent you will have to buy a smaller house than you could if interest rates were at 8 or 10 percent.

One of the biggest problems in buying a house is finding downpayment money. It can come through savings, through loans from friends or relatives, and through your own labor or "sweat equity." In some cases downpayments can be arranged even though you have little or no money. This type of arrangement is referred to as *creative financing*.

A second major problem is where to obtain mortgage money. Mortgage money can come from savings and lending institutions, commercial banks, or mortgage bankers, pension funds, and real estate investment trusts. Take a creative view about the financing of a house, but be sure you have complete knowledge about the implications of financing techniques. A real estate agent can help you find a satisfactory and affordable house.

The major expense of home ownership is the mortgage payment. Most of this monthly payment will go for interest and property taxes, and is deductible from taxable income. Because of tax deductibility, these payments are less expensive than they first appear. Maintenance and operating costs also must be considered. As the years go by, the value of your house will increase and probably exceed the amount of money you have invested in it. Thus home ownership will increase your net worth over time.

Controlling credit and consumer loans

- Consumer credit fundamentals
- Controlling credit
- Major forms of consumer credit
- Cost of consumer credit
- Important credit legislation
- Building and maintaining a credit rating
- Dealing with credit difficulties
- Summary

Consumer credit is both a boon and a curse to Americans. With consumer debt at an all-time high, the regular use of credit to finance everything from durable goods to everyday consumables has never been more pervasive and extensive. The use of consumer credit clearly has a role in your personal financial planning. However, the temptations for abuse of consumer credit privileges have never been greater. Horror stories in the news media concerning overextended families and personal bankruptcies have become commonplace.

It is important for you to become familiar with the major sources and types of consumer credit.[1] You must be aware of the cost of consumer credit, how to control it, and how to use it wisely. If you are successful in controlling credit use, you will increase your assets and net worth. Responsible use of credit will help you work toward financial independence. You will also enjoy a rich life enhanced by wise decisions in the use of credit and in spending your money.

Consumer credit fundamentals

Consumer credit is the use of credit by people to purchase goods and services. It is separate and distinct from business credit, which finances the purchase of productive business assets. In nearly all cases consumer credit is used to finance the purchase of goods (which may be either durable or nondurable) or services which will be used up by individuals. When you charge it at the department store or borrow money to buy a car, you are using consumer credit.

Forms of consumer credit

Consumer credit takes a variety of forms, the commonest of which is service credit. Service credit refers to the credit extended for commonly used services such as home electricity or telephone service. As you use these services, the electric company and telephone company maintain an account in your name. They then send you a monthly bill for the amount of service used. Since you do not pay for electricity or telephone service on a pay-as-you-go basis, you are using credit to purchase these services.

Other common types of consumer credit probably are familiar. They include cash loans, installment sales (also called buying on time), overdraft checking accounts, retail charge accounts, oil company credit cards, bank credit cards, travel and entertainment cards, and so forth. These forms of credit are used by a great many people. The use of such credit, in effect, allows you to trade future income for current consumption. If

---

[1] A glossary of technical terms associated with credit and loans is provided in an appendix at the end of this chapter.

you buy now and pay later, you obtain the immediate use of goods or services in return for your promise to pay for them out of future income. This trading of future income for current consumption is the essence of consumer credit, regardless of its form.

Advantages of credit   To answer questions about why people use credit and why credit is beneficial, we should examine the advantages and disadvantages of credit use. One major advantage is that credit allows you to purchase items requiring a major cash outlay and then pay for these items in small amounts over an extended period of time. The purchase of a new car may be the best example of this use of credit. Most people would be unable to purchase a new car if they had to pay the full cost in cash. Even people with adequate savings to pay cash for a new car are often unwilling to do so. The do not want to deplete their savings account by the $6,000 or more that a new car commonly costs. By using credit, they can pay for the car from current income while they are using it. They also keep their savings intact.

This example illustrates two additional advantages of credit: preservation of savings and a pay-as-you-go system. For most people, building a savings account is a long and difficult process. It often takes years of small deposits to build up a four-or five-figure savings account. Using credit as an alternative to withdrawing savings allows you to preserve these hard-earned savings dollars and still make major purchases.

The pay-as-you-go aspects of credit are also attractive to many people. As noted, the use of credit allows you to have the immediate use of an item and to pay for this item while you are using it. This advantage of credit is also the source of one of the major dangers of credit use, namely, the temptation to seek instant gratification in return for a promise to pay out of future income. Once this type of habit is developed, it becomes very easy to say "charge it" whenever you see any desirable good or service.

There are two other advantages of credit. Access to credit and the maintenance of a good credit record is a great advantage in the event of a financial emergency. In such emergencies credit can provide a very convenient temporary solution to a sudden financial problem.

Credit offers a good bit of convenience. Charge accounts and credit cards allow you to make a number of purchases and receive an itemized bill once a month. Many people find these record-keeping services convenient. They prefer to shop or travel without having to bother with writing checks or carrying large amounts of cash. Retail store charge accounts are also convenient because a charge account often confers preferred customer status on the charge account holder. Preferred customers receive advance notice of sales and are kept on the store's mailing list for shop-by-mail service.

Credit disadvantages   The disadvantages of credit use must also be understood. The two biggest dangers of credit are that credit use ties up future income and often leads to overspending. It is very easy to spend more than you have budgeted when it is not necessary to pay immediate cash for a purchase. Many widely used credit cards allow up to 20 months to pay for purchases. The low monthly payment in relation to the cost of an item can provide an irresistible temptation to overspend for planned items or to buy items that were not planned. For example, a $400 stereo may seem very expensive if you had to pay $400 in cash. But at "only" $20 a month (plus interest, of course) it seems quite affordable. If uncontrolled, these small monthly payments can add up to the point where a large slice of current and future income is obligated to cover past debts. Many families and individuals have learned the hard way that these past debts can mount up. The total monthly payments on indebtedness may grow to be equal to or actually greater than the amount of monthly income. When this happens, you're in trouble. The return trip from the state of insolvency is a long and difficult one.

Another disadvantage of credit use is that it costs money to pay the interest. An automobile ad in a recent daily paper illustrates the high cost of credit. A brand new convertible sports car is advertised at a cost of $499 down and $199 a month for 48 months. The fine print of the ad reveals that the cash price of the car is $7,461. This is the price you would pay if you had available funds to pay cash for the car. On the extended payment terms, you would instead pay a total of $10,051 for the car ($499 down plus a total of $9,552 in monthly payments). The cost difference of $2,590 represents the cost of credit. In this case the annual percentage rate of interest is 16.5 percent (a later section of this chapter will explain the annual percentage rate in detail).

This simple example is a good illustration of the trade-off involved in the benefit of credit use versus its cost. Credit would allow you to own a brand-new convertible sports car without having saved $7,461. You can drive and enjoy the car while you pay for it. This is an obvious benefit. On the cost side, over the four years you pay for the car, you will pay $2,590 more for the privilege of owning it before you have the cash to buy it. You also have a fixed obligation of $199 a month in your budget for the next four years.

The final danger of credit use is the possibility that you might lose the item purchased if you cannot meet your payments in the future. Most contracts for major purchases bought on time give the seller or lender the right to repossess the item purchased if payments are not made on time. Referring to the automobile example, if you are unable to meet your payments after, say, six payments have been made, the seller could repossess the car. The seller then has the right to sell the car to settle your debt. If the car should be sold for more than the amount of the debt, you would be paid the difference between the amount owed and the amount the car was sold for. However, since cars, like many other consumer durables, depreciate rather rapidly, it is unlikely that the sale price would be more than the debt. You would almost certainly lose your downpayment and all payments made up to the time when payments ceased. In this case you would lose a total of $1,693 ($499 downpayment plus six payments of $199 each).

The responsible use of credit is a definite benefit in personal financial planning, but it is not a costless benefit. If not closely monitored and controlled, the indiscriminate use of credit can lead to serious financial difficulties. Therefore you must learn to control your credit.

Controlling credit

With credit readily available to nearly all consumers, the topic of credit control is becoming increasingly important. The first and most important thing to learn about credit control is that *credit does not increase your income.* While this statement may seem obvious, a surprising number of people use credit to purchase items which they know they cannot afford. This kind of rationalization is dangerous to your financial health. It is very important to recognize that if you cannot afford to pay cash or to save for an item, then you cannot afford to buy it on credit either. Most consumer credit plans charge fairly high interest rates. If you think that you are unable to afford to save for an item, you certainly cannot afford to buy it on credit.

Debt guidelines

What constitutes a reasonable debt limit? Some guidance in answering this question is provided by information from the Federal Reserve Board. These data, reproduced in Table 7–1, show that about one third of middle-income families ($15,000–$19,999 gross family income) had no debt at all. Slightly over one third had committed 9 percent or less of their gross

Table 7–1
Average family debt ratios

		Debt repayments as a percent of gross income				
Gross family income	No debt	Under 5 percent	5–9 percent	10–19 percent	20–39 percent	40 percent or more
$10,000–$14,999 ...	42%	8%	14%	24%	9%	*
$15,000–$19,999 ...	34	11	24	23	5	*
$20,000–$24,999 ...	32	19	24	16	5	*
$25,000 and over ...	42	23	21	8	2	*

Note: The debt repayment ratios are lower here than if they had been based on take-home pay.
*Less than 0.5 percent.
SOURCE *Consumer Views*, Citibank, January 1980 (from the Federal Reserve Board 1977 Consumer Credit Survey). By courtesy of *Consumer Views*, published by Citibank, copyright Citicorp.

income to debt repayments, and just under one third had committed 10 percent or more of their gross income to debt repayments. Families with incomes below $15,000 or above $25,000 showed the highest incidence of no debt at all. For both income groups, 42 percent of the families reported no installment debt.

For all income groups, less than 10 percent of the families had committed over 20 percent of their income to installment payments. Overall, the majority of families in the United States have obligated less than 10 percent of beforetax income to installment payments. Over a third of all families actually have no installment debt at all.

The Federal Reserve data are useful in providing a measure of overall indebtedness for average American families. However, when you establish a reasonable debt limit for yourself, you should establish guidelines based on your take-home pay. The amount of payroll deductions you may have for such things as federal and state taxes, Social Security, union dues, and insurance and pension plans may be quite different from those of another person earning the same gross income. Because of this, total installment debts as a percent of take-home pay should be used as a guide to plan your use and control of consumer credit.

A maximum of 20 percent of your take-home pay obligated to meet monthly installment payments is a common guideline. In fact, 15 percent of take-home pay is more easily managable. A debt limit of 10 percent or less would be considered a fairly low level. Since inflation has steadily eaten away at most people's annual pay raises in recent years, we recommend a 15 percent limit as the most appropriate guideline.

Table 7–2 applies this guideline for a married couple who both work

**Table 7–2
Tracking your maximum debt limit**

Sample calculation

a.	Annual take-home income (after taxes and all other deductions)	$18,000
b.	15 percent of annual take-home income	2,700
c.	Monthly installment maximum (item b. divided by 12)	225
d.	Current monthly installment payments	175
e.	Margin of safety	50

SOURCE Adapted from *Consumer Views*, Citibank, January 1980.

General guidelines

Annual take-home income	Monthly installment maximums		
	10 percent	15 percent	20 percent
$ 8,000	$ 67	$100	$133
12,000	100	150	200
16,000	133	200	267
20,000	167	250	333
24,000	200	300	400
30,000	250	375	500

and earn a total of $18,000 per year in take-home income from all sources (including salary, bonuses, dividends, and interest). Calculating 15 percent of annual take-home income shows that they can afford to make $2,700 in annual installment payments. Dividing the annual payment of $2,700 by 12 months shows that their installment payments should be no more than $225 per month. They currently make $175 per month in monthly installment payments. The $50 per month difference shows their margin of safety between what they are now paying and the maximum amount they can afford to pay.

The bottom section of Table 7–2 gives general guidelines for maximum monthly installment payments according to your annual take-home income. The 10 percent, 15 percent, and 20 percent columns show the maximum monthly installment payments you could afford, depending on whether you use 10 percent, 15 percent, or 20 percent of your monthly take-home income as a guideline. For example, if you earn $12,000 per year in take-home income, the 15 percent guideline we recommend tells you that you could comfortably afford $150 per month in installment payments. In no case should your monthly payments exceed $200. In reading these tables, you should keep in mind that the figures represent average guidelines. Your situation may not be at all average. Thus if you have an exceptionally high mortgage payment, extremely high medical bills, a large number of dependents, or some other unusual situation, the guidelines may not apply to you. As with all general guidelines, the application of the guidelines must be tempered with common sense and a knowledge of your own particular situation.

Advantages of paying cash

You should consider the alternative of paying cash versus using credit. One of the immediate and most important advantages of paying cash for purchases is that paying in cash helps fight the temptation to overspend by using credit. Handing over cash for a purchase seems somehow more real than handing over a plastic credit card or just saying charge it. As an alternative to carrying cash, you may want to use your checkbook instead. Using a checkbook is sometimes inconvenient because of time required to obtain a check approval. Deducting the cost of a purchase immediately from your checkbook balance, however, has the same inhibiting effect on overspending as does paying cash. Whether paying by cash or check, the immediate reduction in your available funds has a strong emotional impact and will be a great help in fighting the temptation to overspend.

Many people argue that buying on time is a better way to make major purchases than saving the money required to make the purchase. They argue that the cost of what you want to buy increases faster than the rate at which you can save. In other words inflation pushes up prices so fast that the cost of your purchase will be so much higher by the

Table 7–3
Saving versus buying a car on credit

Credit price of car = $499 down plus $199 per month for 48 months	
Savings plan (6 percent interest):	
a. $499 deposited now will grow in 4 years to	$ 630
b. $199 deposited per month for 4 years will grow to	$10,766
c. Savings balance at the end of 4 years will equal	$11,396
Cost of car:	
Current cost = $7,461	
Cost in four years (10 percent inflation) =	$10,924
Savings account − Future cost =	$ 472

time you save the cash that you would have been better off buying on time. In most cases this is a faulty line of reasoning. The reason this argument is generally faulty is that in periods of high inflation, the amount of interest you have to pay is also very high. The finance charges for buying on time drive the price of your purchase up significantly. A simple example will show how this works.

In the example concerning the purchase of a new sports car, the credit terms were $499 down and $199 per month for 48 months. If instead of paying this money for a car payment, you deposited the money in a savings account earning 6 percent interest, your saving account would total $11,396 at the end of four years. This total would be the sum of two factors. The $499 downpayment earning 6 percent per year interest would amount to $630 at the end of four years. The $199 monthly deposit earning 6 percent per year would amount to $10,766 when the interest is added on. This total of $11,396 should be compared to the probable price of the car four years from now.

As shown in Table 7–3, at current prices the sports car costs $7,461. Recent experience has shown that new car prices should be expected to increase by 8 to 10 percent per year. Assuming that your sports car increases in price by the maximum 10 percent per year, the car would cost $10,924 four years from now. This cost would be almost $500 less than the amount of money you would have saved to buy the car. Thus, by paying yourself, you could buy your new car and have $500 left over. By coincidence, a great car stereo system costs about $500 (or you might even save the money)!

Major forms of consumer credit

Consumer credit comes in a wide variety of packages. One of the most common forms is a cash loan taken out at a bank, credit union, savings and loan, or similar institution. Loans of cash may be either secured or unsecured, and may be repaid in installments or by a single payment. A secured loan is one for which some item of value is pledged as security. If the loan is not paid on time, the lender has the right to take the item that was pledged. Under this type of loan agreement, the item pledged is referred to as the *collateral* for the loan.

Secured loans

Probably the most familiar type of secured consumer loan is a car loan. Like most consumer loans, payments on a car loan are made in installments. If these installment payments are not made on time, the lender may take back the car to satisfy the loan. If this occurs, the car is said to be repossessed by the lender.

Mortgage loans are also a common type of secured cash loan. This type of loan is used to purchase a personal residence, such as a house or condominium apartment. Mortgage loans, and a special type of mortgage loan called a second mortgage, were explained in detail in Chapter six.

Unsecured loans

Unsecured loans of cash are also fairly common. With this type of loan, you do not have to pledge any collateral. Such a loan is often called a *full faith and credit loan* because you are pledging your full faith and credit to repay it. In effect, your reputation and integrity are the only collateral for an unsecured loan.

Whether a loan is secured or unsecured, it may be repaid either in installments or in a single payment. As its name implies, an installment loan is paid back in installments, usually in a series of equal monthly installments. The amount of the loan (called the *principal*) plus interest typically is paid back in 12, 18, 24, 36 or more equal monthly installments.

In contrast to an installment loan, a single-payment loan is repaid by one single payment at the end of the loan period. If you borrow money on a single-payment loan, you are required to repay the principal plus the interest in a single payment at the end of some specified period of time. In most cases a single-payment loan is repaid in a relatively short period of time. Repayment in 3, 6, or 9 months is fairly common, and terms of more than one year are fairly rare.

Figures 7–1 and 7–2 show a sample loan application and a sample promissory note and security agreement. The loan application asks about the purpose of the loan, whether it will be secured or unsecured, and the financial condition of the borrower. The promissory note and security agreement is a statement of the agreement between borrower and lender at the time the loan is made. This particular sample agreement is one of the newer kinds of plain English agreements many lenders are now using. The note clearly explains such things as terms of payment, insurance, amount financed, interest and late charges, and other factors. When you take a loan out, you should read this agreement carefully to be

FIGURE 7-1
Sample loan application form

Page 1

Application for Consumer Loan
The Riggs National Bank of Washington, D.C.

To THE RIGGS NATIONAL BANK OF WASHINGTON, D.C., Consumer Credit Department. _____ 19 ____

I (We) hereby apply for a loan of $ _____ repayable in ☐ _____ equal monthly instalments, ☐ _____

PURPOSE

Personal

☐ Unsecured loan for the purpose of _____

☐ Secured loan, secured by _____ for the purpose of _____

Vehicle, Boat

☐ Instalment loan to purchase ☐ automobile ☐ boat ☐ _____ to be secured by chattel mortgage on conveyance to be purchased, as described herein. Comprehensive, fire and theft and $50/$100 deductible collision insurance will be maintained for term of the loan. Title or Notice of Security Interest Filing will be delivered to Riggs. You may call seller for more detailed description of the property.

MAKE	MODEL	YEAR	TITLE IN NAME(S) OF	TO BE TITLED IN	SERIAL NUMBER IF KNOWN

LIST PRICE	DISCOUNT	COST	TRADE IN	CASH PYT	TOTAL DOWN PYT	AMOUNT TO FINANCE	NAME OF SELLER

INSURANCE COMPANY	POLICY NUMBER	AGENT	ADDRESS	PHONE

Property Improvement

☐ Unsecured loan to improve ☐ my (our) residence as described below on 2nd and 3rd lines of "Applicant" section ☐ property other than my (our) residence,
located at _____ owned by _____ and
described as _____ (Attach copy of estimate, if available.)

DESCRIPTION OF IMPROVEMENTS TO BE MADE	NAME OF CONTRACTOR	ESTIMATED COST

APPLICANT

LAST NAME	FIRST	MIDDLE	BIRTH DATE	NO. OF DEPENDENTS AGES

PRESENT STREET ADDRESS	CITY	STATE	ZIP	HOW LONG	HOME PHONE

☐ BUYING MONTHLY PYT. ☐ RENTING	MORTGAGE HOLDER'S LANDLORD'S NAME	IF BUYING, TITLE IN NAME OF	EST VALUE	MORTGAGE

DRIVER'S LICENSE NO. & STATE	SOCIAL SECURITY NO.	VISA STATUS (IF YOU ARE NOT A U.S. CITIZEN)

PREVIOUS ADDRESS IF AT ABOVE ADDRESS LESS THAN 5 YEARS	HOW LONG

CHECKING ACCOUNT NO.	INSTITUTION	SAVINGS ACCOUNT NO.	INSTITUTION

PRESENT EMPLOYER	POSITION	HOW LONG

EMPLOYER'S ADDRESS	ANNUAL SALARY	PHONE NO.

Alimony, child support, or separate maintenance income need not be revealed if you do not choose to rely on it ———— | OTHER INCOME $ ___ PER | SOURCE

PREVIOUS EMPLOYER	PREVIOUS EMPLOYER'S ADDRESS	HOW LONG

NEAREST RELATIVE	RELATIONSHIP	ADDRESS—NEAREST RELATIVE	PHONE NO.

CO-APPLICANT (Complete only if a joint application)

LAST NAME	FIRST	MIDDLE	BIRTH DATE	RELATIONSHIP TO APPLICANT	NO. OF DEPENDENTS AGES

PRESENT STREET ADDRESS	CITY	STATE	ZIP	HOW LONG	HOME PHONE

☐ BUYING MONTHLY PYT. ☐ RENTING	MORTGAGE HOLDER'S LANDLORD'S NAME	IF BUYING, TITLE IN NAME OF	EST VALUE	MORTGAGE

DRIVER'S LICENSE NO. & STATE	SOCIAL SECURITY NO.	VISA STATUS (IF YOU ARE NOT A U.S. CITIZEN)

CHECKING ACCOUNT NO.	INSTITUTION	SAVINGS ACCOUNT NO.	INSTITUTION

PRESENT EMPLOYER	POSITION	HOW LONG

EMPLOYER'S ADDRESS	ANNUAL SALARY	PHONE NO.

Alimony, child support or separate maintenance income need not be revealed if you do not choose to rely on it | OTHER INCOME $ ___ PER | SOURCE

NEAREST RELATIVE	RELATIONSHIP	ADDRESS—NEAREST RELATIVE	PHONE NO.

LIABILITIES of Applicant and Co-applicant

OUTSTANDING DEBTS AND LOANS (Include Riggs, other Banks, Finance Companies, Credit Unions, credit cards, other lines of credit, and anyone else to whom indebted. If none, so state. Use separate sheet if necessary.)

NAME OF CREDITOR	ACCOUNT NO.	NAMES IN WHICH ACCOUNT IS CARRIED	ORIG. AMT. OR HIGH CRED.	PRESENT BALANCE	MONTHLY PAYMENTS

ARE YOU ENDORSER OR GUARANTOR OF ANY NOTE OR CONTRACT? ☐ NO ☐ YES TO ____ FOR ____	OTHER NAMES IN WHICH YOU HAVE RECEIVED CREDIT

You are hereby authorized to
(1) ☐ Charge my account no. _____ for the monthly payments
(2) ☐ Disburse proceeds of the loan as follows _____

I understand that credit life insurance is not required and will not be provided unless requested by me in writing on your form 884.

Everything that I have stated in this application is correct to the best of my knowledge. I understand that you will retain this application whether or not it is approved. You are authorized to check my credit and employment history and to answer questions about your credit experience with me.

APPLICANT'S SIGNATURE	DATE	CO-APPLICANT'S SIGNATURE	DATE

Form 782 (Rev. 10/79)

Figure 7–1 *(continued)*

Page 2

Supplementary Financial Information
Personal Financial Statement

Statement of the financial condition of _____ as of _____ 19_____

ASSETS				LIABILITIES			
Cash (Schedule A)				Notes Payable to Banks (Schedule A)			
Securities (Schedule B)				Notes Payable to Others			
Accounts & Notes Receivable				Accounts and Bills Due			
Real Estate Owned (Schedule C)				Unpaid Income Taxes			
Real Estate Mortgages Owned (Schedule D)				Real Estate Mortgages Payable (Schedule C)			
Cash Value—Life Insurance (Schedule E)				Instalment Contracts Payable			
Other Assets (Itemize)				Other Liabilities (Itemize)			
				TOTAL LIABILITIES			
				NET WORTH			
TOTAL ASSETS				TOTAL LIABILITIES & NET WORTH			

DEPOSITS IN AND AMOUNTS OWED TO FINANCIAL INSTITUTIONS

Schedule A

NAME OF BANK, SAVINGS AND LOAN, CREDIT UNION (Include Checking, Savings, and Certificates of Deposit)	AMOUNT OF DEPOSIT	AMOUNT OWING	ON WHAT BASIS? (Unsecured, Endorsements, Collateral)

SECURITIES OWNED

Schedule B

NO. SHARES (STOCKS) FACE VALUE (BONDS)	DESCRIPTION OF SECURITY (Issuer, Class of Stock, Rate and Due Date of Bonds)	IN NAME(S) OF	MARKET VALUE	TO WHOM PLEDGED

REAL ESTATE OWNED

Schedule C

DESCRIPTION	LOCATION	TITLE IN NAME(S) OF	PURCHASE PRICE	MARKET VALUE	MORTGAGE BALANCE

REAL ESTATE MORTGAGES (TRUSTS) OWNED

Schedule D

LOCATION AND TYPE OF PROPERTY	TYPE OF LIEN (1st, 2nd)	IN NAME(S) OF	ORIGINAL AMOUNT	PRESENT AMOUNT	UP TO DATE?	FINAL MATURITY

LIFE INSURANCE CARRIED

Schedule E

FACE AMOUNT	NAME OF COMPANY	TYPE OF POLICY	BENEFICIARY	CASH SURRENDER VALUE	LOANS	ASSIGNED?

I hereby certify that the above statement is a true and correct statement of my financial condition as of the date stated above. I understand that any credit now or hereafter extended to me by The Riggs National Bank is made upon the strength of this statement and agree to notify the Bank of any change that materially reduces my ability to meet my obligations.

DATE SIGNED_____ 19_____ SIGNATURE _____

SOURCE   Courtesy of Riggs National Bank, Washington, D.C.

FIGURE 7-2
Promissory note and security agreement

First National City Bank

Consumer Loan Note   Date_____, 19____

(In this note, the words **I, me, mine** and **my** mean each and all of those who signed it. The words **you, your** and **yours** mean First National City Bank.)

Terms of To repay my loan, I promise to pay you_____ Dollars
Repayment ($_____). I'll pay this sum at one of your branches in_____ uninterrupted_____
installments of $_____each. Payments will be due_____, starting
from the date the loan is made.

Here's the breakdown of my payments:

1. Amount of the Loan $_____
2. Property Insurance Premium $_____
3. Filing Fee for
   Security Interest $_____
4. Amount Financed (1+2+3) $_____
5. **Finance Charge** $_____
6. Total of Payments (4+5) $_____

Annual Percentage Rate_____%

Prepayment of Even though I needn't pay more than the fixed installments, I have the right to prepay the whole outstanding
Whole Note amount of this note at any time. If I do, or if this loan is refinanced—that is, replaced by a new note—
you will refund the unearned **finance charge,** figured by the rule of 78—a commonly used formula for figuring
rebates on installment loans. However, you can charge a minimum **finance charge** of $10.

Late Charge If I fall more than 10 days behind in paying an installment, I promise to pay a late charge of 5% of the
overdue installment, but no more than $5. However, the sum total of late charges on all installments can't be
more than 2% of the total of payments or $25, whichever is less.

Security To protect you if I default on this or any other debt to you, I give you what is known as a security interest
in my ○ Motor Vehicle and/or _____ (see the Security Agreement I have given you
for a full description of this property), ○ Stocks, ○ Bonds, ○ Savings Account (more fully described in the
receipt you gave me today) **and** any account or other property of mine coming into your possession.

Insurance I understand I must maintain property insurance on the property covered by the Security Agreement for its
full insurable value, but I can buy this insurance through a person of my own choosing.

Default I'll be in default:
1. If I don't pay an installment on time; or
2. If any other creditor tries by legal process to take any money of mine in your possession.

You can then demand immediate payment of the balance of this note, minus the part of the **finance charge**
which hasn't been earned figured by the rule of 78. You will also have other legal rights, for instance, the right
to repossess, sell and apply security to the payments under this note and any other debts I may then owe you.

Irregular Payments You can accept late payments or partial payments, even though marked "payment in full", without losing
any of your rights under this note.

Delay in Enforcement You can delay enforcing any of your rights under this note without losing them.

Collection Costs If I'm in default under this note and you demand full payment, I agree to pay you interest on the unpaid
balance at the rate of 1% per month, after an allowance for the unearned **finance charge.** If you have to sue
me, I also agree to pay your attorney's fees equal to 15% of the amount due, and court costs. But if I defend
and the court decides I am right, I understand that you will pay my reasonable attorney's fees and the
court costs.

Comakers If I'm signing this note as a comaker, I agree to be equally responsible with the borrower. You don't have to
notify me that this note hasn't been paid. You can change the terms of payment and release any security
without notifying or releasing me from responsibility on this note.

Copy Received The borrower acknowledges receipt of a completely filled-in copy of this note.

            Signatures   Addresses

Borrower:_____   _____

Comaker:_____   _____

Comaker:_____   _____

Comaker:_____   _____

Hot Line If something should happen and you can't pay on time, please call us immediately at (212) 559-3061.

Personal Finance Department
First National City Bank

PBR 668 Rev. 1/75

SOURCE   Courtesy of First National City Bank of New York.

sure you understand the terms of the loan. You should read Figure 7–2 carefully to be sure that you understand the terms explained there.

Education loans

An education loan is a special type of unsecured loan that may be of great interest to college students. Direct government loans or government-guaranteed loans can be applied for at a college's financial aid office. A direct loan is a loan made directly to the student by the government, such as a National Defense Student Loan. These loans are limited to a maximum of $5,000 over four years of college, with no more than $2,500 to be borrowed in the first two years. Government-guaranteed loans are loans made by commercial lenders such as a bank, savings and loan, or credit union, in which the government guarantees repayment. Direct government loans and government guaranteed-loans are for students who can qualify for financial aid on the basis of need. Since each college defines need according to its particular circumstances, it is necessary to obtain details from the financial aid office.

The biggest advantage of government loan programs is that the loans generally carry low interest rates and have liberal repayment terms. Principal payments do not have to be made until after graduation. Interest payments can also be deferred until after graduation on most of these loans. The biggest disadvantage of the programs is that the loans are often hard to obtain. The direct government loan program has been cut back in recent years. Commercial lenders are often reluctant to make loans at low rates, even with a government guarantee. Details as to availability and sources of such loans should be obtained from the college's financial aid office. You can also apply for an education loan that is not part of a government program from any commercial lending source. Such a loan would be a normal unsecured loan for the purpose of education. It would carry market interest rates and normal repayment terms.

Automatic overdrafts

Automatic overdraft accounts are becoming available from commercial banks. Under this type of arrangement, you can arrange for your bank to honor checks that overdraw your account. You may only overdraw up to a certain predetermined limit, and you then have to pay the money back in installment payments. The number of payments allowed to repay your account and the interest rate are negotiated in advance between you and the bank. A typical agreement, for example, might say that you could overdraw your account up to a maximum of $1,500. The amount overdrawn might then be repaid in 18 equal installments plus interest at 1.5 percent per month on the declining balance. There is ordinarily no limit on the number of times you may overdraw your account. However, the size of your monthly installment changes every time you write a new overdraft check. In effect, each new overdraft check sets up on a new loan agreement.

Credit lines

A line of credit with your bank or credit union is somewhat similar to an overdraft account. Under this type of agreement, you again have a predetermined credit agreement. The number of installment payments necessary to repay any money borrowed and the rate of interest are also predetermined. You may borrow cash when you need it up to the total amount of your credit line without any further approval from the lender. You must then pay back the money borrowed according to prearranged terms.

Both overdrafts and credit lines offer a great deal of convenience in borrowing. You know repayment terms in advance, and you can obtain money up to your limit without requesting any further credit approval. In addition, the monthly installment payment is considered the minimum payment. You may make any larger payment, including paying the loan in full, at any time you wish. This convenient feature of overdrafts and credit lines adds a good deal of flexibility to your credit management.

Retail charge accounts

Most people are probably familiar with retail charge accounts. These are the charge accounts you open with a retail store so that you may buy merchandise from that store on credit. These accounts normally charge no interest if paid in full within 30 days of the billing date. An interest charge of 1 to 2 percent per month is paid on balances over 30 days old. Retail charge accounts typically come in one of two common varieties: an open-ended account or a revolving account. An open-ended account is similar to a line of credit. The charge customer is assigned a maximum dollar limit that may not be exceeded. If the entire balance is paid off within 30 days of when the bill is received, no interest is charged. If the entire balance is not paid within 30 days, the balance may be repaid in installments. The customer is then charged interest on the unpaid balance. The allowed number of installment payments may extend over several months or years.

With a revolving account, extended payment terms are automatic. Customer and store agree on the maximum total amount which may be charged on the account. Purchases made on this type of account are automatically billed in installments, usually 12 to 24 monthly installments. These accounts normally charge from 1.5 to 2 percent interest per month. A minimum monthly payment, often $20 to $30, is usually required. Thus if you charge a $100 item on a 24-month revolving account, you normally would be required to pay a minimum monthly payment of $20 to $30.

Some retail charge accounts do not allow installment payments, and always require payment in full within 30 days of the billing date. These accounts, often called *regular charge accounts,* are designed to extend credit for small, recurring purchases consumers may find more convenient to pay on a monthly basis. Oil company charge cards are a special type of regular charge account. They are nationally acceptable rather than limited to a single store or group of stores. Gasoline purchases are recurring in nature, and an oil company credit card generally requires payment in full within 30 days for purchases of gas and oil and other small purchases. For major items, such as tires or repairs, extended payment terms are often allowed.

Bank credit cards

You are probably familiar with bank credit cards, especially the three best-known cards, VISA, NAC, and Mastercharge. Typical terms available on bank cards allow up to 36 months to repay with interest, charged at the rate of 1 to 1.5 percent on the balance of the amount owed. A minimum monthly payment, usually $5 to $10, is required, and the balance may be paid off at any time. The card accounts usually have an upper limit on charges of $500 to $1,500 depending on your needs and credit rating. Normally, there is no interest charge if new charges are paid in full within 20 to 30 days of receipt of the bill. Many people find this feature very attractive and use a bank credit card as an interest-free source of credit. To keep this source interest-free, you must always pay your bill in full and on time.

Bank credit cards offer a great deal of flexibility. The better-known cards are issued by affiliated banks all over the country. The cards are accepted by retail businesses all over the world. In effect, the card serves as a credit line for merchandise purchases. As long as you do not exceed the upper limit on charges, you may charge whatever you want, wherever you want it.

Another useful feature of bank credit cards is that the cards may be used to obtain a cash advance at any one of the affiliated banks that issue the card. This service is convenient in the event of an emergency need for cash. If, for example, you are far away from home on a vacation or business trip and run out of cash, a bank credit card can turn a distressful situation into a very minor inconvenience. However, use of a bank credit card to obtain cash should be reserved for emergencies. Bear in mind that you are in effect charging cash when you use your bank credit card for a cash advance. These types of charges have a way of building up to large outstanding balances if not carefully controlled.

Even if used only rarely, bank credit cards can be quite helpful when paying for something with a personal check. Most retail stores and other commercial establishments require a driver's license and one major credit card for identification when customers write personal checks for purchases. A bank credit card is universally acceptable for this purpose.

Travel and entertainment cards

American Express, Diners Club, and Carte Blanche are the best known of the travel and entertainment cards. As their name implies, travel and entertainment cards (T & E cards) are charge cards used primarily for travel and entertainment purposes. T & E cards are readily accepted around the world by airlines, hotels, travel agencies, restaurants, and the like to charge a wide variety of goods and services. These cards normally require payment in full within 20 to 30 days of receipt of the bill. However, for large dollar purchases it is possible to arrange installment payments, usually with interest charged at the rate of 1.5 percent per month.

It is also possible to arrange a credit line or obtain cash advances through some travel and entertainment cards. These cash advances or credit lines are handled in essentially the same manner as previously described for bank credit lines or bank credit cards.

Travel and entertainment cards have gained wide acceptability for other types of purchases. Many retail stores and service agencies accept travel and entertainment cards as readily as a bank credit card. Because of this added convenience, travel and entertainment cards have become increasingly attractive to consumers in recent years.

There are two disadvantages of travel and entertainment cards relative to bank credit cards: cost and availability. These cards normally charge an annual membership fee of about $30, whereas bank credit cards are usually issued at a lower charge or no charge. In addition to this added cost, travel and entertainment cards are usually more difficult to obtain than bank credit cards. In comparison to a bank credit card, a higher income is normally required before granting credit under a T & E card. Because of these two reasons, many people prefer a bank credit card over a T & E card.

Installment sales contracts

An installment sales contract is commonly referred to as buying on time. It is generally used to finance big ticket consumer durable goods, such as automobiles and major appliances. Most installment sales contracts require a small downpayment, with the balance of the price paid off over a number of months or years. When entering into an installment sales contract, you obtain immediate possession of the item in return for your agreement to pay for it in the future. The automobile purchase terms described earlier in this chapter are an example of an installment sales contract.

Two warnings are appropriate concerning installment sales contracts. First, they are usually quite expensive both in terms of interest cost and restrictive loan agreements. Second, the dealer from whom you buy an item on the installment plan seldom retains your sales contract. The dealer normally sells the contract to a sales finance company in order to obtain immediate cash. This arrangement can present a serious problem if the merchandise turns out to be defective. You may get involved in a disagreement with the dealer over replacement of the defective merchandise. Stopping payment on your sales contract will not put any pressure on the dealer to resolve the dispute. Since the dealer would no longer be holding your contract, you may well end up negotiating your dispute with both the dealer and the sales finance company.

Major sources of consumer credit

Table 7–4 summarizes the major sources of consumer credit. Of the five sources listed in the exhibit, life insurance companies generally provide the lowest cost source of credit. Credit unions are generally the next least expensive. Banks and savings and loans charge very similar interest rates and are usually more expensive than credit unions. The remaining source of financing, consumer finance companies, are generally the most expensive source of the five sources listed. Loans may also be obtained from a variety of other sources. These sources include sales finance companies, pawnshops, remedial loan societies, mail order loans, friends and relatives, and loan sharks.

Commercial banks

Commercial banks are the most common sources of consumer credit. They provide a wide variety of loans, including unsecured cash loans (called *personal loans*), automobile loans and other secured loans, educational loans, mortgage loans, and second mortgage loans. Traditionally commercial banks have preferred to specialize in large dollar-value consumer loans such as automobile loans. However, with the explosive growth in the use of bank credit cards, banks now make a large number of small loans through cash advances on credit cards.

Two special purpose loans available through banks should be mentioned. The first is a passbook loan. Under this type of loan arrangement, you pledge your passbook savings account as collateral for a loan. The interest rate charged is usually a few percent more than the interest earned on your savings account. The interest rate is low because you are in effect borrowing from yourself. There are two good reasons why you might be willing to do this. One is that your savings account is such good collateral that banks are very willing to make this type of loan. If you have not yet established a credit rating, this type of loan is a good first step in doing so. The second reason is that most of us find it quite difficult to save money. Once you build up a sizable balance in your savings account, you may not want to withdraw the money to make a major purchase. A passbook loan may be a good alternative to a large withdrawal. You may find that you are more likely to meet loan payments to a bank than to meet your voluntary savings goal each month. If you withdraw your savings, you may never replace them, but you are almost certain to meet your loan obligations. Because of this, a passbook loan is a good way to preserve hard-earned savings dollars.

The second special purpose loan is the so-called bill-consolidation

Table 7-4
Sources of consumer credit

Credit source	Commercial banks	Consumer finance companies	Credit unions	Life insurance companies	Savings and loan associations
Type of loan	Single payment loans. Personal installment loans. Passbook loans. Check-credit plans. Credit card loans. Second mortgages.	Personal installment loans. Second mortgages.	Personal installment loans. Share draft-credit plans. Credit card loans. Second mortgages.	Single or partial payment loans.	Personal installment loans (generally permitted by state-chartered savings associations). Home improvement loans. Education loans. Savings account loans. Second mortgages.
Lending policies	Seek customers with established credit history. Often require collateral or security. Prefer to deal in large loans such as auto, home improvement and modernization, with the exception of credit card and check-credit plans. Determine repayment schedules according to the purpose of the loan. Vary credit rates according to the type of credit, time period, customer's credit history and the security offered. May require several days to process a new credit application.	Often lend to consumers without established credit history. Often make unsecured loans. Often vary rates according to the size of the loan balance. Offer a variety of repayment schedules. Make a higher percentage of small loans than other lenders. Maximum loan size limited by law. Process applications quickly, frequently the same day as the application is made.	Lend to members only. Make unsecured loans. May require collateral or cosigner for loans over a specified amount. May require payroll deductions to pay off loan. May submit large loan applications to a committee of members for approval. Offer a variety of repayment schedules.	Lend on cash value of life insurance policy. No date or penalty on repayment. Deduct amount owed from the value of policy benefit if death or other maturity occurs before repayment.	Will lend to all credit-worthy individuals. Often require collateral. Loan rates vary, depending on size of loan, length of payment and security involved.
Cost	Lower than some lenders because they: Take fewer credit risks. Lend depositors' money which is a relatively inexpensive source of funds. Deal primarily in large loans which yield a larger dollar income without an increase in administrative costs.	Higher than some lenders because they: Take greater risks. Must borrow and pay interest on money to lend. Deal frequently in small loans which are costly to make and yield a small amount of income.	Lower than some lenders because they: Take fewer credit risks. Lend money deposited by members which is less expensive than borrowed money. Often receive free office space and supplies from the sponsoring organization. Are managed by members whose services, in most cases, are donated. Enjoy federal income tax exemptions.	Lower than some lenders because they: Take no risk. Pay no collection costs. Secure loans by cash value of policy.	Lower than some lenders because they: Lend depositors' money, which is a relatively inexpensive source of funds. Secure most loans by savings accounts or real estate.

Common range of annual percentage rates*	15%–18% credit card and check-credit plans. 11%–18% unsecured loans. (in Canada, 11%–12½%) 8½%–13½% secured loans and passbook loans. 12%–15% second mortgages. (in the U.S., regulated by national and state banking laws; in Canada, there are no legal restrictions on bank rates).	15%–36% personal loans (depending on the size of the loan and state or provincial laws; in Canada, generally from 15%–24%). 13%–20% second mortgages.	9%–15% (limited to 15% under federal and most state credit union laws, but may be higher in some Canadian provinces).	5%–8% (as stated in the policy).	7¼%–14% savings account and other secured loans. 13%–20% second mortgages.
Services	Offer several different types of consumer credit plans. May offer financial counseling. Handle credit transactions confidentially.	Provide credit promptly. Make loans to pay off accumulated debts willingly. Design repayment schedules to fit the borrower's income. Usually offer financial counseling. Handle credit transactions confidentially.	Design repayment schedules to fit the borrower's income. Generally provide credit life insurance without extra charge. May offer financial counseling. Handle credit transactions confidentially.	Permit repayment at any time. Handle credit transactions confidentially.	Often offer financial counseling. Specialize in mortgages and other housing-related loans. Handle credit transactions confidentially.

* Rates applicable at date of printing.

SOURCE This information is taken from the money management booklet *Managing Your Credit*, published by the Money Management Institute of Household Finance Corporation, Prospect Heights, Illinois.

loan or debt-consolidation loan. This type of loan may be familiar from advertisements that urge you to replace all those little monthly payments with one convenient payment. If you have a large number of monthly payments, a debt-consolidation loan may help you get your payments under control. However, you should recognize that a debt-consolidation loan is a sign of poor credit management. If you find yourself in need of this type of loan, you should carefully reevaluate your use of credit.

Credit unions

Credit unions generally offer very attractive loan rates to members of the credit union. Loan terms available at your credit union generally offer better repayment terms and interest rates than the terms and rates available from other sources. Credit unions make secured or unsecured loans, debt-consolidation loans, and overdraft accounts, and offer a wide variety of repayment terms. Credit unions make loans secured by your share account. These loans are similar to the passbook loans made by commercial banks. Many credit unions now also make first and second mortgage loans. Since credit unions are associations of affiliated members, the greatest advantage of a credit union loan is its ready availability and low cost.

Savings and loans

Savings and loan associations concentrate most of their lending in the housing area. Most loans are for first or second mortgages. Savings and loans also make passbook loans, home-improvement loans, and loans for education. In addition, savings and loan associations can now make personal-installment loans unter the new deregulation legislation. Interest rates charged are generally comparable to rates available from commercial banks.

Consumer finance companies

Consumer finance companies specialize in relatively small installment loans to individuals. They make both secured and unsecured loans. A large part of their business is concentrated in unsecured loans. These companies offer very fast service and often take risks that banks, credit unions, and savings and loans will not take. Because they often make loans to people with poor credit histories, interest rates at consumer finance companies are generally quite high in relation to bank rates. Consumer finance companies also make second mortgage loans and often provide financial counseling to borrowers.

Many people like to borrow from consumer finance companies because the service is generally fast and friendly. Loans are often approved in one day, and many people find the atmosphere less imposing than a bank's. Additionally, people with poor credit ratings find that consumer finance companies will grant them a loan when a bank has turned them down. However, you pay dearly for this service in interest rates that are often substantially higher than what a bank would charge. You should also consider that if a bank will not grant you a loan, this may be a good indication that you should not be borrowing money. Banks do not normally turn down loans without good reason. If you are turned down at a bank, you should carefully reexamine your credit management position.

Life insurance companies

Life insurance loans are described in detail in Chapter 9 of this text. Some kinds of life insurance build up cash values as well as provide life insurance protection. If you reach a position where you no longer need life insurance protection, you can turn in your policy in exchange for its cash value. Alternately, if you do not wish to turn in the policy, you can borrow the cash value. The advantage of borrowing the cash value is that the interest rate is generally quite low and the repayment terms extremely flexible. The interest rate is stated in the policy and is usually in the range of 5 to 8 percent per year. You may repay the loan in partial payments, in a single payment, or you may choose to pay only the interest on the loan. In the event of your death, any outstanding balance would be deducted from the face value of your policy. The amount of the loan is limited to the amount of the cash value you have built up on your policy.

Sales finance companies

Sales finance companies do not deal directly with consumers. When you buy big ticket items such as automobiles, furniture, stereo equipment, and major appliances, the dealer will often offer to finance the purchase for you on an installment plan. In fact, dealers can rarely afford to "carry your paper" and wait for you to pay them over the next year or two. Instead, they sell your note to a sales finance company to obtain immediate cash. Your payments are then made directly to the sales finance company. As a general rule, these types of arrangements are quite expensive in relation to loans available from commercial banks, bank credit lines, or bank credit cards. Annual interest rates may be expected to run in the area of 18 to 30 percent per year. If you let the dealer arrange financing for you, you will probably pay more than if you shopped around to obtain your own financing.

The biggest advantage of installment sales arrangements is convenience. Since the seller normally earns a commission on the sale of your note, sales people are extremely helpful in arranging credit for you. If you have a weak credit rating, sales finance companies may be willing to extend credit where another lender might turn you down. In fact, one used car dealer in a major metropolitan area advertises with the slogan "Bad credit, who said it?—walk in, drive out." It is safe to say that you will drive out with a very expensive financing deal to go with your used car.

It is important to read the fine print in an installment sales contract. Installment purchase agreements often contain clauses that are quite restrictive in nature. Until outlawed by the Federal Trade Commission, most installment sales contracts were subject to the *holder-in-due-course* doctrine. This said that if the merchant sold your contract to a sales finance company, the sales finance company had no responsibility in the event of a dispute concerning defective merchandise. Thus if your purchase turned out to be defective and the merchant refused to make any satisfactory restitution, you could not discontinue making payments on the item. Since the sales finance company was considered a holder in due course, your debt was held to be valid, regardless of the quality of the merchandise. Although this clause is now illegal, it is a good indication of the tone of a sales finance agreement and a signal for caution.

Another clause, the *add-on clause,* allows additional purchases to be added on to your original contract. All items added to the contract are held as security for your loan. If you cannot pay for some reason, all the items may be repossessed, even if you only have a few payments left on the last item purchased. An *acceleration clause* requires that the entire loan be paid in full if you miss one payment. A *balloon-payment* clause requires a final payment that is much higher than all the other payments. This makes the contract look less expensive because monthly payments prior to the balloon payment are artificially low. Many people cannot pay the balloon payment when it comes up and have to refinance the contract. If there is another balloon payment in the new contract, the item may never get paid off. A wage-assignment clause gives the lender the right to attach your future wages if you fail to meet the payments on time. As noted earlier, the lender also retains the *right to repossess* the item or items purchased if you do not meet your payments.

Other restrictive agreements may be written into your contract. The only safe guide is to read the contract carefully. Do not sign any contract with overly restrictive agreements. Acceleration clauses and the right to repossess are fairly common. However, you should avoid add-on, balloon-payment, and wage-assignment clauses. As a general rule, a loan from your bank or credit union will probably offer better terms than an installment sales contract.

Pawnshops

Pawnshops loan money against valuable goods that can be easily resold, such as stereo equipment, jewelry, or similar items. To borrow money from a pawnshop, you simply bring in some object of value that is easily stored. The pawnbroker will appraise it, make you a loan for some fraction of its value, and hold the item as security. The broker will give you a ticket entitling you to reclaim the item if you pay off the loan with interest within a stated time. Interest costs are very high for this type of financing. Since most items are never reclaimed, repayment periods are short, usually 60 to 90 days, and the loan is a fairly small percentage of the item's value. If you do not repay the loan, the item will be sold to satisfy the debt. As a lending source, pawnshops should be used only as a last resort. On the other hand, pawnshops are an interesting place to shop for used merchandise if you are able to make a valid judgment of the quality of the merchandise.

Remedial loan societies

Remedial loan societies are pawnshops operated by nonprofit organizations in a number of big cities. The remedial loan society operates in the same manner as a pawnshop, with one major exception. Because the society is sponsored by a nonprofit organization, interest rates are generally quite reasonable. As in the case of pawnshops, if an item pledged as security is sold for more than the amount of the loan, the difference is refunded to the borrower. There are only a handful of remedial loan societies in existence in the United States today.

Mail order loans

You may see magazine and newspaper advertisements for quick, confidential loans by mail. These loans are generally quite expensive and should be avoided except as a last resort. The only advantage of such a loan is that it is quick and confidential. Mail order loan companies may not be required to observe the law in the state in which you live if the company is located in another state. Thus the companies are often loosely controlled and almost always very expensive.

Friends and relatives

Friends and relatives may often loan you money at a low cost or even at no cost. Repayment terms are often loosely defined and quite flexible. However, in principle it is unwise to borrow from friends or relatives. Money difficulties between friends and relatives have been the source of many long-standing disputes. Borrowing from such sources should probably not be considered until other conventional sources have been exhausted.

Loan sharks

The term *loan shark* is applied to persons who operate outside the law. These people prey on victims who cannot obtain money from other sources and are desperate enough to subject themselves to astronomical interest rates and possible physical violence in the event of late payment. Loan sharks may charge as much a 1,000 percent per year or more for a loan. They may even refuse to accept repayment of the principal amount of the loan in order to keep you paying the interest. There is no circumstance that would justify borrowing money from a loan shark. If you are desperate enough to turn to such a source, you would be better off to file for personal bankruptcy, or throw yourself on the mercy of your creditors.

Cost of consumer credit

The cost of consumer credit is normally meausred in terms of its *annual percentage rate* (APR). The APR can be defined as the annual finance charge as a percent of the average amount of credit in use during the life of the credit contract. For example, consider the purchase of a $1,000 stereo system that you finance through an installment sales contract. If you pay for the stereo in 12 equal monthly installments, you would begin the contract with a balance of $1,000. At the end of the year, the loan would be paid off and your balance would be zero. Therefore, the average amount of credit in use would be $500. This is the average of the beginning balance and ending balance ($1,000 + $0 ÷ 2 = $500). If you pay $100 in finance charges, the annual percentage rate would be 20 percent.

Annual percentage rates

Computing the annual percentage rate for credit accounts where interest is charged as a percentage of the monthly declining balance of the loan is the simplest case. In this case, the APR can be determined by multiplying the monthly rate by 12. Most bank credit cards and many retail charge accounts charge interest at the rate of 1½ percent per month on the declining balance of the account. Multiplying the 1½ percent per month times 12 months yields an APR of 18 percent per year.

Table 7–5 lists required monthly payments on a $1,000 loan according to the APR and number of months to repay. The bottom half of the table also lists the sum of the payments on the $1,000 loan. As you can see, the impact of increasing interest rates on the total cost of your loan is quite substantial. Suppose you borrow $5,000 to buy a new car and pay the loan off over four years. At a 12 percent interest rate, your monthly payment would be $131.65 ($26.33 times 5). The sum of your payments would be $6,320 ($1,264 times 5). At a 16 percent APR, your monthly payments would be $141.70 and the sum of your payments over the 48 months would be $6,802. Over the life of the contract, you would pay a total of $482 more in total payments at the higher interest rate. The obvious moral of the story is that it pays to shop around for credit to obtain the lowest cost.

Cash loans and installment sales

The law now requires all lenders to disclose the APR on any loan agreement. However, there is still some confusion in credit contracts because there are a variety of ways to compute interest charges on

Table 7–5
Required payments on a $1,000 loan

| | **Monthly payments** | | | | | |
| | Number of months to repay loan | | | | | |
Interest rate (APR)	12	18	24	36	48	60
12%	$88.85	$60.98	$47.07	$33.21	$26.33	$22.24
14%	89.78	61.93	48.01	34.18	27.33	23.54
16%	90.76	62.86	48.97	35.16	28.34	24.32
18%	91.68	63.81	49.92	36.15	29.38	25.39
24%	94.57	66.71	52.87	39.23	32.60	28.77

| | **Sum of payments** | | | | | |
| | Number of months to repay loan | | | | | |
Interest rate (APR)	12	18	24	36	48	60
12%	$1,066	$1,098	$1,130	$1,196	$1,264	$1,334
14%	1,077	1,115	1,152	1,231	1,312	1,413
16%	1,089	1,131	1,175	1,266	1,361	1,459
18%	1,100	1,149	1,198	1,301	1,410	1,524
24%	1,135	1,201	1,269	1,412	1,565	1,726

cash loans and installment sales. The three most common methods are add-on, discount, and simple interest on the declining balance. Table 7–6 illustrates each of the three methods for a $1,000 loan to be repaid in one year. The interest rate is quoted by the lender as 18 percent.

Under the add-on method 18 percent of the amount borrowed is added on to the principal amount of the loan. The monthly payment is determined by dividing this total by the number of months the contract runs. For this example $180 in interest is added on to the $1,000 payment so that the total amount repaid would be $1,180. The annual percentage rate for this loan is approximately 31.7 percent.

Under the discount method the interest is deducted from the face amount of the loan in advance. The borrower receives only the difference between the face amount of the loan and the interest charge, but has to repay the entire face amount. In this example $180 is deducted from

Table 7–6
Computing interest rates: cash loans and installment sales

	Add-on	Discount	Simple interest on declining balance
Long term	1 year	1 year	1 year
Amount of loan requested	$1,000	$1,000	$1,000
Interest at 18% quoted rate	$ 180	$ 180	$ 100
Proceeds to borrower	$1,000	$ 820	$1,000
Annual percentage rate	31.7%	38.3%	18%

the $1,000 face amount and the borrower receives $820. By paying back $1,000 over the course of a year, the APR on this loan is approximately 38.3 percent.

Simple interest on the declining balance is the easiest method to understand. An annual interest rate of 18 percent charged on the declining balance of a loan is a true APR of 18 percent. In this example interest would be charged at the rate of 1½ percent per month on the declining balance. Total interest charges for the year would be approximately $100, and the APR is 18 percent.

Once again the moral of the story is obvious. When comparing credit terms, you should always compare the annual percentage rates. Under the add-on and discount methods the APR is approximately double the quoted rate of 18 percent. This is because your average loan balance is only about half of the face amount over the life of the contract. However, the interest rate is applied to the entire face amount. The quoted rate will be equal to the true APR only in the case where interest is charged on the declining balance.

Credit cards and charge accounts

For credit cards and charge accounts, interest is normally charged at a monthly percentage rate applied to the account balance. The actual dollar cost of interest depends on the method used to determine it or on what balance the percentage interest charge is computed. Three methods are commonly used: the *adjusted balance* method, the *previous balance* method, and the *average daily balance* method.

Table 7–7 illustrates the application of the three methods to the same account. In each case, the account's opening balance is $200 at the first of the month. A $100 payment is made on the 10th of the month, and a new charge for $50 is made on the 15th of the month. At the end of the month the closing balance of the account is $150. By applying the three different methods for determining the balance for finance charges, a finance charge of 1½ percent of the balance may result in a dollar charge of $2.25, $2.37, or $3.00.

Table 7–7
Computing interest charges: credit cards and charge accounts

Account transactions	Adjusted balance	Previous balance	Average daily balance
Balance, June 1	$200	$200	$200
Payment, June 10	100	100	100
New charge, June 15	50	50	50
Balance, June 30	150	150	150
Balance for finance charge	150	200	158.33
Finance charge at 1½ %	$ 2.25	$ 3.00	$ 2.37

Using the adjusted balance method, the 1½ percent finance charge is applied by first deducting the $100 payment from the opening balance. Then the new $50 charge is added on to obtain the balance for financing charge of $150. Applying the 1½ percent finance charge to $150 yields a finance charge of $2.25.

Under the previous balance method, payments and new charges are ignored altogether. The 1½ percent finance charge is applied to the beginning balance. In this example the 1½ percent finance charge is applied to the opening balance of $200, and the account is charged $3.00.

The average daily balance method is the most complicated to compute but probably the fairest method for both lender and borrower. Using this method, all payments and new charges are taken into account. The finance charge is assessed against the average daily balance of the loan. In this example the daily balance for the first 10 days of the month is $200. After the $100 payment is made on the 10th, the account balance drops to $100. It remains at $100 for five days until the new $50 charge is made on the 15th of the month. The balance then increases to $150 and remains at $150 for the last 15 days of the month. The average daily balance is computed as follows:

$$
\begin{aligned}
(10 \text{ days}) (\$200) &= \$2,000 \\
(\ 5 \text{ days}) (\$100) &= \quad 500 \\
(15 \text{ days}) (\$150) &= \underline{\ 2,250} \\
\text{Total} \qquad &= \$4,750
\end{aligned}
$$

Average daily balance = ($4,750) ÷ (30 days) = $158.33

Applying the 1½ percent finance charge to the average daily balance of $158.33 results in a finance charge of $2.37.

As this example shows, there is a wide variation in the actual finance charge even when the interest rate is the same. The adjusted balance and average daily balance method offer the lowest cost financing. The previous balance method is the highest cost method. Credit cards and charge accounts using this method of computation should be avoided.

Range of annual percentage rates

You have seen that finance charges vary widely, depending on the source of financing. Life insurance loans generally range from 5 to 8 percent APR. Credit union loans commonly charge 9 to 12 percent APR. Savings and loans normally charge APRs in the range of 10 to 14 percent on loans other than savings account loans. Loans secured by savings accounts normally cost about 8 to 10 percent APR.

Commercial bank finance charges vary widely. Credit cards and overdraft plans normally charge an APR of 18 percent at current rates. Secured and unsecured cash loans range in the area of 12 to 18 percent.

Passbook loans range from 8 to 12 percent. Consumer finance company rates for secured and unsecured loans show the widest range of variation. Depending on the size of the loan, the security involved, and the credit rating of the borrower, the cost of the loan may range from 18 to 36 percent APR.

It is difficult to generalize about the costs of other loan sources. Installment sales contracts may range from 18 to 36 percent. Rates at pawn shops are usually the maximum allowed by state law and often run at a 36 percent APR. Remedial loan societies operate at about one half this ratio. Loan sharks, since they operate illegally, often charges rates as high as 1,000 percent per year or higher.

Credit life insurance

Many loan agreements offer the option of purchasing credit life insurance. This type of insurance policy pays off the loan balance in the event that you die before the loan is paid in full. There are only two important things you should know about credit life insurance. First, it is a very expensive form of insurance and should almost always be avoided. Second, it is illegal for a lender to require you to purchase credit life insurance as a condition for granting a loan. You should read all credit contracts carefully before you sign and watch out for credit life insurance. Since sales people earn a commission for selling you this insurance, they often include it automatically in a financing contract. You should clearly specify that you do not want this type of insurance.

Life insurance planning is examined in detail in Chapter 9. When planning your insurance needs, you should allow for a fund to pay off any debts. There are many less expensive ways to meet this need than through credit life insurance.

Important credit legislation

There have been a number of important laws passed in the past few years that are designed to protect your rights as a borrower. The most important provisions of these laws are summarized in Table 7–8. This table also lists the addresses of the federal agencies responsible for enforcing these laws. If you believe that your rights have been violated, you should send a written complaint to the agency in charge of enforcing the law. You should also send a copy of this complaint to the lender who has violated your rights. The fact that you have filed a complaint with the correct authorities will often move the lender toward a speedy resolution of your dispute.

Truth in Lending

Originally enacted in 1969, the Truth in Lending Act is the oldest of the consumer-oriented federal laws governing credit dealings. This law requires specific disclosure of finance charges as an annual percentage rate and a dollar amount. The law has a provision that limits credit card holders' liability to a maximum of $50 in the event of unauthorized credit card use. It also provides for a number of other important rights of credit users.

Fair Credit Reporting Act

The Fair Credit Reporting Act provides important rights in regard to any credit files that are maintained on you. If you are denied credit, insurance, or employment, you must be informed of the name and address of any consumer credit reporting agency that provided a report on you. You are also entitled to inspect the contents of your credit file and to file a rebuttal report concerning any negative information in your file.

Fair Credit Billing Act

The Fair Credit Billing Act establishes procedures to be followed when billing errors or billing disputes arise between you and a lender. This act also allows you to withhold payment on credit cards when the goods or services charges turn out to be defective.

Equal Opportunity Credit Act

The Equal Opportunity Credit Act was a landmark piece of legislation that did away with much of the discrimination against women applying for credit. The act prohibits discrimination based on sex and marital status. It essentially requires that women, particularly married women, must be treated equally with men in the granting of credit. The act requires creditors to report information on an account in the names of both the husband and wife if both use the account and are jointly responsible for payment. It also prohibits creditors from requiring women to reapply for credit upon a change in marital status. In the area of mortgage lending, this act reversed the common practice of counting only the husband's income in determining how much money a couple could borrow for the purpose of buying a house.

In addition to banning discrimination against women, the act forbids other forms of discrimination as well. It also prohibits discrimination based on race, national origin, religion, age, or the receipt of public assistance.

Fair Debt Collection Practices Act

The most recent of the credit laws, the Fair Debt Collection Practices Act, was enacted in 1978. It was passed to curtail abusive, deceptive, and unfair practices employed by some debt-collection agencies. The act has served to curtail such practices as calling a debtor late at night, contacting the debtor's employer, or making threats against the debtor. This act was an important piece of legislation in protecting the rights of borrowers who have been unable to meet their debt payments.

Table 7–8
Summary of U.S. Credit Legislation

Act (date effective)	Major provisions	Penalties for noncompliance	Governing agencies
Truth in Lending (July 1, 1969) (January 25, 1971)	*Provides specific cost disclosure requirements for the annual percentage rate and the finance charge as a dollar amount.* *Requires disclosure of other loan terms and conditions.* *Regulates the advertising of credit terms.* *Provides the right to cancel a contract when certain real estate is used as security.* *Prohibits credit card issuers from sending unrequested cards.* *Limits a cardholder's liability for unauthorized use of a card to $50.*	*Individual suits:* *Actual damages.* *Twice the amount of any finance charge involved (at least $100, at most $1,000).* *Court costs and reasonable attorney's fees.* *Class action suits:* *Up to $500,000 or 1% of the creditor's net worth, whichever is less.* *Criminal penalties:* *Fine of not more than $5,000 and/or Imprisonment for not more than one year.*	The following federal agencies are responsible for enforcing all of these Acts. The agency to contact for information or in case of a complaint depends on the particular creditor involved. If a retail store, department store, consumer finance company, gasoline credit card, travel and entertainment card or a state-chartered credit union is involved, contact: One of the FTC regional offices, or Federal Trade Commission (name of the Act) (Washington, D.C. 20580.)
Fair Credit Reporting Act (April 24, 1971)	*Requires disclosure to consumers of the name and address of any consumer reporting agency which supplied reports used to deny credit, insurance or employment.* *Gives a consumer the right to know what is in his file, have incorrect information reinvestigated and removed, and include his version of a disputed item in the file.* *Requires credit reporting agencies to send the consumer's version of a disputed item to certain businesses or creditors.* *Sets forth identification requirements for consumers wishing to inspect their files.* *Requires that consumers be notified when an investigative report is being made.* *Limits the time certain information can be kept in a credit file.*	*Credit reporting agencies are liable for:* *Any actual financial injury a consumer suffers as a result of the agency's failure to follow proper procedures.* *Any additional penalty the court may impose.* *Court costs and reasonable fees for the consumer's attorney.* *Criminal penalty for those obtaining information under false pretenses and those supplying information to unauthorized persons:* *Fine of not more than $5,000 and/or Imprisonment for not more than one year.*	If a bank is involved, contact one of the following: If it is a nationally chartered bank, contact: Comptroller of the Currency Consumer Affairs Division Washington, D.C. 20219. If it is a state-chartered bank and a member of the Federal Reserve System, contact: Board of Governors of the Federal Reserve System Division of Consumer Affairs Washington, D.C. 20551. If it is a state-chartered bank and is insured by the Federal Deposit Insurance Corporation, but is *not* a member of the Federal Reserve System, contact: Federal Deposit Insurance Corporation Office of Bank Consumer Affairs Washington, D.C. 20429. If a federally chartered or federally insured (FSLIC) savings and loan association is involved, contact: Federal Home Loan Bank Board Washington, D.C. 20552.
Fair Credit Billing Act (October 28, 1975)	*Establishes procedures for consumers and creditors to follow when billing errors occur on periodic statements for revolving credit accounts.* *Requires creditors to send a statement setting forth these procedures to consumers periodically.* *Allows consumers to withhold payment for faulty or defective goods or services (within certain limitations) when purchased with a credit card.* *Requires creditor to promptly credit customers' accounts and to return overpayments if requested.*	*For failure to follow proper procedures, the creditor forfeits the amount of money in dispute and any finance charges computed on that amount, up to a maximum of $50. In this case, a consumer can collect whether or not there has been a billing error.*	

Equal Credit Opportunity Act (October 28, 1975)	Prohibits credit discrimination based on sex and marital status. Prohibits creditors from requiring women to reapply for credit upon a change in marital status. Requires creditors to inform applicants of acceptance or rejection of their credit application within 30 days of receiving a completed application. Requires creditors to provide a written statement of the reasons for adverse action.	*Individual suits:* Actual damages. An additional sum up to a maximum of $10,000. Court costs and reasonable attorney's fees. *Class action suits:* Up to $500,000 or 1% of the creditor's net worth, whichever is less. *Time limits:* A suit may be filed no later than two years from the date the violation occurred. If an agency begins enforcement proceedings within the two year period, cases may be filed up to one year after the proceedings begin. If the Attorney General begins a civil suit within these two years, there is a one year extension on bringing suit.
(March 23, 1977) (June 1, 1977)	Prohibits credit discrimination based on race, national origin, religion, age or the receipt of public assistance. Requires creditors to report information on an account to credit bureaus in the names of both husband and wife if both use the account and both are liable for it.	
Fair debt Collection Practices Act (March 20, 1978)	Prohibits abusive, deceptive and unfair practices by debt collectors. Establishes procedures for debt collectors contacting a credit user. Restricts debt collector contacts with a third party. Specifies that payment for several debts be applied as the consumer wishes and that no monies be applied to a debt in dispute.	*Individual suits:* Actual damages. An additional sum up to a maximum of $10,000. Court costs and reasonable attorney's fees. *Class action suits:* Up to $500,000 or 1% of the debt collector's net worth, whichever is less. *Time limits:* A suit may be filed no later than one year from the date the violation occurred. *Frivolous lawsuits:* Third-party debt collectors may receive court-ordered compensation from a consumer to cover the cost of defending themselves in court against a suit brought in bad faith or for the purpose of harassment.

If a federally chartered credit union is involved, contact:
National Credit Union Administration
Division of Consumer Affairs
Washington, D.C. 20456.
On a state level, contact:
The Attorney General's Office.
State Banking Department.

SOURCE This information is taken from the Money Management Institute Booklet *Managing Your Credit*, published by the Money Management Institute of Household Finance Corporation, Prospect Heights, Illinois.

Building and maintaining a credit rating

Building and maintaining a credit rating is actually a fairly simple process. When you apply for a loan or charge account, you will be asked such questions as the nature of your employment, your salary, whether you own or rent your residence, and so forth. The creditor will base the decision of whether or not to grant credit on your answers to these questions. In assessing your application, lenders commonly base their decisions on what are known as the three Cs of consumer credit analysis: character, capacity, and collateral.

Character

Character refers to the lender's assessment of your personal character. Are you regarded as someone basically honest who may be trusted to make your best efforts to repay your loan? The consumer credit decision is in large part based on a relationship of trust between lender and borrower. Whether or not the lender feels that you are a trustworthy individual plays a major role in the credit decision.

Capacity

Capacity refers to the lender's assessment of whether or not you have the financial capacity to meet the loan payments. Even if the lender is convinced that you are an honest and trustworthy person, a negative decision will be made if you lack the financial capacity to meet your payments. In short, all the good intentions in the world will not repay a loan if you do not have the income to meet the payments.

Collateral

Collateral refers to the security pledged to secure the loan. Although many lenders make unsecured loans, many larger loans require some form of collateral. The lender may limit the loan to the amount that could be recovered by sale of the collateral in the event you do not meet your payments. An automobile loan limited to 75 percent of the retail value of the car purchased is a common example of this provision.

Consumer credit files

Many lenders use reports from centralized credit reporting agencies as an aid in making lending decisions. These agencies specialize in maintaining credit reports on individuals. You can identify them by looking under "credit reporting agencies" in the yellow pages of your telephone directory. Large numbers of lenders subscribe to these services and regularly make reports on their accounts to the agency. If you apply for credit with a lender who uses one of these agencies, the lender requests a report on your credit history from the agency. This report on your past credit history provides much of the basis for the lender's decision on your loan request. If you have a good credit history with a record of paying on time, you will almost certainly get the loan if the lender feels that you have the capacity to repay on time.

Lenders place a great deal of reliance on the information contained in credit files. The Fair Credit Reporting Act requires the lender give you the name and address of the credit reporting agency if you are turned down for credit based on the agency's report. You then have the right to inspect your file to determine whether there is any adverse information in it. If the information is inaccurate or misleading, you have the right to attempt to change it. The agency will be required to change the information if you can prove that it is in error. If the adverse information is the result of a billing dispute, you have the right to put your side of the story in the file. It is important for you to take these steps if you are rejected for credit. Your credit file is an important part of your personal history, and you should protect your credit rating.

If you want to know whether or not a file is maintained in your name, contact your local credit reporting agency. They are required to tell you if they maintain a file on you, and you have a right to see your file. If you have not been rejected for credit but just want to review your file, you will probably have to pay a small fee. This fee, usually about $5.00, is charged to cover handling and administrative costs of making files available for inspection. If you are exercising your right to see the file because you have been refused credit, there is no fee.

Borrowing for the first time

If you are borrowing for the first time, you will obviously not have any credit history. This makes it more difficult for lenders to assess whether or not you should be granted credit. Consequently, you may have a difficult time in getting a first credit request approved. Whether or not you do encounter difficulty depends upon how carefully you lay the foundation for building a credit history.

A good first step in establishing a credit history is to apply for a retail charge account or a bank credit card. Your first account will probably have a fairly low limit. You should use this account sparingly and be absolutely certain to make your required payments on time. If you want to establish further credit, perhaps at a bank, you might consider a passbook loan. These loans are relatively easy to obtain and will help in building your credit rating. Similarly an automobile loan where you make a very sizable downpayment should be fairly easy to obtain.

Establishing credit for young people is often especially difficult. If you are having a hard time in getting credit, you might consider applying for a loan with a cosigner. A cosigner is a person who will pledge to repay the loan for you if you do not pay. If you fail to meet your payments, the cosigner is just as liable for the debt as you are. If you can arrange for a cosigner who has a good credit rating, you may be able to get a loan that would otherwise have been denied. A parent or relative will often agree to cosign for you.

When borrowing for the first time, you may encounter the advice to borrow on an unsecured cash loan and then put the money in a savings account. Loan payments can then be made from the account, and you will have paid only the difference between the interest on the loan and the interest earned on the savings account. By doing this, you will have gained some ground in establishing a credit rating. Although this advice is quite common, it is not particularly good advice. You will end up paying interest charges for no good reason beyond making your file look better. You will also find that nearly all loan applications inquire about the purpose of the loan. Borrowing money to deposit it in a savings account may not impress your banker as a very serious need for a loan. You are better off to build up your credit rating by wise use of retail charge accounts and bank credit cards. If you want to establish bank credit, a first loan for some consumer durable good, perhaps with a cosigner, would be a preferable first step.

Dealing with credit difficulties

Because of inexperience or mismanagement, you may find yourself having difficulty in meeting all your obligations. If this happens, the most important thing is to take prompt corrective action. In particular, you should pay very close attention to the credit danger signals listed in Figure 7–3. If you find yourself at the limit of your credit arrangements, having difficulty meeting payments, chronically late in paying bills, or exhibiting other signs of credit difficulty, act quickly to correct the problem.

One of the most important considerations in dealing with a credit difficulty is to keep open the lines of communication between you and your creditors. If you know that you are going to have difficulty with a loan payment, notify your creditor and see if an alternate repayment plan can be worked out. Many lenders are willing to make alternate arrangements rather than have the loan go into default. If they can see that you recognize the problem and are taking corrective action, they are often quite cooperative.

If you do encounter credit difficulties, the first step you should take is to carefully total up all your monthly obligations and the total amount of money owed. You should then develop a plan which fits into your budget and which allows you to meet your obligations under the credit agreements. In most cases this plan will require you to cut back radically on your normal monthly expenses in order to begin paying off some of your debts. In all cases you should immediately stop using any sort of consumer credit until you have solved your current credit problem. It is important to recognize that you did not get into difficulty overnight and you are certainly not going to get out of difficulty overnight. You will

**Figure 7–3
Credit danger signals**

Danger signals

Is an increasing percentage of your income going to pay off debts?

Are you near or at the limit on your lines of credit?

Are you extending repayment schedules—paying in 60 or 90 days bills that you once paid in 30?

Can you only make the minimum payments on your revolving charge accounts?

Are you paying bills with money earmarked for something else?

Are you borrowing to pay for items you used to buy with cash?

Are you chronically late in paying your bills?

Are you tapping your savings to pay current bills?

Is your savings cushion inadequate or nonexistent?

Do you take out a new loan before the old one is paid off, or take a new one out to pay off the old loan?

Do you put off medical or dental visits because you can't afford them right now?

Are you threatened with repossession of your car or credit cards, or with other legal action?

Are you working overtime just to make ends meet?

If you lost your job, would you be in immediate financial difficulty?

Are you unsure about how much you owe?

Do you worry a lot about money?

A "yes" to any of these questions should give pause for thought. While a single red flag is not a sign of impending doom, it is an indication that you need to proceed with caution for a while—revise and update your spending plan, cut back on credit use and be alert for other signs of overspending.

SOURCE   This information is taken from the Money Management Institute booklet *Managing Your Credit*, published by the Money Management Institute of Household Finance Corporation, Prospect Heights, Illinois.

have to work long and carefully to get yourself back on a firm financial footing. If meeting your obligations requires you to extend payments beyond the length of the original agreement, make arrangements with your creditors to do so. Be absolutely certain to contact your creditors before you miss a payment. Creditors are much harder to deal with after your account is in default than before.

In extreme cases you may have to consider a bill-consolidation loan.

This type of loan allows you to pool all of your outstanding balances into one loan with longer repayment terms. The resulting smaller monthly payment will allow you to meet your monthly obligations on time. This technique will avoid the problem of working out terms with individual creditors and may be advantageous if you can obtain a consolidation loan on reasonable terms. For example, if you owe a total of $3,000 on four charge accounts, your monthly payments might total over $150. If you arrange a three-year bill-consolidation loan of $3,000 at an annual percentage rate of 16 percent, your monthly payment would be about $105. This reduction in the monthly payment may provide the breathing space needed to work your way out of debt.

If you do use a bill-consolidation loan, it is extremely important for you to stop using credit until this loan is paid off. You should not, under any circumstances, use your breathing space to take on new credit obligations. If you do, you will only sink further and further into debt, and you may never get your finances in order.

After working yourself out of debt, you should plan carefully to avoid a repeat of the problem. In particular, you should pay special attention to the guidelines for credit control discussed at the beginning of this chapter. As a proven "creditholic," you should probably limit all future use of credit to the 10 percent guideline suggested. If you restrict future monthly commitments to no more than 10 percent of monthly take-home pay, you should encounter no further difficulties.

Professional credit counselors

If you cannot find a way out of your credit difficulties, you may need to seek out professional assistance. The National Foundation for Consumer Credit operates debt-counseling services throughout the United States. To obtain information on the availability of nonprofit credit-counseling services in your area, you can contact the foundation headquarters at 1819 H Street, N.W., Washington, D.C. 20006. You may also inquire at your local Chamber of Commerce or Better Business Bureau. These credit-counseling services will assist you in working out a plan for getting out of debt. They will also help you in arranging a repayment schedule with your creditors.

If you do decide to seek out a credit-counseling service, be certain that you turn to one of the many nonprofit institutions that offer this service. Many cities also have private companies that specialize in arranging consolidation loans or debt liquidation. These agencies are usually very expensive. In many cases, it would be more accurate to call users of these services victims rather than clients.

Bankruptcy: The court of last resort

If you can find no possible way to repay your debts, you may have to consider filing personal bankruptcy. The Federal Bankruptcy Act, which was revised in October 1979, allows individual debtors to file a petition for personal bankruptcy. A debtor may file a petition for *straight bankruptcy* or a *Wage Earner Plan* (Chapter XIII bankruptcy). In a straight bankruptcy, a debtor files a court petition requesting to be declared legally unable to meet his or her debts. If approved by the court, the debtor is declared bankrupt. Most of the debtor's assets, other than bare necessities such as clothing and furniture, are taken by the court and sold. After all court costs and attorney's fees are paid, any remaining money is distributed to the creditors on a pro rata basis. In most cases the creditors receive a very small portion of what is owed to them.

A Wage Earner Plan is an alternative to a straight bankruptcy. The October 1979 revision of the Federal Bankruptcy Act substantially liberalized the provisions of a Chapter XIII bankruptcy. Under this section of the Act, debtors are allowed to restructure their debts and pay off less than the full dollar amount. Extended payment terms are usually allowed on the amount to be paid back. If this plan is approved, debtors are allowed to keep most of their assets, and cosigners are relieved of their liability. A typical agreement might allow for debts to be repaid at the rate of 60 or 70 cents on the dollar, with extended payment terms. This type of plan extends court protection to an individual's property and also discharges the debts, although at less than the full amount.

Of course, bankruptcy will harm your credit rating and your reputation for handling your finances wisely. Under the revised Act, Chapter XIII remains on your credit record for a period of ten years. Surprisingly enough, you will probably still be able to obtain credit after bankruptcy. Some lenders will reason that now that you have paid off your debts through a bankruptcy, you have the capacity to borrow again. From your own point of view, it should be obvious that you must be extremely careful in committing yourself to credit agreements in the future. You probably should not use consumer credit again for an extended period of time. You certainly should not exceed the 10 percent guideline under any circumstances.

Summary

Consumer credit is at an all-time high in the United States economy. With easy credit increasingly available to all consumers, the responsible use of credit has become more and more important. As a general guideline, monthly credit obligations should not exceed 15 percent of your monthly take-home pay. If your credit payments begin to exceed this limit, you should seriously reevaluate your use of credit.

Major forms of consumer credit include secured and unsecured cash loans, automatic overdrafts, credit lines, retail charge accounts, bank credit cards, travel and entertainment cards, and installment sales contracts. Major sources of consumer credit include commercial banks, credit unions, savings and loan associations, consumer finance companies, life insurance companies, and sales finance companies. While this list of major forms and sources is by no means exhaustive, it is a good indicator of the wide range of credit plans available.

Consumer credit costs are normally expressed in terms of an annual percentage rate of interest. Costs vary widely according to the source of the credit. Life insurance loans generally offer the lowest cost source of consumer credit if you borrow against the cash value of the policy. Credit unions generally provide relatively low cost loans. Commercial banks and savings and loan associations provide a wide variety of consumer loans at reasonable rates. Consumer finance companies and sales finance companies generally charge higher rates than banks do. However, consumer finance companies and sales finance companies offer convenience and will extend credit to persons who might be turned down by a bank or savings and loan.

There are a number of important pieces of federal legislation of interest in the consumer credit area. These include Truth in Lending, Fair Credit Reporting, Fair Credit Billing, the Equal Opportunity Credit Act, Fair Debt Collection Practices, and the Federal Bankruptcy Act. The Equal Opportunity Credit Act has been particularly important in eliminating discrimination against women applying for credit. '

If you do encounter credit difficulties as a result of poor management or inexperience, there are a number of strategies to work your way out of debt. The most important consideration is that action should be taken promptly. Lines of communication must be kept open between you and your creditors. If you cannot find your own way out of debt, you should seek professional help from one of the many nonprofit organizations sponsored by the National Foundation for Consumer Credit or a similar group. As a last resort, you may have to consider filing for personal bankruptcy if there is no way out.

Appendix: The language of credit

Acceleration clause A provision allowing the creditor to ask that all future installments be paid at once if one or more installments have not been paid when due.

Add-on clause A provision for adding new purchases to an existing installment contract.

Add-on charge The finance charge calculated on the amount financed for the term of the contract and added to the amount financed to determine the total of payments.

Annual percentage rate The ratio of the finance charge to the average amount of credit in use during the life of the contract, expressed as a percentage rate per year.

Bank credit card A credit card issued by a bank offering a line of credit and enabling the borrower to make purchases or obtain a cash loan.

Bankruptcy A Federal or provincial court proceeding, under which persons unable to pay their debts in full may be discharged from their legal obligations to do so, with certain exceptions.

Chapter 13 (Adjustment of debts of an individual with regular income) A plan for the repayment of debts which allows a credit user in serious financial difficulty to pay off credit obligations without declaring bankruptcy. In Canada, similar provisions are provided by Part X, Orderly Payment of Debt.

Chattel mortgage An instrument which transfers title to personal property to another as security for the payment of a debt. If the indebtedness is not paid according to the terms of the agreement, the holder of the mortgage has the right to obtain possession of the mortgaged property.

Collateral note An instrument by the terms of which the credit user delivers possession of real or personal property to the creditor as security for payment of the debt. If the credit user fails to make the payments according to the terms of the note, the creditor has a right to sell the collateral and apply the proceeds to the payment of the debt.

Composition A settlement under Chapter 13 by which a potential bankrupt pays off his obligations by paying only a part of the total amount owed to each creditor.

Conditional sales Sales made under a payment contract where security interest remains with the seller until all payments are made.

Consolidation loan Combining several debts into one loan for the purpose of reducing payments into a single lower payment plan over a longer period of time.

Cosigner One who agrees to pay a debt if the credit user does not.

Credit bureau A firm which collects, stores and distributes consumer credit history information to credit grantors under the requirements of the Fair Credit Reporting Act.

Credit history A record of an individual's past performance with credit.

Creditor A person or firm that extends credit services and to whom credit users are indebted.

Credit rating An appraisal made by an individual credit grantor of an individual's credit worthiness—the ability and willingness to pay credit obligations. These appraisals are based upon the credit grantor's own, privately developed criteria for granting credit.

Credit risk The chance of a loss through noncollection of a credit obligation.

Credit worthiness The ability and willingness to repay a debt; having a good credit history.

Default charge   Also called *penalty charge*. An additional charge generally calculated upon an installment payment which is not paid when due.

Defer   To put off until a future time; postpone or delay. Charges made to defer payments on credit contracts are called deferral, deferment or extension charges.

Disclosure   Statement by the creditor to the debtor of all terms relevant to a contract.

Discount charge   The finance charge calculated on the total of payments for the term of the contract and deducted in advance to determine the amount financed.

Down payment   The initial payment on a credit purchase made before the amount to be financed and charges for credit are figured.

Durable goods   Products which provide long-lasting and continuing services.

Extension   An agreement with the creditor which allows a borrower who is having financial difficulties to pay off the debt in smaller payments over a longer period of time.

Face-of-note   Also called *total of payments*. The total amount which the credit user promises to repay, including the finance charge and all additional charges in connection with a credit transaction.

Finance charge   Also called *cost of credit*. The dollar amount of charges for credit, excluding taxes, filing and recording fees, license fees, registration, title and certain other legal fees when authorized; (formerly called interest, carrying charge, service charge or time price differential).

Instrument   A legal document, contract, note or any other type of written agreement.

Interest   The cost of borrowing money; included in the finance charge.

Investment   Anything in which money is or may be invested to earn a return thereon.

Line of credit   The amount of credit a lender will extend to a borrower over a period of time.

Maturity date   The date on which final payment is due.

Note   A written promise to pay a certain sum of money at a certain time.

Obligation   A debt, promise or moral responsibility; a duty imposed legally or socially.

Open-end credit   A credit agreement which provides a line of credit up to a set limit, with the choice of paying in full at the end of each billing period, or paying over several billing periods with a finance charge applied on the unpaid balance.

Outstanding   Still owing.

Principal The amount of a loan or the unpaid price of a purchase before finance charges of any kind are either added or deducted; also known as *amount financed*.

Proceeds Also called the *amount financed*. In borrowing, the actual amount of money given or credited to the credit user; on a time purchase transaction, the balance financed.

Promissory note See **Note.**

Refinance The rescheduling of payments on an installment contract; generally smaller payments extending over a longer period of time.

Refund Unearned portion of a finance charge which is returned or credited to the credit user because of prepayment of the contract.

Repossession Forced or voluntary surrender of merchandise as a result of inability to pay as promised.

Reserve A sum of money or assets set aside.

Retail installment contract and security agreement Also called a *conditional sales contract*. A written agreement between creditor and credit user which permits the credit user to receive goods and services at the time of the purchase but allows the creditor to retain title to the merchandise until payment is completed.

Revolving credit See **Open-end credit.**

Right of Rescission The right of a consumer to cancel, within three business days, a credit contract in which his or her principal place or residence is used as security. This right does not apply to first mortgage loans.

Sales finance agency A financial institution which purchases contracts from retailers, after which the credit user whose contract is purchased usually makes payments to the sales finance company.

Scheduled payment Payment due at a particular time (or times); each of the installments in a credit agreement specified as to amount and date due.

Secured note A note which provides that, upon default, certain pledged or mortgaged property may be applied in payment of the debt.

Security interest The right granted under stated law that allows the creditor to obtain possession of the property covered in the event you do not pay on time or fulfill other contract obligations. Generally the creditor can sell the property, apply the amount received (less expenses) to the balance owed and sue the customer for any remaining amount due. State laws vary regarding creditors' rights and obligations in this area.

Share drafts Similar to checking accounts and offered by some credit unions, they allow members to withdraw funds, pay bills, etc., from their credit union share accounts.

Simple interest The finance charge computed on the principal balances outstanding as long as any portion remains unpaid.

Term The period of time between the date a credit agreement is signed and the date final payment is due.

Terms The conditions written into a note or contract, such as the amount of the loan or purchase, balance financed, charges, size, number and dates of payments, which set forth the rights and responsibilities of either the credit user or the creditor.

Title Proof of ownership.

Unsecured note A credit agreement in which the lender's only security is the credit user's signature and personal financial situation as demonstrated through the credit application.

Wage assignment A signed agreement which permits a creditor to collect a certain portion of a credit user's wages from his employer if payment of the contract is not made according to terms. (Prohibited by law in some states and provinces.)

Wage garnishment A court order requiring that a certain amount of the credit user's wages be paid by the employer directly to the creditor; legal action taken only after a credit user has defaulted. The Consumer Credit Protection Act limits the amount of disposable income subject to garnishment and prohibits the dismissal of an employee for garnishment of any one indebtedness. In Canada, most provinces have a similar law.

SOURCE   This information is taken from the Money Management Institute booklet *Managing Your Credit*, published by the Money Management Institute of Household Finance Corporation, Prospect Heights, Ill.

PART 4

Risk control through insurance

Insurance and risk management

- Personal and insurable risk defined
- General insurance principles
- A personal risk management program
- Risk inventory
- Risk evaluation
- Insurance selection
- Insurance program guidelines
- Impact of Social Security
- Summary

Insurance has been described as a necessary evil that must be borne by the modern family. More importantly, a sound insurance program is a vital prerequisite to realistic and responsible family financial planning. In an era of unrelenting inflation and an increasing tendency toward filing lawsuits, a sound insurance program may well be the single most important aspect of your overall financial plan.

You should reduce the possibility of a financial loss to the lowest practical level. A poor job of insurance planning can subject you and your family to huge financial losses from which your may never recover. Consider, for example, the impact of a $100,000 lawsuit stemming from an automobile accident on a young couple with no auto insurance. If they are required by a court to pay this sum out of current assets or future earnings, it would take them many years to recover from such a financial blow. Proper insurance planning can reduce all or nearly all of this type of risk.

In this chapter we will explore the fundamentals of risk management and insurance planning. The knowledge of fundamental principles gained in this chapter will then be used as a basis for a much more detailed exploration of the various types of insurance coverage in the two following chapters.

Personal and insurable risk defined

In the business world making decisions about which hazards to insure against, which assets to insure, and how much to insure them for is referred to as the process of risk management. Risk management for individuals is just as important as it is for businesses. You should give this aspect of personal finance careful attention. Personal risk management requires a systematic approach to dealing with the fortuitous risks that confront you. You must manage and protect your assets to prevent a loss of net worth caused by a fortuitous act beyond your control.

The concept of a fortuitous risk is important since only fortuitous risks may be insured against. A *fortuitous risk* is a risk that exists solely as the result of a chance happening. It is not the result of any deliberate action on your part. In short, a fortuitous risk is an event that may happen, not one that is certain to happen. For example, the chance of your car being damaged by a hit-and-run driver is fortuitous. But the chance of losing money by investing in an oil well is not fortuitous. In the first instance the damage is not related to any deliberate action on your part. However, the loss of money in an investment is the result of a deliberate choice on the part of an investor to accept a risk.

Personal risks

This distinction is important in determining what risks may be insured against. In order to qualify as an insurable risk, a risk must be fortuitous and must also meet two other criteria—it must be personal, and it must involve only the possibility of financial loss, with no possibility of gain.

A personal loss means that the loss affects people individually and does not affect everyone at the same time. The risk of your house catching fire, for example, is personal because not all houses owned by holders of fire insurance policies will catch on fire at the same time. Most houses will never catch on fire. On the other hand, a major flood will affect all houses in low-lying areas at the same time. Only people living in low-lying areas would be willing to buy flood insurance. This is the reason that flood insurance was not available until recently when it was made available through a program sponsored by the U.S. government's Department of Housing and Urban Development.

Financial loss

The requirement that an insurable risk involve only the possibility of a financial loss is also important. The possibility of losing money through investments or through gambling, although a very real risk, cannot be insured against. These kinds of potential losses also carry with them the possibility of a potential gain. They also violate the requirement that insurable risks be fortuitous.

Insurable interest

In sum, then, an insurable risk is one that is fortuitous, personal in nature, and involving only the possibility of financial loss by the insured person or persons. In order to purchase insurance against such an insurable risk, one very important criterion must be met: the person purchasing the insurance must have an *insurable interest* in the item being insured. An insurable interest simply means that the purchaser of an insurance policy must have a personal or economic interest in the person or thing being insured. For example, you may not purchase a fire insurance policy on a building you don't own since you would not suffer any personal or economic loss if the building should burn down. The requirement of an insurable interest prevents the use of insurance as a means of gambling. This requirement also removes the motivation for a person with no economic or personal interest at stake to take some action that might cause a calamity to happen.

General insurance principles

Insurance is simply a contract called a *policy,* whereby an insurance company agrees to assume the risk of loss resulting from an insurable risk. In return for assuming this risk, you pay the insurance company a fee called the *policy premium.* By collecting premiums from many individuals, the risk of loss is spread over a large number of policyholders. The few policyholders who do suffer losses are reimbursed for their losses out of the premiums collected from all policyholders. You thus share risk with many policyholders.

Indemnification

A key insurance concept is that insurance companies seek to provide *indemnification* against losses. To indemnify means to restore lost value or to compensate for damages or loss sustained. The practical result of indemnification through insurance is that you cannot make a profit through insurance. An insurance policy only restores lost value and does not pay more than the amount of value lost or damages sustained. Thus, for example, if you own a building worth $80,000 there is no point in insuring it for more than $80,000. If the building were insured for $100,000 and subsequently destroyed by fire, the insurance company would only pay the $80,000 that the building is worth, not the $100,000 it was insured for. Because of this indemnification principle, there is no point in insuring any item for more than its value. The indemnification principle also prevents individuals from seeking to make a profit by insuring an item for more than its value and then causing the destruction of the item insured in order to collect on the insurance policy.

One seeming exception to the indemnification principle is in the area of determining the value of a human life. There is no upper limit on the amount of life insurance you may purchase. In regard to the earlier discussion concerning fortuitous risk, it is important to note that life insurance does not provide insurance against death. This is because death is inevitable and therefore not a fortuitous risk. Life insurance provides insurance against the risk of premature death. It is designed to indemnify against lost earnings because of a premature death. Of course, you must have an insurable interest in order to purchase a policy on someone's life. In most cases the insurable interest consists of economic dependence on the head of a household. Most life insurance is, in fact, purchased by heads of households. However, subject to health requirements and the possession of an insurable interest, insurance companies do sell unlimited amounts of life insurance to an individual. Chapter 9, Life Insurance, will explore this topic in detail.

Insurance mechanics

The mechanics of insurance are quite straightforward. The insurance company performs a function called *underwriting*. The company decides which risks will be insured and how much should be charged to insure each risk. Insurance underwriters use a variety of calculations made by statistical specialists known as *actuaries*. Actuaries calculate the probability that a given loss will occur. The rate to charge to insure against such a loss is then based on the probability that the loss will occur. Basically rates are set to allow the company to earn a profit based on the law of averages.

Risk spreading

Insurance companies use the law of averages to spread the risk of loss among many individual policy owners. A simple example will illustrate how this concept works. If you were to start an insurance company for the purpose of selling fire insurance on individual homes, you would need to know the probability that a home would catch on fire. You would also need to know the average damage which could be expected from each fire. Suppose you knew that only one home in a thousand was likely to catch on fire in a given year and that the average damage from a home fire was $50,000. You could then easily calculate how much you would have to charge each homeowner in order to insure 1,000 homes against the chance of fire. In this case you would have to collect $50 per year from each homeowner to cover the expected fire loss on the one in a thousand homes that is expected to catch on fire. This $50 from each homeowner would just cover your expected costs. You would have to charge an additional fee to earn a profit.

Risk pooling

This simple example illustrates the fundamental principles of insurance. If you insure 1,000 homes, you will have spread the risk of a $50,000 loss for one individual among 1,000 individuals. Each individual has in a sense traded the possibility of a very large loss of $50,000 for the certain loss of $50, which is paid as an insurance premium. This is the essence of insurance—risks are pooled by many individuals with everyone in the pool paying a small sum to protect everyone against the probability of having to pay for a very large loss. Your company, in this example, will earn a profit if loss experience is less than anticipated. That is, if no homes catch on fire, you will earn a large profit of $50,000. If, on the other hand, two or more homes catch on fire, or if the damages to one house are more than $50,000 you will incur a loss for the year. These profits or losses are called *underwriting profits* or *underwriting losses.*

Of course, this example is oversimplified. Underwriting is actually much more complicated in actual practice. But the fundamental principles are the same. An actual insurance company spreads the risk of loss over many thousands of policyholders. It must take into account many additional factors such as the exact value of each home insured, the presence or absence of such devices as smoke detectors and automatic fire alarms, and past loss experiences for different types of construction.

Additionally, underwriters commonly classify various insureds as to the probability that they will experience a loss. They charge higher rates for the high-risk categories. For example, in underwriting automobile insurance, young male drivers generally pay much higher rates than middle-aged female drivers because young males on the average have higher accident rates than middle-aged females. Similarly, in underwriting life insurance, an overweight man who is a heavy smoker will pay a higher premium for the same policy than a man the same age who is a nonsmoker and not overweight. Underwriters attempt to take all such relevant factors into account before writing a policy.

Investment income

In addition to earning underwriting profits and losses, insurance companies also earn a profit by investing the money they collect in premiums. Over the years insurance companies build up cash reserves from the profits of prior years. These accumulated profits, along with current premium payments, are invested in stocks, bonds, mortgages on property, and other investments. Profits from these investments are then added to underwriting profits (or losses) to determine the company's overall profitability. Since underwriting profits and losses often show large fluctuations, the stability of investment profits make a major contribution toward allowing the company to stay in business and charge reasonable rates.

A personal risk management program

Given an understanding of the basics of insurance, let's turn our attention to devising a personal risk management program. This overview of risk management for individuals will provide the necessary background against which to structure a personal insurance program.

Developing a personal risk management program requires careful and comprehensive planning. Two recent trends have made effective personal risk management even more important than it has been in the past.

Impact of inflation

The first of these factors is the impact of rapid inflation, which has caused an increase in the size of potential losses that must be covered by insurance. Areas such as life insurance to replace income lost because of premature death, disability income insurance to replace lost income because of illness or accident, health insurance to pay medical bills, and homeowners insurance to protect the rapidly excalating value of a personal residence have been particularly hard hit by inflation. Insurance policies must be larger than in the past, and must be reviewed much more frequently. One insurance feature that has grown rapidly in popularity in recent years has been the use of policies that automatically increase the amount of coverage each year. These types of policies have been particularly popular for homeowners insurance. The face value of the policy can be increased each year to keep pace with the increasing value of the home the policy is written to insure.

Impact of lawsuits

A second recent trend affecting risk management has been an increased societal tendency toward very large awards in personal injury and liability lawsuits. Jury awards of hundreds of thousands of dollars are no longer a rarity in lawsuits involving personal injuries, such as those resulting from automobile accidents. This trend is obviously an important consideration in planning your insurance program.

A personal risk managemnt program may be organized into three major functions: risk inventory, risk evaluation, and insurance selection. Each of these three major functions will be examined in detail.

Risk inventory

A risk inventory simply involves the identification of risks to which you are exposed. These risks are traditionally broken down into three major categories: personal risks, property risks, and liability risks. These categories are summarized in Table 8–1, along with an identification of the type of insurance normally associated with each type of risk.

Table 8–1
Risk exposure summary

Type of risk	Insurance
1. Personal risks:	
a. Loss of income due to premature death	Life insurance
b. Loss of income due to disability	Disability income insurance
c. Loss of financial assets due to cost of illness or injury	Health insurance
2. Property risks	
a. Loss or damage to automobile	Automobile insurance
b. Loss or damage to home and/or its contents	Homeowners insurance, renter's insurance
c. Loss or damage to personal property	Personal property insurance
3. Liability risks	
a. Liability due to home ownership	Homeowner's insurance
b. Liability due to automobile ownership and operation	Autmobile insurance
c. Liability due to negligence or malpractice related to personal or professional activities	Comprehensive liablity insurance Malpractice insurance

Personal risks

Personal risks involve the potential loss of income or financial assets through illness, injury, or premature death. With the rapidly rising cost of medical care, virtually everyone should be insured against the possibility of illness or disability. Two kinds of insurance policies should be carried. First, a health insurance policy will cover the cost of medical expenses such as doctors' fees and hospital charges. Quality health care is extremely expensive and, without adequate insurance, is beyond the reach of all but the very wealthy. Second, anyone who earns an income upon which he or she (or his or her dependents) depends for support should have a disability income policy. These policies are designed to replace lost income in the event that you are disabled by illness or accident and cannot work to earn an income.

The third type of personal risk insurance, life insurance, is used to replace lost income or services because of the premature death of the policyholder. A secondary, and less important, objective of life insurance is to provide a lump sum to cover the cost of funeral expenses. Calculation of the amount of life insurance required is a bit complicated and is afforded extensive treatment in the next chapter. At this point it is important to note that life insurance is a critical requirement for heads of household upon whom other household members are dependent for support. Life insurance should also be carried on spouses who are responsible for child rearing and homemaking. Should the homemaker die, it would be quite expensive to purchase these services. This fact must be considered in planning comprehensive life insurance.

Property risks

Property risks involve the risk of loss of property through such causes as fire, theft, malicious mischief, civil disturbances, and so forth. You should have three or more types of insurance policies to guard against financial losses due to such risks. First, if you own your own residence, you should have a homeowners insurance policy. This policy insures your home and its contents against loss due to the perils noted above. Homeowners insurance policies also typically include protection against personal liability arising from home ownership. If you do not own your own home, you should have a renters insurance policy to provide similar coverage for the property you own within your rented dwelling.

The second common type of property insurance is automobile insurance, which provides protection against the cost of damage to an automobile from accident, fire, theft, or other causes. Automobile insurance normally provides both property and liability coverage in the same policy. Auto liability coverage will be discussed more fully below.

The third common type of property insurance is personal property insurance. This type of policy is often used to supplement your homeowners or renters property insurance. Personal property insurance covers individual items that may not be insured, or may not be insured for full value, through your homeowners or renters policy. This type of policy typically provides a list or schedule of items, such as antiques, jewels, or furs, which are insured by the policy. The policies are therefore often referred to as *scheduled personal property insurance policies*. These types of policies offer important coverage for such items at relatively low cost. For example, if you lost a diamond ring in the ocean surf, a scheduled personal property insurance policy would turn a potentially large financial loss into a minor inconvenience.

Liability risks

Liability risks arise from the possibility of being held legally responsible for injury or damage to another person or persons. In most cases this liability arises as a result of negligence on the part of the persons held liable. One very common type of liability affecting individuals is liability as the result of injuries sustained in automobile accidents. The liability provisions of autmobile insurance policies are designed to insure against such losses.

You can also be held liable for damages sustained by individuals that take place on property you own. For example, a guest in your home might fall over a bicycle left lying in your driveway. You might be held liable for damages to the guest on the grounds that leaving the bicycle in the driveway was negligent behavior. Homeowners insurance policies contain liability provisions to protect against such losses.

You may also be held liable for other types of damages to people stemming from personal or professional activities. In general, any activity in which you engage where a possibility exists for damage or injury to another party may give rise to the possibility of personal liability. Professional people such as doctors or lawyers are particularly vulnerable to lawsuits alleging negligence due to malpractice. Such professionals normally purchase a special purpose liability insurance policy known as *malpractice insurance*. Most other forms of potential liability may be insured against through a comprehensive personal liability policy.

Risk evaluation

Once a risk inventory has been completed, step two in the personal risk management program requires an evaluation of these risks. Risk evaluation requires an assessment of the size of potential losses as a result of the risks identified in your risk inventory. You must also make an assessment of the probability that the potential loss may occur. This evaluation will then form the basis for a decision concerning whether or not you should insure against the potential loss.

It is most important therefore for you to clearly identify those potential losses that might be financially devastating. You should then place first priority on insuring against them. For example, the loss of income because of illness, injury, or premature death will have an enormous financial impact on your family. Similarily, personal liability resulting from an auto accident or other causes can also be financially devastating. If you are like most people, you do not possess immense independent wealth. Therefore, as a general principle you must insure yourself against these potential losses. There is really no decision for you to make. You *must* be insured. The only decision you must make is how much insurance you should purchase.

Other decisions may not be so clearly defined. For example, if you own a car worth $50, it probably makes no sense to insure it against collision damage. The cost of the collision insurance is too high in relation to the total value of the car. In this case, and in other less clear-cut cases, some decision analysis is necessary.

The probability of an event's occurence is important. In most cases the lower the probability of a potential loss, the lower is the cost of insurance against the potential loss. As a general rule, the most cost-effective insurance is that which guards against a potentially large loss that has a low probability of occurrence. If the potential loss is highly probable, the cost will be extremely high. For example, the cost of theft insurance for a citizens band (CB) radio installed in an automobile is so high that insurance is probably not worth purchasing. In fact, many insurance companies will no longer write theft insurance policies for CB radios because recent experience has demonstrated the high probability of theft.

You should not use the low probability of loss as an excuse for failing to devise an adequate risk management program. A 35-year-old man, for example, faces the probability of dying of approximately two chances in one thousand, or two tenths of 1 percent. If he is responsible for the support of himself, a wife, and two children, the financial impact on his family from his premature death would be potentially devastating. He therefore must have adequate life insurance. The fact that his death had a very low probability of occurence would provide little financial comfort to his survivors.

Insurance selection

The final major function to be performed in a risk management program is to decide whether or not to insure against the various risks that have been identified and evaluated. In general, you have three choices for risk management: risk avoidance and loss prevention, risk assumption, and risk transfer through insurance.

Risk avoidance and loss prevention

Risk avoidance and loss prevention is a simple and effective means by which you can deal with risk. Risk avoidance simply means that you avoid engaging in activities that may lead to losses. For example, you may avoid risks of property damage and personal liability associated with owning and operating an automobile by not owning one. This is a reasonable alternative if you live in an area with adequate public transportation. Similarly, you may minimize that risk of contracting a disease such as lung cancer by not smoking. And you may reduce the risk of accidental death by not engaging in risky activities such as operating a private aircraft, hang gliding, or riding a motorcycle. In short, you may avoid personal risks by being careful.

Risk assumption

Risk assumption involves what is commonly called *self-insurance*. Self-insurance means that you assume the risk of loss personally and are prepared to pay the loss out of your own funds or by liquidating financial assets. For example, if you own a car worth $200, you may choose not to buy automobile collision insurance on the car, thereby personally assuming the risk of loss through collision damage. If the car is damaged, you will have to pay the repair cost yourself. This may be a highly acceptable risk when you compare the cost of collision insurance to the maximum possible loss of $200, the total value of the car.

Risk transfer

Risk transfer through insurance is the process whereby individuals transfer risk to an insurance company by purchasing an appropriate policy. Thus you transfer the risk of collision damage to a new $6,000 automobile to an insurance company by purchasing collision insurance that will pay for damages sustained in a collision. Similarly you insure your dependents against the financial consequences of your premature death through the purchase of life insurance.

Many people use a combination of all three techniques for effective risk management. One very common method to reduce the cost of insurance is to combine risk transfer and risk assumption through the use of deductibles. For example, on a $200 deductible automobile collision insurance policy, you are responsible for paying the first $200 in damage resulting from a collision. The probability of experiencing minor damages from minor accidents, or fender benders, is quite high. Assuming responsibility for the first $200, which amounts to assuming all costs if the total damage is less than $200, significantly reduces the cost of collision insurance. Similar techniques are often used to reduce the cost of disability insurance and heatlh insurance.

Detailed guidance concerning the selection of individual policies will be provided in the two following chapters. The present chapter concludes with an overview of insurance buying guidelines and a brief discussion of the role of Social Security in insurance planning.

Insurance program guidelines

General guidelines for personal insurance management may be organized into a six-step process: selecting an agent, selecting a company, reading the contract, reducing cost, reviewing coverage, and reporting losses.

Selecting an agent

Selecting an agent from whom you will purchase your insurance is a key step in the insurance process. Many individuals use two different agents for insurance planning—one who specializes in personal risks (life, health, and disability), and one who specializes in property and liability risks. Agents may work for a single company, or they may work for an independent agency representing many companies. Independent agents do not owe their allegiance to a single company. You may reasonably expect that they will be able to provide more objective advice concerning the relative merits of policies insured by various companies. The yellow pages of your local telephone directory will provide you with a list of independent insurance agents.

Having compiled a list of independent agents, you might solicit the opinions of local friends, relatives, and business people in obtaining recommendations for an agent. Although overreliance on friends' opinions should be avoided, this information can be quite useful. You may also obtain guidance by checking with the local Better Business Bureau, the state insurance commission, and the local branch of the state consumer affairs office.

You can obtain an indication of an agent's competence by finding out if he or she holds a professional designation such as Chartered Life Underwriter (CLU) or Chartered Property Casualty Underwriter (CPCU). These designations indicate that the agent has completed advanced work in the field and has passed professional certification examinations.

Selecting a company

In selecting a company, the most important consideration for you to keep in mind is that rates for identical policies vary widely from one company to another. If you were to select ten companies at random and ask each company for a rate quote on a single policy, it is almost certain that the different companies would quote ten different rates. It is also true that a company offering the best rate for one type of policy may not offer the best available rate for another type. In the insurance business it clearly pays to shop around.

In addition to cost, it is important to consider the financial stability of companies under consideration. Sizable financial losses as well as interruption of coverage may occur to policyholders if a company should go bankrupt. A.M. Best Company's *Best's Insurance Guide,* available in most libraries, provides information on the financial stability of various firms.

In evaluating companies, you should realize that there are two broad categories of insurance companies: stock companies and mutual companies. Stock companies are owned by stockholders; company profits are either paid out to the stockholders in the form of dividends or reinvested as retained earnings. Through stock purchases, stockholders provide capital to the company and the company earns a profit on that capital on behalf of the stockholders. Mutual companies, on the other hand, do not have any stockholders and are owned by their policyholders. Profits are distributed directly to the policyholders as policy dividends at the end of the year.

Policies that distribute dividends at the end of the year are known as *participating policies* because policyholders participate in the profits of the company through dividends. However, stock companies may also sell participating policies that pay some dividends to policyholders. Stock companies may also sell nonparticipating policies. It is therefore very important to know whether a policy is participating or nonparticipating when you compare costs.

People have argued for years about whether stock companies or mutual companies offer lower cost policies. The only certainty in this controversy is that the evidence is not clear. There is no general guide that will tell you which type of company provides the lowest cost for a given policy. The only way for you to be sure of getting the best price is to compare the cost of the same policy among all the companies being considered.

Reading the contract

An insurance policy is a legal contract between insurance company and policyholder. Unfortunately, there is no way of understanding the exact provisions of this contract without carefully reading the policy. Since very few policies are written in plain English, this is a tedious but necessary chore which you should not avoid if you are a responsible financial planner. There are basically three types of provisions in most insurance contracts: the declarations section, the insuring agreement, and the conditions and exclusions.

The declarations section contains such information as the name of the policy owner, the nature of the item being insured, the cost of the insurance, and the time period during which the policy will be in force. The insuring agreement stipulates the obligations of the insurance company under the contract. This section describes the risks covered by the contract and the amount of coverage provided.

The conditions and exclusions section describes the conditions that must be met in order for the insured company to be required to pay. It also describes any exclusions that would result in the company not being required to pay. For example, personal property insurance policies provide insurance against theft but commonly exclude what they call *mysterious disappearance*. They also require that a theft be reported to the police before any payment is made. This exclusion effectively states that the policy will not cover items lost by their owner.

Reducing costs

You may take a number of actions to reduce the cost of your insurance. Two of the major cost-reduction techniques, careful comparison shopping and the use of deductibles, have already been mentioned. These actions are the two most important ones that should be used to hold down costs of many types of insurance policies.

In the area of life insurance planning, cost comparisons and cost-reduction strategies are very complicated. This topic will be delayed until it can receive more extensive coverage in the following chapter.

As a general rule, however, the cost of life insurance, as well as of health and disability insurance, can be substantially reduced through the use of group insurance policies available through your employer, union, or professional association. Group policies are available to cover entire groups of people, such as all employees of a corporation or all members of a union. Group policies usually offer much lower rates than those offered on policies to individuals.

The major disadvantage of the use of group insurance is that you may lose the insurance when you leave the group. Thus, if you resign from a company through which you have purchased group disability insurance, your coverage may lapse. Most group policies have provisions for converting to individual coverage when you leave the group. You should check these provisions carefully before using group rather than individual coverage. Additionally, as with all policies, you should check the cost of the group policy as compared to other policies. It is not a wise idea to automatically assume that group policies always cost less.

You may also achieve some small savings by paying premiums annually instead of monthly or quarterly. Monthly or quarterly payments involve more administrative expense on the part of the company and are more costly. However, this technique does carry the danger that unless you are an effective budgeter, you may find it difficult to pay a large premium once a year. If you are confident that effective budgeting will not pose a problem, then annual payments would be appropriate. If, however, you are not a well-disciplined budgeter, the additional cost of monthly payments may be worthwhile.

Some companies will give you the annual premium rate but allow you to pay the premium by having it automatically deducted from your checking account at the bank. This automatically gives you a budget plan and a lower annual rate.

Reviewing coverage

Once your insurance program is in place, you should review it for adequacy about every two years, or more often if major personal events occur in your life. As noted previously, the effects of inflation make it particularly important to keep your policies such as homeowners insurance, life insurance, and disability insurance up to date. On the occasion of major life changes, such as marriage, divorce, or birth of a child, your overall insurance program should be reviewed in detail. This small review effort will be time well spent in keeping a risk management program up to date.

Reporting losses

When a loss occurs, you must decide whether or not you should report the loss and file a claim with the insurance company. For small losses it may be better to absorb the loss yourself. Your loss experience is an important factor in determining your insurance rates. For example, an individual who parks a car in a crowded parking lot and continually files small claims for damage to the paint may experience an increase in automobile insurance rates. Self-insuring for such small damages may well be more cost effective than filing a series of nuisance claims.

One notable exception to this rule occurs if any possibility of personal liability is involved. For example, in a collision where minimal property damage is involved, the accident should always be reported to the insurance company, even if no claim to pay the damages is to be filed. The reason is that later claims may arise for injuries sustained during the minor collision, such as neck whiplash or back injuries, which were not apparent at the time of the accident. If the accident is not reported to the insurance company within a reasonable time, the insurance company may not be obligated to pay for personal injury or liability damages later assessed against the driver. Since these injuries can be very substantial, it is foolish to take a chance on not having liability protection when it is needed.

Impact of Social Security

A final consideration in planning a risk management program is the impact of the Social Security system on insurance planning. In addition to providing retirement money for members of the system, Social Security can also pay death benefits, disability benefits, and health care benefits through Medicare. These payments must be taken into account by persons covered by Social Security when planning insurance coverage. The specifics of the Social Security system will be examined in the two following chapters, which provide detailed treatment of insurance planning.

Summary

Personal risk management is a systematic approach to dealing with fortuitous risks that confront you. A fortuitous risk is a risk that exists solely as a result of chance and not as a result of any deliberate action on your part. An insurable risk must be fortuitous. It must also be a personal risk that offers no possibility of financial gain. In order to purchase insurance against an insurable risk, you must have an insurable interest in the person or item being insured.

An insurance policy is a contract that provides indemnification against possible losses stemming from insurable risks. Insurance companies use the law of averages to spread the risk of loss among many individual policy owners.

An effective personal risk management program has three major components: risk inventory, risk evaluation, and insurance selection. Insurable risks may be categorized as personal risks, property risks, and liability risks. As a general rule, the most cost-effective insurance is that which insures against the possibility of a potentially large loss that has a low probability of occurence. The three common methods of risk management are risk avoidance and loss prevention, risk assumption, and risk transfer.

The two main categories of insurance companies are mutual companies, which are owned by policyholders, and stock companies, which are owned by stockholders. Policy rates vary widely from company to company, so careful comparison shopping is required when purchasing insurance.

A comprehensive risk management program prevents a major loss of your financial net worth through a realistic expenditure from current income.

Life insurance

- Life insurance goals
- Multiples-of-salary approach
- Needs analysis for insurance planning
- Selecting the right kind of insurance
- Term insurance
- Cash value insurance: whole life
- Cash value insurance: endowment policies
- Special types of insurance policies
- Life insurance cost comparisons
- Major life insurance policy provisions
- Andy and Annette's insurance plan
- Summary
- Appendix: Life insurance language guide

Nearly every American family owns some type of life insurance. Next to a savings account, life insurance is probably the most important financial asset you own. Yet the majority of families are underinsured. In this chapter we will provide guidelines to determine how much insurance you need. You will also learn how to meet that need at a reasonable cost. Your net worth will be increased, your expenditures reduced, and your loved ones protected by selecting the proper type and amount of life insurance.[1]

Life insurance goals

The primary purpose of life insurance is to replace income lost due to premature death. Whether you should consider owning life insurance is primarily determined by whether other people depend on you for support. Traditionally life insurance is purchased to replace the income of a family's primary wage earner. It is common, however, to include the cost of replacing lost services of spouses who are not employed outside of the home. The cost of child care, cooking, cleaning, and so forth is clearly a major expense. It would have to be borne by a surviving widow or widower in the event of premature death of the spouse responsible for providing these services. Insurance is also needed when both husband and wife work outside the home.

To answer the question of whether or not you need life insurance, your primary concern should be the extent to which others depend on you. Young, single persons with no dependents probably need little, if any, life insurance. At the other end of the age spectrum, older retired persons who have accumulated a substantial net worth over the years often do not require large amounts of life insurance either. The argument is often advanced that young people should buy life insurance solely because the premium payment is lowest when the insureds are young. This is not a valid argument. Although it is true that the annual premium is lower for young people, it will have to be paid for a longer number of years, assuming normal life expectancy. The average annual premium is lower, but the total amount paid will probably be about the same as if the young person waited until life insurance was actually needed. The person would then pay a higher annual premium for fewer years.

People who need not protect dependents are often encouraged to buy life insurance as a means of forced savings. This is the wrong reason for life insurance. A number of better means of savings, providing higher rates of return, are available. Some types of life insurance do not provide a means of forced savings. There are some advantages to saving through insurance, but life insurance should never be purchased solely as a savings medium.

---

[1] The appendix to this chapter contains a helpful guide to terms used in life insurance.

In short, life insurance should be purchased mainly for the purpose for which it is intended: to replace lost income in the event of premature death. Any additional uses of life insurance should be given a much lower priority in the insurance budget. You will have to plan for the purchase of life insurance, health insurance, disability insurance, and perhaps more. It should be obvious that careful planning is required to allocate an appropriate portion of your budget to insurance purchases. You must strive to provide an adequate amount of insurance at a reasonable cost.

Some interesting statistics about ownership of life insurance are available from the American Council of Life Insurance. Table 9–1 shows that 72 percent of all adults—80 percent of all men, and 65 percent of all women—own life insurance. About 85 percent of male heads of household and 64 percent of female heads of household own life insurance. The highest incidence of life insurance ownership occurs in families. In 93 percent of all families with children under the age of 18, at least one family member owns life insurance. In most cases the head of the family is the one insured. The average American male owns almost $30,000 worth of life insurance. The average American female owns just under $8,000 worth of life insurance. These data clearly reflect the extensive use of life insurance as an important element in most family and individual financial planning systems.

Determining whether or not you need life insurance is a relatively simple process. If you have sufficient net worth to cover funeral expenses and

Table 9–1
Ownership of life insurance
by adults (1976)

	All types of life insurance	Agent-mar-keted individual life insurance	Employee group life insurance
Total adult:	72%	54%	31%
Men	80%	59%	42%
Women	65%	50%	21%
All household heads:	80%	59%	42%
Male head	85%	62%	48%
Female head	64%	49%	21%
All families*	88%	70%	51%
Husband-wife families	90%	71%	55%
With children under 18	93%	73%	63%
Without children under 18	88%	70%	47%
Average amount of coverage:			
Men	$28,980	$19,210	$20,620
Women	7,640	5,240	8,620
Children	2,630	2,450	2,310

* Data indicate percentage of families where at least one member owns life insurance.
SOURCE: American Council of Life Insurance, *Life Insurance Fact Book 1978.*

no one is dependent on you for support, you probably do not need any insurance at all. If you plan to pay funeral expenses from a life insurance policy, a small policy should suit your needs. If, however, other people are dependent on your income for support, then the problem gets a bit complicated. This problem may be solved by a detailed needs analysis, or it may be solved by a very simple shortcut technique.

Multiples-of-salary approach

The shortcut technique simply says that the amount of life insurance required can be determined by using a simple rule of thumb related to your annual income. One such rule of thumb method has been proposed by First National City Bank of New York. Financial counselors at Citibank have determined that a family can maintain its standard of living following the death of the family breadwinner if the family's aftertax income is equal to 75 percent of what it was before the breadwinner's death.[1] The counselors further concluded that serious erosion in the family's standard of living would occur if income declined to less than 60 percent of the predeath income. Thus as a general goal, bank staffers advise adequate insurance to provide between 60 and 75 percent of current aftertax income in the event of premature death.

Table 9–2 shows the multiples you can use to determine the amount of life insurance you need. The counselors based their plans on a family of four whose breadwinner had died. They also assumed that insurance proceeds would be invested to produce a rate of return of 5 percent after deducting for taxes and the effect of inflation. The percentage of income required would not come from the insurance proceeds alone. The multiples assume that the family also receives Social Security bene-

**Table 9–2
Citibank's multiples-of-salary chart**

Your present gross earnings	Present age of spouse							
	25 years		35 years		45 years		55 years	
	75%	60%	75%	60%	75%	60%	75%	60%
$7,500	4.0	3.0	5.5	4.0	7.5	5.5	6.5	4.5
9,000	4.0	3.0	5.5	4.0	7.5	5.5	6.5	4.5
15,000	4.5	3.0	6.5	4.5	8.0	6.0	7.0	5.5
23,500	6.5	4.5	8.0	5.5	8.5	6.5	7.5	5.5
30,000	7.5	5.0	8.0	6.0	8.5	6.5	7.0	5.5
40,000	7.5	5.0	8.0	6.0	8.0	6.0	7.0	5.5
65,000	7.5	5.5	7.5	6.0	7.5	6.0	6.5	5.0

SOURCE: "Consumer Views," Citibank, July 1976. By courtesy of "Consumer Views," published by Citibank, copyright Citicorp.

[1] *The Wall Street Journal,* December 6, 1976, p. 40.

fits. Finally, the multiples do not take into account the possibility of income from personal savings, investments, or pension funds. However, even with the qualifications implied by these assumptions, the multiples do provide a simple and useful guide to make an approximate estimate of your insurance requirements.

The multiples of salary in Table 9–2 are very easy to use. To determine the approximate amount of insurance required, you simply multiply the appropriate multiple times your present gross income. The result is the approximate amount of insurance required. For example, assume that your spouse is 25 years old and your current gross earnings are $15,000. You should own life insurance with a face value of approximately 4.5 times annual income, or $67,500, if you intend to provide 75 percent of your income to your survivors.

If you earn $15,000 income, 6.5 times income would be required to provide the same 75 percent standard if your spouse were 35 years old instead of 25. At a spouse's age of 45, 8.0 times income would be required, and at a spouse's age of 55, 7.0 times earnings would be required. The large differences in required multiples are due to the effects of Social Security. The chart assumes Social Security coverage for the survivors. If death occurs while the spouse and children are young, a relatively high level of benefits will be available as a result of the aid for dependent children. In the middle-aged bracket, after the children are grown, this aid would not be available. In the higher-aged bracket, the surviving spouse would be close to retirement age. Thus a lower level of insurance would be required to provide income for the relatively short period of time remaining until retirement benefits will be available. As a result of this pattern of Social Security benefits, the required salary multiple first increases and then decreases as the age of the surviving spouse increases.

Needs analysis for insurance planning

Unfortunately the easy way to life insurance planning is not the best way. Most families have some special requirements or different circumstances than those assumed for the "typical" family of four that most insurance rules of thumb are based on. To do a truly effective job of life insurance planning, a detailed analysis of your specific financial needs is required. If you are not willing to invest the time required for a thorough needs analysis, the multiples-of-salary approach is certainly better than no planning at all. However, it is not as good as a thorough needs analysis.

A needs analysis attempts to identify all the financial obligations which would have to be met if your income had to be replaced by your life insurance proceeds. This approach to life insurance planning requires a thorough analysis of your goals and future financial needs. An analysis of this sort is undoubtedly the most effective approach to life insurance

**Table 9–3
Summary of life insurance needs
analysis for Andy**

1. Present value of family income needs
   a. $24,000 per year for 57 years*
      ($24,000) (26.8) $643,200
   b. Less Social Security for 16 years
      ($9,600) (16) .... (153,600)
   c. Less Annette's earnings for 20 years
      ($12,000) (20) .... (240,000)
   d. Less Annette's Social Security
      retirement benefits, age 65–90
      ($4,800) (25) .... (120,000)
         Net family income needs $129,600
2. Debt liquidation
      Consumer debt 6,000
      Home mortgage 75,000
3. Final expenses and taxes 20,000
4. Emergency fund 10,000
5. College fund 70,000
6. Total needs $310,600
   Less savings and investment .... (15,000)
         Total insurance needs $295,600

* Assumes a 3% rate of return after inflation on money invested today. See Table 9–4.

planning. The use of this technique will be illustrated by undertaking a needs analysis for Andy and Annette, a married couple with two children.

Andy and Annette have a son aged 8 and a daughter aged 6. Andy is 35 years old, and currently earns $40,000 per year as a tax manager in a large certified public accounting firm. The family lives in a home with a $75,000 mortgage and has approximately $15,000 in liquid savings and investments. They have consumer debt totaling $5,500, most of which is for an automobile loan. Annette is 33 years old, and is currently devoting full time to raising their children, Arthur and Anne. Andy's only life insurance is a $125,000 policy he purchased through his employer. The Citibank multiples-of-salary chart indicates that Andy should carry a total of $240,000 to $320,000 in life insurance (6 to 8 times annual income). But Andy feels that a careful needs analysis should be undertaken before he commits a large portion of the family budget to life insurance. Because of this, Andy has prepared a thorough needs analysis, which is summarized in Table 9–3.

**Step one: Family
income needs**

The first and largest item on Andy's needs list is the provision of a lifetime income for his wife and children. Using the Citibank guidelines and assuming that adequate insurance will be available to pay off their home mortgage, Andy and Annette have agreed that Annette and the children could maintain their current standard of living on 60 percent of the family's current gross income. They therefore plan to provide an income of $24,000 per year (60 percent of $40,000). To insure that this amount of income will be available over Annette's entire lifetime, the needs analysis assumes that she will live to age 90, and that $24,000 per year will be required for the next 57 years.

Two factors complicate the determination of the amount of money required to provide $24,000 per year for the next 57 years. First, this family does not actually need the total of $24,000 times 57 years. Such a sum, $1,368,000, would be required only if the proceeds of the insurance policy were not invested over the 57 years and thus produced no rate of return at all. The lump sum provided by any insurance proceeds would obviously be invested to produce a rate of return. The actual lump sum required is an amount of money which, when invested at an assumed rate of return, would be sufficient to provide $24,000 per year for 57 years. The $24,000 withdrawn each year, however, would be composed of part principal withdrawal and part interest earned on the lump sum. The net result is that the total of the principal and interest would be exhausted at the end of 57 years.

Annuity tables are used to determine the amount of money needed to provide an annual income for a certain number of years. One such table is shown in Table 9–4. It shows the number of dollars required to be invested at a given rate of return in order to provide one dollar per year of income for a given number of years. The number of dollars required is called an *annuity factor*. For example, the annuity factor for 30 years at 6 percent is 13.8. The meaning of this number is that $13.80 invested at a 6 percent rate of return is adequate to provide $1 per year for the next 30 years. Over the course of the 30 years, a total of $30 would be withdrawn from the original $13.80 investment: $13.80 principal and

Table 9–4
Sample annuity table

	Rate of return on investment			
Years	3%	6%	8%	10%
10	8.5	7.4	6.7	6.1
15	11.9	9.7	8.6	7.6
20	14.9	11.5	9.8	8.5
25	17.4	12.8	10.7	9.1
30	19.6	13.8	11.3	9.4
35	21.4	14.4	11.6	9.6
40	23.1	15.0	11.9	9.8
45	24.4	15.4	12.1	9.8
50	25.7	15.8	12.2	9.9
55	26.4	16.0	12.3	9.9
57	26.8	16.1	12.3	9.9
60 (or more)	27.7	16.2	12.4	10.0

$16.20 in interest earned during the 30 years. The $13.80 is referred to as the *present value* of $1 per year for 30 years at 6 percent.

The second complicating factor in providing $24,000 per year for the next 57 years is inflation. The $24,000 per year will maintain Annette and the children's current standard of living for a while. Yet inflation may be expected to seriously erode the purchasing power (the amount of goods and services a dollar will buy) of $24,000 over the next 57 years. In fact, over the past decade the purchasing power of the dollar has declined by about one half. It now takes about $2 to buy what $1 would buy ten years ago. Because of this decline in purchasing power, Andy should plan to provide the purchasing power equivalent of $24,000 per year. Therefore, Andy must set aside a larger amount now to have enough income every year for the next 57 years to purchase what $24,000 will purchase today.

The solution is for Andy to provide a lump sum of investment capital sufficient to provide the purchasing power equivalent of $24,000 per year. The lump sum will be invested. Income will be withdrawn from this invested capital. In order to determine the amount of the lump sum required to produce the purchasing power equivalent, we will have to use the annuity tables in Table 9–4.

The key to using the annuity table is to select the appropriate rate of return on investment. Results will vary widely, depending on what rate of return is selected. If a return of 10 percent is expected, only $9.00 of investment capital is required to provide $1.00 per year for the next 57 years. If, on the other hand, a return of 3 percent is expected, $26.80 in investment capital is required to provide $1 per year for the next 57 years. This wide variation in results certainly indicates that the expected rate of return on investment must be selected with great care.

Andy and Annette's objective is to provide the equivalent of $24,000 in purchasing power. Thus their appropriate rate of return should be the difference between the actual rate of return they expect to earn on investment capital and the rate of inflation. This choice provides enough investment capital to provide a constant amount of purchasing power. For example, Andy and Annette think that the investment capital may be conservatively invested to produce a 9 percent long-run rate of return. They also think that a 6 percent rate of return will be necessary to keep up with the long-run inflation rate. They therefore will use a "real" rate of return of 3 percent to determine the amount of investment capital required to provide $24,000 in purchasing power per year over the next 57 years. They are assuming that the proceeds of Andy's insurance will be invested to produce a rate of return that is 3 percent greater than the rate of inflation.

Long-term planning, such as planning your life insurance, requires some difficult estimates. You must estimate long-run rates of return on invested capital and future rates of inflation. Available rates of return and the inflation rate are currently very high in the United States. An estimate of 9 percent return on investment and 6 percent inflation may seem extremely low. These estimates represent long-term trends rather than cyclical highs. Historical evidence indicates that the estimate of a 3 percent real growth rate is quite reasonable.

Applying this reasoning to our example, we can multiply the annuity factor of 26.8 times $24,000 to arrive at a required lump sum of $643,200. This figure is about 45 percent of what would be required if the investment capital earned no rate of return at all.

Impact of Social Security

Fortunately Andy and Annette will not have to rely on insurance alone to provide the entire $643,200. Part of the required sum will be provided by Annette returning to work in the event of Andy's death. Social Security benefits payable to Annette and the children following Andy's death will also be of great assistance. Such benefits will provide nearly $300,000 over Annette's lifetime. The law provides support payments to surviving spouses with dependent children until the youngest child reaches 18 years of age, or 22 years of age if the child is a full-time student. The amount payable depends on how long the deceased spouse paid into the Social Security system and the amount that was paid in. To determine the amount to which your survivors would be entitled, a simple request may be filed with your local Social Security office. It is important to recognize that the Social Security office cannot take any action to pay benefits unless a claim is filed.

Table 9–5 provides a brief summary of Social Security death, disability, and retirement benefits. The magnitude of these benefits, which are tax-free, can be quite substantial. Details of eligibility rules and exact determination of the amounts for which individuals are eligible must be determined in consultation with Social Security experts. The summary chart does provide a good ballpark estimate of what can be expected. For more details, you should obtain copies of the publications listed at the bottom of the table from your local Social Security office. To obtain the address of this office, look in the telephone directory under Social Security Administration, or inquire at any post office. You should also obtain a report of your earnings credited to your Social Security number. You can do this by sending post card Form OAR 7004, which is obtainable free at any post office.

On the basis of the number of years Andy and Annette have belonged to Social Security system, the amount they have paid in, and assuming that both children will go to college, Annette will be eligible for approximately $9,600 for the next 16 years. At the end of 16 years, their youngest child will reach age 22. Annette will then no longer be eligible to receive any additional benefits until she reaches retirement age. This period— the middle years after the children are grown but before retirement age—

Table 9–5
Summary of Social Security benefits (1979)

Death:
Lump sum payment: $255.
Monthly payments to survivors: $183 to $949.50 (for three or more surviving dependents).
No payment to surviving spouse without dependent children under age 62.

Disability:
Monthly payments to worker: $129.50 to $533.30.
Monthly payments to worker with dependents (family benefit); $194.30 to $933.30.

Retirement:
Monthly benefit, Age 62: $97.50 to $365.50.
Monthly benefit, Age 65: $121.80 to $534.70.
Family monthly benefit (retired worker plus two eligible family members): $182.70 to $935.70.
Special minimum benefit: if covered by Social Security for more than 20 years, minimum monthly retirement benefit = $230. at age 65.

Inflation:
If annual cost of living increase is 3 percent or more, benefits increase by same amount.

SOURCE: "Your Social Security," U.S. Department of Health, Education and Welfare, Social Security Administration, January 1979; and "Social Security Information for Young Families," U.S. Department of Health, Education and Welfare, Social Security Administration, January, 1979.

is often referred to as the *widow's blackout period.* During this time no benefits are available to surviving spouses from Social Security.

In addition to the support payments for surviving spouses with dependent children, Annette will be eligible for Social Security retirement benefits. Annette expects to return to work about 12 years from now when their youngest child is 18 years old. At that time Annette will be 45 years old. She expects to work until age 65 when she will retire. She will then be eligible for Social Security retirement benefits of approximately $4,800 per year for the remainder of her life.

The total of surviving spouse and retirement benefits must be subtracted from Andy and Annette's original estimate of $643,200 in determining future family needs. In this case no adjustment for inflation is required because, as detailed in Table 9–5, Social Security payments automatically increase to keep pace with inflation.

The final item to be deducted from total family income needs is the total amount of Annette's expected earnings when she goes back to work at age 45. Annette expects to be able to earn the equivalent of $12,000 per year in current purchasing power upon returning to work. She anticipates receiving annual salary increases to keep pace with inflation. In terms of current purchasing power, Annette expects to earn $240,000 during this 20-year working period.

The Social Security benefits and Annette's income are shown as deductions from the original $643,200 estimate in item 1 of Table 9–3. The net result of these calculations is that Andy and Annette need to provide $129,600 to meet family income needs in the event of Andy's premature death.

Step two: Debt liquidation

The next major need for which Andy and Annette must plan is a fund to liquidate all the family's indebtedness. This a fairly large amount of money, but quite reasonable in relation to their income. They have a few small charge accounts and an automobile loan, for a total consumer indebtedness of $6,000. Their largest debt is their $75,000 home mortgage. Andy feels very strongly that he must leave Annette and the children with a debt-free house if he should die. The $75,000 amount therefore is a very high-priority item in their planning. As a general rule, a sound life insurance plan should include a provision to pay off the mortgage. Adding the mortgage to Andy and Annette's consumer debt brings the total required for debt liquidation to $81,000.

Step three: Final expenses and estate taxes

Andy and Annette have budgeted a total of $20,000 for funeral arrangements, administrative expenses involved in distributing his estate, and estate taxes. The last chapter of this book treats estate taxes in more detail. But at this point it's enough to note that an allocation of $3,000 to $5,000 for funeral arrangements and administrative expenses should be adequate for most people. For an estate the size of Andy's, a $15,000 estate tax allocation is more than adequate. It would not be necessary to pay taxes on the current estate. The $15,000 would be available if the estate grows substantially in the future.

Step four: Emergency fund

Andy wants to insure that his family will have an adequate liquid fund available to meet unexpected emergencies. As a general rule, three to six months' income should be available in such a fund. Andy has allocated $10,000 for this purpose and feels this should be enough.

Step five: College fund

Andy and Annette hope to send both their children to a private college for four years. Based on current costs of private colleges, it will cost about $35,000 for each child, or a total of $70,000. By the time the children attend college, college costs will have risen. However, the $70,000 will have been invested to earn a rate of return commensurate with inflation. Therefore, the $70,000 fund should provide adequate purchasing power to send the children to college.

Step six: Total insurance needs

The sixth and final step in the needs analysis is to total up the needs outlined in steps one through five, and deduct any savings and investments currently available to meet these needs. In Andy and Annette's case, their total needs add up to $310,600. They currently have $15,000 in savings and investments available. Thus a net total of $295,600 in life insurance is needed. Since Andy already has a policy for $125,000, he should purchase additional insurance in the amount of approximately $170,000.

In addition to planning insurance for Andy, Andy and Annette must also plan an insurance program for Annette. In the event that Annette should die before the children are old enough to care for themselves, Andy would have to purchase child-care services for the children. He also feels that he would have very little time to devote to housekeeping because of the time pressures of his job. Andy therefore would have to hire a full-time housekeeper to look after himself and the children. It is obvious that a full-time housekeeper is a poor substitute for a full-time wife and mother. However, the housekeeper could at least replace some of the services required to keep the house running.

Insurance experts have suggested that a $25,000 life insurance policy is normally adequate for this purpose. Two factors are of most importance in making this determination. The first is the fact that much of the cost of a housekeeper will be covered by the absence of the normal level of expenditures by the deceased family member. Second, statistics indicate that remarriage rates for widowers with children are high. Most widowers are remarried within five years. Professional services are therefore required for a relatively short period of time in most cases. Because of these considerations, Andy and Annette agree that a $25,000 policy will be adequate.

Now that Andy and Annette have carefully determined the amount of insurance required to meet their financial needs, they must perform one additional important task. They must determine what type of policy to buy and from whom to buy it.

Selecting the right kind of insurance

Life insurance policies are available in a wide variety of forms. Since the insurance business is heavily sales-oriented and highly competitive, major insurance companies offer whatever options, combinations, and variations are necessary to attract customers. To make an intelligent selection from the many possible policies, keep in mind that there are really only two basic forms of insurance protection: *term insurance* (policies that do not build any cash values) and *cash-value insurance* (policies that do build cash values). If you understand the distinction between these two types, you'll be able to eliminate most of the confusion about buying life insurance.

Term insurance

Term insurance is the easiest type of insurance policy to understand. It is generally the most economical way to purchase life insurance protection. In a term policy the insurance company agrees to pay a stipulated sum to the person you name to receive the face value of the policy in the event of your death. The face value of the policy is the amount for which your life is insured. The person or persons named to receive this face value are called your beneficiaries. A term policy is valid for a fixed number of years, the policy's term, and must be renewed at the end of that term if insurance is to continue in force. Term policies generally are available in four major forms: straight term, renewable term, convertible term, and decreasing term.

Straight term

A straight term policy provides insurance coverage for a fixed number of years. Usually terms are 1, 5, 10, 15, or 20 years, or until age 65. These policies usually have a level annual premium that is fixed for the life of the policy. When the policy expires, it is of no value. A new policy would have to be purchased if protection is still required or desired.

Renewable term

Renewable term is term insurance that may be renewed at the end of the term without requiring a new medical examination. The renewal premium rate will be higher than the original rate since the probability of death increases as you get older. A typical policy might be valid for five years at a fixed premium. It might be renewable for another five-year period for a higher premium. Such a policy could be renewed every five years up to some maximum age, usually age 65 or 70. In later years, say, age 55 or 60, the annual premium rates become very high.

Convertible term

Convertible term is term insurance that allows you to convert the policy to a cash value policy at standard rates, regardless of any health change. Term insurance policies are often both renewable and convertible.

Decreasing term

Decreasing term insurance is a term policy with a fixed premium and a declining face value. Over the term of such a policy, the cost of the policy remains constant, but the amount that will be paid to your beneficiary declines. These types of policies are very popular to provide for paying off a home mortgage in the event of premature death. The face value of the policy may be set to decrease at the same rate as the principal amount of money owed on the home mortgage decreases.

Term insurance is generally regarded as *temporary insurance*. Unlike cash value insurance, term policies are valid only for a fixed term rather than a lifetime. The existence of a fixed term and of increasing renewal rates present the primary disadvantage of term insurance. However, term insurance has one major advantage that makes it attractive to young families: term insurance offers the largest dollar value of coverage for the lowest cost. Most young and growing families require large amounts of coverage and have a great deal of pressure on the family budget. Term insurance often represents the only affordable means of providing adequate life insurance.

Cash value insurance: whole life

Whole life insurance (also called straight life or ordinary life) is the most commonly purchased type of life insurance policy in the United States. This type of insurance continues in effect for as long as the premium is paid. The premium remains the same throughout your lifetime.

Because the policy continues in force throughout your lifetime, whole life insurance is often called *permanent insurance*. The premium paid on whole life insurance is higher than necessary to provide insurance coverage alone, and the excess builds up a cash value that belongs to you as the policyholder. At your option you can borrow the cash value of the policy from the insurance company at a very attractive interest rate. You may also terminate the policy and receive its value in cash. A third option also exists whereby you may exchange your policy for a new and smaller policy that is fully paid up.

Because of its cash value buildup, whole life insurance is often said to have living benefits as well as death benefits. If you die, your beneficiary collects the face value of the policy. If you live, you can cash in (surrender, in insurance terms) the policy for its cash value. But if you wish to keep the policy in force even though some emergency requires the use of the cash value, then you can borrow the cash value from the company. If you do borrow, no credit check is required, and the loan may be repaid at your convenience. In fact, you may elect never to repay the loan. In the event of your death, the accumulated interest and principal amount of the loan are deducted from your policy's face value before your beneficiary is paid.

In effect, then, whole life insurance provides insurance benefits along with a forced saving plan. The rate of interest earned on the savings component of a whole life policy is generally far below the rate of return that can be earned on alternative investments. For this reason many people feel that whole life is a poor investment. (The savings aspect of whole life will be explored in some detail in the section of this chapter dealing with cost comparisons of term versus cash value insurance.) The primary advantage of whole life is that the policy remains in force for your entire life at a constant premium cost. Many buyers of whole life insurance also consider the forced savings aspect of whole life a major advantage because most people find saving difficult. Although the interest rate earned is low, a whole life policy does enforce savings discipline. This is a discipline lacking in most of us. There is also a tax consideration because interest earned under the forced savings plan is tax-free to the policyholder. Unless the cash value exceeds the cumulative amount of premiums paid in, cash values are considered to be a return of premium to the policyholder and are nontaxable.

The primary disadvantage of whole life insurance is its cost. Whole life is much more expensive than term insurance when measured over the course of a person's lifetime.

Modified whole life

Like term insurance, whole life insurance is available in a variety of variations and combinations. One very popular variation is modified whole life. Under this type of policy, premium payments are adjusted to be lower than normal in the early years of the policy, usually the first five or ten years, and then higher than normal later on. This type of policy is actually a permanent policy that offers a combination of term and whole life to hold down costs in the early years of the policy's life. The policy uses mostly term in the early years to keep costs low. It then gradually shifts to whole life in the later years. The primary appeal of this type of policy is to young families that expect their income to increase as they grow older. The lower premium in the early years offers an affordable option for permanent insurance.

Limited payment life

Another popular whole life variation is limited payment life. This type of policy provides a permanent insurance policy. Premiums are paid for a fixed term, usually 20 years ("twenty pay life"), or to age 65 ("paid up age 65"), rather than over an entire lifetime. The primary appeal of this type of policy is that even though premium payments stop, the insurance remains in force. Since a fewer number of payments are made, the amount of the individual payments are higher. This increased cost is the primary disadvantage of limited payment life. For most young families, limited payment life is a very poor choice for insurance coverage because its cost is too high.

Family plan insurance

Family plan insurance is a combination of insurance policies. It is usually a mixture of whole life and term, designed to provide coverage for an entire family. For example, such a policy might provide $10,000 for the husband, $5,000 for the wife, and $2,500 for each child. In most cases, the insurance on the husband is whole life and the insurance on the wife and children is term.

Family income policy

Most companies also offer a family income policy, which is a combination of decreasing term and whole life. The decreasing term policy is for a set number of years, often 20 years. If the policyholder dies before the period of 20 years is up, the term portion of the policy is used to pay a regular income to the family. At the end of the 20 years, the face amount of the whole life policy will be paid to the family.

Family income rider

A similar type of policy, called a *family income rider,* pays the face amount of the whole life at the time of death rather than at the end of the term policy. The term policy is still used to pay an income for the fixed number of years.

Family maintenance policy

A final variation, called a *family maintenance policy,* pays an income for a fixed number of years after the policyholder's death. In this case the term portion of the policy is level term instead of decreasing term. If the policy is a 20-year policy calling for 10 years of income payments, the family receives income payments for 10 years regardless of when the policyholder dies. For example, if the policy holder dies 19 years after buying the policy, family income payments are made for 10 years. Under a family income policy, income payments would have been paid for only 1 year.

As a general rule, these combination policies are not necessary for families in which a responsible and knowledgeable person is available to administer the deceased's estate. The primary purpose of life insurance is to replace lost income that otherwise would have been available to support dependents. If the surviving spouse or other dependents invest insurance proceeds wisely and prudently, they will almost always be better off financially than if they let the insurance company invest for them. Insurance companies operate on very low assumed rates of return. Typically they pay very low rates of return on money left with the company. The reason they do this is to insure that they do not overestimate the amount of money that will be available to meet their huge financial committments.

Cash value insurance: endowment policies

Another major type of cash value insurance is the policy that places primary emphasis on the savings and income aspects of life insurance. This type of policy, which is called an *endowment policy,* is set for a fixed term. At the end of the term, the company pays you the face value of the policy. If you die before that time, the policy pays your beneficiary the face value. Endowment policies typically have a limited payment period, often 20 or 30 years, or until age 65.

**Retirement income
policy**

One special variation of an endowment policy is called the *retirement income policy*. Instead of paying a lump sum when the policy reaches the end of its term, a lifetime income is paid monthly to the policyholder. This type of policy combines death protection with an assured income after retirement.

Since endowment policies emphasize savings over insurance and require very rapid accumulation of cash values, *endowment policies offer the most expensive insurance you can buy*. Endowment policies are clearly inappropriate for most families. You can buy much cheaper insurance and you can find much better savings plans. Except for some special purpose types of plans with special tax advantages, endowment policies make little sense for most people.

**Special types of
insurance policies**

Up to this point, the discussion has been limited to what insurance people refer to as *ordinary insurance*. In insurance terms *ordinary* refers to policies sold directly to individuals by insurance agents. Table 9–6 summarizes the most common types of ordinary insurance available. In addition to ordinary insurance, there are three major varieties of insurance that are not easily classified under the heading of ordinary insurance. The first of these, group life insurance, is a very rapidly growing segment of the life insurance market. Group life insurance is nearly always term insurance.

**Table 9–6
Summary of ordinary life insurance
policies***

1. Term insurance
   a. Straight term
   b. Renewable term
   c. Convertible term
   d. Decreasing term
2. Cash value insurance: whole life
   a. Whole (straight) life
   b. Modified whole life
   c. Limited payment life
   d. Family plan
   e. Family combination policies
      Family income policy
      Family income rider
      Family maintenance policy
3. Cash value insurance: endowment
   a. Limited payment endowment
   b. Retirement income endowment

* *Ordinary life* refers to policies marketed directly to individuals.

Group life insurance

Group life insurance, in contrast to ordinary life insurance, is sold to groups of individuals. These groups are commonly all the employees of a given organization, all the members of a professional association, or all the members of some similar identifiable group. The insurance company negotiates an insurance contract with the group. Then its members are given the option of purchasing insurance through the group plan. The insurance company issues one master policy to cover the entire group. Each group member who joins receives a certificate verifying ownership of insurance coverage through the group. Administrative costs to the insurance company are quite low for group policies. Premium rates to group members are correspondingly low.

Low cost is one of the two major advantages of a group policy. In most cases group insurance coverage is significantly lower than the cost of a comparable ordinary insurance policy. You cannot always assume that every group life insurance policy will provide the lowest possible cost. In general, however, these types of policies are quite cost-effective.

The second major advantage of group life insurance is that it is often available to group members without the requirement of a physical examination. This can be a major advantage if you believe that your health might cause an insurance company to raise the rates on your policy above the standard rate charged a normally healthy individual.

Credit life insurance

A second type of life insurance policy in the special category is credit life insurance. The most notable feature of credit life insurance is that it should almost always be avoided because of its high cost. Credit life insurance is an insurance policy sold as part of a debt contract, for example, on an automobile loan. If the borrower dies before the loan is paid off, the credit life insurance pays off the loan. You should know that current consumer protection laws prohibit lenders from requiring a borrower to buy credit life insurance as a provision for granting the loan. If you wish to provide insurance to pay off a loan, you can almost always buy an ordinary term policy for less than the cost of a credit life insurance policy.

Industrial life insurance

The final type of life insurance in the special category is industrial life insurance, which is extremely expensive. Industrial insurance policies are generally sold for very low face value amounts, often less than $1,000. Premiums are collected weekly by an insurance agent who usually visits the policyholder's home. These policies derived their name from the fact that they are generally sold as burial insurance to low-paid industrial workers. Because such workers are better educated than in the past, industrial life insurance sales have shrunk to a small fraction of total insurance sales.

Life insurance cost comparisons

Table 9–7 and Figure 9–1 present some comparative cost and cash value data for four major types of policies: term (five-year renewable and convertible), straight life, limited payment life (20 years), and endowment (20 years). The variation in cost is extremely wide. For a 30-year-old man, the cost of five-year renewable term is less than 15 percent of the cost of a 20-year endowment policy and about one third of the cost of a straight life policy. A 30-year-old man thus could obtain about $3,000 worth of term insurance for the price of $1,000 of whole life. Compared to an endowment policy, he could obtain about $7,500 worth of term life insurance protection for the cost of $1,000 worth of endowment insurance.

Table 9–7
Approximate annual premium rates for $1,000 of life insurance*

Bought at age	Term 5-Year renewable convertible	Straight life	Limited payment (20-payment)	Endowment (20-year)
18	$5.35	$11.95	$20.15	$43.17
20	5.38	12.54	20.93	43.20
25	5.50	14.27	23.11	43.43
30	5.68	16.60	25.83	43.68
40	7.96	23.32	32.87	45.20
50	14.21	34.51	43.06	48.91

* Rates shown are approximate premium rates for nonparticipating life insurance policies for men. Rates for women are somewhat lower because of women's somewhat lower mortality. Rates of participating policies would be slightly higher, but the cost would be lowered by annual dividends. The premium rates shown here are per $1,000 of protection if the policies were purchased in units of $10,000.
SOURCE "Policies for Protection," American Council of Life Insurance, 1978.

The major cost advantage of term insurance is very clear from these comparisons. However, as the policyholder grows older, the cost of renewing term insurance becomes quite high. For example, at age 50, term insurance would cost $14.21 for $1,000 worth of coverage. On the other hand, had a male policyholder bought straight life at age 20, he would still be paying $12.54 for his $1,000 worth of protection. In addition, as Figure 9–1 shows, he would also have been accumulating cash value for the past 30 years. The cash value of his straight life policy would now be approximately $380. This cash value could be borrowed or obtained simply by surrendering the policy if insurance were no longer needed. The term policy would have accumulated no cash value since the purchaser would have been buying only insurance protection for the past 30 years.

Figure 9–1
Approximate cash values for $1,000 of life
insurance taken out at age 18

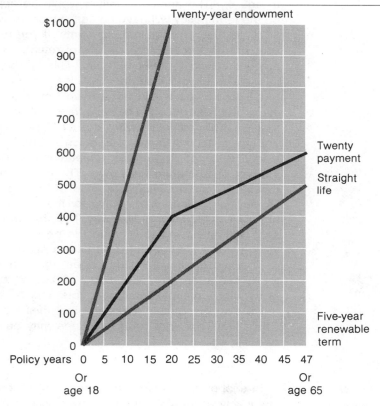

SOURCE "Policies for Protection," American Council of Life Insurance, 1978.

**Term insurance
versus whole life**

Which is better, term or whole life? Unfortunately the answer is not simple. Opinion is divided as to the correct answer to this question. One popular approach to insurance planning says that you should always "buy term and invest the rest." This concept says that you will end up ahead financially if you buy term insurance at a lower premium. You can invest the difference between the term and whole life premium. At the end of your planning horizon, you will be better off with the term insurance plus the invested premium difference.

A simple illustration will clarify this concept. Suppose you are 20 years old and are planning an insurance program through to age 65. You can buy a $25,000 straight life policy for a constant annual premium of approximately $315 per year. This policy will have a cash value of approximately

$15,000 when you reach age 65. Your buy term and invest the rest alternative is to buy a level premium term policy that will remain in force to age 65. The annual premium would be approximately $140. At age 65 the term policy will have no cash value. However, you will have saved $175 per year in premium payments. If you had invested this $175 per year at a 6 percent aftertax rate of return, your total investment would amount to slightly over $20,000. This is about $5,000 more than the cash value of your insurance policy.

Obviously you would have been better off under the buy term and invest the rest option. The only flaw in this concept is that it assumes that you will faithfully invest the $175 per year for the next 40 years and not succumb to the temptation to spend the money on something else. The necessity to resist temptation may be the strongest argument in favor of whole life insurance. The cash value buildup is an effective means of forced savings. In spite of its relatively low yield, the whole life savings buildup is attractive for the forced savings benefit. It is also attractive because of its flexibility. The premium can be borrowed if necessary without having to give up the policy. Thus the resolution of term versus whole life is at least partially a matter of personal preference.

The line of reasoning described above assumes, of course, that a family can afford to make such a choice. With the unrelenting pressure of inflation on most family budgets, this is often not so. Most young families simply cannot afford to meet their life insurance needs through whole life. Therefore term insurance may be the only practical means of doing so.

Comparing costs among companies

In shopping for insurance, cost comparisons among companies are absolutely essential. Unfortunately, such cost comparisons are difficult to make because different companies present their costs in different ways. The problem is further complicated because the company offering the best price on term insurance may not offer the best price on whole life. One factor may be counted on in making cost comparisons: the variation in cost from company to company will be extremely wide.

First, you must distinguish between participating and nonparticipating policies. Participating policies rebate part of the premium in the form of a dividend at the end of the year. Nonparticipating policies do not rebate any dividends. Because of this, the nonparticipating policy may appear to have a higher cost before dividends are taken into account. This fact, combined with the fact that dividend scales and cash values vary widely from company to company, makes comparison even more difficult.

However, difficult or not, the informed consumer must be willing to compare costs. Fortunately the insurance industry provides cost comparison indexes that can be used to make direct comparisons among policies issued by various companies. Two comparison indexes are commonly used to compare policy costs: the *net payment cost comparison index* and the *surrender cost comparison index*. Both these indexes are based on the *interest adjusted cost method*. This method takes into account the time value of money (i.e., the fact that money received in the future is not as valuable as money in hand today). In short, a dollar to be received 10 years from now will not be as valuable as a dollar in hand today. A dollar in hand today can be invested at some rate of interest and grow to be much more than one dollar at the end of 10 years.

Interest adjusted cost method

Interest-adjusted comparison cost indexes combine the premium payments, dividends, and cash value buildup into a single index number for ease of comparison. Cost comparison indexes show you the net cost per $1,000 of life insurance coverage. *The lower the index number, the lower is the actual cost of the policy.* The index number calculation assumes that some rate of return, usually 5 percent, will be earned on money in hand today. Using this assumed rate of return, the cost comparison index takes into account the time value of money. The index adjusts for differences in the timing of dividend payments and cash value accumulations. Policy A, for example, may offer a higher cash value after 10 years than policy B. Policy B, on the other hand, may have a higher cash value at the end of 20 years. Interest-adjusted comparison indexes make adjustments for these timing differences.

Net payment cost comparison index

The net payment cost comparison index provides an index of the average yearly net cost per $1,000 of insurance protection. The index takes into account premium payments, dividends, and the time value of money. This index shows the net difference between premium payments to the company and dividend payments to the policyholder, making an adjustment for the time value of money. This time value of money adjustment is a very important step in the calculation because nearly all participating policies pay dividends that increase over time. Since dividends vary from year to year, the index calculation must be made for some assumed number of years. Companies usually calculate the index for 10 years and for 20 years. For nonparticipating policies the net payment cost comparison index is equal to the annual premium payment. Nonparticipating policies do not pay dividends. In making cost comparisons, the policy with the lowest net payment index offers the best value for your premium dollar in terms of the lowest yearly net payment.

Surrender cost comparison index

The surrender cost comparison index goes one step further than the net payment cost comparison index. This index takes cash surrender values into account. It reflects the average yearly net cost per $1,000 of insurance protection, taking into account premium payments, dividends, cash values, and the time value of money. It is most useful in comparing policies if cash values are most important to you. The calculation of this index assumes that you surrender the policy at the end of 10 or 20 years and take its cash value. The lower the level of this index, the better the return you are getting for your money if you cash in the policy. For term policies that have no cash surrender value, the surrender cost index will be the same as the net payment cost index.

Equivalent level annual dividend

A third measure of life insurance value is the *equivalent level annual dividend*. This figure shows the part played by dividends in determining the net cost of participating policies. Most participating policies pay dividends that increase over time. Dividend dollars received early in the life of a policy are more valuable than dividend dollars that you have to wait 5, 10, or 20 years to collect. Therefore, some means of comparing future value to present value is required. The equivalent level annual dividend shows you what a stream of increasing dividends would be worth if the company were to pay a level dividend each year instead. Taking the time value of money into account, the equivalent level annual dividend coverts an increasing dividend stream into a constant dividend stream. By adding the result to the net payment cost comparison index, you can see the total cost of a participating policy before deducting dividends.

Cost comparison summary

In summary, what do these cost comparison indexes mean? The easiest way to understand the meaning of the indexes is to say that they represent a kind of an average yearly cost per $1,000 of protection of owning the policy for 10 or 20 years. In using these indexes for cost comparison, the most important point to remember is that a policy with a lower index number is a better life insurance buy than a similar policy with a higher index number. Comparisons must be made between policies that are as similar as possible (i.e., for the same age of policyholder, the same face amount, and other similar features). The closer the policies are to being identical, the more reliable will be the cost comparisons. Remember that a low cost comparison index for one policy issued by a company does not guarantee that other policies issued by the same company will offer a similarly low index. In particular, the fact that a given company offers a low cost term insurance policy is no guarantee that it will also offer a low cost whole life policy. The reverse is also true.

Figure 9–2 shows a ledger sheet giving cost data prepared for a $25,000 whole life policy issued to a male aged 35. The policy is a particularly low cost one that is issued by a special-purpose nonprofit corporation, Teachers Insurance and Annuity Association of America (TIAA). This

Figure 9–2
Illustrative ledger sheet for $25,000
whole life policy

PREPARED FOR WILLIAM DROMS   10/17/79   M35   H

$25,000 ORDINARY LIFE POLICY

LEVEL ANNUAL PREMIUM	$429.50*
FIRST YEAR CASH DIVIDEND	$110.50**
FIRST YEAR NET PAYMENT	$319.00

*ALTERNATIVE PREMIUMS ARE—SEMI-ANNUAL $223.25, QUARTERLY $116.00.

THE PREMIUM AND DIVIDEND AMOUNTS SHOWN ABOVE ARE FOR THIS TIAA POLICY ISSUED
TO A MAN AGED 35, NEAREST BIRTHDAY. THE FOLLOWING SCHEDULE SHOWS ANNUAL
PREMIUMS, FUTURE DIVIDENDS, AND YEARLY NET PAYMENTS. IT ALSO SHOWS GUARANTEED
AMOUNTS AVAILABLE FOR LOAN AT 8 PERCENT INTEREST, OR UPON CASH SURRENDER OF
THE POLICY. UNDER THIS POLICY THE INSURANCE PROTECTION IS CONSTANT AT $25,000.

FOR YEAR	ANNUAL PREMIUM	DIVIDEND** END OF YEAR	NET** PAYMENT	LOAN OR CASH VALUE END OF YEAR
1	429.50	110.50	319.00	.00
2	429.50	110.50	319.00	.00
3	429.50	110.50	319.00	270.75
4	429.50	122.75	306.75	634.75
5	429.50	139.00	290.50	1006.75
6	429.50	155.75	273.75	1386.50
7	429.50	173.00	256.50	1773.75
8	429.50	190.25	239.25	2168.75
9	429.50	208.00	221.50	2570.75
10	429.50	226.25	203.25	2980.25
11	429.50	244.50	185.00	3397.00
12	429.50	263.25	166.25	3820.25
13	429.50	282.50	147.00	4250.00
14	429.50	301.75	127.75	4685.50
15	429.50	321.25	108.25	5126.25
16	429.50	341.25	88.25	5572.00
17	429.50	361.25	68.25	6022.00
18	429.50	381.50	48.00	6476.00
19	429.50	402.00	27.50	6934.00
20	429.50	422.50	7.00	7395.00
Age 65	422.75	632.00	−209.25	12043.50

COST COMPARISON FACTORS**	10 YEARS	20 YEARS
LIFE INSURANCE NET PAYMENT COST COMPARISON INDEX	$11.50	$8.96
LIFE INSURANCE SURRENDER COST COMPARISON INDEX	$2.47	$.44
EQUIVALENT LEVEL ANNUAL DIVIDEND	$5.68	$8.21

THE INDEXES SHOWN ABOVE PROVIDE COMMON DENOMINATORS FOR COMPARING THE RELATIVE
COSTS OF SIMILAR POLICIES ISSUED BY OTHER COMPANIES. THE LOWER THE INDEX THE
BETTER THE VALUE. AN EXPLANATION OF THE INTENDED USE OF THE COST COMPARISON
INDEXES, AND THE EQUIVALENT LEVEL ANNUAL DIVIDEND ALSO SHOWN, IS GIVEN IN THE
TIAA LIFE INSURANCE GUIDE, AND IN THE LIFE INSURANCE BUYER'S GUIDE. THE
INTEREST RATE USED IN THE CALCULATION OF THESE FACTORS IS   5.00 PERCENT.

** DIVIDENDS, NET PAYMENT AMOUNTS, AND COST COMPARISON FACTORS SHOWN ARE BASED
ON TIAA'S CURRENT DIVIDEND SCALES AND ARE NOT GUARANTEED.

TEACHERS INSURANCE & ANNUITY ASSOC. OF AMERICA 730 THIRD AVENUE, N.Y., N.Y.

SOURCE: Teachers Insurance and Annuity Association of America, New York, New York.

company issues very attractively priced policies for professors and administrators in higher education. The cost figures shown provide a good
illustration of the cost comparison concepts discussed above.

Table 9–8 presents some additional cost comparison figures from a
recent exhaustive insurance study in *Consumer Reports*. The data shown

Table 9–8
Summary of life insurance net costs

	Lowest cost	Median cost	Highest cost
Term insurance:			
Participating	1.63	3.07	4.26
Nonparticipating	2.44	2.96	5.43
		Surrender cost index	
Whole life insurance:			
Participating	−0.14	2.62	6.63
Nonparticipating	2.10	3.59	6.54
		Net payment cost index	
Participating	6.07	10.49	14.49
Nonparticipating	6.58	9.84	13.75

Illustrative rates shown assume a $100,000 face value policy issued to a male, age 25. Rates for females are generally lower. Rates quoted are per $1,000 of coverage.
SOURCE *Consumer Reports,* February and March, 1980.

in the illustration is only a small excerpt of the total data available in the report. It provides some guidance as to the relative costs of term and whole life policies in terms of net cost indexes. The *Consumer Reports* study (February and March 1980) also lists cost comparisons by company; it is an invaluable source of information for insurance shoppers. You should obtain and read carefully a copy of this report before buying any type of life insurance.

The most important conclusion you should draw from all the data presented here is that life insurance costs vary widely from company to company and from policy to policy. The intelligent purchaser of life insurance must plan purchases and research a potential company and policy very carefully. Life insurance is a long-term financial commitment that should be entered into with utmost care. Shopping wisely and carefully will pay substantial benefits for many years into the future.

Major life insurance policy provisions

When purchasing insurance, you must go through the chore of reading your policy carefully. A brief summary of major policy provisions is necessary. Much of the information that follows has been adapted from an Institute of Life Insurance publication entitled "Plain Talk about your Life Insurance Policy." This publication provides an excellent map to guide you through your life insurance policy.

Additional benefits

When you purchase a policy, you normally obtain a number of additional benefits that are attached to the basic policy as optional features known as *riders.* One such common benefit is the *waiver of premium benefit.* It states that the company will pay your premium payments for you if illness or accident prevents you from working. This benefit normally goes into effect six months after total disability.

A second common additional benefit is the *accidental death benefit,* also called a *double indemnity clause.* This additional benefit is paid to your beneficiary if you die as a result of an accident. It's called double indemnity because the benefit is most often written to pay double the face value of the policy in the event of an accidental death.

These additional benefits result in an added cost to the basic policy. The waiver of premium benefit is clearly desirable and should be purchased as a general rule. The accidental death benefit is questionable. If you have based your insurance planning on a careful needs analysis, your beneficiaries have no need for more insurance solely because of the manner of your death. Many people buy this coverage anyway because its cost is fairly low. It seems an attractive gamble with destiny. But it makes little economic sense and probably should be avoided.

Nonforfeiture rights

If you fail to pay your policy premium by the due date (i.e., the date by which the insurance company requires payment), you will normally be allowed about a month to make the payment without penalty. The exact length of this grace period varies from company to company. It is normally not less than 30 days. If no payment is made by the end of the grace period, the policy is said to lapse. However, if the policy is a cash value type policy, it still has value because of its nonforfeiture rights. Term insurance policies normally do not have any nonforfeiture rights.

Nonforfeiture rights are certain rights and values you cannot lose, or forfeit, even if the policy lapses. It is very important to know what the particular nonforfeiture rights of your policy are. If you should allow the policy to lapse, you will suffer an unnecessary loss if you do not exercise your nonforfeiture rights. You need to become familiar with four major nonforfeiture rights.

The first is your *reinstatement right.* If you can show that you are still in reasonably good health after the policy lapses, you can put the policy back in effect, that is, reinstate it, by paying the past due premiums, with interest. With most insurance companies, you can usually reinstate the policy for a period up to five years after it lapses.

A second important nonforfeiture right is the *surrender value* of your policy. After the policy lapses, if you choose not to reinstate it, you can cash surrender your policy. Cash surrender allows you to cash it in with the insurance company and obtain the policy's cash value. Every cash value policy will have a table in the policy listing the cash value of the policy per $1,000 of insurance at the anniversary date of the policy. Of course, you do not have to let the policy lapse before collecting the cash value. You can cash surrender the policy at any time simply by turning it in to the insurance company. You do not have to surrender the policy to get its cash value. You can borrow the cash value of the policy at a rate of interest provided for in the contract.

The third important nonforfeiture right is called the policy's *extended term value.* After the policy lapses, if you do not take the cash value, you can use the cash value of your policy to buy a fully paid-up term insurance policy with the same face value, which is good for a limited term. The length of the term is specified in a table in the policy. For example, if you allow a typical $10,000 whole life policy to lapse after ten years of payments the cash value would normally be sufficient to provide $10,000 worth of term insurance valid for a term of about 20 years. In most cases, if you do nothing after your policy lapses, the extended term option is automatic.

A final important nonforfeiture right is your policy's *reduced paid-up value.* This is the amount of insurance your cash value will buy that will remain in force for the remainder of your life without payment of any additional premium. On a typical $25,000 whole life policy, if lapse occurs after 10 years, the cash value will buy about $8,500 in paid-up insurance. This $8,500 in insurance remains in force for the rest of your life without any premium payments required. The exact amount of reduced paid-up insurance is specified in your contract.

Settlement options

In the event of the death of the insured, most policies offer one of five basic settlement options. Settlement options represent your choices as to how the proceeds of your insurance policy are to be paid to your beneficiary. They also can play an important role in retirement and estate planning. You can elect the means of settlement yourself or leave it up to your beneficiary to make after your death. The most common option is the *lump sum option,* whereby the face value of the policy, less any outstanding loans, is paid in one lump sum to the beneficiary. Unless you elect some other option, most policies automatically pay your beneficiary in a lump sum.

You can also elect an *income for life* option. Under this option the insurance company pays a lifetime income to your beneficiary. The amount of the payment depends on the beneficiary's age and the amount of the proceeds from the policy. In electing this option, the policy should provide for a minimum guaranteed payment period, for example, 10 years. If the beneficiary dies before the 10 years are up, a lump sum payment will be made to a person designated by the beneficiary. A table in the policy provides payment details.

You can also elect an *income for a specified period* option. This option provides your beneficiary with a regular monthly payment that draws on both the principal and interest over a stated period of time. This option is often used to provide a continuing family income when children are growing up. Once again, a table in the policy provides payment details.

The *income of a specified amount* option provides a regular payment of a chosen amount for as long as the policy proceeds plus interest last. Finally, the *interest only* option elects to leave the policy proceeds with the insurance company. The company then makes regular interest payments to the beneficiary. This option is sometimes elected to create a family fund for emergencies, college expenses, or other future needs. The family can collect the income and leave the principal proceeds intact.

One word of caution is in order in selecting your settlement options. Most life insurance companies pay relatively low rates of interest in calculating settlement options. If your beneficiary is capable of making independent savings and investment decisions, or has access to a reliable family or professional advisor, he or she may be far ahead financially by electing a lump sum settlement and investing the proceeds to provide a family income. Part 5 of this book will cover investment strategies in detail.

Other policy features   In addition to nonforfeiture rights and settlement options, there are a number of additional policy features of which you should be aware. A general understanding of your *policy rights* is one important consideration. Unless you make an *assignment* of your rights, (i.e., sign away some of your rights to someone else), you own the policy and control all aspects of it. This includes the right to change the beneficiary, the frequency of premium payment, the right to borrow on the policy, the choice of how death proceeds are to be paid, and the right to choose how dividends are to be used. You may also name a *contingent beneficiary,* that is, the next person to receive death proceeds in the event your beneficiary should die before you do. You can also split the proceeds between two or more beneficiaries.

Your policy also contains a number of other important clauses. The *incontestability clause* says that after the policy has been in force for a stated number of years, usually two years, the company loses the right to challenge any statement made in your application. Thus if you have misstated the nature of your health in the application, you are home free after two years. The *suicide clause* usually states that if you die by suicide within two years of buying the policy, the company will return only the premiums paid to your beneficiary. After two years the company will pay the death proceeds in full if death occurs because of suicide. Finally, the *age clause* says that if you misstated your age in the application, the company will pay the death proceeds that would have been paid for your correct age.

Two remaining items are of interest in reading your policy. The first is the *automatic premium loan,* which allows you to authorize the company to borrow against the cash value of your insurance to pay any premiums you fail to pay. The *dividend option* allows the election of taking your dividends in cash, using them to reduce your premiums, leaving them with the company in an interest bearing account, or buying more insurance with them.

Now that we have completed our exploration of the major considerations in selecting life insurance, we will conclude this chapter by returning to the case of Andy and Annette and completing their insurance plan. The final step is, of course, to select an appropriate policy or policies to protect the family against the financial impact of Andy's premature death.

Andy and Annette's insurance plan

Andy and Annette's family situation required approximately $295,000 in total insurance protection for Andy and a $25,000 policy for Annette. Group term insurance already provides $125,000 of Andy's needed amount. Andy thus needs to purchase an additional $170,000 in life insurance protection. His group term insurance offers an exceptionally good buy. It is a low-cost policy from the insurance company's point of view, and the cost is partially paid by Andy's employer. Andy's cost for $125,000 of coverage is only $450 per year.

The first policy Andy decides to buy is a decreasing term policy. The policy decreases in face value approximately in line with the decreasing balance on Andy and Annette's home mortgage. This type of policy, which is often called *mortgage insurance,* offers a very good value because the decreasing face value holds down the cost of the policy. This policy costs approximately $450 per year.

Andy still needs an additional $95,000 in life insurance. Because of his relatively high tax bracket, the savings features of whole life and the permanency of this insurance appeal to him. However, the cost of $95,000 in whole life is prohibitive. Andy decides to settle for $70,000

**Table 9–9
Andy's insurance plan**

	Face value	Annual cost
Group term insurance	$125,000	$ 450
Decreasing term ("mortgage insurance")	75,000	450
Term:		
Five-year, renewable		
and convertible	70,000	560
Whole life	25,000	500
Total needs and cost	$295,000	1,960
Less: first year dividend		220
Net cost (first year)*		$1,740

*Dividend will increase after the first year, and net cost will decline.

in five-year renewable and convertible term insurance and $25,000 in whole life. The term costs $560 per year and the whole life costs $500.

Andy's total need of $295,000 is thus met at a total annual cost of $1,960. This cost is partially offset by his dividends, since all policies other than the group policy are participating. His first year dividends of $220 will reduce his net cost to $1,740 per year, or $145 per month. After the first year, dividends will begin to increase, reducing his net cost further. Andy's insurance plan is summarized in Table 9–9.

To provide for Annette's insurance requirements, Andy and Annette settle on a 15-year level term policy in the amount of $25,000. This is the amount they had previously determined would be adequate to insure Annette's life. The policy is nonparticipating and costs $140 per year.

Summary

The primary purpose of life insurance is to replace income lost through premature death. A careful needs analysis should be undertaken to determine the amount of life insurance required to adequately protect your dependents. The needs analysis should consider family income needs, Social Security benefits, debt liquidation requirements, final expenses and estate taxes, an emergency fund for the family, and a college fund for the children, if required. An adequate plan should also provide for life insurance to replace the services of a spouse who is employed full-time as a homemaker.

There is a wide and even confusing variety of available insurance policies. Reduced to the bare essentials, most are variations of one of three basic policies: term, whole life, or endowment. Whole life and endowment policies build cash values and therefore have a built-in savings feature along with insurance protection. Term policies do not build cash values but offer much lower cost protection. For most young and growing families, term insurance is the only financially feasible means of protection. For most families an endowment policy is the worst possible choice of insurance coverage.

Life insurance cost comparisons are very difficult because of the variety of premium rates, dividend payment policies, cash value buildups, and the timing of these dollar streams. The insurance industry offers two cost comparison indexes that should be used when shopping for a policy. They are the net payment cost comparison index and the surrender cost comparison index. When comparing similar policies issued by different companies, the lowest index offers the best insurance value. Policies that pay dividends also provide you with an equivalent level annual dividend index.

In reading a life insurance policy, you need to become aware of a number of important benefits and rights associated with the policy. You should pay particular attention to the waiver of premium benefit, the accidental death benefit, your nonforfeiture rights, and your settlement options.

Appendix: Life insurance language guide

Accidental death benefit A provision that can be added to your policy which will provide an additional amount of money to your beneficiary if you die as a result of an accident. This is referred to as "double indemnity" when the amount of this provision is equal to the face value of your policy.

Agent A person who represents a life insurance company to sell life insurance and service life insurance contracts. Agents are sometimes referred to as "life underwriters."

Applicant The person who applies for life insurance by completing and returning an application. The "applicant" may or may not be the person who will be covered by the life insurance policy.

Annuitant A person who receives periodic payments from a life insurance company under an annuity contract. These periodic payments will often continue for as long as the person is alive.

Annuity A contract that will provide you with periodic income payments for a specific length of time. These payments could be for a certain number of years or for the life of the owner.

Aviation exclusion rider If you fly, and do not choose to pay the "Aviation Extra Premium," your life insurance policy will include this rider. If you die as a result of flying, your beneficiary will receive **only** the premiums that have been paid to the company.

Aviation extra premium An extra premium you pay to have protection if you fly for a living or a hobby. This premium covers you if you should die as a result of your flying. **Only** the basic policy and additional term riders can be protected. Accidental Death Benefits and Waiver of Premium Benefit are excluded from this protection by the extra premium—this is standard throughout the insurance industry.

Beneficiary The person who is designated by the owner of a life insurance contract to receive the policy proceeds when the insured dies.

Cash surrender value The amount of money you are guaranteed to receive if you decide to terminate your permanent life insurance policy before it becomes payable at death, or at maturity if it's an endowment policy. Only permanent policies build cash values; term plans don't.

Cash value of paid-up dividend additions If you decide to use your dividends to buy additional insurance, this insurance also builds a cash surrender value which will be paid to you if you decide to stop the policy. The "cash value" of your dividends increases each year and is never less than the amount of dividends used to purchase the additions.

Contingent beneficiary   The person designated by the owner of a life insurance contract to receive policy proceeds if there is no primary beneficiary living when the insured dies. Sometimes referred to as the "secondary beneficiary."

Contingent owner   The person who owns the life insurance policy in the event of the primary owner's death.

Convertible term insurance   A term insurance policy which allows you to exchange the policy for a whole life policy without having to prove that you are insurable.

Death proceeds   The amount of money that the beneficiary receives when the insured dies. This amount includes the face value of the policy, plus any dividends or dividend additions and/or accumulations credited to the policy.

Disability benefit   An option you can add to any life insurance policy to assure that the company will pay your premiums if you become totally and permanently disabled. The disability must last for at least six consecutive months to be considered permanent. The benefit is often referred to as Waiver of Premium.

Dividends   An amount of money which is refunded annually to the owner of a participating life insurance policy. The amount of the dividend depends upon the mortality, interest earned on investments and expense experience of the company. As the Owner, you may choose how you want to receive your "dividend." The most common choices are: (1) Paid in Cash; (2) Left with Company to Accumulate at Interest; (3) Used to Reduce the Next Year's Premium; or (4) Used to Purchase Additional Life Insurance. Dividends are not guaranteed.

Dividend accumulations   You can ask the company to hold your annual dividends and allow them to grow at the company's current interest rate compounded annually. The annual dividend is not regarded as income for income tax purposes since a dividend is considered to be a return of part of the premium that's already been paid. The interest earned on the dividend is taxable as income. When you die, both the face amount of the policy and the dividend accumulation account will be paid to your beneficiary.

Effective date   The date your life insurance becomes effective. Premiums for your policy are calculated from this date.

Endowment insurance   A type of life insurance that pays a stated death benefit if the insured dies within the specific number of years; or, pays the same amount to the owner if the insured outlives the length of the contract.

Extended term insurance   If you decide not to pay premiums any longer, you may use the cash value of the basic policy and your dividend account to buy a single premium term insurance policy for the same face amount as the basic policy. The length of the new term insurance policy will be for a certain number of years and days.

Face amount The amount stated in the policy that will be payable upon the death of the insured or, if an endowment, at the maturity date of the policy. This amount is subject to adjustments for dividends, extra benefits added to the policy (i.e., accidental death benefit, etc.) or any outstanding loans.

Family rider A provision that can be added to a whole life policy to insure your spouse and children, or just the children. Level term insurance covers the children until each child reaches age 25. At that time each child may buy up to ten times the original amount of term insurance in permanent insurance without having to prove insurability. The spouse's coverage is decreasing term insurance and expires when you are 65 years old.

Insurability option rider A provision that may be added to a permanent life insurance policy. This allows the insured to purchase additional life insurance policies at specified times without having to show insurability. The dates to buy additional insurance are usually ages 25, 28, 31, 34, 37 and 40. You may also buy it when you marry or when children are born.

Insured The person whose life is covered by a life insurance policy. The name of the "insured" is always shown on the first page of the policy.

Issue age The age used when calculating premiums for a life insurance policy. USAA Life's "issue age" is the age that you are at the time you apply, usually referred to as "age last birthday."

Lapsed policy A contract no longer in effect because the premium was not paid.

Level premium life insurance Any life insurance policy that requires the same amount of premium from year to year. This premium is more than the cost of protection during the earlier years of the contract and less than the actual cost during the later years of the contract. The overpayments during the earlier years, together with interest, balance out the underpayments in the later years.

Level term insurance Term life insurance protection that remains the same for a specified number of years—usually 5, 10, or 15 years. Your beneficiary will receive the death benefit if you die before the end of the protection period.

Limited payment life insurance A permanent life insurance policy in which premiums are paid for only a specified number of years or to a certain age, usually 65. The protection under the policy continues after the premium paying years are over.

Military aviation exclusion rider If you fly for military purposes and do not wish to pay the Aviation Extra Premium, your policy will include this rider. If you die as a result of military flying, then the company will pay your beneficiary **only** the premiums that have been paid.

Nonforfeiture option If you decide to stop paying premiums, you can take your cash value (if any) in one sum or use it as a single premium to buy either term insurance equal to the face amount of your policy or to buy a reduced amount of paid-up permanent life insurance.

Owner The person who has the right to request changes guaranteed by the policy (e.g., change of beneficiary).

Ordinary life insurance See permanent life insurance.

Participating life insurance Any life insurance policy that returns a dividend to the owner each year. Non-participating life insurance does not return an annual dividend to the owner. Dividends are not guaranteed.

Permanent life insurance A life insurance policy that continues to cover the insured for his lifetime. The premiums might be paid for the lifetime, or for a specified length of time, depending upon the type of policy bought. There are three words in the life insurance industry that are used interchangeably with Permanent: Ordinary, Straight and Whole Life.

Policy The printed legal document stating the terms of the insurance contract between the life insurance company and the owner.

Policy loan The owner of a permanent life insurance policy may make a loan from a life insurance company using the policy as the security. Interest is charged annually, and if not paid will increase the amount of the loan. The loan cannot be larger than the amount of the cash value of the policy. Any loans that are unpaid at the time of death of the insured are subtracted from the policy benefits.

Premium The amount of money the owner agrees to pay the insurance company to keep his insurance policy in force. The owner pays these premiums at specified times each year. The owner can pay his premiums annually, semi-annually, quarterly, or monthly.

Premium payor The person who has the responsibility of paying the premiums on a life insurance contract to the insurance company.

Reduced paid-up insurance If you decide not to pay premiums any longer you may use the cash value of the basic policy and your dividend account to buy a single premium whole life policy which will be in effect for as long as you live without any further premium payments. The whole life policy will be for a lesser amount of insurance than the original basic policy.

Renewable term insurance Life insurance which is in effect for a specified number of years that can be extended at the end of each term. When the contract is renewed the premiums increase because they are based on the age of the insured. No proof of insurability is required.

Settlement option You or your beneficiary have different choices (besides one lump sum) of how to receive life insurance proceeds. As owner of the policy you may make the choice or you may leave the decision up to your beneficiary. There are six different settlement options to select from.

Special class Paying a higher than standard premium for your life insurance policy due to health condition, flying status, etc.

Straight life insurance See permanent life insurance.

Supplementary contract An agreement between the life insurance company and the owner or beneficiary. The contract requests the company to retain the death benefit and make payments in accordance with the settlement option selected.

Underwriting The process by which the company determines whether or not to accept a person's application and to issue a policy. Items used to decide whether a person is insurable include occupation, health, avocation or hobbies and geographic location.

Whole life insurance See permanent life insurance.

SOURCE USSA Life Insurance Company, USAA Building, San Antonio, Texas 78288. Reproduced by permission.

10

Health, property, and liability insurance

- Health insurance
- Types of health insurance policies
- Important policy clauses
- Shopping for health insurance
- Disability insurance
- Homeowners property and liability insurance
- Homeowners insurance coverage limits
- Automobile property and liability insurance
- Summary

Suppose you have a good job, enjoy your work, and are planning to buy a house or a new car in the future. What would happen to your plans if you became sick or disabled? Would your income continue? If you buy a house or an automobile, how would you protect your property from loss caused by fire, accident, or theft? The assets you have acquired have been purchased with savings from income or from loans. If your goal is to increase your net worth and achieve financial independence, you must protect yourself with insurance. In this chapter we will discuss ways in which you can protect your income and assets through the purchase of health, property, and liability insurance. Proper insurance selection enables you to secure your long-run financial position and maximize your net worth.

Health insurance

Americans spend more than $200 billion a year on health care. Included in this total are public and private expenditures for personal health care, medical research, construction of medical facilities, administrative and health insurance costs, and government-sponsored public health activities. The total spending level is awesome, and the cost of health care is increasing faster than the cost of most other items. The average cost per day for a stay in the hospital is currently over $250. It is no exaggeration to say that most people cannot afford to get sick in America.

Figure 10–1 shows the rapid escalation of health care costs in the past decade. Most people protect themselves from these costs by buying some form of health insurance. They also purchase income disability insurance that pays them an income when they are sick and cannot work.

Your health and disability insurance policies may well be the most important policies you buy. They are certainly more important than life insurance or property insurance. Even if you should die without a dollar of life insurance, your dependents will probably find a way to survive by working and drawing Social Security benefits. If your property is destroyed, you can eventually replace it if you are healthy enough to continue working. But a major illness followed by a long period of disability can deal a financial blow from which you might never recover. Except for the fabulously wealthy, none of us can afford to be without health and disability insurance.

Nine out of 10 Americans under age 65 carry some kind of health insurance. Similarly 90 percent of all civilian workers are protected by some form of disability insurance. Most individuals purchase their insurance through their employer in the form of group insurance. Nearly all of this insurance is subsidized, either partially or fully, by the employer. In fact, group health insurance as a fringe benefit is so common that its absence would be considered most unusual.

Figure 10–1
Medical care cost index

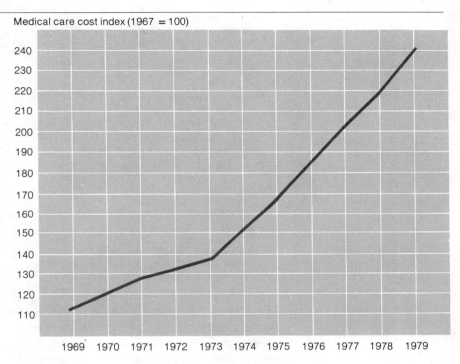

Medical care cost index (1967 = 100)

SOURCE   Department of Labor, Bureau of Labor Statistics.

Types of health insurance policies

There are five common types of health insurance or medical expense policies: hospital expense, surgical expense, physician's expense, major medical expense, and comprehensive medical insurance. The first three of these policies are often referred to as basic plans. In addition to these five common policies, a sixth policy, dental expense insurance, is becoming popular in the United States. Table 10–1 summarizes the types of policies available.

Hospital expense insurance

Hospital expense insurance covers the costs of hospital room and board and the usual charges for hospital services and supplies. Benefits payable under a hospital expense policy are normally expressed as a service-type benefit. A service-type benefit means that the policy provides the required service. For hospitalization insurance the service required is daily room and board in a hospital. Payment is made directly to the hospital by the insurance company. Most hospitalization policies pay the daily room and board cost of a semiprivate (two-person) room and board

Table 10–1
Health insurance summary

1. Hospital expense insurance:
   Hospital room and board.
   Hospital service and supplies.

2. Surgical expense insurance:
   Surgical procedures.
   Anesthetic.

3. Physician's expense insurance:
   Nonsurgical hospital care.
   Physician home or office visit.

4. Major medical insurance:
   Large, unpredictable medical expenses subject to deductibles and coinsurance.

5. Comprehensive medical insurance:
   Hospital expense.
   Surgical expense.
   Physician's expense.
   Major medical.

6. Dental expense insurance:
   Dental services and supplies.
   Examinations, fillings, extractions.
   Bridgework, dentures, oral surgery, root canal.
   Orthodontics.

charge of the hospital. The maximum benefit payable for other services and supplies is usually expressed as a multiple of the daily room and board charge. For example, a policy might specify that hospital services and supplies are paid up to a maximum of two times the daily room and board rate.

Some hospitalization policies provide direct reimbursement to the policyholder. If you have this kind of policy, you pay the hospital and are then reimbursed by the insurance company. This kind of policy normally specifies payment of the actual room and board charges up to some specified amount per day. If charges run over this specified daily maximum, you have to pay the extra cost yourself. With the current rapid inflation in health care costs, these charges could be fairly substantial. Because of this, a service-type policy is generally a better buy. If you do buy a direct reimbursement policy, however, you should be certain to increase the maximum as needed to keep pace with inflation.

Surgical expense insurance

Surgical expense insurance covers the cost of surgical procedures performed as a result of sickness or accident. This policy also covers the cost of anesthetics administered for a surgical procedure covered by the policy. Policy limits are generally expressed as covering the "usual, customary, and reasonable" cost of a surgical procedure. Your surgeon can tell you whether or not the fee for your operation falls within the usual, customary, and reasonable range for your policy. If the fee is not in this range, you will either have to pay the difference or select another surgeon.

Some policies specify payment limits in terms of a fixed-dollar amount for each type of operation. As in the case of medical expense insurance, inflation may cause a problem here. Since costs are escalating rapidly, you are probably better off with a usual, customary, and reasonable policy.

Physician's expense insurance

Physician's expense insurance is also known as "regular medical expense" insurance. It covers the cost of physicians' fees for nonsurgical care in a hospital, doctor's office, or in your home. Policy limits are normally expressed in terms of maximum payments for specific services. For example, the policy might specify a maximum reimbursement of $20 for an office visit to your doctor. Physician's expense insurance may also cover the cost of diagnostic X-rays and laboratory tests.

Medical expense, surgical expense, and physician's expense are commonly referred to as basic policies. If you experience a major illness, your medical costs might quite easily skyrocket well beyond the policy limits of your policy. To insure against this problem, you should buy a major medical expense insurance policy.

Major medical expense insurance

Major medical expense insurance is designed to pick up where basic policies leave off. Major medical provides large dollar amounts of coverage for unpredicted major medical expenses. This type of policy covers a wide range of medical charges with few limits on the types of charges covered. This policy acts as a supplement to the basic hospital-surgical-physician policies and pays expenses over and above the coverage of these policies.

The upper limit on major medical policies is climbing dramatically as a result of rapid inflation in medical costs. Where $25,000 to $50,000 limits were common less than 10 years ago, the majority of new policies have upper payment limits of $100,000 or higher. In fact, unlimited maximum benefits for major medical policies are becoming quite common. A $1,000,000 upper limit is not rare.

If you have the three basic policies, why would you need major medical? The answer to this question is quite simple. Many basic health plans place an upper limit on dollars payable for a given health service. It is quite probable that an extended hospital stay resulting from a major illness or accident could run up a bill far in excess of the amount payable from your basic policies. This is where major medical insurance takes over. Major medical insurance prevents a medical catastrophe from also becoming a financial catastrophe. Table 10–2 provides an illustration of a typical major medical policy that covers 80 percent of major medical expenses. This kind of coverage of such expenses is quite common.

Table 10–2
Combined benefits of major
medical and basic policies

1.	Hospital expense:		
	a.	$250 per day for 20 days	$5,000
	b.	Miscellaneous fees and services	1,500
	c.	Medication and laboratory tests	700
		Total hospital expenses	$6,200
2.	Surgical expenses:		
	a.	Surgeon's fees	1,800
	b.	Anesthetic	600
		Total surgical expenses	$2,400
3.	Physician's expense:		
	a.	Visits in hospital	700
		Total physician's fees	$ 700
		Total expenses	9,300
Payable under basic plans			4,500
Remainder due			$4,800
Payable under major medical			3,840
Balance paid by patient			$ 960

Comprehensive medical expense insurance

Comprehensive medical expense insurance does exactly what its name implies. It offers a single policy that combines the three basic plans and major medical into one package. This is an extremely popular plan, particularly for group insurance offered through employers. Such policies generally offer very good terms and very high limits on major medical. A major medical policy that pays 100 percent of major medical expenses instead of the customary 80 percent is also commonly available. Since most people buy health insurance through an employer-sponsored comprehensive plan, you may expect to encounter this type of policy.

Dental insurance

Dental insurance policies are becoming increasingly common. They have become especially popular as a fringe benefit for employees represented by a union. The basic, major medical, and comprehensive plans described above nearly always exclude normal dental work. These plans do, however, cover mouth and gum diseases and oral surgery in many cases. Dental insurance policies are designed to cover common dental expenses, such as X-rays, fillings, extractions, and orthodontic work.

Since dental expenses are very common and predictable, dental insurance is really more of a prepayment plan than an insurance plan. Nearly everyone incurs dental expenses, and insurance companies can predict these costs rather closely. Therefore, the cost of the insurance must be fairly close to the actual cost of dental work for most people. Because of this, a dental policy is not usually a very good buy unless it is offered as an employee fringe benefit. If it is available to you as a fringe benefit and is partially or wholly paid by your employer, you should certainly take it. However, if you would have to pay the entire cost on your own, you probably should not buy it.

There are two possible exceptions to this rule. First, if you find budgeting for dental expenses difficult, a dental plan may be helpful. A dental insurance policy can act as an effective means of forced payment. By prepaying through a dental insurance plan, you will at least be certain to get the care you need. You will also be forced to budget for it. The second possible exception is if you expect to have extraordinarily high dental expenses. In this case a prepaid dental plan at a fixed price may be a real bargain.

Special-purpose health insurance

You will probably run across advertisements for special-purpose policies such as accident insurance. These policies pay a flat sum of money for injuries or disabilities resulting from accidents. A typical policy may offer to pay a flat sum per day, say, $100, if you are injured and have to go to the hospital. Benefits may also be expressed as a lump sum. For example, the policy may pay $2,500 for the loss of an arm or leg. In general, these policies are a poor buy. You should plan on using your health insurance to cover such costs. In the event you are disabled by accident or illness, you should have a disability policy that will replace lost income.

Another special purpose policy, cancer insurance, has been advertised fairly widely in the last few years. But this policy is an even worse buy than accident insurance. It is ridiculous to think that you would need more insurance for a cancer-caused disability or illness than would be required if the cause were some other disease. You should plan your comprehensive coverage to anticipate any kind of disability or disease. Special-purpose policies have no place in a carefully designed health insurance program.

Important policy clauses

We must all face up to the rather tedious prospect of reading our health insurance contract. Even if you plan to purchase comprehensive group insurance through your employer, you should read your contract carefully. If only one plan is available, it is extremely important to understand exactly what the contract covers. If there are any coverage gaps, you will have to purchase a supplementary contract to fill them. It has also become commonplace for an employer to offer a choice among one or more plans. In this case you must read all the available contracts in order to make an intelligent choice. To make this decision, it is important for you to understand some of the more important policy provisions.

Deductible clause

Most health insurance policies have a deductible clause. This requires you to pay for first dollar coverage, say, the first $100 or $200 of covered expenses for a given year. The insurance company will pay the agreed amount above this level. This provision relieves the insurance company of the need to pay large numbers of small claims. Since processing large numbers of these claims is quite expensive, deductibles also save you money when you buy a policy. The higher the deductible, the lower the cost of your policy.

Deductible clauses vary widely among companies. The most liberal allow you to accumulate the deductible over the course of a year for all family members covered by a policy. This type of a deductible might require you to pay the first $100 per year of your family's medical expenses. Any additional expenses would be paid by the policy. A more restrictive policy might require you to pay the first $100 of expenses for each family member each year. Thus for a family of four, you could pay up to $400 for the four members in a year. An even more restrictive policy might allow less than a year to accumulate the deductible. If the deductible period were three months, for example, you would have to pay the first $100 of medical expenses incurred during each three-month period.

It is impossible to generalize about typical deductible clauses. The only certainty is that for any given insurance plan, a higher deductible will result in a lower cost. You should set your deductible at a level you feel you can afford if you or a member of your family should become ill.

Coinsurance

A coinsurance agreement is one of the most important clauses to look for in reading over your health insurance contract. It is a very common feature of a major medical contract. Coinsurance says that you and the insurance company jointly insure major medical expenses. The insurance company pays the largest share of the expense. A typical coinsurance agreement states that the insurance company will pay 80 percent of major medical expenses and that you will pay the remaining 20 percent. If you should incur a large medical bill, the coinsurance clause will result in a fairly substantial medical expense for you to pay. For example, a $20,000 major medical expense would not be unusual for major surgery and a long hospital stay. If your major medical insurance has an 80 percent coinsurance clause, the insurance policy would pay 80 percent, or $16,000 of the expense. You would have to pay the remaining $4,000.

Employer-sponsored comprehensive medical plans without a coinsurance clause are becoming popular. If one is available through your employer, you should go ahead and take it. If you have to choose between policies with and without coinsurance, you will find the policy without coinsurance more expensive. Since the insurance company's costs are higher if there is no coinsurance costs, your premium must also be higher. However, the extra cost is certainly justified as protection against a potentially devastating major medical expense.

Waiting periods

Health insurance policies almost always require a waiting period before certain medical treatments are covered. The waiting period simply says that some period of time must elapse after the policy is purchased before a specified illness or disability will be covered. This provision is designed to prevent people from postponing medical treatment until insurance can be bought. Nearly all comprehensive policies specify a 9- or 10-month waiting period before providing coverage for childbirth expenses.

Policy exclusions

When choosing among available policies, you should look carefully for clauses that exclude certain types of medical coverage. Nearly all policies exclude elective cosmetic surgery. Maternity benefits sometimes are excluded from policies, although employer-sponsored plans normally provide maternity benefits. If you have to pay for the insurance entirely on your own, however, maternity benefits may not be a good buy. Since maternity coverage is normally purchased only by couples who expect to have children, the cost is quite high. In fact, the cost may be equal to or greater than the cost of paying for maternity costs on your own. As in the case of dental insurance, the major advantage of paying for your own maternity coverage is as an aid to budgeting.

You should also watch out for exclusion of mental illness. If possible, you should not buy a policy with this provision. Finally, be sure your policy covers you worldwide and not just in the United States.

Renewability

You must also read carefully the renewability clause in your health insurance contract. Some contracts give the company the right to cancel your policy at their option. This is obviously an undesirable feature and should be avoided at all costs. You should buy a policy that guarantees renewability at your option. Otherwise, you run the risk of being left without health insurance when you need it most. This is an unacceptable risk.

Policy provision summary

In summary, what should you look for in a health insurance policy? In most cases you will be choosing a policy that is wholly or partially paid by your employer. You should read the contract carefully and purchase a plan that offers comprehensive health expense protection. If a comprehensive plan is not available, you will have to purchase a combination of basic and major medical policies. You should look for a policy with a very high or unlimited ceiling on dollars of coverage available.

You should select the highest deductible you can comfortably afford. If available, you should choose a policy that does not have a coinsurance clause. You should also pick a policy with the least restrictive exclusions and shortest waiting period. You should not buy a policy that allows cancellation at the option of the company.

If there are any gaps in your employer's health insurance plan, you will have to buy a separate individual policy to cover the gaps. If you have to buy insurance on your own, you should shop widely and carefully.

Shopping for health insurance

Adequate health insurance is expensive. It is nearly impossible to make any meaningful generalizations about health care costs because terms of coverage vary so widely. If you have to bear all of the cost of your health insurance, you should expect to pay $800 to $1,000 a year or more for an adequate comprehensive policy. Fortunately, most of us do not have to bear all of this cost because of the availability of employer-sponsored group insurance.

Group insurance

Group health insurance offers the same cost advantages as does group life insurance. Since only one master policy is issued to cover the entire group, administrative costs are minimized. These savings are passed on to you when you buy health insurance through a group. Most employers or other groups arrange a master policy through Blue Cross-Blue Shield or through a major private insurance company.

By far the largest savings to individuals buying group insurance is from employer subsidies. Most employer-sponsored group health programs are paid for partially or even fully by the employer. Employer-subsidized programs are so common that subsidized health insurance is regarded as a standard fringe benefit. Many employers now offer a choice among a variety of policies.

Blue Cross-Blue Shield

Blue Cross and Blue Shield are a group of affiliated health insurance organizations geographically dispersed around the United States. They are nonprofit organizations originated and supported by physicians that exist solely to provide health insurance to individuals and groups. There are about 70 Blue Cross and 80 Blue Shield organizations in the United States. Together, these organizations are the largest writers of group health insurance in the country. Blue Cross and Blue Shield write individual policies as well as group insurance. Under Blue Cross-Blue Shield guidelines, as few as two people may be considered a group for insurance purposes.

The Blue Cross portion of a Blue Cross-Blue Shield policy provides hospital expense insurance. This policy pays all hospital expenses, including room, board, lab fees, X rays, and so forth. Blue Shield provides the surgical expense insurance portion of the Blue Cross-Blue Shield policy. In addition to surgical expense, Blue Shield also covers a number of physician's fees not related to surgery. Major medical supplemental coverage is also available from Blue Cross-Blue Shield.

A standard Blue Shield contract pays surgical expenses on a scheduled basis. This means that Blue Shield has a schedule that lists the amount the policy will pay for a given type of surgical operation. An expanded Blue Shield contract is also available. The expanded contract will pay the usual, customary, and reasonable fee for a surgical operation. Your physician will have a copy of Blue Shield's usual, customary, and reasonable (UCR) fee schedule. If he or she is not willing to accept the Blue Shield fee as full payment, you will be asked to pay any extra fee. Blue Shield normally recommends that you do not sign any agreement to pay more than the UCR fee. Instead, you can refer the fee back to Blue Shield, which will negotiate with your physician for a reduced fee.

Private insurance companies

If you do not buy your health insurance coverage through an employer-sponsored plan or a nonprofit organization, you will have to carefully investigate the offerings of private insurance companies. As a rule of thumb, you should confine your search to large, well-known, multiline insurance companies. You will have to read the policies very carefully, paying particular attention to payment limits, exclusions, and waiting periods.

The best advice in regard to private plans is to shop widely and carefully. Investigate at least three plans from large, reputable companies, and compare the policy provisions carefully. You should then select the policy that provides the best coverage for the price. In comparing prices and benefits, bear in mind that the benefits are more important than the price. If there is a small price difference between policies, you should select the one with the best coverage, even if it is a bit more expensive. A major illness not covered by insurance could bankrupt you. A slightly higher annual premium is a small price to pay to protect yourself from this possibility.

Health maintenance organizations(HMOs)

Health maintenance organizations, or HMOs as they are called, are actually prepaid medical care plans. These organizations provide health care service directly to members by owning clinics and hospitals and employing physicians. The HMO supplies all your medical insurance needs directly. You normally are given a choice of the level of coverage you wish to buy and are charged a flat monthly fee. The broadest form of coverage includes everything from physician's fees and prescription medicine through major medical coverage.

HMOs are fairly expensive, and most members subscribe through an employer-sponsored plan. If your employer offers such a plan, you should consider it very carefully as an alternative to the more conventional forms of health care coverage. Most, if not all, major metropolitan areas have HMOs located in the area. They generally provide excellent service for the price.

As HMOs gained popularity in recent years, they were subjected to a variety of criticisms. One of the most common criticisms is that since the physicians are employees of the HMO, they do not have as strong an incentive to perform well as do doctors in private practice. There does not, however, seem to be any objective evidence to support this contention. Perhaps a more valid criticism is that HMOs do not offer a wide choice in selection of a personal physician. Most HMOs do allow you to select a staff doctor as your personal physician, but your choice is limited. Many people have a family physician with whom they are very comfortable. Therefore they would not be willing to switch to a HMO. This disadvantage is largely offset by the availability at the HMO of a duty doctor or duty nurse at night and on weekends.

Medicare

Medicare is a federally sponsored health care program for people aged 65 and older and for certain disabled Americans. It is financed by contributions of employers and employees through Social Security. There are two parts of the Medicare program. Part A, compulsory hospitalization insurance (HI), covers hospitalization expenses, nursing home care, and some nonhospital medical expenses. Part A is entirely financed by Social Security. Anyone aged 65 or over who is eligible for Social Security benefits is automatically covered by Medicare.

Part B of Medicare is a voluntary program partially financed by the federal government and partially financed by monthly payments from people who choose to join. Part B provides voluntary supplementary medical insurance (SMI), which pays for physician's services and some medical services and supplies not covered under part A. Part B pays 80 percent of covered medical and surgical charges above a $60 deductible amount. The individual cost of part B is $8.70 per month.

Medicaid

Medicaid was established under Title 19 of the Social Security Act. This program provides federal matching funds to states wishing to expand health care services offered under public assistance programs. Medicaid is designed to assist people who cannot afford to provide adequate health care for themselves. Persons eligible for Medicaid include people aged 65 or older, permanently disabled people aged 18 or over, and low-income families with children under age 21. Medicaid provides such services as hospital care, laboratory services, X-rays, nursing and home health services, family-planning services, and physician's services. All states except Arizona participate in the Medicaid program.

Mail-order health insurance

Our advice to you about mail-order health insurance is simple: don't buy it. This type of insurance, notable mainly for the extensive fine print in the contract, is often found advertised in the Sunday newspaper. The policies generally offer to pay a fixed dollar payment for every day you are in the hospital. However, the contracts are often full of exclusions and require a fairly long waiting period. The average length of a hospital stay in the United States is about eight days. However, many mail-order insurance policies specify cash hospitalization benefits to be paid on the 10th day. Thus, the probability of ever collecting on one of these policies is fairly small.

National health insurance

A national health insurance program sponsored by the federal government has been debated in the Congress for many years. Thus far, very little progress has been made in this direction. Medicare and Medicaid are very limited in scope and provide no benefits for the vast majority of Americans. A national health program will probably continue as a discussion topic for many years into the future. At this time it does not appear that any action will be taken soon. You therefore should depend on your own planning efforts without considering the possible impact of national health insurance.

Disability insurance

Adequate disability insurance protection may be even more important than adequate health and life insurance. Insurance experts and planners consider disability insurance a part of the health insurance package. In establishing your insurance budget planning priorities, you should give priority to health and disability insurance over any other type of insurance. If you are disabled by accident or illness, your normal income may be disrupted for many months and years, or even for life. Without health and disability insurance, your entire financial planning system can be destroyed. Disability insurance obviously cannot replace your health, but it can replace your income.

Social Security benefits

Disability insurance planning is not difficult. As is true for life insurance planning, Social Security is the bedrock on which your disability plan should be constructed. If you are employed by an organization that exempts you from participation in the Social Security system, then you should explore the alternative to Social Security provided by your employer. For example, the largest group of employees exempt from Social Security participation are civilian employees of the federal government. In place of Social Security, federal civilian employees are entitled to a variety of government-sponsored retirement, health, and disability benefits.

Under Social Security you are considered disabled if you have a severe mental or physical condition that prevents you from working and is expected to last for at least 12 months. Your Social Security payments would begin in the sixth full month of your disability and continue for as long as you are disabled. It is important to note that under this definition of disability, you must be unable to work at any occupation in order to receive payments. A more liberal interpretation of disability is desirable when purchasing a commercial disability policy.

The amount of disability payments under Social Security depends on the amount of money you have paid into the system and the number of years you have paid in. Monthly benefits for a disabled person range from $122 to $502.60, depending on age and past earnings. For disabled persons with dependents, monthly family benefit payments range from $183 to $879.60. To determine what your monthly benefits would be, contact your local Social Security office to check your individual account.

Workers' compensation

Workers' compensation benefits are state-sponsored programs that provide benefits to people disabled by illnesses or injuries incurred on their jobs. The rules for eligibility and the size of payments vary widely, depending on the state in which you live. If you are eligible for Social Security benefits, however, any workers' compensation benefits may be deducted from your Social Security payment. Payments are made only if you can prove that the disabling accident or illness is job-related. Disability insurance planning requires income replacement regardless of the cause of your disability. You should therefore ignore the possible impact of workers' compensation in your disability insurance planning.

Because of the wide variation in state laws governing workers' compensation, it is not possible to make any general statements about the benefits. If you are concerned, you should check with the workers' compensation office in your state.

Planning your disability insurance

Social Security payments are almost certainly inadequate to meet your total disability income needs. Disability payments under Social Security are fairly substantial for low- and middle-income people. For higher-income people, of course, Social Security disability payments would replace a much smaller percentage of income. But in any case these payments are only one important component in insurance planning.

**Table 10–3
Steve's disability insurance plan***

Current monthly income		$2,000
Less: tax savings		(400)
insurance premiums waived		(50)
Adjusted monthly income		1,550
Sources of replacement income:		
Spouse's part-time employment	$300	
Social Security payments	400	
Total replacement income		(700)
Balance needed from disability insurance		$ 850

* Includes federal, state, and Social Security taxes.

Table 10–3 illustrates a typical disability insurance plan for Steve, a married man in his middle 30s. Steve has a wife and three children who are dependent on him for support. His insurance objective is to preserve his family's standard of living if he should become disabled. Steve's current monthly income is $2,000. If he should become disabled, he would not have to replace all this income because he now pays taxes on the $2,000. Since disability income is tax-free, he only needs to replace the aftertax component of his current income. He now pays a total of $400 per month in federal, state, and Social Security taxes. He will not have to replace this $400 with disability income.

Steve also makes $50 per month in life insurance payments. All his policies have a waiver of premium benefit that waives payment of the premium in the event of disability. Therefore, he will not have to replace the income currently being used to pay these premiums. This $50 saving, along with the $400 tax saving, can be deducted from his current gross income to determine his adjusted monthly income. His adjusted monthly income, in this case $1,550, is the income that will need to be replaced if he is disabled.

Steve should next consider the likely sources of income available to replace the $1,550. Because there are three children at home, it will not be possible for his wife, Carol, to work full-time outside the home. However, she would be able to work part-time and could earn $300 per month after taxes. The second source of income is Social Security benefits. On the basis of Steve's age and past contributions to the Social Security system, he is eligible for a monthly benefit check of $400. This benefit, combined with Carol's earnings, reduces his insurance needs to $850 per month. So he will have to purchase insurance in this amount.

Disability insurance cost

It is difficult to generalize about the cost of a disability insurance policy. One of the most important cost variables is the length of the waiting period before disability payments begin. Most policies specify that you must be disabled for a certain number of days before any payments will be made from the policy. The waiting period may be as short as 30 days or as long as 180 or more days. The longer the waiting period, the less likely it is that you will ever receive any payments from the policy. You should pick a waiting period that is the longest time that you could comfortably replace your income from current assets.

Another key cost variable is the policy's definition of disability. Some policies have a very narrow definition of disability. They pay benefits only if you are unable to work at any job at all. This is the definition used for Social Security benefits. Other policies are very liberal, and define disability as being unable to perform your usual job. The difference is obviously important. The fact that you are unable to perform your current job as a watchmaker, for example, would not necessarily mean that you could not do office work. The more liberal your policy's definition of disability, the more expensive it will be.

The length of benefit payment is important in determining costs. Some policies pay benefits for a fixed number of years, some pay to age 65, and some pay for life. Your occupation is also a key cost variable. The cost of disability insurance would obviously be much higher for a construction worker than for a secretary. Your age and general state of health are additional factors to be considered. The better your health and the younger you are, the lower is the cost of your policy.

With all these factors to consider, it is easy to see why no general statement can be made about costs. To give some rough idea of the cost level, however, let's consider one example. A policy written by a private company for professional people provides disability income if an insured person is unable to perform his or her normal job. This particular policy covers a limited number of professional groups, such as lawyers, business executives, college professors, administrators, and so forth. A policy that provides $1,000 per month income after a 90-day waiting period would cost you about $400 per year.

Impact of inflation

In planning disability income, inflation is obviously a major concern. As the purchasing power of the dollar declines, the fixed income provided by most disability policies becomes less valuable. Some companies offer policies that increase payments along with increases in inflation. But these policies are in the minority. As noted in Chapter 9, Social Security benefits increase with inflation, which is some help. However, the bulk of your benefits will probably come from a disability policy.

Nearly all disability policies limit their maximum payment to no more than 60 percent of your current gross income. Policies normally also limit the total amount you can collect from all sources. If you have more than one policy, the combined policies will not pay a total of more than 60 percent of your gross income. The companies share this total in proportion to the amount of insurance you have purchased from each. Thus you cannot normally buy insurance of more than 60 percent even if you go to more than one company.

Once you have purchased a policy, most companies allow you to increase the amount of benefits payable up to some maximum total coverage. One common rule allows an increase in the benefit up to twice the original amount of the policy. Thus a policy paying $1,000 per month may be increased each year up to a maximum policy limit in benefit payments of $2,000 per month. The cost of the policy will increase along with the increased benefits.

Ideally you would want to buy a policy with benefits that increase each year with inflation. If you cannot buy such a policy, you should review and increase your coverage each year. Increasing your coverage each year to stay at or near 60 percent of your gross income is the next best choice.

Sources of disability insurance

About 90 percent of all civilian workers have disability insurance. Most people purchase this insurance through an employer-sponsored program. If you do not have an employer-sponsored program, you will have to purchase insurance from a private company. Most companies that sell health insurance also sell disability insurance. In fact, you may be able to buy disability insurance as part of your health insurance package.

You can also buy disability insurance through many life insurance companies. If you buy whole life, you can often buy disability insurance as a rider to your whole life policy. A typical policy might allow you to buy $100 in monthly disability benefits for every $1,000 in life insurance owned.

Regardless of where you buy your insurance, you should shop carefully. The same rules for carefully comparing costs and benefits of health insurance policies should be followed. Unfortunately another health insurance rule also applies: adequate disability insurance is expensive.

Homeowners property and liability insurance

Whether you rent a home or apartment or own your own home, property and liability insurance is an important component of your overall insurance plan. There are a number of forms of homeowners insurance. There is even a special form of policy for renters. Even though this policy is for people who rent, it is still called homeowners insurance.

In shopping for homeowners insurance, you can buy a number of separate policies or you can buy a comprehensive policy. For example, you might buy a fire insurance policy, a burglary and theft policy, a liability policy, and so forth. Instead of buying all these separate policies, you can buy a comprehensive policy that would protect you against all these risks and more. This type of package deal is what homeowners insurance offers. Most people prefer this package deal because it offers the broadest form of coverage at the best price. One comprehensive policy is almost always less expensive than a collection of individual policies.

Comprehensive homeowners policy

Comprehensive homeowners policies are available for one- and two-family personal residences, or *dwellings* as they are called in the policy. The policy covers the dwelling itself and any *appurtenant structures* on the property, such as a garage, toolshed, or other structure. The policy also insures your household furnishings and personal property. An important feature of personal property insurance is that the insurance is valid both at home and away from home. Thus, if your personal property is stolen or damaged, you are protected regardless of the location of the property. For example, one of the authors had a new pair of skis stolen at a ski resort. The loss was covered by his homeowners personal property insurance.

Another important feature of a homeowners policy is an additional living expense benefit. This benefit pays your added living expenses if damage to your home makes it necessary for you to live somewhere else temporarily. For example, if your home is severely damaged by smoke, you might have to live in a hotel while your home is being repaired. Your homeowners insurance policy would pay the difference between your normal living expenses and the cost of living in a hotel. Of course, there are limits on the total amount that the insurance company will pay. As we will see, these limits are keyed to the total amount for which your property is insured.

The number of perils against which your policy insures depends upon how broad a policy you choose to buy. The narrowest coverage is provided by what is called the Basic Form (HO–1) policy. This form insures you against the 11 perils identified in Figure 10–2. A broader form of coverage, called the Broad Form (HO–2), insures you against seven additional perils, which are also identified in Figure 10–2.

The broadest form of coverage is called the Comprehensive Form (HO–5). This insurance provides protection against loss or damage from all perils except for perils specifically excluded in the policy. All HO policies exclude loss or damage caused by flood, earthquake, war, and nuclear accidents. Additional perils may also be specifically excluded. Although the HO–5 policy is commonly referred to as an all-risks policy, it does not really insure you against all risks. You should read your policy carefully, and make certain that you understand which risks are excluded from your HO–5 policy.

Renters insurance

If you are a renter, a Tenants Form (HO–4) policy is available. This policy is also known as a Contents Broad Form policy. An HO–4 policy

Figure 10–2
Homeowners policy coverage

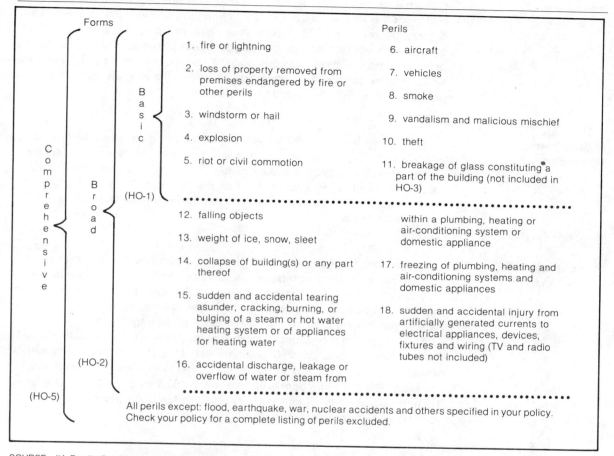

SOURCE "A Family Guide to Auto and Home Insurance," Insurance Information Institute, 1978, p. 16.

insures your household contents and personal property against virtually all the same perils as does the HO–2 Broad Form policy. This policy also provides coverage for additional living expenses and personal liability. An additional policy for homeowners is also available. This is called a Special Form (HO–3) policy. An HO–3 policy provides the same coverage for your dwelling and appurtenant structures as does the HO–5 Comprehensive Form policy. However, your personal belongings are afforded less coverage. They are insured only against perils identified in the HO–4 Tenants Form policy. The advantage of this policy is that you can reduce your annual premium by reducing your personal property coverage slightly. Your actual dwelling, however, will still have the broadest form of coverage available.

Condominium insurance

If you own a condominium apartment unit or townhouse, the condominium association normally buys a master property and liability insurance policy for the entire unit. A Condominium Unit Owners Form policy (HO–6) may be purchased to insure your personal property and household goods. This policy also will insure you against damage to any additions or alterations you make to your unit that are not insured by the association's master policy. The coverage is approximately the same as that provided by an HO–4 Tenants Form policy.

Mobile home insurance

If you own and occupy a mobile home that is at least 10 feet wide and 40 feet long, you can purchase a special mobile home insurance policy. This policy provides essentially the same coverage as an HO–2 Basic Form policy. Premiums for this policy are quite a bit higher than for a conventional home because of the greater possibility of wind damage to a mobile home.

Flood insurance

Up until about 15 years ago, you could not buy flood insurance for your home. Insurance companies would not sell flood insurance because only people who were likely to suffer flood damage would be willing to buy it. If only houses in flood-prone areas were insured, insurance companies would not be able to take advantage of risk spreading.

There is now a program available that is sponsored by the U.S. Department of Housing and Urban Development (HUD). If your community meets certain requirements, you can purchase flood insurance through the HUD program. The premium cost is approximately $35 for $15,000 of coverage. To find out whether or not you are eligible for flood insurance, contact your homeowners insurance agent.

Earthquake insurance

Earthquakes cause damage mainly in the Pacific Coast area of the United States, especially in California. They can strike in many other parts of the United States as well, and most families are not insured against this type of damage. Earthquake insurance is specifically excluded from an HO–5 Comprehensive Form policy. However, it can be purchased as an addition to a homeowners policy. In most areas of the country, the cost is fairly small.

Liability insurance

Liability insurance protects you against losses due to a lawsuit or claim against you for accidental injury to another person or damage to their property. This coverage applies whether the damage or injury occurs in your home or away from home. A liability policy covers you for physical damages arising from most causes except automobile accidents. You must buy separate coverage for automobile accidents as part of your automobile insurance package.

Liability insurance is automatically included as part of your homeowners insurance policy. All forms of homeowners policies include liability coverage that protects you and any family members who live with you. The coverage also extends to damage which might be caused by your pets. The standard insurance provisions include personal liability insurance, medical payments to others, and several supplementary coverages for physical damage to other people's property.

If you should accidentally injure another person or someone should be accidentally injured on your property, you could be financially devastated. Suppose, for example, that your newspaper carrier steps in a hole on your property and suffers a serious back injury. You could be sued for a large sum of money that might exhaust all your assets and even place a claim against your future earnings. A personal liability policy protects you from loss by paying for your legal defense in a lawsuit and paying any subsequent judgement against you. Of course, the policy pays only up to the limit of the coverage you elect to buy. Your homeowners policy automatically covers you for a minimum of $25,000, but you can buy higher limits. Given a society where lawsuits and large dollar settlements are becoming increasingly common, a large limit seems advisable. Since liability insurance is relatively inexpensive, a policy limit of $100,000 or more is not unreasonable.

Medical payments coverage provides for payment of medical expenses for persons accidentally injured by you or on your property. Like liability coverage, this insurance covers you, members of your family, and injuries caused by pets. Your homeowners policy automatically includes coverage up to $500 per person, but you can buy larger amounts. Once again, accounting for inflation is important in selecting your coverage limits. Medical payments coverage of $2,000 should be considered.

Unlike liability insurance, medical payments coverage makes payments regardless of who is at fault. If you or members of your family accidentally injure someone, medical payments coverage will pay that person's medical expenses immediately. You do not have to be adjudged at fault for the accident for this payment to be made. If, however, the injured person later sues you for additional damages, liability coverage immediately pays your legal defense fees. No liability payments will be made, however, unless a court finds you legally liable for damages. In essence, medical payments insurance provides immediate payment for minor injuries. Liability insurance provides coverage for major payments stemming from a lawsuit.

Supplementary coverage on your homeowners policy pays for minor damage to someone else's property. This insurance covers you and your family members, regardless of who is at fault. Damage caused by children under age 13 is covered, even if intentional. If you or your child should hit a baseball through your neighbor's picture window, for example, your policy would pay for the damage. The maximum amount payable for any one accident is $250.

Homeowners insurance coverage limits

If you should suffer a total loss of your home, homeowners insurance will pay no more than the market value of your property. Thus there is obviously no need to insure your property for more than its actual value. However, there are two good reasons to insure your property up to its full value. First, the rapid increase in the value of property makes full value insurance almost mandatory. If your home should be completely destroyed by fire, the replacement cost would be quite high. It would almost certainly be higher than what you originally paid for the house. If you are not insured to full value, your share of the replacement cost could be financially devastating.

Impact of inflation

You should review your policy annually to insure that your coverage limits are keeping up with inflation. Most insurance companies now offer an inflation guard endoresment on a homeowners policy. This endorsement automatically increases the amount of insurance on your home each year. However, there is some danger in relying on this endorsement to keep pace with inflation. On a typical policy, the inflation guard increases your coverage by 3 or 4 percent per year. With inflation in property values running at 10 percent or more per year in many parts of the country, a 3 or 4 percent automatic increase is obviously inadequate to keep up with inflation. Therefore, whether or not you have inflation guard, you should still review your policy annually.

Coinsurance

There is a second good reason to insure for full value. This is because of a unique coinsurance feature of all homeowners policies. If you should suffer a partial loss, your insurance company pays the full amount of the loss only if you have insured your home for at least 80 percent of its replacement value. If you are not insured for at least 80 percent, you will have to share any partial loss with the insurance company. The amount you would share is determined according to the ratio of your insurance coverage to the required 80 percent limit. For example, if your home is worth $60,000, 80 percent of this value is $48,000. If you carry only $40,000 insurance, the insurance company would only pay 83.3 percent ($40,000/$48,000) of any partial loss.

You should insure your home for at least 80 percent of its value to avoid this coinsurance clause. The additional cost to insure for full value

Table 10–4
Sample homeowners insurance
coverage limits

Property coverage: Policy limits
  Dwelling $60,000
  Appurtenant private structures . . . . .   6,000 (10% of dwelling)
  Personal property . . . .   30,000 (50% of dwelling)
  Additional living expenses . . . .   12,000 (20% of dwelling)
Liability coverage:
  Personal liability . . . . $25,000 (each occurence)*
  Medical payments . . . .   500 (each person)*
  Property damage . . . .   250 (each occurence)

* Larger amounts are available

SOURCE   Adapted from "A Family Guide to Auto and Home Insurance," Insurance Information Institute, 1978, p. 24.

is fairly small. Given the necessity of constantly keeping pace with inflationary increases in the value of your home, insuring to full value seems worth the added cost.

The property insurance coverage limits you select for your home automatically determine some of your other coverage limits. The dollar coverage for appurtenant private structures, personal property, and additional living expenses is determined as a percentage of the amount of insurance on your dwelling. Appurtenant private structures are insured for 10 percent of the dwelling insurance. Personal property is insured for 50 percent of the dwelling, and the allowance for additional living expenses is set at 20 percent of the dwelling insurance.

As noted earlier, minimum levels of coverage for personal liability and medical payments coverage are automatically included in your homeowners policy. These minimum coverage levels are not set as a fixed percentage of your dwelling insurance. The minimum coverage of $25,000 for personal liability and $500 for medical payments may not be adequate in these inflationary times. The higher limits suggested earlier should be seriously considered. Table 10–4 presents a summary of the coverage limits for a hypothetical home that is insured for its full value of $60,000.

Cost of homeowners
insurance

In comparison to other types of insurance, homeowners insurance is relatively inexpensive. The chart in Table 10–5 illustrates the cost of insurance for our hypothetical $60,000 home. Of course, costs vary according to the type of construction, the location of the home, and the company from whom the policy is purchased. The costs illustrated in the exhibit are for a frame home located in a midwestern city. As you can see from the table, insurance costs are quite modest in relation to the large dollar value of insurance coverage purchased.

Table 10–5
Illustrative homeowners insurance costs

Coverage	Cost per year	Cost per month
Basic Form (11 perils)	$290	$24.40
Broad Form (18 perils)	$330	$27.80
Special Form (dwelling: "all risk") (personal property: 18 perils)	$336	$28.00
Comprehensive Form ("all risk")	$480	$40.00

All policies assume $100 deductible.
SOURCE   Adapted from "A Family Guide to Auto and Home Insurance," Insurance Information Institute, 1978, p. 24.

Supplementary property insurance

Many people buy a supplementary personal property insurance policy in addition to the basic homeowners policy. The reason for this is that a homeowners policy always has some dollar limitation on the amount payable for loss or damage to high-cost items. These limitations normally apply to watches, jewelry, cameras, silverware, furs, antiques, coins, and so forth. A separate policy that insures these items for full value is often necessary. As noted in Chapter 8, such a policy provides a list or schedule of items insured by the policy. Such policies are therefore referred to as *scheduled personal property insurance*. These policies are also sometimes called *personal articles floater policies*. The personal property insurance portion of a homeowners policy is often referred to as *unscheduled personal property insurance*.

The cost of a scheduled personal property insurance policy is quite low. For example, a policy insuring $5,000 worth of scheduled personal property generally costs about $60 per year. If you own any items that qualify as scheduled personal property, you should certainly buy such a policy.

Whether you rely on your homeowners policy exclusively or buy an additional policy, an accurate inventory of your personal property is important. In the event of loss or damage, an inventory assists you in filing a quick and accurate claim. For example, if your home should burn to the ground, it would be almost impossible to remember every item of personal property in the home. An accurate inventory would make it possible for you to obtain payment for all the items that were destroyed or damaged. The inventory should be kept in your safe-deposit box or a fireproof file.

Supplementary liability insurance

In addition to the liability insurance provided by your homeowners policy, you will also need to purchase automobile liability insurance. This insurance is part of a standard automobile insurance policy. Automobile insurance details are provided in the concluding section of this chapter. A third type of liability coverage has also achieved increased popularity in recent years. This type of policy is called *personal catastrophe insurance* or *umbrella liability insurance.*

An umbrella liability policy acts as a supplement to the liability insurance coverage provided by your homeowners and automobile insurance policies. This policy expands your coverage to include more potential sources of liability, such as slander or libel. It also expands the dollar amount of your coverage in the same way that major medical insurance expands the dollar amount of your medical coverage.

Most insurance companies write umbrella policies in minimum amounts of $1,000,000. In addition, they almost always require you to have at least $50,000 worth of comprehensive liability insurance in your homeowners policy. On your automobile insurance policy, you are required to have bodily liability insurance of at least $250,000 per person ($500,000 per accident) and property liability insurance of at least $25,000.

Umbrella liability insurance is relatively inexpensive. You can buy a $1,000,000 policy for less than $100 in most states. Determining a reasonable coverage limit is quite difficult, however. A personal liability lawsuit could potentially wipe out all of your personal net worth as well as make a claim on your future earnings. Depending on your personal asset and income situation, you may want to purchase anywhere from $1,000,000 to $5,000,000 in coverage. Given the relatively low cost, a $1,000,000 policy seems quite reasonable.

A final liability policy is of limited interest to certain professions, such as law or medicine. This is a special form of personal catastrophe insurance called *malpractice insurance.* It provides insurance against a major lawsuit related to a person's professional practice. Malpractice insurance is very expensive but indispensable for people in sensitive professions.

Automobile property and liability insurance

If you own an automobile, automobile property and liability insurance is an absolute necessity. Not only is auto insurance required under the law in most states, but driving without it would be sheer stupidity. The cost of property damage and injury as a result of automobile accidents in the United States is about $150 million *per day.* Driving without automobile insurance could expose you to a potentially devastating lawsuit from which you might never recover. Most drivers buy a comprehensive policy that includes the following six major coverages: bodily injury liability, property damage liability, medical payments, uninsured motorists protection, collision, and comprehensive physical damages. Of the six coverages, bodily injury and property damage liability are the most important.

Bodily injury liability

Bodily injury liability provides liability coverage for injuries or deaths stemming from an automobile accident. This insurance covers you, members of your family, and other people who drive your car with your permission. You and members of your family are also covered when driving someone else's car with the owner's permission. Like your homeowners liability insurance, this policy provides funds for your legal defense if you are sued. If you are judged legally liable for an injury or death, the policy pays the damages assessed against you up to the limit of your policy coverage.

Bodily injury liability coverage is stated in terms of the amount of insurance available for any one person injured in an accident and the total amount payable to all people injured in an accident. Insurance quoted as 25/50 (25, 50) would provide a maximum of $25,000 to any single person injured or killed in an accident. A maximum of $50,000 would be provided for all people injured in any one accident. Most states require bodily injury coverage of at least $10,000 per person and $20,000 per accident (10/20). Many states require more than that amount. Your insurance company or state department of motor vehicles can tell you what the required minimum is in your state.

Property damage liability

Property damage liability is the second type of liability coverage needed in your automobile insurance package. Like bodily injury liability, this coverage applies to you, members of your family, and others who drive your car with your permission. Property damage liability provides funds for legal defense and payment for damages done by your car for which you are legally liable. This includes damage to other people's cars and other property, such as buildings, telephone poles, trees, and so forth. Property damage liability does not cover damage to your own car. Damage to your own car is covered under the collision insurance section of your policy.

Most states require some minimum level of property damage liability insurance. Many states require a minimum of $5,000 insurance, although some states require a higher limit. Property damage liability insurance is often referred to in conjunction with the limits on your bodily injury liability policy. Thus, a 25/50/10 policy refers to $25,000 bodily injury liability per person, $50,000 bodily injury liability per accident, and $10,000 property damage liability. This policy would be referred to as a 25, 50, and 10 liability policy.

Medical payments insurance

Medical payments insurance pays your medical expenses if you are injured in an automobile accident. It also pays the medical expenses of any member of your family who is similarly injured or any guests in your car who are injured. Unlike bodily injury liability, you do not have to be judged at fault for the accident to be paid under medical payments insurance. The reason for this is that bodily injury liability insurance pays for injuries to other people for which you are at fault and declared legally liable. Medical payments insurance pays for your own medical expenses. If someone else is responsible for the accident, medical payments coverage pays for your medical costs immediately. Your insurance company then recovers this expense from the other party.

Medical payments insurance is sold in minimum amounts of $500, but most people need a higher amount of coverage. In selecting your coverage limits, you should consider the medical payments coverage available for you and your family through your health insurance policy. You want to be certain that adequate coverage is available, but you also do not want to pay for duplicate coverage. A $5,000 limit is probably adequate for most people.

Uninsured motorists protection

Uninsured motorists protection provides payment for medical expenses resulting from an accident caused by an uninsured driver. This protection applies to you, members of your family, and guests in your car. It also covers you and members of your family if you are injured while riding in someone else's car or hit by a car while walking.

It is important for you to have uninsured motorists protection as part of your automobile insurance package. Not all states require everyone who operates a motor vehicle to have auto insurance. In some states a driver can pay an uninsured motorists fee instead of showing proof of insurance. In such states there will always be some drivers on the road who choose to drive without automobile insurance. Also, even in the majority of states where auto insurance is required, there are always some people who break the law. You might become involved in an accident with someone who does not have automobile insurance.

Uninsured motorists coverage is generally sold to provide payment up to the amount specified by the state's financial responsibility law. Every state has a financial responsibility law. The law simply states that if you are involved in an automobile accident causing substantial damages, you must present proof of your ability to pay these damages. The maximum amount you must be able to pay varies according to each state's law. Most people meet this requirement by showing proof of insurance. Without insurance, you would have to show proof of adequate personal wealth to pay damages.

Coverage above the minimum required by the state's financial responsibility law may also be purchased. You should be certain to buy an amount of coverage adequate to pay medical expenses and property damage in the event of an accident. Coverage of at least $10,000 should be considered.

Collision insurance

Collision insurance pays the cost of repairing damages inflicted on your car in an automobile accident. It pays for these damages regardless of who is at fault for the accident. If the accident involves another motor vehicle, your insurance company collects from the other driver's insurance company if the other driver is responsible for the accident. This procedure is very convenient because you can have your car repaired immediately, even if you believe that the other driver will ultimately be judged legally liable for the damages. Without collision insurance, you would have to wait until liability was established before you could collect the repair costs from the other driver.

Collision insurance is normally sold on a deductible basis. Most policies are written with a minimum deductible of $100 on collision insurance. This prevents people from filing small claims for very minor damages. It also reduces the cost of collision insurance. Many people buy an even higher deductible limit. The reason for this is that collision insurance is relatively expensive. The higher the deductible, the lower is the policy premium. You should carefully consider how much risk you can afford to take when selecting your collision coverage.

A second cost consideration for collision insurance is the make, model, and year of your car. Newer, more expensive cars naturally cost more to repair than older, less expensive cars. Therefore, collision insurance on a more valuable car is much more expensive than on a less valuable car. In fact, as your car gets older, there comes a point where you may not want to pay for any collision insurance at all. If you own a car that has a very low market value, you may want to consider doing without collision insurance.

Comprehensive physical damage

Comprehensive physical damage insurance pays the cost of damages resulting from causes other than automobile accidents. Perils insured against include such things as fire, theft, glass breakage, hail or wind damage, vandalism, collision with a bird or animal, and so forth. The cost of comprehensive physical damage insurance varies widely according to the area of the country in which you live. Earthquake damage, for example, is much more likely in San Francisco than in New York. Similarly hailstorm damage is more common in the Midwest than in the South. Premiums vary accordingly.

Like collision insurance, comprehensive physical damage insurance is normally sold with a deductible. A $50 or $100 deductible is common, although higher deductibles are available. Full comprehensive (i.e., no deductible) is also available. Also, like collision insurance, you should balance the cost of the insurance against the value of your car. If you are driving a brand new Porsche, you may well want to consider full comprehensive. If, on the other hand, you own a 1967 Chevy, you may not need any collision or comprehensive insurance.

No fault insurance

Table 10–6 summarizes the various categories of automobile insurance policies available and their applicability. In addition to this traditional type

Table 10–6
Automobile insurance summary

	Principal applications	
Coverages	Policyholder	Other persons
Bodily injury:		
Bodily injury liability	No	Yes
Medical payments	Yes	Yes
Protection against uninsured motorists	Yes	Yes
	Policyholder's Automobile	Property of others
Property Damage:		
Property Damage Liability	No	Yes
Comprehensive Physical Damage	Yes	No
Collision	Yes	No

SOURCE "A Family Guide to Auto and Home Insurance," Insurance Information Institute," 1978, p. 6.

of automobile insurance, some states have now enacted *no fault automobile insurance.* During recent years the traditional auto insurance system has been subjected to a good deal of criticism. Most of this criticism was aimed at the expensive and time consuming process of determining who was legally liable (at fault) for damages suffered in an automobile accident. The process of suing or being sued is very expensive, and final settlements often take years. In addition, jury awards vary widely and sometimes bear no relationship to the actual amount of damages suffered. As an approach to solving some of these problems, several states have passed no fault legislation.

Essentially, no fault insurance requires that the cost of property damages and personal injuries be paid by the injured party's insurance company, regardless of who is at fault for the accident. In theory, this procedure should eliminate the need for long and expensive court proceedings. In practice, injured parties are free to sue to recover real or perceived damages above the maximum payable under the state's no fault legislation.

Since no fault legislation is passed by the states, the provisions vary widely among the states in which no fault legislation is in effect. In general, however, nearly all states prescribe some maximum payment amount for medical expenses and loss of income. They also prescribe the conditions that would give an injured party the right to sue. Such conditions normally include death, permanent injury, or disfigurement. In buying insurance for your car, it is obviously important to know whether or not your state is a no fault state. Your insurance agent or state department of motor vehicles can provide necessary details.

Cost of automobile insurance

The cost of automobile insurance varies widely according to geographic location, age and driving record of drivers, type of car, and so forth.

Because of these many factors, it is very difficult to generalize about the cost of auto insurance. However, a few guidelines can be established.

One general consideration relates to the comparative costs of automobile insurance. As the data in Table 10–7 show, the cost of auto insurance does not generally increase in proportion to the amount of coverage purchased. In fact, the cost of increasing your policy limits is quite small in relation to the increased coverage for bodily injury and property damage liability. For example, increasing your bodily injury coverage from 10/20 to 100/300, an increase of a factor of 15, less than doubles the cost of the policy. Similarly the data indicate that you can increase your property damage liability insurance by five times (from $5,000 to $25,000) at a cost increase of only 7.5 percent. This information certainly should be carefully considered when selecting liability coverage limits.

A second general consideration can be seen in Figure 10–3. These data clearly show that the age and sex of the driver play a major role in determining insurance premiums. In general, young, unmarried, male operators pay the highest rates for automobile insurance. The reason is that young, unmarried males have very high accident rates. Rates decline rather sharply as male drivers approach the age of 30 or get married. Married males pay about the same rates as married females.

A number of other factors also influence automobile insurance rates. Your individual driving record is, of course, a key consideration. A driver with a clean record pays lower rates than one with a record of accidents and moving violations. High-performance or "muscle" cars are also charged a premium in most cases.

Table 10–7
Automobile insurance comparative costs

Comparative costs of bodily injury liability:

In an area where	10/20	costs	$55 per year
you can buy	25/50	for	$76 per year
and	50/100	for	$90 per year
or	100/300	for	$104 per year

Comparative costs of property damage liability:

In an area where	$5,000	costs	$67 per year
you can buy	$10,000	for	$70 per year
and	$25,000	for	$72 per year

Comparative costs of medical payments insurance:

In an area where	$500	coverage costs	$8 per year
you can buy	$1,000	coverage for	$10 per year
and	$2,000	coverage for	$12 per year
or	$5,000	coverage for	$15 per year
or	$10,000	coverage for	$23 per year

SOURCE "A Family Guide to Auto and Home Insurance," Insurance Information Institute," 1978, pp. 4–5.

Figure 10–3
Insurance rates and driver age*

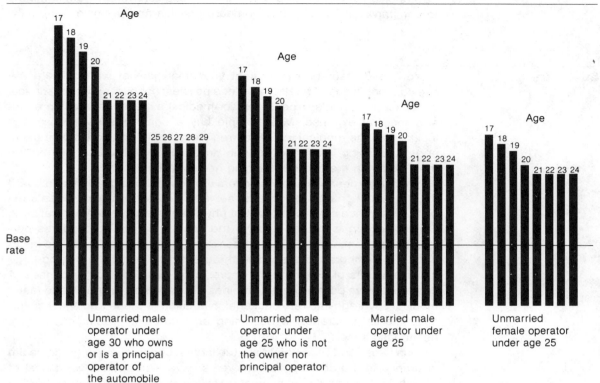

*Based on a driver classification plan used by a large segment of the business in many states. These comparisons of gradations are for private passenger cars used for pleasure where all operators have "clean" driving records. Adjustments in premiums are made for cars used to drive to work, used for business, or used on a farm. Adjustments are also made for youthful operators with driver training credit, drivers with "unclean" driving records, and owners of more than one car. In many states, premium discounts are available to students with outstanding scholastic records.

SOURCE "A Family Guide to Auto and Home Insurance," Insurance Information Institute, 1978, p. 10.

Discounts from base rates are also available. Most families who insure more than one car on the same policy are eligible for a discount on insurance premiums for multiple cars. Many insurance companies offer discounts for people who have completed a driver education course or a defensive driving course. A number of companies are now offering good student discounts to high-school and college students with a B or better average. Discounts are also available to families where a youthful driver is a resident student at a school or college away from home. At the other end of the age spectrum, many companies offer senior citizen discounts to drivers over age 65.

Overall, it would seem that the only valid generalization about auto insurance rates is that it is not possible to generalize. Rates vary widely and are dependent on a number of factors. As is true for all kinds of insurance, you should shop wisely. Rates also vary widely from company to company, and you should compare policies and premiums carefully.

Summary

You need insurance to protect your financial net worth. There are five common types of health insurance policies: hospital expense, surgical expense, physician's expense, major medical expense, and comprehensive medical expense. Most people buy a comprehensive policy that includes all the medical insurance requirements in one convenient package. Purchasing insurance through an employer-subsidized plan is the most common method of obtaining health care insurance.

Hospital expense insurance covers the cost of hospital room and board and the usual charge for hospital services and supplies. Physician's expense insurance covers the cost of physicians' fees for nonsurgical care. Surgical expense insurance pays the cost of surgical procedures performed as the result of illness or accident. Major medical expense insurance supplements the preceding three basic policies by providing large dollar amounts of coverage for unpredicted major medical expenses. A comprehensive policy simply combines the three basic policies and major medical coverage into one package. In addition to these traditional coverages, dental insurance is becoming an increasingly common form of health insurance.

Blue Cross and Blue Shield are the largest underwriters of group health insurance in the country. Recent years have also seen a good deal of growth in the popularity of health maintenance organizations (HMOs) that provide prepaid medical care plans. For older Americans, Medicare and Medicaid provide substantial medical benefits.

Disability insurance replaces lost income if you are disabled by accident or illness. Social Security plays a key role in most people's disability insurance planning. Like health insurance, most people purchase this insurance through an employer-sponsored program.

Homeowners property and liability insurance protects you against a large number of potential perils affecting your home and personal property. The liability insurance portion of this policy protects you against potential lawsuits involving claims against you for accidental injury to another person or damage to their property.

Automobile property and liability insurance protects you against loss of property through damage to your automobile. It also provides liability insurance protection against possible claims against you arising out of an automobile accident. Most drivers buy a comprehensive policy that provides six major coverages: bodily injury liability, property damage liability, medical payments, uninsured motorists protection, collision insurance, and comprehensive physical damage insurance.

PART 5

Investing for the future

11

Investment risks, financial prerequisites, and investment alternatives

- Some questions about putting savings to work
- The search for investments—the investment process
- Investment risks
- Can you accept the risks of investment?
- Applying the tests to Bob and Shirley
- Knowledge of investment alternatives
- Sources of information
- Summary
- Appendix: A glossary of investment terms

Your financial goal is to increase your wealth over time. You do this by saving first and then investing in more profitable investments. We discussed the difference between saving and investment in Chapter 4. You should save in order to establish an emergency fund and to work toward short-term financial goals. Your investments, on the other hand, should be more oriented toward the long term. This long-term orientation allows you to assume more risk in your investment program than you can accept in your savings program. In return for this increased risk, you can earn a higher rate of return on your investments.

In this chapter we will suggest some questions you should raise in attempting to put your savings into more profitable investments. The risks of investments are discussed along with the financial condition you should achieve before you consider more risky investments. We apply these standards against the financial condition of a young couple, Shirley and Bob, so that you may see how the standards are applied in a practical setting.[1]

Some questions about putting savings to work

In Chapter 4 you learned where you could put your savings to earn interest while you accumulated a large enough amount of money to invest in more profitable (and more risky) investments. You have to work hard to save. You have to discipline yourself to give up some consumer goods so that you will have more future wealth and financial independence.

It is difficult to save when you are constantly being bombarded by "sellers' hype." A major publisher, we are told, has a new and excellent set of books just off the press that will enlighten and educate us. A large auto company offers us a $300 rebate to buy a new car. A major airline provides us with a bargain air fare to escape to "sun land" for the time of our lives. Radio and TV constantly offer us wonderous bargains that will make us happier. Even when you go on vacation to relax and get away from it all, as you lie in the sand looking skyward, your reverie is broken suddenly by a low-flying airplane trailing a long snakelike mesh sign. The sign tells you to hurry to a local discount house to take advantage of new low prices. Most of the time you could do without these products and services. But you must force yourself to resist their appeal because everyone doesn't believe that happiness is a six-figure bank account or 1,000 shares of IBM.

If you have been fortunate enough to save a goodly sum of money, you reach a point where you seek investments that are more profitable than a savings account, yet not so risky that you might lose all your hard-saved dollars. Two things will happen when you build up a large

---

[1] The appendix to this chapter contains a glossary of investment terms. The glossary terms are in the order in which they appear in this chapter.

amount of savings. First, once you have achieved a saving goal (say, $10,000) that will be available for investment, you realize how small the sum is to do the job. Second, your federal income taxes increase. The savings account that paid 5½ percent interest is now offering less than 4 percent interest after federal income taxes are deducted. It is offering even less after state income taxes are taken out. You have less simply because your ordinary income and your tax rate have gone up.

You should search out investments that offer a higher yield after taxes but without the fear of taking undue risk. But what investments? If you choose common stocks, how do you select among all the available stocks? When do you buy common stocks? Where do you obtain information? Do you have to pay for this information? Should you buy tax-exempt securities? Who can advise you about them? Where do you buy them? Maybe Treasury bills (whatever they are) will allow you to earn a higher yield with less risk. Should you buy gold and where? Why not invest in diamonds, silver, or gold coins? Why not invest in real estate? Inflation seems to be so strong that you might benefit more if you bought a real asset rather than securities. And how will these investments fit into your retirement program and meet your financial goals? You may feel too confused, uncertain, and afraid to risk your money. Chances are you won't do anything—and in the process you'll lose more ground to inflation.

You lose by paying higher taxes than you should. You lose as inflation eats away at your purchasing power. This is because an 8.75 percent saving certificate cannot overtake a 10 percent inflation rate. You lose because you are unfamiliar with other investment outlets and are afraid to take the risk. Lack of information and fear, however, should not be mistaken for risk. Often people confuse fear of investment with possible loss.

You must be informed enough so that you know the nature of each investment, can reduce fear, and can assess the risk of each alternative. Information about new investment outlets is no farther away than a local newspaper and *The Wall Street Journal*. A subscription to *The Wall Street Journal* is a "must" for all investors. A list of other sources of information appears at the end of this chapter.

The search for investments—the investment process

What do you need to know before undertaking an investment program? First, you should understand the risks associated with investment. Second, you must be in a financial posture to accept these risks. Third, you must know the yield and risk aspects of each investment and the part each will play in your investment program. Fourth, you must have good information that is simple and yet accurate. Fifth, you must know the principles of investment or portfolio management so that you can meet your investment goals. Sixth, you must know about the marketplace where securities are bought and sold, and who can buy and sell these securities. Seventh, you must know how to analyze and value investments. All this might seem a difficult task. But a small amount of work over a long period of time can transform a layman into an informed investor.

Investment risks

Most investors are risk averse and dislike the idea of losing money. But there are risks associated with all investments. As an investor you should understand the nature of the risks and attempt to minimize them. Your overall investment objective will then be to earn the maximum possible rate of return consistent with the level of risk you are willing to assume.

Inflation—the number one risk

Inflation is public enemy number one. The risk of inflation is the risk of loss of purchasing power of your investment dollars. This is known as the *purchasing power risk;* it refers to the risk that your invested capital will earn a lower rate of return than the rate of inflation. The problem of inflation has been very difficult during the past decade. The annual rate of price increases, as measured by the consumer price index, rose from 3.30 percent in 1972 to 10.97 percent in 1974 at the height of the OPEC oil embargo. It ended the decade with a 13.3 percent increase in 1979. The behavior of consumer prices is seen in Figure 11–1.

One way to beat inflation is to purchase real assets or common stocks that increase in price along with the increase in the general price level. Real estate in most major metropolitan areas of the United States has been a good hedge against inflation, except for brief interludes of recession when prices became stable or declined. Gold coins and gold bullion, if bought at the right time, also would be a good antiinflation investment. Diamonds have done well, as have some stamps and antiques.

Many common stock groups have done well during the past few years. Over the long run, common stock investments have substantially outpaced the inflation rate. The variation in stocks shows that the stock market is risky. Investors must be careful to select stocks that will perform better than inflation, even though this is difficult to do.

The price patterns of the Standard & Poor's 500 Stock Index appear in Figure 11–2. The index is a good guide to the general level of the market. It is composed of 500 companies in various industry groups. The industry groups contained in the index appear in Table 11–1.

Fixed-income securities that yield 15.00 percent are good investments relatively, in spite of inflation, if you are in a low tax bracket. Under conditions of rapid inflation, real estate and other scarce assets would be a better hedge against inflation than common stocks.

Figure 11–1
Consumer price index

Index, 1967 = 100 (ratio scale)

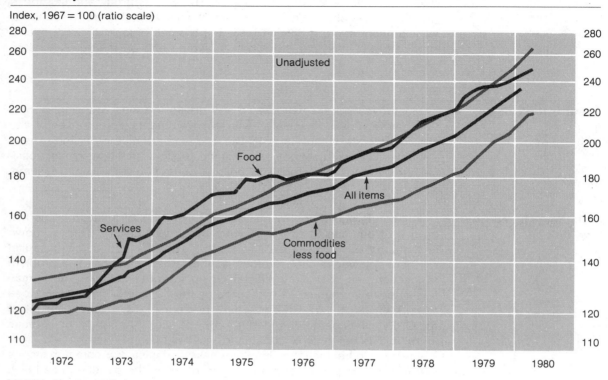

SOURCE   Department of Labor.

**Business failure—an
important risk**

The risk of business failure is another risk you must guard against as an investor. Business risk, in its absolute form, is the complete failure of a business in which you invest. In a relative sense the loss of earnings per share is also a form of business risk. In general, *business risk* can be defined as the risk of an earnings decline in a company in which you invest your money. Thus business risk appears as a loss of earnings per share or in the variation of earnings per share. Business risk also appears in investor expectations. If investors expect higher earnings and are disappointed with lower earnings, they will sell their stock and push the price of the stock lower. Therefore, if a company's sales decline and earnings per share drop, the market price of the shares might drop dramatically. Some companies are cyclical in character, and their earnings rise and fall with the business cycle. Auto companies are good examples. The price of the shares of stocks also fluctuate in value. Investors expect the price to vary because of the business cycle. The business cycle consists of periods of expansion and contraction (prosperity and recession) of business activity.

Companies with growing or stable earnings are more attractive to investors than companies with fluctuating earnings. Generally investors pay a higher price for a dollar of stable earnings or a dollar of earnings expected to grow at a constant rate per year. However, there is danger in paying too high a price for earnings per share. If earnings do not grow as expected, the price might fall, and the investor would lose. None of the common stocks is immune from all forms of business risk.

The best way to protect yourself from loss in market price created because of business risk is by careful analysis of the companies in which you invest. This requires analysis of the future earnings of the company, analysis of the price behavior of the stock, and a recognition of the character of earnings growth of the company. The business risk, by the way, is usually related to investment in common stocks. It also may affect the price behavior of preferred stock and lower quality bonds.

The risk of price change—market risk

The price of common stocks and other securities is affected by events unrelated to their earnings or dividend changes. A great deal of emotion is associated with ownership of stock. Price is also susceptible to the psychology of the marketplace, whether rational or irrational. News events—for example, the rate of inflation, war or peace in the Middle East, a military regime taking control in Iran, the death of the President, drought in the West, heavy snow storms in the Midwest, or a labor strike— all have their momentary and long-term effects on the movement of stock prices. These events are basically unpredictable. When they occur, they are transmitted to the market place and cause stock prices to fluctuate.

It is normal for the price of stocks to fluctuate. Prices have a range much higher than most people would suspect. The Standard & Poor's 500 Composite Index shown in Figure 11–2 has a price range of a high of 120 in 1973 and a low of 62 in 1974. In 1975 the range of values was 15 percent around the average of 83. Between 1976 and 1979 the index ranged between 87 and 110. In 1980 it moved to a new high of 124. This suggests the possibility of high returns and risks.

It is difficult to determine why stock prices are so variable. Yet as an investor purchasing stocks, you must understand that stock prices will continue to fluctuate. If you don't like the variability of stock prices, you can avoid the risk by not buying common stock. But bonds also vary in price, as do gold, silver, diamonds, and antiques. If you don't like variability, then your best alternative is savings certificates. They don't offer a high yield, but they are stable.

Not only do stock prices vary, but the magnitude of the change and the direction of change are almost impossible to predict in the short run. Price movements in the short term are said to be "random" in charac-

Figure 11-2
Stock market and business history since 1926

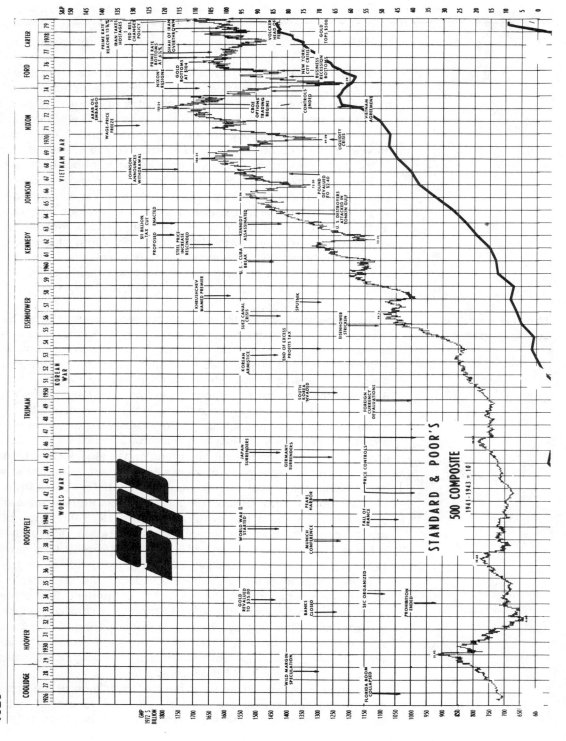

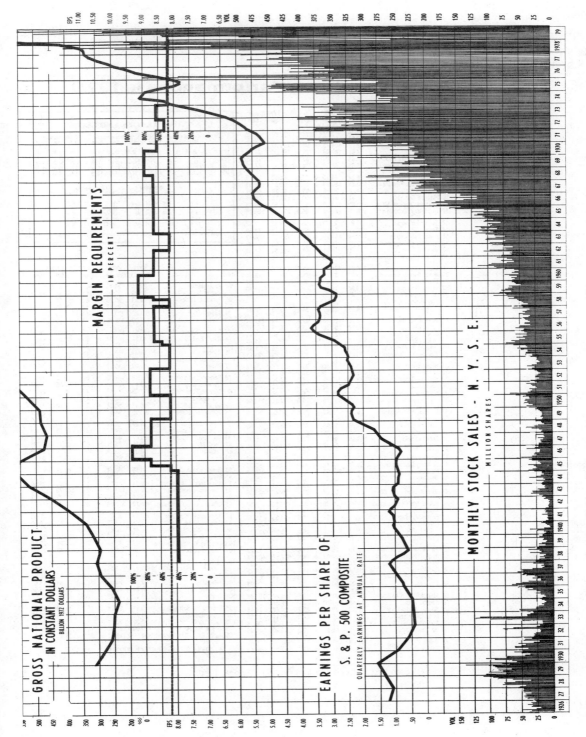

GROSS NATIONAL PRODUCT
IN CONSTANT DOLLARS
BILLION 1972 DOLLARS

MARGIN REQUIREMENTS
IN PERCENT

EARNINGS PER SHARE OF
S. & P. 500 COMPOSITE
QUARTERLY EARNINGS AT ANNUAL RATE

MONTHLY STOCK SALES - N. Y. S. E.
MILLION SHARES

SOURCE   Standard & Poor's Corporation, Trendline Division, 1980.

Table 11-1
Stock group performances in 1979

Stock Group Performances In 1979

Rank	1978 Dec. 31	1979 Dec. 31	% Change	1979 Range High	Low
1 Crude Oil Producers ...	264.32	532.91	+101.6	545.04	272.56
2 Fertilizers	9.63	19.25	+ 99.9	19.25	10.18
3 Machine Tools	53.79	104.75	+ 94.7	106.00	53.15
4 Gold Mining	97.61	185.06	+ 89.6	185.06	94.89
5 Can. Oil & Gas Expl.	12.33	23.06	+ 87.0	23.06	12.52
6 Metals: Miscellaneous	46.68	81.56	+ 74.7	81.56	47.80
7 Copper	25.54	44.10	+ 72.7	44.10	26.19
8 Natural Gas Pipelines	119.65	199.96	+ 67.1	202.25	121.50
9 Offshore Drilling	54.68	90.46	+ 65.4	92.29	43.89
10 Finance Cos.	57.91	92.74	+ 60.1	110.13	58.36
11 Textiles: Apparel Mfrs.	28.60	44.82	+ 56.7	44.82	29.03
12 Oil: Integr. Domestic	170.76	265.76	+ 55.8	271.61	168.23
13 Sugar Refiners	17.81	27.72	+ 55.6	29.42	17.52
14 Toys	10.78	16.56	+ 53.6	18.13	11.20
15 Metal Fabricating	119.34	181.29	+ 51.9	181.29	126.25
16 Hospital Management	13.04	19.63	+ 50.5	19.63	11.85
17 Gaming Cos.	11.70	16.81	+ 43.7	22.64	11.63
18 Oil Well Equip. & Svce.	1029.12	1474.89	+ 43.3	1485.16	998.71
19 Coal: Bituminous	285.21	408.16	+ 43.1	444.26	303.25
20 Home Furnishings	23.22	32.86	+ 41.5	35.17	19.84
21 Chemicals (Misc.)	9.18	12.89	+ 40.4	12.89	9.24
22 Discount Stores	13.94	19.52	+ 40.0	23.91	14.40
23 Oil Composite	161.43	225.88	+ 39.9	231.72	161.31
24 Electronics (Semi./Comp.)	18.55	25.62	+ 38.1	25.93	18.21
25 Beverages: Distillers	128.79	176.98	+ 37.4	179.79	131.51
26 Railroads	42.22	56.50	+ 33.8	58.33	43.67
27 Low Price Stocks	169.32	225.87	+ 33.4	247.50	179.44
28 Indus./Spec. Mach.	100.92	134.62	+ 33.4	137.19	101.74
29 Heating & Plumbing	70.53	93.38	+ 32.4	99.80	71.56
30 Electronics (Instrum.)	25.85	34.17	+ 32.2	34.35	25.13
31 Brokerage Firms	8.81	11.60	+ 31.7	12.55	9.18
32 Containers: Paper	142.62	187.76	+ 31.7	196.47	142.71
33 Natural Gas Distributors	78.73	100.47	+ 27.6	102.72	77.83
34 Aerospace	110.76	140.69	+ 27.0	140.69	99.86
35 Multi-Line Insurance	14.34	18.12	+ 26.4	18.96	14.46
36 Oil: Integr. Intl.	152.26	191.55	+ 25.8	197.16	152.58
37 Roofing & Wallboard	59.36	74.42	+ 25.4	80.42	62.20
38 Investment Cos. (Closed End)	44.28	55.34	+ 25.0	55.42	42.38
39 Conglomerates	16.46	20.49	+ 24.5	21.31	16.66
40 Entertainment	159.50	197.82	+ 24.0	197.82	150.21
41 Property-Casualty Insur.	104.07	126.70	+ 21.7	127.60	106.40
42 Hotel-Motel	45.73	55.54	+ 21.5	64.32	46.99
43 Building Composite	54.70	66.12	+ 20.9	71.04	56.21
44 Publishing	256.34	309.23	+ 20.6	310.14	255.58
45 Cement	28.51	34.35	+ 20.5	36.95	28.57
46 Railroad Equipment	60.11	72.45	+ 20.5	74.81	57.52
47 Sav. & Loan Hold. Cos.	23.53	28.27	+ 20.1	34.80	23.39
48 Publishing (Newspapers)	22.83	27.30	+ 19.6	27.30	22.54
49 Aluminum	103.30	123.26	+ 19.3	127.01	102.71
50 Forest Products	18.95	22.51	+ 18.8	24.85	19.30
51 Office & Bus. Equip.: Excl. IBM	235.44	279.07	+ 18.5	285.09	227.10
52 Real Estate Inv. Trust	1.91	2.26	+ 18.3	2.69	1.97
53 20 TRANSPORTATION	12.79	15.07	+ 17.8	16.52	12.83
54 Radio-TV Broadcasters	428.14	492.03	+ 14.9	517.22	407.57
55 Retail Stores (Drug)	21.10	24.19	+ 14.6	25.18	19.58
56 Chemicals	50.94	58.12	+ 14.1	61.04	51.75
57 Electrical Equipment	271.63	309.65	+ 14.0	327.18	267.72
58 Tobacco	76.02	86.00	+ 13.1	86.00	72.93
59 400 INDUSTRIALS	107.21	121.02	+ 12.9	124.49	107.08
60 Capital Goods	107.58	121.20	+ 12.7	122.31	108.99
61 Mach.: Agricultural	70.13	79.02	+ 12.7	84.42	71.15
62 Hospital Supplies	34.77	39.11	+ 12.5	39.11	31.53
63 500 COMPOSITE	96.11	107.94	+ 12.3	111.27	96.13
64 40 FINANCIAL	11.22	12.57	+ 12.0	13.90	11.05
65 Drugs	162.44	181.73	+ 11.9	183.14	156.19
66 Textile Products	44.36	49.56	+ 11.7	49.65	42.84
67 Restaurants	23.74	26.44	+ 11.4	28.87	21.32
68 Mobile Homes	47.70	53.00	+ 11.1	54.87	40.24
69 Personal Loans	78.53	85.20	+ 8.5	101.14	79.07
70 Pollution Control	26.30	28.42	+ 8.1	29.81	24.12
71 Paper	204.02	220.17	+ 7.9	242.26	208.30
72 Department Stores	123.80	133.20	+ 7.6	141.42	121.77
73 Banks: Outside N.Y.C.	100.64	107.87	+ 7.2	119.79	96.06
74 Steel: Excl. U.S. Steel	42.21	45.04	+ 6.7	52.31	43.37
75 Electronic Major Cos.	78.35	82.89	+ 5.8	90.14	75.97
76 Containers: Metal & Glass	34.16	35.99	+ 5.4	39.47	33.68
77 Shoes	46.02	48.39	+ 5.1	53.68	46.47
78 Banks: New York City	42.18	44.30	+ 5.0	49.92	40.92
79 Homebuilding	20.13	21.13	+ 5.0	26.05	19.45
80 Leisure Time	27.22	28.48	+ 4.6	28.61	23.16
81 Life Insurance	199.27	207.65	+ 4.2	246.07	192.49
82 40 UTILITIES	48.47	50.24	+ 3.7	52.85	47.14
83 Consumer Goods	82.09	84.57	+ 3.0	89.23	79.82
84 Auto Parts—Orig. Equip.	15.02	15.46	+ 2.9	17.29	14.66
85 High Grade Stocks	72.48	74.52	+ 2.8	77.05	71.14
86 Tel.: Excl. A.T.&T.	39.87	40.77	+ 2.3	43.75	37.71
87 Food Chains	55.15	55.21	+ 0.1	63.45	54.31
88 Truckers	73.31	73.39	+ 0.1	86.10	68.96
89 Foods	69.90	69.71	- 0.3	73.73	65.75
90 Retail Stores Comp.	73.70	73.51	- 0.3	82.58	71.38
91 Steel	39.98	39.36	- 1.6	48.10	38.13
92 Auto Trucks & Parts	42.24	41.51	- 1.7	51.90	38.66
93 Elec. Household Appl.	126.69	123.44	- 2.6	147.78	120.63
94 Auto Parts—After Mkt.	15.40	14.80	- 3.9	17.12	14.57
95 Constr. & Mat. Handling	389.19	372.28	- 4.3	411.98	342.73
96 Beverages: Brewers	34.14	32.57	- 4.6	38.38	29.88
97 General Mdse. Chains	7.08	6.73	- 4.9	7.85	6.66
98 Air Conditioning	32.41	30.62	- 5.5	36.28	28.55
99 Office & Bus. Equip.	1209.57	1139.62	- 5.8	1292.86	1056.12
100 Vending & Food Service	25.92	23.84	- 8.0	28.58	22.98
101 Electric Companies	31.38	28.44	- 9.4	33.48	27.97
102 Investment Cos. (Bond Funds)	8.97	7.96	- 11.3	10.12	7.96
103 Automobiles	68.82	60.94	- 11.5	78.62	60.74
104 Telephone	27.25	24.04	- 11.8	28.84	23.60
105 Air Transport	46.64	40.73	- 12.7	52.35	38.54
106 Soaps	166.62	145.48	- 12.7	167.80	140.69
107 Beverages: Soft Drinks	112.51	95.26	- 15.3	116.66	90.42
108 Cosmetics	64.49	54.05	- 16.2	67.44	53.73
109 Air Freight	31.32	26.21	- 16.3	35.76	25.97
110 Tire & Rubber	113.09	91.96	- 18.7	126.72	86.45
111 Auto: Excl. Gen. Motors	24.59	19.21	- 21.9	26.95	18.29

An alphabetical list of these groups appears on page 1000.

ANNUAL RANGES AND CLOSES

	400 Industrials High	Low	Close	20 Transportation High	Low	Close	40 Financial High	Low	Close
1979	124.49	107.08	121.02	16.52	12.83	15.07	13.90	11.05	12.57
1978	118.71	96.52	107.21	18.20	12.40	12.79	13.18	10.14	11.22
1977	118.92	99.88	104.71	15.46	12.43	13.85	12.67	10.57	11.15
1976	120.89	101.64	119.46	15.34	12.63	15.34	12.79	10.21	12.79
1975	107.40	77.71	100.88	12.17	9.97	12.09	11.47	8.64	9.78

	40 Utilities High	Low	Close	500 Composite High	Low	Close
1979	52.85	47.14	50.24	111.27	96.13	107.94
1978	54.47	46.47		106.90	86.90	96.11
1977	57.56	51.90	54.73	107.00	90.71	95.10
1976	54.24	44.70	54.24	107.83	90.90	107.46
1975	45.81	35.31	44.45	95.61	70.04	90.19

*Ranges prior to July 1, 1976 are based on weekly rather than daily indexes.

SOURCE   Standard & Poor's Corporation, *The Outlook,* 1980.

ter, that is, independent and unpredictable. This is known as the *random walk hypothesis* and is widely accepted by stock market analysts. Some experts suggest it might explain the price of a security. Over a long period of time, prices tend to vary around a level determined by earnings and dividends.

The problem you face as an investor is that the market could move in a direction opposite to that which is expected. This would result in the loss of a substantial sum of money if you have to sell suddenly. The only way to protect yourself is to be able to hold you investment position and not sell in a weak market. Or you should be careful to buy at a low point in the market. In short, you must exercise good timing.

The 1973–74 period was a time when an investor with limited financial means could have been wiped out. In 1974 the Standard & Poor's 500 Index declined from 99 to 62, a drop of more than 37 percent. The market declined because of an expected recession brought about by inflation in energy prices and an attempt by the Federal Reserve Board to raise interest rates. The Federal Reserve Board hoped in this way to restrict the growth of the money supply; this, in turn, would control inflation. As a result, interest rates increased and stock and bond prices declined. Both professional and amateur investors lost large sums of money.

Such price changes cannot be predicted with certainty. But they will happen some time, and you must be prepared to accept this risk. You should try to avoid the purchase of securities when they are over-priced.

The interest rate risk   When the general level of interest rates in the money and bond markets changes, the yields change on individual bonds. As yield or interest rates increase, bond prices decrease. As yields decrease, bond prices increase. Therefore investors face a risk of loss of principal because of changes in the general level of interest rates. The change in the level of interest rates affects bond prices directly. Common stocks are indirectly affected since higher interest rates should require higher common stock yields. Bond and stock prices tend to move in the same direction but not necessarily at the same rate. As yields on bonds increase and bond prices fall, stock prices tend to fall as well.

As an investor you must estimate the direction of interest rates if you hope to reduce risk. All investors face a loss in price if they purchase 7 percent bonds at par ($1,000) only to hold them for a year to have yields rise to 9 percent. The interest rate paid on a 7 percent bond is $70 per year, and it remains fixed over the life of the bond. As other new bonds are issued to yield 9 percent, the bond contract calls for the payment of $90 per year per $1,000. Therefore if another investor were to buy your bond, the amount paid would be the present value of

Figure 11-3
Interest rates and bond yields

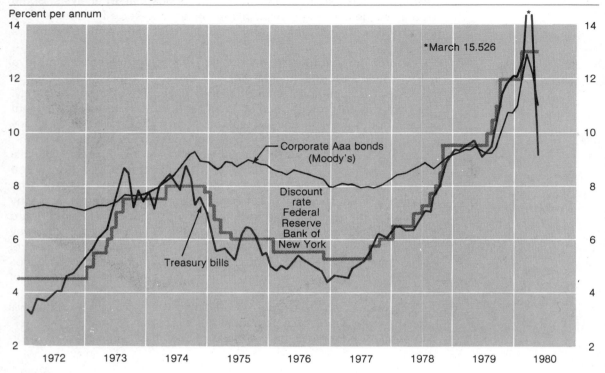

Percent per annum

SOURCE   Department of the Treasury, Board of Governors of the Federal Reserve System, Moody's
Corporation.

the $70 a year interest and $1,000 maturity value discounted at a 9 percent rate. This value is approximately $900. Therefore as yields in the market rise, bond prices drop. As yields fall, bond prices rise. If it were necessary to sell the bond, you could lose a substantial amount of money.

You should try to prevent a substantial loss by carefully analyzing the trends in interest rates. If rates are expected to increase, invest in short-term securities. If rates are expected to decrease and are high, then purchase long-term bonds. Loss is also prevented if you are in a position to hold securities until prices recover. Even fixed-income securities are not riskless. The patterns of interest rates are shown in Figure 11-3.

Can you accept the risks of investment?   In order to accept the risks associated with the purchase of any investment, you must be in a strong financial position. The stronger your financial position, the greater is your ability to profit by intelligent investment management and diversification.

The first thing you must do is to take stock of your financial assets and liabilities. You need to know what you own and what you owe. The simplest way to do that is to construct a personal balance sheet summarizing your assets, liabilities, and net worth. You will recall the detailed discussion of balance sheets in Chapter 3. An analysis of your balance sheet will indicate whether or not you can really accept investment risks.

To illustrate an assessment of financial strengths, we will look at the financial position of Bob and Shirley. They are a married couple in their middle 40s. Their personal balance sheet appears in Table 11–2. Their checking account is at a commercial bank. Savings are divided between a 6 percent $5,000 time deposit at a commercial bank and the remainder in savings certificates yielding 11 percent at a savings and loan association. They also have $21,000 in common stock and $12,000 in life insurance cash value. The $1,000 asset is a 10 percent loan to their church. The $4,500 asset is money owed to Bob from a consulting contract.

Bob and Shirley own a $12,000 auto, and two houses worth $235,000. Furniture and personal assets are worth $40,000. Total nonfinancial assets are $287,000.

Bob and Shirley's liabilities represent claims against their assets (and their income). The $5,000 bank note represents an open line of credit

Table 11–2
Bob and Shirley's balance sheet

BOB AND SHIRLEY
Balance Sheet

Assets			Liabilities		
Financial:			**Current:**		
Checking	$ 2,500		Bank Note		$5,000
Savings	22,500		Accounts payable		800
Common stock	21,000		Income taxes		3,000
Life insurance			Total current		$8,800
cash value	12,000		**Long-term:**		
Debts owed by			8 percent mortgage		
others	1,000		on residence		$ 38,000
Accounts			12 percent mortgage		
receivable	4,500		on condominium		60,000
Total	$63,500	$63,500	12 percent auto loan		10,000
Nonfinancial assets:			Total long-term		$108,000
Auto	$ 12,000		Total, long-term		
Furniture	25,000		and current		116,800
Personal assets	15,000		Net worth		$233,700
Residence	150,000				$350,500
Florida condominium	85,000				
Total	$287,000	$287,000			
		$350,500			

with their commercial bank. The $800 represents current charge accounts at department stores. The $3,000 income taxes owed is paid quarterly by Shirley on her income. Bob and Shirley's long-term liabilities include two mortgages, one on each house. These were obtained from a savings and loan association. The 12 percent auto loan is for the new car they purchased. The total debt owed by Bob and Shirley amounts to $8,800 in current liabilities and $108,000 in long-term liabilities. Their total debt burden is $116,800, which is paid off periodically from current income. If they should have difficulty meeting their payments, they could sell their assets to pay their debts, if necessary.

What Bob and Shirley own after their debts are subtracted is their net worth. In Bob and Shirley's case, their net worth is $233,700 ($350,500 − $116,800). This level of net worth is probably more than most of us will have in a lifetime, even with inflation. But to determine whether or not their financial position is strong, we must apply the financial prerequisite guidelines. We will first establish a set of general financial prerequisites. We will then return to Bob and Shirley to apply the tests of financial prerequisites.

The financial prerequisites

Before you invest, you should meet the following standards of prerequisites: (1) you must have adequate life insurance; (2) you should have equity in a home; (3) you should have a modest amount of consumer debt; (4) you should have a satisfactory level of money in your checking account; (5) you should have adequate savings for an emergency; and (6) you should have enough money for investment to make it profitable and economical. You must also have a plan that will allow you to accumulate funds for investment on a regular schedule.

Adequate life insurance   One important prerequisite for investment is an adequate amount of life insurance. The main purpose of life insurance is to replace income that would be lost if the insured should die. Ordinary life insurance also provides savings as long as the insured lives. What is considered an adequate amount of life insurance will vary from person to person. Guidelines for life insurance planning were discussed in detail in Chapter 9. Before you even consider an investment program, carefully analyze your life insurance needs. You need to take care of these needs before you can start investing.

The purchase of a home   If a family decides to purchase a home when interest rates are relatively high, the downpayment should be as large as possible. The larger the downpayment, the smaller the mortgage and the less onerous the burden of the principal payment and interest charge. Certainly a 10 percent downpayment should be the minimum downpayment for most families. The higher the value of the house, the larger the downpayment. For houses above $50,000, a 20 percent downpayment normally would be appropriate. It is desirable both economically and financially for any young family to consider home ownership as soon as they can afford it. In an inflationary economy, ownership of a home provides a substantial inflation hedge. Done properly and within your income, it is a must for most people. It will allow you to improve your financial well-being in the long run.

There are some who think that a house should be purchased with a minimum downpayment and a maximum mortgage. Actually the lending institutions dictate the amount of money you can borrow and the rate of interest you pay. In times of tight mortgage market conditions, savings and loan institutions and all lenders ration the amount of money they lend to a single borrower. In the early 1980s some lending institutions were lending a maximum of $75,000 to a single family. They were not making loans for investment purposes. Mortgage money was very scarce. The idea that you should borrow as much as possible to buy a house when interest rates are low is sound. When interest rates are very high, the idea loses its appeal. If you seek a maximum mortgage, make certain you can put money to work elsewhere at a higher aftertax yield than the mortgage interest rate. You will find it difficult to earn 10 percent over long periods on other investments after taxes. In fact, several research studies indicate that common stocks provide an investor with an average total yield (dividends and capital gains) of 9 percent before taxes over long periods of time. If you are in the 30 percent bracket, you would earn approximately 6.3 percent after taxes.

There is one aspect of real estate ownership that might support the maximum loan theory. During inflationary periods the value of real estate increases, and capital gains on real estate therefore are substantial. When you compare the advantages of capital gains from real estate against even a 13 percent mortgage, the real estate transaction may be more profitable than any alternative. However, it is not always possible to sell a house quickly for a large profit. Prudence therefore suggests a cautious attitude about the level of debt on a home. The proven principles of conservative finance should not be ignored. You should not incur excessive debt, even on your family home.

The advantages of home ownership were discussed in detail in Chapter 6. In financial planning it is important that your housing needs be satisfied before you invest in securities. You should buy a house you can afford. Start small, and then move up as your income grows. This will help you maximize your net worth in the long run.

Minimum installment debt Prudence suggests that you keep consumer installment purchases to a minimum. It does not make sense to borrow money at 12 to 18 percent with the idea that you are going to take your excess cash and put it to work to earn 9 percent. As explained in Chapter 6, in no case should your monthly consumer debt payments exceed 20 percent of net monthly income after taxes. In most cases 10 percent of monthly net income is a better guide. Therefore, if your net income is $1,000 a month, you should not spend more than $100 to $200 a month for installment debt. It is extremely important for you to check this simple rule to make certain it is not exceeded. If you develop a system to limit installment debt, you will be in a much better position to invest. And you can do so with less risk.

Adequate checking and savings as an emergency fund Before investing you should have adequate savings that can serve as an emergency fund. Such savings can provide for temporary needs or be a financial reserve to take advantage of opportunities to buy business or personal assets at attractive prices. Such a reserve can solve financial problems before they occur without difficulty. The amount needed in ready cash is determined in part by your habits. Some people say they do not need a large amount of cash because they rely on personal loans from a commercial bank. This might be dangerous. Under the conditions of national financial restraint (tight money) that occurred in 1974 and 1980, it might be impossible to obtain a loan at a reasonable price. Under these conditions an adequate emergency reserve would be wise.

The size of your emergency fund should be based on your income, other assets you have, and your attitude about financial security. As a general rule, you should have between three and six months' after tax salary in an appropriate savings account.

These funds will be put to productive uses. They can be kept in a savings account at a commercial bank, a mutual savings bank, or a savings and loan association. If the amount is sufficiently large, it can be invested in United States government bonds or tax-exempt municipal bonds. These should be liquid investments, that is, have a short time before maturity. Our previous discussion about savings and savings instruments in Chapter 4 can be used as a guide on the placement of funds. Investment in short-term government securities—a topic that will be discussed in Chapter 12—will serve as another guide to your investment in liquid emergency funds.

Money to invest Once you have met the financial prerequisites for investment, you can make investments in securities and other productive assets. One question often raised is "Where can I get money to invest?" After all, you must have money before investment begins. The bulk of the money invested comes from savings accumulated from past and current income. In fact, several plans have been designed to help people convert their savings into financial or real assets. These assets would be more profitable over the long term than keeping money in a savings account. One way of achieving this is through an annual investment plan.

This plan requires you to make regular amounts of investment each year. You put money aside each month in savings. Then you purchase securities once or twice in the year. For example, $100 saved every month would accumulate to $1,200 at the end of the year. A stock purchase of $1,200 is more economical than 12 purchases of $100 each. You get the benefit over a long period of time of dollar averaging, that is, of buying at different prices. You have lower brokerage commissions, and you accumulate a good sum of money.

Some people join investment clubs to begin the accumulation process. The National Association of Investment Clubs was created to provide investment information to people in the United States who are not informed about security investment. A substantial amount of information has been distributed by this organization. Some people have, indeed, formed investment clubs that help investors learn about common stock investment. Modest individual sums invested collectively soon accumulate to large sums. The results for many investment clubs have been most gratifying.

You need not wait until you have amassed a fortune to begin an investment program. In fact, it is prudent to invest periodically on a regular basis. In this way you can take advantage of market swings; you can reduce the problem of timing of the sale and purchase of securities. You stand a good chance of earning a satisfactory yield with less risk by buying regular dollar amounts of securities over a long period of time.

Applying the tests to Bob and Shirley

Insurance

Let us apply the tests of financial strength to Bob and Shirley. First, they do have an adequate amount of life insurance. They have $200,000 in insurance with a cash value of $12,500. Their combined income is $60,000, and their children are grown and have graduated from college. The amount seems adequate even with mortgage loans of $98,000. The insurance is carried on Bob's life. If anything happened to Bob, there would be enough insurance to pay off the mortgages and still provide money for living expenses. Shirley should consider taking out a $20,000 insurance policy on her life for the benefit of the children since she too is working. The bulk of their insurance is term. This makes sense on a cost basis.

Housing

Bob and Shirley have substantial equity in both houses. The mortgage on their residence is 23 percent of value, and it is 70 percent of value on their Florida condominium. Their income is adequate to support their residence. The Florida house is rented in season and has been a good investment. They have adequate income to pay for the Florida house with rental income and additional income from their combined earnings.

Consumer debt

Bob and Shirley's consumer debt is not high. They have a $10,000, 36–month auto loan that requires a monthly payment of $332.15. This is a new car loan. They put $2,000 down on the purchase price of the auto. They have, in addition, their monthly charges for gasoline and a few small, recurring bills from a local department store. Their debt payment is well below the 10 percent limit. So they are in a good financial position.

Savings

The savings position of Bob and Shirley is adequate. On the basis of their after income they should have between $10,000 and $20,000 in savings. Their basic goal is to increase the amount of money in savings to 50 percent of their annual income. (Whether you earn $3,000 a year or $30,000 a year, these ratios must be met!) Realistically, their current asset position is quite adequate to undertake the risks of investment.

The investment fund

Bob and Shirley's personal investment fund appears to be $21,000 of common stock. In the broader sense their investment should include their second house in Florida. It should also include the antiques they purchased, which have increased in value. The gold jewelry that has been purchased or received as gifts, the sterling silver received as wedding presents, and even a part of the family residence are investments.

Bob and Shirley have done well over the years because of their wise practice of buying assets and their ability to save as well as earn. They have accepted investment risks, and they continue to be in a position to accept these risks. Our definition of investment includes not only securities but also real assets, including real estate and personal property. Remember that they are interested in maximizing their net worth, not just their ownership of securities. And in the process they wish to maximize their enjoyment of life too.

Knowledge of investment alternatives

You must understand each type of investment security before investing. It is important to know the expected return and risk associated with each. You should know the investment characteristics of the various alternatives, and keep your list up to date. Then you can make intelligent decisions about your investments. This requires knowledge about the amount of return, the time period of the investment, and the variability of return that is a measure of risk. Return and risk do change. You must be able to anticipate changes in expected returns. Investment success requires, in part, the correct analysis of future events.

A summary of some investment alternatives appears in Table 11–3. The list starts with defensive, income investments subject to the money rate risks. It ends with investments in real assets, such as houses and more speculative investments like gold and silver. It would be a good idea to become knowledgeable about these investment alternatives since they are the building blocks of any investment program. Not all of them will be usable. Treasury bills require minimum purchases of $10,000. Commercial paper requires minimum purchases of $100,000. Even though you might be unable to buy these securities, it is good to know that they exist. Each of these securities will be discussed in the following chapters.

Table 11–3
Investment alternatives

	Investment objective and risk
Short-term debt investments:	
Treasury bills, 91 days	Defensive, income
Federal agency securities	Defensive, income
Money market funds-mutual funds	Defensive, income
Certificates of deposit	Defensive, income
Commercial paper	Defensive, income
Longer-Term debt investments:	
Treasury notes	Income, money rate risk
Treasury bonds	Income, money rate risk
Federal agency bonds	Income, money rate risk
Corporate bonds	Income, money rate risk
Convertible bonds	Income and growth, money rate and business risk
Bond mutual funds	Income and growth, money rate risk
Tax-Exempt investments:	
Treasury bills and bonds, exempt from state income taxes	Defensive, income, money rate risk
Municipal bonds	Tax-exempt income, money rate risk and business risk
Tax-exempt municipal bond funds	Tax-exempt income, money rate risk
Ownership securities:	
Preferred stock	Income, money rate and business risk
Convertible preferred stock	Income, growth, money rate and business risk
Common stock	Income, growth, money rate and business risk
Common stock mutual funds	Income, growth, money rate and business risk
Real asset investment:	
Real estate	Growth, money rate and business risk
Gold	Growth, money rate and business risk
Silver	Growth, money rate and business risk

Sources of information

It was suggested that you should learn about sources of information. You should develop a simple information system that helps you select the appropriate securities to meet your return and risk needs. You can be overwhelmed by the data available to you. Therefore you must be selective. Your goal is to select securities in the economy that are in strong industries and that represent strong companies. Therefore you should develop your sources in these areas: (1) the economy; (2) the industry and; (3) the security as well as an overall news source.

Background and general information sources

Let's first of all take a look at background information sources:

The Wall Street Journal   This publication serves as a basic source of information about all business topics. You can refer to it for specific sources of information, but it is also a good idea to get in the habit of reading the *The Wall Street Journal* every day. It not only provides information about common stock and debt securities but it also offers a broad spectrum of information about the economies, industries, and companies of the whole world.

Barron's   This weekly publication contains pure data, market statistics, company reports, industry analysis as well as information about the market. It is a readable, timely, and reliable source of information available at newstands and public libraries.

Business Week   This outstanding weekly publication covers a broad range of subjects, from the economic outlook to restaurants you may want to visit in the world's leading cities. It can keep you informed and help you find attractive investment opportunities. It is published by McGraw-Hill Book Company.

The economy

There are many sources of information about the national economy, both federal and private. Let's look at some of the publications put out by the federal government:

Federal Reserve Bulletin   Published monthly by the board of governors of the Federal Reserve System, Washington, D.C., it contains a summary of business conditions as well as the Federal Reserve Board Index of Industrial Production. It provides a compilation of statistics that show trends in business, interest rates, money supply figures, production, construction, employment, retail sales, prices, and the behavior of the securities market. It gives data on the gross national product (GNP) and its components.

The Survey of Current Business Published by the U.S. Department of Commerce, it tells about business trends. It includes an elaborate set of data on economic statistics, business activity, and prices and production.

Business Conditions Digest This publication, issued monthly by the U.S. Department of Commerce, presents many economic indicators. Its presentation of data reflects work done by the National Bureau of Economic Research. One of its main features is the publication of information on leading, coincidental, and lagging indicators. Such data on the composite leading indicators help you anticipate future movements of the economy and stock market.

Economic Indicators Prepared for the Joint Economic Committee by the Council of Economic Advisors, this publication provides excellent data about the national and international economies. Published by the U.S. Government Printing Office, Washington, D.C.

Private reports *Business Week, Dun's Review, Forbes, Fortune,* and the *Nation's Business* publish useful reports about the economy.

Industry information

Standard & Poor's provides an excellent industry service in its *Industry Survey.* It periodically reviews more than 85 different industries. *Value Line Investment Survey* provides information about a broad list of industries; its basic data are first-class. Both of these services are usually available in the public library. Standard & Poor publishes *The Outlook,* and Moody's Investor Services produces *The Stock Survey.* Both contain general recommendations about securities and the stock market.

Company information

An excellent source of information about industrial companies is Standard & Poor's *Stock Reports,* which is concerned with the New York Stock Exchange, the American Stock Exchange, and the Over The Counter market. *Value Line* and Moody's *Stock Survey* also offer similar information about selected companies.

Standard & Poor produces a compact *Stock Guide* and *Bond Guide.* Moody's *Handbook* and *Weekly Bond Survey* furnishes information about companies and securities. All of these materials are available in many public libraries. These publications offer to investors reliable, up-to-date information.

If you read all—or some—of these sources of information regularly, you should quickly become an informed investor.

Summary

You have learned that there are real risks associated with putting your savings to work. If you wish to maximize your wealth, you will be required to accept more risk. The risks of investment are: inflation that robs you of your purchasing power; business failure that can take away dividends on stocks and interest on debt securities; security price changes brought about by changes in company earnings and dividends or other factors; and interest rate changes that cause bond and stock prices to change.

If you are in a strong financial position, you can accept these risks. To be in a strong financial position, you need to have adequate life insurance, a substantial equity in a home of your own, an adequate balance in your savings and checking accounts, minimum consumer debt, and a sum of money available to invest for the long term.

You can invest in Treasury bills and certificates of deposit. If you have a lot of money, you might also consider commercial paper. You can invest in federal, state, municipal, and private debt securities, in common and preferred stocks, and in real assets, including real estate, gold, silver, diamonds, stamps, coins, antiques, and objects of art. You should become familiar with all these investment alternatives, including their reward and risk characteristics. The next four chapters will take up each of these investment possibilities in greater detail.

Appendix: a glossary of investment terms

Investment   The purchase of an asset for an increase in value and income over the long term.

Risk   The possibility of a loss in the value of an asset or the variation in the expected income or gain.

Current yield   The price of the asset divided into the income from the asset.

Total yield or total return   The price or average price of the investment divided into the income plus the annual gain.

Portfolio   The list of investment assets purchased by an investor.

Portfolio management   Changing investments to increase yield or reduce risk.

Inflation   A general increase in the price level caused by too many dollars chasing too few goods.

Investment principles   Guides to investment decisions.

Securities   Investments in financial assets represented by shares of common stocks or bonds.

Shares   Ownership of common stock as evidenced by a stock certificate.

Common stock   The ownership of a business corporation divided into shares.

Bonds Long-term loans sold by a business or government, usually divided into units with a minimum value of $1,000; bonds bear interest.

Notes A promise to pay an intermediate term loan within 1 to 10 years; notes bear interest.

Interest The payment for the use of borrowed capital.

Dividend The payment of a share of the profits for the use of common stock or ownership capital.

Risk averse Most investors try to avoid risk.

Fixed-income securities Usually bonds; but also any security that pays a constant or fixed rate of interest or dividend.

Business risk The possible loss created because of a decline in earnings or the failure of a business.

Market risk A possible loss resulting from a decline in the price of a security.

Random walk hypothesis Prices of common stock move randomly in the short run; the price cannot be predicted since prices are independent of past price movements.

Interest rate risk Risk of change in the price of a fixed-income security because of an increase in the market level of interest rate.

Financial assets Securities you own and savings.

Financial liabilities Debts you owe.

Financial strength Substantially more financial assets than financial liabilities.

Long-term liabilities Debts owed by you that will be repaid in 10 years or longer.

Total debt Long-term and short-term debt.

Net worth Assets minus total debt.

Balance sheet List of assets, liabilities, and net worth.

Equity That part of an asset that you own; for example, if you own a $100,000 house with a $60,000 mortgage, the $40,000 is your equity or ownership.

Mortgage money Money available from lending institutions for mortgage loans.

United States government bonds Long-term bonds and short-term notes and bills issued by the U.S. government.

Tax-exempt municipal bonds Bonds sold by state and local governments to raise money; the interest is exempt from federal income taxes, the state exempts these bonds from state income taxes.

Real assets In contrast to securities or financial assets; included are real estate, land, gold, coins, stamps, art, and antiques.

Investment club   A group of people contribute monthly sums of money that are accumulated, and then invested in securities.

Dollar averaging   The purchase of securities at regular intervals at various prices.

Investment fund   Money available to purchase investment assets.

Expected yield   The total yield expected to be earned over the life of the investment.

Treasury bills   Short-term debt sold by the U.S. Treasury to raise money to run the federal government.

Federal agency securities   Securities sold by the various agencies of the U.S. government to raise money to finance their activities.

Money market funds   Mutual funds that invest in short term debt securities.

Certificate of deposit   Money borrowed by commercial banks to provide money to lend at a fixed rate for a stated period of time.

Commerical paper   Short-term loans by large businesses with excellent credit ratings, sold to financial institutions or wealthy individuals to raise money for working capital.

Corporate bonds   Long-term debt sold by corporations to investors.

Convertible bonds   Corporate bonds convertible into common stock.

Warrant bond   A warrant gives the bondholder the priviledge to buy common stock at a certain price for a specified period of time.

Bond funds   Mutual funds that buy bonds.

Mutual funds   Companies that sell shares to investors, and then invest the money in securities of other companies.

High-grade bond fund   A mutual fund that buys only the top quality bonds.

Salomon Brothers   A well-known and well-respected investment banking firm in New York.

Tax-exempt municipal funds   A mutual fund that invests in tax-exempt bonds.

Ownership securities   Securities that represent ownership in the company, including preferred and common stock.

Preferred stock   Ownership that has a prior claim over common stock earnings and usually pays a fixed dividend.

Convertible preferred   Preferred stock that is convertible into common stock at a fixed price for a stated period of time.

Investment in short-term and long-term debt securities

- Short-term U.S. government securities—Treasury bills
- Short-term Treasury notes and bonds
- Short-term agency bonds
- Money market funds
- Commercial paper as a short-term investment
- Certificates of deposit
- Long-term government and agency bonds
- Tax-exempt state and municipal bonds
- Corporate bonds
- Summary

During periods of high interest rates, you awaken to the fact that your savings at the local savings and loan association or commercial bank are only paying 5½ percent on your passbook account. You soon learn that Treasury bills, certificates of deposit, and money market funds are paying 10, 11, 12, and 13 percent interest. You may know vaguely that they exist, but you are busy and don't take the time to learn about these new outlets for investments. You may be fearful that your money will not be protected by the federal government. Besides, you have a comfortable banking relationship that includes a checking account, a credit line, and an auto loan plus a savings account, so why change?

The answer to this question comes at the end of the year when you receive a notice from the bank informing you that you have paid $500 in interest on your auto loan at an annual rate of 12 percent. You shrug and say, "Well, it's tax-deductible." You are in the 30 percent tax bracket, and you can write off the loan. Thus the loan only costs you $350 after taxes (reducing your taxable income by $500 saves $150 in taxes, i.e., .30 × $500 = $150 = the tax saving).

At about the same time you receive another statement from the bank saying you have been paid $500 interest on your savings of $9,090 on deposit. Since interest is subject to the 30 percent federal income tax, you have only $350 left after taxes. Then you realize something else: the auto loan costing $500 is for only $4,166, and it takes you over $9000 in savings to earn $500 in interest.

At this point the 10 to 13 percent return from other investment opportunities becomes more attractive. But what are they? What rate will they pay? Are they safe? How do you go about buying them? Who can provide information about them? These are very real and legitimate questions. You should not invest in any of these securities unless you know what you are getting and unless you are completely comfortable with them.

In this chapter we will answer these important questions. We will describe in detail investment opportunities available in debt securities. Information will be provided on government securities, money market funds, commercial paper, certificates of deposit, and corporate bonds.

Short-Term U.S. government securities: Treasury bills

The U.S. government must borrow money to run its activities, just as a business borrows money to finance its activities. The U.S. Treasury is the agency that handles the job of financing the government's debt. After all, even the federal government must borrow if its income is less than its expenditures. In fact, many people have criticized the federal bureaucracy because of its propensity to spend too much.

Whatever the reasons for the growth in federal expenditures and an ever-growing federal debt, the bulk of financing has been through the issuance of Treasury bills. Treasury bills are sold primarily to commercial banks, financial institutions, foreign investors, and an ever-growing number of individual investors. The reasons for this growth in individual interest in T-bills, as they are sometimes called, is, first, their relatively high current yield (above 15 percent in mid-1981). Second, they are backed by the unquestioned financial integrity of the U.S. government. Third, such securities are highly liquid, marketable, and easily converted into cash. Fourth, the price is least susceptible to changes in interest rates because the typical maturity date is 91 days to 1 year. And fifth, income from Treasury bills is exempt from state and local income taxes. These are powerful advantages for owning these top-quality securities.

Yet Treasury bills have some disadvantages. First, the yields are fixed only for the life of the security (91 days). Yields have fluctuated widely in the past. Treasury bill yields were as low as 3.0 percent in 1963, for example, and were over 15 percent in 1981. Therefore Treasury bills are most attractive to investors for periods when yields are high compared to other investment and saving alternatives.

A second disadvantage is the $10,000 minimum purchase requirement, with additional amounts available in $5,000 increments. This means that T-bills are unavailable for an investor who has only a few hundred or a few thousand dollars to invest.

A third disadvantage is the cost involved in buying treasury bills in the secondary market and the general inconvenience surrounding the purchase of securities directly from the Federal Reserve Bank. Treasury bills may be purchased directly from the Treasury bill window of the Bank. If purchased directly from the Federal Reserve Bank, no commission payment is required.

You can also buy Treasury bills from a commercial bank or brokerage firm in what is known as the *secondary market*. In this case a fee of $30 is normally charged. If the securities are kept in custody by a bank or brokerage firm, an additional charge is made (as much as $30 for custodian fees). These charges reduce the amount of interest earned. On a single $10,000 Treasury bill the charges cause a significant drop in yield.

Therefore the cheapest way to buy Treasury bills is at the Treasury bill window of the Federal Reserve Bank. You should plan to keep the securities at home or in some safe place. When the T-bills mature, they may be presented to the Federal Reserve Bank (or a commercial bank acting as agent for the Treasury) for payment a few days in advance of the maturity date. If the proceeds are to be reinvested (without a commission cost), the Treasury will send the investor a check for the difference.

If you are not in a position to buy directly from the Treasury or the Federal Reserve Bank, then the next least expensive method is to buy through your broker or commercial bank. After Treasury bills are purchased, they cannot be sold to the Treasury or Federal Reserve until they reach maturity. Before maturity, they can only be sold in the secondary market through a broker or commercial bank.

In spite of these disadvantages, Treasury bills provide the investor with an excellent short-term liquid investment of excellent quality.

Treasury bill yields

Treasury bills are sold on a discount basis. This means that you do not receive a separate check for interest. The maturity price of the bond is $1,000, and you pay less than this (the discount) when you buy it. The discount rate in effect is the interest rate or yield you receive. If you bought a 91-day Treasury bill with a $10,000 maturity value for $9,750, the $250 represents the discount or your yield in dollars for the period. The annual rate of yield is found as follows: the interest of $250 is divided by the principal of $9,750, and then multiplied by 4. Thus:

$$\$250/\$9,750 \times 4 = 2.564 \times 4 = 10.256 \text{ percent}$$

The prices of Treasury bills are quoted in *The Wall Street Journal* and many leading newspapers. Table 12–1 from *The Wall Street Journal* provides a list of yield quotes for each Treasury bill issue from July 22, 1980 through June 18, 1981. Notice that the quotes are yield or annualized discount rate and not price. This is because T-bills are traded on a discount basis. In Table 12–1 maturity date (mat. date) indicates the date when the security reaches maturity. Bid represents the yield from a bid price. The *bid price* is the price at which a dealer is willing to buy the security. The *asked price* is the yield from a price at which a dealer is willing to sell. The *yield column* gives the true bond equivalent yield if

Table 12–1
Representative Treasury bill yields

	U.S. Treasury Bills						
Mat. date	Bid	Asked Discount	Yield	Mat. date	Bid	Asked Discount	Yield
-1980-				10-30	7.93	7.77	8.05
7-22	8.10	7.46	7.57	11- 6	7.93	7.77	8.07
7-24	8.00	7.38	7.49	11-13	7.94	7.78	8.09
7-31	8.08	7.40	7.52	11-20	7.93	7.73	8.05
8- 7	8.02	7.62	7.75	11-28	7.93	7.75	8.08
8-14	7.67	7.31	7.44	12- 4	7.94	7.70	8.11
8-19	7.69	7.43	7.58	12-11	7.87	7.77	8.13
8-21	7.68	7.32	7.47	12-18	7.94	7.74	8.11
8-28	7.70	7.38	7.54	12-26	7.93	7.75	8.13
9- 4	7.82	7.54	7.72	-1981-			
9-11	7.44	6.82	6.98	1- 2	8.02	7.86	8.27
9-16	7.94	7.64	7.84	1- 8	8.02	7.88	8.30
9-18	7.92	7.72	7.93	1-15	8.00	7.94	8.38
9-25	7.94	7.74	7.96	1-29	8.01	7.81	8.25
10- 2	7.93	7.77	8.00	2-26	7.99	7.81	8.26
10- 9	7.93	7.77	8.02	3-26	7.98	7.82	8.29
10-14	7.95	7.75	8.00	4-23	7.99	7.83	8.33
10-16	7.96	7.90	8.17	5-21	7.97	7.81	8.34
10-23	7.95	7.77	8.04	6-18	7.93	7.83	8.40

SOURCE   *The Wall Street Journal*, July 18, 1980.

an investor pays the asked price. The true bond equivalent yield is annualized to a 365-day year rather than the 360-day year used in the discount equation.[1]

In order to find the dollar price of a $10,000 Treasury bill, the formula used is $10,000 − (discount rate in basis points[2] × days to maturity × $0.0027778). The $0.0027778 number is the value of one basis point in dollars per day for a $10,000 Treasury bill. An example can be found by examining the September 25, 1980 Treasury bill issue that is selling at a discount rate of 7.74 percent. If you bought this bill on July 22, the dollar price would be

$$\$10,000 - (774 \times 65 \times \$0.0027778) = 10,000 - \$139.75 = \$9,860.25^3$$

The bond equivalent yield for a Treasury bill is comparable to the yield of other bonds or any other semiannual compound interest rate. Once you know the discount rate (it is safe to use the asked discount rate in the case of Treasury bills), the annualized compounded yield can be easily calculated. Without using an equation, all you need do is to check *The Wall Street Journal* for the yield figure when making comparisons with other investments.

How the investor uses Treasury bills

Treasury bills are usually attractive when their yields are higher than the typical passbook savings rate and the rate on certificates of deposit or other short-term investments. They can be used as a defensive haven for funds under conditions of rising interest rates when long-term yields are expected to increase. As discussed in Chapter 11, when bond yields increase, bond prices fall. Once bond yields have risen, a reverse shift can be made by investing in long-term bonds.

Treasury bills also can be used as a haven from an uncertain stock market. If common stock prices are expected to decline, you can sell your common stocks and invest the proceeds in Treasury bills. In this manner Treasury bills can be used as a profitable and liquid reserve awaiting the commitment of investments to other areas.

Information about Treasury bills

Obviously the most important source of price information about Treasury bills is *The Wall Street Journal*. The *good part* about investing in Treasury bills is that you know that they are top quality. With this knowledge you can then focus on the yield or discount. Quotes in *The Wall Street Journal,* however, are only an indication of the market price, yield, or discount. Actual trades at the Federal Reserve Bank or through an

---

[1] David M. Darst, *The Complete Bond Book* (New York: McGraw-Hill, 1975), p. 122.

[2] There are 100 basis points in 1 percent.

[3] Darst, *Bond Book,* p. 119.

agent in the secondary market establish the exact discount rate and yield.

Probably the best procedure for learning the current yield is to call a customer representative of a brokerage house or an officer of a commercial bank who can provide that information along with the costs of the transaction. And if it is not convenient to buy directly from the Federal Reserve Bank, the order can be placed through your broker or a commercial bank.

Short-term Treasury notes and bonds

There are other securities issued by the U.S. government and its agencies that you can purchase as short-term investments. As Treasury notes and bonds and the bonds of agencies are one year from maturity, they begin to trade like short-term securities. These securities were originally issued as long term and intermediate term bonds and notes. These bonds and notes pay interest by check if they are registered, or by the redemption of a coupon if they are bearer bonds. Bearer bonds do not have a registered owner, and interest and principal are paid on presentation of the bond or coupon. Treasury bonds and notes are absolutely safe; they enjoy the same credit rating as Treasury bills and have the same strong following among institutional investors. Yet they do suffer from the interest rate risk, and the price in the market can indeed change. This can result in a gain or loss for the investor.

Table 12–2 is a list of Treasury bonds and notes found in *The Wall Street Journal*. The short-term bonds maturing in January 1981 (under the second two columns) have a coupon or interest rate of 9.75 percent (first colums 9 3/4s where the *s* is the possessive, and the quote is read *nine and three quarters*). The bid price of the bond is 100.16, or 100 and 16/32s. Federal government bonds are quoted as $1,000 units and in $\frac{1}{32}$ of a point, a point being $10. Therefore, 100.16 is $1000 and $^{16}\!/_{32}$s of $10, or $5.00. Therefore the bid price of the bond is $1,005.

The asked price in the fifth column is 100 and $^{20}\!/_{32}$s or $1,006.25—the price you would pay for the bond. The next column (Bid Chg.) is the change, in 32nds, in the bid price from the previous day. Thus the bid price of the issue is $^{2}\!/_{32}$s larger than the previous day.

The last column is the indicated annualized yield of 8.45 percent. This is the bond yield comparable to the bond yield calculated for the T-bills.

The unit of trading in these issues varies from $1,000 to $10,000, depending on the issue. This would be determined at the time of purchase.

Short-term agency bonds

Table 12–3 provides an abbreviated list of agency bonds, some of which are short-term. These quotes are also found in *The Wall Street*

Table 12–2
Yields on U.S. Treasury issues

Treasury Issues

* * *

Bonds, Notes & Bills

Monday, July 28, 1980
Over-the-Counter quotations; sources on request.
Decimals in bid-and-asked and bid changes represent 32nds; 101.1 means 101 1/32. a-Plus 1/64. b-Yield to call date. d-Minus 1/64. n-Treasury notes.

Treasury Bonds and Notes

Rate	Mat.	Date	Bid	Asked	Bid Chg.	Yld.
6¾s,	1980	Aug n	99.28	100	+ .1	6.55
9s,	1980	Aug n	100	100.4	+ .1	5.91
8⅜s,	1980	Aug n	99.29	100.1	.....	7.74
6⅞s,	1980	Sep n	99.22	99.26	.....	7.82
8⅝s,	1980	Sep n	99.31	100.3	+ .1	7.84
8⅞s,	1980	Oct n	100	100.4	.....	8.19
3½s,	1980	Nov	98.12	98.20	+ .2	8.24
7⅛s,	1980	Nov n	99.15	99.19	- .1	8.42
9¼s,	1980	Nov n	100.3	100.7	- .2	8.46
5⅞s,	1980	Dec n	98.29	99.1	+ .1	8.23
9⅞s,	1980	Dec n	100.15	100.19	- .3	8.34
9¾s,	1981	Jan n	100.16	100.20	- .2	8.45
7s,	1981	Feb n	99	99.4	- .1	8.68
7⅜s,	1981	Feb n	99.8	99.12	- .1	8.57
9¾s,	1981	Feb n	100.18	100.22	- .2	8.53
6⅞s,	1981	Mar n	98.28	99	- .1	8.44
9⅝s,	1981	Mar n	100.20	100.24	.....	8.45
9¾s,	1981	Apr n	100.22	100.26	- .2	8.62
7⅜s,	1981	May n	98.29	99.1	- .3	8.66
7½s,	1981	May n	99	99.4	- .1	8.66
9¾s,	1981	May n	100.26	100.30	- .2	8.57
6¾s,	1981	Jun n	98.10	98.14	- .3	8.56
9⅛s,	1981	Jun n	100.11	100.15	- .3	8.59
9⅜s,	1981	Jul n	100.16	100.24	- .4	8.58
7s,	1981	Aug	98.4	98.20	.....	8.40
7⅝s,	1981	Aug n	98.25	98.29	- .3	8.74
8⅜s,	1981	Aug n	99.19	99.23	- .3	8.66
9⅝s,	1981	Aug n	100.23	100.31	- .3	8.67
6¾s,	1981	Sep n	97.22	97.26	- .4	8.76
10⅛s,	1981	Sep n	101.14	101.18	.....	8.69
12⅝s,	1981	Oct n	104.4	104.8	- .6	8.89
7s,	1981	Nov n	97.22	97.26	- .2	8.82
7¾s,	1981	Nov n	98.20	98.24	- .2	8.79
12⅛s,	1981	Nov n	103.26	103.30	- .4	8.94
7¼s,	1981	Dec n	97.24	97.28	- .4	8.88
11⅜s,	1981	Dec n	103	103.4	- .6	8.98
11½s,	1982	Jan n	103.6	103.10	- .6	9.10
6⅛s,	1982	Feb n	95.20	95.28	- .6	9.04
6⅜s,	1982	Feb	95.24	96.8	- .4	9.03
13⅞s,	1982	Feb n	106.14	106.18	- .8	9.33
7⅞s,	1982	Mar n	97.24	98.5	- .9	9.27
15s,	1982	Mar n	108.14	108.25	- .7	9.35
11⅜s,	1982	Apr n	103.2	103.6	- .10	9.37
7s,	1982	May n	96.10	96.14	- .6	9.20
8s,	1982	May n	98	98.8	- .5	9.08
9¼s,	1982	May n	100	100.4	- .11	9.18
9⅜s,	1982	May n	100.2	100.6	- .7	9.26
8¼s,	1982	Jun n	98.12	98.20	- .4	9.05
8⅝s,	1982	Jun n	98.29	98.31	- .7	9.22
8⅛s,	1982	Aug n	98.4	98.12	- .3	9.01
9s,	1982	Aug n	99.16	99.20	- .8	9.20
8⅜s,	1982	Sep n	98.12	98.16	- .6	9.15
7⅛s,	1982	Nov n	95.17	95.25	- .5	9.20
7⅞s,	1982	Nov n	97	97.8	- .6	9.23
9⅜s,	1982	Dec n	100.6	100.14	+ .2	9.17
8s,	1983	Feb n	96.15	96.23	- .19	9.49
9¼s,	1983	Mar n	99.16	99.24	- .13	9.36
7⅞s,	1983	May n	95.31	96.7	- .13	9.45
11⅝s,	1983	May n	104.18	104.26	- .16	9.63
3¼s,	1978-83	Jun	87.16	88.16	- .12	7.79
8⅞s,	1983	Jun n	98.14	99.22	+ .14	9.40
9¼s,	1983	Aug n	99.5	99.13	- .11	9.48
11⅞s,	1983	Aug n	105.20	105.28	- .11	9.60
9¾s,	1983	Sep n	100.8	100.16	- .14	9.56
7s,	1983	Nov n	92.30	93.6	- .10	9.45
10½s,	1983	Dec n	102.13	102.21	- .16	9.58
7¼s,	1984	Feb n	92.24	93.8	- .16	9.54
14¼s,	1984	Mar n	113.12	113.20	- .13	9.75
9¼s,	1984	May n	98.28	99.4	- .17	9.53
8⅞s,	1984	Jun n	97.14	97.22	- .17	9.60
6⅜s,	1984	Aug	89.12	90.12	- .18	9.28
7¼s,	1984	Aug n	92.6	92.14	- .16	9.55
8s,	1985	Feb n	93.28	94.4	- .15	9.64
3¼s,	1985	May	87.11	88.11	- .10	6.09
4¼s,	1975-85	May	87.20	88.20	- .2	7.09
10⅜s,	1985	May n	102.6	102.14	- .19	9.73
14⅜s,	1985	May n	116.14	116.22	- .20	9.92
8¼s,	1985	Aug n	94.8	94.16	- .18	9.65
9⅝s,	1985	Aug n	99.13	99.17	- .22	9.74
7⅞s,	1986	May n	91.4	91.12	- .26	9.86
8s,	1986	Aug n	91.14	91.22	- .28	9.86
6⅛s,	1986	Nov	84.19	85.19	- .16	9.49
9s,	1987	Feb n	95.6	95.14	- .23	9.97
12s,	1987	May n	107.31	108.7	- .21	10.28
7⅝s,	1987	Nov n	88.2	88.10	- .22	9.91
8¼s,	1988	May n	89.18	89.26	- .25	10.17
8¾s,	1988	Nov n	91.27	92.3	- .19	10.18
9¼s,	1989	May n	94.6	94.14	- .24	10.22
10¾s,	1989	Nov n	102.1	102.9	- .23	10.36
3½s,	1990	Feb	88.8	89.8	- .8	4.93
8¼s,	1990	May	89.14	90.14	- .11	9.79
4¼s,	1987-92	Aug	88.22	89.22	- .8	5.43
7¼s,	1992	Aug	79.16	80.16	- .11	10.08
4s,	1988-93	Feb	87.28	88.28	- .16	5.22
6¾s,	1993	Feb	78.24	79.24	- .17	9.55
7⅞s,	1993	Feb	82.12	82.28	- .10	10.34
7½s,	1988-93	Aug	79.12	80.12	- .16	10.26
8⅝s,	1993	Aug	86.16	87	- .16	10.48
8⅝s,	1993	Nov	86.18	86.26	- .13	10.49
9s,	1994	Feb	88.31	89.7	- .15	10.51
4⅛s,	1989-94	May	88.4	89.4	- .4	5.24
8¾s,	1994	Aug	86.30	87.6	- .16	10.52
10⅛s,	1994	Nov	96.22	96.30	- .20	10.54
3s,	1995	Feb	88	89	- .6	4.01
10½s,	1995	Feb	99.8	99.16	- .18	10.57
12⅝s,	1995	May	113.13	113.21	- .28	10.78
10⅜s,	1995	May	98.12	99.16	- .29	10.57
7s,	1993-98	May	72.14	73.14	- .17	10.26
3½s,	1998	Nov	88.17	89.17	- .8	4.34
8½s,	1994-99	May	84.2	85.18	- .22	10.38
7⅞s,	1995-00	Feb	78.5	78.21	- .25	10.47
8⅜s,	1995-00	Aug	82.5	82.21	- .23	10.46
8s,	1996-01	Aug	78.23	80.7	- .19	10.46
8¼s,	2000-05	May	81.4	81.20	- .14	10.31
7⅝s,	2002-07	Feb	76.4	77.20	- 1.6	10.18
7⅞s,	2002-07	Nov	79.3	80.3	- .9	10.02
8⅜s,	2003-08	Aug	81.17	82.1	- .27	10.34
8¾s,	2003-08	Nov	84.26	85.10	- .30	10.36
9⅛s,	2004-09	May	87.5	88.21	- 1.23	10.49
10⅜s,	2004-09	Nov	98.23	99.7	- .27	10.46
11¾s,	2005-10	Feb	109.5	109.21	- 1.3	10.64
10s,	2005-10	May	96.6	96.14	- .26	10.39

SOURCE *The Wall Street Journal*, July 29, 1980, p. 43.

Table 12-3
Yields on agency issues

Government, Agency and Miscellaneous Securities

Monday, July 28, 1980
Over-the-Counter quotations; sources on request.
Decimals in bid-and-asked and bid changes represent
32nds; 101.1 means 101 1/32. a-Plus 1/64. b-Yield to call
date. d-Minus 1/64. n-Treasury notes.

FNMA Issues

Rate	Mat	Bid	Asked	Yld
7.50	9-80	99.24	99.28	8.39
8.75	9-80	99.28	100	8.46
8.70	10-80	99.26	99.30	8.79
6.60	12-80	99.3	99.7	8.75
8.00	12-80	99.19	99.23	8.71
7.05	3-81	98.22	98.30	8.85
7.35	3-81	98.28	99.4	8.83
6.85	4-81	99.8	99.20	8.91
10.00	4-81	100.16	100.24	8.82
7.25	6-81	98.12	98.20	8.92
7.95	6-81	99.30	99.6	8.93
8.85	7-81	99.22	99.30	8.91
7.25	9-81	98	98.8	8.93
9.38	9-81	100.6	100.14	8.94
9.70	9-81	100.16	100.24	8.96
7.88	10-81	98.14	98.22	9.03
6.45	12-81	96.14	96.30	8.88
7.30	12-81	97.18	98.2	8.83
15.25	2-82	107.30	108.14	9.20
7.15	3-82	96.12	96.28	9.27
8.88	3-82	99.2	99.18	9.16
7.38	4-82	96.20	97.4	9.23
15.30	4-82	108.20	109.4	9.34
6.65	6-82	94.20	95.20	9.25
7.10	6-82	95.26	96.10	9.29
9.45	7-82	99.20	100.4	9.37
6.80	9-82	94.12	95.12	9.25
8.40	9-82	97.22	98.6	9.36
8.60	10-82	98	98.16	9.36
9.00	10-82	99	99.12	9.31
7.35	12-82	94.16	95.16	9.51
7.75	3-83	95.2	95.18	9.71
9.50	4-83	99.2	99.18	9.69
8.75	4-83	97.8	97.24	9.71
9.25	4-83	98.14	98.30	9.70
9.50	5-83	99.4	99.12	9.67
6.75	6-83	91.30	92.30	9.63
7.30	6-83	93.6	94.6	9.61
8.10	6-83	95.22	96.6	9.65
10.85	7-83	101.24	102.24	9.75
6.75	9-83	92.4	93.4	9.34
8.50	9-83	96	96.16	9.82
9.70	8-83		NL	0.00
9.25	10-83	98.12	98.28	9.66
8.00	12-83	94.4	95.4	9.73
8.40	12-83	95.12	96.12	9.68
14.10	2-84	111.4	111.28	10.02
9.50	3-84	98.16	99.16	9.66
7.35	4-84	91.20	92.20	9.77
8.20	4-84	93.20	94.20	9.97
14.25	5-84	112	112.24	10.07
6.25	6-84	88	89	9.73
9.25	6-84	97.20	98.20	9.68
8.20	7-84	93.24	94.24	9.83
9.05	7-84	97.4	97.20	9.79
11.10	8-84	102.28	103.12	10.02
7.95	9-84	92.16	93.16	9.91
9.75	9-84	99	99.16	9.89
11.70	10-84	104.16	105.16	10.05
6.90	12-84	88.20	89.20	9.88
7.55	12-84	90.20	91.20	9.96
9.90	1-85	99.8	99.20	9.99
7.65	3-85	90.16	91.16	9.99
8.60	6-85	93.24	94.24	9.98
9.95	6-85	99.8	99.16	10.03
7.25	7-85	88.20	89.20	9.96
7.45	9-85	89	90	9.99
7.90	10-85	90.16	91.16	10.03
8.80	10-85	94	95	10.05
8.20	3-86	90.4	91.4	10.32
9.50	3-86	95.20	96.20	10.30
9.20	4-86	94.20	95.20	10.23
7.95	7-86	88.24	89.24	10.30

Federal Land Bank

Rate	Mat	Bid	Asked	Yld
8.70	10-80	99.29	100.1	8.35
7.10	1-81	99	99.8	8.74
6.20	4-81	97.30	98.6	8.82
6.70	4-81	98.10	98.18	8.77
9.10	-7-81	99.26	100.10	8.75
6.65	10-81	98.2	98.10	8.92
6.65	1-82	96.8	96.24	9.05
7.80	1-82	97.22	98.6	9.14
6.90	4-82	96	96.16	9.13
8.15	4-82	97.24	98.8	9.26
7.80	7-82	98.14	98.30	9.30
7.30	10-82	95.14	95.30	9.36
8.00	10-82	97.2	97.18	9.23
7.20	1-83	94.22	95.6	9.43
7.95	1-83	96.20	97.4	9.53
8.65	1-83	97.8	97.24	9.54
7.30	10-83	92.28	93.28	9.55
7.35	10-83	93.4	94.4	9.50
7.10	7-85	91.20	92.20	10.02
7.95	10-85	90.16	91.16	10.08
8.80	10-85	94	95	10.05
7.60	4-87	86.12	87.12	10.24
7.25	7-87	84.12	85.20	10.18
7.85	1-88	86.4	87.20	10.26
8.20	1-90	86.8	88.8	10.16
6.95	4-91	83	85	10.29
7.95	10-96	78.20	80.20	10.45
7.35	1-97	73.28	75.28	10.45

World Bank Bonds

Rate	Mat	Bid	Asked	Yld
8.35	9-80	99.28	100	8.35
4.75	11-80	99	99.16	6.66
8.35	12-80	99.16	99.24	8.94
9.85	3-81	94.8	94.24	10.14
8.00	7-81	98.12	99.4	8.99
9.40	9-81	100	100.16	8.91
3.25	10-81	94	96	6.85
4.50	2-82	93.24	94.8	6.66
12.65	3-82	104	104.16	9.58
7.00	5-82	95.16	96	9.52
7.13	8-82	95.4	95.20	9.67
8.15	1-85	92.20	93.4	10.11
5.00	2-85	83.12	84.12	9.29
8.60	7-85	93.20	94.4	10.13
8.85	12-85	94.4	94.24	10.13
8.38	7-86	91.12	91.28	10.24
7.80	12-86	88.12	88.28	10.22
7.65	5-87	86.16	87	9.38
7.75	8-87	86.24	87.8	10.35
4.50	2-90	64.24	65.24	10.22
5.25	7-91	66.28	67.28	10.35
5.38	4-92	65.24	66.24	10.34
5.88	9-93	67	68	10.40
6.50	3-94	70.8	71.8	10.52
6.38	10-94	68.24	69.24	10.52
8.63	8-95	83.8	83.24	10.84
8.13	8-96	79.4	79.20	10.83
9.35	12-00	85.28	86.12	10.64
8.85	7-01	82.4	82.20	10.99
8.38	12-01	78.16	79	10.93
8.25	5-02	77.16	78	10.91
8.35	8-02	78.4	78.20	10.99

FIC Bank Debs.

Rate	Mat	Bid	Asked	Yld
7.90	1-81	99.14	99.22	8.61
7.00	4-82	96.2	96.18	9.26
7.95	4-86	89.20	91.4	10.04
6.95	1-87	83.20	85.20	10.04

PNMA Issues

Rate	Mat	Bid	Asked	Yld
7.75	3-87	86.28	88.4	10.26
11.15	5-87	101.28	102.12	10.64
7.65	6-87	86.8	87.8	10.28
9.10	7-87	92.4	93.2	10.41
7.50	10-87	84.2	85.28	10.32
10.50	6-88	98.24	99.8	10.64
8.55	9-88	88.4	89.12	10.53
9.30	6-89	91.20	93.4	10.51
7.80	10-91	79.20	81.20	10.64
7.00	3-92	73.28	75.28	10.67
7.05	6-92	74.4	76.4	10.64
7.10	12-97	70	72	10.67

Fed. Home Loan Bank

Rate	Mat	Bid	Asked	Yld
7.30	8-80	99.25	99.29	8.39
9.75	8-80	99.31	100.3	8.05
7.80	11-80	99.22	99.26	8.52
6.70	11-80	99.7	99.11	8.71
7.75	11-80	99.17	99.21	8.73
9.30	11-80	100	100.4	8.75
7.60	2-81	99.10	99.18	8.39
10.00	2-81	100.16	100.20	8.83
13.25	3-81	100.14	100.22	8.64
9.55	5-81	100.16	100.24	8.66
9.65	5-81	100.16	100.20	8.68
15.80	7-81	106.12	106.20	8.68
7.05	8-81	97.30	98.6	8.85
12.85	8-81	103.6	103.14	8.84
12.85	10-81	104.4	104.12	8.95
8.65	11-81	99.10	99.26	8.79
6.60	11-81	96.18	97.18	8.57
7.95	2-82	97.22	98.6	9.21
8.63	2-82	98.18	99.18	8.92
7.45	5-82	96.14	96.30	9.31
9.15	5-82	99.8	99.24	9.29
9.60	7-82	100.4	100.12	9.35
11.25	8-82	102.18	103.18	9.31
8.25	11-82	97.8	97.24	9.34
9.00	2-83	98.18	99.2	9.41
7.30	5-83	93.18	94.18	9.54
11.60	5-83	104.10	104.26	9.60
9.30	8-83	98.20	99.20	9.44
12.25	8-83	106	107	9.56
14.05	10-83	111.4	112.4	9.57
7.38	11-83	93.4	94.4	9.47
9.50	11-83	99	100	9.49
9.05	2-84	97.12	98.12	9.59
9.85	3-84	100.12	100.24	9.59
7.75	5-84	93.24	94.24	9.41
8.75	5-84	97	98	9.38
11.00	5-84	103.4	104.4	9.67
7.85	8-84	93	94	9.66
7.38	11-84	91	92	9.68
7.38	2-85	90.4	91.4	9.83
8.13	5-85	92.24	93.24	9.77
9.35	8-85	97.12	98.12	9.76
8.10	11-85	91.24	92.24	9.88
11.30	11-86	103.24	104.24	10.25
10.45	2-87	100.4	100.28	10.26
7.65	5-87	87.8	88.16	10.01
7.60	8-87	86.16	87.24	10.06
7.38	11-93	76.28	78.28	10.33
7.88	2-97	76.28	80.28	10.30

Bank for Co-ops

Rate	Mat	Bid	Asked	Yld
6.85	4-81	98.6	98.22	8.89
7.75	1-86	89.12	90.28	9.97

Asian Development Bank

Rate	Mat	Bid	Asked	Yld
8.50	1-81	99.12	100	8.50

Inter-Amer. Devel. Bk.

Rate	Mat	Bid	Asked	Yld
4.25	12-82	89.12	90.12	8.76
4.50	4-84	84.24	85.24	9.15
4.56	11-84	82.28	83.28	9.65
4.50	1-85	93.12	93.28	9.98
8.00	3-85	92.8	92.24	10.19
8.38	2-86	92	92.16	10.19
5.20	1-92	75	76	8.53
6.50	11-92	75.16	76.16	9.83
6.63	11-93	75.12	76.12	9.82
6.50	10-95	83	83.16	10.89
9.00	2-01	83.28	84.12	10.92
8.75	7-01	81.24	82.8	10.92
8.38	6-02	78.24	79.8	10.88
9.63	1-04	88.12	88.28	10.95

GNMA Issues

Rate	Bid	Asked	Yld
8.00	81.8	81.24	10.80
8.50	84.4	84.20	10.84
9.00	85.20	86.4	11.12
9.50	87.26	88.10	11.28
10.00	90.8	90.24	11.40
11.00	95.3	95.11	11.67
12.50	100	100.16	12.33

Federal Farm Credit

Rate	Mat	Bid	Asked	Yld
13.15	8-80	99.31	100.3	4.42
14.35	8-80	99.31	100.3	5.34
12.25	9-80	100.5	100.9	8.39
15.30	9-80	100.14	100.18	8.40
12.80	10-80	100.16	100.20	8.43
8.00	10-80	101.8	101.12	8.53
9.90	10-80	100.3	100.7	8.66
13.05	11-80	100.29	101.1	8.43
13.25	11-80	101.1	101.5	8.40
8.45	12-80	99.27	99.31	8.43
15.35	12-80	101.29	102.5	8.24
7.90	1-81	99.17	99.21	8.67
17.00	1-81	103.1	103.9	8.61
12.80	2-81	101.23	101.27	8.72
8.55	3-81	99.22	99.26	8.76
8.00	9-81	99.14	99.18	8.64
10.00	7-81	100.18	101.2	8.83
8.90	1-82	99.8	99.24	9.08
8.45	4-82	98.2	99.4	9.01
7.20	9-82	95.20	96.4	9.28
9.65	9-82	100.8	100.24	9.24
10.95	10-82	102.24	103.8	9.24
8.05	3-83	95.28	96.28	9.43
10.90	4-83	102.24	103.8	9.50
13.40	4-83	108.4	108.20	9.70
9.30	12-83	99.6	99.6	9.60
9.00	1-84	97.24	98.24	9.43
9.50	1-84	98.24	99.24	9.58
9.45	4-84	98.8	99.8	9.69
9.70	6-84	98.20	99.20	9.81
9.55	12-84	99.4	99.12	9.72
10.65	12-84	101.20	102.20	9.88
10.90	1-85	102.4	103.4	10.01
13.25	4-85	110.4	111.4	10.21
9.20	6-85	97.4	97.12	9.93
10.75	10-86	101	102.16	10.19
10.00	12-86	99	99.8	10.17
12.65	8-89	109.16	110.16	10.62
7.75	9-89	83.16	85	10.33
10.60	10-89	98.28	100.12	10.53
10.95	1-90	100.24	102.8	10.57

SOURCE *The Wall Street Journal*, July 29, 1980, p. 43.

Journal and the bonds are traded in 32ds of a point. Thus the Federal National Mortgage Association (FNMA) 7.35 percent issue (in percent and not 32ds) is selling at an 98.28 asked price, that is, 98 and $^{28}\!/_{32}$, to yield 8.85 percent to maturity in March 1981. You should select the yield on short-term bonds in the desired maturity range that provides you with the highest yield.

There is a commission charge for buying short-term bonds in the secondary market. Such transactions are handled by a broker or through a commercial bank. The minimum fee is $25 to $30, and the commission fee per bond declines as the number of bonds increases.

Money market funds

What is a money market fund?

Money market funds handled by mutual fund managers have captured the public's imagination. Investment companies and mutual funds that invest in stocks and bonds of other companies will be discussed later.

One of the fastest growth areas of the mutual fund industry is the area of money market funds or cash management funds. Managers of these funds invest in short-term money market investments, such as government securities, bank certificates of deposit, and corporate commercial paper.

A list of money market funds obtained from *The Wall Street Journal* appears in Table 12–4. Forty four funds are listed, which represents a truly phenomenal growth. Five years ago there were less than a dozen funds managing a few billion dollars. Today money market funds manage more than $120 billion and dominate the growth in the mutual fund industry.

Not only has there been a growth in money market funds but several brokerage firms have also started their own cash management operations. One of the best-known and largest brokerage firms in the country, Merrill Lynch, Pierce, Fenner & Smith has opened up a new consumer banking account, which is called a *cash management account,* or CMA. Merrill Lynch has been very active in providing a broad range of consumer products, such as bill paying and record keeping as well as checking and credit, that can be extended to their customers.

How to find out about money market funds

One way to learn about money market funds is to call your local stock-brokerage firm or commercial bank. These firms have money market funds available that might fit your needs. It is important for you to understand that the funds can only perform as well as the instruments in which they invest. Some take more risks that others. Some limit themselves

Table 12–4
Selected money market mutual funds

American funds group	Keystone custodian funds
Cash management	American liquid trust
American general group	Lexington group
A.g. reserve	Money market
Cash reserve	Lord Abbott
Capital preservation	Cash res.
Control capital	Lutheran brotherhood
Daily cash	Brotherhood money market
Daily income	Mass financial services
Delaware group	MCM (mass cash management)
Cash reserve	Merrill Lynch
Dreyfus group	Ready asset
Dreyfus liquid asset	Money market asset
Money managements	Mutual of Omaha funds
Federated group	Money market
Money market management (MMM)	National securities funds
Money market	Liquid reserve
Fidelty group	Oppenheimer funds
Cash reserve	Money bi
Daily income	Price Rowe
First investors fund	Prime reserve
Cash management	Putnam funds
Franklin group	Daily divided trust
Liquid asset	Reserve funds
Funds incorporated group	Scudder funds
Current interest	Cash investment
Grad cash reserve	Shearson funds
Holding trust	Daily dividend
Intercap	Stein Roe funds
Investors group funds	Cash reserve
IDS cash	Temporary investment
Johnston cash	Union service group
John Hancock funds	Union cash
Cash management	Value line funds
Kemper funds	Cash funds
Money market	Vanguard group
	Market money

SOURCE *The Wall Street Journal,* January 15, 1980, p. 37.

to top-quality short-term investment outlets, others take greater risks. Some of them invest their funds in short-term securities with average maturities of 30 days; others buy longer-term securities.

Rating money funds

The price stability of securities owned by money market funds is one of the great appeals of the funds. Since the value of the securities bought by funds does not fluctuate much, the funds are able to keep their share value constant. All the money market funds have a constant share value of $1. If you buy 1,000 shares today for $1,000, you know that you can sell those 1,000 shares for the same price a month or a year from now. Interest is calculated daily and automatically reinvested in the fund. If there is a decline in market value because of rising interest rates, the decline is deducted from that day's interest. Similarly an increase in value because of falling interest rates is added to that day's interest. Not all funds exactly follow this system, which is called *marking to the market,* but the net result is about the same.

In addition to price stability, another appeal of the money market funds is that they pay interest much higher than that available from a savings account. Interest rates on money market funds follow the economy overall, and tend to keep pace with the rate of inflation. For example, most funds listed here paid about 12½–13 percent interest for the 12-month period ending with the first quarter of 1981. Compared to the 5½ percent available from local banks, that's a very good rate of return. Of course, your deposit is not insured by the federal government. But these funds are about as safe as you can get other than a bank passbook account. If you buy from a brokerage firm, however, your account is insured by the Security Investors' Protection Corporation (SIPC) against the possibility of the firm going bankrupt. SIPC does not insure you against losing money. But the chance of losing money is so small that even the most conservative investor can feel safe.

If you do decide to invest in a money market fund, be sure to write for a prospectus (description of the fund), and read it carefully. One of the key variables to look out for is the average maturity of the fund (i.e., the average length of time until securities in the fund mature). The longer this time period, the more volatile will be the fluctuation in market value. Some funds have average maturities of less than 50 days; others have a much longer time span. During a period of falling interest rates, the longer maturity funds do better. However, the reverse is true as rates rise.

How a money fund works

Most funds require you to invest a minimum amount of money. The amount varies from $1,000 to $5,000. Normally there is no withdrawal penalty, there are no redemption fees, and there are no sales charges. The funds offer an extremely valuable tool for the small investor because small amounts of money can be invested in rather sophisticated investment areas. Without a money market fund, you would have to have a minimum of $10,000 to buy Treasury bills, for example. A smiliar minimum would be required to buy more sophisticated investments. Even bank certificates of deposit require you to invest minimum amounts of money.

Most funds send you a monthly statement as to the number of shares and the amount of interest you have earned for the month. Each month you receive your interest in the form of new shares. If you earn $200 in interest in a month, you receive 200 shares at $1 each, which are added to your previous balance of shares at $1 apiece. Even though the price of the fund does not change, the number of shares you own does change. Therefore you can see investment growth in terms of the number of shares you own. This also means that you need some other source of information about performance other than those quoted in *The Wall Street Journal*. One useful source of information is *Money* magazine. *Money* publishes a monthly list giving the performance of the ten largest money market funds.

Another advantage of a money market fund is that you can obtain your funds through a checking system as easily as you write checks against a commercial bank account. Most funds stipulate that a minimum amount of money has to be withdrawn—usually $500. In addition to writing checks on your account, you can withdraw money in any amount by mail or telephone without loss or penalty at any time. In addition, you keep the earnings on your money in your account until a check is presented for payment or until you withdraw funds from your account. A money market fund can be used as a custodial account for minors. It can also be a joint partnership owned by several individuals.

How to open a money market account

To open a money market fund, all you need to do is to request complete information about all charges and expenses. One expense that has not been mentioned is the management fee charged by money market funds. That fee is a percent of the fund's value. Actually, for the small investor, this is a minor consideration when you consider the fees involved in those kinds of trades. A short-term money market fund can probably do a much better job of earning money for you than you can yourself by putting money directly into CDs or government securities. You receive the benefits of professional management and a higher rate of return at a cost of less than one half of 1 percent. If you assume that the fund earns 12 percent and that a one half of 1 percent fee is paid on the total value of the fund, then the management cost of the fund is approximately 4.1 percent of income received. This is quite low in comparison with ordinary fees charged by mutual funds, and the advantages seem to outweigh the costs.

Use of a money market fund

Money market funds may be used in the same way as Treasury bills to assist investors in meeting their investment goal of maximizing return and minimizing risk. As we have seen, money market funds and short-term investments are particularly attractive when interest rates are high. If interest rates are expected to climb, investors might want an alternative to extending their investment maturities in bonds or of looking at common stock for investments. In general, liquid trusts, money market funds, government securities, and short-term agency securities offer an excellent way of helping investors earn a high rate of return while they reduce their risk and maintain a highly liquid position.

Commercial paper as a short-term investment

Money rates are listed daily in *The Wall Street Journal*. Such a series of quotes appears in Table 12–5. It is a good idea to refer to this figure in the *Journal* periodically to find out what is happening in the money market. Since the wise investor must be aware of all the investment alternatives available, this is a quick reference. A variety of money rates are listed in Table 12–5. Some are relevant to investors, other are not. Certainly investors cannot buy at the prime rate because that is the rate at which banks lend money to their prime customers for short periods of time. Investors cannot invest in federal funds because these are inter-

**Table 12–5
Money rates**

Money Rates

Monday, July 28, 1980

The key U.S. and foreign annual interest rates below are a guide to general levels but don't always represent actual transactions.

PRIME RATE: 10¾% to 11%. The charge by large U.S. money center commercial banks to their best business borrowers.

FEDERAL FUNDS: 19% high, 8¾% low. 9¼% closing bid, 9½% offered. Reserves traded among commercial banks for overnight use in amounts of $1 million or more.

DISCOUNT RATE: 10%. The charge on loans to member commercial banks by the New York Federal Reserve Bank.

CALL MONEY: 10%. The charge on loans to brokers on stock exchange collateral.

COMMERCIAL PAPER: placed directly by General Motors Acceptance Corp.: 8⅜%, 30 to 270 days.

COMMERCIAL PAPER: high-grade unsecured notes sold through dealers by major corporations in multiples of $1,000: 8⅜%, 30 days thru 90 days.

CERTIFICATES OF DEPOSIT: 8¼%, one month; 8.40%, two months; 8½%, three months; 8½%, six months; 8½%, one year. Typical rates paid by major banks on new issues of negotiable C.D.'s, usually on amounts of $1 million and more. The minimum unit is $100,000.

BANKERS ACCEPTANCES: 8.55%, 30 days thru 180 days. Negotiable, bank-backed business credit instruments typically financing an import order.

EURODOLLARS: 9 11/16% to 9 9/16%, one month; 9 3/16% to 9 1/16%, two months; 9 5/16% to 9 3/16%, three months; 9 9/16% to 9 7/16%, four and five months; 9 11/16% to 9 9/16% six months. The rates paid on U.S. dollar deposits in banks in London, usually on amounts of $100,000 or more.

FOREIGN PRIME RATES: Canada 12½%; Germany 11%; Japan 9.69%; Switzerland 5¾%; Britain 17½%. These rate indications aren't directly comparable; lending practices vary widely by location. Source: Morgan Guaranty Trust Co.

TREASURY BILLS: Results of the Monday, July 28, 1980, auction of short-term U.S. government bills, sold at a discount from face value in units of $10,000 to $1 million: 8.221%, 13 weeks; 8.276%, 26 weeks.

SAVINGS RATES: on instruments offered to individuals; minimum amounts vary. Money market fund-a, 7.36%; six month money market certificate, 8.406%; 30-month savings institution certificate-b, 9½%; savings institution passbook deposit-b, 5.5%; U.S. savings bond, 6.5%.

a-Annualized average rate of return after expenses for past 30 days on Merrill Lynch Ready Assets Trust, the largest of such funds; this isn't a forecast of future returns. b-Commercial banks are limited to paying one-quarter percentage point less than savings and loan associations and savings banks.

SOURCE *The Wall Street Journal*, July 29, 1980, p. 36.

bank loans. Similarly, you cannot invest in the discount rate because that is the rate the Federal Reserve Bank charges commercial banks for direct loans. You also cannot become involved in call money because call money really consists of very short-term loans to brokers on stock exchange collateral. But you can invest in commercial paper.

Commercial paper is a fairly simple type of short-term money market security. It is simply an unsecured corporate IOU. Major corporations sell these IOUs through commercial paper dealers. The corporations pay interest on these securities just as they would on any other short-term loan. Commerical paper is considered a very safe form of investment because the securities are sold only by the financially strongest corporations.

Price quotes for commercial paper

The first quote listed for the yield on commercial paper is for commercial paper placed directly by General Motors Acceptance Corporation. The rates are given for 30 to 60 days, 60 to 90 days, 90 to 180 days, and 180 to 270 days. Unfortunately an investor must invest a minimum of $25,000 in 30–day paper.

How to buy commercial paper

The rather large minimum purchase requirement probably means that you will not be able to purchase commercial paper directly through a dealer or broker. Instead, the most practical way for you to earn the high yields available on commercial paper is by buying a money market fund that invests in commercial paper. For all intents and purposes, the direct purchase of commercial paper is limited to institutions and very wealthy individuals. However, it is important for you to know what commercial paper is because many money market funds invest a substantial portion of their assets in it.

Certificates of deposit

Two types of certificates of deposit are available to individual investors. The first is the relatively small-size certificates described in Chapter 4. These certificates may be purchased directly from commercial banks, savings and loan associations, mutual savings banks, and credit unions. They come in a variety of maturities and offer attractive rates of return.

The other type of certificate of deposit is the large, negotiable certificates issued by major financial institutions. These certificates, sometimes called *jumbo certificates,* normally come in minimum amounts of $100,000. Rates paid on jumbo certificates are generally higher than Treasury bill rates.

Certainly you should examine all alternatives when considering short-term investment. However, those that are familiar, such as Treasury bills and money market funds, give investors a high yield and maximum liquidity. They can also be purchased in fairly small amounts. As a practical matter, a money market fund that invests in certificates of deposit, commercial paper, and federal securities offers you the best opportunity.

Long-term government and agency bonds

All the investment media discussed up to this point have been short-term investment opportunities in fixed-income securities. The U.S. government also issues long-term debt securities. These securities, unlike Treasury bills that sell at a discount, pay interest semiannually. These bonds and notes sell at face value and have coupons attached. When interest payments are due, you simply detach a coupon and present it to any commercial bank acting as an agent for the U.S. Treasury. If the bond or note does not have coupons attached, it is called a *registered bond*. Such a bond is registered in your name when you buy it. Interest payments are then paid directly to you as they become due. *Agency bonds* are bonds issued by various government-related agencies to finance their activities. You may recognize such agencies as the Federal National Mortgage Association and the World Bank.

Some long-term bonds available for purchase are listed in Tables 12–2 and 12–3. In moving to long-term government securities, the investment quality of the security does not change. Only the investment maturity changes. When interest rates are high, some people invest heavily in federal fixed-income securities to obtain unquestioned bonds of superior quality and relatively high interest rates. Under normal circumstances long-term bonds of the U.S. government sell at higher yields than Treasury bills. The higher yield compensates you for the interest rate risk. All you need do is to pick out the maturity you are willing to accept, and then decide whether or not the yield is satisfactory. Ordinarily the yield on a U.S. government agency bond is only indirectly guaranteed by the government of the United States. It has a somewhat lower credit rating and therefore offers a higher yield. Historically these securities have not defaulted. They have paid their interest on time, and the government has guaranteed some of the agencies directly. Therefore, if it is possible to earn a higher yield for the period of time you select, you might want to consider agency bonds.

Analysis of longer-term bonds

In an analysis of longer-term bonds you will find that U.S. government securities and their agencies enjoy an excellent credit relationship with investors, particularly institutional investors. Therefore detailed credit analysis is unnecessary except to analyze very carefully the direction of interest rates. If interest rates decline from present levels, then the price of the bond chosen will increase. In this case you will earn a somewhat higher rate of return for the period invested. For example, let's assume you choose a five-year bond that offers a yield of 10 percent. Also assume that interest rates decline to 8 percent. The price of that bond will rise in the market, and an investor will have a capital gain on the bond. The price rises because your bond is still paying 10 percent interest while new bonds are only paying 8 percent interest. Your bond, being more valuable than new bonds, will rise in price. In a short period you might earn 15 percent. To earn 15 percent, you would have to sell the bond prior to the maturity date, reap the benefits, pay a tax on those benefits, and then reinvest the money at the new and lower rate. But for short periods of time you might earn an excellent return on bonds of the federal government or federal agencies.

The danger of rising interest rates

The major danger in owning long-term bonds stems from the interest rate risk. The interest rate risk was described briefly in the previous chapter. It is the risk of loss of capital and interest as a result of rising interest rates. If interest rates rise in the future, the price of bonds will decline. If you own long-term bonds, you will lose out on the value of your bonds. You will also lose out in the sense that you will earn a lower rate of return than new bonds pay.

To illustrate this risk, let's return to the example of the 10 percent bond. If you buy a bond today paying 10 percent interest, and interest rates increase in the future, the value of your bond will decline. For example, suppose you hold that bond for five years while interest rates on new long-term government bonds increase to 12 percent. You will now own a five-year old bond paying only 10 percent interest. Other investors who wish to buy bonds can now buy new bonds paying 12 percent interest. If you have to sell your bond, you would have to sell it for less than the price of new bonds. In fact, you would have to sell it for a price at which someone buying it would earn the same rate of return as new bonds pay. Thus, if your bond has a face value of $10,000, you would probably have to sell it for about $9,500. How far the bond might decline in value would depend on how many years remain until it reaches maturity. The longer the maturity, the bigger will be the discount from face value. The interest rate risk points out the most serious risks of purchasing long-term bonds. As a matter of practice, you might lose a few points in interest income, but you would be better off to stick to shorter maturities. Or simply stick to Treasury bills because you then would not have to worry about a decrease in capital. All you would have to worry about would be making sure that your money is invested periodically.

No inflation protection

The other basic disadvantage of investing in fixed-income securities is that they offer no protection against the risk of inflation. Although you might earn a 10 percent return over the life of a bond, if the inflation rate is 11 percent, you have actually lost purchasing power. Certainly an ideal investment would be one that provides a 10 to 12 percent yield. But historically it has been extremely difficult to obtain a return of 10 to 12 percent when the national economy is only growing at 2½–3 percent annually. Therefore, if you are going to purchase long-term bonds, you should make sure that interest rates are close to their peak or at least stable. Unfortunately these conditions are difficult to achieve, and in an inflationary economy your dollars constantly buy less and less.

Interest rate trend

The reality of interest rates increasing is demonstrated in Table 11–3 of Chapter 11, which shows the pattern of yields or interest rates on long-term government bonds. It indicates that the trend has not always been up. But certainly in the last decade long-term interest rates have tended to rise. Ideally, if you are going to commit your funds to long-term bonds, you should do so at the peak of interest rates. On the other hand, if you can buy a top-quality long-term U.S. government security yielding 13 percent for a long period of time, it will provide you with substantial income. It will also be stable over the life of the bond. Your investment will not grow each year, but it will be good for an income investor who needs a substantial amount of current income. Of course, the interest income on such bonds is exempt from state taxes.

Tax-exempt state and municipal bonds

State and municipal bonds are exempt from federal income taxes. They thus offer investors, particularly people in high income tax brackets, an attractive investment alternative. State and municipal bonds have some business risk, and they bear the interest rate risk and inflation risk. The amount of state and municipal securities in existence is not as great as the amount of federal debt securities outstanding. But the growth of municipal securities outstanding has been far greater. Well over $225 billion of state and municipal debt are outstanding, with annual additions amounting to over 10 percent of this amount.

This growth might not continue in the future because of a growing opposition to property tax increases and a general increase in government spending. We can expect many more cases where property tax limits similar to California's Proposition 13 will be passed. At the same time limits will be imposed on the amount of debt that state and local communities can issue. The growth of state and local government financing will probably diminish in the future. This is because the growth of such financing in the past has been associated with increased expenditures for education, roads and bridges, utilities, housing, veterans' benefits, and similar items. We expect such expenditures to grow more slowly. The tremendous number of new facilities built since World War II resulted in the increase of outstanding state and municipal securities. Private investors have lent the bulk of these funds to states and municipalities. Individuals and commercial banks are the largest suppliers of funds. Both are about equal in size, and together provide about 78 to 80 percent of the funds. Insurance companies have supplied about 14 percent of these funds. The rest has been received from corporations, mutual savings banks, and other investors.

States, municipalities, special schools, and road and park districts, with the consent of the people, can issue bonds that have the distinct advantage of being exempt from federal income taxes. Such bonds are also usually exempt from income taxes levied by the municipality selling the securities. This feature makes state and municipal securities uniquely attractive to wealthy individuals and institutions in the high-tax brackets.

There are two basic types of state and municipal bonds; general obligations bonds and revenue bonds. These bonds are usually issued as *debenture contracts.* This means that they are without a specific pledge of real or personal property other than a pledge of revenues from a project with the taxing ability of the issuing agency. The bonds are in either straight maturities or serial maturities. In the case of serial maturities, they are paid off or retired every six months. When the bonds are issued, a schedule is published showing the amount of interest charges and debt retirement to be paid every six months.

General obligation bonds

General obligations bonds are fully tax-supported. They are considered to be "full faith and credit bonds" guaranteed by a political unit with the power to levy taxes. The base for the tax that supports debt is usually the assessed value of real estate. Income taxes and sales taxes might also be pledged. The investment quality of each issue or bond depends on the legality of the issue and the ability of the issuing community to pay the debt and interest and retire the debt when it is due. Obviously this varies from community to community.

Legality

The legality of a bond issue is determined by legal counsel to make certain that political leaders have the right to issue a particular debt and that they have the approval of citizens in the taxing jurisdiction. The ability to pay debt service interest with repayments of principal is a function of per capita income and the amount of debt outstanding. A guide to repayment is the income level of the citizens, the existing debt per capita, the relationship of debt to assessed valuation, and the issuer's past record. Many communities place limits on the amount of debt that can be issued with a rule of thumb suggesting that such service not exceed 25 percent of the annual budget. Obviously a wealthy and growing community is in a better position to pay its debt than a mature community that is declining in population. Debt is also limited by law to from 1 to 20 percent of the assessed value of property with a 7 percent limit common. The state of California in 1978 passed Proposition 13, which limited the amount of tax on property to 1 percent of the value of the property. This created a substantial change in direction for expenditures and taxation for the state. The full effect of the tax limitation on property has not yet been determined.

Price quotes

Prices of general obligation bonds are not usually available in either local papers or *The Wall Street Journal.* State and municipal bonds are traded in a local, over-the-counter market. Such trading is handled by members of the brokerage community and by specialists who trade in, and make markets in, these securities. Major national brokerage firms also provide both price information and advice.

Table 12–6 provides a list of bonds by state, maturity, and rating. Group 5, the base group, provides the yield to maturity for various ratings and years to maturity. The yield on AAA, California, five-year maturity, is 6.00 percent. The AAA, Missouri bonds for the five-year maturity would yield 5.85 percent (−.15). The Delaware AA− bonds in Group 12 would yield 6.50 percent (+.50) for the five-year maturity. The rates in Table 12–6 change from time to time on the basis of market activity. Yield differentials also change.

Trading unit

You would be wise to trade in units of 25 bonds for the best marketability. Trading becomes a little sticky at less than that amount, although units of $5,000 (five bonds) trade more easily than $1,000, which is really an odd-lot purchase.

Dealers trade the bonds on a net basis, with a variable per bond commission that declines as the number of bonds increases. We can expect to pay $5 per bond, with a minimum commission of perhaps $25.

Revenue bonds

Revenue bonds are bonds of a political subdivision, government unit, or public authority whose debt service is paid solely out of revenues from the project. Bridge, tunnel, and tollway bonds are excellent examples of this kind of bond. A complete list of such bonds would include a broad group of economic and business activities. Revenue bonds have the advantage of not increasing the debt burden on general revenues of a municipality; they can be issued when the debt limit has been reached. They follow the principle of benefits received, which means that the project is paid for by those who use it. This enables communities to provide facilities even though few or no general revenues are used to support specific projects.

Table 12–6
Yields of general obligation bonds

State General Obligation Bonds
Comparative Value Trading Chart

Moody's	S&P		5 Years	10 Years	15 Years	20 Years
		GROUP 1				
Aaa	AAA	Missouri	−.15	−.15	−.20	−.20
Aaa	NR	Oklahoma	−.15	−.15	−.20	−.20
Aaa	AAA	Utah	−.15	−.15	−.20	−.20
Aaa	AAA	Virginia	−.15	−.15	−.20	−.20
		GROUP 2				
Aaa	AAA	North Carolina	−.15	−.15	−.15	−.15
Aaa	AAA	Texas	−.15	−.15	−.15	−.15
		GROUP 3				
Aaa	AA	Georgia	−.10	−.10	−.10	−.10
Aa	AA	Kentucky	−.10	−.10	−.10	−.10
Aaa	AAA	Minnesota	−.10	−.10	−.10	−.10
Aaa	AAA	South Carolina	−.10	−.10	−.10	−.10
Aaa	AA+	Tennessee	−.10	−.10	−.10	−.10
		GROUP 4				
Aa	AA	Alabama	−.05	−.05	−.10	−.10
Aaa	NR	New Hampshire	−.05	−.05	−.10	−.10
Aa	AA	New Mexico	−.05	−.05	−.10	−.10
		GROUP 5 (BASE GROUP: YIELDS TO MATURITY)				
Aaa	AAA	California	6.00%	6.10%	6.40%	6.75%
Aaa	AAA	Illinois	6.00%	6.10%	6.40%	6.75%
Aa	AA	Louisiana	6.00%	6.10%	6.40%	6.75%
Aaa	AAA	Maryland	6.00%	6.10%	6.40%	6.75%
Aa	AA−	Mississippi	6.00%	6.10%	6.40%	6.75%
Aaa	AAA	New Jersey	6.00%	6.10%	6.40%	6.75%
Aaa	AAA	Wisconsin	6.00%	6.10%	6.40%	6.75%
		GROUP 6				
Aa	AAA	Maine	0	+.05	+.05	+.05
Aa	AA	Michigan	0	+.05	+.05	+.05
Aa	AA+	Ohio	0	+.05	+.05	+.05
Aa	AA	Rhode Island	0	+.05	+.05	+.05
Aa	NR	Vermont	0	+.05	+.05	+.05
Aa	AA+	Washington	0	+.05	+.05	+.05
		GROUP 7				
Aa	AA	Florida	+.05	+.05	+.10	+.10
Aa	AA	Nevada	+.05	+.05	+.10	+.10
		GROUP 8				
Aa	AA	Connecticut	+.10	+.10	+.15	+.15
A-1	AA+	West Virginia	+.10	+.10	+.15	+.15
		GROUP 9				
Aaa	AA+	Oregon	+.10	+.10	+.20	+.20
		GROUP 10				
A-1	A+	Alaska	+.15	+.20	+.25	+.25
		GROUP 11				
Aa	AA	Hawaii	+.20	+.25	+.30	+.30
		GROUP 12				
A	AA−	Delaware	+.50	+.65	+.60	+.50
		GROUP 13				
A	AA	New York	+.50	+.90	+.85	+.65
		GROUP 14				
A-I	AA	Massachusetts	+.75	+.90	+1.00	+.75
		GROUP 15				
A	A+	Pennsylvania	+.75	+1.00	+1.10	+.85

NR-Not rated.

Arizona, Arkansas, Colorado, Indiana, Iowa, Kansas, Nebraska, South Dakota and Wyoming haven't any general obligation debt. Idaho, Montana and North Dakota are excluded because of current thin secondary market supply.

SOURCE *Merril Lynch Pierce Fenner & Smith, Bond Market Commentary*, January 3, 1980.

Are revenues sufficient?

The basic question investors must raise about revenue bonds is whether revenues from a project will be sufficient to pay the debt service, both interest and principal repayment. A careful analysis must be made to determine the business risk. Certainly some securities have been issued by revenue authorities that have not been particularly good investments. Investors must analyze the business situation surrounding revenue bonds as well as the integrity of the issuing unit to make certain both are secure and adequate. Investors must examine revenue bond issues by municipalities just as they would a private corporation. In other words there must be enough revenue from the project to pay the debt when it comes due and to pay interest charges. In addition, there must be sufficient revenue to maintain the economic strength of the revenue project. Otherwise, the project should not be considered a viable investment alternative for most investors.

Active bonds are quoted

Some of the more actively traded tax exempt bonds are quoted in *The Wall Street Journal.* If you want to find a price quote for "Big Macs," for example, you will find them there. Big Macs are bonds issued by the Municipal Assistance Corporation of New York, which was created to help New York City survive financially. These tax-exempt securities pay a high yield because the risks are high. Notice in Table 12–7 that the Big Macs 9¾s of 92 are selling at a bid price of 101 and an asked price of 104. The coupon is 9¾ percent on the bond, which means that the interest stated in the bond agreement is $97.50 annually per thousand dollars of par value. The bonds mature in 1992, and you will pay the asked price if you want to buy them. The change column refers to the number of points change from the preceding day. In the case of the 9¾s of 92, there was a −1 change from the previous day.

Unfortunately the newspaper does not calculate the bond yield to maturity. If you want to calculate the yield, you should divide the average investment into the average annual income. The average investment is 104 + 100 = 102, or $1,020.

The annual income is $97.50. Since you have paid 104 for the bond, you must write off the $40 loss over the 12 years to maturity ($1,040 − $1,000 = $40). If you divide 12 into 40, you get a loss of $3.33 per year. Thus the average annual income is $97.50 − $3.33 = $94.17. Dividing $1,020 (1,000 + 1,040)/2 into $94.17 provides an approximate average yield of 9.232 percent. This is a good yield when you realize that it is tax-exempt. Of course, the risks are also high.

Rating municipal bonds

It is extremely difficult for the average investor to rate municipal bonds, either a general obligation bond or a revenue bond issued by a municipality. Even if you live in the community, you will find it hard to determine

Table 12-7
Price quotes of tax-exempt bonds

Tax-Exempt Bonds

Here are current prices of active tax-exempt revenue bonds issued by toll roads and other public authorities.

Agency	Coupon	Mat	Bid	Asked	Chg.
Bat Park City Auth NY	6⅜s	'14	65	69	.....
Chelan Cnty PU Dist	5s	'13	70	73	+ ½
Chelan Cnty PU Dist	6⅜s	'29	76	80	+ ½
Chesapeake B Br&Tun-f	5¾s	'00	70	73	− ½
Chi Calumet Skyway-f	3⅜s	'95	51½	53½	.....
Columbia S.P.E.	3⅞s	'03	72½	74½	.....
Dallas-Ft Worth Airport	6¼s	'02	77	81	.....
Dela. River Port Auth	5⅝s	'09	65½	67½	− ½
Douglas Cnty PU Dist	4s	'18	53½	55½	.....
Florida Turnpike Auth	4¾s	'01	82½	84½	.....
Grant Cnty PU Dist	3⅞s	'05	67	70	.....
Illinois Toll	3¾s	'95	78½	80½	.....
Indiana Toll	3½s	'94	86	88	+ ½
Jacksonville Exp	4.1s	'03	72	75	.....
Kentucky Turnpike Auth	6⅛s	'08	73	77	− ½
Munic. Assist. Cp. NY	9¾s	'92	101	104	−1
Munic. Assist. Cp. NY	9¼s	'90	114½	118½	.....
Munic. Assist. Cp. NY	9s	'85	105½	109½	.....
Munic. Assist. Cp. NY	8s	'86	99	103	.....
Munic. Assist. Cp. NY	8s	'91	91	95	.....
Munic. Assist. Cp. NY	8⅜s	'08	88	92	.....
Munic. Assist. Cp. NY	8⅝s	'99	92	96	.....
Munic. Assist. Cp. NY	10¼s	'93	105	109	.....
Munic. Assist. Cp. NY	7½s	'95	86	90	.....
Maryland Br&Tun	5.2s	'08	83	86	.....
Mass Port Auth	6s	'11	81	84	.....
Mass Turnpike Auth	3.3s	'94	93	95	− ½
Massachusetts	9s	'01	115½	117½	.....
Nebraska P.P.D.	6⅛s	'13	73	76	.....
NJ Turnpike Auth	5.2s	'08	66	68	.....
NJ Turnpike Auth	6s	'14	75	78	+ ½
NJ Sports Auth	7½s	'09	107	110	.....
NY State Power Auth	6⅝s	'10	76½	79½	− ½
NY State Power Auth	8⅛s	'10	92	95	− ½
NY State Thruway	3.1s	'94	63	66	.....
NY State Urban Devlp	6s	'13	62½	66½	.....
NY State Urban Devlp	7s	'14	72½	76½	.....
NY State Urban Devlp	9⅜s	'99	98	102	.....
Penn Turnpike	3.1s	'93	94½	96½	.....
Port of NY Auth	4¾s	'03	60	63	.....
Port of NY Auth	6s	'08	71	74	− ½
Port of NY & NJ Auth	7s	'11	84	88	.....
Valdez (Exxon)	5½s	'07	74	76	− ½
Valdez (Sohio & B.P.)	6s	'07	75	77	.....
West Virginia Turnpike	3¾s	'89	56½	58½	.....
Washington P.P.S.S.	6½s	'10	74½	78½	.....
Washington P.P.S.S.	7¾s	'17	88	92	.....

f-Trades flat without payment of current interest.

SOURCE *The Wall Street Journal,* July 29, 1980, p. 37.

the credit worthiness of a particular bond issue. Even rating agencies have found it difficult to accurately rate such bonds. Many rating agencies are just catching up to the economic realities of a community. For example, when New York City was in difficult financial straits, the rating agencies did not begin to change their ratings until the city was almost bankrupt. Yet in hindsight it was apparent that the city's expenditures were rising at a more rapid rate than its revenues. This statement is not intended as a criticism of the rating agencies. When information is difficult to come by and requires time to be translated into the marketplace, it is not easy to determine a community's credit worthiness.

It is important, therefore, that for investors to examine the behavior of yields in the marketplace for municipal securities they have purchased.

Such analyses by the investors themselves, along with those of the rating agencies, will serve as a guide to the relative attractiveness of the securities. You must rely on bond ratings as a first guide to the investment quality of securities. Moody's *Municipal and Government Manual* provides factual rating services. Bonds are rated from Aaa to C. Aaa bonds are the best quality and carry the smallest risk. Interest payments are covered from revenues well above those needed to maintain the solvency of the particular bond issue. C bonds are the lowest rated bonds; they are neither highly protected nor adequately secured. Obviously C bonds have a higher yield than Aaa bonds because of the increased risk. Information about bonds may be found in the *Bond Buyer: Prices and Yields National Municipal Review, Municipal Yearbook,* and *Census Report on Government Debts in the United States.* If you stay within the ratings from Baa to Aaa, you will be safe from the risk of default.

Bond information

Bond quotations and information about state and municipal bonds may be obtained from a municipal bond dealer, as mentioned previously. A partial list is carried in Standard & Poor's *Weekly Bond Outlook* and Moody's *Weekly Bond Survey.* Prices are listed in the pink sheets quotations of brokerage offices. This is where you must go to find quotations on local securities.

Historical yields

Historical yields on municipal bonds may be found in current issues of the *Federal Reserve Bulletin.* Over the past decade yields on state and local government AAAs have ranged from 2.9 percent to almost 11 percent. A person in the 50 percent tax bracket would have to earn 5.8 percent to 22 percent in fully taxable income to achieve the same aftertax results. We can calculate what a comparable fully taxable yield would have to be by dividing one minus the investor's marginal tax rate in the tax-exempt yield. Thus a person in the 50 percent tax earning an 11 percent aftertax return on a municipal bond would need to earn a full taxable yield of 22 percent. This is found by dividing 1 minus .50 into 11, which comes out to 22 percent. A yield conversion table is given in Table 12–8.

Risk and reward

The risk and reward on municipal securities are still there because yields do fluctuate. Tax-exempt municipals are unique, but they carry risks—they are subject to the money rate risk and the purchasing power risk. Revenue bonds are also subject to the business risk. At a yield above 6 percent, they are attractive for income investors in high-income tax brackets. The historical trend of the yield has been up, and investors who purchased these bonds early in 1970 would have a capital loss.

Table 12–8
Fully equivalent taxable yield

Tax-exempt yield	Fully equivalent taxable yield			
	Tax bracket			
	20	30	40	50
4	5.00	5.71	6.67	8.00
5	6.25	7.14	8.33	10.00
6	7.50	8.57	10.00	12.00
7	8.75	10.00	11.67	14.00
8	10.00	11.42	13.33	16.00
9	11.25	12.86	15.00	18.00
10	12.50	14.29	16.67	20.00
11	13.75	15.71	18.33	22.00

The only time you can prevent a capital loss is when you buy municipal bonds for the long term at very high interest rates. Since this is difficult to do, you must be careful to assess the risks involved in the purchase of municipal bonds before committing your funds. An upward increase in yields causes a loss in the price of the bond. State and municipal bonds, however, offer stability of income. For the most part they are quality investments, appealing to investors in the high-tax brackets.

All the same, you need to undertake a careful analysis of the credit worthiness of a community before you purchase its securities. Keep in mind the fact that risks are involved in the ownership of both long-term and short-term state and municipal bonds.

Corporate bonds

In the last decade U.S. private corporations raised more than $200 billion through the issuance of debt securities. Corporate bonds represented more than two thirds of the total capital raised. For the most part they provided investors with sound and safe investments. Yields ranged from 7.5 percent to 9.5 percent for most of the decade.

The nature of corporate bonds

Corporate bonds are a long-term, written promise to pay the amount borrowed in a set time at a fixed and specified rate of interest. The corporate bond is in reality a loan made by buyers of the bond to the corporation. Such a loan is usually large; it is divided into many parts and then sold to investors. The parts, usually $1,000 in denomination, make up the total bond issue. A business corporation issuing bonds is in effect selling its credit to an individual or a financial institution willing to invest in its securities. The borrowing corporation promises to do two things. First, it will pay the interest when it comes due, either quarterly or semiannually. Usually the greater the risk involved with the bond, the higher the interest paid. Second, the corporation will pay the face amount of the loan when it matures, or when it is called for redemption by the corporation at what is referred to as the *first call date.*

Bond indentures

Bond indentures are agreements containing the terms and conditions of a lending arrangement between corporations issuing the bonds and corporate trustees representing the bondholders. The items covered in a bond indenture are the interest rate, or coupon rate, the trustee's certificate, the registration and endorsement, any property pledged as security, and agreements, restrictions, and remedies of trustees and bondholders in case the company should default on its two promises. If the bondholders have any special rights, such as the right to convert the bond into stock at some future time, the terms are stated exactly in the bond indenture.

One of the first promises made in a bond indenture is a statement concerning the time of repayment of the principal and concerning the security pledged to ensure that the debt will be paid when it comes due. Bonds are retired at maturity date, typically after 20 years or longer for a long-term bond issue. In other cases the bonds are subject to call or are retired serially. Most bonds today are callable at the option of the issuing corporation. The term *callable* means that the corporation has the right to recall the bonds by paying off its debt. This gives the company an opportunity to retire the debt before maturity, a step that might be necessary in order to take advantage of surplus funds or lower interest rates, or to clean up the capital structure of the company if new financing is anticipated. The investor should know the time of a possible call, as this will have an effect upon the yield that will be received. This is important when you purchase bonds at a premium (that is, at a price above the face value). This is particularly the case when the call price is substantially below the market price of the bond. Bonds may be retired serially, which is usually the case in municipal financing. Thus every six months of a 20-year bond issue one 40th of the issue is retired, along with the payment of interest. Investors purchasing these bonds know the exact date of repayment and the yield for the period. Hence such investors can calculate what is referred to as the *yield to maturity.* The calculations we did for the approximate yield to maturity on government bonds indicate how to measure the yield to maturity over the life of a bond. The equation we used was average price divided into average income. The average price is found by adding the purchase price to the maturity value and dividing by two:

$$(P + MV)/2$$

The average annual income is found by adding the average annual capital gain or loss to the annual interest income. This is:

$$(MV - P)/\text{years to maturity} + I$$

If you pay more for the bond than the maturity value, you have a loss that is written off over the life of the bond. If you buy the bond for less than the maturity value, you have a gain that must be added to interest income.

Security of principal and types of bonds

A statement is made in the bond indenture about the security of principal. Debenture bonds are considered to be full faith and credit obligations. The company simply says, "I'm selling my credit. I promise to pay the claim when due. You have all my resources to support this pledge or bond." The pledge of security takes different forms. Subordinated debentures are junior to an existing or senior bond issue. Mortgage bonds carry, as specific security, a pledge of real property. There might be more than the pledge, which investors must examine carefully. This is because the risk of first mortgage bondholders and second or junior mortgage holders must be assessed. Obviously a first mortgage bond is senior in the claim of assets and income to the junior mortgage bond issue. Often mortgage bond issues have an after-acquired clause, which pledges all new property acquired after issuance as further security for the debt. This supposedly prevents the dilution of the first mortgage holder's position and security. Equipment trust bonds are quite common in the railroad industry, where equipment or rolling stock is pledged as security for bond issues. Sometimes corporations issue collateral trust bonds, which have personal property, other bonds, or common stock as security for the principal. Some bond issues are guaranteed by another company, or jointly, in that they are jointly secured by two or more companies. Receivers' certificates, in spite of their "poor" name, are really prime securities of corporations in receivership when new securities are sold to raise money to continue business operations. The securities issued take first claim over other existing debt.

Payment of interest

It is important to know whether your capital and interest payments are secure. Therefore you need to know your legal position if the company defaults, that is, does not pay interest or principal when it becomes due. Investment analysts suggest that a careful security check be made. Most important, you should undertake a careful analysis of the firm's ability to pay interest as it comes due and of its ability, over time, to generate a sufficient flow of cash or funds to repay the debt. Often a sinking fund is required to assure that debt will be retired from current funds. The sinking fund requires the firm to make annual payments into a fund that will accumulate sufficient money to pay off the bond at maturity. This gives the investor greater assurance that the bonds will be paid off when due.

The interest to be paid to the bondholder is fixed in the bond indenture.

The dollar interest rate is known as the *nominal rate*. The dollar rate as a percent of the par value or maturity value of the bond is called the *interest rate*. If the interest is paid by coupon, it is called the *coupon rate*. A bond issued at par ($1,000) with a $60 nominal rate and a 6 percent interest rate also has a yield to maturity of 6 percent. If the bond should drop in price subsequently, the current yield would increase, but the nominal rate and the interest rate stated in the bond indenture would remain constant. This, of course, is one of the risks you accept when you purchase any fixed-income obligation, that is, the risk of a change in interest rates.

Additional protection for investor

Protective convenants like the after-acquired clause are sometimes added to afford further protection. Often common stock dividends are limited by the bond indenture; if cash falls below a certain level, no dividends may be paid. Sometimes mortgage bonds are limited to no more than 50 percent of the value of the property, which is another example of investor protection.

The investment quality of bonds and bond ratings

The quality of a bond depends upon the overall credit position of the company, the ability of the company to repay principal and interest, the pledge of other assets as security, and a number of other factors. These factors are analyzed by professional analysts. The analysts' judgement is reflected in what is kown as *bond ratings*.

The two best-known rating agencies are Moody's and Standard & Poor's. These corporations specialize in judging the credit worthiness of corporations, states, and municipalities issuing debt securities. The highest rating they give is "triple A," which is noted as AAA on Standard & Poor's scale and Aaa on Moody's scale. This rating is assigned only to the best-quality debt obligations where the timely payment of interest and repayment of principal is unquestioned. Very few corporations qualify for a triple A rating. Bonds may be rated from a high of AAA to a low of D. A D rating is assigned to bonds actually in default.

There are four rating categories for what are considered investment grade bonds: AAA, AA, A, and BBB (Standard & Poor's) or Aaa, Aa, A, and Baa (Moody's). Commercial banks are prohibited by law from investing in any debt securities rated lower than BBB. Bonds rated BB and lower are considered speculative, and are best avoided by unsophisticated investors. If you intend to invest in corporate bonds, you would be best advised to follow the same rule applied to commercial banks: buy bonds only if they are in the top four rating categories. Nearly all libraries and all brokerage offices have available a copy of Moody's and Standard & Poor's bond guides.

Yields and investment quality

Yields on bonds have increased over the past decade, reaching a peak during the credit crises of 1974 and 1980. Bond yields increase with increased risk, that is, the lower the bond rating, the higher the yield. And except for AAA bonds, yields have been higher on public utility and railroad issues than on industrial bonds. Because these relationships change over time, you need to reexamine them before making an investment decision.

Price quotes, information, and buying

Corporate bonds are purchased through a broker for a fee that ranges from $25 per bond for one bond to $2.50 per bond for the purchase or sale of many bonds. If you want to buy 10 bonds of American Telephone and Telegraph Corporation (ATT), you can check the price and yield in *The Wall Street Journal*. If you want a bond selling at a discount, you could buy ATTs 8¾ percent bonds, which become due in the year 2000. Table 12–9 contains sample price quotations of bonds listed on the

Table 12–9
Price quotes of corporate bonds

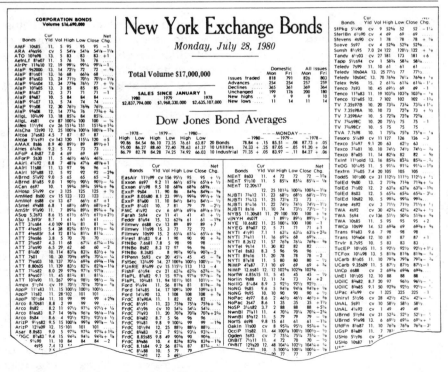

SOURCE *The Wall Street Journal*, July 29, 1980, p. 44.

New York Stock Exchange. The first column gives the name of the bond, its interest rate, and the year the bond issue matures. One of the quotations for ATT reads ATT, 8¾, 00. ATT is the name of the company, 8¾ the interest or coupon rate, and 00 the year the bond matures, which is 2000.

The second column is the current yield (cur yld), which is 10 percent. It is found by dividing the current price into the coupon in this case, 8¾, divided by 83½.

The third column is volume, that is, the number of bonds traded, which in this case is 114.

The next three columns represent the high and low prices for the day, and the closing price for the day. In this case the high was 83⅞, the low 83¼, and the closing price 83½.

The last column shows net change from the previous day. This means that the closing price was ⅛ of a point higher than on the previous day. One eighth is $1.25.

Unfortunately, no yield to maturity (YTM) figure is provided. We must estimate it. The average investment is 91.75 (83½ + 100)/2 or $917.50. Average income is $87.50 + ($1,000 − $835.00)/20 = $87.50 + $165.00/20 = $87.50 + 8.25 = $95.75. Therefore, the approximate yield to maturity is $95.75/$917.50 = 10.436 percent. Rounded off, it equals 10.4 percent. Whether this yield is acceptable or not depends on your need for income, your tax bracket, your attitude toward risk, and the yield and rating of other securities.

Before you make a decision, you should check the rating of the bond. ATT's is AAA. You could find this rating in Standard & Poor's *Bond Guide,* in a Value Line Information sheet, in a Standard & Poor's *Fact Sheet,* and in company information found in Moody's or Standard & Poor's manuals.

Investment advantages of corporate bonds

Corporate bonds are an attractive investment for institutional investors and individuals desiring income, particularly if bonds can be purchased that yield 10 percent, 12 percent, or higher. Risk is involved, however, notably the money rate risk, and to some extent the business risk that is associated with lower-rated bonds. These bonds suffer from the purchasing power risk. As inflation increases, the purchasing power of the principal and the interest declines. As a result, investors will suffer in an inflationary environment. Such bonds are not particularly attractive for people in high-income tax brackets since much of the interest will be taxed away. Thus care must be exercised in purchasing corporate bonds. If yields in the market increase, investors must be prepared to accept the fact that the principal has decreased, and that a capital loss will result if the bonds are sold.

Bonds also can be used for trading purposes. If you anticipate correctly the movements in the money markets, you may purchase bonds at a low price when yields are high and sell them at a high price when yields are low. If you purchased bonds in early 1980 and held them through mid-1980, the returns you might have earned would have been in the magnitude of 20 percent. This is attributed to the high-interest rates paid in early 1980 on long-term bonds. In addition, interest rates declined rapidly in 1980, providing investors with a capital gain on the principal of the bond. This extremely difficult feat attests stimply to the shrewdness of hindsight. At least, you should be aware that this pattern does develop in the bond market for traded bonds.

The Bond Markets and Financing Business columns of *The Wall Street Journal* help inform investors about conditions in the money and bond markets. In addition, these columns furnish general news about the national economy, Treasury, Federal Reserve system, and current political environment. Moody's *Manuals* and Standard & Poor's *Bond Guide* provide ample financial information about specific bond issues. *The Wall Street Journal* and Standard & Poor's *Trade and Security Statistics* provide substantial factual data about bond yields and prices. Investors should become familiar with these sources of information.

Convertible and warrant bonds

Convertible bonds and bonds with warrants are special types of bonds. They offer an opportunity to share in the growth of earnings of a particular company by allowing an investor to convert the bonds into shares of common stock or to buy shares of common stock at a fixed price. Convertible bonds may be converted into the common stock of a company at a fixed price for a certain number of years. This conversion price is established by the company issuing the bonds. A bond can be converted into, say, 20 shares of common stock. A conversion rate 20 shares of stock per each $1,000 of bonds is equivalent to investing into shares of stock at a price of $50 a share. If the shares of common stock increase in price, the price of the convertible bond will also increase.

A warrant attached to a bond gives the bondholder the right to buy a share of stock at a fixed price in some future year. If the stock increases in price, the holder will gain. These participating features eliminate the major disadvantage of corporate bonds, which is the fact that bonds have a fixed and limited yield. Such bonds therefore are attractive. Purchased at a relatively high yield relative to common stock yield, they also allow the investor to share in the future growth of the common shares. Convertible bonds generally have a lower rating than nonconvertible bonds of the same company. Convertible bonds are usually rated Baa, and have a lower interest rate than a Baa bond without a conversion rate. In buying bonds with warrants or convertible bonds, investors hope to participate in the company's earnings and growth through the increased value of its common stock.

Convertible bonds

The conversion features stated in the bond indenture allow bondholders to convert their bonds into a certain number of shares of common stock. The conversion price or number of shares is determined by the company. The agreement tells you how many shares you receive for each bond, or the price at which the common stock is convertible. If the price is $20, then the $1,000 bond is convertible into 50 shares. When the bond is issued, the conversion price is above the market price for the stock. Let's assume that the market price of stock is $18 per share, but that the conversion price is $20. This means that the value of the bond in terms of stock is $900, that is, 50 shares times $18, since the bond is convertible into 50 shares of stock. It is only when the market price of stock increases in the future that the bond will increase in price. Thus, if the price of stock increases to $25 per share, we would expect the price of a convertible bond to move to $1,250 at least. Since the bond usually sells at a premium over the common stock conversion price, we might assume that if the stock goes to $25 a share, the convertible bond will probably move up to $1,300 or higher.

If the price of the stock falls, so will the price of the convertible bond. However, since the bond still pays interest, it will sell as other bonds sell. It will move with the market price of other bonds of comparable quality, even though the price of the stock falls substantially.

Thus an investment in convertible bonds increases in value when the market price of the stock increases. But it does not decline proportionally if the market price of the stock decreases. The advantage of the convertible bond then is its defensive-aggressive characteristic.

Yields of convertible bonds vary, and prices change much like common stock. These bonds have a potential for a high yield, but they also have a high risk. Excellent sources of information about convertible securities are found in the Kalb, Voorhis and Company's weekly *Convertible Factfinder* and *Convertible Bond Chart Book*, RHM Associates' *Convertible Survey*, and the Convertible Bond Section of Standard & Poor's *Bond Guide*.

Bonds with warrants

Warrants to buy stock are usually associated with both bonds and preferred stock. A warrant is an option to buy a certain number of shares of common stock at a set price for a limited number of years. A warrant attached to a bond gives the owner the right to buy stock in the company. If the common stock price increases, the holder can either sell the warrants—they move up in price too—or exercise the warrants and buy the stock. Because a substantial risk is involved, you may not profit if the common stock does not increase in value.

Summary

Treasury bills, government bonds, bonds of federal government agencies, and money market or liquid asset funds offer liquid and profitable investments. These financial assets may be used as a part of your total investable assets. The yields on such investments are usually quite attractive when compared to those of savings accounts and certificates. These financial assets provide more liquidity. They also provide temporary, short-term outlets for funds when common stocks and long-term bonds are sold because of an expected decrease in the stock or bond market. These financial assets are easy to learn about, and you should not hesitate to consider them as a possible investment.

Long-term bonds usually offer a higher yield. They are attractive to people seeking stable income at a high rate of return. Unfortunately long-term bond prices are unstable. You can suffer a loss in the price if yields in the market move up. An investor should make long-term commitments only when yields are high. It is necessary to diversify your holdings by maturity dates to avoid the risk of changing bond prices. Of course, if yields decline, you will benefit through an increase in the price of the bond.

Convertible bonds and bonds with warrants offer a fixed income plus an opportunity to share in the growth of common stock if the common stock increases in value. They offer you the hope of protecting yourself from the ravages of inflation. The lack of inflation protection is the single most important disadvantage of any type of fixed-income security.

13

Investing in preferred and common stocks

- Equities and the balance sheet and income statement
- Preferred stock as an investment
- Common stock for investment—higher risk and higher reward
- Analyzing the investment climate and selecting companies for investment
- Buying and selling securities and selecting a broker
- Summary

Equities and the balance sheet and income statement

Preferred and common stocks of private corporations are referred to as *equities,* or ownership securities. Such securities are in contrast to debt securities that reflect what private corporations or governments owe. Owners of preferred and common stock receive dividends as payment for the use of their capital in the corporate business. The ownership or equity position of preferred or common stockholders is reflected both in the balance sheet (a summary of assets and liabilities) and the income statement, which is sometimes called a *profit and loss statement.*

The relationship of preferred and common stock to assets and other liabilities can be understood by reference to Tables 13–1 and 13–2. No figures are provided since it is the relationships that are important, not the numbers. Table 13–1 shows the preferred and common stock as a part of net worth. Both have a claim against the assets, but only after the debt holders, both short-term and long-term, has been satisfied. That is why owners are risk takers. However, some owners—the preferred stockholders—have a preferred position over common stockholders who are the residual owners.

You can see in Table 13–2 that dividends of preferred stock are paid before common dividends and after corporate taxes have been paid. Interest on debt is paid before taxes and before any dividends on preferred or common stock. The amount of money retained in the business by earnings increases the assets of the business and the net worth. This benefits common stockholders directly. It only indirectly improves the security of lenders and preferred stockholders. We should keep these relationships in mind as we consider preferred and common stock for investments. Common stock, in particular, offers a *potential* for higher yields but with substantially higher risks.

Table 13–1
Simplified corporate balance sheet

Balance Sheet	
Assets *What Company Owns*	*Liabilities* *What Company Owes*
Current assets: 　Cash in banks and in securities 　Accounts receivable from customers	Current liabilities: 　Accounts payable— 　　Charges for purchase of material 　Loans from banks
Inventories for production	
Fixed assets: 　Buildings and land 　Equipment to produce the product	Long-term debt: 　Long-term bonds 　Borrowed capital
	Net worth—what is provided by the 　owners: 　　Preferred stock 　　Common stock 　　Retained earnings
Assets =	Liabilities and net worth

Table 13-2
Simplified corporate income statement

Sales or revenues

— Cost of goods (use of inventory sold)
= Gross profit

— Selling expenses
— General expenses
— Depreciation (use of fixed assets)
= Net profit

+ Other income (interest and dividend)
— Other expense (interest expense) — use of debt capital
= Net income before federal income taxes

— Federal income taxes
= Net income available for owners

— Preferred dividends
= Net income available for common stockholders

— Common dividends
= Net income reinvested in business assets
(Increases retained earnings and increases assets)

Preferred stock as an investment

Preferred stock represents a part of the permanent ownership capital of a business. This type of security has two attributes that make it appealing for some investors. First, the dividend is usually fixed in amount. Second, it must be paid before dividends on common stock are paid. Hence the notion that such dividends are "preferred." The stock is more secure than common stock. Preferred stock owners have preference to assets before common stockholders if the company should fail, be liquidated at sale, or be reorganized. If a company's assets are sold to pay the claims of creditors because of failure or bankruptcy, the assets must first be used to satisfy claims of secured creditors: bondholders would be paid first, and then preferred stockholders would receive their share. What remains would be distributed to the common stockholders.

The amount of the dividend on preferred stock is usually stated as a dollar amount or as a percent of the par value. Usually it is a fixed amount or rate that is set forth in the preferred stock agreement. The dividend is paid from net income after taxes and after the bond interest has been paid but before any dividend payments on common stock.

The preference with respect to assets and dividends is an attractive inducement for some investors. Investors seeking security of principal—possibly a yield higher than bond interest and with less risk than common stock—would be attracted to preferred stock.

Usual features of preferred stock

Although holders of preferred stock enjoy preferential treatment with respect to assets and earnings, they are usually nonvoting with respect to ownership decisions. However, they have the right to vote for the election of some directors if the payments of preferred dividends are in arrears (that is, unpaid). Preferred stock has no maturity date but is normally callable at the option of the company management. Investors should check this feature carefully, since a high-yielding preferred might be called by the company in times of low interest rates. The typical preferred dividends are *cumulative,* that is, if the dividends are not paid, they accumulate and must be paid before common stock dividends are paid. Preferred dividends are usually nonparticipating, that is, the preferred holders do not share in the earnings of the company, as do holders of common stock. Preferred stock is usually nonconvertible, that is, it is not convertible into common stock. Those preferred stocks that are convertible—about one third of the total—offer a special attraction to investors to share in the future earnings of the common stock.

Preferred stock yields and prices

How would you find out about preferred stocks available for investment? You would want to know their price, yield, quality, rating, and risk—and the place of all these factors in the reward-to-risk investment spectrum. Let's begin with the subject of information and price.

The first thing you need to discover is information about the current price and dividend of a preferred stock. Then you can estimate its current yield (dividend divided by price). Price information can be obtained in *The Wall Street Journal.* Table 13–3 is part of the price quotes for the New York Stock Exchange Composite in an edition of the *Journal.* To find a preferred stock that might be a possible investment candidate, let your eyes move down one of the columns until you note a *pf.* This is the abbreviation for the term *preferred stock.* The first *pf* you see is a *dpf* for Alabama Power (AlaP dpf). A definition of each abbreviation is found in the footnote section at the end of the price quotes. *Ala P* stands for Alabama Power; *d* stands for a new low price; and *pf* stands for *preferred.* The closing price of the stock is 6¾ (close), the dividend (Div.) is $.87. The current yield is found by dividing $.87 by 6¾, which comes to 12.89 percent. This is an attractive yield because it will continue for the life of the stock. The only problem with this preferred stock is its potential for price change. About one year ago its price was 8⅜ and its yield was 10.74 percent. The price has since declined. Therefore we find one of the major risks of preferred stock ownership—it is susceptible to changes in interest rates. If interest rates move up, the price declines. Preferred stock is also subject to business risk. If the company has a bad year or becomes insolvent, it could elect to not pay a dividend.

Continuing down the column, we find another Ala P pf, which pays a $9 dividend and shows a closing price of 68, or $68. Dividing price into dividend provides a current yield of 13.23 percent. This, too, is an excellent yield and would be attractive for investors who are not in a high income tax bracket.

Table 13-3
Price quotes of New York Stock Exchange Composite

NYSE-Composite Transactions
Wednesday, January 30, 1980
Quotations include trades on the New York, Midwest, Pacific, Philadelphia, Boston and Cincinnati stock exchanges and reported by the National Association of Securities Dealers and Instinet.

SOURCE   *The Wall Street Journal*, 30 January 1980.

As we move our eyes down the list of stock transactions, we find an excellent list of preferred issues from which to select a suitable investment. Note that American Airlines preferred (AAir pf) pays $2.18 in dividends; it could be purchased at $17 to yield 12.82 percent. The $1.75 ACan (American Can) pf is priced at $17.25 to provide a current yield of 10.14 percent, as indicated in the yield column. The yield, rounded, is provided for us. Thus it is easy to generate a diversified list of preferred stocks.

Which preferred issue should we select? Just remember one principle: the higher the yield, the higher the risk. Therefore, we conclude that the Ala P $9 issue is the most risky with a current yield of 13.23 percent. It is followed by Ala P dpf .87 with 12.89, American Airlines with 12.82 and American Can with 10.14 percent. To answer this question, however, you need more information. At this point we turn to the *Stock Guide* published by Standard & Poor's to find the ratings of these stocks.

Preferred stock ratings and information

Standard & Poor's preferred stock rating system ranges from the highest rating of AAA down to C. Obviously no rating system or advisory source is perfect, but the information in the *Stock Guide* all   you to make an informed decision about the rewards and risks of preferred stocks. Of the stocks mentioned above, Alabama Power preferreds are rated BB; they offer a higher yield and more risk than American Airlines' preferred, which has an A rating and a lower yield. Standard & Poor's *Stock Reports* and *Fact Sheet* are readily available sources that provide even more information about companies.

More detailed sources of information about companies and their preferred stocks are the following Moody's publications: Moody's *Industrial, Transportation, Public Utility* and *Banking* and *Finance* manuals. They contain sufficient historical data to enable you to analyze companies and make certain that their preferred stocks are adequately secured by assets and earnings. Annual reports of companies as well as interim reports on them also provide data about the financial soundness of their preferred stocks.

Analysis of a preferred stock

You should check two important pieces of information before making an investment in a preferred stock: the amount of net assets per share and the amount of earnings per share. Such data allow you to determine if the dividend is secure. The net asset value is found by subtracting the stated value of the liabilities from the value of the total assets of the company, and then dividing by the number of shares of preferred stock. The higher the net asset value, other things equal, the more secure is your investment.

Just remember that creditors must be paid before the preferred stockholders of the company if the company should fail and have to be liquidated. Therefore, the amount of the debt outstanding will have an effect on the security of the preferred stock. The greater the debt, the less secure is the preferred stock. Net income before preferred dividends, divided by the number of shares of preferred stock outstanding, provides earnings per preferred share. The amount and stability of earnings per share for each preferred share outstanding must be determined. The greater the number of times net income covers the preferred dividend and the greater the earnings per preferred share, the more secure is the preferred stock investment. In your analysis you must note the trend of earnings per preferred share and the earnings to dividend coverage. If earnings per share are increasing and dividend coverage ratio is stable or increasing, this is a sign of strength and of a secure investment.

Preferred stock: An income investment subject to the interest rate risk

Ordinary preferred stock is purchased for income, since most preferred stocks pay a higher current dividend yield than common stock. Since interest rates change because of changing conditions in the long-term capital and money markets, the price of preferred stocks changes. If interest rates or yields are rising, the market price of the preferred stock

Figure 13–1
Yields on preferred stocks

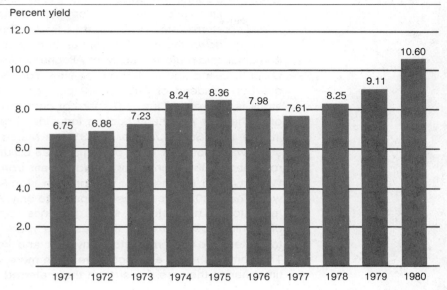

Percent yield

will tend to fall. On the other hand, if yields are falling, the price of the preferred stock will rise and you will benefit. It is important for you to understand the risks associated with preferred stock investment. Not only might the company fail but interest rates might also change. This would cause the price of preferred stock to fall if yields rise.

Figure 13–1 shows the trend in preferred stock yields. Notice that the trend of yields since 1977 has been up. This means that prices of preferreds have declined. This also means that a heavy investment in preferred stock four years ago would have given you today lower prices and a capital loss. Therefore, if yields are expected to continue to rise, you should avoid a commitment to preferred stocks.

Convertible preferreds

There is a class of preferred stock that offers you both current income and the possibility of sharing in the growth of a company. Convertible preferred stock is convertible into common stock at the option of the preferred stockholders at some predetermined ratio of preferred to common stock. But keep in mind that there are not many convertible preferred stock issues available for investment.

Information about convertible securities is not easily obtained. Price information is available in *The Wall Street Journal*. But you cannot just go down the listings of preferred stocks to find one that is convertible. Even if you could, you would not find the terms of conversion from preferred to common. You can find information about companies issuing convertible preferred stock in Standard & Poor's *Stock Guide*. As an example, if you go down the list of securities in a recent issue, you will find the $3 cumulative preferred stock of Allegheny Ludlum Industries ($3.00 Cm Cv pfd). Listed and traded on the New York Stock Exchange, it pays a quarterly dividend of $.75 ($3.00 per year). This convertible preferred stock is convertible into 1.0 share of common stock. The closing price of a share of Allegheny Ludlum Industries preferred stock was quoted in *The Wall Street Journal* at 33¼ on March 23, 1979. The common stock was quoted at 16½, paying a $1.28 dividend. If the common stock rose above 33, an investor would benefit from the conversion feature. While waiting for the price of common stock to improve, the investor would earn 9.02 percent, as compared to only 7.7 percent from the common stock. The preferred stock dividends appear secure. The amount of earnings per share for the past five years appears to be adequate to protect the preferred stock investor and keep the dividend secure. The common stock earnings have been more variable and cyclical over time; hence they are riskier than the preferred stock.

Common stock for investment—higher risk and higher reward

In the past common stock captured the financial imagination of many people in the United States. At one time over 30 million Americans owned common stock, directly or indirectly. Common stock was looked upon as a hedge against inflation. People saved diligently to buy it. There was excitement and riches in the equity markets. The stock market performed well during the period of the late 1950s and early 1960s. For short periods in those decades it was not uncommon to buy a stock and see its price double in a few months. This fact by no means suggests that this was the normal behavior for all stocks. But it does suggest that there once was a time when profits could be made easily in the purchase of equities. During this period conditions were favorable for equities. It was a time of generally low inflation, lower interest rates, and growing corporate profits.

This condition changed with the quadrupling of oil prices by the Organization of Petroleum Exporting Countries (OPEC) in 1973–74. A continuous rise in all prices occurred during the rest of the decade. Inflation was out of control. The monetary policy of the United States attempted to combat this problem by raising interest rates through the Federal Reserve system.

As interest rates rose, the price of equities fell. During 1973 and 1974 the stock market suffered one of its most precipitous drops. This created such enormous instability that people became frightened about the ownership of common stock.

The inflationary conditions that began in the 1970s have continued into the 1980s. Energy costs have increased, interest rates are higher, and a high level of inflation goes on. The amount of real output of energy has declined. What once appeared to be a land of economic opportunity has become a land plagued with rising costs, high interest rates, and a disinterest in equities as a viable place to invest funds. These severe inflationary conditions have created losses in common stocks owned by Americans and others. You can hardly blame the average American investors who see their income increasing but also find that the dollars they receive in income do not buy as much as in the past. In the past decade the stock market has become more volatile, more erratic, and more subject to wide variation. This has taken place in spite of the fact that institutional investors, that is, banks, pension funds, life insurance companies, and casualty companies, have become the dominant force in equity markets.

Increasingly investors have turned away from common stocks as investments. They have put their money into real estate and other physical assets that have a tendency to increase along with the general increase in prices. For a time gold and silver bullion attracted investors' attention, as the price of gold rose briefly above $850 an ounce. Real estate has had a lasting appeal to individuals because it has proved a hedge against inflation. In the past 10 years Americans saw their purchasing power erode by 7 percent per year. During this same period the value of real estate has increased 15 percent per year. Some Americans have examined objects of art and gold as investments. Such assets increased in value, too. Small wonder that American investors became dissatisfied with common stocks!

In spite of all the negative factors, common stocks still offer opportunities for profit. Currently there is a resurgence of interest in common stock investment. It just takes more work and care in the management of common stock investments to provide good results. But good results can make common stocks an excellent inflationary hedge.

Characteristics of common stock

Common stock is the way in which investors can participate in the ownership of large corporations and increase their rate of return. Ownership is evidenced by a stock certificate, which is freely transferrable by an owner at any time during the ordinary business day. Shares are traded by brokers who are trained to buy and sell shares for the benefit of owners. This share ownership is reflected in the net worth section of a business, as shown in Table 13–1.

As a common shareholder, you have a share in the assets of the company and a share in control of the company. As an owner you may vote your shares on matters that affect you. Your share in the business gives you a right to a pro rata amount of earnings per share in the future. Therefore, as a common stockholder you have a right to future earnings in the corporation. This right of ownership gives you a right to receive dividends. It also gives you a right to maintain your proportional share of ownership in the company. As owner of shares of common stock of a corporation, you may receive two sources of income in the future: (1) dividends from your common stock as long as you remain an owner on the books of the corporation; and (2) the sale price of the shares if you sell them at some future time. If you hold the shares forever, that is, without selling, the only income that you will receive is dividends per share. Dividends per share are a function of the growth of earnings of the corporation and the decision of its management to pay dividends to shareholders who have risked their own capital.

Dividends on common stock—cash dividends

More elaboration is necessary to understand how you as an investor benefit from dividends of a company. Usually dividends paid to stockholders are in cash. The amount of the cash dividend is determined by the directors of the corporation. Many corporations have paid regular dividends to their stockholders for 50 years or more. You want to find out the amount of the current dividend on any common stock you might consider for investment. To do this, you need only examine *The Wall Street Journal*. It lists the most recent dividend paid out by the company along with the price of the stock.

Table 13–3 provides the information you need. For example, notice that Air Products (Air Prd) pays an $.80 per share dividend for a current yield of 2.1 percent on the current price of 37⅞ per share. The calculation to find the dividend rate is as follows $.80/$37.875 = 2.11 percent. Air Products is rated A+ by Standard & Poor's, and is an excellent growth stock. Its earnings and dividends have grown in the past and are likely to continue to grow; yet it pays only a 2.1 percent yield. Since its yield is low, an investor would not buy this stock for current income. By way of contrast, the stock of American Brands (ABrands) pays $5.50 in dividends and provides a current yield of 8.2 percent on a price of 67¼. This company, which is also rated A+, might be used for income purposes.

The distinction between an income and growth stock is important. An income stock provides an investor with the highest income with stability so as to meet the investor's current living requirements. A retired person, for example, usually requires maximum income.

A growth stock, on the other hand, provides a small current income, but offers the promise of capital appreciation. A person planning on retirement in 10 years might do well to invest in growth stocks.

Business firms in the United States, on the average, pay out approximately 50 percent of their earnings in dividends to stockholders. But the dividend payout is not automatic. Often a company with a substantial growth in earnings may pay out only a modest current dividend. This is because the company needs the money for expansion. If you want to examine the investment merits of a common stock, you must explore the earning potential of the company in the past, and then estimate what its earning potential is likely to be in the future. For it is the future stream of earnings that will determine the amount of the company's future dividends. At the same time the amount of future earnings will actually determine the future price of the common stock. The combination of expected dividends and expected price determines whether a common stock is going to be an investment success.

Stock dividends

Some companies that are primarily growth companies pay dividends in the form of stock. Approximately 5 percent of companies listed on the New York Stock Exchange pay stock dividends as a regular policy. The advantage of receiving stock dividends rather than cash dividends is that you do not pay an income tax on stock dividends until you sell the stock. As long as the stock dividend is held, it becomes part of your asset base and is not subject to federal income tax. Investors in a high-income tax bracket would be wise to consider stocks paying stock dividends.

Stock dividends are only as good as the ability of the company issuing them to earn money in the future. Even though a company follows a policy of paying stock dividends, its shares may not increase in value. This is because its earnings and dividends have not increased. If you wish to avoid paying federal income taxes on dividends in the form of common stock, do not be deluded by your tax position alone. Make certain that the company can provide you a future growth of earnings that will result in higher dividends and higher prices. Otherwise you will be placing your emphasis incorrectly. If a declared stock dividend is in the form of stock that differs from the security owned, the stock dividend remains subject to federal income tax.

Stock and cash dividends

Some companies pay a combination of stock dividends and cash dividends. More and more, stockholders are becoming interested in higher cash dividends, however. This is because of current inflation, even though investors might be better off with a smaller amount of cash dividends. The smaller amount would reduce their taxes. At the same time, if the investors reinvested their cash dividends in the company, they might increase their gains substantially in the future. Often the decision to pay out a small cash dividend is related to the tax position of state and local governments.

Property dividends

Other forms of dividends are also paid on common stock, such as property dividends. In this case the stockholder receives a portion of the products of the company. In the past companies sometimes did not have money to pay a dividend. Instead, they issued script, which was eventually paid off in cash. Some companies have paid bonds as dividends. This did not give the investors an immediate amount of cash but a bond or debt to be paid in the future. In a sense the investors were receiving an interest-paying dividend. This was fine as long as investors felt confident about the credit worthiness of the company. Otherwise it was not a particularly good investment. You should carefully examine the amount, type, and timing of the dividend before buying common stock.

Declaration of dividends

Dividends are declared by the board of directors to stockholders of record. A public announcement is then made, indicating the amount of the dividend payable, when it is payable, and who is to receive it. There are three dates to remember when you receive a dividend: the announcement date, the date of record, and the date when the dividend is actually paid. After the date of record, the stock will be sold without the dividend attached. So if you plan to sell your stock, you should check to see when the next dividend is to be paid. You can then sell your stock either before or after the date of record. In this way you may benefit either by receiving the dividend in cash or by selling the stock before the dividend is declared and thus obtaining your benefits. Usually a stock price will decline the day that it is selling *ex-dividends* (that is, without dividends). You should normally make sure that you don't sell your stock the day before the date of record and thus lose your dividend. It is a simple matter to check the *Stock Guide,* which will tell when the dividend is of record and when the dividend is paid. When in doubt, you can ask a broker, an investment adviser, or a trust officer at a bank to verify the dividend date.

In maintaining your right of ownership as a common stockholder, you are entitled to maintain your proportionate share in the earnings, and assets, and voting control of the company. From time to time corporations raise money by offering for sale new stock in the company to existing stockholders. In investment banking circles this practice is known as a *rights offering*. Current stockholders are given an opportunity to subscribe to the new stock on the basis of their previous holdings. They have the right to maintain their proportionate share of ownership in the company. Therefore, when a company elects to sell stock, some states require the company to allow existing shareholders to subscribe to the new shares. In this way they can maintain their proportional share of assets, voting power, and future earnings.

A company selling stock, usually with the help of an investment banker or underwriter, gives its current stockholders an opportunity to buy more stock at a price below that available to the general public. Each share of stock has attached to it a right that has a value. When the company announces its intention to sell stock, a right is attached automatically to each share. This right is given to the stockholder as of the date of record.

When a rights offering takes place, you as an investor are afforded an excellent way to purchase common stock. If you use your rights, you can buy stock for less than what it would cost to buy 100 shares (a round lot transaction) through a broker. Since the rights cost less and since the brokerage commissions are lower on rights, a person not owning stock can go into the marketplace, buy the rights, and then exercise these rights with the company before they expire. This becomes an inexpensive way to buy stock. We also find that the banking system offers stockholders an opportunity to borrow money to buy common stock through a rights offering at more attractive rates than usual. This lending opportunity is more attractive than the one set up by the Federal Reserve Banking system under margin requirements for borrowing money against pledged common stock. It is important to remember that rights do have value; they should either be sold or used to purchase stock.

The future price of a stock—the other part of value

The other source of income for common stock investors is the expected price of the share at some future time. Therefore, in deciding to buy common stocks, you must be concerned about its future price since this determines the return you receive from the investment. The future price of the stock depends first and foremost on the future earnings of the company at the time the stock is going to be sold. The price is also determined by conditions in capital markets when the stock is to be sold. Conditions depend on the level of interest rates. The higher the level of interest rates, the lower will be stock prices. The price also depends on the level of inflation. Ordinarily the higher the expected rate of inflation, the lower the stock price.

A number of other variables are important. The price depends on the value of the dollar in international markets. The higher the value, the higher will be the stock price in the future. The future price depends on the general confidence level of all Americans with respect to the economic outlook. Prices depend on the government's attitude toward the future. Are we faced by a stable, conservative fiscal plan, or by a recklessly inflationary program? Prices depend on the state of the economy with respect to war or peace. Since all these factors affect the future price of a stock, it is extremely difficult to forecast with accuracy, the price for a common stock three years in the future. No one really knows what the future will bring. But we do know that the future price revolves around future earnings. It will vary with the basic earning trends established by the company.

Measuring the expected yield from common stock

If you can estimate your future dividends and the future price of your stock, you can also estimate the return you might receive from your investment. Let's assume that the current price of the stock is P_0, and that the future price of the stock is P_3. (P_3 represents some function of the earnings in year three and the expected earnings thereafter.) Assume that P_0 is $25 and P_3 is $34. Assume that the annual dividend paid in each of the next three years in the future is $1. What then is the total return you will earn on your investment?

The approximate total return is found by calculating first the annual capital gain. You add it to the dividend income, and then divide the total by the average investment. In this case you have purchased the stock at $25. After you hold it for three years, it is worth $34 a share. If we ignore any commission charges for buying or selling the stock and any income taxes, the capital gain on the stock for the three-year period is $9. Therefore the average annual capital gain is $3. If we add the annual dividend of $1 to the $3 capital gain, we have a total gain per year of $4 per share. This figure includes capital gains and dividend income.

The average investment for the period is found by adding $25 (the investment at the beginning of the period) to $34 (the investment at the end of the period). This gives a total of $59, which we divide by two. The average investment, therefore, is $29.50 per share. The $4 average annual gain, divided by a $29.50 average annual investment, results in a total return of 13.6 percent. This is an excellent rate of return from a common stock investment, even though common stocks are risky.

As an investor you wish to know the estimated future return from your stock. You wish to maximize its total annual return and minimize its risk. Unfortunately you must make these estimates yourself. Some investment services provide estimates of total annual return, but they do not make them readily available to all investors. *Therefore you should make the estimates yourself.* Otherwise you'll have to rely on estimates by professional investors you consider reliable. You will make errors, but at least in the end you will learn to rely on yourself.

You must be the judge of what the future will bring. No one else can do it for you. Actually a lot of people may offer their opinions about future prices and dividends. But you'll be better off if you think your own thoughts about the future and draw your own conclusions.

Past returns from common stocks

The example just cited indicates what you might expect to earn from an investment in common stock. It is important for you to be realistic in your expectations. What can an investor reasonably expect to earn from an investment in common stock? Five, 10, 15, or 25 percent? What's reasonable? We will assume that while you are not greedy, you are confident that you can attain some of the historical limits with respect to earnings. An examination of past trends and past returns will provide some clue as to what reasonable expectations you might hold for the future.

Several studies have tried to determine what a common stock will provide in the way of total return for an investor over a given number of years. If you were to use a single figure in estimating what the average common stock might earn over a very long period of time, take the figure of approximately 9 percent. In the 1980 economy, with 12 percent bond yields and 13 percent short-term yields, a 9 percent return on a common stock return would not be considered very high. That is one reason why the 1979 stock prices were low in relationship to the high 1979 corporate earnings. Since a great deal of risk is involved in common stock, the 12 percent interest rates in that year forced stock prices down so that they would provide a return of 14 to 15 percent. Over long periods of time it is possible to earn 9 percent from common stocks but difficult to earn the same return from bonds. Table 13–4 reveals that over a 53-year period common stocks provided higher rates of return than other forms of investment securities. But for segments of time the stock market and common stocks might not perform as well as fixed-income obligations.

A recent period will give us some idea of the profitability of common stocks. Between 1969 and 1979, the Standard & Poor's 500 Index—a composite average—earned an average annual return of approximately 5.75 percent. That isn't very high when you consider that you could have earned almost as much by simply keeping your assets in a savings account at your local savings and loan association. When we examine the individual companies in the Dow Jones Industrial Average (DJIA), an old favorite for measuring the direction of the market, we find that many common stocks did much better than average. Even though the

Table 13–4
Investment rates of return, *Summary of Ibbotson-Sinquefield data* (1926–1979)

Investment series	Average annual compound return	Year-end 1979 cumulative wealth index*
Common stocks	9.0%	$106.11
Long-term corporate bonds	3.8%	$ 7.48
Long-term government bonds	3.1%	$ 5.28
U.S. Treasury bills	2.7%	$ 4.12
Consumer price Index	2.7%	$ 4.28

*Year-end 1925 = $1.00.

SOURCE Roger G. Ibbotson and Rex A. Sinquefield, *Stocks, Bonds Bills, and Inflation: Historical Returns (1926–1978)* (and 1979 summary update sheet) Charlottesville, Va.: Financial Analysts Research Foundation, 1979.

market average for that 10-year period earned slightly less than 6 percent, you might have selected, with care and luck, a group of stocks that would have earned a much higher return. This is really the crux of the problem you face in selecting common stocks. You must try to select the right stocks and hold them for the right period of time in order to achieve a return higher than what you might have earned by keeping your money in a savings account or other fixed-income securities.

Risk and return

There is a substantial amount of risk associated with common stock investment. The risk is indicated by the variability of the past annual returns from common stock. For example, over the 53-year period from 1926 through 1978, the return for the Standard & Poor's 500 Composite Index was 8.9 percent.[1] The variation from year to year averaged 22.2 percent. This means that during about two thirds of the period, the return ranged between −13.3 and 31.1 percent. For those who might not be familiar with statistics, this set of numbers can be interpreted in the following way: the average return for the period was about 9 percent. In some years it was much lower and in others it was much higher. In fact, two thirds of the time you would have expected the returns to be between approximately −13 percent and +30 percent. It is important to know that stock prices fluctuated so much to provide this variability of return. It is also discomforting to know that if you buy some common stock, its price might bounce around by as much as 10 to 20 percent in a single year.

This variability of return can be used as one measure of the riskiness of ownership of common stock. It tells you that you must be prepared for the risk of ownership. It also suggests that you should attempt in some way to use the variability of price to earn a higher return. Of course, you have to recognize the fact that attempting to obtain higher returns means that you will have to buy and sell the security; you can't just buy it and hold it. You know that you will not always be right, that you will probably make some mistakes. But at the same time if you are to improve your return and improve your stability of return, you must be willing to take advantage of what you perceive as low or high prices.

The returns mentioned for Standard & Poor's Composite Index came about because of price variability. In 1968 the Standard & Poor's 500 Index was about 90. In 1970, however, the index declined to 80. It rose to a high of 110 in 1972, dropped to 105 in 1973, declined to 90 in 1974 and to approximately 82 in 1975. The years 1974 and 1975 were dismal for the stock market. Standard & Poor's 500 Index reached a low of 62.28 in 1974. What a wonderful time to have purchased stocks!

---

[1] Roger G. Ibbotson and Rex A. Sinquefield, *Stocks, Bonds, Bills and Inflation: Historical Returns (1926–78)* (Charlottesville, Va.: Financial Analysts Research Foundation, 1979).

By the middle of 1981, the index had rebounded to 130 again. But if you had been investing in the period 1973–74, you would have faced a recession and inflation. Could the economy ever recover from the oil embargo and the quadrupling of oil prices imposed by foreign governments through the International Oil Cartel of the OPEC countries?

Thus you face real risks in investing in common stocks. You must have knowledge of these risks on the basis of past returns and past variations of returns. The past variations provide a measure of risk when combined with your estimates of future return. Your estimates are powerful tools to tell you what the risks and profitability will be in the future. In fact, a word of advice to investors tells them: don't think of the past, but of the future. The future is where you will achieve success or failure.

Appraisal of risk—stock ratings

Professional sources of information provide help in determining the riskiness of a common stock. Although not perfect, Standard & Poor's *Stock Guide* and similar publications use a ranking system that emphasizes earnings, dividend stability, and growth. A company ranked A+ has the highest stability in growth of earnings and dividends. A company ranked C has the lowest stability. In between, you have gradations of risk categories that emphasize stability of earnings, dividends, and growth. Obviously the ratings established by Standard & Poor's are only an approximate guide to value. But they give the investor some idea of how risky and profitable investment in a particular common stock might be.

Advantages and disadvantages of common stock ownership

The major reason for purchasing common stock is to obtain a higher return than you can obtain from any other type of security investment. It is impossible to obtain over long periods of time higher returns from investment in long-term bonds than from stocks. Individual common stocks have the potential for a higher total return as a result of their higher dividends and higher capital gains. Higher profitability of common stock is enhanced by the tax structure. Common stock capital gains are taxed at a lower rate than ordinary income. If a person is in a high income tax bracket, a bond that might for the moment yield 10 percent is taxed as ordinary income. A person in the 50 percent tax bracket would have to pay half of the income from interest to the federal government in the form of taxation. But the same return in the form of capital gains would be taxed at a much lower rate. Therefore, there is a potential tax advantage for investment in common stocks. Of course, the increased potential for profits from common stock ownership rests on an assumption that common stock earnings will increase in the future. If earnings do increase, the value of the shares will increase in value. This will benefit the investor.

The major disadvantage of common stock ownership is the added risk you take in attempting to earn a higher return. This risk is reflected in a substantial lack of stability of price, dividends, and yield. Not only are dividend yields and total returns unstable but common stocks ordinarily do not pay a high level of current dividends. In order to obtain a high level of income in present market conditions, you would need to look to fixed-income securities.

A major point must be made about common stock as a hedge against inflation. Some common stocks are a very good hedge against inflation. But in periods of rapid, double-digit inflation, interest rates increase and stock prices fall. As we look back in history, the late 1950s and early 1960s had the most profitable stock market on record. This was a period of low interest rates, high price stability, and very little inflation. Under these conditions the investment advantage was with common stocks. Prices soared and investors made money. But under conditions of high rates of inflation in 1973, 1974, and 1979, the prices of common stock declined substantially. When the economy of the United States or the world is faced with rapid inflation—perhaps an inflation caused by scarce oil and a need for energy—the end result is to reduce stock prices. The best hope of improving common stock prices is through improved productivity, increased national output in real terms, and reduced inflation. Lower yields on fixed-income securities in turn increase common stock prices. Common stocks then become the preferable investment media they were under more stable world conditions.

In spite of the warning that common stock prices are not likely to perform well in an inflationary environment, they have still tended over long periods of time and despite their extreme variability to outperform long-term bonds.

Information about stocks

You already know that you can read *The Wall Street Journal* to obtain price information and current dividend yields. The *Stock Guide* published by Standard & Poor's provides information about the past earnings of a company, the price variability of its stock, the company's capital structure, and the products it produces. An example of this information is found in Table 13–5.

This information gives some insight into investment opportunities; its ratings are very helpful. However, the information supplied is insufficient for you to make a value judgement about future earnings, dividends, and price action of a company.

In order to obtain these future estimates, you should examine Standard & Poor's *Stock Reports* or *Fact Sheets*. A typical *Stock Report* is contained in Table 13–6. You should also consider an analysis of other investment services. Standard & Poor's *The Outlook,* for example, gives an in-depth analysis of industries and companies and some clue as to their future. But in addition you need to make your own analysis on the basis of available sources of information. Let us discuss briefly the type of analysis you should make, the available sources of information, and the way you can use your analysis in a valuation equation to determine what a stock's future price and dividend are worth in relationship to its current price.

Analyzing the investment climate and selecting companies for investment

It is difficult to make a rational decision to buy a specific common stock. The best way to begin your investment decision process is to examine the national economy and the economic environment in which we operate. You should invest in industries that are strong and competitive—industries that will grow in the future. You will want to invest in strong companies within those industries. You should also attempt to buy common stock at an attractive price. This will offer you a fair rate of return for the risks you are assuming.

An examination of the national economy

Most people in American society are untrained in economics. They have a knowledge of their own personal finances. They know when a budget of the federal government is in deficit. But they do not have the skill or time to analyze thoroughly the economic environment in which they live. Economic analysis is usually left to trained economists employed by Wall Street brokerage firms and large financial institutions throughout the United States. This information is communicated to individual investors by the financial press, including *The Wall Street Journal, New York Times,* your local newspaper, and national periodicals like *Business Week* and *Forbes.* This is an efficient way to find out about what is going on in our society.

Most people are not economic forecasters. As a result, they must rely on the thinking of experts to obtain the right information at the right time. Unfortunately experts are often wrong and often differ among themselves. Therefore you must learn to judge and analyze the future for yourself. You might begin by asking yourself what would be a desirable—as well as an undesirable—set of economic circumstances for common stock investment.

First of all, a strong dollar in international terms is generally a plus for common stock values. Next, a balanced federal budget when inflationary pressures are high is also a plus. Conversely, a deficit spending policy is a positive sign when the resources of our country are less than fully employed and when there is no inflation. Third, stable prices are a plus for common stocks. This does not mean just stock prices, but it means all commodity prices, including the price of goods and services in our daily lives. Another factor of strength is a stable and growing gross national product (GNP). A real economic growth rate close to the

Table 13-5
Standard & Poor's Stock Guide: an information source

STANDARD & POOR'S CORPORATION

116 Int-Int

Index	Ticker Symbol	Name of Issue	Market	Principal Business
1	ICFT	Intercraft Indus	N	Metal, wood frames; art repro
2	INTR	Interface Mechanisms	N	Mfr printing/reading prdts
3	IFIN	Interfinancial, Inc.	N	Insur hldg; instal lend'g
4	ISLD	Inter-Island Resorts	N	Hawaiian hotels, foods, transp
5	IK	Interlake, Inc	NY,M,P	Integrated steel producer
6	IMI	Intermark, Inc.	AS	Operating-holding co
7	INMT	Intermountain Gas Ind		Sells nat gas: southern Idaho
8	IAL	Int'l Aluminum	NY,P	Extrusion & fabricating
9	IBKWA	Int'l Bank, Wash DC A	AS,Ph	Hldg insur, bank, mfg, invest
10	IBK	Int'l Banknote		Mfr securities & currencies
11	IECO	Int'l Basic Economy	N	Contr by Rockefeller family
12	IBM	Int'l Bus. Machines	NY,B,C,M,Ph,P	Lgst mfr business machines
13	ICLA	Int'l Clinical Labs	N	Regional lab systems
14	INC	Int'l Controls	AS,P	Electronics/aerospace
15	INDQ	Int'l Dairy Queen	N	Lmtd menu stores: franch'g
16	IFF	Int'l Flavors/Fragr.	NY	Creator & mfr, used by others
17	IFS	Int'l Foodservice	AS	Food service: inst'l/office
18	IGI	Int'l General Ind'l	AS	Packaging mchy: auto, elec eq
19	IHR	Int'l Harvester	NY,B,C,M,Ph,N	Truck mfr: farm mchy: constr
20	IKNG	Int'l Kings Table	N	Family style restaurants
21	IHLD	Int'l Life Hldg	AS	Life, accident, health insur
22	IGL	Int'l Minerals/Chem	NY,B,M,Ph,P	Phospate rock: chemicals
23	Pr	4% cm Pfd (110) vtg	NY,M	potash, hydro-carbons
24	IMC	Int'l Multifoods	NY	Flours, durum prods, feeds
25	IP	Int'l Paper	NY,B,C,M,Ph,Mc	World's largest paper maker
26	PRO	Int'l Proteins	AS	Mfr & dstr fishmeal: shrimp
27	IRF	Int'l Rectifier	NY,P	Semiconductor, drugs, alloys
28	IRDV	Int'l Research & Dev	N	Safety evaluation eq/svs,
29	INS	Int'l Seaway Trading	AS	Brand name import'd footw'r
30	IST	Int'l Stretch Prods.	N	Mfr tricot & elastic fabrics
31		Int'l Sys/Controls	OC	Mfr agric, contr&process eq
32	ITT	Int'l Tel & Tel	NY,B,C,M,Ph,P	Diversified int'l concern
33	Pr H	$4.00 cm Cv H Pfd vtg	NY,B	A major mfg & supplier of
34	Pr I	$4.50 cm Cv I Pfd vtg	NY	telecommunications eq/svs,
35	Pr J	$4.00 cm Cv J Pfd vtg	NY	provides financial & insur-
36	Pr K	$4.00 cm Cv K Pfd vtg	NY,B	ance services, and makes
37	Pr N	$2.25 cm Cv N Pfd vtg	NY,B,M	industrial & consumer prod
38	Pr O	$5.00 cm Cv O Pfd vtg	NY,P	coal, oil & gas producer
39	INP	Interpace Corp	NY,P	Concrete pipe: ceramic: bldg
40	Pr	5% cm Cv Pfd (110) vtg		insulator, dinnerware
41	IPH	Interphoto Corp	AS	Dstr cameras, photo eq: lites
42	INT	Interplastic Corp	C	Synthetic resins, plastics
43	IPPF	Interprov Pipe Ln	N,Mc,Tc	Line runs east from Alberta
44	IPG	Interprov Grp Co's	NY,Tc	Worldwide advertis'g agencies
45	IFGR	Inter-Regional Fin. Gr.	N	Hldg co: security dealer

Uniform Footnote Explanations—See Page 1. Other: ¹Mc,Tc. ²Ph. ³Ph,P. ⁴ASO.13,'77. ⁵Incl $1163M retire plans. ⁶$2.12;'77. ⁷$0.41,'78. ⁸Merger talks with Int'l Bank. ⁹$12 Mo Dec'77, Fiscal Jun'77 earned $0.97. ⁱ⁰@$2.38,'78. ⁱⁱ@$1.35,'78.
**Accum on Pfd. **Incl ⁱ²$2.12;'77. **Mobil offers $800M for General Crude Oil Unit. **@$1.31,'78. **Pension. **Credit default:excludes $39M cur.maturities. **@$4.49,'78. **To 8-31-79,scale to $100 in'80. **F.C. & Pfd divds, Times Earned. **@$3.02,'78.
**To 8-31-79,scale to $100 in'85. **To 8-31-79,scale to $100 in'82. **To 8-31-79,scale to $100 in'89. **To 8-31-79,scale to $100 in'81. **@$1.32,'78.

Table 13-5 (continued)

COMMON AND PREFERRED STOCKS

	DIVIDENDS					FINANCIAL POSITION				CAPITALIZATION				—$ Per Shr—EARNINGS—$ Per Shr—						INTEREST EARNINGS OR REMARKS $—Per Share—$		
	Latest Payment			So Far 1979	Total Ind. Rate	Paid 1978	Cash& Equiv.	Curr. Assets	Curr. Liabs.	Balance Sheet Date	Long Term Debt Mil-$	—Shs. 000— Pfd. Com.			1975	1976	1977	Years 1978	1979	Last 12 Mos.	Period	1978	1979

Index 1–45, with company data rows.

SOURCE Standard & Poor's Stock Guide, 1980.

◆ Stock Splits & Dirs By Line Reference Index [1] 2-for-1, '75,'77. [2] 2-for-4, '77. [3] 4-for-10, '79. [4] 2-for-1, '76. [5] 3-for-2, '76. [6] 3-for-1, '77.
[7] 5-for-4, '77. 2-for-1, '78. [8] 100%, '75. [9] 3-for-10, '79. [10] 2-for-1, '78. [11] Adj to 5%, '78. [12] 3-for-1, '77. [13] 10%, '75,'77.

Table 13-6
Standard & Poor's *Stock Report:* El Paso Natural Gas

El Paso Co. 822

NYSE Symbol ELG Options on ASE

Price	Range	P-E Ratio	Dividend	Yield	S&P Ranking
Aug. 4'80	1980				
21 1/8	30 1/2-15 3/4	9	1.48	7.0%	A–

Summary

This holding company owns a major gas pipeline operator serving the West Coast and has diversified interests, including oil and gas exploration and chemicals. While near-term earnings will continue to be adversely affected by the April, 1980 suspension of deliveries of LNG from Algeria, the long-term earnings outlook remains favorable.

Current Outlook

Reflecting suspension of Algerian LNG deliveries in April, share earnings for 1980 will probably decline to about $1.90–$2.20 from 1979's $2.99.

Dividends are expected to continue at a minimum of $0.37 quarterly.

Substantial profit potential exists in the Algeria I project, which at full deliveries will supply three eastern pipelines with the LNG equivalent of one billion cf. of natural gas per day over a 25-year period. ELG's supply situation should also benefit from the recent U.S./Mexican natural gas agreement.

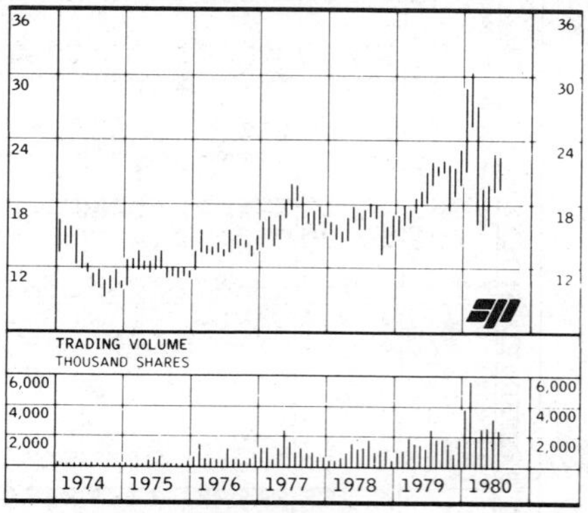
36
30
24
18
12
TRADING VOLUME
THOUSAND SHARES
6,000
4,000
2,000
1974
1975
1976
1977
1978
1979
1980

Operating Revenues (Million $)

Quarter:	1980	1979	1978	1977
Mar.	1,028	599	442	398
Jun.	925	751	490	425
Sep.		832	517	417
Dec.		906	581	455
		3,088	2,030	1,695

Operating revenues for the six months ended June 30, 1980 rose 45%, year to year. Discontinuance of LNG deliveries from Algeria and lower chemical manufacturing profits penalized margins, and net income fell 43%. Share earnings were $0.87, versus $1.57.

Common Share Earnings ($)

Quarter:	1980	1979	1978	1977
Mar.	0.74	0.69	0.54	0.67
Jun.	0.13	0.88	0.53	0.66
Sep.		0.83	0.53	0.31
Dec.		0.59	0.82	0.60
		2.99	2.42	2.24

Important Developments

Jun. '80—The FERC approved El Paso Natural Gas' rate settlement proposal extending the provisions of a 1979 settlement through May 31, 1981. Under the agreement, EPNG will refund $55 million to its customers and reduce its rates by about $30 million.

Apr. '80—El Paso's Algerian unit failed in its efforts to extend an agreement with Sonatrach (the Algerian national oil and gas company) to receive LNG from Algeria beyond the March 31, 1980 termination date. Sonatrach advised El Paso that it would not continue deliveries of LNG beyond March 31 at the current $1.95/MMBtu price authorized by U.S. authorities. El Paso purchases about 700 million cf. of LNG per day for resale.

Next earnings report due in late October.

Per Share Data ($)

Yr. End Dec. 31	1979	1978	1977	1976	1975	1974	1973	1972	1971	1970
Book Value	**23.50**	20.18	20.02	17.73	20.54	19.88	18.30	18.33	17.30	16.19
Earnings[2]	**[1]2.99**	[1]2.44	[1]2.24	[1]1.98	[1]1.88	[1]2.66	[1]2.05	[1]1.64	[1]1.88	[1]1.33
Dividends	**1.36**	1.15 1/2	1.10	1.10	1.10	1.00	1.00	1.00	1.00	1.00
Payout Ratio	**45%**	47%	49%	379%	59%	38%	49%	61%	53%	75%
Prices—High	**23 1/4**	18 1/4	20	15 3/4	13 3/4	16 5/8	21	21 1/4	22 1/8	20
Low	**15 1/8**	13 3/8	14	11 3/4	10 1/4	9 1/8	12 3/4	16 5/8	15 3/4	14 3/4
P/E Ratio—	**8–5**	7-5	9-6	48-36	7-5	6-3	10-6	13-10	10-7	15-11

1. Ful. dil.: 2.93 in 1979, 2.36 in 1978, 2.13 in 1977, 1.74 in 1976, 1.60 in 1975, 2.17 in 1974, 1.80 in 1973, 1.47 in 1972, 1.71 in 1971, 1.23 in 1970. **2.** Bef. results of disc. opers. of −1.30 in 1978, −1.69 in 1976, bef. spec. item(s) of +0.13 in 1973, −0.26 in 1971, −0.29 in 1970.

Standard NYSE Stock Reports
Vol. 47/No. 155/Sec. 10

August 11, 1980
Copyright © 1980 Standard & Poor's Corp. All Rights Reserved
Standard & Poor's Corp.
25 Broadway, NY, NY 10004

Table 13-6 *(continued)*

822

El Paso Company

Income Data (Million $)

Year Ended Dec. 31	Total Oper. Revs.	Cap. Exp.	Depr.	% Depr. Revs.	% Oper. Taxes/ Revs.	Oper. Ratio	[12]Fxd. Chgs.Tms. Earns.	[4]Net Inc.
1979	3,089	420	149	4.8%	5.4%	92.0	2.05	138
1978	2,031	317	126	6.2%	6.4%	90.9	2.16	109
1977	1,695	325	108	6.4%	7.8%	89.4	2.11	92
1976	1,351	331	104	7.7%	7.9%	88.0	1.93	73
1975	1,389	445	106	7.7%	8.2%	89.0	1.64	58
1974	1,251	237	105	8.4%	7.6%	86.7	1.93	74
1973	983	184	91	9.3%	6.5%	87.0	1.61	65
1972	902	111	87	9.6%	7.1%	86.1	1.48	53
1971	1,037	163	93	9.0%	6.7%	86.4	1.60	58
1970	925	120	92	9.9%	4.7%	87.4	1.45	41

Balance Sheet Data (Million $)

Dec. 31	[3]Gross Prop.	Depr. Res.	% Earn. on Net Prop.	Long Term Debt	—% Long Term Debt of— Net Prop.	Oper. Revs.	Invest. Cap.	Total Invest. Cap.	% Earn. on Inv. Cap.	Common Equity Ratio
1979	4,029	1,531	9.9%	1,587	63.5%	51.4%	55.4%	2,865	9.4%	31.1
1978	3,578	1,376	8.4%	1,409	64.0%	69.4%	56.5%	2,492	8.1%	30.8
1977	3,398	1,275	8.5%	1,415	66.6%	83.5%	59.0%	2,396	7.9%	31.3
1976	3,066	1,174	8.6%	1,380	72.9%	102.2%	62.9%	2,193	7.6%	27.9
1975	2,925	1,192	8.8%	1,202	69.3%	86.5%	65.5%	2,012	8.4%	28.9
1974	2,575	1,109	11.4%	850	58.0%	67.9%	55.9%	1,521	11.3%	32.2
1973	2,322	1,011	9.8%	878	66.9%	89.3%	57.9%	1,517	8.1%	29.3
1972	2,649	1,096	8.1%	1,130	72.8%	125.3%	63.5%	1,782	6.2%	26.5
1971	2,584	1,037	·9.1%	1,116	72.2%	109.5%	65.1%	1,715	8.0%	26.5
1970	2,496	1,001	7.8%	1,062	71.0%	114.7%	64.9%	1,637	7.4%	24.8

1. Reflects change in FERC method of accounting for allowance for funds used during construction in 1977 & 1970. 2. Fixed chgs. & pfd. divs. times earns. prior to 1974. 3. Excl. funds held by trustee. 4. Bef. loss on disct. opers. in 1978 & 1976.

Business Summary

The El Paso Company is a holding company whose principal subsidiaries are engaged in natural gas transmission, chemical manufacturing, liquefied natural gas activities, oil and gas production, and development of coal properties. Revenues (including intersegment sales) and operating income contributions in 1979 were:

	Revs.	Profits
Natural Gas	72%	62%
LNG	13%	17%
Chemicals	11%	14%
Oil & Gas production	3%	12%
Other	1%	(5%)

El Paso Natural Gas operates an interstate pipeline system primarily serving California, New Mexico, Texas and Nevada. Gas sales in 1979 amounted to 1.14 trillion cf., versus 1.08 trillion cf. in the prior year.

El Paso Products manufactures a variety of chemical products, including butadiene, styrene, ammonia, ethylene, propylene, polyethylene, and polypropylene.

Deliveries of LNG from Algeria, initiated in March, 1978 to serve the eastern section of the U.S., were suspended April 1, 1980.

Dividend Data

Dividends have been paid since 1936. A dividend reinvestment plan is available.

Amt. of Divd. $	Date Decl.	Ex-divd. Date	Stock of Record	Payment Date
0.37	Nov. 2	Nov. 9	Nov. 16	Dec. 14'79
0.37	Feb. 1	Feb. 15	Feb. 22	Mar. 31'80
0.37	May 2	May 12	May 16	Jun. 30'80
0.37	Aug. 1	Aug. 18	Aug. 22	Sep. 30'80

Next dividend meeting: early Nov. '80.

Finances

Capital expenditures for 1980 are projected at $426 million, down from 1979's $446 million.

Capitalization

Long Term Debt: $1,539,200,000, incl. $16,427,000 6% Series A debs. due 1993 conv. into com. at $16.94 a sh.

Subsid. Pfd. Stock: $168,174,000.

Common Stock: 47,285,771 shs. ($3 par). Institutions hold about 19%. Shareholders: 109,841.

Office—2727 Allen Parkway, Houston, Texas 77019. **Tel**—(713) 525-9400. **Chrmn & Pres**—T. H. Petty. **VP-Secy**—J. B. Megahan. **VP-Treas**—M. B. Bracy. **Investor Contact**—P. R. Ferretti. **Dirs**—H. Boyd, A. C. Glassell, Jr., W. V. Holik, Jr., J. R. Hubbard, L. E. Katzenbach, B. F. Love, W. D. Noel, T. H. Petty, W. F. Rockwell, Jr., K. Rush. **Transfer Agents & Registrars**—Chase Manhattan Bank, NYC; Continental Illinois National Bank & Trust Co., Chicago. **Incorporated** in Delaware in 1928.

Information has been obtained from sources believed to be reliable, but its accuracy and completeness are not guaranteed.

SOURCE Standard & Poor's *Stock Report*, August 11, 1980.

long-term trend level of 3 percent would be an ideal growth rate and favorable for equities. In addition, stable long- and short-term interest rates, reflected in a monetary policy neither restrictive nor expansionary, would be a positive factor. Relatively low interest rates designed to stimulate economic growth help the equity market. And, of course, full employment with minimal inflation would be a favorable ingredient for common stock valuation.

The forces cited above would be favorable for common stock prices. The reverse of these conditions would be unsatisfactory. For example, a weak dollar on the international money exchange, a budget deficit under conditions of inflation, substantial inflation, a stringent or restrictive monetary policy, and rising unemployment—all these would be signs of weakness in the national economy. As you assess the economic environment in which you live, you must look for factors that seem to point toward favorable conditions for the equity market. You must think ahead to see how these factors might change. Then you must make investment decisions in accord with the facts, remembering that unfavorable circumstances anticipated in the future are giving you a warning. They are telling you to avoid common stocks. On the other hand, if you expect a favorable economic environment in the future, you should favor common stock investment. A typical forecast is found in Table 13–7.

Look for the strong industries

Standard & Poor's *Industry Surveys* provide investment information for a wide range of industries. This same information is available periodically at brokerage firms, university libraries, and public libraries in most cities. You can obtain it by simply checking it out of your local library. In *Industry Surveys* you will find a list of the following industries you might consider for investment: aerospace, air transport, autos and auto parts, banking, building, beverages, Canadian industries, chemicals, containers, communications, electronics, finance, food processing, food processing including bakery, health care, drugs and cosmetics, home furniture, insurance, investment companies, leather and shoes, liquor, leisure time activity, machinery, metals, office equipment, oil and gas, oil, paper, publishing, rail equipment, railroads, retailing, retailing foods and restaurant chains, rubber fabricating, soft drinks, steel and coal, telephone, textiles, tobacco, trucking, and utilities, electric and gas. An example is given in Table 13–8.

The list does not provide an exhaustive definition of subindustries within each group. This is because the subindustries are defined by the products they sell. Yet within each industry you can quickly learn which subindustries appear to be strong and which appear to be weak. This is simply done by comparing the relative size and growth of the subindustry to the size and growth of the national economy. It has become apparent in the early 1980s that the electronic computer industry is a leading industry, that drug and health care is an outstanding industry, and that many savings banks and commercial banks present excellent investment opportunities. You could learn this from information in *Industry Surveys*. Again, the best way to determine the strength of an industry is by comparing its size and growth to the national economy's size and growth. You could

Table 13–7
Forecast of the U.S. economy

	S&P 500 INDEX ANNUAL RANGE			
	—Our Forecast—		——Actual——	
	High	Low	High	Low
1980	123	95	...	..
†1979	113	92	*112	*95
‡1978	110	90	108	86½

†Forecast made December, 1978. ‡Forecast made December, 1977. *To date.

Buying opportunities ahead

THE first year of the new decade promises to be an exciting and challenging one for investors. The major market "averages" may well move in a wider range than in any year since 1975.

The S&P 500-stock index in 1979 has ranged between 95 and 112—a difference from the low to the high of 18%. In 1978, the spread was 25%. In each of the two preceding years, it was about 20%.

We are forecasting a range of 123-95 in 1980 (the current level of the "500" is about 107), which would be a spread of nearly 30%. The low may be seen before midyear, perhaps in the first quarter; the high, in either the third or fourth quarter, depending importantly on the direction of interest rates and inflation at the time.

High volatility in 1980 is suggested by the large number of "unknowns" in the investment equation, with all of the uncertainties inextricably intertwined.

An economic recession seems finally to be taking shape, to the unusual accompaniment of sighs of relief. Investors, businessmen and consumers have been fearful that the strains on our monetary system, if not soon relieved by moderation of demand for goods and services in the economy, would have serious consequences.

Recession should end by midyear

S&P economists are saying that the recession will end around the middle of the year. And, as shown in the table on the next page, results for all of 1980—taking into account a gradual recovery in the second half—won't look too bad.

A saving grace, they point out, was the long period of advance notice given the current slump. While consumers have continued to spend actively in anticipation of higher prices, businesses have been exercising a good deal of restraint. Inventory levels are far less dangerous than they were at the start of the 1973-74 recession.

Our economists are quick to warn, however, that all bets would be off should the Middle East situation deteriorate markedly.

With or without "punitive" military action by the U.S. in Iran, the spate of terrorism directed against our country throughout the world seems likely to continue. Such goading, with a backdrop of concern about Russia's growing military capabilities, could lead to much heftier defense spending. It would be a mistake to assume that

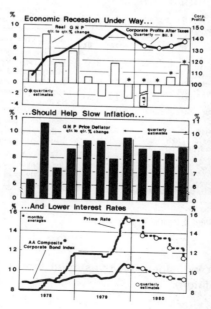

Table 13-7 *(continued)*

this would be good for our economy. It is not further stimulus that we need in the existing inflationary environment.

Our energy lifeline, meanwhile, is being threatened. Iranian oil is not the key, though if it stops flowing completely—rather than just to the U.S. directly—there would be serious disruptive effects on the economy. Actions that might be taken by other leading oil-producing nations could be more critical. If Saudi Arabia, for instance, were to choose or be forced to cut oil shipments substantially, not only would most of the western world suffer a major economic blow, but the risks of military action also would be greatly heightened.

At the least, we should be prepared for further hikes in oil prices arising out of the nearby OPEC meeting and indicated continuing tight supply conditions. Unsettled currency markets are also to be expected.

To keep inflation under control and provide support for the dollar, the Federal Reserve will be unable to let up very much on the credit reins, notwithstanding a weakening economy. The Fed can only hope that oil and defense—and perhaps premature tax reduction in the forthcoming Presidential election year—don't compound its problems.

In the circumstances, we see interest rates easing only moderately in 1980. The yield on the S&P index of AA-

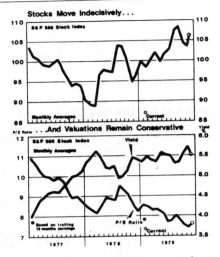

rated bonds, currently around 10.8%, may get no lower than about 9.3%.

This suggests that institutions and other investors will continue to channel sizable sums into the bond market, to the disadvantage of stocks. Currently, the yield spread in favor of fixed-income instruments over equities is the widest in modern history (see page 409).

Healthy recovery possible

The market is vulnerable to disappointments on the Middle East, inflation or interest-rate fronts. But if current concerns prove to be overblown, a healthy recovery in stock prices could occur before too long.

There are, moreover, good reasons to be optimistic from a longer-term standpoint. Stocks today are quite modestly valued on a historical basis. The P/E ratio on the S&P 500 index, at 7.4 times estimated 1979 earnings and 7.8 times the 6% lower profits we are projecting for 1980, is near its lows of the past 30 years. In addition, the Middle East crisis should spur efforts to reduce dependence on imported energy, and the underlying drift toward fiscal conservatism in the U.S.—including new investment incentives—seems likely to continue.

Thus, while it is advisable to play it close to the vest for the time being, attractive investment opportunities could develop as 1980 progresses. Industry groups and individual stocks we favor for above-average performance appear on the following pages.

KEY PATTERNS IN THE ECONOMY
Standard & Poor's Projections

	Est. 1979	Est. 1980	Est. 1979	Est. 1980
	—(Billions)—		—% Change—	
Gross National Product	$2,363	$2,538	+11.1%	+ 7.4%
Inflation Rate for Year ...	8.9%	8.8%	...	...
GNP in 1972 Dollars	1,428	1,409	+ 2.1	− 1.3
Basic Components of GNP:				
Personal Consumption ...	1,503	1,635	+11.3	+ 8.8
Gross Private Investment .	389	387	+10.8	− 0.6
Net Exports	−3	−4	...	...
Government Spending	474	520	+ 8.8	+ 9.6
Three Major Spending Areas:				
Personal Buying of Durables	211	215	+ 5.2	+ 1.8
Business Capital Outlays .	255	271	+15.3	+ 6.2
National Defense	108	119	+ 8.9	+10.2
Corporate After-Tax Profits..	142	134	+17.1	− 6.2
Other Key Indicators:				
Indus. Product. ('67=100)	151.7	146.4	+ 3.8	− 3.5
Unemployment (ann. avg.).	5.9%	7.7%	...	...
Housing Starts (thousands)	1,745	1,588	−13.1	− 9.0
*†Corporate Bond Yields ...	9.73	9.75	...	...
†3-Mo. Treasury Bills	9.96	9.14	...	...
Increase in Consumer Prices	11.2%	10.7%	...	...

*S&P index of AA-rated corporate bonds. †Average for year.

SOURCE Standard & Poor's, by permission.

then select industries for investment that appear to be attractive now and in the future.

**Selecting companies
for investment**

Once you have selected an industry for investment consideration, you must then examine individual companies within the industry to see if they have the characteristics that might lead to success. You need to analyze several areas before considering a company for investment.

First, select companies that are competitive leaders within the industry. This is extremely important. Competitive leaders have achieved a size and dominance that make them attractive for investment opportunities. They are large enough to be strong, but not so large that they lack

**Table 13-8
Strong industries**

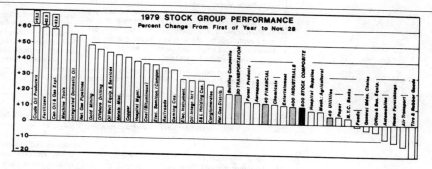

Industries best situated for 1980

The value of selectivity in investment is dramatically illustrated in the 1979 group performance chart above. Our choices of groups likely to do best next year are shown below, including favored stocks in these areas. Industries well-positioned for the decade of the eighties are discussed in the box on the next page.

Energy-related groups should continue in the investment spotlight, although a somewhat more selective approach toward the stocks is now called for. Well-situated *oil companies* should be able to extend their earnings gains of 1979, despite the proposed windfall profits tax. Worldwide production is likely to be held at levels that keep prices rising. Although U.S. price ceilings on gasoline and certain crude oil categories will have a restraining influence, the price decontrol program for U.S. crude that began June 1 should provide increasing relief for domestic producers. Among our favorites at this time are ATLANTIC RICHFIELD, a Stock for Action, as well as Master List issues EXXON, STANDARD OIL OF INDIANA, MOBIL CORP. and ROYAL DUTCH PETROLEUM.

The outlook for *drillers* is also favorable. Rising worldwide prices for oil and gas and the phased decontrol of new domestic natural gas prices are stimulating both offshore and onshore drilling. Also spurring activity is the fact that major oil companies are spending more funds on exploration to comply with President Carter's directive to lessen dependence on Mideast crude and to quiet public opposition to price decontrol. Worldwide footage drilled in 1980 is projected to rise about 8%, vs. an estimated increase of less than 1% this year. Prospects for offshore drilling are the best since late 1975, when overcapacity was experienced. Land drilling also should do well, with the U.S. rig count expected to climb 12% in 1980, after dropping around 4% this

year. WESTERN CO. OF NORTH AMERICA is a promising speculation in the group.

Increased oil exploration will, moreover, benefit the major *oil well equipment and service companies* next year. Profits should be enhanced by a continuing shift to premium-priced products needed for deeper and more complex drilling. The cost of major expansion in personnel and assets by many of the companies should be readily absorbed, with U.S. rig activity again on the upswing. Our favorite in the group is SCHLUMBERGER (a Stock for Action).

With prices expected to rise and no supply disruptions foreseen, the *natural gas* industry should also experience a banner year. Support is coming from the increased importance the government is placing on natural gas, as well as from a growing trend of residential conversions to gas heating systems. The recent agreement between the U.S. and Mexico in which the latter will export 300 million cubic feet of natural gas daily removes a roadblock to the future supply of supplemental sources of natural gas to the U.S. market. It is an important step in making gas available from a variety of sources at a price competitive with other fuels. SOUTHERN NATURAL RESOURCES (a Stock for Action) is one of the best positioned in the group.

Aerospace—Prospects for the *defense* sector of the aerospace industry are being strengthened by increasing concern over Russia's growing military capabilities and by recognition of our vulnerability to terrorist activities around the world. With large defense programs already in place, the industry will be little affected by next year's anticipated economic downturn. Our favorite in the group is GENERAL DYNAMICS (a Stock for Action). In

Table 13–8 *(continued)*.

Groups we favor for the eighties

The **forest products** and **building materials** industries should be stimulated in the coming decade by a strong new housing market, the result of an expected surge in new household formations because of the baby boom of the late 1950s. Building materials should receive further support from increased demand from remodeling and energy-conservation.

The **oil services** industry should enjoy above-average profit growth until at least the 1990s, when alternate fuels may begin to play a greater role. With most of the world's easily accessible crude reserves already discovered, the search for new oil and gas will likely move to deeper levels onshore and to harsher physical environments offshore. These are more profitable for the industry, since greater emphasis is placed on product reliability and on service, with price playing a lesser role.

As world food needs become more pressing, there will be greater demand for the most efficient **farm machinery**. As a result, there should be a continuous worldwide upgrading of agricultural equipment.

Health care spending in the next decade will continue to outpace growth in the overall economy. Hospital management companies will benefit, and with the steady rise in the number of older persons, so will nursing homes. Medical technology, with emphasis on new diagnostic equipment and surgical techniques (laser surgery, for example), is also an emerging growth area.

Sophisticated new products will again keep **high-technology** industries in the growth forefront. Especially promising areas are instrumentation and semiconductors. Computers will continue to dominate technology in the 1980s, with emphasis on distributed data processing (DDP, or the processing of information at sites remote from a mainframe computer), communications, word processing, and microcomputers.

---

the *commercial* sector of the industry, we prefer Master list BOEING, which should continue to increase its share of the market in coming years.

Hospital Management—Essentially recession resistant, the industry could show an earnings gain of more than 25% in 1980. The major chains are in a position to cope with the need to keep down operating costs, and in fact are benefiting to some extent from these pressures because a growing number of less efficient hospitals are finding it best to sell out to the chains or to turn over operation to them via management contracts. Master List HOSPITAL CORP. OF AMERICA and Stock For Action AMERICAN MEDICAL INTERNATIONAL are two favored issues in the group.

Leisure/Entertainment—Outlays for leisure pursuits should continue to increase next year, although the slow economy will limit growth to selected areas. We expect most of the gain to be concentrated in *gaming, movies* and *cable television*. Casino gambling in 1980 should be boosted by the ongoing expansion of Atlantic City and the Nevada markets (Las Vegas, Reno and Lake Tahoe). Legislators have recognized the potential economic benefits from gaming, and several states, including New York, Massachusetts, Illinois, Pennsylvania and Florida, are considering legalization of casino gambling.

The *movie* industry could be aided by next year's expected recession, since consumers generally "trade down" to movies from more costly leisure activities as plays, concerts, sporting events and the like. In fact, 1980's box-office receipts, helped by scheduled major releases and non-theatrical distribution of films to television, are expected to exceed 1979's level (currently running above 1978 by a good margin). METRO-GOLD-WYN-MAYER, offering representation in both gaming and movies, is an appealing speculation.

The *cable television* (CATV) industry next year is expected to benefit from continued brisk demand for pay-TV services and recent favorable FCC decisions. Subscribers currently number about 15 million, which represents a relatively small percentage of the potential market. An attractive speculation in the group is WARNER COMMUNICATIONS, which also has major interests in other types of entertainment and in publishing.

Technology—With productivity improvement continuing as a key business priority, demand for *analytical instruments* and *testing and measuring (T&M) instruments* should show further above-average growth next year. Prospects are also brightened by increasing governmental regulations in the areas of environment, health and safety. Companies are being forced to more accurately measure and identify potential hazards in their products from the standpoint of workers, consumers and the environment. Our current choices in the group are TEKTRONIX and PERKIN-ELMER, both Stocks for Action.

SOURCE   Standard & Poor's, by permission.

growth potential. These candidates have survived the test of time and are likely to continue to do so in the future. This does not mean you must confine yourself only to the giants of an industry. In the subindustry listings you might discern from reading *Industry Surveys* some competitive leaders as excellent investment candidates. If you select a subindustry category, make certain to select a company that has been a leader for some time. Table 13–9 provides information of this sort.

Second, sit down with a pencil and paper, and estimate what the earnings of the company might be over a future investment period. Professional analysts tend to limit their forecasts to three years because they can only estimate that far ahead. Beyond three years it is difficult for

Table 13–9
Strong companies for growth and income

SUPERVISED MASTER LIST OF RECOMMENDED ISSUES

GROUP 1: FOUNDATION STOCKS FOR LONG-TERM GAIN

These issues are basic building blocks for the portfolio. They offer the prospect of long-term appreciation, along with moderate but growing income. The investor seeking to build an estate should start with stocks from this list, augmenting them with issues from other groups according to his objectives and temperament.

Earnings Per Share ($) 1977	1978	E1979	Indicated Div. $	1977-79 Price Range	Recent Price	P/E Ratio	Yield %		Annual Growth Rates —for Latest 5 Years— Sales	Earn.	Div.	▼Price Action vs. Mkt. 9-21-76 to 3-6-78	Since 3-6-78	Listed Options Traded	Last Page Ref.
[2]2.72	[2]3.53	[2]4.20	1.32	31 - 20⅝	27	6.4	4.9	BankAmerica	..	16%	9%	1.02	1.02	C	491
2.41	2.60	2.85	1.20	28⅜- 19¾	21	7.4	5.7	Beatrice Foods (*Feb.)	16%	11	11	1.03	0.74	A	454
[2]3.05	[2]3.88	[2]4.20	1.30	34 - 18⅞	22	5.2	5.9	Citicorp	..	11	10	0.74	0.89	C	482
3.01	3.16	3.75	1.40	43¾- 22	32	8.5	4.4	Dow Chemical	15	11	23	0.60	1.14	C	435
3.99	5.59	6.00	2.90	86¾- 41⅛	48	8.0	6.0	Eastman Kodak	11	5	4	0.56	0.93	C	425
5.41	6.20	9.25	4.00	61¼- 43	58	6.3	6.9	Exxon Corp.	17	−0.2	8	0.99	1.04	C	469
4.25	4.80	5.75	2.20	44¼- 28	38	6.6	5.8	Heinz (H.J.) (*Apr.)	10	14	19	1.49	0.82	..	469
4.58	5.32	4.80	3.44	80½- 58¾	65	13.5	5.3	Int'l Business Machines	14	14	21	1.06	0.85	C	505
4.98	[4]4.94	[5]5.90	2.80	69⅝- 35⅛	38	6.4	5.8	International Paper	11	3	3	0.63	0.85	C	491
6.19	6.99	7.60	3.40	93⅝- 70¼	74	9.7	4.6	Procter & Gamble (*June)	13	13	12	0.99	0.78	A	612
4.34	5.14	5.35	1.50	52 - 24⅞	52	9.7	2.9	• Southern Nat. Resources	19	14	9	1.45	1.38	..	402
6.90	7.36	10.50	3.00	85⅞- 43¾	84	8.0	3.6	Standard Oil (Ind.)	21	11	17	1.02	1.51	C	542

GROUP 2: STOCKS WITH PROMISING GROWTH PROSPECTS

These stocks promise to enjoy well above average growth rates in earnings per share for the foreseeable future. Stocks in the second category carry a higher degree of risk, but by the same token offer greater reward potential. Income is not a consideration here.

Established Growth

Earnings Per Share ($) 1977	1978	E1979	Indicated Div. $	1977-79 Price Range	Recent Price	P/E Ratio	Yield %		Latest 5-Year Growth Rates Sales	Earn.	No. of Earn. Gains '74-'78	Interim ▪Earn. Trend	▼Price Action vs. Mkt. 9-21-76 to 3-6-78	Since 3-6-78	Listed Options Traded	Last Page Ref.
1.98	2.48	2.95	1.00	42⅝- 19⅜	41	13.9	2.4	Abbott Laboratories	18%	25%	5	+20%	1.22	1.24	Ph	482
2.46	2.83	3.30	0.80	44½- 27⅞	38	11.5	2.1	Big Three Industries	29	28	5	+10	1.01	1.05	..	505
2.69	3.08	3.45	1.44	40⅜- 28	36	10.4	4.0	Bristol-Myers	12	14	5	+13	0.93	1.02	MW	469
2.15	2.43	2.85	1.14	33⅞- 21⅞	26	9.1	4.4	PepsiCo, Inc.	20	18	5	+20	1.08	0.84	C	425
2.80	3.39	4.05	1.25	38⅝- 25¾	35	8.6	3.6	Philip Morris	20	20	5	+21	1.17	0.99	A	478
3.12	3.94	5.00	1.10	100⅜- 37⅜	96	19.2	1.1	• Schlumberger Ltd.	24	39	5	+27	1.22	1.79	C	402

More Speculative Growth

Earnings Per Share ($) 1977	1978	E1979	Mill. Shs. Outst.	1977-79 Price Range	Recent Price	P/E Ratio	Yield %		Latest 5-Year Growth Rates Sales	Earn.	No. of Earn. Gains '74-'78	Interim ▪Earn. Trend	▼Price Action vs. Mkt. 9-21-76 to 3-6-78	Since 3-6-78	Listed Options Traded	Last Page Ref.
4.18	5.86	7.50	4.1	101½- 17½	101	13.2	...	Datapoint (*July)	48%	36%	5	+43%	1.53	2.14	..	579
3.40	4.10	5.00	40.2	69½- 36⅝	68	13.6	...	Digital Equipment (*June)	35	30	5	+27	0.91	1.38	C, A	600
1.82	2.22	2.75	11.0	25⅛- 10	22	8.0	3.1	• General Cinema (Oct.)	18	23	5	+11	1.58	1.23	..	478
1.95	2.39	3.00	17.0	41½- 13	42	14.0	1.2	Hospital Corp. of Amer.	30	24	5	+26	1.58	1.87	..	454
3.10	4.28	4.95	18.1	64 - 28¼	60	12.1	1.4	• Tektronix (*May)	23	29	5	+36	1.27	1.47	..	402

•Best situated currently for the objectives described in the paragraph introducing each group of stocks.

EARNINGS are for calendar years or for fiscal years ending as indicated after names. Unless otherwise noted, they are based on common and common share equivalents, excluding nonrecurring items and including restatements. A—Actual. E—Estimated. ↑Estimate revised upward since last publication of the Master List; ↓estimate revised downward. *Of the following year.

Listed options traded: C—Chicago Board Options Exchange; A—American Stock Exchange; Pa—Pacific Stock Exchange; Ph—Philadelphia Stock Exchange; MW—Midwest Options Exchange.

INDICATED DIVIDENDS include actual or possible extras. ↑Dividend increased; ↓dividend decreased. PRICE/EARNINGS RATIOS are based on latest shown estimated or actual earnings. GROWTH RATES for sales and earnings are through latest completed years reported; for dividends, through 1978.

All stocks currently in the Supervised Master List are listed on the New York Stock Exchange.

▼A figure above 1.0 indicates that the stock outperformed the S & P industrial stock price index in this period. It is computed by taking the ratio of the stock's price at the end of the period vs. the beginning of the period and dividing it by the corresponding ratio of the index. The time periods covered are updated periodically to conform to the latest major market cycle.

▪This column compares share earnings of the latest six months with those of the corresponding year-earlier period.

Table 13-9 *(continued)*

GROUP 3: CYCLICAL/SPECULATIVE STOCKS

This group comprises stocks selected for high reward potentials stemming from a variety of considerations—including emerging opportunities, turnaround situations, stocks to benefit from cyclical upswings, and the like. Readers can expect to see more frequent changes in this list than in the others. The risk factor in some of the issues in this group may be high and the stocks recommended may not be suitable for those concerned with income or with investment grade securities.

Earnings Per Share ($) 1977	1978	E1979	Indicated Div. $	1977-79 Price Range	Recent Price	P/E Ratio	Yield %	Listed Options Traded	Last Page Ref.		Remarks
3.78	4.07	↑4.25	1.60	28 -18⅝	24	5.6	6.7	..	430	Allied Stores (*Jan.)	Margin-improvement program continuing.
5.62	7.23	9.00	3.00	58¼-25¾	55	6.1	5.5	..	425	American Standard	Modestly valued on strong profit trend.
2.83	5.05	7.85	2.40	53 -16⅝	47	6.0	5.1	C	430	•Boeing	Heavy new commercial jet orders aid long-term prospects.
1.04	1.31	1.55	0.60	16¼- 7½	14	9.0	4.3	..	505	Browning-Ferris (Sept.)	Regulation of waste disposal methods aids growth prospects.
5.74	8.52	11.50	2.10	65 -35	58	5.0	3.6	C	443	Burlington Northern	Superior rail and natural resource potentials.
2.11	2.45	2.85	0.72	37 -14	31	10.9	2.3	..	542	Harris Corp. (*June)	Growth in electronic communications enhances outlook.
[2,3]6.64	[2]8.37	↓[2]9.20	3.00	49¾-34	48	5.2	6.3	C	518	INA Corp.	Rising investment income providing thrust.
2.29	2.93	3.50	0.66	20⅛- 7¼	14	4.0	4.7	..	454	Morse Shoe	Rapidly expanding Fayva shoe store chain.
2.76	3.23	↓3.25	Nil	34⅝-10½	30	9.2	..	C, A	430	Tandy Corp. (*June)	Dominant in its field; above-average growth.
2.30	3.18	4.15	1.30	46½-20¾	29	7.0	4.5	C	435	Weyerhaeuser Co.	Timber self-sufficiency enhances long-term prospects.
2.82	3.56	3.75	1.20	41 -23½	33	8.8	3.6	..	446	Wheelabrator-Frye	New refuse-to-energy process adds speculative kicker.

GROUP 4: LIBERAL INCOME WITH INFLATION PROTECTION

If high yield alone were the goal, it would be easy to compile a list of high-grade bonds returning 10% or more. But bonds afford no protection against inflation. While it was hard to beat inflation in the past decade, the list below comprises quality stocks that in our opinion offer the prospect of dividend growth sufficient to compensate for the degree of inflation we envisage for the period ahead.

Earnings Per Share ($) 1977	1978	E1979	Indicated Div. $	1977-79 Price Range	Recent Price	P/E Ratio	Yield %		Dividend History: 5-Year Growth Rate	No. of Ann. Incr. 1974-78	5-Year Avg. Payout	Latest Increase	Inflation Hedge Ratio††	Listed Options Traded	Last Page Ref.
6.97	7.74	8.05	5.00	65⅝-51⅝	54	6.7	9.4	American Tel. & Tel.	10%	5	61%	4- 2-79	1.09	C	446
3.81	4.54	4.20	2.40	29 -24⅛	26	6.2	9.2	Florida Power & Light	10	5	47	6-15-79	0.93	..	469
4.75	5.31	9.00	3.00	56 -29 11/16	52	5.8	5.8	Mobil Corp.	8	5	39	3-12-79	1.01	C	446
[6]4.36	[6]4.50	[6]5.45	2.10	35 -26⅛	34	6.2	6.2	•Reynolds (R.J.) Indus.	6	5	40	12- 5-78	1.21	C	401
11.73	10.55	↑25.00	5.53	80¾-51¼	79	3.2	7.0	•Royal Dutch Petrol.	14	5	29	6-20-79	1.50	..	425

††This figure shows the degree to which the stock's dividend and price change offset the sharp increase in the consumer price index in the 5 years through 1978. A figure of 1.0 would indicate that the impact of inflation was completely offset.

[1]Consolidated, GAAP accounting basis. [2]Net operating earnings. [3]Before losses of $0.17 in 1977 from discontinued operations. [4]After nonrecurring charges. [5]From continuing operations—not counting gains from the sale of certain assets. [6]Adjusted for 2-for-1 split effective Dec. 10.

even the most astute analysts to arrive at an estimate of earnings. In order to anticipate the growth of earnings in the future, you need to know something about past earnings. Therefore, you must examine the trend of earnings as well as the future expected level of earnings before making an investment decision. You should revise your forecast on a quarterly basis.

Third, select an efficient firm. Operating efficiency refers to the firm's ability to produce goods and services at a reasonable price. Other things being equal, the higher the cost of producing a dollar of sales, the less efficient the firm; the lower the cost, the more efficient the firm. The operating efficiency of a company can be measured in terms of sales per employee, profits per employee, or possibly of sales per dollar of plant investment and of profits per dollar of plant investment. But it is extremely important for you to estimate how efficient the company is among its competitors.

The fourth factor has to do with the firm's current financial position. It ought to have a strong current financial position, that is, its current assets should exceed its current liabilities by a substantial margin. Liquid assets—cash and accounts receivable—should be equal to or exceed current liabilities. The firm ought to have adequate current funds to meet its operating expenses. This is another reason why you should select a firm that is a competitive leader and has developed a record of financial soundness.

Fifth, make an examination of the company's capital structure. You want to select a company that has adequate financing. Long-term debt should not be excessive, and there should be a reasonable amount of equity to support the company's debt. As a stockholder you want to make sure that the business of the firm is sound. You want to make sure that its debt is adequately covered by assets owned by investors. If its debt is exorbitant, this means that the firm's long-range financial position is in jeopardy.

Sixth, you need aggressive, able, and intelligent managers running the firm. Therefore, one item on your checklist for investment is for you to learn how well the management is doing. It has to bring together land, labor, and capital to produce a good or service at a profit for the shareowners. Without efficient operations the firm cannot or will not be able to earn a profit. And a profit is needed in order to turn the company's stock into a profitable investment for the future.

Finally, you must estimate somehow the future return you expect to earn from your investment. As shown previously, the relative attractiveness of the current price of a stock is only in relationship to its expected dividends and price in the future. Let's assume that in analyzing a company, you find that the dividend growth and expected price of its stock three years from now are not likely to provide a 12 to 14 percent total return. Perhaps you should then ignore that stock as a possible investment candidate. Assume a stock is selling at $50 a share in the marketplace and paying a dollar per share in dividends. To make this stock an attractive investment, you would have to receive a dollar of dividends in each of the next three years, which is a 2 percent annual rate. In addition, you would need a 10 to 12 percent growth per year in the price. Since the current price of the stock is $50, it needs to increase in three years to about $67 a share. The only way the price per share can increase this way is for it to be in an environment where the stock market fully reflects the future estimated earnings of a company. If there is no chance of the company increasing its price over the next three years or of increasing its dividend to provide you with at least a 12 to 14 percent rate of return, then you should no longer think of the stock as an investment.

Of course, this discussion is designed only to highlight some of the factors you need examine as you select common stocks. You can explore these subjects in greater depth in other investment books. But we need to put our analysis into a frame of reference that sums up the factors to look for in your analysis of a firm: its competitive position; its operating characteristics; future profitability; its financial condition and capital structure; what kind of management is running it; and the firm's future earnings in relationship to its present price. These factors will help you estimate if the rate of return will be adequate for the risks you are assuming. Without such a simple analysis it would be difficult for anyone to make an adequate financial decision about any company.

Some questions to ask   You must estimate the future earnings of a company for a three-year period. Then you'll need to compare the stream of income you expect to receive with the current price, and ask the following questions:

1. Are the sales numbers realistic?
2. Are the earnings realistic?
3. Are the dividends realistic?
4. Is the price realistic?

And lastly, does it appear that the stock's current price when compared to its future price, future earnings, and future dividends will provide an adequate rate of return? This simple process requires you to examine the national economy, a particular industry, and a particular company. You then must reach an estimate as to the future rate of return from the company's stock over a three-year period. You will need to make use of this very powerful tool of analysis over and over again to help you in making sound investment decisions. Without it you are likely to operate only on tips and guesses. And you do not want to have to make your investment decisions on the basis of uncertainty.

Buying and selling securities and selecting a broker

The role of brokers   Like bonds, common and preferred stocks are purchased through brokers on a commission basis. Thus if you decide to buy 100 shares of IBM, you are required to buy them through an agent, the *stockbroker*. Actually, if you were able to find someone wanting to sell 100 shares of IBM, you could conceivably handle the sale yourself. But first a broker or banker would have to guarantee that the owner of the shares actually could legitimately sell them. But how would you find a seller? Should you call on your friends? Advertise in a newspaper? Shout out your needs on the street corner in the financial district? Such procedures would be highly unlikely and very inefficient.

Finding a broker

Probably you would end up by finding a broker who would buy the shares for you. Many shares are traded on the New York Stock Exchange or American Stock Exchange. Prices are quoted in *The Wall Street Journal* under New York Stock Exchange Composite (NYSE-Composite Transactions) or American Stock Exchange Composite (Amex Composite Transactions). Shares are also traded in the Over the Counter market (OTC) or at a regional exchange. If you know what stock you want to buy, you must ask a broker to handle the purchase for you.

You need to know something about the brokerage firm and the broker before you place your order. One way to find a broker is to seek the advice of knowledgeable friends and members of the financial community with whom you are already familiar. Most likely it will be officers of your commercial bank or a local savings and loan association. You can ask them to recommend three brokers. Then call each of the three and discuss your intended purchase and future needs. After this, you make a decision as to which broker you will use.

When you talk with brokers, keep in mind the following points: Will they give you prompt and efficient service? Are they persons of unquestioned integrity? Are they experienced? Will they serve you well without trying to "push" for business? Do they share your investment philosophy? Will you enjoy and respect your mutual relationship with the brokerage firm? Does it have an unquestioned credit rating? Does it provide good information? Can it provide service in all markets, including options and commodities?

When you open an account with a brokerage firm, you should explain your investment objectives in detail so that your broker understands your investment needs.

Brokerage commissions

The cost of buying securities can be substantial. Your broker's commission is based on the dollar amount of each transaction and the number of shares involved. The greater the number of shares and the greater the dollar amount, the lower the commission percentage. This is shown in Table 13–10, which is a typical partial schedule of commission fees in the brokerage community for 100 and 200 share orders. Since May 1, 1975 the Securities and Exchange Commission has required negotiated commissions. This means that commissions can no longer be fixed for all members of the New York Stock Exchange.

For example, in buying common stocks, a purchase of 100 shares is considered a *round lot purchase*. A purchase of less than 100 shares is called an *odd lot*. If you purchase an odd lot, you pay an odd lot fee in addition to the usual commission. The cost of buying 10 shares of a $75 stock, including the $1.25 odd lot fee, might be $23 or 3.07 percent. The cost of buying 100 shares at $75 would be approximately $103

Table 13–10
Schedule of broker's commission fees

1 0 0 S H A R E T A B L E

PRICE		1/8	1/4	3/8	1/2	5/8	3/4	7/8
1	10.00	11.25	12.50	13.75	15.00	16.25	17.50	18.75
2	20.00	21.25	22.50	23.75	25.00	26.25	27.50	28.75
3	30.00	30.00	30.00	30.00	30.00	30.00	30.00	30.00
4	30.00	30.00	30.00	30.00	30.00	30.00	30.00	30.00
5	30.00	30.00	30.00	30.00	30.00	30.00	30.00	30.00
6	30.00	30.00	30.00	30.00	30.00	30.00	30.00	30.00
7	30.00	30.00	30.00	30.00	30.00	30.00	30.00	30.00
8	30.00	32.09	32.29	32.49	32.69	32.89	33.09	33.29
9	33.50	33.70	33.90	34.10	34.30	34.50	34.70	34.90
10	35.10	35.30	35.50	35.70	35.90	36.10	36.30	36.50
11	36.71	36.91	37.11	37.31	37.51	37.71	37.91	38.11
12	38.31	38.51	38.71	38.91	39.11	39.31	39.51	39.71
13	39.92	40.12	40.32	40.52	40.72	40.92	41.12	41.32
14	41.52	41.72	41.92	42.12	42.32	42.52	42.72	42.92
15	43.13	43.33	43.53	43.73	43.93	44.13	44.33	44.53
16	44.73	44.93	45.13	45.33	45.53	45.73	45.93	46.13
17	46.34	46.54	46.74	46.94	47.14	47.34	47.54	47.74
18	47.94	48.14	48.34	48.54	48.74	48.94	49.14	49.34
19	49.55	49.75	49.95	50.15	50.35	50.55	50.75	50.95
20	51.15	51.35	51.55	51.75	51.95	52.15	52.35	52.55
21	52.76	52.96	53.16	53.36	53.56	53.76	53.96	54.16
22	54.36	54.56	54.76	54.96	55.16	55.36	55.56	55.76
23	55.97	56.17	56.37	56.57	56.77	56.97	57.17	57.37
24	57.57	57.77	57.97	58.17	58.37	58.57	58.77	58.97
25	59.18	60.39	60.54	60.69	60.83	60.98	61.13	61.27
26	61.42	61.57	61.72	61.86	62.01	62.16	62.30	62.45
27	62.60	62.75	62.89	63.04	63.19	63.33	63.48	63.63
28	63.78	63.92	64.07	64.22	64.36	64.51	64.66	64.81
29	64.95	65.10	65.25	65.39	65.54	65.69	65.84	65.98
30	66.13	66.28	66.42	66.57	66.72	66.87	67.01	67.16
31	67.31	67.45	67.60	67.75	67.90	68.04	68.19	68.34
32	68.48	68.63	68.78	68.93	69.07	69.22	69.37	69.51
33	69.66	69.81	69.96	70.10	70.25	70.40	70.54	70.69
34	70.84	70.99	71.13	71.28	71.43	71.57	71.72	71.87
35	72.02	72.16	72.31	72.46	72.60	72.75	72.90	73.04
36	73.19	73.34	73.49	73.63	73.78	73.93	74.07	74.22
37	74.37	74.52	74.66	74.81	74.96	75.10	75.25	75.40
38	75.55	75.69	75.84	75.99	76.13	76.28	76.43	76.58
39	76.72	76.87	77.02	77.16	77.31	77.46	77.61	77.75
40	77.90	78.05	78.19	78.34	78.49	78.64	78.78	78.93
41	79.08	79.22	79.37	79.52	79.67	79.81	79.96	80.11
42	80.25	80.40	80.55	80.70	80.84	80.99	81.14	81.28
43	81.43	81.58	81.73	81.87	82.02	82.17	82.31	82.46
44	82.61	82.76	82.90	83.00	83.00	83.00	83.00	83.00
45	83.00	83.00	83.00	83.00	83.00	83.00	83.00	83.00
46	83.00	83.00	83.00	83.00	83.00	83.00	83.00	83.00
47	83.00	83.00	83.00	83.00	83.00	83.00	83.00	83.00
48	83.00	83.00	83.00	83.00	83.00	83.00	83.00	83.00
49	83.00	83.00	83.00	83.00	83.00	83.00	83.00	83.00
50	83.00	88.00	88.00	88.00	88.00	88.00	88.00	88.00

Table 13–10 *(continued)*

200 SHARE TABLE

PRICE	1/8	1/4	3/8	1/2	5/8	3/4	7/8
1	20.00	22.50	25.00	27.50	30.00	30.00	30.00	30.00
2	30.00	30.00	30.00	30.00	30.00	30.00	30.00	30.83
3	31.47	32.11	32.75	33.39	34.04	34.68	35.32	35.96
4	40.60	41.25	41.89	42.53	43.17	43.81	44.46	45.10
5	45.74	46.38	47.02	47.67	48.31	48.95	49.59	50.23
6	50.88	51.52	52.16	52.80	53.44	54.09	54.73	55.37
7	56.01	56.65	57.30	57.94	58.58	59.22	59.86	60.33
8	60.73	61.13	61.53	61.93	62.34	62.74	63.14	63.54
9	63.94	64.34	64.74	65.14	65.55	65.95	66.35	66.75
10	67.15	67.55	67.95	68.35	68.76	69.16	69.56	69.96
11	70.36	70.76	71.16	71.56	71.97	72.37	72.77	73.17
12	73.57	73.97	74.37	74.77	75.18	76.54	76.83	77.13
13	77.42	77.72	78.01	78.30	78.60	78.89	79.19	79.48
14	79.78	80.07	80.36	80.66	80.95	81.25	81.54	81.84
15	82.13	82.42	82.72	83.01	83.31	83.60	83.90	84.19
16	84.48	84.78	85.07	85.37	85.66	85.96	86.25	86.54
17	86.84	87.13	87.43	87.72	88.02	88.31	88.60	88.90
18	89.19	89.49	89.78	90.07	90.37	90.66	90.96	91.25
19	91.55	91.84	92.13	92.43	92.72	93.02	93.31	93.61
20	93.90	94.19	94.49	94.78	95.08	95.37	95.67	95.96
21	96.25	96.55	96.84	97.14	97.43	97.73	98.02	98.31
22	98.61	98.90	99.20	99.49	99.79	100.08	100.37	100.67
23	100.96	101.26	101.55	101.84	102.14	102.43	102.73	103.02
24	103.32	103.61	103.90	104.20	104.49	104.79	105.08	105.38
25	105.67	109.10	109.40	109.69	109.99	110.28	110.58	110.87
26	111.16	111.46	111.75	112.05	112.34	112.64	112.93	113.22
27	113.52	113.81	114.11	114.40	114.70	114.99	115.28	115.58
28	115.87	116.17	116.46	116.75	117.05	117.34	117.64	117.93
29	118.23	118.52	118.81	119.11	119.40	119.70	119.99	120.29
30	120.58	120.87	121.17	121.46	121.76	122.05	122.35	122.64
31	122.93	123.23	123.52	123.82	124.11	124.41	124.70	124.99
32	125.29	125.58	125.88	126.17	126.47	126.76	127.05	127.35
33	127.64	127.94	128.23	128.52	128.82	129.11	129.41	129.70
34	130.00	130.29	130.58	130.88	131.17	131.47	131.76	132.06
35	132.35	132.64	132.94	133.23	133.53	133.82	134.12	134.41
36	134.70	135.00	135.29	135.59	135.88	136.18	136.47	136.76
37	137.06	137.35	137.65	137.94	138.24	138.53	138.82	139.12
38	139.41	139.71	140.00	140.29	140.59	140.88	141.18	141.47
39	141.77	142.06	142.35	142.65	142.94	143.24	143.53	143.83
40	144.12	144.41	144.71	145.00	145.30	145.59	145.89	146.18
41	146.47	146.77	147.06	147.36	147.65	147.95	148.24	148.53
42	148.83	149.12	149.42	149.71	150.01	150.30	150.59	150.89
43	151.18	151.48	151.77	152.06	152.36	152.65	152.95	153.24
44	153.54	153.83	154.12	154.42	154.71	155.01	155.30	155.60
45	155.89	156.18	156.48	156.77	157.07	157.36	157.66	157.95
46	158.24	158.54	158.83	159.13	159.42	159.72	160.01	160.30
47	160.60	160.89	161.19	161.48	161.78	162.07	162.36	162.66
48	162.95	163.25	163.54	163.83	164.13	164.42	164.72	165.01
49	165.31	165.60	165.89	166.19	166.48	166.78	167.07	167.37
50	167.66	167.95	168.25	168.54	168.84	169.13	169.43	169.72

without an odd lot fee. This amounts to a percentage commission of 1.37 percent. If 500 shares were purchased, the cost would be approximately $422. The percentage charge would be 1.125 percent. Thus you should buy in round lots and large dollar values to keep brokerage costs to a minimum.

In the past few years many large discount brokerage firms have grown up. These firms charge a lower commission than large, well-known firms charge. They also provide less service in the way of financial advice and investment counseling. Most of these firms provide only one service—they execute your orders when you call them. If you feel that you do not need the advisory services of a larger firm, you may want to consider using a discount broker.

Giving orders to a broker

You must learn how to communicate with your broker. Many orders can be given, but the most direct, and simplest order is the *market order*. It simply tells your broker to buy or sell a certain number of shares at the existing market price. The broker is required to sell at the highest price or buy at the lowest price available in the market when the order is given. Therefore, you are protected to a certain extent by the rules and regulations of the brokerage industry. Sometimes a broker is given an order to buy or sell at a set price. It is difficult to execute such an order with precision. That is why a market order is the easiest to follow; it assures either a purchase or a sale.

Sometimes you might use a *limit order* to your advantage. This kind of order specifies the price at which a stock is to be bought or sold, for example, an order to buy General Motors (GM) at 42 when the current price is 47. If and when the price of GM declines to 42, the limit order goes into effect. If the price does not decline to 42, the order is not exercised. Even if the market declines to 42, the order might not be filled if stock is not available.

A *stop order* might be a way to insure that you will be able to buy the stock. If the price drops to 42, the order becomes a market order. In that way the order is executed. Of course, the stock might never drop to 42, and then you might not buy the stock. That is why if you think a stock is fairly priced, you should insure a purchase by giving a market order.

Summary

Common and preferred stock represent an ownership share in a company. Preferred stock pays a fixed dividend that can be attractively high. In addition, some preferred stocks can be converted into common shares that might improve their profitability. The typical preferred stock is cummulative as to dividend and nonconvertible.

The common stock of a company offers the prospects of higher return and risk. Common stocks are one of few ownership securities that offer you the possibility of earning a return greater than the rate of inflation. You can choose either income or growth stocks. Price quotes for common stocks are found daily in *The Wall Street Journal* or any good newspaper.

Careful analysis must be made to determine the growth of earnings. Future earnings determine a stock's future price. It is also helpful to find the Standard & Poor's rating on a stock in order to determine the risk involved in making a purchase. You must also estimate the future yield.

You should select a broker who is efficient, honest, and able to provide you with information at a reasonable price. You need a broker who will understand your goals and be willing to work with and for you. You must learn to communicate with the broker. The simplest and least confusing kind of order is a market order. At least, it insures that you will be buying or selling the stock somewhere close to the quoted price.

To analyze investment opportunities you must use the following procedure:

1. Form an overall view of the national economy.
2. Select those industries that are strong.
3. Select good companies for investment that are:
   a. Competitive.
   b. Profitable.
   c. Financially strong.
   d. Possess a strong balance sheet.
   e. Have good management.
   f. And whose shares sell at a reasonable price based on future dividends and earnings.

In short, you need to buy common stock when the return that is expected is equal to or greater than the risk assumed.

14

Portfolio management and the use of mutual funds

- Goals and objectives of portfolio management
- Establishing your income portfolio
- The growth stock investment portfolio
- The use of mutual funds in portfolio management
- Summary

Once you have a sufficient sum of money to invest, you should choose securities that meet your objectives. We assume that you know your objectives or what you want from an investment. We further assume that you are sufficiently informed about the expected return and risk of various securities. You can thus combine them in such a way to provide you with a return and risk that will meet your established objectives. The process of selection and continuous management of many securities to meet your needs as an investor is referred to as *portfolio management.* As Table 14–1 suggests, no recipe can be used by all investors.

What you are doing is matching the reward and risk characteristics of yourself as an investor with the reward and risk characteristics of securities. Securities put together to meet your objectives and goals are referred to as a *portfolio of securities.* A portfolio is simply a collection of securities owned by an investor. Records are kept so that from time to time you can appraise the situation to see if your objectives are being met. From time to time securities in any portfolio should be reviewed as a part of the portfolio management process. Portfolio management really includes several activities. The first and perhaps most important is constructing a plan to meet your objectives. Second comes the selec-

Table 14–1
Investment recipes for different investors

Income investor	Growth and income investor	Growth investor	Risky-growth investor	Tax-exempt investor
4 parts: Income common stocks with some growth	4 parts: Growth stocks		4 parts: Risky-growth stocks	2 parts: Growth stocks
5 parts: Bonds with short to medium maturities	2 parts: Income stocks	8 parts: Growth stock	5 parts: Growth stocks	2 parts: long-term tax-exempt bonds
	2 parts: bonds			4 parts: Medium-term tax-exempt bonds
	2 parts: Cash*			
1 part: Cash*	2 parts: Cash*			1 part short-term tax-exempt bonds
		2 parts: Cash*	1 part: Cash*	1 part: Cash*

* Savings, money market funds, or short-term government securities.

tion process, which assumes that you have some criteria for choosing investment securities to meet your objectives. The final activity is supervision. Supervision is required to assure you that you are meeting your objectives and that your portfolio's stocks and securities are performing as expected. If not, you will need to change them. Supervision assumes that you will be making a constant appraisal to see whether the reward and risk characteristics of each security continue to meet your goals and objectives.

The art of investments, or the practice of investments, is simply carrying out the three most important phases of portfolio management: planning, selection, and supervision of securities in the portfolio.

Goals and objectives of portfolio management

Before discussing the planning, selection, and supervision of a securities portfolio, let's examine some or all the objectives you as an investor might have. If you have $10,000 or $100,000 to invest, what would you want from your investment? Your objectives will go a long way to determine the selection of securities. Later they will shape the planning and supervision of the securities.

Security of principal

One of the major objectives of investment is to maintain security of principal. This means that as an investor adverse to risk, you will wish to maintain the value of the securities in your portfolio. In fact, you will seek to increase their value over time in order to compensate for the decline in the real purchasing power of the dollar as a result of inflation. The maintenance of principal implies that the value of your portfolio should increase. As you already know, this is difficult at a time of rampant inflation. If you already have a large sum of money for investment purposes, you should take good care of it because it is difficult to accumulate such a sum from scratch. Once a sizeable investment has been achieved, you should protect it.

As the size of your investment fund grows, you will discover that your attitude toward risk also will change. For example, an investor some time ago began a retirement fund with a $2,000 annual investment. There was little fear of risk or loss when the amount was below $10,000. Then one day this investor totaled the share value of the fund and found it to be over $25,000. Shortly thereafter she sold all her common stocks and put the proceeds in a money market fund. The fear of loss had caught up with this investor; her sense of caution had overtaken her desire for a higher return.

Growth as a goal

Some investors emphasize not only protection of their investments but also their growth. They seem to prefer growth of principal over growth of income. What they desire is a substantial growth of capital in the future, which can then be converted into either a larger income or the use of capital for other activities. Such investors are in a high tax bracket and have enough income to meet all their current needs. If you are in this situation, you will want to emphasize capital growth through capital gains. At the same time you will require a substantially different type of security than an income investment portfolio. In fact, you will need to concentrate on the growth of the value of your principal. Perhaps you will want to take advantage of short-term moves in stock prices. The focus on capital growth requires a philosophy of buying low and selling high. It also suggests that you will benefit from paying lower capital gain taxes on growth stocks rather than higher taxes on current income of high-dividend stocks. Therefore, as an investor in growth shares, you will be substantially interested in a high total return of both dividend income and capital gains. Your main emphasis will be on capital gains. Over time you hope to increase your asset values, and in a sense you will ignore current income.

Income as an objective

Some investors are primarily concerned with stability of income. In fact, most investors like the idea of receiving some income from their investments, even though it might be only a small amount. Most investors hope that the principal amount of their investment will be stable and actually grow over time. And that is why, if your main concern is income, you should purchase common stocks for income and growth. You know that over time many companies' dividends will increase. Thus you will share in an increased growth of income. Even some growth investors like the idea of current income to help defray their expenses and to provide them with a bird in the hand that will grow over time and enhance their growth portfolio. Dividends can be reinvested, and dividend reinvestment should not be ignored as an additional future value of your portfolio.

Many investors need current income to maintain their livelihood. If you are a retired person living on a modest pension plus Social Security, you would benefit from an investment portfolio providing a high current income. Therefore, your major goal would be to achieve the highest possible income for each dollar invested. This requires securities that pay a higher current dividend rate in comparison to that of growth stocks. In addition, you may set great value on stability of income and growth of income. Therefore, in meeting your income needs, you should diversify between fixed-income securities and common stocks paying a high dividend rate and having some potential to grow in the future.

Marketability of securities as a goal

Marketability is an objective that all investors should meet. Marketability is the ability to sell a security easily and quickly. To achieve this, you might be wise to confine your purchases to better-known stocks with a large number of shares outstanding. There have been cases where investors have attempted unsuccessfully to sell stocks of small companies in a declining market. That is because the shares did not possess marketability.

The liquidity goal: Selling securities without loss

Liquidity is a stronger form of marketability and should be an important investment objective. If the securities in your portfolio possess liquidity, you can convert them into cash with little or no loss of value. The best example of liquid securities is short-term Treasury bills. Certificates of deposit have liquidity. Unless they are negotiable, however, you might be at a disadvantage in converting them into cash because of a penalty clause. Often such a penalty clause stipulates that the rate of return will be lower if you cash the certificates before they reach maturity. Savings accounts have liquidity, but you may not always be able to convert them into cash at an instant's notice. In some cases you might have to wait as much as three or four or more days to convert a large savings account into cash. A demand deposit with a commercial bank is completely liquid, but it is unprofitable. Even your checking account may require three days to clear. This might not seem to be an important point, but if you are involved in a commercial transaction you will need to have the money available to meet your requirements.

Probably most investors are guilty of being illiquid. This is because most of us do not wish to keep money in demand deposits that pay no interest (except perhaps for NOW accounts). As an investor, you should place a certain portion of your funds in such short-term liquid investments as short-term government securities, certificates of deposit (CDs), or money market funds.

Favorable tax treatment: an important goal

As an investor you should seek investments that minimize your tax burden. This is simply in accord with the principle that investors should try to obtain the highest aftertax return from an investment, whether it is a growth or an income portfolio. You must be aware of the tax implications of all your investments. For some investors the purchase of tax-exempt securities might provide the highest aftertax income. In fact, tax-exempt securities might provide a higher aftertax yield than growth stocks. Keep in mind that tax-exempt income can be reinvested in other tax-exempt investments that may provide an excellent rate of return. The solution to your investment needs is a function of your marginal tax bracket. You can make one or all of the following decisions to reduce your tax burden:

Purchase tax exempt bonds;
Purchase bonds with a tax free covenant;

Purchase securities providing capital gains that will be taxed at a lower rate than your current income.

You might consider the possibility of swapping investments without paying any income taxes. This is possible when you trade one asset for another. Under certain cases some of your securities might be traded for other securities on a tax-free basis.

Another way of reducing taxes is to postpone income until after retirement when you will probably be in a lower tax bracket.

Taxes also may be minimized by making certain that capital gains are taxed at long-term rather than short-term rates. The tax rate on short-term gains is higher than that on long-term gains. Federal income taxes should be kept at a minimum along with state and local taxes.

You might examine the possibility of legal trusts where income to the trust is taxed at a lower rate than your other income. You should also consider taking advantage of tax-deductible annuities that reduce your taxable income.

Finally, you might seek tax shelters that reduce your current tax burden. All of these steps might be important ways of reducing your taxes and increasing your aftertax income.

The vital necessity of diversification for all investors

Another basic principle that you must follow in portfolio management is diversification. The *diversification principle* makes it certain that you will reduce your risk even though you might at the same time reduce your expected rate of return. In other words you should not put all your eggs in one basket.

Growth investment diversification

One way of discussing diversification is to examine it both from the viewpoint of yourself as a growth investor and an income investor. Let's begin by considering your problems as a growth investor. In this situation you are interested primarily in long-term capital gains. You are willing to consider short-term gains only insofar as they work well for you in the long term. You will wish to reduce your taxes to a minimum in the hope that you can realize some gains later on. As a growth investor you will not be particularly interested in current income because of the ordinary taxes that must be paid on it. Therefore, you will be interested in the three following types of diversification.

Security diversification

In order to reduce risk, you will include in your portfolio several common stocks designed to provide the highest return and the lowest risk. If you have only a small amount of investment money, you will find it difficult to diversify. For a small portfolio the number of common stocks included would be somewhere between 6 and 10. As your portfolio grows in size, the number of securities purchased could be increased.

Diversification based on the timing of your purchase and sale of securities

Since it is impossible to buy low and sell high consistently, you would be wise to purchase the same stock at more than one time over several months, or a year, to make certain that you are paying a fair price. You should attempt to time your purchases carefully. Even if you think a stock is underpriced, it still might be wise to buy it more than once since the market price does fluctuate because of unexpected events.

Diversification based on your defensive-aggressive position

Finally, there is a third kind of diversification—one based on your defensive-aggressive position. This type is related to timing. As a growth investor you will at times be defensive in the management of your portfolio. If you anticipate a market decline, you can sell some of your stocks and place the proceeds in a reserve of fixed-income short-term securities that will not decline even if the market is expected to do so. Defensive securities would include short-term government securities, money market funds, and certificates of deposit. If you think the market is too high, then the reserve position might be as high as 30, 40, or 50 percent of your portfolio. On the other hand, if you are optimistic about the stock market, then the amount that might be diversified into risk-free securities, as they are called, would be somewhat smaller.

The schedule in Table 14–2 provides an example of defensive-aggressive investment for you as a growth investor with different amounts of money.

Table 14–2
Defensive-aggressive portfolios

	$20,000 Fund		$100,000 Fund	
	Aggressive	Defensive	Aggressive	Defensive
Short-term debt	$ 2,000	$10,000	$10,000	$50,000
Equity securities	18,000	10,000	90,000	50,000
Number of securities	6–10	5	6–15	6–10

Income investment and diversification

On the other hand, if you are an income investor, you are faced with a different kind of problem. Ordinarily if you have a sum of money to invest for income, you might put all of it to work at one time. This creates a problem of management. What should you do if you want to maximize current income and minimize risk?

If you invest in short-term securities, the yield normally is not very high, although yields have been high in 1980 and 1981. If you put all your investment in long-term fixed-income securities, you might earn a higher yield. However, if interest rates go higher in the future, the value of your investment will decrease, and you will suffer a capital loss.

If you buy income stocks paying a high dividend, you are confronted by the same basic problem because common stocks do fluctuate in value. With common stocks at least you have the possibility of dividend growth, which cannot be achieved with fixed-income long-term investments. In these circumstances you should diversify your income investments in stocks that promise dividend growth over a period of time. You should buy income stocks offering a high current dividend yield. At the same time you should have a portion of your portfolio in fixed-income securities providing stability.

If there is some uncertainty about the future, you might maintain a defensive position as well as a position favoring income growth. For example, if you have $100,000 to invest and interest rates are expected to rise, you should invest the fund in short-term fixed-income securities. When interest rates peak, you can buy long-term bonds or common stock. In this situation you buy when bonds and stocks are low. Of course, this is a difficult timing task to accomplish. Recognizing the difficulty of timing, you might want to stagger your investment in both fixed-income securities and in common stocks.

The following example explains the situation more fully. Let's assume that you are interested in income growth and have $100,000 to invest. You think that interest rates may rise but are not positive on this score. Your portfolio could be divided between fixed-income securities and common stocks (50 percent in each). If common stocks are somewhat over-priced at present, you might establish a reserve for the purchase of common stock over the next few months, or perhaps even over the next year or two. (You need to maintain a long-term attitude in considering how to put your money to work.) In this way you will dollar average your purchase of shares. Later on you can buy income stocks that are expected to go up in terms of dividend income. As far as the fixed-income securities are concerned, the half you invested in fixed income securities could be diversified one fifth in short-term securities maturing within one year, one fifth in securities maturing from two to three years, one fifth in securities maturing from three to four years, one fifth in securities maturing in four to six years, and one fifth in securities maturing in six to 10 years. You can then reinvest the proceeds as the money becomes available on the basis of the outlook for interest rates at the time that reinvestment takes place. Although you might ignore the problem of diversification if a lump sum of money is available for investment, the problem is there, and must be solved. Table 14–3 reflects this diversification.

Diversification is a problem for the income investor as well as the growth investor. If you are an income investor, you must diversify just as a growth investor would to protect your principal. Assured of a steady

Table 14–3
Diversification for an income investor

Fixed-income securities:	
1 year	10%
2–3 years	10%
3–4 years	10%
4–6 years	10%
6–10 years	10%
Common stocks	
Income and growth	50%
Total.....................	100%

income, you need not worry about anticipating the long-term and short-term interest rate market.

In summary, diversification is designed to reduce risk and maintain return for both income investors and growth investors. Without diversification you are accepting too many risks. Ordinarily small investors tend to underdiversify and maintain too high a degree of selectivity. If you are wrong, your losses can be substantial. On the other hand, institutional investors, pension funds, commercial bank trust departments, and mutual funds tend to overdiversify. They have so many securities in their portfolios that they find it extremely difficult to research and follow all those securities. Smaller portfolios tend to have fewer stocks. Timing diversification is also important. But it is important, very important, for you to practice all forms of diversification. This is the way for you to weather the storms of stock market price fluctuation.

The need to supervise your investments

Supervision is an extremely important part of portfolio management. It can be assumed that as an investor you will make decisions rationally and without undue emotional pressure from the stockmarket or your broker. You should aim to acquire a conservative attitude that takes into account timing and diversification. Once your portfolio has been set up, you must constantly monitor, reassess, and reevaluate it to make certain that your securities are doing what they are supposed to do. Also, it is important to realize that prices of securities do change. You should take advantage of price changes if your portfolio in the long run is to outperform the stock market. This applies whether you are an income investor or a growth investor.

A case in point is appropriate to illustrate this concept of supervision. Let's assume that you are a large investor with a number of shares of General Motors common stock in your portfolio. The price reached $85 per share just before the oil embargo. GM is considered to be an income stock with growth possibilities. If you purchased GM stock, you would not expect it to grow substantially in price over time, but at least you would benefit from a growing dividend income. In the past GM's dividends have grown, and many investors have benefited from the growth of the dividend. At $85, however, the stock was overpriced. If you had GM in your portfolio as an income stock, when it reached $85 you should have seriously considered selling it. You might have put the money into a different income security, or you might have put it into short-term Treasury bills to await a time when the price of GM stock would come down. Later on, in fact, the price of General Motors dropped to between 45 and 55. At this level GM would be considered an excellent value for an income investor. But now let's assume that later on GM's stock for some unknown reason increases from 55 to 75. What should you do as an income investor? At this point it might be wise to sell GM, take the profits, and invest them in short-term securities. Another possibility would be to put the money in savings accounts until the price of the stock declines. In this way you would realize some gains on this cyclical, income stock. At the same time you would continue to have income from your temporary investments. Of course, you can't expect to be right on all these trades. But supervision means that you will try to trade shares judiciously over time to improve your profitability.

Supervision certainly doesn't mean that you have to trade shares every week. It means, however, that you must monitor your portfolio on a monthly basis, keeping particular watch of price changes of individual shares and maintaining an awareness, based on all your information about the shares. In this way you will know when the market is underpriced, overpriced, or fairly priced, and you can act accordingly. Obviously decisions of this type will not be perfect, but you must try to make them.

Let's take another example of supervision to demonstrate the need to manage your portfolio carefully. Some years ago a large institutional investor in Washington, D.C., had an investment in First Pennsylvania Corporation, a large bank-holding company in Philadelphia. The company's earnings declined because of bad results from real estate loans. There was some concern among investors about whether the company would recover. A careful examination and forecast of the earnings, however, indicated that the company's earnings would increase in the future despite management problems that might give concern to an investor. The investing institution owned other bank stocks, including Bank of America, Chase Manhattan, and Citicorp. A careful analysis suggested that the risks in First Pennsylvania Corporation were somewhat high, and that its earnings were vunerable. First Pennsylvania might be considered a growth stock or an income stock, depending on how you viewed it. At one time it had been a growth stock. But more recently it looked more like an income stock, paying out a somewhat larger dividend than many growth stocks. After further analysis the risks seemed to be too large. As a result, a decision was taken to sell the stock at 16 because the institutional investor did not want to accept these risks. Subsequently the price of the stock declined to 13. Now this was only $3 a share decline, and you might say that this wasn't very much. But $3 as a percent of a $16 stock is almost 20 percent. Therefore the decision to sell at the correct time prevented a 20 percent loss in the stock price. Of course, this does not take into account the cost of trading. Nonetheless, you have to undergo costs of this type in order to manage your portfolio well. (When last checked, that particular stock was listed at 8.)

In addition, you must appraise companies to determine the risks and rewards of their common stock, and thus estimate whether they are overpriced, underpriced, or fairly priced. As indicated above, this is a continuing process. If a stock for some reason moves up in price beyond its proper level, you should sell it and reinvest the proceeds in other securities. An excellent example of this situation is the market in the late 1970s when many companies became takeover candidates of larger companies. Exxon, for example, announced its intention to take over Reliance Electric. It wished to develop a new electric motor that would vary the amount of electricity going into the motor rather than the amount coming out. There were substantial savings of efficiency in this concept. Since Exxon had the concept and Reliance had the capacity to produce the product, it seemed a logical merger. Prior to the announcement, the price of Reliance Electric was $35 a share, and the company's stock was considered a growth stock.

Upon the bona fide announcement that Reliance was to be acquired by Exxon, the price of Reliance's stock moved up substantially to $65 a share. If you made a careful analysis of the situation at that time, you would have realized that this price was much too high. Since the stock was selling at that price, a wise decision was to sell it and take a profit. As an investor you had no way to know if the company would actually be acquired by Exxon. There was a chance that the deal might fall through, causing the price of Reliance's stock to decline. If Reliance was actually acquired by Exxon, Reliance would then become Exxon's subsidiary. You would no longer own Reliance Electric because your Reliance shares would be traded for Exxon shares. At this point you ought to raise the following question. Do you really want to own more shares in Exxon, a major oil producer? The decision to sell, whatever might happen to the price of the stock, seemed correct. This is the type of decision that you as an investor are called on to make.

Let's now consider another decision that confronts all investors. What should you do about a sharp rise in a stock's price for no apparently good reason? Assume that the price of one of your stocks suddenly increases so that you have a 40 percent capital gain. A gain of this magnitude is what you might have expected over the next three years. Just on the very merits of this fact alone, you might be wise to sell the stock and take a profit. People sometimes hesitate to do this in their portfolio management, but it does make sense. You can always reinvest proceeds from the sale of a stock, even though it means putting your money temporarily into savings or investing it in short-term defensive securities. Thus it is critical for you as an investor to understand the principle of supervision. If you act accordingly, you can take advantage of market opportunities.

Performance and portfolio management

In carrying out portfolio supervision, you should measure the actual performance of your portfolio. It is extremely important to appraise it on a quarterly basis. Price the stocks from price quotations in *The Wall Street Journal,* total their value, and then find out the percentage gain or loss in your portfolio for the quarter. Take the list of stocks you own, price them, multiply the price times the number of shares held, add them together, and then find the total value of the portfolio at the end of the three-month period. It is unnecessary to do it any more frequently than that, although mutual funds value their investments on a daily basis. For most investors quarter-to-quarter yields are adequate as long as supervision moves along on a month-to-month basis.

Once you determine the value of your fund and have calculated its return, compare the present figure to the value at the end of the previous quarter. Let's assume that your fund is now worth $10,500, and that at the beginning of the quarter it was worth $10,000. The portfolio has increased $500 over the quarter. If you divide $500 by $10,000, you come up with a 5 percent rate of return for the quarter. This is a return for the year of approximately 20 percent. Obviously the gain in your portfolio is going to include some dividend income. Certainly you want to include this income in the yield. However, if you have made investment contributions to the fund during the period, you should subtract them so that you can be sure that you are actually measuring the performance of the money invested and not the total, overall growth of your portfolio.

How well have you done? Two criteria can be used to determine this. The first is to decide how well you have done on the basis of your own objectives. Did you expect to earn a 5 percent gain during that quarter? If the answer is no, then you did better than expected. If the answer is yes, then you have achieved your objective. If you earned less, then you ought to take another careful examination of the portfolio to make certain that it is invested in the right securities.

The second criterion is how well you have done relative to the market. That is, how well have you done in comparison with Standard & Poor's 500 Index? You can find this out by determining the price of the S & P 500 Index at the end of the previous quarter, comparing it to the price at the end of the most recent quarter, calculating the percentage gain or loss, adding in the dividends, and then calculating the percentage gain or loss of the market. You should then compare your percentage gain or loss with the performance of Standard & Poor's 500. Over time you will not only have an adequate measure of the performance of the fund but you will also be able to keep track of your money and learn what is going on in the marketplace. You will have a good measure of how well your portfolio has performed. This will give you a good excuse to reexamine each security in your portfolio to make sure that it is doing a satisfactory job in relation to the risk of holding it.

Establishing your income portfolio

You can carry out the selection of stocks for your income or growth portfolio through information available in *The Wall Street Journal.* In addition, you need to do a little thinking and analyzing with the help of Standard & Poor's *Industry Survey.*

Setting up a conservative income portfolio

You might establish a very conservative income portfolio if you are seeking highest-quality securities with diversification. At the same time you could still earn a yield that will provide a substantial amount of income, provided you do not encounter any special problems or have to pay high income taxes.

As a first example, let's begin by setting up an income portfolio with government securities. Such securities do not provide a hedge against inflation because the interest income on them does not grow. On the other hand, if the income is substantially above trend, as was the case in June 1979, you could obtain, even without much expertise, an income of almost $8,500 a year on a $100,000 investment. To do this, you would need to maintain liquidity and diversification and at the same time keep the number of securities in your portfolio at a minimum.

Let's see how this works. With $100,000 to invest, you might diversify your investments according to maturity. First, you could put $20,000 into short-term securities ($20,000 worth of Treasury bills). On June 25, 1979 Treasury bills provided a return of 8.903 percent for 26 weeks. You would need to turn these securities over at the end of 26 weeks and reinvest them. When the Treasury bills mature, you might decide to move out longer in the maturity spectrum or remain in Treasury bills. You could purchase such bills directly, through a broker or a commercial bank. In order to get slightly higher yields, you would have to go out a little bit further in the June 1979 market. Therefore, it would have been a good idea to go to two-year maturities to pick up extra yield. In June 1979 two-year Treasury obligations yielded 8.93 percent. This was not much different from the yield of six-month Treasury bills. But the obligation paid slightly higher interest rates and was fixed for that time. Therefore, you could have put $20,000 or 20 percent of your fund into these obligations. This issue matured in June 1981 and yielded 8.93 percent.

Carrying out a system of diversification, you would then put 20 percent into issues maturing after 1981. For example, the issue maturing in June 1983 provides a yield of 8.70. The issue maturing in August 1985 provides a yield of 8.71, and obligations maturing in May 1988 provide an 8.76 yield. You have not gone out more than eight years. Yet you have maintained your liquidity and are still receiving a nice income from your portfolio.

Now let's compare this portfolio with other investment possibilities. If you keep your money in a savings passbook, you would earn 5.50 percent. In 1979 you would not earn much more than 8.0 to 8.5 percent on investments in a savings and loan association, without as much liquidity as your Treasury portfolio. Thus you have improved your yield at little or no risk. In fact, should the interest rates change, you can reinvest your money, as it becomes available, in other government securities at even higher rates. For example, in January 1980 when Treasury bills came due, they provided income for the investor at the end of six months of $445. This $20,000 could then be reinvested in longer-term securities or invested in short or intermediate securities, depending on the outlook for interest rates.

So as your securities mature, you can reinvest the proceeds and maintain your income from the portfolio. Any change in interest rates would be automatically adjusted into the investment mix. There is liquidity in your portfolio if money is needed. Yet the money isn't so far from the maturity date that you are going to lose a substantial amount through price fluctuations. Therefore you have a very high-quality bond income investment portfolio offering an excellent return with little or no risk. The yield is approximately 8.80 percent, ignoring any commission cost on the purchase of the bonds. This is summarized in Table 14–4. Ordinarily your cost in buying the bonds would be relatively small.

Table 14–4
Conservative government securities
Income portfolio 6/25/79

Maturity	Amount	Percent
1979 180-day Treasury bills	$ 20,000	8.90
1981 2-year Treasury security	$ 20,000	8.93
1983 4-year Treasury security	$ 20,000	8.70
1985 6-year Treasury security	$ 20,000	8.71
1987 8-year Treasury security	$ 20,000	8.76
Total	$100,000	
Average yield		8.80

Setting up a more aggressive income portfolio

You can obtain a higher yield at a slightly higher risk by investing not just in government securities but also in a number of high-quality private corporate securities. Periodically *The Wall Street Journal* publishes a list of recent prices of new bond issues issued by various corporations.

Table 14–5
Fixed-income diversification guide

		A	AA	AAA
Short-term (91 day) government	10%			
1-year (government)	30%			
2- to 5-year	30%	=10%	10%	10%
5- to 10-year	30%	=10%	10%	10%
	100%			

Corporate bonds may be added to your portfolio to increase yield. You should diversify these securities from AAA to A, and vary them in maturity length from short term to intermediate term. Adding these corporate bonds will allow you to increase your yield without adding undue risk to your portfolio. Long maturities should be avoided.

Even though you are willing to accept an additional risk, you should diversify on the basis of maturity and type of security. Table 14–5 reflects the basic diversification pattern for a conservative fixed-income investment stategy.

The portfolio in Table 14–6 was set up to meet the diversification needs of an investor who needs maximum current income from a portfolio. Note that the portfolio has been invested 20 percent in 12.57 Treasury bills with a maturity of 91 days. This provides some protection so that you could take advantage of interest rate changes if they continue to rise. Another $20,000 is invested in one–year Treasury bills that offer a high yield and liquidity. The balance of the portfolio has been divided among AAA, AA, and A rated securities that offer different maturities to obtain a higher long-term yield. In addition, a portion of intermediate term securities was used to eliminate the hazard of changing yields that might result in a decline in price. An increase in price might develop if interest rates fall at a later date.

Long-term bonds with extended maturities have been used in part.

Table 14–6
Conservative high-quality income
portfolio 1/21/1980

90-day Treasury bills	$ 20,000	12.57%
One-year Treasury bills	20,000	12.05
Private corporate bonds:		
AAA (varying maturities)	20,000*	11.10
AA (varying maturities)	20,000*	11.50
A (varying maturities)	20,000*	11.69
Total	$100,000	11.78%

* Based on an average of varying yields found in *The Outlook* published by Standard & Poor's Corporation, January 28, 1980, p. 963.

Although there is a risk that these securities might decline in price because of a trend toward higher yields, the assumption is that a 11.10 to 11.69 percent average yield fairly compensates for the long-term business and inflation risks that the portfolio faces. Overall 40 percent of the portfolio is invested in two different Treasury securities covering essentially two different time periods. The remainder is invested in six different securities. This portfolio thus provides time diversification, credit diversification, and industry diversification.

Overall you can expect to receive a yield of 11.78 percent on $100,000 invested in these securities, thus yielding a return of $11,780 per year. Your portfolio provides a higher return than long-term government securities. The only real risk is that you have not hedged against inflation. But with little or no effort, just by examining *The Wall Street Journal*, you can select a portfolio that will provide adequate diversification and a good yield without a great deal of risk. You should think about this process and apply it to your own income needs.

Since this portfolio of fixed-income securities does not provide a substantial hedge against inflation, even though it provides maximum current income, you might want to diversify into common stocks. The common stock return might be a bit lower as a percent of investment, but over a long term common stock dividends will grow to provide a higher rate of return than fixed-income securities. The rate of return might even be higher than that of the bond portfolio discussed above. Therefore, it might be well for you to examine high-yielding common stocks that could be added to your investment portfolio. Such common stocks might offer assurance that the dividends would grow over time and compensate you for inflation. Some people might say that this means compromising current income for future income, which is true. The one major disadvantage of a fixed-income portfolio is that over the last two decades interest rates have fallen and risen, but the general trend has been up because inflation has been higher. In examining income portfolios of the past, you will find that the fixed-income portion is selling at a substantial discount over current price.

Selecting an income portfolio with growth potential

The task of selecting an income portfolio that is likely to grow is difficult. The best position you should take is to buy quality investment securities with a high current yield and growth potential. This means buying good industrial, public utility, and transportation company securities that have a high current payout but will also continue to grow. At present, American Telephone and Telegraph Corporation (AT&T) is a good example of a dividend-paying stock that has increased in value over time and pays a fairly stable and high yield. The process of selecting the income stock is a little bit more complex than selecting bonds because you have a broader range of securities from which to choose. Nonetheless, as you take up *The Wall Street Journal,* you can go over the stocks traded on the New York Stock Exchange and find some that are paying a rather good dividend in growing industries. However, you must carefully examine the current income that can be generated from these stocks, although all the percentages are given in the newspaper. The only thing that you need do is to verify that the dividend has grown over time, and that it can be expected to continue growing in the future.

In addition, you might want to consider the addition of preferred stock in an equity portfolio. As you go down the stock listings in *The Wall Street Journal* of June 29, 1979, you suddenly realize that it is difficult to find stocks offering high income as well as growth potential. You will also note that preferred stocks seem to offer the highest current income. For example, the Alabama Power preferred would provide you with a yield of 11 percent. Certainly you might wish to consider this offering. Allegheny Ludlum Steel has a $3 preferred stock that pays approximately 9 percent while a $2.19 preferred stock pays 10 percent. But these are more in the nature of fixed-income securities without offering the security of principal characteristic of fixed-income securities.

American Telephone and Telegraph Corporation offers a common stock that fits the bill. This common stock pays a $5 dividend for a yield of 8.6 percent. AT&T dividends have grown over the past 10 years at the rate of 7 percent each year. This 7 percent growth rate has gone a long way to compensate for inflation. Proceeding down the list, you will discover that Arizona Public Service pays a 9.6 percent dividend. The dividend growth of this company also has been fairly good over the last few years. Since the southwestern part of the United States is expanding all the time, you can anticipate that this stock will have an increase in dividends over the years. Thus it would be an excellent stock to include in an income portfolio. Atlantic City Electric, although not the most dynamic growth area, might benefit from the anticipated increase in gambling on the East Coast. Its common stock pays a dividend of $1.74 a share to yield 9.2 percent. In checking Baltimore Gas and Electric, you will find that stock yields 9.9 percent. However, over the long range the growth of that company will probably be limited. As you can begin to see, many income stocks are in public utilities that pay a high dividend but do not show a substantial growth of earnings.

The Boston Edison Company cannot be ignored for its substantial dividend. Its stock pays $2.44 in dividends. On a price of 22½, this offers a yield of 11 percent, which is not bad for a stable utility stock. However, you cannot expect substantial growth from this particular company. Generally speaking, you would be prudent not to invest your entire portfolio in public utilities. Many of them, particularly electric utilities, have a high yield, but there isn't a substantial amount of growth. Therefore you should compromise and find issues like AT&T that have a fairly good current dividend as well as some growth potential. Esmark, a food company, seems to fit the bill for an income portfolio offering a dividend yield of 6.8 percent, with a dividend of $1.84. Esmark has experienced a growth of dividends over time, and should be a good holding if you are interested in income and some growth.

You might go through the entire list of securities on the New York Stock Exchange with the idea of selecting income stocks that offer a high current income and some growth potential. Just by going through the first part of the New York Stock Exchange Composite Transactions, you can come up with a group of stocks offering on the average approximately a return of 8.6 percent with the possibility of a substantial future. You should, however, avoid public utilities that have not shown substantial past growth. It has been difficult for many utilities to increase their earnings, cover their interest charges, and increase their rates.

If you are interested in income, the common stock portfolio, which offers a lower return, might be combined with the long- and intermediate-term bond portfolio. On the average you would earn a good yield, and you would have some possibility for growth and a hedge against inflation. A guide to this diversification is found in Table 14–7. The weakest part of this portfolio would be the money rate risk. This could be solved partially by keeping a 20 percent reserve in short-term investment securities.

Table 14–7
Income portfolio with fixed-income securities and common stock

Short-term securities	20%
Fixed-income securities: 　20% short-term, 　20% intermediate-term, 　divided equally between AAA, AA, 　　and A securities	40%
Common stocks: 　Divided among income 　　growth stocks	40% 100%

These portfolio solutions to the varying income needs of investors are illustrative only. They were selected from a list of securities that did not reflect every security available for income. When you wish to establish an income portfolio, you should look at a broader list of securities suggested by Standard & Poor's Corporation and Value Line Investor Services. You should also consult with a broker who has good research capabilities.

Income portfolios for high-income investors　　Often you can find attractive income securities from municipal bonds on which it is unnecessary to pay federal income taxes. If the bonds are issued in the state where you reside, then your income will be exempt from state income taxes as well as from federal income taxes. As a matter of principle, it is wise for you to invest in tax-exempt securities issued in your own state, provided these securities enjoy a rating of A or better.

The Wall Street Journal provides you with a list of tax-exempt bonds that are actively traded. However, many bonds are not even listed, and are sold through brokers who have information about current prices and yield not found in *The Wall Street Journal* or a local newspaper. In order to find the price of such a bond, you must consult a broker familiar with and knowledgeable about tax-exempt bonds.

Most large brokerage firms in the country have special municipal departments that are happy to provide investors with some idea of the direction of yields on a municipal bond portfolio. The trend in municipal bond yields for the years 1976 through 1980 has been up. It reached a new high in 1981, as inflation rose. In mid-1979 long-term tax exempt bonds yielded close to 6.7 percent free of taxes. This means that a person in the 50 percent tax bracket would have to earn a fully taxable yield of 13.4 percent to equal the yield on municipal bonds.

A list of state obligation bonds in Table 12–6 in Chapter 12 ranks the states from highest to lowest. The base Group 5 provides a yield to maturity for various years to maturity and various ratings. The 10-year AAA bonds rated by Standard & Poor's would provide you with a yield of 6.10 plus 0.05 percent, or 6.15 percent. Certainly you could find enough bonds on this list to set up your portfolio.

In doing so, you should follow the principle of diversification. Diversify rating and maturity, and be sure not to extend beyond the 10-year maturities. Make certain that you keep a 10 percent reserve.

Diversification by maturity and investment quality is important in minimizing risk and maximizing yield. A tax-exempt portfolio should be considered much like the corporate bond portfolio with maturities staggered and ratings diversified. The only difficulty with tax-exempt bonds is finding high yields in shorter maturities. You must bear in mind that municipal bonds might not be available in the quantity and maturity you wish. Nonetheless, if you happen to be in a very high tax bracket and are in need of income, tax-exempt bonds would make an excellent solution to your income problems.

The growth stock investment portfolio

Often investors do not wish to attach maximum importance to current income. Because of high taxes, they may postpone the receipt of current income in order to build up a larger fund in the future. If you are interested primarily in growth, you might wish to examine a broad selection of growth stocks. Unfortunately you cannot easily find such a list in *The Wall Street*

Journal. Even if you select growth stocks on the basis of the usual criteria of earnings and dividend growth, some growth stocks just won't grow. In fact, over the past decade the so-called growth stocks have been among the worst performing stocks because people have become more interested in dividends. The principle of a "bird in the hand is worth more than two in the bush" is being applied. Stocks that pay a high dividend rate as well as offer some capital growth are favored. Let's examine what growth stocks are, and then find out how you can select them.

Concept of growth

In the simplest terms a growth stock is one whose earnings, dividends, and price have grown faster than the overall market. A growth stock generally pays out a lower current dividend than an income stock, but the total return (dividends plus capital gains) is usually higher. In selecting growth stocks, you should look for securities that have had a history of high growth in rates of earnings and dividends, and that provide a low but growing current yield. This combination helps insure gains in the future. At the same time it offers low current income so that you need not pay a great deal of taxes on your dividends. Most of your return from growth stocks will be in the form of capital gains. These gains will be taxed in the future at lower rates.

Security selection

Table 14–8 provides a list of stocks with the largest total market value, some of which have attributes associated with those of growth stocks. Of the companies on the list, IBM, Schlumberger, Ltd., Eastman Kodak, Procter & Gamble, Minnesota Mining and Manufacturing, Halliburton, Du Pont, Sears, Xerox, Merck, Caterpillar Tractor, Johnson & Johnson, and many of the oil companies are regarded as growth stocks. All of them have a low current dividend yield. Some of them would make ideal investments.

Growth stocks and diversification

In setting up a growth portfolio, it is not necessary for you to invest in all the companies on the list in Table 14–8. Nor should you confine your selection only to companies on the list. You would be wise to examine industries that appear to be growing, to select dominant firms in an industry, and to make certain that the growth of earnings and dividends is expected to be high in the future. Then you should buy a diversified list of such securities.

To obtain this information, you need to examine more than just price, earnings, and dividend information in *The Wall Street Journal.* You should also obtain some historical information about the earnings growth of these companies from Standard & Poor's manuals, from the Standard & Poor's

Stock Guide, and possibly from *Value Line.* This information will give you useful hints about securities that show a good rate of growth in earnings and dividends. In this way you would be following the principle of investing in dominant companies of dominant industries. You would be investing in quality stocks, and you would be diversifying your interests. Assuming that you have $100,000 to invest, you ought to limit your funds

Table 14–8
Advice on highest-value NYSE issues

Our latest recommendations on the most prominent of big-capitalization, widely-held stocks are presented for quick reference in the accompanying table of NYSE issues. They are ranked in order of market values (stock prices times shares outstanding), ranging upward from $4.6 billion.

The group of 32 makes up the top tier of the 256 companies identified by a recent S&P computer screening as having common-stock investment values of $1 billion or more.

In the nine months since we conducted a similar study, IBM and AT&T remain in first and second place, respectively, as the stocks with the greatest market values. Some notable changes among the leaders include the jump by STANDARD OIL (INDIANA) from 9th to 5th and the slides by GENERAL ELECTRIC to 9th place from 5th and KODAK to 18th from 7th.

Not surprisingly in view of the runup the oils have experienced over the past year, this group makes up more than half the list.

NYSE Stocks with Highest Total Market Values

Recent Market Value (Bil. $)	% of Shrs. Owned by Institutions	Earn. $ Per Share 1979	Earn. $ Per Share E1980	Current Price	†P/E Ratio	Yield %	Company	Recommendations
40.3	18	5.16	5.90	66	11.1	5.2	★Int'l Bus. Machines	Should remain the dominant factor in a market with superior growth potential. Shares are attractive for long-term total return.
35.2	15	8.04	8.30	51	6.1	9.8	★American Tel. & Tel.	Near four-year low, stock is a sound holding for income; price should strengthen after interest rates peak.
27.7	8	9.74	11.00	64	5.8	7.5	★Exxon Corp.	Stock does not fully reflect company's outstanding position in all major petroleum areas.
15.6	20	10.04	7.50	54	7.2	8.5	General Motors	See page 938.
14.1	29	10.23	11.25	104	9.2	3.5	★Standard Oil Indiana	Growing emphasis on oil-gas production augurs well for continuing good profit gains, and shares have long-term appeal notwithstanding a recent runup.
13.6	26	E5.00	6.25	112	17.9	1.0	★Schlumberger, Ltd.	Brisk demand for oil well drilling services should continue to buoy earnings; despite high P/E, stock has superior appreciation potential.
12.6	1	E10.00	8.00	36	4.5	2.8	British Petroleum	Possible lower inventory profits this year would be a dampener on earnings; shares could underperform other energy issues over short term.
12.5	27	9.48	10.50	63	6.0	4.8	★Mobil Corp.	See page 939.
12.4	33	6.20	6.50	55	8.5	5.1	General Electric	Shares of this largest electrical equipment producer may be held for long pull, but they lack near-term appeal.
11.9	3	E25.00	18.00	87	4.8	6.4	★Royal Dutch Petrol.	Sound commitment for income and capital gains, as company's fundamentals are good.
11.7	13	9.83	14.00	100	7.1	2.0	Standard Oil of Ohio	Principal producer of domestic crude should show strong earnings gain this year; shares are one of more attractive in energy group.
11.0	34	9.48	11.00	103	9.4	3.3	Atlantic Richfield	To be split 2-for-1, the stock is conservatively valued in relation to potential earnings from oil and other natural resources.
10.9	31	10.44	11.00	74	6.7	4.3	Standard Oil of Cal.	With its good position in both crude production and refining, the shares are a solid total-return investment.

Table 14–8 (continued)

Recent Market Value Bil. $	% of Shrs. Owned by Institutions	Earn. $ Per Share 1979	Earn. $ Per Share E1980	Current Price	†P/E Ratio	Yield %	Company	Recommendations
9.8	7	7.32	8.00	69	8.6	3.5	**Shell Oil**	The shares of this number two U.S. marketer of gasoline are well worth holding.
8.8	....	8.00	6.00	34	5.7	3.4	**Shell Transport/Trad.**	The inactively traded stock of the owner of 40% of Royal Dutch-Shell Group has less appeal than Royal Dutch Petroleum.
9.7	21	6.48	7.00	38	5.4	6.3	**Texaco Inc.**	Selling at an historically low P/E, the stock is a sound holding for rising dividends and long-term growth.
8.5	40	5.77	6.50	60	9.2	3.0	**Phillips Petroleum**	This integrated crude producer with an important stake in the North Sea is an attractive long-term investment.
7.8	31	E5.75	6.25	48	7.7	6.0	**★Eastman Kodak**	Likely to be a sluggish market performer near-term due to high price of silver; long-term prospects favorable, however.
7.6	24	6.78	7.25	44	6.1	5.1	**Gulf Oil**	Merits retention for rising income and long-term price appreciation potential.
7.5	32	7.34	8.25	95	11.5	1.7	**Getty Oil**	The shares offer sound value, despite recent strength.
6.2	29	4.33	3.65	34	9.3	4.7	**★Dow Chemical**	One of better-situated chemical companies; long-term prospects are favorable and stock is a sound holding.
5.9	28	56.99	57.60	70	9.2	4.9	**★Procter & Gamble**	At their lowest P/E of the past ten years, the shares offer good value and should work out well in the long run.
5.9	47	5.59	6.15	50	8.1	4.8	**Minn. Mining & Mfg.**	Stock is at historically low valuation; has long-term appeal for total return.
5.9	39	6.42	7.50	106	14.1	1.9	**Halliburton Co.**	Earnings are expected to pick up, after falling last year; we would hold the shares.
5.8	43	6.42	6.15	40	6.5	6.9	**Du Pont (E.I.)**	Profits are expected to drop slightly this year, so shares may underperform market; however, longer-pull prospects are favorable.
5.6	31	7.58	7.60	56	7.4	3.4	**Conoco Inc.**	Focusing on primary crude exploration in the U.S., North Sea and Canada, the company's outlook is bright; coal interests add to appeal.
5.4	17	E42.65	42.85	17	6.0	7.5	**Sears, Roebuck & Co.**	Stock at lowest level in more than a decade; near-term potential limited but good recovery is probable over next few years.
5.3	35	6.69	7.30	63	8.6	3.8	**Xerox Corp.**	New products introduced in 1979 should contribute to earnings progress; strong foreign business should limit vulnerability to any domestic softness. Long-term total-return investment.
5.1	40	5.06	5.65	67	11.9	3.4	**Merck & Co.**	Although stock is at a high P/E, strong R&D and good earnings visibility make it a worthwhile holding.
4.9	37	5.69	7.00	56	8.0	3.8	**Caterpillar Tractor**	Number one position in earthmoving machinery makes stock a hold for long-term growth.
4.7	41	111.15	111.25	86	7.6	3.5	**Sun Co. Inc.**	Broad domestic oil/gas exposure enhances appeal for growth over the long haul.
4.6	31	E5.85	6.65	75	11.3	2.7	**Johnson & Johnson**	Shares have long-term attraction based on company's widespread representation in growing health care field.

†Based on 1980 estimated earnings. ★Master List issues. E-Estimated. N.E.-No estimate. 1Fully diluted. 2Excluding non-recurring gains. 3Year ends October. 4Year ends January of following calendar year. 5Year ends June.

SOURCE Standard and Poor's *The Outlook*, February 11, 1980.

to approximately 10 companies. If you exceed this number, you will find that the principle of diversification works against you. This is because you would have to spend too much of your time analyzing, managing, and measuring the performances of too many investments.

Let's see how you might wish to diversify your investments among some of the securities listed in Table 14–8. You might consider the following companies: IBM, AT&T (more for income purposes than growth, even though AT&T is an excellent firm), Exxon, Schlumberger, Eastman Kodak, Procter & Gamble, Minnesota Mining and Manufacturing, Halliburton, Sears, Xerox, Caterpillar Tractor, and Johnson & Johnson. All these securities represent dominant firms in dominant industries; they are extremely well-managed companies; and they offer diversification.

Growth stocks and timing

To insure the proper timing of your purchases or sales of stocks, you should maintain some cash reserves. Do not commit all of your money at one time in the stock market. In setting up your investment portfolio from among the stocks mentioned earlier, you would be wise to analyze the current market and your own expectations about the future. You can then decide whether to maintain a defensive or an aggressive position. Let's assume that you were considering an investment policy as of February 1980. You would note that the market had risen but might decline. The United States was suffering from rampant inflation. Interest rates were high and expected to come down, but not to their historic levels. In those conditions you would be somewhat hesitant about committing all your funds to the stockmarket. Therefore, it would seem that a 30 percent reserve in short-term securities for the later purchase of stocks would be appropriate. You might invest other money in some of the companies listed above. Since the uncertainties are high, your money should be put to work slowly. Ten thousand dollars should be kept in a reserve.

The guidelines above do not represent the only way to handle a growth portfolio. The stocks listed are not the only growth stocks. You need to measure the expected earnings and dividend growth over time as well as the magnitude of this growth. You should select stocks that are dominant in an industry and give evidence of higher growth than the Standard & Poor's 500 Index. In setting up the portfolio, you should diversify among a number of stocks. Keep a cash reserve. If market conditions are uncertain, increase your cash reserve in anticipation of buying common stock if the market goes down. This kind of portfolio will provide a 3 to 5 percent current income and a growth of dividends and capital appreciation over time. You should earn a total rate of return in the area of 11 to 15 percent over the next three years. Thus in your growth portfolio there would be less current income compared to an income portfolio. On the other hand, you would have the possibility of substantial growth.

Managing a growth portfolio

As an investor you should find out what a firm's growth rate has been in the past, and whether or not the firm is expected to maintain its position of dominance in the future. You should average your investments so that you don't put all your money to work at one time. Do not forget investment strategy and timing. If the stock market is expected to decline, you certainly would want to keep your money in short-term securities. If the market is expected to rise, you would want to keep your money fairly well invested. Since it is difficult to estimate exactly when the market is low or high, you should simply keep some money invested at all times. No intelligent investor would put together a growth portfolio and just allow it to sit there. It must be managed. Sometimes growth stocks become overpriced. You must sell them if you really want to take advantage of changes in the market. There is no such thing as all stocks being too high or all stocks being too low. Sometimes stocks may be overpriced and sometimes underpriced. This is true of all growth stocks.

Performance measurement

A quarterly review of the value of the portfolio should be made. Compare the return of your portfolio to the return of the market. If the behavior of your portfolio is poorer than the market's, then you ought to take steps immediately to correct the problem.

The use of mutual funds in portfolio management

Often investors seeking to invest funds do not have the expertise to analyze and select securities. They rely on people who are expert portfolio managers to invest their funds. Companies that invest in the securities of other companies are referred to as *investment companies* or *mutual funds*. These companies simply purchase existing common stock, bonds, or short-term debt securities for the benefit of the owners of the company.

Types of mutual funds

Closed end funds Essentially there are two basic types of investment companies. One is referred to as a *closed end investment company*. Such a firm acts much like a corporation that produces a service for its owners. The closed end company buys assets that are common stock or debt securities of other companies. It has a fixed number of shares outstanding. It can borrow long-term money from the sale of bonds, or it can borrow short-term money from the sale of short-term securities. Money raised is invested on behalf of the owners of the closed end investment company.

Some closed end investment companies use *leverage*. Leverage comes about when this kind of company borrows money to invest for its owners. This borrowed money is added to money contributed by the owners, and securities are purchased. A simple illustration will explain how leverage works. Let's assume that a closed end investment company sells $1 million of common stock to various investors. The company issues $1 million worth of stock, and then its managers invest the money in the securities of other corporations. If you examine the balance sheet of the closed end investment company, you will see that the company has $1 million worth of common stock owned by its owners. In addition, it has $1 million invested in the stocks or bonds of other corporations.

Assume that the managers of the closed end investment company decide to borrow money to invest for their stockholders. Suppose they borrow $500,000 in the form of long-term bonds. Now the company has $500,000 worth of debt. Next the managers invest this money in shares of other business corporations. The bond indebtedness is a fixed claim that does not share in the profits. The bondholders receive only their interest and eventual principal repayment. Any profits earned on the borrowed money over and above the interest payments will accrue to the benefit of the common stockholders.

Assume the money is invested in common stock that goes up in value, and the value of the half million dollars worth of securities purchased with borrowed money increases to $700,000. The $200,000 gain over the $500,000 purchase price increases the share value of the common stockholders. This is a form of asset leverage, and the gain goes to the shareholder of the closed end investment company.

Unfortunately reverse leverage also takes place. If the value of the assets should decline, then the loss goes against the common stockholders of the closed end investment company. There is no guarantee that the shares purchased by the closed end investment company management will actually increase in value. But it is possible with the closed end investment company to have the leverage principle take effect. This can be a benefit to owners of the company.

Mutual funds   The second type of investment company is referred to as an *open end investment company* or mutual fund. A mutual fund sells shares in the company at net asset value. Net asset value is the value of all of the securities owned on the basis of a daily market appraisal. (In some cases the appraisal may be even more frequent.) This reflects the book value of the mutual fund. In other words the open end mutual fund invests in the common stock and fixed-income securities of other corporations, which are appraised daily. Such securities fluctuate in price. The value of the shares of the open end mutual fund can be found by simply dividing the number of mutual fund shares outstanding into the net asset value of the fund to arrive at the fund's net asset value per share. This is also the fund's selling price per share. Thus, as the value of the fund goes up, the value of the owners' shares also goes up. If the value of the fund goes down, the value of the shares of the open end mutual fund also goes down. Again, there is no guarantee that the shares will go up or down. But the mutual fund selling these shares can sell all of the shares it wants at the net asset value. The mutual fund takes the money paid by the owner of the mutual fund and invests it in assets similar to those already owned. Thus you as an investor have a way of buying a widely diversified group of assets selected by experts in their fields for their benefit.

Cost of buying mutual funds

The cost of buying a mutual fund can be as low as nothing or as high as 8½ percent of the value of the shares. Some funds called *load funds* charge a commission when you buy shares. The maximum commission that may be charged is established by the National Association of Security Dealers. As you increase the dollar amount of shares purchased in a load fund, the percentage amount of the commission generally decreases.

Funds that do not charge you a commission when you buy shares are called *no-load funds*. These funds may be purchased directly from their sponsors at net asset value. A simple example will demonstrate the difference between a load fund and a no-load. Suppose you have $1,000 to invest and you want to buy a mutual fund. Suppose further that you are comparing two funds, both of which have a net asset value per share of $10.00. Finally, suppose one fund is a no-load fund, and the other is a load fund charging a commission of 8½ percent.

If you buy one of these funds, what will you get for your $1,000? If you buy the no-load fund, you will get 100 shares of the mutual fund worth $10.00 per share. If you buy the load fund, however, the 8½ percent commission will be deducted from your $1,000 before any shares are purchased. Thus your $1,000 will buy $915 worth of shares after deducting the commission. You will therefore receive 91.5 shares worth $10.00 each if you buy the load fund.

It would be reasonable for you to ask why the one fund charges a commission and the other does not. The answer to this question is really quite simple. Load funds are actively sold by securities sales people, including stockbrokers, insurance agents, and even salespeople who sell mutual funds door-to-door. Since these salespeople expend a great deal of time and effort in selling mutual funds, they must be compensated. The commission is used to pay them for selling the mutual funds.

No-load funds, on the other hand, do not employ commission salespeople. These funds are sold directly by the organization sponsoring the fund. The funds are advertised in the financial press and sold by mail. They are not normally available through salespeople or stockbrokers.

One exception to this rule, however, is the money market funds. All of the large money market funds are no-load funds, and many of them can be purchased through brokers. In fact, the country's largest money market fund is sponsored by the brokerage firm of Merrill Lynch, Pierce, Fenner & Smith and can be purchased through any Merrill Lynch office.

Obviously, if you want to buy a no-load fund, you will have to do your own research. A salesperson who sells mutual funds on commission will be eager to explain the advantages and disadvantages of funds that pay a commission but not very interested in explaining a fund that does not pay one. This is the main reason you pay a commission on a load fund. If you are willing to do a little research on your own, you can save this cost.

Researching mutual funds is a fairly easy job. There are two widely available publications you can consult to obtain information. One is Wiesenberger Financial Services' *Investment Companies,* published by Warren, Gorham, and Lamont of New York. The other is Standard & Poor's *Investment Survey of Investment Funds.* These publications are available at most large public and university libraries. They provide a wealth of information to help you become an "instant expert" on mutual funds. When you find a fund in which you are interested, you can request the fund's managers to send a prospectus. The prospectus will provide complete information about the fund. After reading it, you can make a decision about the suitability of the fund in meeting your investment goals.

You should also check another important source of information about mutual funds. *Forbes* magazine publishes an annual performance survey of nearly all American mutual funds in August or September each year. This survey rates the funds with a grade of A to F for performance in up markets and performance in down markets. If you are planning to buy shares in any kind of mutual fund, you should certainly check the fund's performance in the most recent *Forbes* survey in your library.

A final word is appropriate about load versus no-load funds. There is no convincing evidence showing that load funds perform better (i.e., provide a higher rate of return) than do no-load funds. People who sell load funds often claim that this is true, but it cannot be proven. The fact that you pay a commission for a load fund does not therefore mean that you are buying a superior product. It only means that you are buying less assets for your money. It should be fairly obvious, therefore, that you should do your own research and save the commission charge. As a general principle, you should look for a no-load fund that meets your investment objectives.

Management fees

Whether you buy a load fund or a no-load fund, you will have to pay a management fee. This fee compensates the managers of the fund for their professional services in buying and selling securities. It also covers the cost of such administrative functions as keeping records, mailing statements, running the fund's offices, and so forth. Most funds charge a management fee of about one half of 1 percent of the fund's assets. When selecting among various funds, you should compare their management fees. If you find a fund that charges an extremely high fee, you may want to search out a similar fund with a more reasonable fee.

Functions of a mutual fund

The most important function of a mutual fund is that of providing diversification and professional management for small investors. With as little as $1,000 or even less, you can open a mutual fund account. Your account will be part of a very large sum of money managed by professional investment analysts. Since these analysts study the securities markets as a full-time job, they bring a degree of knowledge and professionalism to the task of managing your money you probably lack. Also important is the fact that the mutual fund manages many millions of dollars and thus can achieve broad diversification among securities. It is very difficult to buy a large number of securities with a small amount of money. However, by buying shares in a mutual fund, you can buy a part of a large pool of diversified investments.

When shopping for a fund to meet your investment objectives, you should bear in mind that mutual funds come in many different varieties. You can buy funds that invest primarily in growth stocks (called *growth funds*). You can invest in funds whose major objective is to maximize current income *(income funds)*. You can also buy funds that invest in common stocks and try to achieve a balance between growth and income *(balanced funds)*. *Bond funds* that invest only in various types of bonds are also available. You can even buy special types of bond funds that invest only in municipal bonds or U.S. government bonds. As mentioned earlier, you can also invest in funds that invest solely in money market instruments (money market funds). The important point is that you must shop carefully to find a fund that pursues investment objectives consistent with your own investment objectives.

A new type of mutual fund called a *unit investment trust* has grown in popularity in recent years. Unit investment trusts are sponsored by some of the larger brokerage firms. They are generally unmanaged funds sold in units of $1,000. By *unmanaged* is meant that these trusts buy some type of securities and hold them to maturity. Once the trust is established, no securities within the trust are bought or sold. Income earned on the trust is paid out to the trust certificate holders as it is earned. The principal amount is refunded when the certificates mature. In the meantime no management is required because no securities are traded within the trust. These types of trusts generally are sold at a very low commission rate, usually less than 1 percent.

A simple example of one type of unit trust will show how these investments work. One large brokerage firm offers a unit investment trust that specializes in investing in certificates of deposit issued by foreign banks. These certificates usually come in large denominations of $1 million or more and pay fairly high interest rates. The brokerage firm sells unit investment trust certificates in units of $1,000 to many individual investors, and then buys a portfolio of these large certificates of deposit. When the certificates mature, usually in six months, the individual investors are repaid their $1,000 investment plus interest. By using unit investment trust certificates, the brokerage firm can pool many small investments and buy $100 million or more in bank certificates.

Many different types of unit investment trusts exist. Some invest in municipal bonds, some in special types of government agency certificates, some in foreign bank certificates, some in corporate bonds, and so forth. You should check with your broker to find out what is available.

Mutual funds and your investment strategy

The role of mutual funds in the formation of a strong investment portfolio has been the subject of some controversy. Some time ago a group of prominent physicians, lawyers, and business executives listed a number of mistakes they themselves had made. In reflecting on their past experiences, they admitted that they had either failed to develop a sound investment plan or, if they had some kind of a plan, they had failed to stick to it. They had often been too impatient of success and too greedy. Speculation rather than investment had frequently been their goal. And finally they had not understood very clearly what expectations they ought to have for the common stock shares of mutual funds in their portfolios. They blamed this combination of attributes for the lack of success of their investment efforts.

If you talk to the average American investor, you may hear that he or she has no interest in mutual funds. The complaint may be raised that most mutual funds perform poorly and cause people to lose money. Such a disabused investor may go on to assert that you should skip mutual funds and stick to well-known investment possibilities, such as real estate, gold, silver, antiques, and other collectible items. You will be told to keep your money in a savings account. Perhaps you should try making an investment for a brief period of time in a short-term liquid trust or mutual fund. As you discuss the matter further, you will discover the need to develop your own investment plan that will include the correct perspective about mutual funds. The following strategy might work for you.

First, select three complimentary mutual funds: a money market fund, a bond fund, and a common stock fund that provides both dividend income and growth. Your bond fund should be a balanced fund primarily emphasizing intermediate term securities. Your short-term fund should provide liquidity. Once the portfolio has been selected, you should make regular monthly contributions to each of the three funds. From time to time you can vary the amounts. Generally speaking, when short-term interest rates are high, you should put more money into the money market fund than the bonds or common stock fund. Most of the time, however, you should invest a third of your monthly investment into each one of the three funds. You should continue this plan independent of the movement of the stock market or of the outlook for the economy. In other words, as the funds increase in price, you would buy fewer shares. As the funds go down in price, you would buy more shares. The assumption is that you should add money to these funds on a regular basis until you have reached your objective of having a certain amount of money available for your retirement or to meet other goals. This could be a part of your own retirement program. You would not try to anticipate changes or alter your portfolio mix in order to take advantage of changes in the market. The important thing is for you to maintain a long-range perspective.

If you follow this plan over a period of years, you will be startled by the amount of money you have accumulated. You will be pleased to discover how much the value of your fund has grown.

It would be wise for you to reinvest the income of your fund in stock, bond, or money market funds. You would be diversifying and maintaining liquidity. You would be taking advantage of opportunities to invest in common stocks that in the long run will probably turn out to be a better hedge against inflation than any other financial asset. If you select funds carefully in the first place, you will have a chance of making money by investing in mutual funds. But don't speculate, don't gamble, and don't try to anticipate the highs and lows of the stock market. It is extremely difficult to guess what it will do. Put your money to work. If you let it work for a long period of time, you will have a substantial amount of assets that will add to your life's savings and comforts.

This plan will probably do more for your investment habits than selecting the right mutual fund. But don't begin with the idea that you are going to buy low and sell high. Few people have the ability to do that.

In the last analysis, if you follow the practice of dollar averaging, if you select several funds, and if you maintain a long-term perspective, you will benefit from your investments in mutual funds. You will not join the chorus of many greedy pseudosophisticates who say, "I bought a mutual fund once. I lost money, and I will never do it again." You can turn the tide in your favor by simply being prudent, long-term, and logical in your approach.

Summary

You often hear the question "Where is the best place to invest my money?" There actually is no one best place to invest. Rather there are several recipes that can meet the variety of needs of many investors.

First, you must establish your goals or objectives. All investors want security of principal, marketability, liquidity, favorable tax treatment, and diversification to reduce risk as an objective. Once these objectives are met, then you must decide if you need income, a combination of income and growth, growth, growth with more risk, or tax-exempt securities that meet your needs if you are in a high tax bracket. You also must decide if you are going to be aggressive, that is, assume a great deal of risk, or be defensive, that is, reduce risk. Whichever you choose, you still must diversify by industry, security, maturity of debt, and your cash position.

Once your goals and objectives are established, you must supervise your investments. This suggests a quarterly review and action if securities no longer meet your objectives. You should measure the performance of your securities on a regular basis. Various portfolios can be constructed to meet your income and growth goals.

It requires skill to manage a growth portfolio. Often people find management a difficult task. If this is the case you can select a few mutual funds. One solution would be to invest in three mutual funds on a regular basis. In that way you have security diversification as well as time diversification. If possible, select no-load mutual funds. Select one for liquidity, a money market fund; one for income; and one for growth. Then invest regular amounts in each. In this way you will add to your net worth, which will increase over time.

15

Investment in real assets

- Real estate investment as an inflation hedge
- Investment in a vacation home
- Interval ownership—buying the use of a condominium for a few weeks
- Investment in land or farms
- Investment in real estate investment trusts (REITs)
- Investment in precious metals and art objects
- Return and risk of investment in real assets
- Summary

Until recently Americans have not been interested in investing in such real assets as gold, silver, coins, antiques, and other valuable goods. This is not true in many other countries where families hold their wealth in the form of gold coins, silver, or jewels. For example, when some Vietnamese refugees reached our shores a few years ago, they brought along their most valuable possessions, which included gold in all forms and jewels. Diamonds also have a high value, and are both easily stored and transported. By way of contrast, only a minority of Americans historically have been collectors of coins, stamps, and antiques. Until 1975 we were not legally entitled to possess gold bullion.

Along with the rest of the world, however, Americans have always been willing to invest in real estate. In Chapter 6 we discussed home ownership, its tax advantages, and its impact on net worth. In fact, it is not only the price increases in houses that have begun to attract the attention of investors. The rapid rise in the price of many commodities, particularly the dramatic increase in the price of gold and silver, has also appealed to investors.

Of course, the speculative surge in prices may not last for a long time. But it has made countless people around the world aware of a way of investing that is growing at a rate often above the general rate of inflation.

The long-run solution for inflation requires a bundle of constraints, including high-interest rates, a balanced budget, more capital investment, more saving, less dependence on imported energy, and no indexation of wages and prices. But until a utopian environment is reached, you must find ways as an investor to protect yourself from the ravages of inflation. At the same time you realize that the attempt on the part of all investors to hedge against inflation is itself a major cause of inflation. You should consider investment in real assets to protect the purchasing power of your investment dollars. You may begin by examining the investment characteristics of real estate.

Real estate investment

Real estate investment as an inflation hedge

In most areas of the United States, inflation has caused a substantial increase in the price of real estate. In some areas prices of homes have risen dramatically. In Hawaii, California, and Washington, D.C., annual rates of price increase have been in the magnitude of 15 to 20 percent per year or more. In Georgetown, a fashionable area of Washington, D.C., an eight-foot wide, two-story row house with no backyard sold for $72,000 in 1979. Just 10 years earlier the same property had sold for only $12,000. It was not uncommon for real estate investors to buy a house for $100,000 and sell it six months later for $125,000. One woman sold her house for $160,000. Then two days after it was put back on the market, she realized she had sold it too cheaply, and she bought it back for $165,000. After painting the house inside and out, she sold it for $190,000.

The speculative fever in housing—and it is speculation—was so high in Los Angeles in 1977 that builders, flooded with buyers, sold houses by lottery. The lucky winners could then buy the house and move in. Or they could sell their option at a profit and get in line for the next auction.

In Washington, D.C., there has been a substantial amount of renovation of houses on Capitol Hill close to the Congress and in other areas of the city. It is not uncommon for investors to buy a house for $30,000 and invest an additional $15,000 in renovation work. They can then either rent the house for $6,000 per year or sell it for $70,000, realizing a gain of $25,000 in just six months. Such a feat is difficult to duplicate in the stock market. But the lure of profit, in spite of some negative social implications, has resulted in a noteworthy redevelopment of Washington, D.C., at a substantial profit to investors.

After observing all the activity in real estate, many potential investors might like to learn how to do the same thing: make a profit in real estate. We shall now trace briefly the steps you will need to take to get started in this form of investment.

The importance of location

The first step is to locate a property that has the potential of maintaining or increasing its value. This means that you must study trends in real estate prices and values in your area. An analysis of the price of houses in various neighborhoods will reveal the magnitude of price changes as well as the stability of prices. This may require a bit of work, but it will pay off by helping in the decision-making process. One U.S. metropolitan neighborhood, for example, experienced an 8 percent per annum increase in prices over a five-year period. Houses increased in price from $50,000 to $73,500. In another section of the same city, slightly more expensive houses increased from $60,000 to $96,700—a 10 percent annual increase. Such an analysis suggests that the more expensive area is more desirable financially than the first area. Obviously the past is not going to repeat itself exactly in the future, but such an analysis of trends will reveal clues to the better housing areas of a community. Remember that as these two neighborhoods were rising in value, houses in other neighborhoods of the same city were being abandoned. So it pays to look carefully at neighborhood trends.

An analysis of real estate as a business indicates that the three most important factors in selecting real estate are: (1) location, (2) location, and (3) location. A careful price analysis will reveal the best location in a community. Having a good location involves buying a well-constructed house on an attractive lot that meets peoples' living requirements from a physical and an aesthetic viewpoint. You should buy in a neighborhood close to public transportation, stores, schools, and recreational facilities. The area should be pleasant, quiet, properly zoned, and well protected by police and fire fighters.

In most large U.S. cities the center of town has declined, unless massive efforts have been made to redevelop it. Where these efforts have been carried out, there has been a reversal of the former trend, resulting in increased values for the city center. Washington, D.C., Boston, and New York City are examples of this turnaround situation. Certainly investors can find opportunities for investment in these areas. Such a change reverses the trend to suburbia; a countertrend toward urbia is going on in some areas. If the cost of energy increases and public transportation improves, there will be a continuation of this new trend.

If you still have any doubts about the value of a neighborhood, lot, or house, consult a real estate agent at a reliable firm or a mortgage banker familiar with trends in property values in metropolitan areas.

Buying at a fair price

As a buyer of real estate, you should try to acquire property at a fair price. Of course, you must be able to afford the property. Just because you do not have $200,000 to purchase a house doesn't mean the house is overpriced. The financial aspects of real estate will be discussed shortly. Whether the price of the property is fair or realistic can be determined by the selling price of comparable properties. In the real estate business, these are referred to as *comparables*. Your agent can supply you with a list of comparable sales in the neighborhood.

Once armed with a comparable list, you can determine if a home's price is realistic. Most sellers establish the price in the same way. They determine what they think is a fair price. Then they add on a 6 percent real estate commission. Finally they add on something extra for negotiation purposes. For example, assume that six houses in the same neighborhood, all slightly different, sold for $54,500, $53,500, $56,000, $55,000, $57,500 and $53,000 within the past six months. You determine that the house most like one you wish to buy sold for $55,000 six months ago. You also discover that current sales prices are 5 percent higher than six months ago. The seller's asking price is $59,000. A realistic price would be $57,500 which would include a 6 percent real estate commission. You could begin negotiations for the house by making a written offer to buy through your agent. If the market is tight, that is, if few houses are available, it would be wise to offer close to the asking price. In that case you might offer $57,750. If the house has been in the market for a few months, if the market is slow, and if there are other similar houses on the market, you might offer less.

Contract for purchase　　The *contract for purchase* requires an offering price, a good-faith deposit, and a settlement date. This date is the day when the title and ownership of the property are to be transferred to the buyer. A clean contract would contain an offer to purchase the house for $57,000. Along with a deposit of $5,700, there would be included a statement that the balance will be paid when title passes in 60 days. An "unclean" contract would be one where the contract is made contingent on a number of factors, such as a proviso that the seller must paint the house inside and out. Putting these conditions on the purchase contract is proper if market conditions warrant them. If the market is tight and you really want the house, then the simpler and cleaner the contract the better.

Deposit money　　In addition to supplying a signed contract and deposit money, you will also be required to provide a credit sheet for the purchaser. This sheet tells the seller about your financial background, that is, your present assets and liabilities, and your income level. Obviously the seller wants to learn whether you have the financial ability to purchase the house. The seller can then make a reasonable judgment about whether or not you will be able to obtain a mortgage on the property.

Analyzing the investment　　But let's back up a bit. Before you decide to buy the house, you must determine if it is a good investment. In order to do this, you must estimate its future growth of income, expenses, rents, the amount of property taxes, insurance charges, and costs of management and maintenance. As you analyze the situation, you may learn that property taxes have increased 8 percent per year; rents have increased 10 percent every two years; maintenance expenses have increased 7 percent per year; and insurance costs have increased 5 percent per year. The insurance rate must be adjusted periodically because of the increased property value. Your insurance cost will increase an additional 10 percent in three years because your property will increase in value at the rate of 12 percent per annum. In addition, you will have mortgage and depreciation expenses, which are an important part of the rate of return estimates. Since this is a commercial investment, the lending institution will provide a 25-year mortgage loan for 75 percent of the value of the property. The interest rate is assumed to be 11 percent, which is 10 percent higher than it would be if you were going to occupy the house yourself. If the house sells for $57,000, then the mortgage would be $42,750, and the downpayment would be $14,250. The monthly cost of the mortgage payment, including principal and interest payments, would be $419. This payment will remain constant over the 25-year life of the mortgage. Depreciation of the house is assumed to be straight line, that is, an equal amount each year. The land value is $10,000, and the value of the premises is $47,000.

Closing costs

Many house purchasers only think about the amount of the down payment and monthly mortgage and tax payments. They fail to consider the closing costs, which can be sizeable. For example, examine the closing costs for a $52,000 house with a mortgage of $42,750 in Montgomery County, Maryland, in 1978, which are listed in Table 15–1.

Table 15–1
Sample closing costs

Recording fees	$ 12.00
Revenue stamps	250.80
Transfer tax	
State	285.00
County	245.00
Tax certificate	
County	5.00
Survey	
Minimum—$60.00	60.00
Plat	2.50
Notary fees	4.00
Title examination	132.50
Settlement fee	57.00
Preparation of papers	
Note and deed of trust	65.00
Title insurance	166.50
Taxes, real Subtotal	$1,285.30
Taxes, real estate (county & state)	
Prorated from June 31 to July 1	
Assume January 1, settlement and	
six-months taxes	400.00
Total taxes and closing costs	$1,685.30

Closing costs represent more than 10 percent of the down payment, when real estate taxes are included. Some of the fees and taxes associated with closing costs are tax-deductible. Certainly real estate taxes are deductible along with state and county transfer taxes, revenue stamps, settlement fees, and possibly title insurance. For purposes of illustration, we will assume that all settlement costs are deductible as a business expense. But in an actual case, you will need to check this point with a tax consultant.

Making the income and expenses estimate

In the purchase of investment property, let's assume that you are in the 50 percent tax bracket, and that the aftertax cost of settlement expenses is one half of $1,685.30, or $842.65. The aftertax amount must be added to your initial investment. You might also have to pay points. Let's assume that you pay $1,000 for points. The after tax cost of points would be $500. As the investor you must have the total amount available at settlement.

Once the house is purchased, the rental income and expense data are as shown in Table 15–2. Note that there is an operating loss of $2,631 the first year and a $2,107 loss the fifth year. This results in a reduction of income taxes on ordinary income and an aftertax loss of $1,316 the first year and of $1,054 the fifth year. The amounts of these loses will vary in each of the other years. In effect, this reduces the ordinary taxes you have to pay and adds to your cash flow. Table 15–3 recaps the cash effect. No depreciation is deducted in calculating the cash flows because depreciation is a noncash charge. The net effect is a savings in aftertax dollars that reduces the net cash outflow. The net cash loss after taxes is estimated to be $517 the first year, and $478, $472, $580, and $447 in the next four years. This means that you as the investor must make an additional investment of these amounts in each of the forecast years.

Table 15–2
Income and expense estimate of investment property

	Base year 0	Annual rate of increase (percent)	Year				
			1+	2	3	4	5
Annual rental income	5,400	(10)‡	$5,400	$5,400	$5,900	$5,900	$6,400
Net rental income§	4,950		4,950	4,950	5,410	5,410	5,870
Annual expenses							
Taxes	800	(8)	800	864	933	1,008	1,088
Insurance	200	(5)	200	210	221	232	243
Additional value						23	24
Maintenance	750		750	802	859	919	983
Depreciation	1,175		1,175	1,175	1,175	1,175	1,175
Interest	4,704		4,656	4,608	4,560	4,512	4,464
Total tax expense			7,518	7,659	7,738	7,859	7,977
Operating loss			(2,631)	(2,709)	(2,328)	(2,449)	(2,107)
Aftertax operating loss			(1,316*)	(1,355*)	(1,164*)	(1,225*)	(1,054*)

* Assumes 50 percent tax bracket.
† Assumes no change the first year.
‡ Every two years.
§ After 10% rental commission.

Table 15–3
Recap of cash income and expense*
of investment property

	Year				
	1	2	3	4	5
Cash income	$4,950	$4,950	$5,410	$5,410	$5,870
Cash expenses					
Taxes	800	864	933	1,088	1,088
Insurance	200	210	221	232	243
Maintenance	750	802	859	919	983
Principal repayments plus interest	5,033	5,033	5,033	5,033	5,033
Total expenses	6,783	6,783	7,046	7,215	7,371
Cash gain or (loss)	(1,833)	(1,833)	(1,636)	(1,805)	(1,501)
Annual tax saving†	1,316	1,355	1,164	1,225	1,054
Net cash loss aftertax effect.............	(517)	(478)	(472)	(580)	(447)

* With tax effect.
† See bottom line of Table 15–2.

If you bought the house as an investment, your investment schedule would be as follows:

Base year	$15,593*
Year 1	517
Year 2	478
Year 3	472
Year 4	580
Year 5	447
Total cash invested ...	$18,087

* $15,593 = $14,250 downpayment +$843 aftertax settlement costs +$500 aftertax cost of points.

Table 15–4 shows your net worth at the end of five years, assuming the property increases in value as shown in the table. For this investment

Table 15–4
Property value and net worth Projections
for investment property

	Base year	1	2	3	4	5
Property value	$57,000	$63,000	$71,501	$80,081	$89,691	$100,454
Mortgage value	42,750	42,323	41,896	41,469	41,042	40,615
Net worth	14,250	$21,477	$29,605	$38,614	$48,649	$ 59,893

* With tax effect.

your net worth is simply the difference between the value of the property and the amount of the outstanding mortgage. Your net worth thus represents your equity in the property.

The maximum capital gains tax is assumed to be 30 percent. If the house is sold five years from now at $100,454 less a 6 percent sales commission, the net sales price would be $94,427, and the gain on the sale would be $37,427 ($94,427 − $57,000). A maximum tax of 30 percent on this amount would be $11,228, leaving you a net profit of $26,199. In addition to this net profit, you would also recover your $14,250 down payment. Your total cash proceeds for the sale would then be $40,449 ($14,250 + $26,199).

In summary, you would put down $15,593, and add an additional investment of $517 in the first year, $478 in the second, $472 in the third, $580 in the fourth, and $447 in the fifth. The value of your investment would increase to $40,449 after allowances for federal income taxes, assuming that you sell the house at the end of the fifth year.

Estimating the return on the investment

You can now estimate the rate of return, from your investment by discounting the revenue back to the original value. To do this, you would use the present value tables introduced in Chapter 9. In this case the discounted value of the additional annual investment is added to the down payment. The value of the investment in five years is discounted back to the present at the same rate. When the discounted present value of the investment stream equals the discounted present value of the future value of the investment at the end of five years, you have obtained the rate of return on the investment.

In the case of the purchase of the real property, the aftertax investment flows are as follows:

	PV of $1 at 20 percent	Present value at 20 percent
Initial investment, $15,593	1.0	15,593
Additional investment		
Year 1 = 517	.883	431
Year 2 = 478	.694	332
Year 3 = 472	.579	273
Year 4 = 580	.482	280
Year 5 = 447	.402	180
Sum of present value of investment at 20%		17,089
Present value of $40,449* at 20 percent (× .402)		$16,260

* This is the value of the investment at the end of the five-year period.

The present value of your investment at the end of five years will be slightly lower than the present value of the original investment plus your annual investment. This means that the discount rate is slightly high, and that the estimated true return is between 18 and 20 percent. For all practical purposes the investment provides you as an investor with a return of 20 percent after taxes, compounded annually for the five-year period.

Avoiding taxes on capital gains

It is impossible to avoid paying taxes on income from a real estate venture forever. However, it is possible to postpone taxes for a long time. Most real estate ventures under current economic conditions have an annual loss after taxes, and the investor must supply additional investment capital, as in the above example. Capital gains taxes are paid when the asset is sold, but it is not necessary to sell the real estate to enjoy the increase in price. As the property increases in price, you can increase the size of the mortgage on the property by refinancing it. (That is, if a lending institution will agree to do so.) In the case of the house investment under discussion, the value of the property will have increased to $80,081 (see Table 15–4) at the end of three years. You can then mortgage this property with a mortgage value of 75 percent of the amount, or approximately $60,000. By increasing the mortgage to $60,000, you would have available an additional $17,250 toward the purchase of another house. You could also use this money to buy a boat, auto, airplane, or vacation home for investment purposes. Many Americans have done so.

The only problem with this plan is that you are increasing your indebtedness and monthly mortgage costs in the process of increasing your debt. Money from rental income or other income must be available to pay the increased costs. Some lending institutions might be unwilling to increase the mortgage on the property, particularly at a time of tight money. Lending policies of financial institutions do change, and they might decide to make loans only to owner-occupants, rather than to owner-investors. This means that the real estate investor must be certain to reinvest the borrowed money in profitable investment outlets.

The possibility of borrowing an increased amount of money from a mortgage in order to make an additional real estate investment suggests substantial profits. It represents a form of pyramiding. Let's see how this would work on the basis of enough equity to buy a new house every three years for every house that is owned. The schedule is at top of page 409.

There is only one limitation: the amount of income from rents and other sources must be enough to carry the mortgages. If not, you as the investor must be able to make up the difference from other sources. But if you are successful at buying houses, you will have assets valued

	Year				
	0	3	6	9	Total
First house	First house	Second house	Third house	Fourth house	4
Second house		Second house	Third house	Fourth house	3
Third house			Third house	Fourth house	2
Fourth house				Fourth house	1
Total houses	1	2	3	4	10

at from $600,000 to $1 million at the end of 9 to 12 years. Some of these assets could be sold to cover your additional investment. That isn't a bad outcome when you only invested about $15,593 to begin your real estate empire. It won't all belong to you, of course. The properties will all have heavy mortgages, but on the basis of our assumption, you could make a fortune. Maybe the author of *How To Make a Million in Real Estate* was right.

What could go wrong?

The description of your real estate investment and pyramid is excitingly profitable. Our projections seem reasonable for costs. Values have gone up in the past. Your debt as a percent of value is not excessive. But the only thing that can go wrong is that our estimates might be wrong. Of course, in addition we might have another recession.

Recessions

The American economy tends to be cyclical. Every three or four years there is an economic slowdown that disrupts business and results in losses to real estate investors, business people, and workers. We had such a slowdown in 1969, in 1974–75, and again in 1980. In 1980 unemployment rose to above 8 percent, the inflation rate was above 10 percent, and the mortgage interest rate increased to as high as 16 percent. There were several quarters of negative growth in the economy, and corporate profits declined during this recession.

In the 1974–75 recession, billions of dollars were lost by institutions. Mortgage lenders borrowed cheap funds in the money market to invest in high-priced mortgages, only to find out later that the cheap short-term money cost 12 percent. They couldn't make a profit by investing in 8 to 9 percent mortgages. Real estate investment trusts (REITs) had the same experience, and lost millions of dollars. Many investors thought they could make money in real estate by buying the common stock of REITs. Some even borrowed heavily against the common stock, thus increasing their leverage and the amount of their anticipated profit. To their dismay the shares did not increase in price but declined. Their sought-after fortune became a millstone around their necks. Financial embarassment was followed by collapse and for some by complete financial failure and poverty. If you ask, "What can go wrong?" just remember the recession of 1974–75, and you'll have your answer. We might have another recession.

Poor estimates

Since all those comments are based on estimates, the more practical answer to the question "What can go wrong?" is that your own estimate can go wrong. The market price of property might not increase as rapidly as you expect. In fact, something might happen to cause a substantial loss, for instance, an uninsured mud slide, flood damage created by an act of God, or a neighborhood blight caused by a change in zoning. An example of this would be the placement of a landfill garbage and trash collections area near your house. This actually happened in one affluent county in 1978. Fortunately for the county residents, it was found that a landfill attracts birds. Since birds are a menace to air traffic and since the landfill site was in the path of commercial and general aviation flights, the courts did not allow the development of the site. Instead, the county authorities now plan a sewage treatment plant, which might also reduce property values.

Rents may not increase according to your expectation because of market limits or rent control. And, of course, you could be plagued by high tenant turnover even though you make your tenants sign a lease. This is one of the major risks of owning rental property. You may have to suffer through periods when your rental properties are vacant. Since rental income then ceases altogether, you will have no cash inflows to offset your mortgage and other costs. For example, a friend of the authors owned four single-family rental properties. One year all four of them were vacant for four consecutive months. The owner had to pay all the mortgage expenses out of his own pocket, thus increasing his investment faster than he had anticipated. If you do invest in real estate, it is essential to establish a reserve fund to cope with such unexpected contingencies.

Your expenses might be higher than originally expected, and your real estate taxes might increase. Maintenance expenses might be higher, particularly if there is high turnover of tenants. Insurance costs increase with inflation and could reduce profits. One or all of these expense increases might result in lower profits and an unfavorable investment.

In principle, real estate investment offers relatively high yields. However, there are risks connected with this form of investment. Caution must be exercised, or else you could turn the lure of high speculative profit into loss and end up in bankruptcy.

Investment in a vacation home

Many couples of all ages dream of owning a second vacation villa on a beach, a mountain retreat near ski slopes, or a winter home in Florida, California, Antigua, or the Bahamas. "Wouldn't it be great," they romanticize, "to have our own place for get-away weekends, for a long summer vacation, or for four-day holiday breaks? And it won't cost us very much. We don't have to finish it all at once. When we're not using it, we can rent it to friends or put it in the hands of local realtors, who, for a small fee, will manage the property for us. Our home-away-from-home will be ours, and someone else will help pay for it."

There is some merit to this idea. Owning a second home can be fun, enjoyable, and profitable. But it also becomes another financial responsibility. It may reduce your family cash flow, since taxes and other expenses are rising. The changing tax laws are also making it less attractive to own vacation properties. Remember one thing: if only you or your family use the house, there are few or no business expense deductions you can claim, except for interest and property taxes. If you use the property for more than two weeks per year, then expenses must be prorated on the basis of the percentage of time the property is used by the investor.

To be an investment, your vacation home must be profitable in the long run. Estimates of trends in revenues and expenses must be made, just as you would do when considering a single-family house as an investment. Again, location is everything in making an investment in a vacation home. Care must be exercised in estimating revenues, expenses, taxes, insurance, maintenance, length of the rental season, and a potential increase in the value of your property.

Many investors depend on the tax-shelter benefits of vacation properties. That is, even though the annual rental income is insufficient to cover all expenses, the annual loss from the property can be written off against ordinary income with a substantial reduction of income taxes. Later, when the value of the property increases, the investor benefits and a substantial capital gain is obtained.

The 1976 Tax Reform Act changed all of this for owners of vacation properties. If you are contemplating an investment in a vacation property today, you had better make very careful estimates. In the past all expenses, including depreciation, could be written off, even if you used the property. Under the new law, if you use the property no more than 10 percent of the time available for rental (or 14 days, whichever is greater), all expenses may be deducted. Expenses include utilities, fees paid to brokers, property insurance premiums, mortgage interest, property taxes, casualty losses, and other costs legitimately attributable to the effort to generate rental income. Under these conditions the property is a business. However, you must demonstrate that the property is indeed a profit-motivated venture. This can be done if you earn a profit for two years out of five, or if you can convince the IRS that your losses are legitimate.

If your use of the property exceeds 14 days, the property is considered a residence for the portion of the year used. If your property is rented for as little as 15 days or less, rental income need not be reported. However, in this case only mortgage interest, property taxes, and casualty losses may be deducted.

If you use the property more than the 14 days, your total deductions for expenses cannot exceed your gross rental income, reduced by the portion of mortgage interest and property tax expenditures related to the rental use. The point of all this is that if the 14 day/10 percent limit is exceeded, you can no longer write losses off against personal income. This is because your property is being used for personal occupancy.

The case of a beach house in Maine

Let's consider a beach property in Maine (see Tables 15–5 through 15–8) and learn how the economics of vacation property work. This is an actual case of a summer property under management in Maine.

Table 15–5 shows income and expenses for the property. The gross income represents income for a period of six weeks. This is more than one half of a 10-week rental season at the rate of $425 per week. Gross rental income was $2,550. A rental commission of 10 percent is paid to the real estate agent for finding the renters. This leaves a net rental income of $2,295.

On the expense side, property taxes in 1977 were $1,320; they had increased substantially after a complete revaluation in 1976. The low interest expense of $200 per year is based on a $9,000 mortgage that has only three years to go before it is paid off. The owner pays $76

**Table 15–5
Income and expenses of Maine summer rental property**

Income and expenses

A. $2,550 Gross rental income
     − 255 Rental commission

B. $2,295 Net rental income

C.   Expenses

a.	Property taxes	$1,320
b.	Mortgage interest	200
c.	Maintenance	200
d.	Utilities	277
e.	Depreciation	1,000
f.	Furnishings-depreciation	900
g.	Travel costs to and from	300
	Total expenses	$4,197

D.   Profit or (loss) .... ($1,902)

per month principal and interest. The original cost of the property, including land, was $17,500 in 1966.

Maintenance expenses are low since the owner has sons willing and able to paint and repair at a low cost. This figure would be much higher if professional artisans were employed for maintenance. Utilities include the telephone, water, and electricity. The house is electrically heated. Depreciation includes the original cost of the building ($15,000 − $2,500 for the land) as well as improvements that have been made to the building. The depreciation for furnishings includes writing off new furniture, carpeting, and appliances purchased in recent years. The travel expense covers the cost of travel to the cottage in the spring to open it for the rental season. Two such trips are allowed each year by the IRS as a legitimate tax deduction.

The total expenses of $4,197 result in an operating loss of $1,902. Since the owner used the property 26 days, the expenses must be prorated to reflect what can be deducted as legitimate expenses. Table 15–6 indicates how taxes and mortgage interest payable are prorated on the basis of 38 percent to the owner and 62 percent for the tenants. Realty taxes and interest totaled $1,520, of which $942.40 (62 percent) was an expense against the property. The remainder of $577.60 would be written off against the owner's income taxes. The difference between net rental income of $2,295 and the business expenses of $942.40 is $1,352.60. This difference is the maximum amount of business expenses that can be written off against ordinary income. The prorated amount of business expenses incurred by the owner, as seen in Table 15–7, is $1,660. Since the adjusted rental income was only $1,352.60, the owner can only write off $1,352.60 against business income. The excess cannot be written off against ordinary income. However, excess taxes and interest paid by the owner can be deducted ($577.60) against ordinary income.

Table 15–6
Calculation of expense limits of Maine property

How to calculate limits on losses
A. Net rental income $2,295.00
B. Minus prorated portion of taxes and
    mortgage (based on total occupancy
    of 68 days)
    Owner 26 days
    Rental 42 days
    26/68 + 42/68 = 38 percent + 62 percent
    or 38 percent for owner *and* 62 percent for
    renter .... $ 942.40*
C. Adjusted rental income and limit
    on deductions and expenses $1,352.60

* 62 percent of $1,520 (taxes and interest).

Table 15-7
Tax-deductible expenses
of Maine property

Actual expenses that normally would be fully deductible as business expenses under Sec. 162 of the Internal Revenue Code

A.	Maintenance and utilities	$ 477.00
B.	Depreciation	1,900.00
C.	Travel	300.00
		$2,677.00
D.	62 percent of $2,677, allocable to rental business, or $1,660.	$1,660.00

The net effect of this is to reduce the amount of write-off against the business rental income. The only way the owner can claim all deductions is by not using the property for more than two weeks. If more rental income is received, then more of the taxes, interest, and expenses can be written off against income from the cottage.

The Maine property
brought up to date

The expenses are distorted somewhat on the Maine beach property because it was purchased at a low price. The mortgage is low, and the usage by the owner is high. Table 15–8 shows the trend in value and expenses for the property.

Let's assume that the owner sold the property to a new owner for $95,000, which is the fair market value of the property, including two building lots valued at $12,500 apiece. The value of the land and building without the two extra building lots is $70,000, the land being valued at $12,500. The value of the building and contents for depreciation purposes

Table 15-8
Trends in value and expense
of Maine property

	1966	1977
Price	$17,500	$95,000*
Mortgage balance		
15-year at 6 percent	9,000	3,350
Taxes	525	1,320†
Mortgage, second	820	200
Maintenance	100	200
Utilities	185	277
Depreciation	500	1,000
Furniture	250	900
Travel	200	300
Rental income per week	200	425

* Includes one building site acquired for $2,500 in 1969 and another site purchased in 1974 for $3,200, both lots being adjacent to property.

† Includes taxes on lots acquired in 1969 and 1974.

is $57,500 ($70,000 − $12,500) over a life of 20 years. The new owners decide to rent the cottage for the entire season of 10 weeks for $425 per week, less the 10 percent rental fee. They plan to use the cottage only one week in the fall and one week in the spring to make certain that the IRS will consider the property a business venture. Closing costs are $500, and the down payment is $29,500. The mortgage is $65,500 at 10 percent interest. The monthly mortgage costs are $603.25. Approximately 90 percent of the monthly mortgage payment ($543) is interest. Annual interest is therefore $6,516.

Since the owners are absentee owners, they require the services of a real estate agent. Their income and expenses are shown in Table 15–9.

Table 15–9
Updated income and expenses on Maine property

Gross income	$ 4,250
Less 10 percent rental commission	425
Net income, 10 weeks at $382.50 =	$ 3,825
Maintenance, annual	200
Utilities, annual	277
Depreciation ($57,500/20)	2,875
Travel costs	300
Taxes	1,320
Interest	6,516
Total expenses	$11,488
Net loss	($ 7,663)
Tax saving at 50 percent	$ 3,831
Net loss after tax	3,831
Minus depreciation (a noncash expense)	2,875
Annual cash loss	$ 956

Thus the owners have to dip into their pockets for $956 each year to subsidize their cottage ownership. This means that their two-week vacation costs them about $478 per week. And, if they don't mind going to the same place every year, they will have an asset that will appreciate 10 percent per year and provide them an excellent return on their investment. Over the long run this will help them maximize their net worth.

Interval ownership

Many people cannot afford to purchase a vacation home, but they like the idea of having their own place. Instead of buying a vacation condominium and renting it to others to help carry the costs, you can buy only one or two weeks' use of a condominium. This kind of interval ownership is sweeping the country. Under the interval ownership concept, you are actually buying a share of a condominium residence. If shares are sold in two-week units, 26 shares are owned by 26 owners. Each of the owners of the residence is entitled to use the residence for the two-week period they purchase.

Let's assume that you purchase two week's use of a condominium at Sanibel Island, Florida, for the first two weeks in March. You could also do the same thing in a number of other popular vacation spots. What will it cost you? What are the advantages and disadvantages of such an arrangement?

Purchase cost—the first expenditure

The amount you pay for the condominium apartment varies according to the time of year in which the apartment use is purchased. High season in Florida begins after Christmas and lasts until Easter. Low season in Florida runs from June to September. The remainder of the year, that is from September to December and from April to June, are intermediate periods. In Sanibel the winter season begins in September and extends into June; the summer season includes the months of June, July, and August. Rental costs are lowest during summer.

The first two weeks in March are an attractive time. Your cost for a two-bedroom condominium at this time would be close to $6,000 per week, or a total of $12,000. You could finance this purchase with a mortgage along conventional lines. With a 25 percent down payment and a 30-year mortgage at 14 percent, the costs would be a $3,000 down payment and a $9,000 mortgage. The mortgage will cost $106.64 per month for the next 30 years. Almost all the payment during the first 10 years is for interest, and interest payments are deductible from income. Looked at in another way, the mortgage payment of principal and interest amounts to $639.84 per week for your two-week vacation. If you are in the 50 percent tax bracket, the cost after taxes for the first year is approximately $320 per week.

The cost of investing in the summer months would be lower. It might be possible to buy the use of an apartment for two weeks in July for a total of only $6,000 ($3,000 per week). This might not be the best time, but you would have a place for your vacation. Cost might take precedent over convenience if you schedule your vacation to correspond with your ownership period.

You should raise the following question: "How do I know if the price is fair?" Not too many interval ownership apartments are available. Finding a comparable weekly cost is difficult. One way to do this is to obtain from the seller the cost schedule for each week in the year. If you add the weekly costs, you can arrive at the total cost of the condominium compared to that of other apartments in the area. In the present case the twelve summer weeks would cost $3,000 a week, or $36,000. The remaining 40 weeks will vary in cost; the average cost will be $5,000 per week, or $200,000. Thus the estimated price of your apartment is $236,000.

The value of your apartment in Florida will vary, depending on its floor level, view, and sun exposure. An apartment on the beach or second floor with a water view and a southern exposure to the sun is most desirable for rental purposes. (Year-round residents prefer the north side, but one with a view.) People renting for a short period appear to like the security of an upper-floor apartment, and a penthouse apartment is regarded as the most desirable of all.

Costs of operation and maintenance

You must also pay operating expenses. They include the following estimated weekly expenses:

Insurance	$ 20
Utilities	20
Phone	10
Maintenance and management	50
Taxes	45
Cleaning	40
Total	$185

Expense estimates, which are based on reasonable estimates as of March 1980, will change. Taxes are deductible as an expense; they will cost only $22.50 after taxes for an investor in the 50 percent tax bracket. Thus the weekly cost (after deduction of the federal income tax) is $162.50 for operating expenses, plus $320 for mortgage costs after taxes, or $482.50. This compares favorably with rentals in the area, which range from $450 to $600 per week. These figures are illustrative only and should be verified for each case.

Condominiums that offer interval ownership to investors also offer worldwide rental exchanges as well as "time swaps" for the use of the building among the owners. Although the mechanics are available for such exchanges, it is not always possible to work out an exchange because of a lack of time. However, if investors cannot use the time period they own, they can ask the condominium management to rent their period to others. (Twenty percent of the rental will go to the management for arranging this service.) This puts the owners-investors in the position of recalculating income and depreciation in order to determine the tax liability. It is not known how the IRS would look upon this arrangement.

Probably no tax liability would be incurred because of the depreciation and operating expense deductions, which would offset the rental income and still allow a deduction against ordinary income.

The owner-investor benefits if the price of a condominium rises in the future. This is one reason why you as an investor might want to purchase an interval of time in a condominium.

Advantages and disadvantages of interval ownership

The major advantages of interval ownership are:

1. Guaranteed availability of space.
2. Tax deductibility of interest and taxes.
3. Potential capital gain as an inflation hedge.
4. Proprietor's interest and pride of ownership.
5. Flexibility of exchanging time periods.
6. Possibility of worldwide exchange program.
7. Some costs are fixed (i.e., mortgage costs).

The major weakness of interval ownership appear to be:

1. The price is usually higher.
2. Management costs are higher.
3. The investor must go to the same place every year at the same time.
4. The sense of having your own apartment with an exchange potential might not come about in reality, since your apartment is a commercial venture.
5. Your anticipated gain might not occur, and you might be able to rent an apartment in other places with enough planning without making a $6,000 to $12,000 investment. In fact, some interval ownership units require you to sell back the property to the managers at the original price, with no gain going to the investor.

Investment in land or farms

It has been said that Carl Yastremski of the Boston Red Sox bought a farm in northern Maine several years ago. But it wasn't his new home. It was an investment in land for the future—a form of protection against inflation. This piece of improved property was a working farm. Not only would it probably increase in value in the future but it could also serve as a vacation retreat and profitable hobby as well.

Many people are interested in land because it is scarce, and in fact, the value of land has increased in the last decade in spite of a deep recession in the mid-1970s.

Even though land has appreciated generally, you need to choose the right piece of land, in the right location, and at the right time. In addition, the carrying costs of ownership, including taxes and interest on loans used to purchase the property, can comprise a substantial burden. Therefore you should attempt to keep carrying costs to a minimum if you decide to purchase land.

The selection process

In selecting land as an investment, you need to follow several well-known principles. First, it is wise to buy land well ahead of the path of development. There are two dangers in applying this principle: if you buy too far ahead of development, the carrying costs will eat up your profit. Or the wrong path might be chosen, and the anticipated development might never take place. The second principle concerns the period of time over which your land is to be developed. The shorter the time, the higher the return. The third principle is for you to be patient about profits. In order to be sure that your patience will be rewarded, make certain that you can meet all payments on the property, including taxes, interest, insurance, and development costs. The fourth principle is to obtain adequate financing. Often an owner will sell property for a 29 percent down payment; the mortgage of 71 percent is then to be paid over several years. (This arrangement is in accord with current IRS rules.) Usually such an arrangement is made to stretch out the capital gain. This is because the capital gain must be paid only when the property has been sold. Each time a payment is made on the mortgage, a part of the property is "sold," and some of the gain is taken. In this way the seller doesn't pay all of the tax in a single year, and the investor has a built-in financing arrangement.

The unit of land investment is high. In large metropolitan areas large tracts of land with 200 acres close to the city sell for as high as $10,000 per acre, or $2,000,000 for the tract. Closer in, smaller tracts intended for residential development may sell for $18,000 an acre. A small tract of land well beyond the ordinary metropolitan commuting boundaries might sell for less.

Land partnerships

One of the big problems of land investment is that it requires a lot of money and the right financing. Unless you can afford to finance a purchase of from $240,000 to $2 million it might be difficult to play the game. This problem also forces smaller investors into other avenues, for example, buying developed lots and holding them for later resale. This may require a long holding period since the lots are often overpriced to begin with.

Another way to invest is to become involved in a land syndicate or partnership. Before entering into a syndicate arrangement, make certain it's legitimate, fraud-free, and economically sound. Make sure you know the other players or else don't play the game.

Don't borrow large sums of money with short-term repayment agreements. It's a great idea to borrow at low short-term rates and renew every 180 days. Yet in periods of high and rising interest rates, the cost of borrowing on a short term note will increase. Your loan might be renewed—but at a very high and unprofitable rate. Therefore, arrange your financing so that the costs and income are in balance, which means that you need to arrange long-term financing.

Real estate investment trusts (REITs)

Real estate investment trusts (REITs) are another way to participate in real estate investment. The REIT is a form of closed-end investment company. The trust sells a limited number of shares to investors, borrowing heavily to obtain maximum leverage. The funds obtained are invested in real estate ventures, including the purchase of buildings and mortgages.

Be careful in selecting a REIT. Buy more than one company in order to provide adequate diversification. The shares of REITs must be analyzed like any other security. Avoid ventures that invest only in mortgages if you want an inflation hedge.

Several REITs failed in the mid-1970s because the cost of borrowed money was higher than earnings from real estate mortgages. Ordinarily long-term mortgages pay a higher interest than short-term loans. In a period of tight money or of a credit crunch, short-term rates rise much higher than mortgage rates. In a time of high-interest rates, business turns bad and firms fail. Mortgage holders cannot make their payments and mortgage lenders fail. It isn't a cheerful thought, but these things have happened.

Investment in precious metals and art objects

Because of inflation investors are lured to assets that increase in value at a greater rate than inflation. They like the idea that precious metals are not subject to taxes like real estate, and yet they increase in value. Of course, you do have to pay capital gains taxes if you sell at a profit. We will look at a few ways in which investors may share in the real growth in value of precious metals and objects of art.

In gold we trust[1]

Why not begin with gold? Gold—that soft, lustrous, yellow metal—has served at various moments in history as the wealth of primitive people; as a material for artistic expression by the artisans of ancient Egypt; as a lure for riches by alchemists who labored to turn the base metal lead

[1] Nicholas Deak's motto. He directs Deak & Co., the largest foreign-exchange business in the Western Hemisphere.

into gold; as an early monetary system based on gold coins; and as a basis for the world's monetary systems (i.e., the gold standard). Today gold is still a valuable commodity that serves as a private store of value, a hedge against inflation, and a substitute for depreciating paper currency. It's a commodity that now can be owned by all citizens and governments of the world. The acceptability and love of gold are so universal that the more gold is produced, the more men and women everywhere seek to possess it.

How to own gold

You can own gold in the form of jewelry, coins, bullion, and shares of mining companies. The easiest way to buy gold is to buy gold jewelry including necklaces, bracelets, rings, chains, earrings, watches, medallions, and objects of art. Unfortunately this is the poorest way if you only want to share in the increased price of gold. There are two basic value components in jewelry. First, there is the purity of the gold; second, there is the artistic value of the gold object. The purity of gold is measured in karats, the purest being 24 karat gold. Pure gold is soft and is mixed with other metals to increase its strength and reduce the karat content. Therefore, 12, 14, and 18 karat jewelry is quite common. Solid gold jewelry is more valuable than gold plate or gold-filled jewelry. Since you are interested in the value of pure gold in a piece of jewelry by weight (i.e., by grams and ounces), you need to know the pure gold equivalent.

The price of gold jewelry has increased in recent years with the dramatic increase in the price of gold. It is instructive to compare the price of a gold watch or chain today with its price a few years ago. A gold necklace purchased for $125 in 1976 was worth over $460 in 1980. This growth is unlikely to continue at the same rate because the gold price will fluctuate. Yet it is gratifying to think that an asset purchased or given will have lasting value and increase its owner's net worth.

Ordinarily buying jewelry is an inefficient way to buy gold. Yet if gold continues to rise in price, the value of the jewelry will also increase.

Gold coins

One way to have your cake and eat it too is to make useful jewelry items out of gold coins and bullion. Gold coins and five-gram wafers of pure gold make excellent pendants with gold chains. Five-gram wafers also make excellent cuff links that will increase or decrease in value along with the price of gold. And, of course, such objects are attractive and interesting to wear or use. Twenty-, 10- and 5-dollar gold pieces also make attractive bracelets and pendants. But they lose their value as the coins suffer wear from exposure.

A new gold coin minted by the U.S. Treasury is an excellent way to own gold. In the past "gold bugs" could own gold only by buying coins from dealers. One of the most popular coins is the South African Krugerrand, which contains 1.00 troy ounces of gold (916.66/1000 fine). The coin itself is sold for its gold content rather than its value as a collector's item. You can also buy a two-Rand South African coin that has about one fourth the gold content of the Krugerrand.

The $20 U.S. double eagle of the Liberty and St. Gaudens types are popular as collectors' items. Each contains .9675 troy ounces of gold, which is 900/1000 fine. Circulated coins make fine pieces of jewelry. In 1974 a coin of this type sold for $90. By 1980 the same coin sold for over $600 if it was in reasonable condition. The $10 and $5 gold coins are also easy ways to own gold.

The following coins are also considered appropriate for purchasing:

Coin	Fineness	Weight oz.
Mexican 50 peso	900/1000	1.2056
Austrian 1 ducat	986.66/1000	.1109
Austrian 4 ducat	986.66/1000	.4438
Austrian 100 corona	900/1000	.9802
Hungarian 100 korona	900/1000	.9802
English old sovereign	916.66/1000	.2354

Each coin will vary in price, depending on its quality and gold content. If a purchase is contemplated, you should obtain expert advice.

Gold bars

Americans may now own gold bars, the cheapest and most direct way of owning gold. The price of this yellow metal has risen and fallen erratically since December 31, 1974. On that date American citizens were given the right to own, buy, and sell gold bullion. This was the first time since the United States went off the gold standard in 1933—41 years earlier—that this practice was legal here. From 1933 to 1975, gold could be owned by individuals only in the form of coins, jewelry, and objects of art. The federal government owned the gold, and for a time used it as a monetary base and reserve for U.S. currency.

Historically the price of gold was fixed by the U.S. government. Even under regulation the price moved from $20.66 an ounce before 1934 to $42.22 in 1974. The free market price of gold rose to $175 an ounce during this time. On 6 January 1975 the Treasury of the United States sold 2 million ounces of the country's 276-million ounce stockpile. After the initial offering the price of gold declined steadily until it reached a low point of $116.50 per ounce. It then began a dramatic rise in 1978, moving to $230 in the fourth quarter of 1978. The price finally rose to over $800 per ounce in 1980 in a speculative flurry not seen for many years. By the middle of 1980, the price of gold had declined to the $630 per ounce level. (Check your local newspaper or *Business Week* for the latest price. The National Broadcasting Corporation (NBC) gives the daily price of gold on its evening news program.)

The price movement of gold has been most erratic since it again became legal in the United States in 1975. If bought and held over the five-year period up to 1980, its price would have increased from $175 to $630. The approximate annual compound rate of growth would have been 22 percent. But the high degree of variation indicates also a high degree of risk. There was greed, madness, and panic in the market when gold went above $800 an ounce.

The return on gold tends to move opposite to the return on common stocks. That is, when common stock yields are high, the yield on gold is low. Actually this is a good quality. What it really means is that gold is a good inflation hedge. It compensates for a stockmarket that declines with inflation and high interest rates. Buying gold, an unproductive asset, is risky. Its price changes quickly, sharply, and erratically because it is susceptible to international money market speculation and the whims of world markets. But it is something of a hedge against the behavior of stock price movements.

Swiss banks sell gold bars in denominations of from 5 grams to 10 ounces. U.S. dealers also sell gold bars. One of the best-known of them, the Deak-Perera Group, sells its own gold bars in 1.5 and 10 ounce sizes, 9999/1000 fine. Each bar is numbered and sealed in a clear plastic package. The Deak-Perera Group offers a repurchase agreement. The statement on the back of each package reads:

> Should the Deak-Perera Group repurchase this bar, we will do so at the prevailing spot price of gold. We will charge the customer no assaying or refining costs provided that the packaging or the security paper within is not disturbed, altered or damaged in anyway. January 1975 [Signed] N. L. Deak.

This statement provides Deak's customers with a simple, inexpensive, and safe way of buying gold bars.

Gold-mining shares

Gold-mining shares are another way of participating in the potential profit of owning gold. The process is indirect, and the price of gold shares does not always follow the price of gold. The unfortunate part about buying shares in mining companies is that it is not easy to translate a rise in gold price into a dollar of common stock profits. When you buy a share, you are buying profits and not so many ounces of gold.

Silver as an investment

Silver has been an excellent inflation hedge over the years. People owning silver coins, sterling silver flatware, tea services, or sterling silver jewelry have been protected from inflation. At the same time they have enjoyed the beauty and use of silver items during their period of ownership. You can buy silver and share in its price increase in much the same way that you can invest in gold. In order to give you some idea about the inflation in silver, its price increased from $1.79 per ounce in 1969 to $5.40 per ounce in 1978. In 1979 the price increased dramatically to over $40 per ounce. But by the middle of 1980, the price had moved down to the $15 to $20 per ounce range.

It is almost impossible to keep up with price changes for silver objects. But a few examples can give you a notion of what has been happening over the past 30 years. One four-place International Sterling pattern cost $34 a setting in 1950. In 1980 the same pattern sold for $500. A sterling tea service purchased for $600 in 1960 now costs $4,000. And a U.S. silver dollar costing $1 in 1950 now sells for $15 or higher, just on the basis of its silver content.

Owning sterling silver will increase a family's net worth and provide daily use (if the family is not afraid to use it). This is certainly an excellent combination. It is interesting to examine the attitude of colonial families toward silverware. A wealthy family in colonial Deerfield, Massachusetts, might own several silver mugs—one perhaps made by Paul Revere, which has now become priceless. A poor family might have only one silver mug or dish, but this object represented a major part of the family assets. Therefore, you need not buy a 12-place setting of silver to benefit. You can begin your collection with the purchase of just one spoon.

Coin and stamp collecting

Coin collecting can be an interesting, educational, and profitable way of improving your net worth. The dean of a leading school of business once told why he collected coins and stamps. He said he knew of no other hobby where he could always keep the money he spent.

It is impossible to indicate how all coins have changed in price. Popular coins minted in 1980 have only their monetary value. Old coins like Eisenhower dollars have a high silver content; they are valuable both as silver and collector's items. Early in 1980 silver dimes sold for over $1.50 each, quarters for $3.75, halves for $7.50, and Kennedy halves (1965–69) for $2.50 each.

Individual collector items sell for higher prices. A 1909 SVDB penny sold for $45 in 1969 and for $130 in 1978. A 1955 Doubled Die penny sold for $100 in 1969 and for $220 in 1978. Certainly these would have been profitable investments.

Stamps have had a similar increase in value. A 1925 horse American sold for $2.25 in 1969 and for $4.25 in 1978. Even when a dollar was a dollar in 1969, most of us could have afforded to pay $2.25 for a stamp.

A higher-priced stamp is the 1892 $5 Black Columbian. It sold for $235 in 1969 and for $650 in 1978. This stamp would also have been a good investment. However, you would have to study this subject area carefully before making an investment commitment. It would be wise to limit the amount of money invested in this area, since stamps tend to be risky investments.

"Diamonds are a girl's (and a boy's) best friend"

Most people like diamonds. They're beautiful and have been a good inflation hedge in the past. Diamonds purchased through a retail jeweler might not have the best investment potential since the markup on diamonds (more than 100 percent) is high. Yet a top-quality gem will increase in value over a 10-year period.

If you want to invest in diamonds, the best way would be to buy them at wholesale. This can be done in the gem markets of New York, London, and Amsterdam. The only problem with diamonds is that the unit of investment is high. A one-half karat diamond might range in price from $500 to $2,000, and a one karat might range from $5,000 to $10,000 and up, depending on quality. As a general rule, the best stones become the most profitable investment over time. Since you might only buy one diamond in a lifetime, you should buy the biggest, highest quality stone you can find at the lowest possible price. And buying a diamond engagement ring wholesale shouldn't be a sin. In the long run this type of ring will bring much satisfaction as well as monetary value.

Paintings and antiques

Almost anything that is scarce, attractive, and useful in the art and antique world has increased in value. Two examples will suffice to indicate the monetary gain of these assets. Andrew Wyeth was a successful and well-known artist. One of his paintings sold for $5,500 in 1969. The same painting brought in $16,000 in 1978. The amount of investment in paintings can be high, but the gains can be substantial.

The area of antique furniture is boundless and requires a great deal of study. Yet money can be made in utilitarian objects that you can use every day. An antique O.G. clock, for example, could have been purchased for $20 in 1955. Today these clocks range in price from $175 to $350. They keep good time (you have to wind them every eight days) and look attractive. Not a bad way to keep track of time. This seems to be the kind of investment that appeals to most people.

Return and risk of investment in real assets

Just what would you expect to earn from investments in real assets such as coins, stamps, and precious metals? That is, what return and degree of risk would you accept in buying such assets? In an attempt to estimate their historic return and risk, a study was untertaken to provide a partial answer to the question. Table 15–10 provides estimated yields

Table 15-10
Return and risk of selected real assets,
1969-1978*

	Return†	Risk‡
Gold	21%	28%
VDB penny	13	11
Silver	13	30
$5 Black Columbian stamp	12	9
Paintings	10	14
Diamonds	10	14
Double Die penny	9	5
Horse American stamp	7	7
Standard & Poor's	6	14

* Based on a graduate study by Barton Raplan, George Washington University, June 5, 1979.

† Rounded to significant whole number. The return is the 10-year annual average return.

‡ This is the variation of the annual return around the average.

for selected real assets from 1969 through 1978. These yields are selected and do not represent all real assets.

The yield in Table 15-10 represents the 10-year average return and risk. During that period gold, the VDB penny, silver, paintings, and diamonds were more profitable than the stockmarket, which had the same amount of risk or perhaps a greater amount.

The $5 Black Columbian, the Double Die Penny, and the Norse stamp were more profitable than Standard & Poor's Index and less risky. Gold and diamonds were found to have a small negative correlation to Standard & Poor's 500 Index, which means that some gold and diamonds would balance the return from common stock and tend to reduce the risk. In other words it isn't a bad idea to invest in a combination of real assets and common stock.

Summary

Investment in real assets is one way you can protect your purchasing power against the ravages of inflation. Real estate investment is one of the best forms of real assets investment.

The most important consideration in selecting investment property is its location. Once a satisfactory location is identified, you should concentrate on finding a house at a fair price. The most effective way to do this is to arm yourself with a list of comparable sales in the neighborhood you are considering. When you locate a possible house, you will then have to carefully analyze its investment merits. This requires you to weigh carefully the required down payment, closing costs, and annual operating and maintenance costs. These costs have to be compared to the annual rental income and appreciation in the value of the property. The resulting comparison will tell you whether or not the house is a good investment.

You may also invest in real estate in other ways. You may want to consider buying a vacation home. You can use the home for a few weeks each year as a vacation retreat. You can then rent the home when you are not using it. The rental income will offset part of your cost of owning the property. You will be providing yourself with a nice annual vacation at a reasonable cost. And you will also be contributing to the growth of your net worth.

Interval ownership of a condominium property also provides a way to buy a part interest in vacation property. There are a number of advantages and disadvantage to interval ownership. You have to examine these arrangements closely.

You can also participate in real estate investment by buying shares in real estate investment trusts (REITs). These companies invest money in real estate on behalf of their stockholders. In this sense a REIT is much like a mutual fund.

As with any investment, there are real risks associated with real estate ownership. Your estimates could be wrong, there could be a housing recession, or your property could remain vacant. Although real estate offers the possibility of high rewards, these risks have to be considered.

There are a number of other possible investments in real assets. Many people invest in precious metals, coins, stamps, objects of art, antiques, and other forms of collectibles. You can earn good returns from these types of investments. But you must also be aware of the risks involved.

PART 6

Planning for retirement and estate transfer

16

Financial planning for retirement

- Retirement planning principles
- Social Security and financial planning for retirement
- A private pension as part of your retirement program
- Employee Retirement Income Security Act (ERISA)
- What happens to retirement income when the breadwinner dies?
- Keogh Plans and Individual Retirement Accounts
- Summary

Planning for financial security at all ages has been emphasized throughout the book. The assumption has been made that financial independence at any age is a worthwhile goal, but the earlier the better. Financial independence is not a function of earning the highest income but of doing the best you can with your income, no matter what the level. Therefore it is as possible for a person earning an income of $10,000 a year to achieve financial independence as for a person earning $40,000 per year. Of course, the problem is simple: as your income increases, so do your tastes and expenses. Whatever your income level, careful planning is required to live within that income. One way of putting this principle is: "Earn a little, spend a little less." It is always startling to learn of people who earned millions ending up penniless, whereas people with modest incomes who were frugal were able to achieve financial independence.

Retirement planning principles

The principles to follow in planning for retirement are simple to state but difficult to follow. The following seven principles provide a general guide to retirement planning:

1. Start financial planning for retirement early.
2. Learn to estimate and plan for your income needs.
3. Learn to estimate and plan for your liquidity needs.
4. Plan to fill in the deficit between working income and retirement income. This is the retirement income deficit (RID).
5. Consider the inflation factor in your planning.
6. Plan for your emotional and physical needs as well as for your financial needs.
7. Discipline your spending habits to provide a fund for future retirement income.

Life cycle of earnings

Figure 16–1 depicts a typical income pattern over a life cycle of an individual who receives a college education and then goes on to graduate school. After graduate school it is assumed that the person worked from the age of 26 until the typical retirement year, age 65. The successful worker starts out after graduate school with an income above $15,000 a year. Over the years the income gradually increases to $40,000 a year. In some cases income might peak at age 50, and then remain constant until age 65. It is assumed that the income of the individual increases every year until his or her retirement.

The negative income pattern exists in the early years, particularly the education years when annual educational expenditures range from $5,000 to $10,000. The negative income shows that there are costs of supporting children from the time of their birth until they are able to stand on their

Figure 16-1
Income over a life cycle

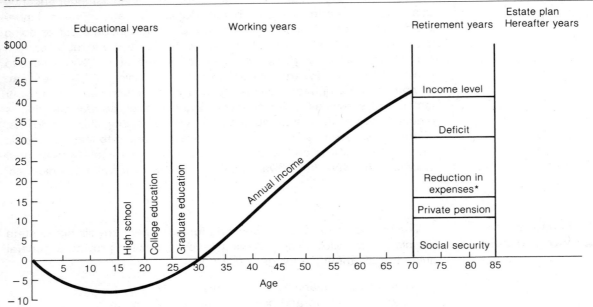

* Includes reductions of taxes, pension contributions, and a reduction in living expenses.

own and earn a living wage. Because of the high cost of education and the time required to obtain a marketable skill, the period of the education years (when a person is trained and educated to make a contribution to society) has been extended. When a career-motivated person begins working, income increases. The benefits of living in a highly complex industrial society provide tremendous excitement. However, you must be realistic about the future because you must plan emotionally and financially for your retirement years. You must plan for the later years when you may fulfill your greatest dreams of being free from the responsibility of daily employment. You will then be able to branch out into new arenas and pursue new hobbies and interests. Your retirement years should be golden years—"golden" in the sense that you are physically able to enjoy them and at the same time have enough money to provide variety and joy.

Maintaining a physically active life-style

A highly important consideration for your retirement years is planning your physical activities. You should plan an active rather than a sedentary life-style. It has been demonstrated that people over 55 enjoy life more if they:

1. Maintain a sensible weight.
2. Maintain a physically active schedule of home and yard work.
3. Maintain a regular physical fitness program centered around sports.
4. Maintain a life-style of moderation in the use of tobacco and liquor.
5. Maintain an active sex life.
6. Maintain and extend an active religious life.
7. Maintain and stimulate interest in others and continue to be of service to others.

The myth that old age brings only the rocking chair has been disproven over and over again.

Prepare for the retirement income deficit (RID)

Unless you are independently wealthy, your income will decline in your retirement years. The worker in Figure 16–1 experiences an income drop from $40,000 to $20,000 in the retirement years. Income will continue to come in from Social Security pension payments. However, there will also be a reduction in expenses. Income taxes are reduced, and you need not deduct for pension contributions. In addition, your cost of not working is less than that of working. Expenses for such things as parking, transportation, and food away from home will cease.

On the other hand, some costs will increase, including greater expenditures for health and travel. Therefore, you must estimate your retirement income deficit (RID) and plan for it.

As a first step, you should examine your savings position. You need to determine just how much income you will have in your retirement years, what will happen to your expenses, and what must be done to improve or provide extra income when it is needed. It is very important for you to do this analysis early in your life. In this way you'll have sufficient time to build up a fund of money in various ways to provide for the retirement income deficit. You must consider when and where you will retire, and how much income you will have when you retire. Unlike most people, you should begin your planning when you begin your first job. Thus when Johnny or Mary start out on their first job, they can look forward to the usual Social Security benefits as part of their retirement program. They will see to it that they have a pension plan that will provide income after retirement. And they will develop a savings program in addition to these formal pension programs that will allow them to have a sufficient sum of money in their retirement years to make up for RID and provide financial independence.

Should you retire?

Not all people want to retire. A former dean of a major business school in the United States felt that retirement was a form of punishment created by humanity for itself. He did not like inactivity, and he did not like the lack of involvement in the day-to-day activities of running a school. He needed something more than just financial security. He needed emotional security—the feeling that what he was doing was appreciated and worthwhile. For people like him, it is perfectly logical not to retire. If they cannot continue in their present job, they should find a new one or become involved in other activities. There is no reason why people cannot continue employment until age 75 or 85. They may retire from their jobs, and then look about to find satisfying activities that require their skills and allow them to make a contribution to society. There is no reason why a person aged 65, 70, 75, 80, or 85 cannot make a contribution to society. Take for example a friend of ours who was a successful lawyer, judge, and community leader. After his formal retirement he continued to maintain his law practice and involvement with the financial and educational community of his city. Thus he was able to go on living a very active and satisfying life. He did not report every day to an office. But he certainly was able to enjoy active semiretirement years when over 80 years of age.

Planning as a joint effort of both spouses

Instead of viewing retirement as a transition from when you are doing something to when you are doing nothing, you should look upon it as a time when you change your activities. It's a time when you have more freedom to do things that you never had time to do when you were fully employed. It might be as simple as playing more golf. It might be more complex in that you may want to become involved in the arts and in community and cultural activities of all types. Or you may just wish to become creative in your own way without the pressures of day-to-day activity. Certainly as you plan for financial retirement, you must not ignore the fact that you have to plan your activities.

If you are married, these activities must be worked out for both husband and wife. Together they must decide not only where they are going to live but what they are going to do in their retirement years. Are they interested in travel, work, or simply recreational activities? These proposals have to be decided hand in hand with your financial planning for retirement.

Social Security and financial planning for retirement

The Social Security system has grown substantially over the years. It was formally introduced through the Social Security Act of 1935. This act has been amended many times over the years to meet the changing needs of our society. In fact, it seems as if the benefits and the contents of the act are amended almost annually to provide benefits for workers. Certainly over the years the benefits have risen, along with the cost of the Social Security system to workers and to employers. Because the income level established originally has been eroded by inflation, the Congress of the United States from time to time has attempted to raise Social Security benefits to compensate for inflation. Certainly inflation—the rising trend of prices in the United States and the world economy—must be one of the first and foremost thoughts of your financial planning. As you look forward to Social Security planning, you must anticipate changes in Social Security that will adjust for inflation. At the same time your planning should allow you to add to these benefits if they will not be adequate to meet your retirement needs. Understanding the Social Security system will allow you to estimate RID.

Social Security as a partial retirement income

The Social Security system was not meant to be a complete retirement program. It was always and still is only a supplemental contribution to your income when you are no longer gainfully employed. Social Security income will provide only a part of your retirement income and only a fraction of the income you earn just before retiring. You must also provide for other forms of income in addition to Social Security in retirement so that you will be able to live a comfortable life.

Breadth and depth of the Social Security system

The Social Security Administration, in its various offices throughout the country, has a series of pamphlets explaining the Social Security system in detail. Generally speaking, the pamphlets are clearly written and understandable and provide a basis for estimating what your Social Security income will be if you are covered by the system. One impression must be cleared up about Social Security. You are not buying into an annuity program when you participate in it. In fact, the Social Security system, even though it covers 9 out of 10 workers in the United States, must be looked upon as a way of taxing people in the higher income groups to provide benefits for people in the lower income groups. In 1979 Social Security deductions from workers and employees in the United States was based on an annual income up to $22,900. Out of that $22,900, a person would pay $1,403.17 on the basis of a Social Security tax rate of 6.13 percent. If a person made the minimum contribution to the Social Security system from its inception in 1937, he or she would have contributed a total of $11,302.97 through the end of 1979. The person would then be ready for retirement. The person's average annual income over that period would have been $6,295. A male worker retiring under the Social Security system would receive approximately $446 a month income. If we assume that his wife was 62, she would receive approximately $167, for a total of $613 a month, or $7,356 a year. This income is greater by almost 15 percent than the average income the couple earned over their lifetime of earnings. In a sense they have a very attractive deal, except that their retirement income of $7,356 is only

33 percent roughly of the maximum income of $22,900 they earned in 1979. The Social Security income they receive is substantially below what they are currently earning, even though it is dramatically above their average earnings for the period they have worked.

The tendency today is for the minimum income covered by Social Security to increase every year. As Table 16–1 shows, the Social Security income base subject to Social Security taxes was $25,900 in 1980. In 1981 it was increased to $29,700. The obvious implication is that Social Security income will increase in 1982 and beyond to a higher and higher level.

There has been some speculation recently that Social Security payments or Social Security income might be reduced. Thus, if this should happen, payments to the Social Security system might be reduced. But this has not happened. Essentially the problem that the Social Security system is facing is that it does not have an adequate amount of revenue to satisfy the claims of the people who have retired in the past. There is a danger that the Social Security system might collapse unless large amounts of money are collected to provide these benefits. The Congress will not allow the system to collapse, and thus it must increase the taxes necessary to pay for it.

Nearly one out of every seven persons in the United States receives a monthly Social Security check. There are more than 24 million people over 65 who have health insurance under Medicare, which is a part of the Social Security system. There are about 3 million disabled people under 65 who also have Medicare. To pay these benefits, there is a tendency to increase the income base subject to the tax. People in upper-income brackets are unlikely ever to get back anywhere near the amount of contributions they put into the Social Security system. In fact, it would

Table 16–1
Social Security tax rate and maximum wages taxable, 1980–1990

Year	Employer and employee will each pay	On earnings up to
1980	6.13%	$25,900
1981	6.65%	$29,700
1982	6.70%	*
1983	6.70%	*
1984	6.70%	*
1985	7.05%	*
1986	7.15%	*
1987	7.15%	*
1988	7.15%	*
1989	7.15%	*
1990	7.65%	*

*The applicable wage base will increase in the future to average wage level increases.
SOURCE   U.S. Department of Health, Education, and Welfare, Social Security Administration.

be to the advantage of people in higher income brackets not to participate in the Social Security system. However, under current law most people are required to belong to the system.

The benefits of the Social Security system are being indexed. For example, benefits were increased 9.9 percent along with other federal retirement programs in 1979. This increase of almost 10 percent is an inflationary factor designed to allow older people living on a fixed income to survive in an economy severely eroded by inflation. But, in fact, the cost-of-living index in the Social Security system makes the economy somewhat more inflationary.

It is important for you to know how you can participate in the Social Security system, when you will be eligible for benefits, and the amount and timing of those benefits. Obviously the dollar amount of these benefits will change over time. Generally speaking, however, the types of benefits available will change much more slowly.

Who belongs to Social Security?

Most people in the United States are covered by Social Security. Almost all employed people are required by law to belong to the system. Nearly all self-employed people also must belong to the system. If you don't know whether your work is covered by Social Security, all you have to do is ask your local Social Security office to find out if you are indeed part of the system.

Most people learn whether they are covered by Social Security when they apply for a job. The employer usually asks for a Social Security number before a person can be hired. If you need a Social Security card, you can call your local Social Security office or pick up a form at the post office.

Husbands and wives who both work are covered by the Social Security system. Both are required to join and pay Social Security taxes, although they cannot both receive primary retirement benefits under Social Security. If you are a domestic employee in a private household, your wages are covered by Social Security. If someone hires you to do farm work, including domestic work on a farm, you are subject to Social Security. If you receive at least $150 in cash from an employer during a year, or if you are employed on 20 or more days during a year, you are subject to Social Security coverage. Work done by a child under 21 for a parent, by a husband for his wife, or by a wife for her husband is not covered by the Social Security law. However, if work is done by a parent for a son or daughter in connection with a son or daughter's business, then this employment is covered.

Quarters of coverage needed

You may elect to receive Social Security retirement benefits at age 62 or 65. In order to receive these benefits, you must have what is known as a minimum of calendar quarters in which you have worked and contributed to the Social Security system. These are referred to as *quarters of coverage.* Of course, you cannot have more than four quarters of coverage in any one year. In 1979 you would have earned one quarter of coverage for each $260 of covered annual earnings. The amount of earnings subject to Social Security payments will increase automatically each year to keep pace with increases and levels of average wages.

Generally speaking, to be fully covered for Social Security retirement benefits you need 40 quarters of coverage. If you became 65 in 1971, you needed 20 quarters of coverage if you were a man. You needed 17 quarters if you were a woman. As noted in Chapters 9 and 10, you should use your Social Security center to obtain information about the system. Medicare benefits, survivor benefits, and disability benefits are all a part of the system. Disability and survivorship benefits are an important part of the Social Security system that we discussed in Chapter 10.

If you are self-employed, the amount of your contribution is somewhat different from that of employees. A self-employed person is both employer and employee. The total Social Security contribution for a self-employed person is higher than the payment required of an employee of other kinds of organizations. However, the payment is not as high as the total employer and employee contribution required for Social Security system members who are not self-employed. In recent years a self-employed person's contribution has been approximately 11 percent. Therefore people who are self-employed may expect to pay more to be fully insured.

Income from Social Security

What are you going to receive from your Social Security retirement income? Many people think that if they always earned the maximum amount covered by Social Security, they will get the highest benefits shown on the basic chart, but this really isn't so. Although retirement benefits as high as $534.70 a month are shown in Table 16–2, payments this high can't be made to a worker retiring at 65 today. The maximum retirement benefit generally payable to a worker who was to become 65 in 1979 was $503.40 a month, based on an average yearly earning of $8,730. The reason the average could be no higher in 1979 is that the maximum covered earnings were lower in the past. Those years of lower limits must be counted in with the higher ones, the recent years, to figure the average covered yearly earnings. This average determines the amount of your check.

Table 16–2 indicates what a person might have expected to receive from Social Security at various levels of income for people retiring before 1979 or reaching age 62 before 1979.

Asking for your money

To collect Social Security retirement benefits, you have to file a claim with your local Social Security office. Paying benefits is not an automatic

**Table 16–2
Examples of monthly Social Security
retirement payments***

	Average yearly earnings after 1950 covered by Social Security						
Benefits can be paid to a:	$923 or less	$3,000	$4,000	$5,000	$6,000	$8,000	$10,000†
Retired worker at 65	121.80	251.80	296.20	343.50	388.20	482.60	534.70
Retired worker at 62	97.50	201.50	237.00	274.80	310.60	386.10	427.80
Wife or husband at 65	60.90	125.90	148.10	171.80	194.10	241.30	267.40
Wife or husband at 62	45.70	94.50	111.10	128.90	145.60	181.00	200.60
Wife under 65 and one child in her care	61.00	133.20	210.00	290.40	324.00	362.00	401.00
Maximum family payment	182.70	384.90	506.20	633.80	712.10	844.50	935.70

*For workers who reach 62 before 1979.

† Maximum earnings covered by Social Security were lower in past years and must be included in figuring your average earnings. This average determines your payment amount. Because of this, the amount shown in the last column generally won't be payable until future years. The maximum retirement benefit generally payable to a worker who is 65 in 1979 is $503.40.

SOURCE   Department of Health, Education, and Welfare Social Security Administration.

action on the part of the government or the Social Security Administration. You must activate the system. This means that you should have a Social Security card and an accurate record of your earnings. Then you must notify the Social Security office two or three months before you intend to retire. You can apply in person or by telephone. Once you have been interviewed by telephone, the rest of the procedure can be done by mail.

In order to activate your Social Security retirement benefits you need: (1) a Social Security card or a record of your Social Security number; (2) proof of the date of birth, i.e., a birth or baptismal certificate; and (3) your latest W-2 wage and tax statement form. If you are self-employed, you will need a copy of your latest self-employment tax return. You must provide this information because the most recent reports on you may not yet be in the Social Security records. If your husband or wife is also going to apply for benefits, he or she will need the same documents. It would also be a good idea to have your marriage certificate available, although this document is not usually required.

What will you receive?   The checks you receive from Social Security may vary from $182.70 to approximately $935.70, if you are 65 and supporting a family. (See Table 16–2.) If you are 62, the range may be from $97.50 to $427.80 for an individual. Benefit rates will change in the future, and the best thing is to apply to your Social Security office to find out about your benefits. You must apply two or three months before retirement so that payments can start the month of your retirement. Otherwise checks won't start until six to eight weeks after the application with all its supporting evidence has been filed.

**Social Security
benefits for workers**

What happens if you continue to work after retiring? Under the Social Security system you can earn up to $4,500 a year without a reduction in your retirement benefits. This sum of $4,500 does not include any other pension plan you might have. If your income from work exceeds $4,500, then for each $2 of earnings above the exempt amount you will have a reduction of $1 of benefits. If you earn $900 beyond the $4,500 of exempt income, for example, you will lose $450 of Social Security benefits. Therefore you should be very careful about the type of work you do and how much you earn after you begin receiving Social Security payments.

For more information on the topic mentioned above, request a pamphlet entitled "If You Work After You Retire." You can obtain a copy from any Social Security office. One question answered in the pamphlet is "What is an employed person?" This seems a straightforward question, yet there are different rules defining whether or not you are employed. In general, if you work more than 45 hours a month in a business, you are considered employed. Even though you work fewer than 45 hours, the work may be considered "substantial" if you are involved in the management of a sizeable business or a highly skilled occupation. Thus the definition *substantial* determines whether or not you are working. If you work fewer than 15 hours a month, your services are never considered substantial, regardless of the size of the business or the value of its products or service.

Sources of funds not included under income and not counted against Social Security earnings are the following: (1) investment income in the form of dividends from stock you own, unless you are a dealer in securities; (2) income from Social Security benefits, pensions, other retirement pay, or Veterans Administration benefits; (3) interest from savings accounts: (4) income from annuities; (5) gains from the sale of capital assets; (6) gifts or inheritances; (7) rental income from real estate property; (8) royalties received in or after the year you become 65 from patents or copyrights obtained before that year; and (9) if you are a retired partner, retirement payments paid from the partnership don't count if the retirement payments are to continue.

If the partnership provides for payment to all the partners or to a class or classes of them; if your share of the partnership capital was paid to you in full before the end of the partnership taxable year; if there is no obligation from the partnership to you except to make retirement payments; and if you have income from a limited partnership, then you need not consider this payment as earned income. Starting in 1978, such a payment is considered investment income rather than self-employment income. It does not affect your Social Security income.

In addition to the foregoing, other types of payments do not count as wages that will reduce your Social Security benefits. These include: (1) sick pay under a plan or system; (2) payments from certain trust funds; (3) payments from certain annuity plans; (4) sick pay received for more than six months after the employee last worked; (5) moving expenses; (6) travel expenses; and (7) pay for jury duty. You must pay income taxes on these amounts, but your Social Security benefits will not be reduced because of them.

Activities that do not reduce Social Security income

As you plan for retirement and incorporate Social Security payments into your program, you must estimate the amount of income you will receive in your retirement years from Social Security. More important, you should emphasize other activities that are not considered to be employment activities. In this way you can build your estate in ways that maximize nonworking income and minimize working income. In other words, before retiring, you really need to be an entrepreneur with assets, royalties, partnership income, or investment income that will add to your income but not reduce your Social Security benefits. Otherwise you may not benefit fully from the Social Security system. Keep in mind the fact that you can participate in another retirement system, a private pension plan, or a Keogh Plan that will supplement the Social Security system. In fact, you should try to build up a private pension program to supplement Social Security income so that you will be able to live comfortably during your retirement years.

A private pension as part of your retirement program

It is apparent that Social Security benefits will not provide you with a sufficient amount of money to retire and still receive the same income you earned while gainfully employed. This is true unless you expect to have a substantial amount of royalty income, income from investments, or some other income that will provide you with income independent of employment. In addition, a private pension plan should be an important source of income in your retirement program. In fact, for many people payments from a private pension program will be more important than Social Security payments.

A typical pension plan

It is impossible for us to look at all the retirement programs available in the United States. But we can describe a few general characteristics of private pension plans.

The highlights of a pension plan should usually include the following features: (1) a monthly income at retirement for a person's life and/or the life of the spouse; (2) benefits based on the amount of annual income; (3) benefits based on the length of service for the organization paying the pension; (4) an assumption as to the normal retirement age; (5) a provision that the person might retire at an earlier age for a lesser amount of money, say, at age 55 or between 55 and 65; (6) survivorship options, that is, if the principal employee dies and leaves a survivor, the surviving person will receive benefits as long as he or she lives; (7) a provision to refund your previous contributions if your employment is terminated; and (8) some statement to the effect that you are vested in the retirement fund after 10 years of continuous service. Vesting means that the fund cannot be diminished and will provide retirement benefits at age 55, even though the pension holder no longer works for the organization. Let's examine the provisions in a representative plan.

Eligibility for a private pension

Usually a retirement income pension program (RIPP) contains the following conditions of eligibility:

Minimum service Most private pension plans require a minimum amount of service. As a rule, to participate you need to have one full year of continuous service. If you are at least age 25 and no older than 60 or 61 at the time you are hired, you must be allowed to join. Some plans put restrictions on who may become a member. In some cases membership in the plan is automatic. You need not do anything to join the system except complete one full year of continuous service.

Paying for the pension There are many ways of paying for pensions. In some cases, where the total cost is borne by the company, the plan is called noncontributory. In the case of contributory plans, employees contribute part of the money and the employer another part. Under a fully contributory plan, employees contribute all of the money.

Once each year an independent firm of pension consultants analyzes the plan to determine the size of contribution required to meet the retirement needs of all the employees. This is done to insure that the necessary funds will be available in the pension fund when the individual employees retire. The pension consultants must observe guidelines and requirements established by the Employee Retirement Income Security Act (ERISA), which has made a dramatic and positive contribution to the way in which pension funds are invested and managed.

Continuous service After an employee's 22d birthday the term *continuous service* must be defined. Obviously certain absences from duty are approved by the company. An authorized leave of absence would be part of continuous employment. Periods of absence after termination of employment are included if the employee is rehired within 12 months. If you leave the company and are rehired more than 12 months later, this would be regarded as an interruption of your continuous service. If under a previous program, there was an opportunity to contribute to a retirement plan and you made no contribution, this period of service would not be counted toward the required continuous service.

A base period In a pension program a base period for calculating the amount of benefits to be received is quite common. In cases where employee and employer make the same contribution, some way must be found to establish a basis for the pension. If the employer pays the entire amount (a noncontributory plan), there must be some way to calculate how much income will be received at the normal retirement age of 65.

A typical way to calculate benefits to be received is based on the final five-year average earnings of the employee. This concept is based on an assumption that earnings for the last five years of employment will be the highest. The base period is calculated only on regular earnings. It usually does not include extra earnings for overtime or any bonuses that might be paid. Typically, with retirement at age 65, the average annual earnings are determined by the last five consecutive years of employment just before retirement, that is, service from age 60 to 65. If a person worked less than five years, the average will be based on the amount of earnings during the years worked. If there was a leave of absence during the period, then the average income will be calculated on the basis of total earnings. Leaves of absence will be eliminated from this calculation.

Normal retirement Retirement is usually fixed as the first day of the month after the employee's 65th birthday. If the employee was born on the first day of the month, the birthday and retirement would coincide and a normal retirement pension would begin. At any time after reaching age 55, an early retirement may be elected, usually at a reduced payment. Also, retirement at age 55 might take place with payments starting at age 65. This allows employees some flexibility in changing jobs and going in a new direction.

Marriage and retirement benefits If an employee is unmarried when the pension program begins, a life benefit payment will be received for the employee's life only; no benefits will be paid to any survivor. This is referred to as the *life only* benefit. However, if the employee is married when the pension payments begin, a somewhat smaller monthly pension may be elected for as long as the employee lives. Some fraction of this pension (often one half) will be paid to the employee's surviving spouse for the rest of his or her life. This type of payment, which provides protection for the spouse, is sometimes referred to as a *survivor benefit.* If the amount of the survivor benefit is 50 percent, it is called a *50 percent survivor benefit.*

These are the normal terms for the payment of retirement benefits. In most companies you must notify the personnel department within 90 days prior to your retirement. They will advise you about the options available, and you may elect the form of payment you wish.

Instead of selecting the single-payment plan or the 50 percent survivor benefit, you may decide on a plan known as the *surviving annuitant benefit plan*. This is somewhat different from the program where the surviving spouse receives 50 percent of the employee's pension. Under this program you might designate any amount of the survivor benefit to another beneficiary.

The person retiring can receive the maximum income by accepting a retirement annuity on the basis of his or her life alone. If he or she takes the option where 50 percent goes to the surviving spouse, then the amount received while both live is smaller than if the annuity is paid out over the life of the retired person. An option where the annuity is paid over the lives of both husband and wife will be even less. Yet in principle this option seems to be the option to use since it guarantees the same level of income for both parties even though it might be a lower amount.

Sometimes an option is used where the annuity will be paid for a certain period of time, say, for 10 years. In this plan the employee selects a payment for the life of the husband and wife with 10 years certain. The amount paid is less than under a joint annuity. If, however, both husband and wife died within five years, the estate or the heirs would receive the income for the remaining five years.

The size of your retirement income Under any retirement program the question always asked is "How much will be paid in retirement income?" The amount paid is a function of how much income was earned in the last five years of employment and the length of employment. Under the final five-year formula plan, the pension is based on the five-year average earnings in the final five years of employment. Calculations of benefits vary, but one typical calculation is as follows: your pension payment is equal to 1 percent of your final five-year average earnings up to $4,200, plus 2 percent of your final five-year average earnings in excess of $4,200 multiplied by your years of credited service up to a maximum of 25 years. This calculation encourages workers in two ways. First, they are encouraged to stay with a company as long as possible, at least for 25 years. Second, they are encouraged to earn as much as they possibly can with the company. Now let's assume that a person stays with a company for 25 years and averages $30,000 in income over the last five years' employment. Such person would receive approximately $13,950 in retirement income.

If the retired person should die, then both the Social Security benefits and benefits under the private pension plan to the surviving spouse decline. Under a typical private plan, the amount paid to the spouse will decline to 50 percent of the original benefit. The amount of the typical private pension payment does not increase after retirement. As a rule, a person retiring at age 65 will earn about one half the income he or she earned prior to retirement. When you consider that income taxes on the income received will be lower than what was paid on preretirement income, the combination of a private pension plan and Social Security benefits provides a fairly good income in retirement. When you assume that a person's living expenses most likely decline, then the combination of a private pension plan and Social Security income allows a husband and wife to live in dignity and with a fair income. If it were not for inflation, they could live a good and comfortable life in retirement. Since inflation does exist other sources of income must be found. The two most common sources are part time employment and investment income.

Death benefits before retirement and after. In some private pension plans, death benefits are paid when the retired individual dies after retirement. However, this benefit is relatively rare, and ordinarily no death benefits are paid as part of pension plans established by companies. Death benefits are provided through life insurance offered to the employee by the company, usually at little or no extra cost. Let's assume that an insured person dies between the ages of 55 and 65 and leaves a spouse (a widow or widower) to whom the employee was married a minimum amount of time (at least one year). Then the surviving spouse will be entitled to some monthly benefits, starting the first day of the month after the death of the insured and continuing for the rest of his or her life.

In a contributory plan the employee receives some guarantee of getting back his or her contributions. If the company has contributed the total amount of contributions, no lump sum benefit need be paid to the estate of an employee who dies without leaving a surviving spouse. However, if the employee has made contributions to the pension plan, the difference between what was paid out and the amount remaining in the fund will go to the estate of the deceased.

A few bits of information about retirement

Under the usual retirement plan a beneficiary must be named in the pension program. The pension plan cannot be assigned, garnisheed, or attached by the courts. It belongs to the employee alone and cannot be used for any other purpose.

There are other methods of establishing retirement benefits. One pension program follows that in existence in the state of Ohio. In programs that follow the Ohio format, retirement income is determined by the employee's length of service and highest five-year average annual salary. The employee receives 1½ percent times the five-year annual average salary times the number of years worked. Thus a person who is 62 or older, has worked 25 years, and has earned an average annual salary of $30,000, will receive 1.5 percent $\times$ 30,000 $\times$ 25 or $11,250 per year. The maximum amount paid is limited to 80 percent of the average annual salary of $30,000 ($24,000). Ordinarily the pension is vested after 10 years of service. It is also possible to retire before age 62 if the employee has achieved 25 or 30 years of employment.

The TIAA–CREF retirement program is a good example of a comprehensive retirement plan. TIAA–CREF was established to provide a retirement program for college and university teachers and administrators and for certain other nonprofit organization employees. TIAA stands for Teachers Insurance and Annuity Association. It represents pension money invested in fixed-income securities to establish a fund providing retirement income. CREF, which stands for College Retirement Equities Fund, provides for investment in equities. A person may select the way in which pension contributions are to be invested between debt securities (TIAA) and equity securities (CREF). The amount paid in retirement benefits depends on the value of the invested funds. This value is a function of the amount invested based on salary, the investment returns earned in the invested funds, and years of employment. Together the plans form a variable annuity. The amount of money to be paid in retirement is estimated each year, but the exact amount is not known until the day of retirement.

Employee Retirement Income Security Act (ERISA)

The participants of a pension plan today are entitled to certain rights and protections under the Employee Retirement Income Security Act of 1974, commonly referred to as ERISA. The provisions of this act are administered by the United States Department of Labor. The ERISA program requires that all participants in the pension plan shall be entitled to:

1. An examination without charge at the company's personnel office, of all plans and documents pertaining to the pension program, including insurance contracts and copies of all documents filed by the company's plan with the U.S. Department of Labor. Participants are also entitled to detailed annual reports and plan descriptions.

2. Copies of all plan documents and other plan information upon written request to the director of personnel of the company or to some appointed representative of the company. The company may make a reasonable charge for supplying copies to the participant.

3. A summary of the plan's annual financial report.

4. A statement detailing whether the individual has a right to receive a pension at the normal retirement age of age 65; and if so, what the benefits would be at the normal retirement age if work is begun immediately under the plan. If a person does not have a right to a pension,

the statement will explain how many more years a person must work to have a right to a pension.

The information available under ERISA is for your financial planning and security. People involved in retirement planning should begin at least a decade or more before retirement to make certain that their pension program is in order. You need to make your request in writing for the detailed statement about your pension. And your company is not required to furnish this statement to you more than once a year. Such statements are to be provided to participants in the program free of charge.

In addition to creating rights for plan participation, ERISA imposed duties upon the people who are responsible for the operation of a benefit plan. Fiduciaries of the plan have a duty and a responsibility to act prudently in the interest of participants and their beneficiaries.

No one, including an employer or any other person or individuals, may fire an employee or otherwise discriminate against an employee in any way so as to prevent the employee from obtaining a pension benefit or exercising his or her rights under ERISA. If a claim for a pension benefit is denied in part or in whole, a written explanation or reason for the denial must be supplied. The employee has a right to have some committee of the company review and reconsider the claim.

Under ERISA certain steps can be taken to enforce the above rights. For example, if a person should request information from the pension committee or other appropriate committee and the information is not received within 30 days, the employee may file suit in a federal court. In such a case the court may require the pension committee to provide these materials. The company can also be required to pay the employee up to $200 a day until the materials are received unless the materials cannot be furnished for reasons beyond the control of the appropriate committee.

If a claim for benefits is denied or ignored in whole or in part, an employee may file suit in a state or federal court. Also, if the people who are managing the money misuse it or if the employee is discriminated against for excercising his or her lawful rights, then the employee may seek assistance from the U.S. Department of Labor. If a lawsuit is filed, the court will decide who should pay the court costs and legal fees.

An example of a retirement plan—John and Mary Bundt

Let's examine what would happen if a couple retired in 1979 under a combination of Social Security and a private pension plan. John L. and Mary Bundt planned to retire on January 1, 1980, when John was to be 65 years of age and Mary 62. John and Mary had full coverage under the Social Security system and were to receive maximum income under that contract. John had earned Social Security credit beginning in 1937 at $3,000 a year to $22,900 in 1979. John's income in 1979 was $40,000 a year, and he had earned an average annual income of

$35,000 for the five previous years. John had worked 40 years for the company where he was then employed. Mary had not worked full time outside the home for a salary. She spent her working years as a full-time homemaker, raising three children and managing her family. She had, however, worked part time on occasion and did qualify for some Social Security benefits.

Mr. Bundt was concerned because he had not yet found out how much additional income he would need in retirement beyond what he was earning. He knew that his income would decline after he retired, and he thought that he might have to work in order to maintain the same standard of living. He was concerned further about the inflation that would certainly continue in the future. He was thinking about a 10 percent inflation factor over the next few years.

Estimating Social Security benefits

The first thing that John had to do was to estimate what he would receive from Social Security. John earned the maximum income for the covered years, that is, he averaged $8,730 a year. He would be entitled to $503.40 a month from Social Security when he retired in 1980. On an annual basis he would receive $6,040 of income. Mary was entitled to a maximum of $187.80 per month, or $2,253.60 a year. Together they would receive approximately $8,294 per annum from the Social Security system. This only represented a little more than 20 percent of their 1979 income. There were some advantages, however, because this sum of $8,294 was not subject to income taxes. The Bundts' income could be charted as was done in Figure 16–1. The base would be the $8,294 that was to be payable to John and Mary from Social Security.

Fortunately the Bundts had a retirement plan from John's company. Under the plan (which has been described in this chapter), John's average income for the past five years immediately prior to retirement was $35,000. He had more than 40 years service with the company. His pension would be 25 percent of his average earnings up to $4,200, and then 50 percent of his earnings in excess of $4,200. (The 25 percent comes from 1% × 25 years.) John and Mary would receive the following income:

$$25\% \times \$4,200 = \$\ 1,050$$
$$50\% \times \$30,800 = \underline{\$15,400}$$
$$\text{Total} = \$16,450$$

Therefore, their total retirement income would be $24,744, which is $15,256 below what they earned in the year just before retirement. In other words they have an indicated deficit $15,256.

This was bad, but not as bad as it seemed. The Bundts would pay less income taxes on a lower income. They would not have to make Social Security payments out of that income since they were no longer planning for retirement. However, they would have to pay taxes on the pension they receive from the company. So this pension would be taxable income unless they had actually contributed to the plan. It is assumed that this was a noncontributory plan and that the company provided everything. If the Bundts contributed, they would pay no income tax on the amount of their income that they contributed.

The Bundts also had to adjust their gross income of $40,000 in the year in which they retired to account for income taxes. At the time they filed their tax returns they were both under 65, they had no dependents, and they took a straight standard deduction. In that case their federal taxes were $9,568. The contribution they had to pay for city tax was $3,435. (We are using the Washington, D.C., tax rate.) Their tax bill was $13,003. If you add onto that a contribution for Social Security in the year in which they retired, they paid an additional $1,404 for Social security. Therefore, after deducting all taxes paid on the $40,000 income, the Bundts ended up with $25,595 that they could use to buy goods and services while they worked.

When they retired, their income would be substantially below what it was before retirement. But how much would they have left to spend? The $8,294 from Social Security would be tax-free. Therefore, the only income subject to taxes would be the pension plan income, which would be $16,450. John received a double deduction in his retirement year (one extra deduction for being age 65 or over). Mrs. Bundt was only 62. They would have to pay taxes to the federal government of $1,940 and taxes to the city government of $898. The total cost would be $2,838, which would leave them $13,621 of spendable pension income after taxes in addition to their Social Security income. These two figures would provide the Bundts with $21,906 of income from Social Security and their pension plan. When this was compared with their previous aftertax annual income ($25,595), the difference was only $3,689. This wasn't as bad as it first appeared. In other words RID (retirement income deficit), that appeared to be $14,000, became only $3,689 after taxes and Social Security payment reductions were considered. Although RID was not very large, if the Bundts wanted to maintain their standard of living and hedge against inflation, they would have to augment their retirement income in some way.

Getting rid of RID

One way John and Mary Bundt could reduce RID was by working part time. Under the Social Security system John could earn up to $4,500 a year without reducing his Social Security income. He would be subject to federal income tax. In his business capacity where he has earned $40,000 a year, John could probably develop a consulting arrangement or another job that would provide him with up to $4,500 a year. This would probably just make up for the difference between the income that he would receive from a pension plan and Social Security and what he had received when gainfully employed after adjusting for taxes.

An investment fund to eliminate RID

John and Mary Bundt were not in bad shape. When you consider that they would not have to spend as much money on parking in the city or for business entertainment, they would be fairly well off in their retirement years. Unfortunately inflation had not yet been considered. The Bundts' income would decline in purchasing power as they got older. All they could do would be to work more to provide more income. Perhaps they could accumulate more money through additional savings and investments to make up for their loss of purchasing power and provide them with supplemental income.

In discussing financial planning, we suggested that you put aside some money regularly in mutual funds, real estate investments, or other assets that have a chance of increasing in value. The Bundts' case points out that a savings plan, in addition to a pension plan and Social Security, is really needed to provide liquidity and extra income for the retirement years. This is particularly important if one or both of the parties should fall into ill health. John and Mary should have an investment fund that will provide income to make up for RID, the difference between their aftertax income before retirement and their aftertax income after retirement. They must also allow for inflation. That means they need a minimum of about $3,700 extra income initially. Because of inflation, John and Mary want to be able to provide an average of $5,000 per year from investment income during their retirement years.

The Bundts need not save $2,000 a year during their working years because interest will be earned on savings. Therefore, a saving of $1,000 per year or $83 per month would produce close to $50,000 in 25 years, assuming only a 5 percent compounding rate.

What will John and Mary need in the way of investments to provide $5,000 worth of income? Let's assume that they could earn at least 10 percent income on their investments. (There's no need to assume that they would convert their savings into an annuity that would provide both interest income and a return of capital.) Then the question is how much would they need to provide $5,000 of additional income without either of them having to work? Dividing 10 percent into $5,000 (to capitalize that money perpetually), we find that the amount of money needed for that purpose is approximately $50,000. Therefore, over their working years John and Mary are required to save approximately $1,000 a year to provide them with a cash nest egg when they retire.

Do John and Mary have $50,000? Well, if they had followed our savings advice, they would have a half year's salary in savings, or $20,000. Therefore, the amount they need would be $30,000 in addition to their regular savings. Since they do have a deficit, they will either have to work or cut back somewhat on their expenditures. This will affect them negatively, but they will not be in too bad shape because of their reduced expenses. Chances are that both of them will enjoy much the same kind of life they lived before John's retirement. But they will have a great deal more freedom. They certainly will be more secure financially in their retirement years than many people.

Let's summarize what we have covered. First, you must estimate the Social Security income you'll receive in retirement. Second, you must estimate your pension benefits. Third, you must compare your total income to your preretirement income after taxes and Social Security payments. Fourth, you must estimate taxes on your retirement income. Fifth, you establish RID, your retirement income deficit, taking into consideration future inflation. Sixth, you then make up RID by:

1. Income from savings or other assets;
2. Working part time;
3. Cutting back your expenditures.

If you do this kind of study well in advance of retirement, you will find it easier to solve the problem of RID.

What happens to retirement income when the breadwinner dies?

Death isn't a subject most people like to face. One of the big questions that arises in the minds of older persons is what happens to the pension and Social Security income if the main breadwinner of the family should die? What would the surviving spouse do? It is a good question that needs to be answered frankly.

Let's look at the figures. At age 65 John has a life expectancy of 12 years and Mary, one of 17 years. Therefore, at the end of 12 years what is going to happen to the income from the pension and Social Security if John dies? If John dies in 12 years at age 77, Mary will be 74 and she will have a right to survivor's benefits. Therefore we can count on the fact that Mary will continue to receive income from Social Security even after John has passed away. She will also receive some death benefits. Although modest in amount, these benefits will help her financially. She does have Medicare benefits in case she should become sick.

The next question we have to ask is what will happen to the income from the pension plan. The terms of John and Mary's private pension assume that after John's death 50 percent of the pension will go to Mary. There is, therefore, a surviving spouse benefit. Actually, if you want to provide assurance of a continuing income for your spouse or anyone else on your death after retirement, you will have to elect the contingent annuitant option. By electing this option, you have a specified percentage of your retirement income paid to the person named as your beneficiary for the remainder of his or her life. Your retirement income will be reduced in order to provide the money for these payments to your beneficiary. The size of the reduction in retirement income depends on the percentage you wish to have continued for that purpose.

You may choose the contingent annuitant option at any time before retirement. If the election is not made more that 31 days before you are eligible for retirement benefits, the election cannot be effected unless satisfactory evidence of good health is furnished. This option has to be applied for in writing. If you want the same income for Mary, you must reduce the amount of income that John and Mary will receive while both are alive. If Mary were to receive the same amount of income, John would have to take a lower amount for both while he lives. This lower amount would be $12,329 a year, compared to the $16,452 a year he would receive under the straight option. In this particular case John has the option of taking a lower amount and providing his wife the same income as long as she lives, or he can opt to receive the higher income as long as he lives and then provide Mary with half the income. The difference would be made up from savings or other funds that could be used or from life insurance proceeds. If we were in John's place, we would opt for the higher income now. Then he could supplement Mary's income by providing funds through life insurance or savings. That would at least give Mary the security of knowing that she would receive an income from the pension, Social Security, and life insurance income.

Of course, John might elect not to retire at age 65. By so doing, he might be able to build up a greater retirement income. If he has $50,000 of savings, this will help. He might also consider moving to another community where living costs and expenses are lower. This would be another way of balancing the income deficit.

Even if John opts to have the lower income paid to him and his wife forever, whether he survives or not, the sacrifice of 20 percent less income after taxes in retirement is not all that great. Doing a certain amount of work for income, even when a person reaches age 65, isn't a bad idea. It gives people some purpose in life, keeps them actively interested in the community, and is less onerous than working full-time. In fact, part-time work can be very enjoyable. Many retired people continue to work when they are 70 or 75. They remain hale and hearty, carrying on a host of activities for their community and in their profession. Indeed, they continue to earn a wage even though they are retired. Because they work less and enjoy themselves more, they can have a fuller, better life than they would if they were doing nothing.

Keogh Plans and Individual Retirement Accounts

What if you don't have a pension plan? You may be a self-employed writer, author, consultant, salesperson, customer's representative, or insurance representative. Or you may work for an organization that does not have a retirement plan. What can you do to provide for retirement?

There are a number of retirement programs available to individuals who work for themselves or do not have a pension plan available where they work. In fact, even people who have a full-time job subject to Social

Security and pension plans can take additional retirement benefits if they should care to augment and supplement their retirement income.

An Individual Retirement Account (IRA) is available for persons employed by organizations that do not have a pension plan for their employees. You may put up to $1,500 a year into such an account to pay a future retirement income. Up to $1,750 can be invested in an IRA, which is set up for a working person and a nonworking spouse. These plans are called *spousal IRA accounts.*

Self-employed people can set up what is referred to as a *Keogh Plan* to provide income when they retire. During the working years, a self-employed businessperson can set aside up to 15 percent of net earnings after expenses for a retirement program, up to a maximum of $7,500 a year. This money can be put into a savings account, common stocks, bonds, or money market funds. In fact, it can be invested almost anywhere as long as the plan is recognized by the Internal Revenue Service and there is some provision for an independent trustee to handle the funds on behalf of the beneficiary. Starting at age 55, or anywhere up to age 65, an individual can take the money from the Keogh Trust. A lump-sum payment, payment of interest only, or payment of a combination of both interest and principal may be elected. Whether you have an IRA or a Keogh Plan, money contributed to the plan is deducted from current taxable income. The individual businessperson or self-employed person then pays income taxes on income from the fund at the time that income is received in the form of future pension payments. In addition, income taxes will be paid on capital gains earned by the fund. As long as the funds are in the IRA or Keogh Plan account, they are not subject to federal income taxes. The amounts invested are allowed to accumulate tax-free to provide for your future retirement income.

Income from Keogh or IRA

How much will a Keogh or IRA plan provide in the way of retirement income? The amount of retirement benefits is uncertain because it depends on the amount of money contributed and the manner in which the retired person elects to receive money from the fund. Let's assume a woman who was self-employed for the last 20 years has put aside $7,500 a year into the Keogh Plan. Let's assume further that she was conservative and bought only short-term money market instruments, that is, Treasury bills, commercial paper, certificates of deposit, and the like. Chances are that over the past 20 years, she has earned anywhere from 6 to 15 percent on her money. At the end of 20 years, she will have $150,000 of contributions to the fund plus the interest accumulation on the $7,500 per year invested at 6 to 15 percent for 20 years. If she earned an average of 6 percent, she would have earned a total of $188,100 in interest over the 20 years. Adding $188,100 to the $150,000 worth of capital contributions, the value of the Keogh account is approximately $338,100.

At age 65, the woman could retire. She could use the money accumulated in her Keogh Plan to set up an annuity similar to the insurance annuities discussed in Chapter 9. She could also withdraw only the interest or profits earned on her fund. Assuming her money could be invested to earn 10 percent per year, she could withdraw $33,810 per year from the fund. In this way she could provide for her retirement income and leave the principal of her fund intact. The $33,810 withdrawal made each year would be subject to income taxes. In addition to the $33,810, the woman would probably also be eligible for Social Security payments.

The income seems rather large. Yet it is probably a good deal less than she was earning as an entrepreneur. As an entrepreneur, she had to earn $50,000 after expenses to put aside $7,500 a year. The $50,000 is a good income, but remember that it will be lessened by taxes from the federal government and state or local government. After the tax adjustment, her annual retirement income is probably not too far away from her preretirement income. Keogh is a way of deferring current income and providing a retirement income benefit. Needless to say, a self-employed individual should invest in a Keogh Plan to provide for future retirement security.

Summary

The major reason for a discussion of private pension plans and the Social Security system is to force the financial planner to look at the future well in advance. Once you estimate what your RID will be, you can take steps early enough to provide for RID and a liquidity fund when you retire. It is your job, perhaps 10 years before retirement, to assess future benefits and learn what your income needs will be. You will be able to provide for the needs by:

1. Working;
2. Saving;
3. Reducing expenses; and
4. Life insurance benefits.

But first you must know what your financial position will be. Second, you must have the desire to do something about it. Third, you must plan to meet these indicated goals. Fourth, you must activate the plan; and fifth, you must control the plan once it is enacted.

This discussion paves the way for the following important questions: What will happen to an estate when one spouse dies? What will go to the surviving spouse? What will go to the children, if there are any children? These questions require a detailed analysis of estate planning, a subject that will be taken up in the next chapter as the final phase of personal financial planning.

17

Estate planning

- What is estate planning?
- Objective
- The estate plan—transfer through a will
- Reducing estate taxes
- How to reduce estate taxes through a trust
- How to reduce an estate through a federal gift tax
- Short-term living trusts—a way to reduce taxes
- Charitable giving—a way to reduce taxes
- Some special financial problems of the aged
- Summary

Throughout this book we have emphasized ways in which you can maximize income, minimize expenses, increase your wealth and net worth, and protect your assets. Ordinarily you tend to think in terms of only your lifetime. But you must also consider what will happen to your wealth in your old age and when you are no longer on earth. You must be concerned about who will receive your assets, how they will be transferred to your loved ones, and what is the best and cheapest way of passing on your wealth. Estate planning is an important and complex subject. Many of the problems and the processes of estate planning will be presented in this chapter. In addition, we'll take up some of the problems facing you as you become older.

What is estate planning?

Estate planning is the process of creating an estate (your assets), preserving your estate, and transferring it to your survivors. This suggests that there are three different stages involved in planning your financial life:

First, there is the creation of your estate by means of saving, and investment, gift, or inheritance.

Second, there is the stage of preserving or conserving your estate.

And third, there is problem of transferring your estate either during your lifetime or after your death to those you designate.

Creation of the estate

The creation of the estate is what this book has been about. We have suggested ways in which you could manage your income to maximize your net worth. This meant that you would start the savings process to build up your net worth. With your savings you bought a house, perhaps two; you invested in securities; you bought antiques; you protected yourself and your family with life insurance. Whether married or single, a person can with control, care, and conservatism accumulate a substantial amount of assets.

We have stressed how you should manage your income to increase your wealth. This will make your future more secure. You might be lucky, in addition, to inherit assets or receive gifts from parents, relatives, or friends. This could increase your assets greatly and speed the day when you are financially independent.

Preservation of the estate

The second phase of estate planning deals with the preservation or conservation of the estate. We have assumed that you have worked hard, saved, and invested successfully. You now want to make certain that your assets continue to grow for the benefit of yourself or your loved ones. This means that your assets must be managed and protected for your benefit while you are living as well as for your beneficiaries when you are no longer around. After all, your assets must continue to provide income and capital growth, and must be protected from the risks of investment, including inflation.

Transfer of the estate　　The third phase of estate planning is the transfer of your assets. You should be concerned with the possible erosion of your estate from high taxes, probate costs, legal fees, and other costs that could reduce your estate assets. Most married people want to transfer their assets to their spouses, children, grandchildren, or friends. Or they might wish to transfer their assets to a school, college, church, or favorite charity. Single persons, too, might wish to leave their assets to friends, relatives, or religious or charitable institutions. Those with families might have a higher goal in protecting hard-earned assets. You might wish to perpetuate your family name by providing for those yet to come. In a sense you are creating a family heritage, not in the dynastic or royal sense, but in the sense of family loyalty and tradition. And you must be concerned with high taxes on your estate as well as the possibility of its mismanagement after you are gone.

There are several ways in which you can transfer assets to your loved ones. As a matter of principle, you should try to keep the benefit of your assets for yourself as long as you may need them. Then you will wish to transfer them at the lowest cost and with the greatest tax advantage to your loved ones. We shall now describe briefly five frequent methods of transferring assets.

Will　Your estate may be transferred by a will. This legal document should provide details of how you want your assets to be distributed at your death.

Gifts　The transfer of your property to spouse, children, relatives, or friends need not wait until your death. Property can be transferred by gift while you are alive. The Internal Revenue system allows assets to be transferred up to a certain amount without paying a gift tax. This means you can reduce your taxable estate and pay no transfer taxes on the legal amount given.

Charitable giving　You may also transfer assets by a gift to your favorite charity or religious organization. Such a gift reduces your estate for tax purposes. It also may be taken as a deduction from federal income taxes.

Gift in trust　Property may be transferred by an irrevocable trust. This kind of trust places, permanently or irrevocably for a 10 year period, your assets in the hands of a trustee. The trustee, who is an expert in these matters, will manage the assets for your spouse, children, or other beneficiaries. In this way estate assets in the trust are not subject to probate, nor are the trust assets subject to estate or inheritance taxes. Examples of irrevocable transfers in trust would be: (1) trusts for the benefit of a minor or an incompetent person; (2) trusts that shift income to a beneficiary for a period of years, with the remainder reverting to the creator (this is called a *Clifford Trust*); and (3) Charitable Remainder Trusts in which the income from the trust goes to its creator and the remainder goes to a charity. This arrangement will be discussed more fully in the section dealing with charitable trusts.

Objective of estate planning

The phase of estate planning we will emphasize is the transfer phase. As you think about your estate plan, keep in mind the overall objective of estate planning. Generally the objective of your plan will be to transfer your assets to or for the benefit of your beneficiaries. You wish to effect this transfer at the lowest cost, with the least amount of tax, and in the shortest amount of time.

Key elements in the objective are therefore the transfer, the beneficiary, administrative costs, tax savings, and time.

Transfer

The transfer aspect is important in estate planning. You must identify what you have in your estate and what you wish done with it. Then you must decide the best and most efficient way of transferring your assets. As noted, the estate may be transferred by will, gift, ownership, or some form of trust. You must decide the best way to do this. How you transfer your estate will depend on the people you wish to benefit, the size of the estate, and the taxes you might be required to pay.

Beneficiary

You must decide on the person or persons you wish to receive your estate. You might wish to have the entire estate transferred to your spouse, and then to your children. If the estate is sizable and if the taxes are onerous, you might establish a trust with the income going to your spouse and the remainder to your children. When selecting the person or persons to receive your estate, you must decide carefully and clearly on those you wish to benefit and the best and least expensive way of accomplishing your goal.

Administrative costs

The best way to reduce administrative costs is to have a properly drawn will or trust agreement. The will or trust should anticipate administrative difficulties that may arise in the administration of the estate or trust. In general, legal counsel should be consulted to determine the best way of reducing administrative costs.

Tax saving

The tax aspect of estate planning is important. You should certainly try to keep tax costs of the transfer to a minimum. Yet for most Americans the size of the estate is relatively small and the federal exemptions so large that estate taxes are not a problem. For wealthy people taxes do play a dominant role. As we shall see, this group might consider a trust or charitable giving. In this way they can reduce their tax bill, maintain their estate intact, and still transfer the estate to the right beneficiaries.

Time

In the transfer process you want your beneficiaries to receive your estate in the shortest amount of time. This also means that you want them to receive the benefits of your assets in a way that is least disruptive to their lives.

A trust might be set up before your death to provide for an uninterrupted flow of income and use of assets. The estate might be gifted before death to achieve the same objectives. A tax lawyer can be very helpful in establishing an estate plan to accomplish this objective.

In the last analysis *you* must decide what you want to do with your estate. You must decide what you have and the best way to accomplish the transfer for the least cost, in the shortest period of time, and with the smallest reduction of the estate by taxes and other expenses. Once you have your objectives clearly in mind within the overall objective of estate planning, then you must decide which plan is best.

The estate plan—transfer through a will

A will is one important way in which you can transfer your assets. In order to understand how a will works, you must understand what is meant by the term *probate* and you must also understand the duties of the *executor*, the person who administers the provisions of the will for your estate and its beneficiaries.

Probate

Probate is the court process by which assets of a deceased person are inventoried, debts and taxes are paid, and property is distributed to beneficiaries named in the will. The process begins by the presentation of the will to the court in the form of a *petition by the executor*, which is normally prepared by a lawyer. The court usually appoints the executor named in the will. If there is no will, the court appoints an administrator or executor in accordance with local state law or statute. The court issues what is called a *letter testamentary* to the executor, or evidence of the executor's authority to act on behalf of the decedent (dead person).

Next, the executor prepares an inventory of the assets and their value.

Third, with the court's approval the debts of the deceased are paid when they become due.

Fourth, it is necessary to determine and pay the estate and inheritance taxes as well as to file federal and state income tax returns for the decedent and the estate.

The last step is to file the final account and distribute the assets once the account has been approved by the court. (See duties an executor in Table 17–1.)

Cost of probate   The cost of this procedure can be significant. In Maryland, for example, the cost of probate is set at 10 percent on the first $20,000, and 4% on the excess of the value of the assets subject to probate. As a rule of thumb, probate fees, including those of the executor and an attorney, range from 5 to 10 percent of the assets subject to probate. Not included as assets in computing the costs is the value of real estate, except where real estate must be sold to pay estate taxes or when the sale of real estate is directed by the will. A $25,000 estate may have probate costs ranging from $1,250 to $2,500. An estate valued at $500,000 may cost from $25,000 to $50,000. Therefore, most people feel a great deal of concern about avoiding probate or at least keeping its costs as low as possible.

Avoiding probate   The best way to avoid probate is not to have an estate. This can be done in one of several ways. Joint ownership passes the estate on without probate since the estate is not owned by the deceased. A trust places legal title to the assets of an estate in the hands of a trustee. As a result, there is no probate estate owned by the deceased. Therefore trusts, gifts, and joint ownership can reduce or eliminate your estate for probate purposes.

Duties of the executor   The duties and responsibilities of an executor are demanding. They are outlined in Figure 17–1 and Table 17–1.

Why have a will?   The reasons for having a will may be summarized as follows:

1. The state has a will for you if you don't write one yourself.
2. You may select your own executor through a will.
3. A will may allow the waiving of a bond premium.
4. A will may allow you to waive the statutory limitation on funeral expense.

Figure 17-1
Outline of executor's duties

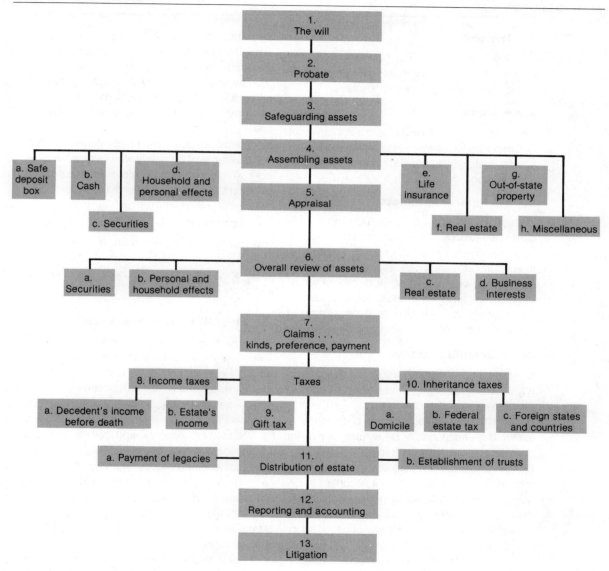

© MCMLXXVII Kennedy Sinclaire, Inc.
SOURCE   Kennedy Sinclaire, Inc.

Table 17-1
The Duties, Responsibilities, and Problems
of an EXECUTOR

1. The will

Find; read; arrange funeral, if asked; confer with attorney-draftsman, members of family and others familiar with the decedent's affairs.

2. Probate

Have will probated; if delay, obtain appointment as temporary or special administrator; file petition for statutory support allowance for widow and children.

3. Safeguarding assets

Protect and preserve property pending qualification as executor: arrange for protection of business interests of decedent; arrange, if needed, for adequate casualty insurance coverage; obtain possession of all decedent's records, papers and memoranda; collect valuables for safekeeping; take charge, if necessary, of personal property.

4. Assembling assets

a.   Safe Deposit Box: Remove contents (usually by judicial authority). Inventory contents and place in executor's control.

b.   Cash: Transfer to executor cash found in known bank accounts, or elsewhere; search for cash in accounts in area banks.

c.   Securities: Obtain custody of securities; re-register in name of executor all securities in decedent's name, or held by brokers, or in safe deposit box; collect interest and dividends; in "margin" account, liquidate any outstanding indebtedness.

d.   Household and personal effects: Inventory; protect; store; obtain appraisals; dispose of perishables.

e.   Life insurance: If payable to estate, obtain proof of death and collect proceeds.

f.   Real estate: Take possession of all records, including deeds, mortgages, leases, tax data,

insurance policies; if income-producing, arrange for continued insurance coverage, management of property, collection of rents.

g.   Out-of-state property: Arrange ancillary administration; obtain possession of personal property; arrange for management of real estate.

h.   Miscellaneous: Collect debts owing decedent; ascertain if decedent was involved in litigation which is pending; determine extent of decedent's interest in other estates, or trusts.

5. Appraisal

Inventory all assets; establish, by qualified appraiser, values on date of death, including values of closely held business interests; file inventory and appraisal.

6. Overall review of assets:

Determine amount of cash needed to pay legacies, taxes, claims, fees and other charges; set up bookkeeping procedure and records; review will as to testator's wishes concerning liquidation of certain assets; when possible, distribute legacies promptly.

a.   Securities: Analyze and review portfolio; determine whether to sell or retain securities after consideration of, among other things: beneficiaries' desires; investment powers under will; market conditions; quality of securities; estate's cash requirements; yield on each security. Make reinvestments, as authorized by will, or law, or both.

b.   Personal and household effects: Distribute without undue delay; if sale is necessary, decide most advantageous time and method; endeavor to obtain true value in case of items or collections of unusual nature.

c.   Real estate: Examine encumbrances, leases, condition of property; where sale is ad-

Table 17-1 *(continued)*

visable, obtain appraisal from qualified person; list for sale and evaluate offers.

d. Business interests: Obtain complete picture of business operation; consult with counsel as to any direction in will with respect to sale of business,or continuation of it; arrange for interim management.

7. Claims—kinds, preference, payment

1. a. Funeral, administration expenses; b. Obligations arising under leases and decedent's business contracts; c. Taxes; local, state, Federal; d. Current expenses; e. Statutory or other allowance for surviving spouse and children; f. Miscellaneous claims; pledges; subscriptions.
2. Payment procedure. a. Advertise for claims as required by statute; b. Ascertain claims, entitled by law to preference and priority in payment, in solvent or insolvent estate; c. Determine validity of claims; d. Require proof of any claims which seem doubtful; e. Reject improper claims, defend estate against them in court if necessary; f. Pay all valid claims as soon as possible.

Taxes This is a highly technical field. It requires precise knowledge and wide experience. The tax liability of the decedent and his estate should be determined by an expert familiar with the statutes, regulations and decisional law pertaining to taxes.

8. Income taxes

a. Decedent's income before death: File state and Federal returns for portion of year prior to death; obtain waivers; pay taxes promptly to avoid penalties; protest assessments deemed unlawful; if necessary, arrange with attorney to challenge them in court.
b. Estate's income: File state and Federal fiduciary returns; provide beneficiaries of distributed income with tax data on their income tax liability; pay taxes on rest of income; make analysis of income, and deductions, during administration.

9. Gift tax
Check for possible gift or estate tax liability as a result of gifts made before 1/1/77.

10. Inheritance taxes

1. Domicile: Determine the decedent's domicile; file timely state inheritance tax return and pay as much of tax as is advisable to obtain discount, if available; collect portion of tax, if any, which is to be paid by others than residuary legatees.
b. Federal estate tax: decide most advantageous date for valuation of estate (either date of death, or 6 months later); decide how deductions can best be used; calculate ''adjusted taxable gifts'' made by decedent; determine amount of appreciation and gift tax paid on gifts made within 3 years of death; file return (not later than 9 months after death); file affidavit on valuation of estate assets, together with detailed appraisal; pay tax when due, or obtain extension if necessary; assist attorney in defending estate against claims for additional tax.
c. Foreign states and countries: Arrange for ancillary administration; determine liability for taxes on real and personal property outside state of domicile, and arrange to pay those taxes.

11. Distribution of estate

a. Payment of legacies: Before a final accounting, there can be partial distribution of legacies. If the estate is solvent, legacies are to be paid and property subject to specific bequests is to be delivered to legatees; rest of estate to be distributed as provided by decree of court; obtain from recipients receipts and final releases.

Table 17-1 *(continued)*

b. Establishment of trusts: Where will creates a trust, property to constitute trust, as provided in will, must be ascertained by executor and turned over to trustee.

12. Reporting and accounting

Provide appropriate parties with pertinent and/or required information regarding the cost or other basis of property in the estate. Where required, prepare and submit for approval of beneficiaries and the appropriate court a statement setting forth in exact detail every item of receipts and disbursements of the estate.

13. Litigation

Assist attorney in defending estate in actions brought by creditors, claimants, dissatisfied beneficiaries, the tax authorities, disinherited relatives, and others who challenge either the validity of the will, or the meaning of its contents, or the manner of execution, or any other matter connected with the estate. Also, the executor assists the attorney in actions brought by the estate to collect property due it, or for any other lawful purpose.

5. A will may lower administrative costs by giving the executor power to act without having to go to court each time for approval.
6. A will may allow you to have your inheritance taxes paid out of the residue of the estate.

One inviolate principle to follow in estate planning is to make sure you have an up-to-date will. There are many reasons to have a will. In spite of the fact that this is sound advice, it is often not followed. Thousands of people die each year intestate, that is, without a will. As a matter of practice, you should write a will as soon as you are married, or as soon as you are gainfully employed and have an estate to leave to your wife, children, parents, friends, church, or charity. The main reason for having a will is to make sure that the rightful beneficiaries will receive your property.

If you don't leave a will, the state in which you live has a will already made out for you. The state will appoint an administrator for your estate. State laws will determine how your assets are to be divided among your surviving heirs. In the case of a married parent dying without a will, a part of the estate will generally go to the surviving spouse and a part to the children. For example, a spouse and two children each receive one third of the estate in California. This is fine if this is the way you want your assets to be divided. However, you might have a different idea about how they should be distributed. Ordinarily a parent will wish to take care of the surviving spouse first, and then provide for the children. Depending on the size of the estate, one spouse may leave all assets to the surviving spouse. The surviving spouse would then care for the children. But children from another marriage who are not legally related to the deceased spouse might be excluded from a share in the inheritance. If there are brothers, sisters, mothers, or fathers who should share in your estate, or if there are friends who should receive some gift as a token of your esteem for them, then you need a will to assure that the people you designate will receive your assets.

As completely and precisely as possible the will should direct the executor how to carry out the wishes of the deceased. A simple will is all that is required for many people. It indicates how the assets are to be distributed. Surviving children, spouses, and relatives have different claims on an estate. Those differences should be considered in the will Therefore, you need to draw up your will with care so that the executor can carry out your wishes. The will allows you to distribute your assets to those whom you wish to care for or remember. It lets you maintain the asset value of your estate, protect the heritage of your family, and keep the costs of settling the estate to a minimum. If you are concerned about giving specific assets, such as sums of money, securities, or real estate to specific persons, your lawyer will need to be as specific as possible in the written terms of the will.

You ought to make your decisions known to your beneficiaries while you are still alive and able to explain what will happen after your death. This is particularly important if a child is to be excluded from a will. As a case in point, we know of a generous mother who gave a substantial amount of her personal jewelry to friends and relatives while she was still alive. During the last 10 years of her life, she was most kind and charitable. But she failed to tell her children that she had given some valuable jewelry away. Her reason was that she didn't want her children to feel sad at not receiving these jewels as gifts. Actually, she was just as generous to her children as she was to her friends and other relatives. Upon the woman's death her children couldn't understand what had happened to her jewelry. They were unpleasantly surprised to learn that their mother had informally given away part of the estate during her lifetime. This caused hard feelings, pitting sister against brother. It created the suspicion that one member of the family might have stolen the assets without the knowledge of other members. Therefore, you should instruct your lawyer to draw up the will in such a way that your wishes are clearly understood.

You need to prepare your family for what will happen after your death. If certain members of your family admire some of your possessions, you might want to bequeath those assets to specific persons as symbols of your love and affection. Jewelry and objects of art fall into this category. But you need to list specific major gifts in your will so that you can pass them on to specific survivors. Even better, why not distribute these assets before death with the approval and knowledge of all concerned? Of course, in this case a gift tax might be required. But this is a small price to pay for smoothing the transition of wealth to others at a most distressing and unhappy time. This assumes, of course, that you will no longer need the assets during your lifetime.

The best intentions should be written down and communicated to all concerned parties. Let's consider the case of a loving mother who says to her oldest daughter, "I will give you my jewelry for taking care of me during my illness." But six months before she had assured her younger daughters that they would receive all her jewelry as a reward for looking after her. In addition, the mother had told the two sons that they would share and share alike all of the assets she possessed, including the jewelry. In this case the mother was making rational statements, but at different times and under different circumstances. This created hard feelings among her children after her death.

A sample will

A sample will gives some idea of the form to follow in writing your will. (See Figure 17–2.) But you should seek legal counsel, since your will becomes legal, valid, and binding as soon as it is endorsed and witnessed.

The will usually begins with the words "Last Will and Testament of . . . ," and then your name.

The first item directs that all funeral expenses and debts be paid as soon as practical. Some states have limitations on funeral expenses that are to be approved by the court. You may want to waive such limitations.

The second item lists the name of your executor, and empowers that person to sell your real estate and dispose of all your personal property, if necessary. You should give broad powers to your executor.

The third item identifies who is to get what. Here you list the people

Figure 17–2

LAST WILL AND TESTAMENT

of

_____

I, _____, a resident of _____

city   state

being of sound and disposing mind and memory, do hereby make, publish and declare this to be my last will and testament, hereby revoking any and all wills by me at any time heretofore made.

Figure 17–2 (continued)

FIRST: I desire my funeral expenses, regardless of any statutory limitation, and all my just debts to be paid as soon as practicable after my death.

SECOND: I hereby name, constitute and appoint _____

name

to be the execut ____ of this, my last will and testament, and I hereby give to my said execut ____full power and authority in the management and control of my estate and the right and power to sell all or such part thereof, without application to any Court, as it may deem necessary or advisable for the payment of my just debts or the advantageous settlement and protection of my estate.

THIRD: I give, and bequeath _____

_____ to _____

if _____ shall survive

me. _____

_____

_____

_____

_____

All of the rest and residue of my estate, real and personal and mixed, I give, devise and bequeath to

_____

IN WITNESS WHEREOF I have hereunto affixed my signature and seal to this, my last will and testament,
on this _____ day of _____, 19 ___ .

_____ (SEAL)

Signed, sealed, published and declared by the above-named testator, as and for her Last Will and Testament, in the presence of us, who at her request and in her presence and in the presence of each other, have hereunto subscribed our names as attesting witnesses on the day and year last hereinbefore written.

WITNESS   ADDRESS

_____   _____

_____   _____

_____   _____

who are to receive specific assets and any donations to charities, churches, colleges, or other institutions. You might even wish to leave funds to an individual in trust for the care of friends or pets. Alternative bequests are important in the event that your primary beneficiary is deceased at the time of your death.

The last item is a list of witnesses who can assure the court that this document is truly your will. It is important to not only have your lawyer draw your will, but to make sure that your will is executed according to the formulations in the jurisdiction in which the will is signed. Keep in mind that Figure 17–2 is only a sample will. Let us emphasize once again that you'll need legal help when you write your will.

Nominating an executor to settle your estate

To look after your assets, you will have to come to grips with a very important problem: the nomination of your executor. Often this responsibility is given to a son or daughter, a spouse, a relative, or a friend of the family or bank trust department. The job is time-consuming and can be complicated. It normally takes someone with professional experience as well as a level head. You may want to appoint a co-executor who is a family member if you name a fiduciary as your executor. With the court's approval, the executor is entitled to compensation for performing these duties. An executor must be concerned with the many facets of handling an estate. He, she, or it will need legal assistance in probating the will, in following the procedures established to protect the assets of the deceased, and in protecting the heirs' rights. Many executors find that the details of their assignment are so time-consuming that they regret agreeing to accept the burden. You need to appoint someone close at hand to give full attention to the details of your estate, not someone from a distant state. In fact, in some states an executor must be appointed who is a resident of the state in which the will is to be probated.

Some executors try to save money in handling an estate by doing everything themselves. This is possible. But a professional executor can save money in the handling of a complex estate by proper post mortem estate planning and administration. Of course, it is desirable to keep settlement expenses of an estate to a minimum. On the other hand, if professional legal services are needed, they may prove to be a very good investment saving money in the long run.

Advantages of a professional executor

Some people find it appropriate to appoint a financial institution as executor of an estate. The reasons for this decision are listed by one financial institution in Figure 17–3. Obviously there are costs involved in settling an estate with the aid of a trust institution. But this arrangement will relieve the burden on an individual executor and provide expert service. An executor unfamiliar with the process of estate settlement may

**Figure 17–3
Advantages in naming a bank to serve as
executor or trustee**

1. **Knowledge and experience:** Our people have made a career of the areas to which they are assigned. We carefully select and train our Trust Department personnel and are well informed on all current developments affecting trust service.

2. **Financial responsibility:** The capital funds of Riggs, the largest bank in our city, attest to our financial responsibility.

3. **Permanence and continuity:** While years may elapse between the time a person makes a Will and the time his estate is settled, while trusts may continue for several generations (or even perpetually under certain circumstances), Riggs is always here. Not only is Riggs permanent, it does not suffer disability, does not travel, is not preoccupied with other responsibilities, and does not die.

4. **Personal concern:** We strive to maintain satisfied customers and beneficiaries as this is our best advertising as well as providing us with a sense of personal satisfaction.

5. **Objectivity and impartiality:** As Executor and Trustee we are obligated to carry out **your** wishes. Accordingly, we proceed in an objective, impartial atmosphere which serves to maintain harmony among your various beneficiaries.

6. **Ability to meet changing needs:** We are alert to economic conditions and investment climate changes as they occur. Should the requirements of your beneficiaries vary with changing times, we can adapt our services, within the limits of whatever discretion you grant to us, to offer new solutions to meet their needs.

7. **Group judgment:** Due to the depth of our administrative, investment, accounting and income tax staffs, a number of able people may be involved in reaching decisions on the varied and complex problems which may arise during the administration of your estate or trust.

8. **Reasonable cost:** Our fees for serving as Executor and Trustee are reasonable in view of the services rendered, are usually deductible for tax purposes, and are governed by either statute or published fee schedule. Also, the Bank maintains several Common Trust Funds, exclusively for our Trust customers, designed to provide all of the benefits of Pooled Investments. Reduced trust fee rates are applied to trust accounts fully invested in one or more of our Collective Investment Funds.

SOURCE The Riggs National Bank of Washington, D.C.

find his or her efforts thwarted. There may be unnecessary delays. Conflicts and disagreements among beneficiaries might be handled better by a financial institution or a bank with a trust department. As a matter of course, if you are naming an executor, you should name a person or institution that will carry out the goals and objectives of your will. It should be some person or institution that can be trusted by the beneficiaries as well as by the creator of the will. A member of the family who is also a beneficiary might be thought by other family members to have a preferential position in settling the estate. Such a distrust may cause problems. In selecting an executor, make certain that the executor:

1. Is willing and able to do the job.
2. Will devote a great deal of attention to the estate.

3. Is financially responsible and trustworthy.
4. Is familiar with all assets, securities, antiques, and objects of art in the estate.
5. Has had prior knowledge and experience in settling a complex estate.
6. Is objective, impartial, and completely reliable with respect to the beneficiaries of the estate. The executor must be able to defend all actions taken in the event a dispute arises.
7. Has good investment judgment.

Impact of estate taxes

One of the big questions you must solve is "How much of an estate will you leave your beneficiaries after the estate taxes are paid?"

Let's start with a few questions. How much will the taxes be? Let's assume that a high proportion of your estate will have to be paid in taxes. Is there anything you can do to protect your estate and minimize these taxes? How large an estate do you have to have in order to benefit from estate planning? At what point should you utilize professional help in your estate management? Your desire to minimize the tax burden on the estate is justified. The notion that estate taxes are a problem only for the wealthy is untrue. You should not believe people who tell you, "If you are married, the exemption of your spouse is so large you don't have to worry about estate taxes." It is true that the Tax Reform Act of 1976 reduced the estate tax rate. Yet you still need careful planning to keep your tax bill at a minimum. That is why estate planning is important.

To provide some idea of the tax implications of an estate, let's assume an estate with property is worth $250,000. Its owner is single. The estate is to be left to one person, and after that person's death, to a second beneficiary. That is, there will be two transfers. Federal estate taxes on the estate from both transfers amount to approximately $36,000. A $300,000 estate under the same assumptions would require taxes of about $62,000; a $400,000 estate, taxes of $115,000; and an estate worth $600,000, a tax bill amounting to $221,000.*

If you are married and must pay estate taxes, with two transfers involved, you would have to pay estate taxes of about $21,000 on a $250,000 estate; $37,000 for a $300,000 estate; $68,000 for a $400,000 estate; and $157,000 for a $600,000 estate. Therefore, it is important for you to study the tax laws before writing your will. In this way you can arrange the transfer of property to your loved ones at the lowest possible cost. You should find out about rates so you will know whether your estate will be subject to taxes. Several years ago a trust officer of a large bank was asked by a customer if his $150,000 estate required

* As of July 1, 1981 the Congress of the U.S. is considering extensive federal estate tax changes which will change the amounts subject to the tax.

a trust or some kind of estate planning. The trust officer replied that estate planning should start when the estate reached $250,000. This bothered the customer somewhat because he thought that he already had a good-sized estate. But he should have been happy, since he learned when to take estate planning seriously. For a married couple, under the Tax Reform Act of 1976, a $250,000 estate is large enough for estate tax purposes.

Estate taxes as a cost of settling an estate

A lot of married people with children use trusts to reduce the payment of estate taxes. Depending on your objective, this can be an important part of estate planning. But before we take up the topic of trusts, let's discuss taxes on estates without a trust.

First of all, you must make an accurate assessment of your estate's value. If you have a will, your executor will do this task. While you are still alive, an inventory of your estate should be drawn up. You can use the inventory to determine the likely impact of taxes on your estate.

What is subject to estate taxes?

Your starting point is finding out your *gross estate* for federal estate tax purposes. This includes everything you own, such as securities, personal property, and real estate. Life insurance, for example, has often been thought to be excluded from the insured person's estate if it is payable to a named beneficiary. Nevertheless, federal tax laws include insurance as part of an estate where ownership of the insurance belongs to the decedent. The full value of the property you own jointly will probably also be included, except to the extent that the surviving owner has contributed to the purchase of the asset.

Gifts as a part of the estate

Effective January 1, 1976, all gifts made within three years of the doner's death are included in the estate for tax purposes, except for amounts under $3,000 per year per donee. Estate and gift tax rates have been combined or "unified," so that in computing the estate tax the estate generally includes any lifetime gifts made after 1976 on which a tax would be required. If gifts were made and taxes paid on them, the amount that the donor paid in taxes that weren't made within three years of his or her death can be deducted from the estate. Assets will be valued at the date of death or six months after the date of death, depending on the executor's choice under the federal estate tax. For planning purposes you need to make a periodic update of the value of the estate every year or two. In this way you will make certain that the value of your estate has not changed in such a way as to affect the estate plan. You need a realistic evaluation of this matter. If taxes must be paid on your estate, you need to know the amount of cash that will be required, even though the Tax Reform Act of 1976 makes it easier to pay estate taxes by stretching out the payments under certain limited circumstances. As a matter of principle, cash can be provided for the payment of estate taxes from the proceeds of your life insurance. These proceeds can also augment the income of your spouse.

Once you have established the value of the estate, it will not be too difficult to calculate the tax. Debts, funeral expenses, and administrative cost are deductible. So, too, is a certain amount of the assets that go to your spouse. Under the Tax Reform Act of 1976, a marital deduction of up to $250,000 or one half of the estate, whichever is larger, can be deducted from the estate before taxes are assessed. Therefore, if an estate is worth $400,000, the spouse has a marital deduction of $250,000. For tax purposes the estate amounts to $150.000. Taxes would have to be paid on that amount, after reducing that amount by the unified tax credit of $47,000.[1]

Paying an estate tax— an example

Let's take a typical example of an estate to show how this procedure works.[2] Assume that Mr. Abbott died in 1981, owning assets worth $600,000. His will leaves $250,000 to his wife, $25,000 to a charity, and the balance of the estate to his children. The tax due on his estate would be computed as follows:

Gross estate	$600,000
Less estimated debts, funeral expenses, and costs	− 30,000
Leaving a net amount	$570,000
Less a marital deduction for property passing to the spouse	−250,000
Leaving an estate net of	$320,000
Less a charitable deduction of	− 25,000
Leaving a net estate subject to tax of	$295,000

Under the new tax rules the tentative tax on $295,000 would be approximately $60,000. If assets in the estate are tied up in real estate and are not liquid, then the funds must come from somewhere to pay the

[1] The unified credit in the Tax Reform Act has been phased in over a period of five years. In 1977 it amounted to $30,000 for transfers occurring in 1977, $34,000 for transfers in 1978, $38,000 for transfers in 1979, $42,500 for transfers in 1980, and $47,000 for transfers in 1981 and the years that follow.

[2] This example was obtained from Kennedy Sinclaire, Inc. in a book called *Tax Talk,* and published by the Riggs National Bank, Washington, D.C. The publication is designed to provide accurate, authoritative information. It is sold with the understanding that its publisher is not engaged in rendering legal, accounting, or other professional services. If legal advice or other expert assistance is required, the services of a competent, professional person should be sought, in accord with a declaration of principle jointly adopted by a committee of the American Bar Association and a committee of publishers and associations.

taxes. This might mean a new mortgage on the house to pay the taxes. Or it might mean actually that the assets must be sold. This could disrupt the life of Mrs. Abbott.

From this $60,000, the estate is entitled to subtract what is referred to as a *unified credit* of $47,000 and thus the actual tax due on Mr. Abbott's estate would be $13,000. The $13,000 is not a large amount of money for a $600,000 estate. The thing that you must guard against is making certain that you obtain all the deductions from the estate. If Mr. Abbott's marital deduction was not allowed for some reason, it would increase the value for tax purposes by $250,000, and the tax, instead of being $13,000, would exceed $90,000. The marital deduction and any other deduction cannot be taken for granted. Sometimes charitable deductions are disallowed for legal purposes because of a change in the law. It is, therefore, important for anyone creating an estate plan to have the plan checked periodically to make certain that the charitable deduction may be allowed, for the type of charity involved.

How to reduce estate taxes through a trust

Excessive estate taxation will erode the family capital over successive transfers. The goal in reducing taxes through trusts is to give your beneficiaries the use of the assets, but have part of the assets excluded from taxes in the estate. For example, it is possible to establish a trust that allows Mrs. Abbott to use the estate while she lives. The remainder of the estate would then pass to the children at her death. By setting up a trust, the amount of taxes that would be paid on Mrs. Abbott's death is greatly reduced. Thus the children would receive substantially more from the trust.

For example, by leaving $250,000 outright to Mrs. Abbott and by setting up a $295,000 remainder trust in which the income goes to Mrs. Abbott and the children, the estate taxes are reduced by $13,000. Otherwise if Mr. Abbott leaves his entire estate to his wife and she, in turn, upon her death, leaves the estate to the children, the estate is taxed twice, once when Mr. Abbott dies and again when Mrs. Abbott dies.

Let's assume that Mr. Abbott learns that he can leave the estate to his wife and that there will be only $13,000 of federal estate tax due on his estate if he leaves it all to his wife. He learns, however, that when his wife leaves the estate to the children, approximately $105,400 will be owed in taxes before it passes to the two children, assuming no reduction in the size of the estate. Legal counsel is consulted (someone familiar with the tax laws). Mr. Abbott discovers that by letting $250,000 of the estate pass outright to Mrs. Abbott and by putting $295,000 in a trust for the benefit of Mrs. Abbott for her life, taxes will be reduced when she dies. When Mr. Abbott dies, the available credit plus the marital deduction will reduce substantially the taxes due on the estate. Then when Mrs. Abbott dies, the tax that she will pay on the $250,000 that she received outright would be $21,400. This represents a tax saving in excess of $82,000 over the original plan that Mr. Abbott had set up. What is more important, Mrs. Abbott has the use of the entire estate. Also, Mr. Abbott is assured that at least half of his estate will go to his children if Mrs. Abbott should remarry.

Under the federal estate tax laws, the estates of married people qualify for favorable treatment, as we indicated in the case of the Abbotts. In the *community-property states* of Arizona, California, Idaho, Louisiana, Nevada, New Mexico, Texas, and Washington, half of the property acquired by a married couple is, in general, assumed to be owned by each partner. Therefore, when one dies, only half of the property is subject to the tax, as was true in the case of Mr. and Mrs. Abbott.

This arrangement does not apply to the other so-called *common-law states*. But in those states the marital deduction provisions enable husbands and wives to leave to a surviving spouse, free of tax, up to $250,000, or one half of the estate, whichever is larger. The effect of the favorable provisions is to greatly reduce the tax cost of leaving property to your husband or wife. Couples worth as much as $425,000 can pass their property outright to each other utterly tax-free. That sounds almost too good to be true. Unfortunately, as we found in the Abbotts' case, the payment of the tax will come in the second transfer, when the surviving spouse leaves the family property to the children.

Setting up a living or testamentary trust

In order to obtain tax advantages for Mr. and Mrs. Abbott, a living or testamentary trust must be set up and its assets managed by a trustee. A living trust is created when Mr. and Mrs. Abbott are alive. Its assets are placed in the hands of a trustee. A testamentary trust is established at the death of Mr. Abbott under his will. Of course, the job of the trustee under such an arrangement is to invest the trust assets in a prudent manner. The trustee must pay income from the trust to the surviving spouse or children, and then pass on the remainder of the trust to the person named in the trust agreement upon the death of the spouse. This means not only that you can save estate taxes in the use of the trust but also that in the transfer process you can have professional management of the assets while the trust is in effect. An investment plan is tailored to meet the needs of the beneficiary. A trust agreement may specify how the money is to be invested. Usually broad investment discretion is given. Since the trust often lasts for many years, the trustee is given the broadest powers to adjust to a continuously changing investment environment. The agreement will indicate how the income and principal are to be used for the benefit of the beneficiaries, including how the funds are to be handled in special circumstances. An example would be when money is needed to take care of a spouse who becomes ill.

When we set up a trust, the trustee is working for the benefit of the surviving family.

There are other advantages to a trust. The trustee not only provides experienced management for the property, but can also prevent the waste of the family's valuable property. If the property is professionally managed by the trustee, this might prevent unscrupulous persons from taking advantage of a bereaved spouse. Widows and widowers are prime candidates for con artists, promoters with speculative investment schemes, and well-meaning but ineffectual family members. In addition, if you have a trust, the trust will see to it that your beneficiaries receive proper care in case of financial need. The trustee may be an individual or a trust company that is always available to handle these problems. In addition, the trust agreement assures you that your property will be distributed as you wish. But there are costs to the administration of a trust—a factor you cannot ignore. The creator of a trust must balance the cost of trust administration against its benefits.

Potential tax savings of a trust

To get some idea of the cost of estate taxes, look at Table 17–2. It indicates the amount of taxation at first transfer and over two transfers for either a single person or a married person. To make use of this vital information, you must first of all find out the total value of property. That means adding up the value of your life insurance, real estate, stocks and bonds, cash in the bank, your interest in jointly held property, and any other assets you own or control. In addition, you must add gifts you have given out. Finally, you must include any gifts above and beyond the limits of the federal gift tax. (We shall discuss the federal gift tax in more detail later in this chapter.)

Second, in order to use the table, you must find the gross value of your property subject to the tax in the far left column. Then, as you read across the appropriate columns—married or single person, taxation at first transfer, and taxation over two transfers—you can determine the amount of tax your estate will have to pay without a trust. You can also determine what will happen if the property is left under a tax-saving trust. These calculations are based on the assumption that no lifetime gift will be subject to tax at death. The calculations incorporate the full credit allowed against an estate tax. If we assume that you are married, you can determine both the taxation over two transfers, and the total amount saved as a result of the trust.

Jurisdictional taxes

People must pay taxes in the tax jurisdiction where they live. For example, if you live in the District of Columbia, your heirs will have to pay an inheritance tax to the District of Columbia. The tax is computed at graduated rates on the value of the share of the estate passing to each

Table 17–2
Federal estate tax

1. Federal Estate Tax — Tax shown is the Federal estate tax reduced by the unified credit and the maximum credit for State death taxes.

	TAXATION AT FIRST TRANSFER				TAXATION OVER TWO TRANSFERS					
	Single Persons (Or married persons with no assets qualifying for marital deduction)		Married Persons (Assuming full marital deduction)		Single Persons — Total tax, assuming that single person leaves property to primary beneficiary, who leaves it in turn to successor beneficiary (other than spouse)			Married Persons — Total tax, estates of husband and wife, assuming that first spouse to die owns all property and		
Value of property subject to tax	Tax	Rate on next bracket	Tax	Effective rate on next bracket	...if property is left outright to primary beneficiary	...if property is left to primary beneficiary in a tax-saving trust	TAX SAVED BY USE OF TRUSTS	...entire estate is left to survivor outright	...half of estate is left to survivor in a tax-saving trust	TAX SAVED BY USE OF TRUSTS
$ 178,290	$ —	30.4	$ —	—	$ —	$ —	$ —	$ —	$ —	$ —
180,000	520	30.4	—	—	882	520	362	520	—	520
200,000	6,600	29.6	—	—	11,194	6,600	4,594	6,600	—	6,600
220,000	12,520	29.6	—	—	21,334	12,520	8,814	12,520	—	12,520
250,000	21,400	31.6	—	—	36,466	21,400	15,066	21,400	—	21,400
300,000	37,200	30.8	—	—	62,645	37,200	25,445	37,200	—	37,200
350,000	52,600	30.8	—	—	88,978	52,600	36,378	52,600	—	52,600
356,580	54,627	30.8	—	—	92,429	54,627	37,802	54,627	—	54,627
400,000	68,000	30.8	—	—	115,056	68,000	47,056	68,000	13,200	54,800
428,290	76,713	30.8	—	30.4	129,799	76,713	53,086	76,713	21,574	55,139
430,000	77,240	30.8	520	30.4	130,690	77,240	53,450	77,600	22,080	55,520
450,000	83,400	30.8	6,600	29.6	141,113	83,400	57,713	87,967	28,000	59,967
500,000	98,800	33.	21,400	15.8	167,170	98,800	68,370	113,609	42,800	70,809
550,000	115,300	33.	29,300	15.8	193,988	115,300	78,688	134,931	58,600	76,331
600,000	131,800	33.	37,200	15.4	220,806	131,800	89,006	156,724	74,400	82,324
650,000	148,300	33.	44,900	15.4	247,661	148,300	99,361	178,383	89,800	88,583
700,000	164,800	32.2	52,600	15.4	275,216	164,800	110,416	200,042	105,200	94,842
750,000	180,900	34.2	60,300	15.4	302,503	180,900	121,603	221,701	120,600	101,101
800,000	198,000	34.2	68,000	15.4	330,460	198,000	132,460	243,104	136,000	107,104
850,000	215,100	34.2	75,700	15.4	358,417	215,100	143,317	264,911	151,400	113,511
900,000	232,200	33.4	83,400	15.4	386,374	232,200	154,174	287,077	166,800	120,277
950,000	248,900	33.4	91,100	15.4	414,054	248,900	165,154	309,244	182,200	127,044
1,000,000	265,600	35.4	98,800	16.5	441,477	265,600	175,877	331,401	197,600	133,801
1,100,000	301,000	34.6	115,300	16.5	498,658	301,000	197,658	375,790	230,600	145,190
1,250,000	352,900	36.6	140,050	16.5	584,108	352,900	231,208	444,493	280,100	164,393
1,400,000	407,800	36.6	164,800	16.1	670,795	407,800	262,995	512,579	329,600	182,979
1,500,000	444,400	38.6	180,900	17.1	729,682	444,400	285,282	559,091	361,800	197,291
1,600,000	483,000	37.8	198,000	17.1	789,882	483,000	306,882	606,532	396,000	210,532
1,800,000	558,600	37.8	232,200	16.7	908,524	558,600	349,924	702,771	464,400	238,371
2,000,000	634,200	41.8	265,600	17.7	1,029,483	634,200	395,283	799,403	531,200	268,203
2,100,000	676,000	41.	283,300	17.7	1,092,584	676,000	416,584	848,213	566,600	281,613
2,200,000	717,000	41.	301,000	17.3	1,155,178	717,000	438,178	897,022	602,000	295,022
2,500,000	840,000	45.	352,900	18.3	1,345,680	840,000	505,680	1,048,211	705,800	342,411
2,600,000	885,000	44.2	371,200	18.3	1,411,470	885,000	526,470	1,100,008	742,400	357,608
3,000,000	1,061,800	48.2	444,400	19.3	1,672,640	1,061,800	610,840	1,309,420	888,800	420,620
3,100,000	1,110,000	47.4	463,700	19.3	1,740,420	1,110,000	630,420	1,364,745	927,400	437,345
3,200,000	1,157,400	47.4	483,000	18.9	1,809,407	1,157,400	652,007	1,419,714	966,000	453,714
3,500,000	1,299,600	51.4	539,700	18.9	2,016,764	1,299,600	717,164	1,583,953	1,079,400	504,553
3,600,000	1,351,000	50.6	558,600	18.9	2,088,090	1,351,000	737,090	1,640,355	1,117,200	523,155
4,000,000	1,553,400	54.6	634,200	20.9	2,371,506	1,553,400	818,106	1,870,189	1,268,400	601,789
4,100,000	1,608,000	53.8	655,100	20.9	2,444,720	1,608,000	836,720	1,928,583	1,310,200	618,383
4,200,000	1,661,800	53.8	676,000	20.5	2,518,990	1,661,800	857,190	1,987,936	1,352,000	635,936
		(Rates are higher on larger estates)		(Rates are higher on larger estates)	Some of the amounts shown in this column will be reduced if primary beneficiary survives for less than 10 years.	The amounts shown in these columns assume that the generation-skipping trust rules do not apply.		Some of the amounts shown in this column and the next will be reduced if wife survives husband less than 10 years.	For estates between $356,580 and $500,000, use of the full marital deduction may benefit the spouse, while in some cases affecting overall tax savings.	

SOURCE   The Riggs National Bank of Washington, D.C.

beneficiary in excess of the basic exemption that is provided. In the District of Columbia, an exemption of $5,000 is provided for a spouse, children, parents, adopted children, lineal ancestors or descendants. The tax is 1 percent of the first $5,000; 2 percent of the next $25,000; 3 percent of the next $50,000; 5 percent of the next $100,000; 6 percent of the next $500,000; and 8 percent on the next $1 million. In calculating the tax, life insurance proceeds must be included if they have been paid to the estate. If these proceeds were taken out to provide for the payment of taxes or other charges against the insured's estate or to benefit the insured's estate, or if the main beneficiary predeceased the insured, then the proceeds must be included. Any property owned jointly with a right of survivorship must pay its fractional interest and is subject to tax. In computing the tax in the District of Columbia, the federal estate tax is deductible from the inheritance tax. In addition, a District of Columbia estate tax absorbs the maximum credit for state tax allowed by the Federal Estate Tax Law. It is important, therefore, for you to have good advice about taxes.

Cost of managing a trust

A trust can possibly save your estate a substantial sum of money, as has been shown. But there is a cost involved in managing a testamentary trust. A person setting up a trust must take into consideration the following costs before committing his or her beneficiaries to such a course of action.

Principal fee The first cost of setting up a testamentary trust is the principal fee, which is a fee on the principal value of the trust. This is based on the current market value of the estate, quarterly, semiannually, or annually, however the billing process works. A typical cost on the first $300,000 is $5 per thousand; the cost on the next $200,000 is $3 per thousand; and above $500,000 up to $5 million, it is $2 per thousand. For values beyond $5 million, a reasonable fee will be charged on the basis of all factors. The principal fee is illustrative. It obviously will vary from one financial institution to another.

If you decide to leave a $600,000 estate to be managed by a trust department of a commercial bank, on the basis of the above schedule the principal fee would be $2,300: $1,500 on the first $300,000, $600 on the next $200,000, and $200 on the next $100,000. This amounts to approximately .38 percent of the value of the trust.

Income fee A typical income fee, is 3½ percent on the first $50,000 of annual income from the estate, 2½ percent on the next $200,000, and 1 percent on any excess income over $50,000. If you assume that the proceeds are invested in bonds and stocks that provide current income at 8 percent, then the income on $600,000 would be $48,000, and the income fee paid would be 3½ percent, or an additional $1,680. The cost of the administration of the $600,000 estate would be $3,980, which is $2,300 for the principal and $1,680 for the income fee.

Viewed another way, the $3,980 represents 8.29 percent of the $48,000 income. This seems reasonable since you will get expert service, the estate will be handled well and prudently, you will protect your heirs and assigns, and the fee will be tax-deductible as a business expense, to the extent there is taxable income.

In setting up a living trust that avoids probate, you might save 2 percent of the probate cost, or $12,000 for an estate of $600,000. This saving must be compared to the annual cost of managing the trust. If the annual fee is $3,980, in three years the annual cost of the trust will have equaled the estimated savings on probate. You will have had, however, the benefit of a living trust during the three-year period.

Minimum fee   Usually a financial institution imposes a minimum fee, which may be as low as $500, up to several thousand dollars.

Termination fee   One other item needs to be noted in the fee schedule. There usually is a termination fee, which is a percent of the market value of the assets held. In the case of the $600,000 estate, a termination fee of as much as 2 percent might be levied on the estate. This would amount to $12,000. This fee is meant to cover the cost of asset distribution at the time the trust is terminated, plus any additional duties performed beyond investment management during the life of the trust. As an aside, individuals not accustomed to working in legal and financial circles will find that the management of a small trust or of a small investment fund requires a great deal of time and effort. The compensation level discussed, that is, $3,980 a year to manage a $600,000 testamentary trust, seems a modest fee. If you consider the expense of financial management, upkeep, and other attendant charges that are necessary, plus the time involved, it might be a bargain.

Costs if more than one trustee is involved   There are situations when a co-trustee is involved with an estate. A co-trustee may provide a liaison with the family regarding your personal objectives. This will add to the cost of trust administration. When setting up a trust, the trustor or the testator should keep in mind the additional cost related to a situation where there is a successor trustee. A bank may make an additional charge for acting as successor trustee. This charge is made where the trust company must review the activities of the prior trustee. The additional charge is known as an *acceptance fee*. It can amount to as much as 1 percent of the current market value of the estate at the time of the opening of the trust.

Advantages and costs of professional help   The advantages of naming a professional executor to handle the estate have been discussed. Certainly an executor with knowledge or experience is necessary to protect the beneficiaries of an estate, their heirs, and assigns. Financial institutions have trained lawyers and financial experts to perform these services quickly and efficiently. The professional executor or trustee has a financial responsibility to protect the interests of the heirs and assigns. A corporate executor or trustee offers permanence and continuity. The corporation does not die, as might be the case when a single individual is appointed an executor or trustee. Professional trustees are likely to be objective and impartial, which can be important in some family situations. And financial institutions have the ability to meet changing needs.

There is a group judgment rather than the judgment of a single individual, and there is personal concern.

Our work in trust activities has revealed the amount of personal concern that trust and investment officers of large financial institutions show for their clients. They treat them with respect and dignity, do an able job, and, in addition, are friendly and courteous. Of course, all these activities that are considered to be advantages are done at a cost. You must weigh the benefits against the cost before you obtain professional help.

How to reduce an estate through gifts

A federal gift tax is due on the amount transferred to children, relatives, or friends in excess of $3,000 per donee each year. The purpose of the gift tax is to prevent lifetime transfers being used to avoid estate taxes. In 1976 the federal estate tax and federal gift tax rates were merged. Prior to that time, the rates were independent. Thus if you make lifetime gifts of over $3,000 per year per person or a total lifetime gift of over $60,000 per person the amount must be added to your estate in computing the federal estate tax. Before you give eveything you own away make certain that you will not need the funds later in life for your own needs.

The first gift tax exclusion—charitable gifts

Let's assume that you want to calculate the amount of federal gift tax you will have to pay. In effect, this means that you are trying to reduce the size of your estate on which taxes must be paid. First of all, you should deduct from the total gifts any allowable charitable gifts. Gifts to qualified charities are not taxable up to certain limits. In addition, charitable gifts to an appropriate institution can be taken as a deduction from your federal income tax. This reduces the value of your estate, and you still get credit for the gift as a deduction against income. It is important to realize this. It might be wise to consider giving part of your estate to a charity, since this is a legitimate deduction from inheritance taxes. In addition, while you are still alive, such a gift is a deduction from your federal income tax. Also, you might consider using specialized trusts, called *charitable remainder trusts.* Such trusts allow you to make payments to individuals during their lifetime; after their death, the remainder of the bequest will go to a charity. These trusts are known also as *pooled income trusts, unitrusts,* or *annuity trusts.* Because they are highly specialized, you should use them only in consultation with your attorney and perhaps with a qualified representative of the specific charity.

The second gift tax exclusion—$3,000 donee exclusion

The second exclusion is on the basis of $3,000 to each donee in a calendar year. This means, for example, that you and your spouse together could give each child $6,000 a year without paying any federal gift tax, since you can combine both spouses' $3,000 exemptions. Gifts made by a husband and wife to a third party are usually taxed with the spouse's consent as though each gave one half. In effect, this doubles each spouse's annual exclusion from $3,000 to $6,000. As an example, if a husband and wife should decide to give a child $6,000 in one year to buy a car, it would be unnecessary to pay a gift tax on this amount. On the other hand, if the couple gave $12,000, then $6,000 would be subject to the gift tax.

The third gift tax exclusion—the marital deduction

The third kind of gift tax exclusion is a marital deduction. The first $100,000 of lifetime gifts given by one spouse to the other spouse would qualify as a marital deduction. In addition, 50 percent of lifetime gifts in excess of $200,000 would also be exempt from the federal gift tax.

In order to find the tax on gifts made in the years since 1976, you should compute your tax on the basis of the rates listed in Table 17–3. Calculate the total of all net taxable gifts you have made since 6 June 1932, including the current calendar quarter. Then compute the tax, at the rates listed below, on such gifts made prior to the current calendar quarter. The difference between the two resulting figures is the gift tax due before deducting the allowable credit. The allowable credit schedule listed in Table 17–3 is as follows:

Table 17-3
Federal gift tax

Net taxable gifts	Gift tax (before deducting credit)*	% on excess
Under $10,000	18% of amount	—
$ 10,000	$ 1,800	20%
20,000	3,800	22
40,000	8,200	24
60,000	13,000	26
80,000	18,200	28
100,000	23,800	30
150,000	38,800	32
250,000	70,800	34
500,000	155,800	37
750,000	248,300	39
1,000,000	345,800	41
1,250,000	448,300	43
1,500,000	555,800	45
2,000,000	780,800	49
2,500,000	1,025,800	53
3,000,000	1,290,800	57
3,500,000	1,575,800	61
4,000,000	1,880,800	65
4,500,000	2,205,800	69
5,000,000	2,550,800	70

SOURCE   The Riggs National Bank of Washington, D.C.

For gifts made in January/June 1977, the maximum credit is $6,000.

For gifts made in July/December 1977, the maximum credit is $30,000.

For 1978, the maximum credit is $34,000.

For 1979, $38,000.

For 1980, $42,500.

For 1981 and thereafter, $47,000.

The maximum credit must be reduced by any previous credit claimed prior to the present deduction. Of course, it is not easy to figure out gift taxes, which are somewhat complicated. But essentially they offer you leeway in paying your taxes as well as credits against which you pay no tax. It is important, therefore, for you to learn about the federal gift tax. The rate varies from 18 percent for an amount under $10,000 to 70 percent for an amount above $5,000,000. If you give $5 million away in gifts on a lifetime basis, the amount you have to pay in taxes to Uncle Sam amounts to $2,550,800. This is because you are now paying 70 percent on the excess of the amount of the gift over $5 million. And that is a lot of money.

Short-term living trusts—a way to reduce taxes

A short-term trust called a Clifford Trust is an irrevocable trust governed by federal statute. The time period of the trust must be for 10 years and one day or longer. It is primarily a tax device to shift income from a person in a high-income tax bracket to a person in a lower tax bracket. Its application is limited to a very small group of individuals whose financial circumstances warrant its use. For example, let's assume that John and Alice have set aside an investment nest egg of $200,000 for their retirement years. They have had this amount for some time; under no circumstances will they need it over the next 10 years. But they would like to use the nest egg to help their children, Jeff and Scott through college. Perhaps they might wish to help their children pay for a house, for furnishings, for a new addition to a house, or for the purchase of an automobile. John and Alice would also like to reduce their income taxes. They plan to retire in 10 years and want to have the use of the $200,000 as income.

What options are open to Alice and John? They might set up a short-term trust and achieve the objective of helping their children. At the same time they can provide for their own retirement. They can set up a short-term trust of $200,000 for 10 years. Income from the trust would be divided between the children. The principal of the trust would revert to John and Alice at the end of the 10-year period. It really doesn't make any difference where the money is invested, although that fact can be specified. The trust would provide that under no circumstances should income from it be used to satisfy a legal obligation of John and Alice to their children. It is assumed that the money will be kept under management for the full period. Its income goes to Jeff and Scott instead of to John and Alice. At the end of the period, the money reverts to John and Alice.

Let's assume that the average current income from the trust is 6 percent, or $12,000 per year. That income is no longer taxed to John and Alice, but rather to Jeff and Scott, who are in a lower tax bracket. John and Alice haven't given up the asset under the trust agreement. But what is the advantage of giving the children the income? Is there a gift tax? Who pays the income tax on income from the trust? First, the income tax is to be paid by those who receive the income. Therefore, Jeff and Scott, each of whom receives $6,000 a year, will each pay an income tax on $6,000 per year. Let's assume that both sons are in the 30 percent tax bracket. That means that they will each pay $1,800 a year on the income. They will have $4,200 a year available to do whatever they wish. What is the advantage of this procedure? If John and Alice had kept the $200,000, they would have received the same $12,000 income. Because they are in the 50 percent marginal bracket they would have to pay $6,000 in income tax and would have $6,000 left. So by setting up a trust, they have increased the income they can keep and save by $2,400 ($6,000 minus $1,800 for each son's tax). Simply because of the tax, they save $2,400 a year. Of course, they have lost control of the money for 10 years. But they wanted to help their children anyway, and the net result is that they have paid less out in taxes. This type of arrangement is an excellent way of reducing your income tax while you are still alive and recovering the principal of the trust when you need it to provide retirement income. The danger in the plan is that you might need the money for yourself during the 10-year period. If you die, the trust money will become part of your estate. Therefore, the trust is not a gift and does not reduce your estate or estate taxes.

Charitable giving—a way to reduce taxes.

Let us now take a look at what is meant by estate planning and charitable giving. When you reach retirement years and are concerned about what is going to happen to your estate, you may have a superabundance of assets. Your children may be well-to-do and in no need of financial help. You find that you have accumulated an adequate sum to take care of your own needs. So you decide to leave a part of your estate to a university, church, or some other private charity. You want to achieve the benefits of giving while you are alive, but also retain the income on the assets you give.

The basic principle of charitable giving through a trust is simple to follow. You give assets to your favorite charity, church, or university. This is in the form of a charitable remainder trust and you must follow the legal rules established for such purpose. But you continue to receive income from these assets as long as you live. Usually income can be received as long as one of the parties involved in making the charitable gift is alive, but it is also possible to do so for the lifetime of two parties. This means that income from a charitable gift could go to your spouse, and then to your children. At this point the assets would revert to the charity. The only limit is on the amount of assets that can be deducted. Depending on the charity, the deduction for the corpus of the estate, that is, for the amount given, may be taken over six years. The amount of the deduction is limited to 50 percent of the adjusted gross income of the person creating the trust. At the end of the period, the total amount contributed goes to the charity.

Let's assume that you earn $50,000 a year (adjusted gross income). At this income level you could give away $25,000 a year for six years (a total of $150,000) as a charitable gift under the charitable deferred-giving plan. The $150,000 invested at 8 percent would provide $12,000 of income per year. Since you can write off $25,000 a year against income, that would mean that the $12,000 would be tax-free. The additional $13,000 could be written off against ordinary income, which would further reduce your income tax.

This gift has the advantage of providing you with a substantial amount of tax-free income. It gives your charity a substantial donation. All of this assumes that you, the individual who is benevolent, would like to benefit some institution. It assumes that your family is well cared for financially and doesn't need the additional income. In a sense it becomes a monument to your remembrance of the activities you were involved with as you went through life. There are many motives involved in charitable giving. Certainly you cannot ignore the tax implications. Charitable giving might fit fairly well into plans for your preretirement as well as your retirement years.

Charitable giving and the marital deduction

Charitable giving might also bridge the gap completely between marital deduction and the taxable amount of an estate. Let's assume that there is a limit on the marital deduction of $250,000 and the estate is $500,000. Taxes will have to be paid on $250,000 of your estate. However, if a charitable trust is created, it might be possible for you to pass the estate on to your spouse with no taxes. Half of the estate is tax-free because of the marital deduction. The other half could be set up as a charitable trust, or unitrust. Income from the trust (an annuity) would go to your spouse for life. The remainder would go to some charitable institution. In that way a substantial sum of money can be given to your favorite charity, and estate taxes can be greatly reduced. This device is particularly attractive if there are securities in the estate that have substantial capital gains. If stocks were purchased at $2 per share, and are now selling at $60 a share, there is a substantial capital gain. Capital gains taxes are not paid on these shares if they are put into a charitable trust.

Most people are not in the enviable position of being able to pass on substantial amounts of money. But there is certainly no harm in considering ways to reduce the cost of passing on substantial amounts of money in a large estate. One way of reducing the tax burden is by charitable giving. The person giving the money does eventually lose the use of his or her assets. At the same time the donor gains goodwill for the family from people or institutions that are recipients of the benefit.

Some special financial problems of the aged

You must be realistic about estate planning and your financial ability to accomplish these goals: (1) beat the inflation rate that has persisted at a high level for the last decade; (2) retire with your full Social Security benefits, a substantial private pension, and a large estate; and (3) use your estate for your own needs while planning how to transfer it to someone else. Many people earn substantially less after retirement. They may find it difficult to provide adequately for their retirement. In addition, they may have accumulated only a modest estate. In fact, a substantial number of people may not be able to retire at all, or may find retirement undesirable. They must maintain some form of employment. Some people have grand dreams of traveling, studying, and moving about the country free of financial worry after they retire. But when they reach old age, they may find that their pension is too small and inflation too great to allow them the luxury of doing as they had planned. Costs for food, housing, and running an automobile have skyrocketed. Even on a once generous pension fund, they can't balance their budget. Under these circumstances many people decide to go back to work. But there are special problems to be considered in old age.

Retirement as a mixed blessing

At first blush you might consider going back to work a tremendous sacrifice. Inflation has forced you back into the job market. You are resentful. But let's take another look at what happens when a person retires. Many people experience what is known as the retirement letdown. For a short period of time they are able to enjoy themselves as they play golf, read, and live the good life. But they find after a while that this life can become dull and boring. They need a creative activity that gives them a purpose in life—something that reduces their anxiety over inflation and the depression brought about by feeling that they are less than first-class citizens. For many the loss of a job is a loss of identity. They just can't take the emotional problems related to retirement. They miss their old friends and habits, and want to continue being active. So they decide to go back to work.

It might be wise for you to plan on working as long as you are physically and mentally able to do so. In some families you may hear parents and grandparents complain that they have to take in sewing, do extra typing jobs, handle special probjects, or work in a store. Even though these people complain about the work, it gives them an outlet. It makes them feel wanted. It also brings them out again into the world.

The Social Security system has favored the desire of older Americans to continue working by providing benefits that continue after retirement. Under the Social Security program, the ceiling has been raised to allow retirees to earn $6,000 in 1982 without suffering a reduction of Social Security benefits. After 1982, the amount that retirees may earn will increase in proportion to national average wages. This arrangement will provide an incentive for people to work in their retirement years and thus beat inflation. They will also live more interesting lives. Many of them may not work a full week. But working just three days a week or a half a day a week for three days will provide extra income, a new interest in life, and a help against inflation.

People in this way may discover the pleasures of a second career. One career is given up as another is found. New needs and talents are needed to begin a new career that may turn out to be both exciting and profitable. This proves a new thesis: life does not begin at 40 but at 70 for a fortunate group of older Americans who are able to help other people and themselves.

Financial planning for sickness and old age

As you grow older and go into retirement, you will feel more and more concern about what will happen to you if you become sick. You may have enough income, but you may not have anyone to look after you. In some cases children can take care of their parents in the parents' home. This seems to be the best way for the elderly. But often this is impossible. Elderly people may need health care in a home for the elderly. Many of these homes are associated with nonprofit and profit-making organizations that are attractive for the elderly. We know a former professor who after retirement bought into a housing complex for the elderly that provided excellent accommodations, recreation facilities, food, and medical facilities. Although expensive, the complex gave to the professor and his spouse the security they needed in their old age. They knew that there would always be someone at the complex to care for them if they needed help.

Whether or not elderly parents go into a nursing home or a home for the elderly is a matter to be discussed by parents and their children. To a great extent the parents' wishes should dictate what happens to them. In one case an elderly parent was in and out of the hospital during the last six months of her life. She did not want to go to a nursing home or a hospital. But it was impossible for members of her family to care for their mother. They had to put her in a hospital, where she could have constant care.

Looking after a parent or loved one at home is a round-the-clock job. It is impossible for a single person to do it alone, as this would create undue hardship and sacrifice. Under ideal circumstances members of the family can care for a loved one in their own surroundings. However, if all members of the family cannot help out, then the family must obtain outside help. Visiting public nurses can sometimes come in two or three times a week. This kind of care can be costly. Most expensive are the services of round-the-clock nurses or nurses working eight hours a day, seven days a week.

For all these reasons, your financial plans should include some provision for the possibility of your becoming sick in your retirement years. Funds must be available to the extent possible to care for you when you become old and infirm. Medicare and Medicaid, Blue Cross and Blue Shield, and other forms of pension and health benefits should continue in force. Certainly, as you prepare your estate plan, you must prepare for the eventuality of becoming sick and incapacitated. You should try to provide a financial plan that offers medical care.

The role of the family in care of the elderly

If you are called on to look for a medical or nursing home to care for an elderly person, you should try to select a place that is acceptable to the elderly person. Children of parents who are becoming elderly have to plan their financial careers and their economic lives for the benefit of their own spouses and children. But they have to understand that they may be called on to help their own elderly parents. This is a matter for discussion among all concerned parties. When selecting outside help or a home, the children should listen to the wishes of their parents. The financial burden will not be as great for the children whose parents have planned ahead for all contingencies. But if the parents do not have enough money, their children must bear part of the financial burden. No one wants to see an elderly parent become a ward of public charity.

A living trust as a possible solution

One solution might be for you to establish a living trust with your assets. Your estate would be managed in such a way as to protect your interests. Your trustee would see to it that you receive proper medical and nursing care. This would relieve your family of the burden of looking after you. You would control your own financial destiny. Other advantages are:

1. it is not subject to public records as a guardianship or conservatorship would be
2. you are protected against your own incapacity

3. you have proper investment management
4. you avoid probate and
5. you have accurate records of your financial affairs

Predators of the elderly

There are people who prey on the elderly. As people grow old, they often become easy prey for ripoffs. Sometimes they are fleeced of their life savings. We suggest that you beware of con games and crooks who offer to provide a secure life in return for your money.

A 1979 article in *The Wall Street Journal* was entitled "Predators Find Elderly Are Often Easy Prey for an Array of Ripoffs."[3] Jim Montgomery, author of the article, quoted from a deceptive advertisement:

> Retire from inflation at any of seven Pacific Homes . . . delicious meals, medical care, superb facilities for recreational and cultural activities, and a lifetime lease on a modern apartment or cottage are all provided through fees that can never be increased once you become a resident.

Montgomery commented that this promise of inflation-immune retirement actually turned out to be too good to be true. But many people believed the ad because it was placed by Pacific Homes, a church-affiliated, non-profit corporation. They thought, "If it's church-related, we can believe it."[4]

A court-appointed trustee who finally took charge of Pacific Homes uncovered what "may well be the longest running, largest ponzi scheme in history." Some people may ask, "If you can't trust a church, what can you trust?" In this case there was deception and fraud designed to fleece older Americans of their savings. The article did not just touch on retirement homes. It touched on every scheme and scam in the book designed to hit the old folks and take their money away from them:

> It is done by telephone, by peddlers door-to-door, in advertising, at the old folks' home. Widows and widowers are deluded with misleading sales pitches for worthless or overpriced insurance policies, home repairs, quack remedies, dance lessons, earn-money-at-home deals, vacation certificates at discount clubs, investment plans, unordered merchandise, and cemetery plots."[5]

It is grief, loneliness, and despair of "pain, destitution and death that make the elderly easy marks for these and other ripoffs that exploit their susceptibility to confusion and forgetfulness as such diminished by age."[6]

You must plan for your old age and face the fact that one of your loved ones might not be around to help and protect you after your spouse

---

[3] *The Wall Street Journal,* November 9, 1979.
[4] Ibid.
[5] Ibid.
[6] Ibid.

has died. You need to understand the pitfalls set for the elderly and develop some sort of warning system that will protect you from the cheats and swindlers that prey upon the unsuspecting.

One of the classic schemes that can be perpetrated on the elderly as well as the greedy of all ages is known as the *pigeon drop*. In this classic con a younger man or woman tells an older person that she or he has just found an unmarked bag full of money. She or he persuades the older person to withdraw a large sum of money from the bank to prove good faith in order to share in the find. The elderly person gives the money to the younger person in good faith. The younger perpetrator then leaves with the old person's money and is never seen again. We must not listen to people who offer to provide something for nothing. Most of the time people who are greedy enough to become involved in a scam lose their money. Montgomery reported that even worse things can happen:

> Sometimes, tragically, the victims lose more than their money. A few months ago, police and a banker in the Bronx helped thwart a pigeon drop aimed at fleecing two sisters, ages 68 and 72 of $17,000 in savings. But, in the mistaken belief that the money was gone, the women jumped from the roof to their deaths.[7]

Scams are not confined to the poor. A wealthy 80-year-old Park Avenue woman handed over $1 million in jewelry, securities, and cash to a team of New York operators. Fortunately, when one of the operators returned to get even more money (she, too, was greedy), arrests were made and the loot was recovered.

Checking nursing homes

Some nursing homes are involved in ripping off their patients. There are 18,000 nursing homes in the United States. Residents of some homes are too weak and confused to know that they are being ripped off. After all, residents of nursing homes have an average age of 80 years.[8] They are afflicted with chronic diseases; half of them are senile; and three out of five are widowed. In effect, they are living at the mercy of their keepers. One home was discovered to be billing a 92-year-old woman 85 cents for a 22 cent package of toilet tissue. One home charged an elderly man $30 for using his own wheelchair. When he complained, they charged him $30 for cleaning it. Elsewhere, nursing homes may be found bilking an 80-year-old person's bus fund of $42,000.

Somehow the elderly must guard against these fraudulent practices. Someone must help the elderly in case members of his family are not available. Before the elderly are sent to a nursing home, the home should

---

[7] Jim Montgomery, quoted in *The Wall Street Journal*, November 9, 1979, p. 1.
[8] Ibid.

be thoroughly checked and some protection should be established for them.

Another way of fleecing the elderly is to sell them too much health insurance. This is one of the greatest ripoffs of all.[9] A congressional committee estimated that about $1 billion per year is spent for health insurance that the elderly people don't need at all, or can't use, or won't collect on. An elderly woman in Pennsylvania spent $50,000 for 30 policies in three years. An 85-year-old blind man bought 26 policies in three years. An 87-year-old Wisconsin woman paid $4,000 on 19 policies sold by six agents representing nine companies. A couple, aged 78 and 82, who couldn't afford refrigerator or television repairs, were trying to keep up annual premiums of $2,882 on 19 policies.[10] Sometimes the elderly are bilked of their savings.[11] Thousands of elderly Floridians were wiped clean by promoters of 14 percent corporate promissory notes that turned out to have been secured by lies instead of by first mortgages. One victim, a retired dentist, lost $200,000. He couldn't take it and committed suicide. There's more at stake than the loss of money in these ripoffs.[12]

Medical quacks also defraud people of their money and their health. Doctors offering "get-well" schemes that cost a fortune often turn out to be complete frauds. There is no fountain of youth. Another scam involves selling dance lessons to the elderly. A 73-year-old arthritic Atlanta woman signed up for more than $4,000 worth of dance lessons. She had to borrow $1,500 from a bank to pay for them before the studio agreed, under pressure from a state agency, to refund $3,000. Of course, you also have health-care homes that promise the world, take virtually all the life savings of the elderly, and then do not provide what they say they are going to provide. There isn't any easy solution to the problem of scams, ripoffs, frauds, and deception against the elderly. But as we prepare for our retirement and old age, we need wise counsel to protect us from our own weaknesses. We must plan ahead.

Summary

There are three phases in estate planning: creation of the estate, conserving the estate, and transfer of the estate at death. An estate may be transferred by joint ownership, through a will, by gift, or through a trust. The basic objective of estate planning is to transfer your estate to your beneficiary (or beneficiaries) at the lowest possible cost, with the least tax burden, and in the fastest amount of time. Of course, specific objectives of each person differ.

[9] Ibid.
[10] Ibid.
[11] Ibid.
[12] Ibid.

One major step in the direction of estate planning is to prepare a will. You should begin at an early age (legally 21) to keep a will on file. In this way, even if you have only a modest amount of personal assets, these assets will be passed on to your loved ones. In writing a will, make certain that you have legal counsel and that you select a competent executor to carry out your wishes. Such a person must have the competence and integrity to meet the charges and responsibilities created under the will. He, she, or it will be compensated for these services. If you cannot find someone close to you who has the ability, interest, and time to do a proper job, then you might consider the possibility of hiring a professional manager. When you create your will, make certain in writing that all persons close to you are aware of the will's provisions so that they know what to expect. Some uninformed heirs have been put in such a position that they are defrauded by unscrupulous persons. Some families, despite the best of intentions, have misunderstood the provisions of a will because there was a conflict between written statements in the will and verbal statements made by the person creating the will.

Another step in providing for the logical transfer of assets is to have an inventory of all assets in the estate. This inventory should include personal assets, furniture and fixtures in the house, works of art, and any identifiable physical items. The best way to insure an orderly transfer of assets is to prepare a list of the various items, their approximate value for estate tax purposes, where they are located, and who is to receive each one of these assets. You should know the approximate market value of your real estate. This can be done by obtaining periodic appraisals, or simply by judging the relative value of the real estate in the neighborhood in which the house is located. At the time of death, real estate will be appraised by a real estate appraiser for estate tax purposes. The list of assets should include all bank accounts (their amounts and location); checking accounts (their amounts and location); cash reserves (their amounts and location); and all proceeds of life insurance. Remember that life insurance owned and paid for by a surviving spouse is not a part of the estate. However, life insurance policies owned by the deceased are a part of the estate, and taxes must be paid on their proceeds.

It is not a bad idea for both spouses to have life insurance. The money is helpful for settling an estate, paying taxes, and providing general liquidity for the heirs.

Once you know the value of your estate, you can determine if there would be a substantial estate tax burden. If this is the case, then you can very carefully decide if you should establish a trust to reduce the estate taxes or if you should pass the assets directly on to your heirs. You should also consider lifetime gifts. If you give money away three years before your death, these gifts will be considered part of your estate. If you make gifts to your loved ones well in advance of your death on the basis of a normal life expectancy, you can reduce your estate. You can give up to $3,000 per person without paying any gift tax. Such a gift also reduces your estate. When you give, you must be certain that under all circumstances you will not need the $3,000 in the future. You can look at the gift tax as a way of transferring your estate while you live without worrying about paying any estate taxes. But you must plan ahead to take advantage of this part of your estate plan.

The marital deduction reduces your estate. It is the most important estate planning tool for married individuals. Estate planning must be done when both spouses are alive to get the maximum benefits when trying to save taxes over successive transfers. You can then explore the advantage of generation skipping transfers to reduce the federal estate tax impact.

We discovered that by charitable giving you can give everything away and still have more. It is almost like a parable from the Bible. You give away your assets, take credit against your ordinary income, and still have more on which to live. If you have a large estate and have properly taken care of your loved ones, then you might seriously consider charitable giving. It will reduce your tax burden and allow you to live well in your remaining years.

You must reckon with the problems of sickness in your old age. You hope that your family will help you, but there is a possibility that you might have to go to a nursing home, where you will be cared for by professionals. At that time you must make certain that your assets are properly handled. You must have someone who can help you in financial matters. You must be aware that there are predators who prey upon the elderly and who will fleece them of their money. So long as you can, you must prevent this from happening later on, after you have no control over your existence. This is extremely important for estate planning. If you have followed all the principles we have described, you should have a substantial estate. You will want to protect that estate for yourself and others to enjoy. You don't want a stranger fleecing your loved ones and denying them the benefits of your hard-earned wealth.

**ADDENDUM:
Economic Recovery
Tax Act of 1981**

As this book went to press in August 1981, the Economic Recovery Tax cleared Congress and was sent to President Reagan for signature. The act is the cornerstone of "Reganomics"—the administration's economic program designed to reduce inflation and unemployment and increase productivity. The central thrust of the act is to substantially reduce the tax burden of individuals and businesses. At the same time, government spending will be drastically reduced to counterbalance the loss in tax revenues to the government. This program is clearly the most radical shift in government fiscal policy since President Franklin D. Roosevelt's New Deal program of the 1930s. Major changes which will impact on personal financial planning are as follows:

1. Individual tax cuts The centerpiece of the act is a 25 percent cut in individual income taxes beginning October 1, 1981. Withholding rates will be reduced by 5 percent in October 1981, 10 percent in July 1982, and 10 percent in July 1983.

2. Indexing The 25 percent tax cut will be fully absorbed in 1984. Beginning in 1985, the amount allowed for personal exemptions ($1,000 in 1981), the zero bracket amount, and the income tax brackets will be indexed for inflation. This means that personal income taxes will be adjusted for inflation to offset "bracket creep." Under the present system, if your income increases to keep pace with inflation, your marginal tax rate increases over time. If inflation increases by 10 percent and your income also increases by 10 percent, for example, you will pay more federal income taxes even though your purchasing power remains constant. With indexing, your taxes will be adjusted for changes in the consumer price index. A pay increase equal to the consumer price index increase will no longer push you into a higher tax bracket.

3. Tax reductions on investment income Tax rates on unearned income, such as stock dividends and bond interest, currently go as high as 70 percent. Effective January 1, 1982, the maximum tax on all sources of income will be reduced to 50 percent.

4. Capital gains tax reductions The change in tax rates on unearned income causes a change in the maximum capital gains tax rate. Income taxes are paid on only 40 percent of any net long-term capital gains. The maximum tax on net long-term capital gains will be reduced from 28 percent (.4 times 70 percent) to 20 percent (.4 times 50 percent).

5. "Marriage penalty" reduction Under the current system, married couples who both earn a salary pay higher taxes than two single people earning the same total amount. Beginning in 1982, such couples may deduct 5 percent of the first $30,000 of the lower-earning spouse's earned income. In 1983 and subsequent years, the deduction increases to 10 percent of the first $30,000. Thus, a maximum of $1,500 may be deducted in 1982. The maximum increases to $3,000 in 1983 and later years.

6. Savings incentives   In order to attract capital into financially ailing thrift institutions, the act authorizes the "All Savers Certificate." Money raised from the sale of these certificates must be invested mainly in home and farm mortgages by the issuing institution (mainly savings and loan associations). One-year certificates may be issued between October 1, 1981, and December 31, 1982. Interest earned on the certificates between 1981 and 1983 will be exempt from taxation, up to a maximum of $1,000 for single persons and $2,000 for joint returns. The certificates will pay 70 percent of the yield on one-year Treasury bills. In 1985, the certificates will be succeeded by an interest exemption of up to $450 on single returns and $900 on joint returns.

7. Dividend exclusion   Beginning in 1982, individuals may exclude $100 of dividend income ($200 on a joint return) from taxation. This provision replaces the current exemption of $200 ($400 on a joint return) for interest and dividend income. For the four-year period 1982 to 1985, there is an additional special dividend exclusion. Single taxpayers may exclude up to $750 of stock dividends received from a domestic public utility corporation, even if the stockholder had the option to receive cash. On a joint return, the maximum is $1,500. When the stock is later sold, capital gains taxes will be paid on the stock dividend.

8. Retirement savings deductions   Employees covered by an employer-sponsored retirement plan may now also have an Individual Retirement Account (IRA). A maximum of $2,000 or 100 percent of compensation, whichever is less, may be contributed to the IRA. The new limit on spousal IRAs is $2,250. In lieu of an IRA, employees may also elect to make voluntary additional contributions to their employer-sponsored pension plan. For self-employed individuals, the maximum allowed contribution to a Keogh Plan has been raised from $7,500 to $15,000. The limit of no more than 15 percent of earnings remains in effect for Keogh Plans.

9. Sale of personal residence   The time period for deferring the gain on the sale of a personal residence is increased from 18 months to two years. For persons aged 55 or older, the once-in-a-lifetime capital gains exclusion for the sale of a personal residence has been raised from $100,000 to $125,000.

10. Estate and gift tax changes A major reduction in estate and gift taxes is provided by the act. Estate and gift taxes are unified, and a single progressive rate structure is applied to cumulative taxable gifts and bequests. A unified credit is then allowed against gross estate and gift taxes. The new unified credit will be increased over a six-year period from its current level of $47,000 to $192,800 for 1987 and successive years. Under present law, a unified credit allows otherwise taxable transfers of up to $175,625 to be exempt from tax. A unified credit of $192,800 will allow transfers of up to $600,000 free of estate tax. The maximum rate bracket will also be reduced, from 70 percent down to 50 percent. This reduction will be phased in over a four-year period. Tables A–1 and A–2 summarize these changes.

The gift tax exclusion has also been raised. Effective in 1982, a taxpayer may give up to $10,000 each year to any individual donee free from gift taxes. Married couples may give up to $20,000. The current limit is $3,000 for individuals and $6,000 for married couples. The act also allows unlimited tax-free transfers between spouses. Under the old law, the estate tax marital deduction was limited to $250,000 or one half of the gross estate. Deductions for gifts between spouses were limited to the first $100,000 of gifts plus 50 percent of lifetime transfers over $200,000.

Table A–1
Unified estate tax credit

Year	Amount of credit	Amount of estate eligible for tax-free transfer
1981	$ 47,000	$175,625
1982	62,800	225,000
1983	79,300	275,000
1984	96,300	325,000
1985	121,800	400,000
1986	155,800	500,000
1987 and later	192,800	600,000

Table A–2
Maximum estate tax rate

Year	Maximum rate	Applicable to transfers transfers exceeding
1981	70%	$5,000,000
1982	65	4,000,000
1983	60	3,500,000
1984	55	3,000,000
1985 and later ...	50	2,500,000

Index